REASON AND BELIEF

BY BRAND BLANSHARD

The Nature of Thought
Reason and Analysis
Reason and Goodness

REASON
AND BELIEF

BY

BRAND BLANSHARD

New Haven   Yale University Press   1975

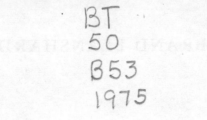

Printed in Great Britain

To
R. Y. B.

PREFACE

When I began the study of philosophy, most philosophers were deeply interested in the problems of religion. Indeed many of them had taken up the study, as I did myself, largely as a means of clearing up religious difficulties. Religion has now drifted from the centre to the periphery of philosophical interest. The younger men who have been brought up in linguistic or analytic schools of thought are likely to look upon the traditional Christian dogmas as meaningless. If they do not so regard them, they commonly take them as superstitions natural enough in a pre-critical age but no longer to be taken seriously.

I hold neither of these views. The verifiability theory of meaning by which theology and metaphysics were to be disposed of as meaningless has not stood up well under examination. And though I can only agree that much traditional dogma is heavily charged with superstition, I do not think it is adequately dealt with by assigning it to a pre-scientific era or by citing Frazer or Freud. Catholics like Gilson and Maritain, Protestants like Kierkegaard, Brunner, and Barth have brought too much learning and acuteness to the defence of their creeds to deserve such treatment, and these creeds continue to commend themselves intellectually, emotionally, and practically to large numbers of thoughtful minds. Views so held and so advocated should receive a respectful hearing from philosophers. Such a hearing I have tried to give them.

This book has had a long and somewhat abnormal gestation. In 1948 I was invited to give the William Belden Noble Lectures at the Harvard Divinity School, and I took as subject 'Present-Day Leaders of Ethical Thought'. Before these lectures were ready for publication I was invited to give the Gifford Lectures at St Andrews in 1952–53. Before this series of twenty lectures had been revised to my satisfaction, I was invited by the American Philosophical Association to give the Carus Lectures for 1959. All this left me deep in manuscripts and with a rather complicated set of liens upon them. Through much shuffling of paper on my part and untiring patience on the part of

9

my sponsors, three books have now emerged. I can only hope that they have gained in quality by not having gone more promptly to the press. Harvard permitted me, for purposes of publication, to incorporate my Noble Lectures with the Giffords. St Andrews permitted me to detach the epistemological side of my Giffords for use in the Carus series, where it was clearly more appropriate; and I promised in return to round out the theological side of my Giffords into a volume that could stand by itself. The three volumes, *Reason and Analysis*, *Reason and Goodness*, and *Reason and Belief* make a sequence in which I have tried to sketch the office of reason in the theory of knowledge, ethics, and religion respectively. They all continue a line of reflection begun many years before in *The Nature of Thought*.

BRAND BLANSHARD
June 1973

ACKNOWLEDGEMENTS

One of the following chapters has appeared in print, and selected parts of two others. Chapter VIII on Karl Barth was presented as a symposium of philosophers and theologians at Princeton Seminary in December 1962, and was printed among the papers of this conference in *Faith and the Philosophers*, edited by Professor John Hick and published by St Martin's Press and the Macmillan Company. It is reprinted with the publishers' permission. An article based on Chapter VI, on Kierkegaard, appeared in the winter number of *The Personalist* in 1968, and permission has been granted by the editor for the re-use of this material. The substance of Chapter XI on 'The Ethics of Belief' was used in a presidential address to the American Theological Society in 1956, and was printed by the Center for Philosophic Exchange in its journal *Philosophic Exchange*, Vol. 1, No. 2, issued in 1972; it is here reprinted with the permission of the editor. These permissions are gratefully acknowledged.

In a work so largely critical as this, it has been necessary for the sake of accuracy to make numerous quotations from the books and authors dealt with. I have sought to make due acknowledgement for these in the notes at the end of the book by giving the publisher, place, and date of each volume on the occasion of the first reference to it.

CONTENTS

For Analytical Table of Contents see pp. 599–609

Preface   *page* 9
Acknowledgements   11

PART I: REASON AND FAITH: THE
CATHOLIC VIEW

Chapter I: Catholic Teaching on Faith and Reason   23

Reason and Revelation   24
The Channels of Revelation   26
The Content of Revelation   28
The Acceptance of Revelation by Faith   30
Grounds for Belief in the Fact of Revelation   32
The Line between Philosophy and Theology   33

Chapter II: Reason and Revelation   37

Their Alleged Harmony   37
The Claim to a Scripture Inspired Throughout   38
Scriptural Inconsistencies   39
Possible Defences   41
    Authentic vs Quoted Statements   41
    Literal vs Metaphorical Statements   42
The Compromise of Vatican II   43
    Corruptions in the Text   46
    The Confinement of Inerrancy to Faith and Morals   49
The Paradox of a Veiled Revelation   52
The Doctrine of Infallibility   53
Inconsistency in Papal Pronouncements   55

Chapter III: Catholic Teaching on Revelation and
    Natural Knowledge   58

Nulla inter Fidem et Rationem Vera Dissensio   58
Revelation and Astronomy   59
Revelation and Biology   62
Revelation and Psychology   66
Science, Lourdes, and Fatima   68
Scientific vs Religious Faith   72

Miracles   74
Problems of the Miraculous   75

Chapter IV: Catholicism on the Marks of the Church   80

'Motives' and 'Marks'   80
  1 *The Unity of the Church*   81
Inconsistencies in Teaching   82
Additions to the Teaching   83
Purgatory   85
New Doctrines Regarding the Virgin   88
The Theory of Development   89
Subtractions from the Teaching   91
  2 *The Sanctity of the Church*   92
Morality Not Based on Authority   92
A Flawed Ideal   93
  3 *The Universality of the Church*   96
  4 *The Apostolicity of the Church*   98
The First Link in the Chain   98
Was 'Thou Art Peter' Ever Uttered?   99
The Attitude of the Apostles   101
The Attitude of the Fathers   101
The Attitude of the Councils   103
The Expected Second Coming   103
The Rise of the Papacy   104
The Second Meaning of Apostolicity   106
The Dialectic of Authority   108
Belief and Desire   110
Belief and the Intellectual Climate   111
Catholic Dogma in the Modern World   114

PART II: REASON AND FAITH: THE LUTHERAN
   SUCCESSION

Chapter V: Reason and Faith in Luther   121

What Luther Inherited   122
The Character of Luther   124
Reason as the Enemy of Faith   129
The Creed as Foolishness to Reason   132
Reason Unsafe in Morals   133
God and Evil   134
The Meaning of Faith   136
Faith and Works   138
Scripture   141
Is Scripture the Final Authority?   144
Is Scripture Coherent?   145
The Arrogance of Philosophy   147
The Meaning of Original Sin   150
A Doctrine without Basis in History, Scripture, or Science   151

A Doctrine That Is Morally Indefensible 154
God and Original Sin 156
The Failure of Reason in Religion 159
The Wall between the Realms 161
The Crumbling of the Wall 163
The Attack on Reason Self-Defeating 165
'Justification by Faith' : Who Is Justified? 167
Luther's Doctrine a Moral Depressant 168
Belief as the Essence of Faith 171
Knowledge of 'the Heart' 173
Faith May Mislead 174
Confusions of 'the Heart' 176
Fate as Dependent on Faith 179
An Immoral Ethics of Belief 180
Faith and Intellectual Integrity 182

Chapter VI: Reason and Faith in Kierkegaard 187

The Kierkegaard Revival 187
The Advance of Rationalism 188
The Existentialist Strategy 190
The 'Stages on Life's Way' 192
The Aesthetic Stage 193
The Ethical Stage 194
The Religious Stage (A) 197
Resignation 198
Suffering 199
The Cloud of Morbidity 201
Guilt 203
Guilt and Irrationality 206
Humour 209
The Humorous and the Inhuman 210
The Religious Stage (B) 212
Objectivity: the Failure of Philosophy 213
Individuals and Abstractions 214
Thought and Existence 216
The Failure of Objective Thought to Give Certainty 219
Belief as Commitment of the Will 220
Subjectivity: Its Meaning 223
Subjectivity as Truth 225
The Failure of Subjectivity 227
Subjectivity as Passion 229
The Leap of Faith 232
Faith as Non-rational 233
The Crucial Case of Abraham and Isaac 234
Kierkegaard as a Moral Nihilist 236
Rational Morals Repudiated 238
Rational Theology Repudiated 240
The Thinker and His Thought 242
Concluding Unhappy Postscript 245

Chapter VII: Reason and Revelation for Emil Brunner   248

The Revolt against Liberalism	248
Brunner on Human Nature	251
Brunner on Faith	255
Brunner on the Good Life	257
Brunner on Revelation and Reason	260
Revelation and Reason in Conflict	261
The Failure of Reason	264
Reason as Unavoidable	265
Theology vs Psychology	268
Theology vs History	270
The Relation of the Two Orders	271
Tension between the Orders	274
The Primacy of Reason	276
The Divine Imperative	278
Moral Nihilism Again	279
Moral Sanity	280
The Dangers of Misplaced Divinity	282
Error in High Places	283
The Analogy to Mysticism	285

Chapter VIII: Reason and Revelation for Karl Barth   288

The Neo-orthodox Position	288
What Revelation Is Not	290
Revelation vs the Bible	292
What Revelation Is	293
Barth's Achievement	294
In What Sense Is Reason Untrustworthy?	295
Knowledge as Incoherent	296
The Abandonment of Natural Reason Disastrous	297
Barth's Irrationalism	299
The Expropriation of Philosophy	301
Unintelligibility Rampant	302
Non-ethical Ethics	304
Strange Affinities	305
The Morality of the Sphinx	306
Barthianism and the Non-Christian World	308
The Futility of Moral and Religious Effort	309
Neo-orthodoxy and Science	311
Pride	316
The Temptation of Irrationalism	316

PART III: ETHICS AND BELIEF

Chapter IX: Rationalism and Christian Ethics (I)   323

Creed and Conduct	323
Central Stresses in Christian Ethics	326
The Claim to Finality	330

Christianity and the Good of Knowledge 333
Christianity and the Natural Man 335
Christianity and Wealth 337
Christianity and Art 340
Christianity and Civic Duty 341
Christianity and Non-resistance 342
Courage 344
Christianity and Nationalism 348
Christianity and Slavery 350
Christianity and the Position of Women 351
St Paul on the Position of Women 356

Chapter X: Rationalism and Christian Ethics (II) 360

Christianity and Justice 360
Christianity and Work 365
Christianity and Family Relations 367
Christianity and the Love of God 369
The Love of God as a Motive 372
Christian Humility 375
Jesus: God or Man? 377
Limitations in Knowledge 381
Limitations in Power 388
The Originality of Jesus 390
The Claim to Moral Perfection 391
Christianity and the Regard for Reason 394

Chapter XI: The Ethics of Belief 400

Is Belief Voluntary? 402
Are Our Beliefs Our Own Concern Only? 404
Social Importance and Social Control 407
The Right to Believe: a Crucial Case 408
Science and the Ethics of Belief 410
Religion and the Ethics of Belief 411
The Gospel Teaching 412
The Pauline Teaching 413
The Coming of Rationalism 416
The Conflict of Principle 416
James's Revolt against Rationalism 418
James and the Will to Believe 419
The Love of Truth and Its Repression 421
Truth or Consequences 424
Pascal's Gamble 424
The Stakes of Religious Belief 427
Truth the Compass of Thought 428
Scepticism and Morality 429
The Use of Authority 430
Certainty and Probability 431

Chapter XII: Myth in Religion — 434

Religion as a Threefold Response — 434
The Animistic Origin of Religion — 436
The Primitive Idea of the Soul — 438
The Birth of Mythology — 439
Myth as Incipient Science — 440
The Manifold Offices of Myth — 441
What Makes a Myth Live — 442
The Mythology of the Hebrews — 445
Myth as Edited by Morality — 447
Christianity and the Liberation of Morality from Myth — 449
Morals as the Shifting Base of Theology — 451
The Autonomy of Christian Insight — 452
The Lost Opportunity of the West — 453
Return of the Church Fathers to Mythology — 454
A Sample: the Myth of the Virgin — 456
The Rational Appraisal of Dogma — 464
The Melting Away of Dogma — 466

PART IV: A RATIONALIST'S OUTLOOK

Chapter XIII: Cosmology — 477

The World a Coherent Whole — 479
The World a Causal Whole — 482
The Uniformity of Nature — 483
The Law of Causality — 484
Objections to the Sway of Causality — 484
All Events Causally Interrelated — 490
Causality Involves Necessity — 493
Causal Necessity in Inference — 495
A Priori Elements in Causation — 496
Joseph and Ayer on Causation — 498
Common Sense and the Perceptual World — 502
The Perceptual World Dependent on Mind — 503
Science and the Physical Order — 508

Chapter XIV: Human Nature and Its Values — 511

Mind as a Packet of Propensities — 512
Need and Impulse as the Basis of Value — 513
Cognitive Evolution — 513
Conative Evolution — 515
Morality and Intrinsic Value — 517
The Nature of Goodness — 517
Rationalism in Morals — 519

Chapter XV: Goodness and the Absolute — 522

God and the Absolute — 523
The Absolute as Fulfilment — 524

Bradley   525
Royce   529
Bosanquet   530
Is the Absolute Morally Good?   532
Is the Absolute Intrinsically Good?   533
A Neutral World   534

Chapter XVI: Religion and Rationalism   538

The Tension between Supernaturalism and Rationalism   538
The Purposive Root of Morality   540
Thought and Length of Vision   541
Thought and Breadth of Vision   541
Thought and Coherence of Aim   542
The Moral Republic   544
The Religious Protest   545
The Theology of Evil   546
Two-storied Man   547
The Transformation of Instinct by Thought   549
Sentiments   552
The Religious Sentiment   552
The Sentiment of Rationality   554
The Rational Impulse in Religion   555
Being Moral and Being Rational   558
Reasonableness as a Motive   560
The Reasonable Temper   561
Faith   565
Reverence   566
Humility   567

Notes   573

Analytical Table of Contents   599

Index   610

PART I

REASON AND FAITH: THE CATHOLIC VIEW

CHAPTER I

CATHOLIC TEACHING ON FAITH
AND REASON

---

1 In this and the three chapters that follow we shall study the relations of reason, faith and revelation as conceived by the Catholic church. There are advantages in beginning with the Catholic position. For one thing, it has been defined with care and precision by the doctors of the church. No similar statement is possible for Protestantism, since there are more than two hundred Protestant sects, each varying slightly in doctrine and attitude from its neighbours. Perhaps also, in beginning with Catholicism, we may profit from the renewed and widespread interest in it aroused by the World Council of the sixties. That Council fastened the eyes of mankind on the Roman church—its ancient creed, its impressive ritual, its incomparable history. The waves of interest then generated have still not died wholly away.

In some minds, the thought of the Council will raise a doubt. Has not Catholicism also become a house divided against itself? Did not the Council admit that the dogmas of the church must be accommodated to the new insights of changing times, and hence that there is no body of teaching that can any longer be put forward as the essential teaching of the church?

No; this is to misunderstand what the Council intended and what it achieved. It did, to be sure, make changes in Catholic practices and attitudes. It decreed that English, French and other local languages could henceforth be used in the mass. Over the demurrers of the Spanish bishops, it decreed that liberty meant liberty not only for Catholics in non-Catholic countries, but for non-Catholics in Catholic countries. It retained the Holy Office, but changed its somewhat tarnished name and limited its powers of censorship over persons suspected of heresy. It condemned anti-Semitism. It strengthened the voice of the bishops, as distinct from that of the Pope, in church administration. Above all, it opened long-closed windows to the circulation of ideas from the modern world—about birth control, about the celibacy of the clergy, about the value of

23

Biblical criticism, about the importance of science—and in the spirit of its convener, Pope John, it sanctioned dialogue and co-operation with those of other faiths. It changed the temper of Catholicism from one of tight-lipped isolation to one of greater friendliness with those outside its walls and readiness to look critically at itself and at its image in the eyes of the world.

These are notable achievements. The Council will mark an epoch in church history, and to belittle it would be myopic. But the nature of its accomplishment has been widely misconstrued. While the Council did change the liturgy, the temper, and some of the practices of the church, it did not change in any important particular the corpus of Catholic belief. The dogmas, for example, that have given special difficulty to Protestants remain substantially what they were. Papal infallibility was less questioned at Vatican II than at Vatican I. Tradition, as a channel of revelation distinct from Scripture, was reaffirmed, though the reciprocal support of the two sources received more stress. The veneration of Mary, which to Protestants appears without any sound basis, was reasserted un-equivocally, the main difference of opinion in the Council being on the question whether the Virgin should have a chapter to herself; and Pope Paul in his concluding address expressed a wish that she should be 'still more honoured and invoked by the entire Christian people' under the title 'the mother of God'. As for the core of Catholic teaching—those relations of reason, revelation and faith with which we shall be concerned in this study—the Council left it conspicuously intact.[1]

REASON AND REVELATION

2 On the question whether that core of teaching is today accept-able we shall have much to say. But on one point let us be clear at once. The Catholic church is not anti-rational; it has a profound respect for reason. Any fair critic must admit that it has made a larger use of reason, that it has a creed more closely articulated intellectually, and that it has engaged in its service a more dis-tinguished succession of philosophic minds, than any other religious body, Christian or pagan. It is far more distrustful of emotion than Protestantism, which has sometimes been content to hold that religion is 'a feeling of dependence' or 'morality touched with emotion' or 'a way of life'. For Rome religion has an intellectual base. The church can say, as Newman did, 'dogma has been the fundamental principle of my religion: I know no other religion; I cannot enter into the idea of any other sort of religion; religion, as a mere sentiment, is to me a dream and a mockery'.[2] Indeed,

Catholicism grants to reason a larger role than would be given it by many or most of the secular philosophers of our day. It holds that reason can show the existence of God with certainty, and trace with a like certainty his principal relations to man and the world. 'The holy mother church,' said the First Vatican Council, 'holds and teaches that God can be certainly known from created things by the lights of human reason to be the beginning and end of all things.'³ At no time has there been so universal a belief in the power of mere reflection to illumine all things in the heavens above or the earth beneath as at the time when the church was in its ascendancy. Whitehead has noted that this was the truly rationalistic period in the history of thought, and that in the scientific period that followed reason was by comparison in eclipse.

Loyal Catholics would add that even today they are the true rationalists. Their allegiance to reason has remained unaltered while outside their borders, in theology, in science, even in philosophy, distrust of reason has become rampant. As for Protestant theology, they would hold that that ill starred vessel is disintegrating, the stern stranded on the rocks of Barthian anti-rationalism, while the prow is being engulfed by the humanism and naturalism of the day. Physical science itself, they point out, is becoming sceptical of its own foundations. If it is to take one secure step beyond what is given, it must validate the law of induction, and this it has found no way of doing; it is therefore itself living on a kind of faith. Even mathematics, traditionally conceived as giving certain knowledge of the world, has now been invaded by scepticism, since mathematical definitions and axioms have come to be regarded not as statements about the nature of things, but as postulates validated in the end by their advantage in use, or as mere linguistic conventions. As for philosophy, it has so largely lost confidence in the powers of reason that its central discipline, metaphysics, once looked upon as 'the queen of the sciences', has been for decades in semi-hiding. When the Catholic thinker observes this widespread defection from earlier hopes, he contends at times that he alone has kept full trust in reason. Speaking of the main anti-religious factions of the century, Dr D'Arcy has written: 'They are all believers. The difference which I would maintain exists between their beliefs is that the Catholic one is founded on reason, the Nazi and the Communist on messianic expectation, and the Agnostic on disillusionment and an interior disharmony.'⁴ If one looks into the book called *The Flight from Reason*, by the late Sir Arnold Lunn, one will find that the title means not the abandonment of philosophy and science for religious superstition, but on the contrary, the abandonment by philosophers and scientists of the one true rationalism, that of the church.

3 Catholicism thus conceives itself as anything but an enemy of reason. But its reliance on reason has limits. On the hither side of a certain boundary it uses reason freely and confidently; reliance on it beyond that limit is discouraged and indeed proscribed. Where is the boundary drawn? It is at the line of demarcation between two orders of knowledge, that which is attainable by our natural powers on the one hand, and that which is attainable only through revelation on the other. The First Vatican Council puts the distinction clearly:

'The Catholic Church with one consent has also ever held, and does hold, that there is a twofold order of knowledge, distinct both in origin and in object: in origin because our knowledge in the one is by natural reason, and in the other by divine faith; in object because, besides those things to which natural reason can attain, there are proposed to our belief mysteries hidden in God, which, unless revealed, cannot be known.'5

On the Catholic view of secular or natural reason little need be said. There is no discernible difference, outside theology, between the way in which a Catholic would go about it to establish a truth and the way of anyone else. The methods of Mendel in genetics, of Pasteur in physiology, of Gilson in secular philosophy, are the recognised methods of any competent person in these fields. The rules of evidence are common property for Catholics and non-Catholics. One difference only need be noted, a difference in tendency. Of the proper use of reason, particularly in the speculative sphere, Catholics have been provided with an officially approved model. In his encyclical *Aeterni Patris* of 1870, Pope Leo XIII instructed Catholic thinkers that henceforth they were to find their exemplar of thought in Thomas Aquinas; 'reason, borne on the wings of Thomas to its human height, can scarcely rise higher'.6

It is not reason, however, that we are for the moment interested in, but rather that source of knowledge which lies, in the Catholic view, beyond the competence of reason, namely revelation. We have at our command a large mass of *veritates a caelo delapsae*, as the decree *Lamentabili* puts it, truths that have come down from heaven.7 Since these truths derive from a source at once other than reason and above it, and possess the completest sort of certainty, we must be as clear as we can about their nature and apprehension. Let us look at the main points of Catholic teaching about (1) the instruments of revelation, (2) its contents, (3) the way we lay hold of it, and (4) the grounds for accepting it.

THE CHANNELS OF REVELATION

4(1) Revelation has had various channels. The chief of these is the spoken word of Christ, who is conceived as incarnate Deity. But revelation has come through others also in the form of inspiration, in which the mind is moved by divine influence to form certain thoughts and give them utterance in certain words. The persons who have been thus inspired are many. It is often supposed by those who have not looked into the matter that Catholics are less inclined than Protestants to accept the entire body of Scriptural writings as inspired and inerrant. This is incorrect. 'Holy Mother Church . . . holds that the books of both the Old and New Testament in their entirety, with all their parts, are sacred and canonical because, having been written under the inspiration of the Holy Spirit . . . they have God as their author. . . .'[8] The books to which such authorship is ascribed are those enumerated at Trent.[9] This great Council accepted as canonical not only the sixty-six books which now form the Protestant Bible, but also seven others,[10] so that the volume of Scriptural revelation is larger for the Catholic than for the Protestant, and very much larger than for those Protestants who, like Luther, would reject some of the sixty-six.

But numerous as are the Scriptural channels, the Catholic has still others: 'before we can so much as know what Bible it is to which we are appealing, since the Bible itself never enumerates its own component parts, we have to go to an extra-biblical authority to learn what "books" are part of the infallible Bible, and what are not.'[11] This needed guidance Catholics hold to have been provided by tradition. The inspiration of Mark and Paul, of Peter and the church fathers, cannot be supposed to have exhausted itself in what they wrote; if their writing was inspired, part at least of their oral teaching must have been so too, and this touched upon many points of belief and practice not explicitly dealt with in Scripture. In the words of Vatican II: 'it is not from sacred Scripture alone that the Church draws her certainty about everything which has been revealed. Therefore both sacred tradition and sacred Scripture are to be accepted and venerated with the same sense of loyalty and reverence.'[12]

But how do we know which elements in the great mass of tradition are to be regarded as revealed truth and which are not? Here appears the third element of revelation, namely the church itself. Its authority derives directly from the words of Christ to the Apostle, 'Thou art Peter, and upon this rock I will build my church.'[13] The authority given to Peter was transmitted by him to his successors, and it includes the power both to 'govern the universal church' and to define its doctrine; on these matters 'none may reopen the judgement of the Apostolic See, than whose authority there is no greater, nor is it permitted to anyone to review its judgement'.[14]

Great as this authority is, however, it was instituted as a means of preserving and interpreting doctrine, not extending it. 'For the Holy Spirit was not promised to the successors of Peter, that by His revelation they might make known new doctrine, but that by His assistance they might inviolably keep and faithfully expound the revelation or deposit of faith delivered through the Apostles.'[15] When the Pope, in his capacity as vicar of Christ, formally pronounces judgement on the meaning of any passage of Scripture, or on any item in the extensive body of dogma which Catholics are required to believe, or on any problem of morals, he is infallibly guided; on such questions 'this See of Saint Peter remains ever free from all blemish of error. . . .'[16]

THE CONTENT OF REVELATION

5(2)   When we turn from the channels to the content of revelation, we face an immense prospect. Fortunately a review of this content in detail is not necessary for our purpose, for the detail is inexhaustible. All the central dogmas of the church regarding God, the world, and man, every article in the Apostles', the Nicene, and the Athanasian creeds, the entire body of tradition as interpreted by the church, the official teaching about the sacraments, the plan of salvation, and the good life—all these are included within the scope of revelation. But there is a great deal more. Outsiders sometimes believe that only a few statements of cardinal importance are regarded by the church as inerrant. This is true if one is thinking only of official papal pronouncements. It is far from true if one is thinking of 'inspired' statements generally. There are literally thousands of these. We have seen that seventy-three Scriptural books 'have God for their Author'. 'All the books which the Church receives as sacred and canonical are written wholly and entirely, with all their parts, at the dictation of the Holy Ghost,' and as for error, such inspiration 'excludes and rejects it as absolutely and necessarily as it is impossible that God Himself, the Supreme Truth, can utter that which is not true'.[17] No distinction is made in these repeated and sweeping statements between moral and religious teaching on the one hand and factual statements on the other; St Thomas held, for example, that if Samuel was not the son of Elcana, 'the Divine Scripture would be false'.[18] Many persons, including many Catholics, suppose this teaching to have been altered or dropped at Vatican II and to have been replaced by a new freedom of interpretation; one may now accept from Scripture what one's own judgement only, or that of one's favourite archaeologist or historian, may approve as credible. This was certainly not the position of the

Council. It reiterated in almost identical words the earlier teaching about the inspiration of the entire text of Scripture, though with certain qualifying phrases whose import we shall have to consider in the next chapter. Meanwhile it would be absurd to take as authoritative the views of restive and scattered revisionists regarding the true meaning of the ancient creed; if there is a difference of opinion as to what the church teaches, the critic should go to its supreme council and pay it the respect of assuming that it means what it says. And Vatican II said: 'everything asserted by the inspired authors or sacred writers must be held to be asserted by the Holy Spirit.'[19]

Though the details of this large body of revelation are beyond our present concern, there is one distinction within it that we must carefully note. Not all the truths that are revealed come to us by revelation only. Some of them come to us *both* by revelation *and* by the processes of ordinary inquiry; indeed in the view of Aquinas we have this double access to far the larger part of revealed truth. In the *Summa Theologica* and the *Summa Contra Gentiles* he considers hundreds of revealed truths about God, man, and nature, about saints, angels, and demons, for which he proceeds to offer demonstrations. His confidence in the power of reason to establish these things makes the ventures of any modern rationalist seem timid. Indeed, if we are to follow the *Contra Gentiles*, there would seem to be only five doctrines of major importance that prove in the end impenetrable to understanding: the creation of the world out of nothing, the Trinity, the incarnation, the sacraments, and eternal life. The acceptance of these two levels of revelation may at first seem strange. That truths beyond our own capacity should be vouchsafed by revelation may be credible enough, but why should so much be revealed which reason can achieve by itself? Aquinas answers that otherwise we should have discrimination in favour of the philosopher and against the plain man. Many of these truths are needed for the right guidance of life; the philosopher has intelligence, patience, and time to lay hold of them; the plain man has not. They must therefore come to him by revelation or not at all.[20]

6 What is the relation between these two bodies of revealed truth? Is what is above reason also against reason? Aquinas and Catholic tradition are emphatic at this point; they deny that such opposition occurs or ever can occur.[21] To be sure, when we ask how the three persons of the Trinity can also be one person, or how the bread and wine of the eucharist can also be flesh and blood, our intellects are baffled. But not to see how something can be true is a very different thing from seeing that it is not true. The doctrines of the Trinity and the eucharist are beyond reason in the sense that it is beyond our finite powers to understand them, but not at all in the sense that they are inherently unintelligible; they are supra-rational, if you will, but not irrational. The divine mind understands them even if we do not. We have no ground for supposing either that there is any incoherence in them or that, if we understood them, we should find them opposed at any point to the truths we grasp by reason. Indeed such a contradiction may be ruled out as impossible. For the things we clearly see by reason must be truths for God as well as ourselves, and to say that these at any point clash with the truths of revelation would be to ascribe incoherence to the divine mind itself. And that, for Aquinas, would be worse than absurd.[22]

THE ACCEPTANCE OF REVELATION BY FAITH

7(3)   But if a truth is unintelligible to us, how can we call it certain? How, indeed, can we accept it at all? The proposition that triangles with equal sides have equal angles, the proposition that it will rain tomorrow, are statements we can understand, and think we can accept as certain or probable as the evidence warrants. But how can we assert something as certain or probable when we do not know what we are asserting? Floods of ink have been poured out on this question; it has been canvassed by many of the doctors of the church—Augustine, Aquinas, Suarez; Newman devotes some hundreds of subtle though not wholly convincing pages to it in the *Grammar of Assent*. The main features of the accepted doctrine seem to be as follows.

(a) The truths that are above reason are not mere blanks for us. When we consider the three persons in one nature, we know what three means, and what one means, and to some extent what persons are, since we are acquainted with finite persons. To be sure, we do not know what an 'infinite person' means, if that is what is intended, or how he could combine several persons in himself. But to speak in metaphors and analogies is not to speak in mere riddles. We are not wholly in the dark as to what it is we are accepting.

(b) We are very largely in the dark, nevertheless. '*Quis est enim fides*,' asks Augustine, '*nisi credere quod non vides?*' And the question remains why we should assent to that which is unintelligible to us. Not only are the assertions we are supposed to accept obscure in themselves; there is no adequate evidence for them within the range of our experience or reason. If we are to arrive at a certain belief in them, therefore, it must be by a different route from that which leads us to belief when the evidence is compelling. Indeed the leading here is supernatural. The First Vatican Council laid it down that

'no man can assent to the Gospel teaching . . . without the illumination and inspiration of the Holy Spirit. . . . Wherefore faith
. . . is in itself a gift of God.'[23] And again:

> 'this faith . . . is a supernatural virtue whereby, inspired and
> assisted by the grace of God, we believe that the things which He
> has revealed are true; not because of the intrinsic truth of the things
> as perceived by the natural light of reason, but because of the
> authority of God Himself, who can neither err nor lead into error.'[24]

(c) Such faith involves the will as well as the intellect. It is
defined by Aquinas as 'an act of the intellect assenting to the truth
at the command of the will'.[25] The mechanism, so to speak, of our
assent to revelation is thus seen to be still further from that of
belief in what is demonstrated or self-evident. There, once we have
clearly seen, assent follows automatically. Revelation, on the other
hand may present itself as actually repugnant to our reason and
common sense. 'According to its very definition, faith implies assent
of the intellect to that which the intellect does not see to be true.
. . . Consequently, an act of faith cannot be caused by a rational
evidence, but entails an intervention of the will.'[26] To make the
matter painfully clear, Vatican I says, 'If anyone shall say that the
assent of Christian faith is not a free act, but necessarily produced
by the arguments of human reason . . . let him be anathema'.[27]
It is strange to reflect that though Descartes and Aquinas agreed
that belief was an act of the will, Descartes held that resort to this
act before the intellect was clear was the root of all error, while
Aquinas held it an indispensable means to salvation. For the
Catholic, to refuse belief is sin; 'nor will anyone', according to
official decree, 'obtain eternal life unless he shall have persevered
in faith unto the end'.[28]

8   Four points about this act of will should be noted. First, just
as reason requires divine illumination to assure that it is really
confronted by revelation, so the will needs divine assistance to
achieve the act of assent. In the face of a suggested belief which seems
neither clear in itself nor in accord with the evidence, we may easily
find ourselves unable to believe, even if we wish to. If at times we
succeed, it is because, as Aquinas says, our own feeble will 'is itself
moved by the grace of God'. As Canon Smith puts it, 'with the
intellect of a Plato, with the iron self-control of a Stoic, with all
the good-will of which man is capable, he can do nothing to prepare
himself for faith without the help of God's grace'.[29] Secondly, at
some apparent cost of consistency,[30] it is said that this act which is
moved by grace is also a free act of our own. Thirdly, since it is thus

free, we acquire merit by doing it. We likewise acquire demerit if we grant assent to anything contrary to revelation, however reasonable this may seem. In the Syllabus appended to his encyclical *Quanta Cura* of 1864, Pius IX condemned, as Proposition XV, the statement: 'Any man is free to embrace and profess the religion which, led by the light of reason, he thinks to be true.'[31] Hence, fourthly, our intellectual and moral ends seem at times to conflict with each other, since even when something presents itself to our reason as true and necessary, it may be our duty to deny it.[32] When such conflict does seem to occur, the loyal Catholic may fall back on certain reassuring reflections. He may reflect, for one thing, that what seems to be required by reason in such a case could not satisfy it in the end, since it is certainly false; 'the faith is always there and any conflict between his faith and his philosophy is a sure sign of philosophic error'.[33] He may reflect, further, that it can never be morally wrong to believe what duty requires him to believe. What is his duty? To obey the divine will. What does the divine will ask of him? To do that which is needful for salvation. And we are expressly told that belief in certain things is a condition of salvation. To believe them as a means to this end is therefore natural and legitimate; 'we believe divine revelation,' says Aquinas, 'because the reward of eternal life is promised us for so doing. It is the will which is moved by the prospect of this reward to assent to what is said, even though the intellect is not moved. . . .'[34]

GROUNDS FOR BELIEF IN THE FACT OF REVELATION

9(4)   We have seen that the assent of faith is given not because the intellect is clear, but in spite of its not being clear; one believes something because God has said it. But if we are called on to believe something that we do not understand, how do we know that God has said it? Here enter what are called 'motives of credibility', that is, grounds for believing that something really is revealed. Suppose that doubts should arise whether the Bible is genuinely a voice from beyond nature; two distinct lines of argument are open, either of which is enough, we are assured, to provide an unprejudiced mind with overwhelming evidence, a warrant from within, and a warrant from without. The warrant from within consists of the harmony and impressiveness of the Biblical story itself—miracles, the fulfilment of prophecy, the portrait of a figure morally perfect, the coherence of the vast plan of salvation, the growth and triumph of the early church against all human probability. If a mind is too darkened to feel the force of this witness, it may turn to the second warrant, the absolute guarantee of a church which, on all matters of this kind, speaks with infallibility. But the doubter may still doubt. 'How am I to know that the authority of this church is what it says it is? This is the point on which the whole chain of argument seems to hang, and am I to accept it on an *ipse dixit*?' By no means, comes the answer. The authority of the church is itself attested to any reasonable mind by marks or notes which only a divinely assisted body could exhibit. These notes are traditionally four: the unity of the church, that is, the identical form taken by its teaching and organisation in all times; its universality, that is, its identity in all places; its sanctity, that is, the production through the ages of lives pervaded by grace and goodness; and finally its apostolicity, that is, its unbroken descent from, and its fidelity to, the original teaching, spirit, and institution of the Apostles. No secular body can produce a parallel to the church in respect to any of these notes; and when the four are taken together, they offer a mass of converging evidence that will convince any open mind.

THE LINE BETWEEN PHILOSOPHY AND THEOLOGY

10 Why is it that in spite of this extensive appeal to reason, so many philosophers have considered Catholicism faint-hearted in that appeal? It is because, as we have just seen, and by its own emphatic avowal, the church draws a line and says to reason firmly, however respectfully, 'Thus far and no farther'. It makes extensive use of reason and at the same time sharply limits it. It cuts the world into two provinces, in one of which, to be sure, reason is given full scope. But in the other, the province containing those truths which it is most important for us to know, the authority of reason is superseded, and if it ventures to say anything at odds with church or Scripture, then regardless of the credentials it offers, it is trespassing where it does not belong and is conducted back across the border. Theology and philosophy are fundamentally different disciplines with different points of departure and different modes of proceeding, theology moving downward from a fixed and certain revelation, philosophy groping upward from the facts of experience. Properly speaking, theology, 'the science of the truth necessary for our salvation,'[35] is not a science at all, for what it expounds is absolute truth, attained by supra-rational means. Theology and philosophy are not rivals but complements of each other. 'It is, therefore, the inalienability of their proper essences', writes Professor Gilson, 'which permits them to act upon each other without contaminating each other. . . . Thomism has room, by the side of a theology which should be nothing but theology, for a philosophy which should be nothing but philosophy.'[36]

Will this division of labour hold? We need hardly say that if it did, and our perplexed and burdened minds could be brought to see that it did, we should be saved incalculable effort, time, and anxiety. The man who can accept it is to be envied in many ways. Without the difficult, self-critical, tormenting wrestle of the philosophers with truth, renewed only to be followed by another fall, he *knows*—simply, smilingly, and absolutely; 'God, his attributes, his providential designs in man's regard, man's own duties to his Creator and to his fellow men—all this, and much more, he knows with a certainty that is supreme'.[37] He has been transported to somewhere near the end of the long road along which others must trudge laboriously. And the truth that is revealed to him is not some set of bleak abstractions about the structure of matter or the ultimate laws of energy, but an intimate report that behind those laws, sustaining them, using them, at times suspending them as he sees fit, is a Person infinitely wise and kind. Thus his main ground of practical as well as intellectual worry is swept away. From now on he knows that the power which made and controls all the galaxies of the universe broods over him night and day. He knows what he must do to fulfil the will of this Power, and knows that however badly things may go with him for an hour or a year or a lifetime, the whole resources of infinity are pledged to make things right for him in the end, and triumphantly more than right, if only he orders his walk obediently. To any observer with a heart, or with an eye for the parts played by hope and fear in the actual fixing of beliefs, the fascination that this creed has exercised, age after age, can be no matter for surprise. But of course its beneficence in the way of peace and comfort is no evidence of its truth, and we are concerned with its truth exclusively. And not even with its truth as a whole, but solely with that part of the creed which limits the use of reason.

11 For all its attractions, most philosophers, past and present, have declined to accept this limit. They would no doubt admit that in dealing with such dark problems as the nature of Deity and the origin and destiny of the world, reason halts and stumbles, but they would agree that if such things are to be known at all, they must be known by rational reflection which starts from the facts of experience and goes on to draw inferences from them; there is no quick nonrational road which, somehow skirting the infirmities of our natural powers and knowledge, conducts us to absolute truth. Of this they are firmly convinced; but how are rationalists of this persuasion to join issue with the Catholic? If they offer arguments designed to show that the 'certainties' of faith are illusions, he will merely smile at them. Such criticism quite obviously begs the question; it assumes the competence of our reason within the sphere where his theory has declared it incompetent, and however cogent to the rationalist, the argument is thus to the believer no argument at all. He is not to be refuted by naïvely assuming the untruth of his main contention. But if the rationalists are to be denied the use of reason in pursuing him into his city of refuge, what are they to do? He asserts that he has an insight which, since it is not intelligible to reason nor reached by rational means, is inaccessible to rational attack. All he asks, he says, is to be let alone in his supra-rational citadel. He insists that he has no enmity to reason in its own province. He has no wish to sally out on his besiegers, and they seem to have no way of getting at him. Is the high argument to die away in a stalemate?

12 If the Catholic claim were like some other claims to a truth above or below reason, we should have to acquiesce in such frustration. There have been mystics who, on descending from their hill of vision, have reported insights as unutterable as they were certain; but just because they were unutterable they were also incommunicable, unsupportable, and irrefutable. Sceptics have jeered that this sounded remarkably like an insight into nothing at all, and the mystics have replied: 'That, of course, is how it must seem to you people on the plain, just as you yourselves will offend a blind man if you talk of the blue and gold of the morning. But your denial has no standing for us who have seen. It is a denial of you know not what, with the help of arguments that seem absurd at the altitude where we have stood.' Now is it not barely possible that the mystic is right, that he really has had a vision into what is so discontinuous with all we know that we can form no conception of it? It is hard to see how the possibility of such vision can be ruled out a priori. And if so, it looks as if rational discussion with him were bound to end in bafflement.

But this is not the case of the Catholic. He is not an irrationalist. He respects reason enough to hold that nothing in the end can be true if it is not reasonable and intelligible; true reason is the voice of God. The supra-rational is not really above reason, but only above reason as we know and use it—a very different thing; there are no contradictions in revelation, nor yet between revelation and any part of natural knowledge. With a person who conceives the role of reason as generously as this, discussion is possible. If he is convinced that anything is really against reason, he cannot, even as a loyal Catholic, accept it. We have already quoted his highest authority as saying, 'there can never be any real disagreement between faith and reason, since the same God who reveals mysteries and infuses faith has conferred on the human mind the light of reason, and God cannot deny himself'.[38] Thus between the Catholic and the secular philosopher there is a large common ground.

Throughout the discussion that follows, we shall try to proceed upon that ground. In the Catholic account of the relation between reason and revelation, three theses are central. I. There is accessible to us a body of revealed truth which, though transcending reason, is still in accordance with reason. II. Since this revelation contains only what is true, there is, and there can be, no conflict between any of its statements and the truths of natural knowledge. III. To a person who approaches the issue with an open mind, the fact of such a revelation can be convincingly shown by reason. In the three chapters that follow, these theses will be considered in order.

CHAPTER II

REASON AND REVELATION

1 The church, according to Catholic teaching, has received a revelation that is at once above reason and in harmony with it. What does this mean?

'Above reason' does not mean merely beyond our present knowledge, as is the geology of Mars, or beyond our personal powers of understanding, as some proposition of the higher mathematics may be; nor does it mean merely beyond the powers of anyone now living, as some theorem of quantum mechanics may be, which will be demonstrated a millennium hence. The theologian would not accept the suggestion that if some exceptionally intelligent boy were born tomorrow and given suitable training he might manage to understand how the three persons in the Trinity could be one. 'Above reason' means beyond the powers of man as such. The doctrine was elaborated at a time long before the discovery of mental evolution, when man's present state was regarded as the state he would keep till the drama of earthly life was over.

Next, what does 'harmony with reason' mean? It is evidently designed to say something about the intelligibility of revealed truth; it says, not of course that such truth is now intelligible to us, but that it is in accord, nevertheless, with the fundamental conditions of intelligibility. And what are these? Primarily the laws of logic. To take the most obvious of them, we may say of revealed truth, even in advance of knowing what it is, that it does not violate the principle of contradiction; all parts of it are consistent with each other; that is the least that 'being in accordance with reason' can mean. Our question then is: Does the teaching offered to us as revealed, though above reason, form a body of internally consistent truth?

The answer can only be No. For included in revelation are not only the official pronouncements of the church, but the entire content of the Old and New Testaments, so far as the writers are speaking with their own voice and not merely quoting others; and

37

there is no difficulty in showing that the Biblical books do not constitute such a coherent whole.

For the religious liberal, the battle over the inerrancy of Scripture was fought and settled long ago. The value of the Bible lies for him in the expression it gives—an authentic and at best very moving expression—to the moral and religious experience of a greatly gifted people. He knows that the attempt to make of the Bible a document dictated, in Donne's phrase, to 'the secretaries of the Holy Ghost', and therefore errorless in every detail, is a blunder calculated to alienate all thoughtful men. This teaching is sometimes regarded as the almost exclusive property of Protestant fundamentalists. On the contrary, it is in substance the position of the largest and most powerful of Christian churches. This teaching is not nowadays much stressed, and many members of the Catholic church are unaware of it, or even deny it, but they do so at their peril. It is not merely the teaching of the greatest of church philosophers, St Thomas, whose opinion is weighty, though of course fallible;[1] it is a belief that has been made mandatory for all Catholics by the official pronouncements of the highest authority.

THE CLAIM TO A SCRIPTURE INSPIRED THROUGHOUT

2 The ecumenical Council of Trent decreed with Papal approval that 'if anyone receive not as sacred and canonical the said books entire and with all their parts as they have been used to be read in the Catholic church, and as they are contained in the Old Latin Vulgate edition . . . let him be anathema'.[2] Nor is anyone at liberty to take one part as more reliable than another; the Council declared that it 'accepts and venerates all the books of the Old and New Testaments, since one God is the author of both, with equal piety and reverence'.[3] This position was reaffirmed by the Vatican Council of 1870.[4] Leo XIII committed the church to it in unequivocal terms. 'All the books which the Church receives as sacred and canonical are written wholly and entirely, with all their parts, at the dictation of the Holy Ghost; and so far is it from being possible that any error can coexist with inspiration, that inspiration is not only essentially incompatible with error, but excludes and rejects it as absolutely and necessarily as it is impossible that God himself, the supreme truth, can utter that which is not true.'[5] The position was reiterated by Benedict XV in *Spiritus Paraclitus* of 1920. It was emphatically re-affirmed by Vatican Council II.

'Holy Mother Church, relying on the belief of the apostles, holds that the books of both the Old and New Testament in their entirety, with all their parts, are sacred and canonical because, having been written under the inspiration of the Holy Spirit . . . they have God as their author and have been handed on as such to the Church herself. . . . Therefore, since everything asserted by the inspired authors or sacred writers must be held to be asserted by the Holy Spirit, it follows that the books of Scripture must be acknowledged as teaching firmly, faithfully, and without error that truth which God wanted put into the sacred writings. . . .'6

SCRIPTURAL INCONSISTENCIES

3 Now this position is untenable. It requires Catholics to accept as true statements that cannot be true, because they contradict other statements held equally to be true. Let us take first a random sampling of such contradictions, factual, moral and religious. In 2 Samuel 24 : 9, we read that there were 800,000 men in Israel who drew the sword; in 1 Chronicles 21 : 5, the figure is given as 1,100,000. In 2 Samuel 6 : 23, we read that 'Michal, the daughter of Saul, had no child unto the day of her death'. Fifteen chapters later in the same book we find a reference to 'the five sons of Michal, the daughter of Saul' (21 : 8). In 1 Kings 9 : 28, we are told that gold was brought from Ophir to the value of 420 talents; in 2 Chronicles 8 : 18, the same gold has the value of 450 talents. In 1 Kings 7 : 15, the twin pillars of Solomon's temple have a height of eighteen cubits; in 2 Chronicles 3 : 15, the same pillars have a height of thirty-five cubits. In 1 Samuel 15 : 29, we read that 'the Strength of Israel will not lie nor repent'. A few verses later in the same chapter we read, 'the Lord repented that he had made Saul king over Israel'.7 Matthew gives a genealogy of Jesus which represents him as descended from David through Solomon. Luke supplies another genealogy which represents him as descended from another son, Nathan. Matthew has forty-one generations from Abraham to Jesus; Luke has fifty-six. Neither genealogy, if true, accords with the church teaching that Jesus has no human father at all. In Mark and Luke, Jesus lays down an absolute prohibition of divorce; in two passages in Matthew he declines to apply this prohibition to the innocent party where the other has been guilty of adultery.8 In the account of Paul's conversion in Acts 9 : 3–7, those who were with him are declared to have 'stood amazed, hearing indeed a voice, but seeing no man'. In the account of the same event in Acts 22 : 6–10, 'they that were with me saw indeed the light, and were afraid; but they heard not the voice of him that spake to me'. All four of the gospels tell the story of the resurrection, but they differ as to the number of angels seen, the places where they were

seen, the number of visitors to the tomb, and the times at which the visits were made.

4 Here is an array of conflicting statements which are taken impartially from the Old Testament and the New, and which could be multiplied many times. Given any pair of them, one member of the pair must be incorrect. Is it objected that they are all trivial, that they concern only petty details? That is true of most of them, but it is beside the point. The question is not whether the writers of these books, when they made mistakes, made big ones or little ones, but whether they made mistakes at all; the church holds that they did not, since these books 'in their entirety with all their parts . . . have God as their author'. And for the settlement of *this* question, conflicting statements on a trivial point like the height of a pillar are more useful than statements about the ultimate nature of things. We may be sure that no pillar can be at once eighteen and thirty-five cubits high, and that a woman cannot both be childless and have five sons, while it is very hard to be sure that, if the doctrine of predestination is affirmed in one place and denied in another, there is any genuine conflict; in these more nebulous regions, a term may bear different meanings. No one cares about the height of the pillars; granted. But if that height is stated incorrectly, as it obviously has been by one or other of the Biblical writers, what follows is that the book the writer wrote is not infallible, that the collection of books in which this one appears is not infallible, and that the doctors, councils, and popes who pronounced it infallible were not themselves infallible.[9]

5 On these matters, however, the Catholic has a resource not open to Protestants. The meaning he is bound to accept is not necessarily what his own reading would find in the Bible, even when the sense seems plain, but the sense that the church officially imposes on the text. Indeed so anxious has the church been that its own interpretation be accepted that it has often warned against the reading of the Bible except under controls. For example, Leo XII in 1824 issued an encyclical against the activities of the British and Foreign Bible Society, describing its efforts to promote the reading of the Bible in the vernacular languages as a deadly pestilence;[10] and its efforts were still opposed even when the Bibles circulated were in approved Catholic translations, so long as the Catholic annotations were not included.

Incidentally, this insistence that Scripture is authoritative only as interpreted by the church implies that the Bible is hardly recognised as an independent authority at all. It could be thus independent only if its pronouncements, as interpreted by competent scholars free from prior commitments, were accepted as authoritative. But when such scholars have questioned the authenticity of the meaning of passages relied on by the church for validating its own claims, it has had a short and practically effective way of dealing with the questioners: it has ruled that its own interpretation is final. However successful in practice, this procedure is logically costly, since it invalidates the favourite argument for the church's own authority, the argument that rests this primacy on Scripture. If the church is to be accepted as authoritative because the New Testament says so, but the New Testament can be interpreted as saying so only because the church says it must, the argument comes to this, that the church is authoritative because it authoritatively says so. This is not an argument calculated to remove doubts.

Granting for the moment, however, that the church's interpretation is final, how is it to proceed with such passages as we have cited? It is committed by the most solemn Papal pronouncement to the view that passages which on their face are contradictory are still errorless. At least four lines of escape have been employed.

Authentic vs quoted statements
6(1)   One is to draw a distinction between what a writer says himself and what he quotes or reports from someone else. When he says in one place that the daughter of Saul died childless and in another that she had five sons, we may hold that in one place he was saying what he himself believed, which is errorless, while in the other he was reporting what he had heard from someone else, which may be mistaken. Consistency is thus preserved by throwing one statement out.

But this course does not give us what is needed. For (a) both sides of the contradiction are usually stated in the same straightforward way, with no indication in either case that the writer meant merely to offer an unverified quotation; and to read him as meaning to do so is to take a liberty unwarranted by anything in the text. (b) Even if he did mean to do so in one case rather than the other, we have no means of judging which, and hence to take either statement in preference to the other as *the* correct one is likewise unwarranted. To say that a book would be errorless if we had means, which it is admitted that we have not, to dismiss the errors with which it is admitted to be strewn is for practical purposes to abandon the claim to errorlessness. (c) It is incredible that a writer should be so inspired that what he says in his own person should be preserved from all error, and yet that this inspiration should be unable to protect him against the most palpable errors of others. If he was able to see profound truths and remote facts undisclosed to common eyes, how could he report as true, in the mouths of others, statements that flatly contradicted what he had seen to be true without alloy? On the other hand, if he was so confused or careless as to report as true the obvious errors of others, how can we repose confidence in him anywhere? Gullibility is not a convincing witness to infallibility.[11]

Literal vs metaphorical statements

7(2)   Sometimes another tack is taken. It is held that one passage is literal and the conflicting one metaphorical, and that, so read, both may be true. We may still hold, as Aquinas did, that 'there can be no falsehood anywhere in the literal sense of Holy Scripture;'[12] if a passage appears to be false, we can say that the writer was stating a truth, but stating it rhetorically or figuratively.

Such interpretations are, without doubt, often sound. The Psalms and the Song of Solomon are, in the main, poetry, and to take them as chains of literal statements would be impossible for any serious student of literature. But the question is whether the method of metaphor can save the consistency of what appear to be statements of fact. It seems clear on reflection that it cannot.

(a) In the passages we have cited it would involve imposing on one or other of the conflicting texts a meaning to which neither the language nor its tone nor its context gives any support. If a writer says that the Lord is his shepherd, or his shield and buckler, or his high tower, or the shadow of a rock in a weary land, we know at once that he is speaking in metaphor, and may well recall that some of the most exquisite poetry in the language is to be found among these passages. But when the writer is recording historical facts such as the height of temple pillars or the number of years lived by the various patriarchs, it is not very plausible to say, when one of his facts is inaccurate, that he has suddenly abandoned the language of fact and is speaking metaphorically. He gives us no warning of such a change; there is nothing in his matter or manner to suggest it; indeed the suggestion is a purely ad hoc hypothesis with nothing to recommend it except the fact that it cannot be ruled out as a priori impossible.

(b) Furthermore, it has unfortunate consequences. If apparently plain statements of fact do not mean what they say, but something else that is veiled and remote, the Biblical writings in general must be read with uncertainty. In these writings are many thousands of statements, most of them quite incapable of being checked. Some of them we find in conflict with other Biblical statements, and where this happens, we say that one or other of the conflicting statements can at best be metaphorically true. But what of the thousands of other statements for which no check is practicable? Is it not more than likely that an indefinite number of these would similarly turn out to be metaphorical if such a check were open to us? The conclusion seems inevitable. But if accepted, it would spread suspicion over the entire body of the text. If what seems to be offered as the plainest statement of fact may not mean what it says, but something inscrutably different, how can we approach Scripture with any confidence at all? We cannot tell from the text whether what we are offered is fact or poetry.

The compromise of Vatican II

8 (c) The attempt to save Biblical inerrancy by metaphorical interpretation is thus self-defeating. It tends to be self-defeating also in a more important sense. The critic who uses it is committed to the attempt to get inside the mind of the writer, to catch the sort of meaning with which he uses his words; and success in such an endeavour is bound to carry him beyond the confines of Catholic or Protestant fundamentalism. The deliberations of the most recent Council provide an apt illustration.

Vatican Council II made a considered attempt to bring Catholic interpretation of the Bible into line with modern criticism. A protracted struggle between conservatives and liberals ended in a compromise that satisfied neither party. The struggle began in the first session with the presentation by Cardinal Ottaviani, one of the most conservative members of a conservative Curia, of the draft of a 'constitution on revelation' which set out the traditional position of the church. The bishops listened to more than a hundred speeches on this draft and then, by a vote of 1,368 to 822, rejected it and sent it back for rewriting. It was rewritten by a commission which was itself so divided that, some two years later, it submitted both a majority and a minority report. The Council debated these reports for five days through dozens of further speeches, and finally adopted a statement that was essentially a compromise.

In this statement the position of Trent and Vatican I was repeated, namely that the Bible was inspired and errorless, both in whole and in part. This inerrancy applied, of course, only to the Bible as interpreted by the church. But Catholic scholars were now encouraged to adopt a latitude in such interpretation that had not been allowed them before. In what did the new freedom consist? Chiefly in a permission to use certain techniques of literary and historical scholarship in determining what the Biblical writers meant. Interpreters of Scripture, 'in order to see clearly what God wanted to communicate to us, should carefully investigate what meaning the sacred writers really intended . . .'; and 'those who search out the intention of the sacred writers must, among other things, have regard for "literary forms" . . . due attention must be paid to the customary and characteristic styles of feeling, speaking and narrating which prevailed at the time. . . .'[13] It seems clear that the doctors were here recognising that the remarkable succession of German higher critics whose work has culminated in the 'form criticism' of recent years had something important to say.

Unfortunately the compromise achieved by the Council was that unstable sort of compromise that unites the two sides of a contradiction. There is no way of combining the inerrancy of Scripture with the application to it of modern critical scholarship. For what such scholarship reveals is that in the comparatively primitive times before any precise science or history had emerged the line between prose and poetry was loosely drawn. Is the book of Genesis a record of fact or an exercise in creative imagination? To us the difference is clear enough, and since we cannot take the account as history, we should take most of it, with little hesitation, as legendary. But to impute our own sharp distinction between history and legend to Hebrew chroniclers of twenty-five centuries ago is to saddle early minds with modern conceptions in a thoroughly unhistorical fashion. What exactly went on in the minds that produced Genesis and Exodus and Daniel we shall never know. What does seem certain is that in a time when critical history and science did not exist, imagination would be invoked in all innocence to fill the gap. Not that it would be invoked *as* mere imagination or poetic fancy; that again presupposes the firm modern distinction. It is absurd to suppose that the writers of Genesis, who supplied conflicting accounts of the creation, were either indulging in irresponsible rhapsodies or recording deliberate lies. They were reflecting, with limited resources of knowledge, on the origin of things, and saying, 'This is how it must have been'. For the details—the days and nights of creation, man's first parents, with their temptation and fall, the deliverance of the tables of the law on a mountain top—they used their imagination because that was all they had to use. But did they conceive of themselves as merely romancing? Assuredly not. They were giving the most faithful account they could of how the world and man and sin and law began. If we 'search out the intention of the sacred writers,' the dominant one is surely not far to seek. It was to tell the truth as they saw it.

If this was in fact the writers' intention, then the attitude prescribed to us by the Council is also clear. What the writers put forward as truth we must accept as truth. But here comes the difficulty for any fundamentalist, Catholic or Protestant. However simply and seriously it was believed by its authors, we now know that much of it is mythology. The grounds for this judgement will be more apparent when we come in a later chapter to study the nature and function of myth. But we shall not argue the matter here. We shall assume—with a near unanimity of theologically un-committed scholars—that Eden and the apple and the serpent were not historical facts, that the interview between Moses and his Deity through a thick smoke on Sinai never happened. If anyone believes that such things did happen, we shall leave him where he stands. The fact is, however, that many Catholic scholars are as ready as their non-Catholic colleagues to take these recitals as apocryphal. And then they are in trouble. They must manage to believe and disbelieve at the same time. If they follow their church, they must accept as truth what the sacred writers offered as truth, and then they will accept a vast mass of assertions which their modernised minds must reject unhesitatingly. If they follow the lead of their research, they will say that these recitals wear the marks of legend on their face, and then to accept them because their writers meant them as true becomes impossibly naive. The new freedom allowed to scholars by Vatican II thus turns out to be an ineligible kind of freedom, the freedom to contradict oneself. Scholars are at liberty to unearth the meanings or intentions of the sacred writers if only they will take them, however incredible, as altogether inerrant.

Thus the privilege of winnowing out metaphorical or poetic from literal statements gives less latitude than appears. The Catholic scholar resents being called a fundamentalist, and it is true that in sobriety of argument and cumulative intellectual resources he has the advantage of most Protestant fundamentalists. But to suppose that he is really at liberty to accept Freud on Moses, if he thinks the argument convincing, or Frazer on the Pentateuch, or Arnold on literature and dogma is to misunderstand his situation. On such excursions into rationalism his church has spoken formally and unequivocally, and it was beyond the power even of Vatican II to reverse the earlier judgements without undermining the church's authority. The present tension between the church and the 'demythologising' thought of Germany repeats at many points the tension with French 'modernism' early in the present century. That movement was led by the Abbé Loisy, who attempted to explain the Scriptural writings as historical and human products. It was crushed by Pius X in two encyclicals of 1907, *Lamentabili Sane Exitu* and *Pascendi Gregis*, which denounced it in general and in detail. Sixty-five doctrines attributed to it were enumerated for explicit condemnation. No Catholic scholar was permitted to undertake the examination of Scripture as if it were a 'merely human document', and the proposition that 'Divine inspiration is not to be so extended to the whole Sacred Scripture that it renders its parts, all and single, immune from error' was among the propositions condemned.[14] In 1902 Leo XIII had set up a Biblical Commission to advise him about permissible and impermissible interpretations of Scripture. Under the sweeping condemnations of the two encyclicals, the Commission was left very little latitude, and it has acted over the years with extreme caution; in 1909, for example, it pronounced that the first three chapters of Genesis were to be regarded as historical rather than legendary. What else, indeed, could it have done? *Roma locuta erat.* The Second Vatican Council was similarly chained to the authoritative pronouncements of the past.

Corruptions in the text

9(3)   Another obvious way to save the inerrancy of Scripture is to say of passages found erroneous that they are not parts of Scripture at all, but insertions by an unauthorised hand. It is clear that in some of the books that have come down to us as the work of certain authors there are parts done by others: Moses did not write the account of his own death; the book of Isaiah is plainly the product of at least two Isaiahs; the last twelve verses of Mark, by the almost universal admission of scholars, are not by Mark, even supposing Mark to have written the gospel attributed to him. Is there any possibility of preserving a consistent and inerrant Scripture by saying, where error appears, that it has been insinuated into the text by some uninspired and anonymous hand?

Unfortunately there is none. The effect of the church's ruling is that even if insertions have been made by foreign hands these insertions too must be held inerrant. *All* the books with *all* their parts as recognised at Trent must be accepted as true without defect.[15] In the early manuscripts of most reliable texts, the familiar ending of Mark does not occur at all; in some others it is reduced to a few lines; in one, there is a second long ending widely differing from the first. It happened that Jerome, in making his Vulgate translation, had before him a manuscript with the first long ending, now rejected by free scholars. It therefore appears in the Vulgate Bible, and since the content of that Bible was formally pronounced inerrant by a succession of popes, this extraneous appendage was itself inerrant. Whoever wrote it, and even if his appearance in the text was that of an interloper, he possessed, during that brief appearance, the privilege of speaking unqualified truth.[16]

This inerrancy of the Vulgate text did not mean, of course, the inerrancy of any meaning that the reader or even the scholar attached to it, but its inerrancy as interpreted by the church; and so guarded, the claim seemed safe enough. The Council of Trent could hardly have anticipated the curious way in which this claim was soon to be tested. Not long after the meeting of the famous Council, there appeared upon the Papal throne Sixtus V, who thought that Jerome's version was in need of revision and that he himself was uniquely qualified for the task. With a committee of advisers he set himself to the large work, reserving for his own pen the final correction of all readings. In 1590 he published his Sixtine edition with the announcement: 'By the fullness of apostolic power, we decree and declare that this edition, approved by the authority delivered to us by the Lord, is to be received and held as true, lawful, authentic, and unquestioned, in all public and private discussion, reading, preaching, and explanations.' Unfortunately, and to the embarrassment of the scholars whose judgement he had often and arbitrarily overruled, the edition that was to be ultimate was quickly seen to be full of errors; and when the unhappy man soon afterward died, these scholars made it plain to his successor that the edition would not do. The Vulgate was accordingly gone over once again, and a few years later a new version was issued by Clement VIII. Since Clement's version differed from that of Sixtus in more than two thousand places,[17] some explanation was necessary, and a preface was prepared by Cardinal Bellarmine, who sought to save the face of Sixtus by laying the 'imperfections' to the printer. But the fact was beyond concealment that Pope Sixtus had erred, not in words only but in interpretation, and many times over. What, then, was the status of the doctine that Scripture, officially interpreted, was inerrant? Both these editions had been backed by the explicit authority of the head of the church. If Sixtus was right in his way of construing Scripture, Clement must have been wrong; if Clement was right, Sixtus was wrong. One need not attempt the ungrateful business of deciding between them, for whichever was in the wrong, and one of them must have been, the official doctrine was no longer tenable.[18]

10   To modern Biblical scholars, eager to reach the fact behind the words and above all the towering, mist-enshrouded figure behind the New Testament, the dangers of being misled are not, of course, confined to interpolations in the text. There is a question in many cases whether the books themselves, either of the Old Testament or of the New, have been written by the authors whose names have been traditionally attached to them. It is certain, indeed, that Moses did not write the Pentateuch; there are too many recorded facts in it that belong to the period after his death. Scholars have found in it the work of at least four main authors, none of whom can be safely identified with Moses, since all alike record post-Mosaic events. Yet the church has never rescinded its official teaching that Moses was the author. Not only does the decree of an ecumenical council refer explicitly to the five books as those of Moses;[19] the twentieth-century Biblical Commission appointed by the Pope also supported the view. It conceded that Moses may have used secretaries to whom he dictated thoughts rather than words, but insisted that he was the 'principal and inspired author' of the Pentateuch and that it was 'conceived by him under the influence of Divine inspiration'. Catholic scholars became so restive under such direction that in a letter of 1948 to Cardinal Suhard of Paris the Commission wrote that it would not oppose 'further and truly scientific examination of these problems'. The *New Catholic Encyclopedia* of 1967 reports that current conclusions on these matters 'show few differences from those of respected non-Catholic scholars', adding the reassurance that 'most of the differences would not be on the confessional level'. What these 'confessional' differences are it does not say.[20]

As for the New Testament, there is perhaps no better attested result of scholarly work upon it than that the gospels of Matthew and Luke have drawn largely for their material on two prior sources, one of them the gospel of Mark, and the other a book that in its original form has disappeared.[21] Mark, therefore, must have preceded Matthew. The Commission, conscious that such criticism violated tradition, rejected both this theory of dependence and the implied sequence of authors. It held that the synoptic gospels were all written by the apostles whose names they bear, and in the familiar order. As for the Gospel of John, in spite of the controversies that have raged over it for a century, the Commission held that the apostle John was certainly its author and that the events and speeches it recorded, however different in content and tone from those of the synoptic gospels, were nevertheless all true.[22] There is happily little doubt that the life and teaching of Jesus can at least in broad outline be discerned by the comparative study of the gospels, though we may never know with certainty who wrote them, or what degree of credence to attach to their occasionally conflicting accounts. The Catholic can ride through these difficulties on a 'high priori road'. Once the church has officially spoken on a problem of this kind, no historical scholarship on the other side has any standing. As Cardinal Manning wrote:

'The appeal from the living voice of the Church to any tribunal whatsoever, human history included, is an act of private judgment and a treason, because that living voice is supreme; and to appeal from that supreme voice is also a heresy, because that voice, by divine assistance, is infallible.'[23]

The suggestion, then, that errors in an inerrant text may be removed by showing certain books or passages to be unauthentic is not adequate to its end. The church has cut off its own recourse to such an explanation by pronouncements which limit beforehand the results that it can accept. Indeed, drawn in two directions at once, it has manoeuvred itself into an untenable position. If it continues to maintain that all the books of the Old and New Testament, 'with all their parts,' are inerrant, it has on its hands a mass of inconsistencies both sides of which it is committed to accept. If it seeks to explain the inconsistencies away by admitting into the text unauthoritative books or passages, it has given up its main thesis, namely that the whole text is inspired, and inspired equally. The policy it has actually followed is one of unhappy compromise. It has presented itself to the world as at once the guardian of a body of revealed, consistent, and unchanging truth and also the patron of disinterested scholarship. The compromise will not bear examination. The inconsistencies can be removed only by an exegesis so violent as to throw the whole canon into uncertainty. And having committed itself before modern scholarship began to the acceptance of the entire Bible, Rome can grant its inquirers only a freedom so cramped and hedged that many of its ablest scholars have withdrawn or been excommunicated.[24]

The confinement of inerrancy to faith and morals

11(4) Sometimes a fourth method is proposed for dealing with apparent errors. It is suggested that the inerrancy of Scripture is limited in the same way as the church's infallibility, that it does not extend to the geology of Genesis or the precarious history of Chronicles, but invests only those statements that pronounce on faith or morals. There are many persons who would accept unperturbed an exposure of inconsistencies in reports about the height of pillars or in genealogical tables; they would say that they do not read the Bible for information on secular matters, but to gain instruction in the spiritual life. The book is not a textbook of science or history; it is primarily a revelation of the divine mind and will, and secondarily a treasury of suggestions on how to live. So long as its guidance on these vital matters is unimpeached, one may cavil about its science or history to one's heart's content.

12 Now, however appealing this view may be, it is not open to Catholics. The three great councils of modern times, one at Trent

and two at Rome, all insisted on the acceptance of the Biblical books
in toto, 'with all their parts'. Pope after modern Pope has taken the
same line, even more urgently and explicitly. When Leo XIII said,
'it is absolutely wrong and forbidden, either to narrow inspiration
to certain parts of Holy Scripture, or to admit that the sacred writer
has erred,'[25] he did not say 'erred in faith or morals'; he said
'erred' without qualification. Benedict XV, in *Spiritus Paraclitus*
(1920), affirmed as 'common to all the sacred writers, that they in
writing followed the Spirit of God, so that God is to be considered
the principal cause of the whole sense and of all the judgments of
Scripture'. Pius X in *Lamentabili Sane Exitu* (1907) condemned as
false the statement that 'since in the deposit of faith only revealed
truths are contained, under no respect does it appertain to the
Church to pass judgement concerning the assertions of human
sciences'. These popes were writing as heads of the church and
specifying what the faithful were to believe, and they were trying to
write unambiguously. Catholics who hesitate before the vast mass
of statements which the church compels them to take as errorless
have often attempted to wrest themselves free, but it is difficult to
see any valid line of escape. They may say that even if such pronouncements, since formally made on matters of faith, should be
accepted as inerrant, it is only the pronouncements themselves that
are inerrant, not the books that they pronounce inerrant. But this
is incoherent. If the statement that the books are inerrant is itself
infallibly true, then the books *are* inerrant; to admit that they were
not would be to impugn as false the statement that has just been
offered as true and infallibly true. Troubled Catholics may hold,
again, that the Papal pronouncements, though they concern matters
of faith and appear in official decrees, are not infallible in the full
and technical sense. Indeed this might be argued about any decree
ever issued; the Papacy is not accustomed to adding footnotes to its
decrees saying 'here infallibility begins' and 'here it ceases'. But I
do not suppose there is a bishop in the Catholic world who would
not take such encyclicals as those just cited as binding on all the
faithful. And in the light of them, the Catholic is not at liberty to
believe that Biblical inerrancy extends to faith and morals only.

13 Suppose, however, that he made out a case to his own satisfaction that it was so confined; would he be intellectually in the
clear? He need then no longer feel that his faith was threatened if
he uncovered misstatements about ancient pillars or half-legendary
kings. But he would still be mistaken if he thought that, having
contracted the compass of inerrancy, he would be left with consistency within the narrower pale. For the plain fact is, unpalatable

as it may be to both Catholic and fundamentalist Protestant, that
the Scripture does not present, and does not claim to present, a
body of consistent teaching even in faith and morals. We do no
service to the Bible by making claims for it that it would not make for
itself. Enough can be said about the great book to make this sort of
defence needless. There are many notes, indeed, of thanks and
praise that we can sound in all sincerity about the Bible. It has been
a great storehouse of materials on which men have drawn through the
centuries to express their aspiration, worship, prayer, and self-
admonition. It is replete with beauty. It is a mirror of the interior
life of a religiously gifted people. Its tales and allegories, its psalms,
its parables, its meditations on good and evil, the profound seriousness with which it takes the moral life, the set of priceless biographies
in which it has sketched the most influential single life that has yet
been lived—these things and many more give it a unique position
among the books of the world. One thing it is not. It is not a
magazine of *veritates delapsae*, of equally errorless truths dropped
down on us from heaven.

Take a single important example which will serve for the fields
of both faith and morals, the character attributed to Deity. On this
matter liberal scholars would agree that we have in the Bible the
record of a long, slow advance, both religious and moral, from
something like primitive savagery to the Sermon on the Mount, an
advance which gives colour to Feuerbach's thesis that man has
created and re-created God in his own evolving image. If one takes
the discrepant ideas of God in the Old and New Testaments as
reflecting the changes in man's own conception of goodness, his
evolving theologies fall into place along the line of ascent. But if one
'accepts and venerates', with the Roman church, 'all the books of the
Old and New Testaments, since one God is the author of both, with
equal piety and reverence,'[26] one is committed to chaos. The point
is too important to be dealt with in an evasive way. The fact cannot
be blinked that at the lower end of the Biblical scale is a God who is
described as doing things that would strain the standards of a Nazi
prison camp. He orders Saul, in attacking Amalek, to 'slay both
man and woman, child and suckling';[27] he kills thousands in a
pestilence;[28] he commands in the case of a wrongdoer that 'thou
shalt not pity him, but shalt require life for life, eye for eye, tooth
for tooth';[29] he approves slavery;[30] he takes as a 'man after God's
own heart' a king whom it is impossible to acquit of lying, adultery,
treachery, and murder. At the other end of the scale, in the New
Testament, he is represented as a being of infinite tenderness who is
concerned over the fall of a sparrow, who asks that we forgive
seventy times seven, who disapproves not only of violence and

adultery but of the harbouring of anger and lust in the secret places of the heart. 'Look upon this picture and upon this,' and then recall the official injunction to accept all parts of the Biblical record as errorless and equally to be venerated. Is it an injunction that can be obeyed?

The inconsistency of the position may be brought out in another way. If there is any part of the Bible to which the Catholic would be inclined to attach pre-eminent authority, it would be the recorded words of Jesus himself. But it is clear that Jesus himself did not accept the view of the Old Testament writings which the church regards as mandatory. Their prescriptions were repeatedly cited to him as a challenge, and repeatedly he set them aside when he conceived that they stood in the way of his gospel of love and forgiveness. 'Ye have heard it said by them of old time, *but* I say unto you . . .'. If the church takes such sayings with their obvious meaning, it faces a curious alternative. It may recognise that the attitude of its founder conflicts with its own, and in deference to his authority abandon its doctrine that all parts of Scripture are to be revered and accepted equally. Or, taking as its base its own account of what is essential to Christianity, it may conclude that the founder of Christianity was not himself a Christian. This line has sometimes been taken, but it is plainly not open to a Catholic. Indeed the church, at whatever cost of consistency, has flatly rejected both horns. 31

THE PARADOX OF A VEILED REVELATION

14 Suppose, however, that a consistent body of Scriptural teaching were at last achieved. Suppose that by identifying some passages as quotations merely, others as metaphorical, others as interpolations, by contracting the scope of revelation to faith and morals, and by using adroitly the extensive armoury of Catholic apologetics, we could put together the pieces of the vast picture puzzle, collected from many places and many centuries, into some sort of unified whole; what then? Looking at this effort in the large, we could see that we should still be committed to a strange and improbable hypothesis. For our hypothesis would then be that a Deity who desired to communicate the truth to his creatures, and who possessed all the means of doing so, chose to bury that truth beneath such layers of obscurity, ambiguity, and apparent contradiction as to baffle nearly everybody. One cannot refute that theory, because it will absorb every new difficulty placed in its way as just another obstacle planted there by Deity for reasons that are in the end beyond us. It is like the scientific theory held by Edmund Gosse's father, who was a geologist of some repute, though a fundamentalist in religion and an opponent of evolution. When there came to light in deep-lying strata fossils that must have been deposited there before the date when on his reckoning the world was created, he explained them by suggesting that they had been placed there by the Creator to puzzle us, deceive us if deceivable, and so test our faith. Such a theory cannot be disproved, for it is consistent with any evidence that might be adduced against it, but for that very reason also it carries no conviction. Furthermore, a theology of this kind seems really self-defeating. For if God were what it implies that he is, if he were the kind of being who, able to vouchsafe a saving revelation to all mankind, reserved it for a small minority even of those then living, a being who, by granting it at a late stage of life on earth, cut off from it the earlier millions who might have been illumined by it, and even then chose to hide much of it under deceptive veils from those anxious to understand it, he must have a character different from that which in human beings we call good. A theology that offers itself as rational should not drive us into irrationality on the cardinal point of God's goodness.

THE DOCTRINE OF INFALLIBILITY

15 We have seen, however, that the ultimate authority for the Catholic is not Scripture but the church, since Scripture itself is accepted as inerrant only as interpreted by the church. No doubt in the Bible as it appears to the groping individual reader, or even to the accomplished scholar, there are antinomies hard to solve, but if the church assures him that they are soluble, he need ask no more. And the church does so assure him. It goes further. It assures him that regarding not only the Bible, but faith and morals generally, the church speaks infallibly. Its voice is inspired by Deity, and to suppose that Deity can err, or speak with discordant voices, is impious. Once the church has officially spoken on such issues, its pronouncement becomes part of the body of supernaturally guaranteed truth, and one knows that no similar pronouncement that has preceded it or will ever follow can place its truth in jeopardy.

But when does the church speak infallibly? The answer just given—'when it speaks officially'—must be made more precise. In earlier times Catholics believed that the most clearly official pronouncements of the church were those of the general councils, of which there have been twenty-one reaching from Nicaea in 325 to Rome in 1962. The Vatican Council of 1870 laid it down, however, that this view was incorrect, and that infallibility was reserved for the Pope alone. The Council decreed it to be 'a dogma divinely revealed: that the Roman pontiff, when he speaks *ex cathedra*, that is, when, in discharge of the office of pastor and teacher of all Christians, by virtue of his supreme Apostolic authority, he defines a doctrine regarding faith or morals to be held by the universal Church, is, by the divine assistance promised to him in Blessed Peter, possessed of that infallibility with which the divine Redeemer willed that His Church should be endowed in defining doctrine regarding faith or morals; and that, therefore, such definitions of the Roman pontiff are of themselves, and not from the consent of the Church, irreformable.'[32]

This is still not wholly definite. For when is the Pope speaking ex cathedra? An enormous number of documents issue from his office, many of them carrying comments on faith and morals; are all these comments infallible? No. Only statements formally issued to the church are so regarded. But then these formally issued statements are themselves of many kinds. That the decisions of general councils when formally underwritten or promulgated by the Pope are to be taken as infallible seems clear; and it is clear also that 'papal constitutions', used for formal pronouncements regarding heresy or discipline, must be accounted infallible. But are bulls infallible—the documents used to appoint dignitaries, erect dioceses, and canonise saints? Are encyclicals infallible—the letters circulated by the Pope, as occasion demands, by way of warning, exhortation, or the inculcation of true doctrine? Both these types of pronouncement are to be regarded, we are told, with 'infinite respect', but the precise conditions under which they, or their parts, are to be held free from error are still debated by the doctors.

This raises obvious difficulties in interpreting decrees of the far past. The doctrine of infallibility was neither promulgated nor generally accepted till 1870, and how is one to determine the precise degree of authority with which Pope Gelasius announced in 493 that unbaptised children could not go to heaven or Pope Innocent VIII in 1484 forbade intercourse with incubuses and succubuses? The difficulty is increased by the fact that for centuries the Pope was not regarded as infallible, even by the general councils of the church; Pope Honorious (625–638), for example, was anathematised as himself a heretic by the sixth general council at Constantinople (680–681); the acts of this council were confirmed by another Pope, Leo II (682–683), who expressly supported the condemnation of his predecessor, and was himself supported in turn by the decree of the seventh general council, the Second Council of Nicaea (787).[33] When general councils could thus reject Papal statements of doctrine as heretical, it is hardly likely that the popes regarded their own statements as infallible, or put them forth as such. This uncertainty gives the Catholic apologist a useful latitude in argument. For it enables him to hold, when an error or contradiction is pointed out in a Papal pronouncement, that in applying the decree of infallibility retroactively one cannot be sure that the erroneous pronouncement fully complied with the conditions of infallibility, indeed that if the statement is erroneous, then the Pope *could* not have made it officially.

I do not doubt that this argument may be offered in good faith. And it may be thought to rule out beforehand any possible criticism of the claim to infallibility, since every allegation of error can be met by an ad hoc allegation, now irrefutable, that it was not offered in a statement perfectly accredited as ex cathedra. Still, discussion may not be wholly futile. Catholics do prize reason and reasonableness, and they must feel some disquiet over this kind of argumentation. They would no doubt agree that there must be *some* set of conditions under which the head of the church is speaking with full authority. They would agree further, I think, that the most natural interpretation of the Vatican decree is something like this: that the Pope is speaking ex cathedra when, acting as Pope, and not as a private person, he issues a statement on faith or morals, again not *to* a private person but to the church in general. If this is a fair interpretation, we may confront it with a fair question: have Papal pronouncements of this kind been uniformly free from error?

INCONSISTENCY IN PAPAL PRONOUNCEMENTS

16 Statements regarding faith or morals are notoriously difficult to prove or disprove, and a critic of any caution will be slow to embroil himself in controversy over transubstantiation or the efficacy of baptism. Such controversy would be idle in any case, since the church considers that the truth in these matters is inaccessible to human reason, and can be attained only by faith. If the Pope has spoken on them, therefore, *causa finita est*, the case is closed, and no argument on the other side could have the slightest weight. Yet reason is not as impotent here as it may seem. For the Catholic does hold that though reason cannot unaided make out all the truths of revelation, it may rightly insist on one thing: it may require that if a truth is beyond error it should not be contradicted by another truth also beyond error. We may therefore ask regarding Papal, as we did before regarding Biblical, pronouncements whether there are inconsistencies among them. To which the answer is that such inconsistencies exist in profusion. We shall confine ourselves to those of one Pope.[34]

In the sixth century the church was divided by the monophysite controversy, in which one group maintained that the divine and human natures in Christ were eternally one, and the other, the Nestorians, denied this. Pope Vigilius was exposed to pressure from both parties. The fourth ecumenical council (Chalcedon, 451) had put itself on record as recognising the orthodoxy of three leaders of the Nestorians. This placed the Pope in a difficult position. Empress Theodora was a strong monophysite, and he owed to her his election; the Emperor Justinian likewise felt the action of the council in approving the Nestorians to be unfortunate, and was eager to have it annulled. At the same time, this action was that of an ecumenical council and was not to be set aside lightly. What was the Pope to do? What he did in fact was to declare himself, reverse himself, and then re-reverse himself. In 540 he declared his approval of what the Council of Chalcedon had decreed, including its anti-monophysite stand. In 544, in a letter to the empress, he declared that he was a monophysite himself, though this profession, as made to a mere individual, albeit an empress, was perhaps less than official. Later in the year, when the emperor issued an edict condemning the stand of Chalcedon, and invited him to support it, he adhered to his first view and refused. In the next year, however, together with a number of other bishops assembled at Constantinople, he signed a formal document, named *Judicatum, condemning* the action of Chalcedon. Notwithstanding this condemnation, when Justinian, in 551, issued an edict also condemning the action, Vigilius refused to subscribe to it; and in 553 when the fifth ecumenical council at Constantinople supported the stand of the emperor and denounced that of the preceding council, Vigilius again refused to do likewise, even at the bidding of a general council. In 554 he changed sides once again; 'he addressed to Eutychius, patriarch of Constantinople, a formal retractation, declaring that he has been the instrument of Satanic delusion, but that now, delivered by Christ from all confusion of mind, he subscribes to the anathema he had so often resisted. Whether it was the function of his infallibility to discover his delusion, or of his delusion to be sure of his infallibility at last, the sequel does not help us to determine . . . he died on his journey back to Rome.'35 How can it be denied that in formally endorsing and condemning the action of a general council the Pope meant to speak officially on a matter of faith? How can it be denied that what he said officially is self-contradictory? Which of his contradictory statements is the authoritative one? In whatever way this question is answered by official apologists, there is surely another hypothesis open to us that seems to accord well with the facts: namely that a perplexed and honest man, charged with a hard official decision and torn between contending factions, changed his mind.

17 This case has a special interest. Before infallibility was made official in 1870, there were many Catholics who did not accept it, as there are no doubt many who in their hearts do not accept it still. Such persons may feel that in concentrating the wisdom of the church in one person too much treasure is entrusted to one frail basket, and that the voice of the church should have been found not in that of the Bishop of Rome but in that of the ecumenical councils. It may be thought that great bodies of this sort will evince a stable judgement for which a claim to infallibility may be far more credibly urged than for an individual. It is worth noting, therefore, that even this claim cannot be sustained. We have just seen that the Council of Constantinople expressly rejected, as heterodox, teachers whom the Council of Chalcedon expressly accepted as orthodox. Again, the Council of Constance, 1414–18, pronounced a general council to be higher in authority than the Pope; the Fifth Lateran Council, 1512–17, reversed this judgement by declaring the Pope to be higher in authority than a council, and incidentally abrogated the canons of another council, that of Pisa of 1409.[36] The case of Vigilius, which we have cited, is interesting in another way. It may be wondered whether, even though popes have contradicted themselves and each other, and councils have contradicted other councils, popes and councils have ever formally disagreed. The answer is that they have. Vigilius, as we have just seen, repudiated Chalcedon, and this is far from being a lonely instance. To cite but one other: 'Innocent I and Gelasius I, the former writing to the Council of Milevis, the latter in his epistle to the Bishops of Picenum, declared it to be so indispensable for infants to receive communion, that those who die without it go straight to hell. A thousand years later the Council of Trent anathematized this doctrine.'[37]

It will be recalled that the first of the three theses of Catholicism that we set out to examine was that in revelation there is nothing irrational; the truths of revelation, though not now fully intelligible to us, present a body of doctrine that is at the least consistent with itself. We have examined this doctrine, and have seen that whether revelation is viewed as coming through Scripture or through the authoritative pronouncements of the church, the doctrine cannot be sustained. We shall turn in the next chapter to the second of the three theses.

CHAPTER III

CATHOLIC TEACHING ON REVELA-
TION AND NATURAL KNOWLEDGE

1 We set out to examine three theses held by the Catholic church regarding the relation of reason and faith: first, that there was no disharmony between revelation and reason as such; second, that there was no disharmony between revelation and natural knowledge; third, that the credibility of revelation, as traditionally accepted by the church, can be established by argument. The first thesis we have found it necessary to dismiss as untenable. We turn now to the second.

'Nulla tamen inquam inter fidem et rationem vera dissensio esse potest';[1] there can be no true disagreement between faith and reason. Professor Gilson, perhaps the most competent of recent apologists, writes: 'it is necessary to adhere firmly to the principle that, since truth cannot be divided against itself, reason cannot be rational if it is opposed to faith.'[2] A standard manual on church teaching tells us: 'If a truth is certainly revealed by God—and that, through the infallible teaching of the Church, he [the theologian] can always ascertain—then any human conclusion or hypothesis, whether it be philosophical, historical, or scientific, which contradicts it, is most certainly erroneous.'[3] But on an issue of such importance it is well to have the highest authority, and here Leo XIII speaks with the same voice as Augustine and the Vatican councils. Concerning possible disputes between the theologian and the scientist, Leo wrote in *Providentissimus Deus*:

'If discussion should arise between them, here is the rule also laid down by St Augustine for the theologian:—"Whatsoever they can really demonstrate to be true of physical nature, we must show to be capable of reconciliation with our Scriptures; and whatsoever they assert in their treatises which is contrary to these Scriptures of ours, that is, Catholic faith, we must either prove it as well as we can to be entirely false, or at all events we must, without the slightest hesitation, believe it to be so." '

'Between faith and reason there can be no conflict'! One wonders, then, what conflict it was of which President White of Cornell wrote the history in his massive *Warfare of Science with Theology*. One wonders what the conflict was that filled the nineteenth century with its noisy reverberations. Of course, if one cares to, one can prove by mere definition that no such conflict is possible. One can say that whatever doctrine contradicts church teaching is not true, and therefore not science; hence no conflict. Or one can say that whenever the church ventures to pronounce on a scientific issue it is going outside its province and saying what is no part of faith; hence again no conflict. Anyone who regards this as a solution of the problem is welcome to it. But the issue we are interested in is not a verbal one. It is this: whether what is offered us by the church as revealed, and therefore certainly true, does in fact conflict at any point with what scientific specialists, working in the appropriate field, would hold to be established by the evidence. Let us look at a few of these fields.

REVELATION AND ASTRONOMY

2 First, astronomy. Here a name that springs to mind at once is that of Galileo. His famous case is somewhat threadbare now, but it remains important both in history and in theory. The essential facts are as follows. (1) On 26 February 1616, Galileo was commanded 'in the name of His Holiness the Pope and the whole congregation of the Holy Office' to abandon the view that the earth moves. (2) On 5 March of that year the congregation of the Index, at the instigation of Pope Paul V, condemned 'that false Pythagorean doctrine, wholly opposed to sacred scripture, which Nicholas Copernicus [and others] teach as to the mobility of the earth and the immobility of the sun'.[4] (3) 1633, at the urgent desire of Pope Urban VIII, Galileo was brought before the inquisition, and under threat of severe punishment, compelled to recant 'the error and heresy of the movement of the earth'. (4) This condemnation was inscribed in the Index, to which in 1664, a third Pope, Alexander VIII, prefixed a bull *Speculatores Domus Israel*, signed by himself and binding the proscriptions of the book on all good Catholics. In this bull he condemned 'all books teaching the movement of the earth and the stability of the sun'. (5) In 1835 this condemnation was at last and silently removed.[5]

Here is a clear case in which the church, speaking officially, took one view, and science, speaking through the voice of the greatest living scientist, took an opposite one. For centuries Catholic apologists have been trying to explain this opposition away. They have suggested that Galileo was condemned not for his science but for his contumacy and disrespect. They have said that he was condemned not for his astronomy but for an attempt to interpret Scripture as according with his astronomy. They have said that God may have seen fit to test our faith with Scriptural texts difficult of interpretation. Cardinal Newman admitted the conflict, but threw up his hands about it. 'Scripture . . . says that the sun moves and the earth is stationary; and science, that the earth moves, and the sun is comparatively at rest. How can we determine which of these opposite statements is the very truth, till we know what motion is?'[6] He would no doubt have welcomed Einstein as showing that if one body is moving relatively to another there is a sense in which it is arbitrary which we take as at rest. Even so, Newman might have had trouble in fitting into his moral and astronomical system the sun that stood still for a day over Gibeon, neither body moving relatively to the other. The chief recourse, however, has been to the familiar contention that in condemning Galileo the church did not act in a fully official way.

3 It is not a very convincing defence. In the congregation of the Holy Office that condemned his teaching, Pope Paul himself was apparently present, and the demand for abjuration, made through Cardinal Bellarmine, was made expressly in the Pope's name; the congregation of the Index, which also condemned the view, was commissioned by the same Pope to inquire into the doctrine, and again its verdict was issued with his approval; the sentence of the inquisition in 1633 was sent by a second Pope, Urban, to all Apostolic nuncios 'to the end that so pernicious a doctrine' might 'spread no further'; a third Pope, Alexander, republished the decrees in a book which he 'confirmed and approved' both 'as a whole and in its parts'. The spectacle of a powerful organisation threatening and imprisoning a scientist of the first rank, compelling him to recant, denouncing his teaching throughout Europe as heretical, suppressing books that contained it, excluding it from the schools, and then, when it was proved beyond question to be true, maintaining that the three popes had never meant, in condemning it, to condemn it quite authoritatively is not a pleasant passage in the history of apologetics.

Suppose, however, that this extenuation is accepted; where does that leave the church in its relation with astronomy? Unhappily, in an awkward position still. For whether Paul and Urban and Alexander were speaking infallibly or not, their denial of the earth's motion was either true or untrue. Assume that it was true and that Galileo was really wrong. A major thesis of modern science never stands alone. This thesis about the motion of the earth has implications for the whole of astronomy and indeed the whole of scientific method. If, in spite of the thousands of observations and calculations that have verified the theory, the earth does not rotate on its axis or revolve round the sun, then not only will the map of the universe have to be redrawn, but the very method of gaining truth by observation must be rejected as unreliable; and if reason is as unreliable as this, its use in theology itself must be suspect.

Suppose on the other hand that the condemnation was mistaken and that Galileo was right. Then the church must admit not only that the head of the church and his most responsible official advisers may make grave mistakes about matters they expressly designate as matters of faith; it must also admit that the plain sense of Scripture may be in error. For even if Paul, Urban, and Alexander were mistaken in denying the motion of the earth and the fixity of the sun, they were still surely correct in saying that both doctrines are repeatedly denied in Scripture. 'He hath made the round world so fast that it cannot be moved'; that denies the first. The sun 'runneth about from one end of the heavens to the other'; that denies the second; and if these are taken as metaphorical, the sun's halting its motion over Gibeon was certainly no metaphor. Now to admit that Galileo was right would be to admit that such passages were not true. But this would imply that Scripture was untrustworthy, and that would be disaster, since the church has pronounced infallibly that it is inerrant.

Rome has never extricated itself from this dilemma. What it has actually done is to adhere to its principle that the Bible is inerrant, while at the same time dropping its case against modern astronomy. That solves nothing in theory. The Biblical passages are still there, and they still mean what the three popes thought they did. And the earth still moves, as Galileo continued to mutter. The course of the rationalist in this difficulty is straightforward; he says that the Biblical writers were human beings who wrote according to their lights but, knowing little astronomy, made perfectly natural mistakes; further, that to set up their groping opinions as a tribunal by which to judge professional astronomers is to invert the true order of things. The Catholic cannot take this view without sacrilege. As a son of the church, he must bow to an inerrant Scripture. As a citizen of the modern world, he must accept the findings of astronomy. And he is deluding himself if he thinks that he can consistently do both.[7]

Vatican II was not allowed to forget Galileo. Bishop Eichinger of Strasbourg, after reminding his colleagues of the intellectual deficiencies commonly charged to the church's account—limitation of intellectual interest, an assumption that faith, in virtue of its certainty, could extend that certainty to other fields, 'a morbid fear of rationalism and the critical spirit'—went on to say:

'The case of Galileo remains a symbol of all these deficiencies in the history of modern times. Let it not be said too quickly that it is part of ancient history. The condemnation of this man has never been revoked. . . . It would be an eloquent gesture if the Church, during this year [1964] which marks the fourth centenary of Galileo's birth, would humbly agree to rehabilitate him.'[8]

The rehabilitation did not come. How indeed could it come without compromising the teaching authority of the church? To rehabilitate Galileo would be to admit that he was right. If he was right, three popes were wrong, not merely on an issue of fact, but on an issue of faith. For either they had misinterpreted to their flock the meaning of Scripture or, if their interpretation was correct, Scripture itself was in error.

REVELATION AND BIOLOGY

4   Turn next to biology. The main generalisation of modern biology is, of course, the theory of evolution. No living biologist of any standing would deny this theory. There are differences about the detail of the process, but there is no difference, I take it, about Darwin's main contention that man's appearance on earth has been a long, slow emergence from animal forms of life, and that these forms have themselves emerged from others still more remote. Is a Roman Catholic free to accept this theory?

It is instructive to consult Catholic manuals on this point. These assure us that the Catholic scientist is at liberty to accept anything that is true. What exactly do such assurances mean? Do they mean that he is free to accept any theory which the evidence before him requires? Or do they mean that in some areas of his inquiry the church is already in possession of the truth, so that regardless of the evidence he may unearth, his conclusions are determined for him in advance? That the position of the church is the latter, not the former, will be evident from an example or two.

The theory of evolution is a theory not only of physical but also of mental evolution. The affinities of animal with human intelligence and the levels of intelligence within the animal world have been studied illuminatingly by Romanes, Lubbock, Hobhouse, Yerkes, Lashley, Köhler, and many more. The Catholic scientist, in approaching these studies, is met by such absolute prohibitions as the following, transcribed from *The Teaching of the Catholic Church*:

'For a Catholic there can be no question and no debate about the hypothesis or even the possibility of the development of Adam's spiritual soul from the non-spiritual animating principle or soul of any brute, however highly advanced in the scale of animal perfection. The theory of evolution taken universally, as embracing the development of the first man's soul from some non-human faculty of one of the higher animals, is out of court for the Catholic. . . .'[9]

It may be said that while a Catholic cannot believe in the evolution of the soul he can still believe in the evolution of the mind. This is not, I think, logically possible. In the manual just quoted, it is said of the 'soul or mind' (the two terms being used as synonyms) that 'its existence and other powers, such as reasoning and volition,' are 'inseparable from its essence';[10] to be a soul is to have certain powers and functions; its character lies in its activities of thinking, feeling, and willing. To deny that the soul evolves is to deny that its powers and functions evolve, and to deny this is to deny that mind evolves. Thus the Catholic is cut off from the belief in evolution in the full sense in which biologists generally accept it.

What alternative to the biologist's view is open to the Catholic scientist? His theory must be (1) that all men have descended from a single pair of progenitors, Adam and Eve, (2) that man's spiritual faculties, instead of evolving with his body, were attached by God to his body at some point in the past, and (3) that God similarly attaches the soul to each man's body at some point in his pre-natal growth. The first point was made clear by Pius XII in his *Humani Generis* of 1950.

'For Christ's faithful cannot embrace that opinion which maintains either that after Adam there existed on this earth true men who did not take their origin through natural generation from him as from the first parent of all, or that Adam represents a certain number of first parents; since it is in no way apparent how such an opinion can be reconciled with that which the sources of revealed truth and the documents of the teaching authority of the Church propose with regard to original sin, which proceeds from a sin actually committed by an individual Adam and which through generation is passed on to all and is in everyone as his own.'

On the second point, the special creation of the soul, one gains useful light from the account of evolution given in the *New Catholic Encyclopedia* of 1967.

'Man's capacity for culture . . . must be, at root, spiritual. This spiritual capacity cannot have its origins in primate potentialities or in a purely material substrate. The human spirit must have its origin in the immediate creative act of God' (V, 682). 'When the hominid body was so disposed by the natural processes governing the rest of primate development, God created and infused the spirit of man, elevating what was formerly a hominid to the stature of a new, distinct, and unique species' (ibid., 683).

As for the third point, the acquisition of a soul by each individual body, we are informed that God waits until the foetus achieves 'human organs for the organic faculties, the operation of which are indispensable for the exercise of reason'. This is believed to be about the end of the third month after conception. 'It is likely that human animation takes place at this time' (ibid., 684).

In early editions of the *Encyclopedia*, even bodily evolution was rejected; 'there is no evidence in favour of an ascending evolution of organic forms (V, 670). It is clear that the Catholic views on evolution have been slowly adjusting themselves to modern biology. But even in the pronouncement which many Catholics regard as a charter of freedom, Pius XII's *Humani Generis*, two requirements of belief are laid down for the biologist on theological grounds: evolution does not apply to man's higher faculties, and since we have all inherited original sin from Adam, we must all have descended from Adam. I do not propose to discuss this theological biology, nor is it easy to see how any scientific inquiry could either prove or disprove it. It belongs to a theology that rests not on science but on the church's interpretation of Scripture, and its credibility turns on whether the church's authority is decisive. On that we shall have more to say.

The Catholic biologist has certainly attained more freedom than he had at the beginning of the century. But how free is he? The position that Genesis is inerrant is still required of him; it was laid down at Trent and Vatican I by the church's highest authority; and the Pope's Biblical Commission has insisted that Genesis must be taken as history, not as legend or allegory. It uneasily added, however, that one is not bound to seek in it for scientific exactitude of expression; and in spite of its insistence on historicity and inerrancy, the church has decided that 'days' mean 'moments or impulses of God's creative activity rather than any definite periods of time'. We are informed that 'With this interpretation, all the objections brought against the Mosaic account of creation from the physical sciences collapse'.[11] This seems over-sanguine. What about the order in which the various creatures were created? In Genesis light is created on the first day, but the sources of light, namely the sun, moon, and stars, do not appear till the fourth; on the fifth day fish and birds make their entrance, and on the sixth day reptiles, though biologists know, from the record of the rocks, that reptiles came before birds and fish, not after them. It is evident that a large licence must be granted if inerrancy is to be preserved. The following passage suggests what this is:

'When it happened that the inspired writer had, incidentally, to touch upon such matters to enforce or illustrate his teaching, to set it in a framework that should make a deeper impression upon his readers, or for some similar reason, he adapted himself to the level of their intelligence, he conformed his phraseology to their common opinions, he took over their current modes of expression.'[12]

This seems to mean that although the writer, as inspired and inerrant, knew the truth about these matters, he deliberately used language that would convey a false impression to his readers. At times, moreover, he used this deceptive language when there was no point in the deception; there was surely no reason why, if he knew that reptiles preceded fishes, he should have reversed the order of their appearance. This is one of the many places where the Roman church has been caught between the claims of science and of a mythology pronounced inerrant. It can hardly afford to denounce science. It cannot without self-stultification abandon an authoritative pronouncement about an errorless book. So it resorts to the expedient of saying that writers who were presumably in command of the truth set down for no evident reasons statements that they knew would induce false beliefs.

5   It may be said that this elastic exegesis itself gives freedom of movement to the Catholic evolutionist. If he establishes his theories by the evidence, the church will find some way of showing that Genesis never intended to say anything inconsistent with them. As evidence piled up, for example, against the theory of special creation, Catholic scholars began to find the term 'special creation' ambiguous, and held that it may not after all exclude the theory 'that God took one of the higher animals and, by infusing into it a human soul, made it a man'. To be sure, the biologist who adopts this view is yielding unduly to evolutionist pressure, but he can accept it without formal condemnation. Still, if he does, he is at the danger line. He will clearly be passing that line if he questions that Adam and Eve were historical personages, that Adam was made first, or that Eve was made out of Adam.[13] Nor can he hold, whatever the evidence, that the race had more than one set of parents.[14]

Is this scientific freedom? Not if freedom means the privilege of following the evidence in whatever direction it may lead. The demand made on modern science that it should adjust its findings to chronicles twenty-five centuries old, innocent of scientific methods or historical standards, is not notably reasonable to begin with, and those Catholics who have attained distinction in biology —they are not many—have keenly felt the strain. The able biologist St George Mivart, who was a president of the British Association, did remain in the church for many years, but he rebelled increasingly against its restrictions and was excommunicated a few weeks before his death. There are other kinds of pressure, however, than the threat of formal excommunication. There is the refusal of the right to publish, which kept the work on evolution of Teilhard de Chardin out of print as long as he lived. The intellectual atmosphere in which Catholic scientists have been supposed to live is suggested by such statements as the following from the officially approved work I have several times quoted, *The Teaching of the Catholic Church*. It says about evolution: 'if we take it as covering all forms of animal life and so embracing the origin of the human body, the positive evidence in favour of it is, at present, so slight and feeble as to be negligible' (I, 208). Of course many fundamentalist Protestant theologians have taken the same line. But they have not had the support of a hierarchy that could claim ultimacy and unchangeableness for its teaching. It is not surprising that Catholic biologists should have conspicuously dragged their feet.[15]

REVELATION AND PSYCHOLOGY

6 If we may take one more field, consider the attitude to which the church has committed itself toward modern psychology. With the vast increase in our knowledge of the subconscious and of the multiple forms of mental pathology, the old belief in witchcraft and demon-possession seems like sheer superstition. Most educated Catholics would perhaps agree. It is worth reminding them, therefore, that they are committed in no uncertain terms to both these beliefs by repeated and formal Papal pronouncements which, as dealing with matters of faith, must be deemed authoritative. The church did not fail to note that mandate in Exodus, divinely inspired, 'Thou shalt not suffer a witch to live,' and since witchcraft involved deliberate dealing with the Devil, it was in the eyes of the church a most serious offence. In his bull, *Summis Desiderantes* of 1484, Innocent VIII noted that witches were swarming through Germany and that they revelled in the blackest of crimes;[16] he decreed therefore that they be rooted out. Julius II in 1504 and Adrian VI in 1523 followed with similar bulls. Regarding witchcraft, says Lecky, 'the Church of Rome proclaimed in every way that was in her power the reality and the continued existence of the crime. . . . She taught by all her organs that to spare a witch was a direct insult to the Almighty.'[17] The Devil and his angels and minions were officially accepted elements of Catholic faith. Aquinas had no doubt about them; he considered that storms and diseases were often the work of the Devil, who could transport witches through the air and transform human beings into animal shapes; and as for demons, they were so earthily real as to be able to have carnal intercourse with witches. Four centuries later the eloquent Bossuet was declaring that 'a single devil could turn the earth round as easily as we turn a marble'. These beliefs would have mattered less if they had not been accompanied by a sense of religious duty to exterminate the crime of witchcraft. Countless miserable old women were submitted to protracted and pitiless torture before the stake gave them release.

Why recite these 'old unhappy far-off things'? Could not an equally severe indictment be made of modern Protestantism? The answer would seem to be No. Protestant sects have their own superstitions, but they have often changed articles of their creeds, or abandoned them and ceased to be. The creed of the Catholic church is offered as unchangeable truth. (Not that it has in fact remained the same, as we shall see, but it is bound to maintain that it has.) Once an element has been included in the deposit of faith, it is there to stay. Hence the church, having taken its stand in a succession of authoritative pronouncements from its head, declaring the existence of devil, demons, and witches an integral part of the faith, can only believe in them still. And it does. If the reader doubts where it stands, let him turn to the articles, 'Devil', 'Demoniacs', 'Demonology', and 'Witchcraft' in the *Catholic Encyclopedia*. In all of them he will find, along with enough anthropological discussion to make it clear that the writer is very, very sophisticated, the central unmistakable fact: the church accepts all these things.

Indeed the devil has occupied a conspicuous part in the recent thought of Pope Paul VI. On 17 December 1972, the Vatican newspaper *L'Osservatore Romano* devoted fourteen columns to Satan, which churchmen reported as part of a papal counter-offensive against attempts in the Netherlands and elsewhere to dilute traditional teaching about the devil. It reported that in an address of 5 November the Pope had spoken of this 'perfidious and astute charmer' as an actually existing person: 'We thus know', he said, 'that this obscure and disturbing being really exists and that he still operates with treacherous cunning; he is the occult enemy who sows errors and disgrace in human history'. Demonology, the Pope went on, is 'a very important chapter of Catholic doctrine that ought to be studied again, although this is not being done much today'. A leading article that accompanied the statement complained that since Vatican II 'a kind of veil of silence has enveloped the Devil,' and urged priests and theologians to focus attention on him.[18]

No conflict here with modern psychology and medicine? Where would one look for a section on 'Demons' in Osler's *Principles and Practice* or Freud's *General Introduction*? President White, who wrote before modern psychopathology had got well under way, quotes a German alienist who peered into the old records about witches: 'in a most careful study of the original records of their trials by torture, he has often found their answers and recorded conversations exactly like those familiar to him in our modern lunatic asylums, and names some forms of insanity which constantly and unmistakably appear among those who suffered for criminal dealings with the devil.'[19] How many psychiatrists of our time would hold that any one of the pitiable women who went to the stake in thousands in the sixteenth century were the consorts of demons, or that the belief in such creatures, then or now, was anything but superstition? The importance of such a belief in the sixteenth century lay in the implacable cruelty which was its natural by-product. Its importance today happily lies not in that terrible quarter, but in the colour it gives to the bitter dictum of T. H. Huxley that 'ecclesiasticism in science is only unfaithfulness to truth'.

SCIENCE, LOURDES, AND FATIMA

7 It must by now have become apparent that, whatever his concessions to science on particular points, the orthodox Catholic does not and cannot live intellectually in the world accepted by modern science. That world is governed by natural law. The Catholic believes that this law is being continually set aside by miraculous intervention from outside the natural order. Pius XI created at least thirty-one new saints; Pius XII created eight more in seven months; and a condition of accepting a new saint is proof that he has performed at least four miracles. Of these four, two may be wrought after his death with the help of his relics or remains. Such relics have supernatural potency; and since, in every altar in a Catholic church, relics of at least one martyr are supposed to be sealed, the number and variety of these objects is immense, and the possible influence on the course of events portentous. For reasons unknown some relics are far more efficacious than others. By reference to the Catholic Almanac one can find where the more precious and potent of these are to be found. There are pieces of the true cross, for example, in eight European cities; the crown of thorns is at Paris, the sponge at St John Lateran in Rome, the robe at Trèves, and part of the winding-sheet at Turin. The house occupied by the Holy Family is at Loreto in Italy, transported there by angels, between 1291 and 1295; to the delight of believers, there was found in it a pattern of the sole of the Virgin's shoe, and two popes offered indulgences to persons who kissed it three times and said Ave Marias over it. At Naples there are great celebrations at the Cathedral in May, September, and December, when its patron saint, Januarius, shows his continued interest by liquefying a vial of his blood, now more than fifteen centuries old. Sometimes saints who are little known spring into belated activity. St Anne, the mother of Mary, is unmentioned in the Bible and unknown otherwise, but at her shrine of St Anne de Beaupré, near Quebec, she began about 1676 a long succession of miraculous cures. Unfortunately the shrine possessed none of her relics, though her body was preserved at Lyons and a second skull at Berne. The shortage was rectified in 1870 when a cardinal presented the shrine with one of her wristbones.

8 Some of the most far-reaching movements in modern Catholicism have originated in alleged appearances of the Virgin, for example the vast pilgrimages to the shrines of Lourdes and Fatima. The apparitions that initiated both these movements were made to children. On 11 February 1858, a fourteen-year-old girl, picking up wood at the mouth of a grotto near Lourdes, France, had a vision of a beautiful lady in white with a blue sash, who invited her to drink at a fountain. There happened to be no fountain at the spot, but scraping away some earth, the girl uncovered a trickle of water which increased into a spring. She reported her experience; her ecclesiastical superiors put grave heads together; and four years later, her bishop declared: 'We consider that the Immaculate Mary, Mother of God, did actually appear to Bernadette Soubirous.' At the hundredth anniversary of the event in 1958, after the sale of millions of gallons of the sacred water, wistful visitations by millions of pilgrims, and the expenditure of millions of dollars on a great underground basilica, this church, the largest in christendom except St Peter's, was consecrated at the spot.

That cures do occur at such places is undeniable. The scientifically minded person who has seen, as I have, the piles of crutches joyously abandoned at St Anne de Beaupré need not deny that among these cases there are genuine and permanent cures. All he cares to deny is the ecclesiastical account of these cures. He finds no good reason to consider them miraculous. He is of the same mind as the committee of the British Medical Council appointed at the suggestion of the Archbishop of Canterbury to investigate the claims of miracles and spiritual healing. This committee of trained medical men reported that it could find no evidence of organic diseases cured solely by supernatural means.[20] It admitted, as candor required, that in a 'very few' cases cures had been effected that were 'at present inexplicable on scientific grounds', but in the light of man's present ignorance of the subtler relations of body and mind, it refused to equate the unexplained with the inexplicable, the merely unknown with the supernatural. That is surely the right course for anyone not committed beforehand to intervention from beyond nature.

The story of Fatima is curiously similar to that of Lourdes. On 13 May 1917, near a small country place of that name, about seventy miles north of Lisbon, three illiterate children aged ten, nine, and seven, came home saying they had seen a beautiful lady who 'looked about fifteen' and who told them to come back on the same day each month; they would in time see something wonderful. They did so, and more and more of the curious countryfolk came along. On 13 October of that year, rumour and expectation running high, many thousands of them assembled. It was a rainy day. But suddenly there came a rift in the clouds; the sun burst through; it seemed to revolve by fits and starts, and even to draw nearer to the earth. Lucia, the ten-year-old, said she saw Joseph, Mary, the infant Jesus, and 'Our Lord', who was dressed in red. The Virgin gave her a message saying that the war would end that day, but that a further horrible war would come unless the world consecrated itself to her immaculate heart. The other children and some of the spectators also were convinced that they had seen super-normal things, but their visions varied widely. The Pope of the time, Benedict XV, and his successor Pius XI seem to have taken no stock in the 'miracle', but Pius XII, who had occasional visions himself and was especially devoted to the Virgin, was minded otherwise; he interpreted the Virgin's message as a genuine, divine, and timely warning against communism; and with his aid the village became an important religious centre, with a large basilica and hospital, and extensive sales of curative Fatima water.

The story does not stand up well under scrutiny. The message Lucia received about the war's ending that very day proved false. The message regarding communism seems never to have been received at all; it is not mentioned in any of the early reports, and must have been read back into the message from a later time. The peculiar motions of the sun were not confirmed by any observatory. The two younger children both died in the influenza epidemics of 1919 and 1920, so that Lucia became the main pillar of reliance for the tremendous miracle. And Lucia was a frail reed. She had a history that suggested abnormality; her mother reported that three times before she had seen a 'sheeted featureless form which approached and then withdrew';[21] she had a somewhat low order of intelligence, and a confused and plastic memory for what she had seen. She retired into a Carmelite nunnery, where at last report she was still living, but under such close guardianship that she could only be interviewed at the authorisation of the Pope himself. The significant fact has come out that not long before her visions her mother had read her an account of the famous appearance of the Virgin, dressed as a beautiful lady, to a boy and girl at La Salette. Combine such antecedents with a childish imagination, an untrained intelligence, and the pressure upon her of the vivid emotion and expectancy of a superstitious countryside, and the stage would seem to be set for the events that followed, without preternatural assistance.[22]

It will be said that nothing in all this commits the church of necessity to a miracle at Fatima. That is technically true, and no doubt many Catholics who are scientifically inclined regard these incidents and the popular excitement they engender with a wincing distaste. But two comments are called for. First, so far as Catholics do display this attitude, they do so in violation of the will and belief of the head of their church. Pope Paul, at the conclusion of Vatican II, made a deliberate and public point of visiting the shrine of Fatima. In a blaze of publicity and surrounded by 'nearly a million pilgrims', he appeared with the one surviving member of the young trio who had seen the wonders, and gave an address emphasising the desire for peace that the Virgin had somehow communicated to them on that rainy day of half a century before.[23] Secondly, in studying the relations of the church and science, it would be myopic to look solely at the formal pronouncements of popes and councils. Though we have done that for the most part in the interest of fairness to Rome, it must be remembered that the church consists not only of the few at the top but also of the millions at the bottom. Many of these millions embrace, and are winked at from the top in embracing, a credulity that is clearly at odds with the scientific spirit and the scientific view of nature. 'The attractiveness of Catholicism as a cult,' says Dean Inge, 'depends almost wholly on its frank admission of the miraculous as a matter of daily occurrence.'[24] The more versed one is in science, the harder that admission becomes.

If this is true, one would expect the intellectual atmosphere of Catholicism to discourage rather than stimulate devotion to science. This expectation appears to be confirmed by statistical investigation. An American woman psychologist has made an inquiry that bears on the point; she has studied 'the origins, educations, lives and minds of sixty-four American research scientists selected as the leaders in their fields by committees of their peers'. 'The most valuable factor in their family backgrounds seems to have been "a home in which learning is valued for its own sake". Five of the families were Jewish; one was aggressively "free-thinking"; the rest were Protestant. None of the scientists came from a Catholic family.'[25] A similar study has been made by Francis Bello, who questioned 107 scientists forty or under, 'judged by their senior colleagues to be outstanding'. 'About half were brought up as Protestants; more than one-quarter were Jewish; less than 5% came from Catholic families. At present, nearly three-quarters have no religious affiliation (including all the former Catholics).'[26] Such figures can hardly be accounted for except by supposing—what reflection would have suggested in any case—that there is a keenly felt inner tension between scientific and Catholic thought.

SCIENTIFIC VS RELIGIOUS FAITH

9 Where such tension occurs, are we not begging the question if we accept the scientific account as the true one? It must be admitted that nothing we have said about Lourdes or Fatima or the appeal to relics proves that the visions were subjective or the relics impotent. Indeed only one who is logically naïve would ever claim to show conclusively in a particular case either that a miracle has occurred or that it has not. To show that it has he would have to show that what is now inexplicable in it is incapable of explanation by any laws at all, and this of course is impossible. Similarly to show that a given event does *not* involve a miracle would require showing of every one of its component factors, no matter how minute, that it followed by law from some known type of antecedent, and this is again impossible. Seeing this, some Catholic apologists have been inclined to say to the scientist, 'Neither your position nor mine can be established by mere reason. Each of us must appeal to a general postulate about the constitution of the world. My postulate is that there are two orders, a supernatural and a natural, and that some events show a break-through from the one to the other; your postulate is that the world is a single continuous whole. Neither postulate can be proved. The difference is that while both of us must accept our postulates on faith, I recognise what I am doing and you do not. Indeed the rationalist is as truly appealing to faith as the devotee himself, for the ultimate principles on which reason proceeds are as little capable of proof as any dogma of the faith.'

This is plausible but confused. We may well pause on it for a moment to see where the confusions lie. It is true that the principles on which reason proceeds, such as the laws of logic, are not themselves capable of proof; any attempt to prove the law of contradiction, for example, would presuppose the validity of the law at every step. But it does not follow that such laws are articles of faith in the same sense as the dogmas of a creed. They are compulsory, and the dogmas are not. If a thinker denies a law of logic, his thought is paralysed and cannot move. To deny the law of contradiction, for example, would be to say of propositions generally that their truth does not exclude their falsity, but then we could never say that anything was true rather than false, which means that we could not think at all. The suggestion that such a law of thought is accepted on faith in the same sense as the dogma that the Deity is triune is plainly untrue. The first proposition is necessary because its truth is the condition of all meaningful thought; the second has no such necessity, for even though true it could quite intelligibly be denied. To say that the appeal to reason involves the same appeal to faith as the acceptance of a creed is to use 'faith' in quite different senses.

Secondly, even if the two postulates—those of one order and of two—both covered all the facts, they would not do so equally well. The principle of Occam's razor bids us never to multiply entities beyond necessity, always to accept the simpler of two adequate hypotheses. And between one causal order and two, there can be no doubt which is the simpler; the supposition of a single order in which each event is explained by others in the same order is clearly simpler than a double order in which the laws of one are suspended from time to time by incursions from the other. It may be said that here again we are appealing to faith, since the proposition that nature conforms to Occam's razor is itself incapable of proof. This appears to be true. Occam's razor, like the principle of the uniformity of nature (namely, that the same kind of agents, under the same conditions, always act in the same ways), is commonly considered not as a conclusion that has been proved, but as a postulate that experience has progressively confirmed. Still, these postulates are not arbitrary. Though not as plainly undeniable as the law of contradiction, they are principles implicit in the activity of thought, aspects of the ideal that thought as such is seeking to realise. Common sense and science use them, and must use them, continually. The Catholic scientist accepts them as unquestioningly as his colleagues in ninety-nine hundredths of his intellectual work. It is only when he comes to extraordinary cases in which things abandon their familiar behaviour, in which water is reported as turning into wine, or the dead as rising and walking, or portentous apparitions as appearing in field or sky, that he is in the least inclined to abandon the principles on which he relies everywhere else. And because these principles belong to the very idea of explanation and obviously apply over the larger part of his experience, they have the right of way. It would be merely frivolous to discard them for reasons less than overwhelming.

MIRACLES

10 Do such reasons ever present themselves? Since it is perhaps impossible to settle this matter a priori,[27] one must deal with individual cases as they come and rely on comparative probabilities. Here the simple argument of Hume will surely dispose of the vast majority of alleged miraculous interpositions. When a suspension of natural law is reported, such as the sun's standing still over Gibeon or the Virgin's appearance to the children at Fatima, which explanation is the more *probable*: that natural law has been set aside or that in the account of the reporter error or deception has entered in? No doubt most Catholic astronomers would agree with their non-Catholic colleagues that, whatever the church says to the contrary, it is far more probable that the writer of Joshua erred than that the earth in fact ceased for some hours to revolve. Nor is the case in principle different with regard to Lucia's report at Fatima. Which is the more probable: on the one hand that a supernatural disembodied woman, changelessly young, should have materialised herself for human eyes in a Portuguese field and offered a forecast of the future of Europe, or that a wrought-up child of ten and certain emotional fellow-devotees should have 'seen' what they were predisposed to see? When the issue is baldly stated, there would seem to be little doubt where the greater probability lies.

We may so state the argument, of course, as to reduce the probability of miracle to zero, as Hume has been charged with doing. We may place on the one side a set of psychological laws which we have found to govern the appearance of illusions, and on the other the miraculous suspension of one or more of these laws. We may then settle the case triumphantly against the miracle by saying that governance by law *means* governance without exception, since laws would be no laws at all if they were subject to violation; we can thus define the miracle out of existence. So put, the argument begs the question. But there is no need to put it so ineptly. We may admit that all the natural laws we know are probable only; we may even admit that it is a matter of probability whether in a given unexplored area there are laws at all, and still the argument has force. Lucia's experience was perhaps unique in some respects, and at the time inexplicable; would that make the appeal to comparative probability irrelevant? Certainly the scientist would not think so. He has confronted many situations in which, as here, some features were inexplicable by the natural causes known to him. In some such cases these features had been confidently laid in the past to bewitchment or demonic possession or the interposition of saints or angels. Range after range of these cases have yielded their perfectly natural though sometimes deeply buried secrets to inquiry. Is it probable that in the present case no such natural causes are to be found? This must be conceded to be possible; the scientist can hardly rule it out a priori. But how likely is it? How plausible would it be, in the face of the overwhelming success of science in bringing to light causes for the unexplained, to say that its long triumphant march has come to a halt with the event now before us, a halt imposed not by our ignorance but by the failure of natural causation itself? Granting that this is not an impossibility, it would certainly be put down by the scientist as improbable in the extreme. And with this we can only agree.

PROBLEMS OF THE MIRACULOUS

11 We have admitted that the hypothesis is not an impossible one. But even this needs to be said with caution. For just what sort of hypothesis would it be? Suppose that in a given case the supernatural had made an intrusion into the natural order; such an intrusion may be conceived in either of two ways. It may be conceived as itself an event occurring in accordance with law, though not merely natural law, or as an event not governed by law at all.

An ingenious apologist for miracle, Sir Arnold Lunn, has taken the former line. 'A miracle is just as "lawful" . . .,' he writes, 'as a natural event. Everything which happens, happens in accordance with law but not necessarily in accordance with natural law. The supernatural also has its laws.'[28] But how would you go about it, in such a case, to distinguish between the natural and the supernatural? In his definition of 'miracle' Sir Arnold Lunn suggests that we can distinguish the two by the fact that where the supernatural is at work natural law is transcended or set aside; a miracle is 'an event above, or contrary to, or exceeding nature which is explicable only as a direct act of God'.[29] But if what appears to exceed or flout a known natural law is itself a lawful occurrence, how are we to know whether it is truly supernatural or due to undiscovered natural laws? Sir Arnold thinks that there is at times so clear a manifestation of trans-natural will or purpose as to leave us in no doubt, just as the communications of other persons, which also break through into the natural order, leave us in no doubt. We will not raise the question whether the ordinary speech and gestures of those around us are really invasions of the natural order from a non-natural or supernatural realm. But suppose we accept the analogy and follow it through. We do take the speech and gestures of others as expressing thoughts and feelings that we cannot directly perceive. Is this hypothesis a fair one? Yes, because we know clearly what it means, and the sort of consequences that would confirm it. We know what affection means, because we have felt it ourselves, and we know roughly what to expect from a person who likes us, so that we can verify our hypothesis in a great variety of ways. Are we in the same position with regard to the hypothesis that the child Lucia's vision was, as Sir Arnold would presumably call it, 'a direct act of God'?

Unfortunately we are not. We know what affection means in another mind like our own, but we have no clear idea of what it would be like in a mind that was infinite, perfect, and all knowing. The hypothesis that such an affection exists is not definite enough to enlighten us as to how it would act in a particular situation. It may be said that if we cannot conceive the purpose of an infinite mind, we can at least conceive a purpose similar to our own though superior in firmness and extent. But as soon as the hypothesis is made definite enough to enable us to infer and test its consequences, these consequences commonly refute it. Let us see how.

12(1)   The consequences of a moral kind that one would naturally infer from the hypothesis of supernatural interposition do not occur. Assume that the Virgin has the power and the will to heal those who appeal to her in trust and reverence, and one can only believe that she would so respond *generally* to those who came to her in this spirit. But the fact is, of course, that at Lourdes and Fatima she turns the vast majority away. Again, if we suppose her to be just in the ordinary sense, it follows that she would not confine her most important messages and manifestations to subnormal children, but would distribute them with some regard to the understanding, need, or merit of the faithful, or even, since her grace is so bountiful, to those outside the pale. Needless to say, all inferences of this kind are no sooner formed than they are belied by the facts. It may be said that if we knew enough we should see that they are not belied by the facts, that the Virgin has attended to all appeals, neglected none, and indeed dispensed perfect love and justice. That way lies intellectual dishonesty. If, starting from a given hypothesis, one sees that certain consequences follow from it, one cannot, upon finding that they do not follow in fact, revise one's inferences to yield whatever the facts may offer; by that method one can prove or disprove any hypothesis whatever. A hypothesis confirmed by any eventuality is plainly an illegitimate one.

13(2)   The intellectual implications of the hypothesis of miracle are likewise as a rule untenable. Assume that in the Fatima case the Virgin did actually speak to the children, and it follows either that she was ignorant or that she deceived them, for they were emphatic that among her disclosures to them was the fact that the war would end that day. So of other such alleged disclosures. The belief of the Roman church is that whenever its head defines dogma for the faithful, a miracle of supernatural guidance occurs. Assume that it does. Then the unhappy conclusion is forced on us, as we have seen, that such guidance has carried its recipients into repeated error and contradiction. Furthermore, if we assume an intelligence solicitous to communicate its truth to eager minds, we should hardly expect it to limit its communications to those of one community, to select its recipients with such apparent arbitrariness, and to muffle its meaning beneath layers of triviality and ambiguity. We cannot, to be sure, dismiss beforehand the hypothesis of a supernatural mind seeking to communicate with our own. But if dealt with at all, it should be taken seriously; its consequences should be thought out and compared with the facts; it should not dissolve into a vague and pious gullibility, ready to swallow as confirmation whatever in fact may happen.

14(3)   If a miracle is accepted, the sort of grounds on which it is accepted must be accorded the same weight everywhere. One cannot consistently accept a case of spiritual healing performed by an apostle in the first century, and reject one ascribed to Mrs Eddy in the nineteenth century on precisely similar grounds. If the evidence for the miracles of Christian saints is regarded as decisive, similar evidence for the miracles of Mohammed cannot merely be ignored. Nor can one with intellectual fairness profess interest in the scientific inquiry into the miracles of candidates for sainthood and at the same time dismiss as deluded the attempt of psychical researchers to apply scientific methods to the study of the supernormal. The evidence must be dealt with impartially and objectively.

   If this is done, one or other of three attitudes toward miracles seems bound to follow. First, it might be recognised that for many of the miracles claimed by non-Catholic faiths there is evidence at least as conclusive as for many or most Catholic miracles. Suppose these non-Catholic miracles to be accordingly accepted. Since they have been wrought in the interests and under the auspices of other faiths, they offer the same sort of confirmation of these faiths as the Catholic miracles do of the Catholic faith. But to admit this would be to take them as confirming truth conflicting with Catholic truth. Such impartiality would for a Catholic be self-destructive. Secondly, finding this consequence intolerable, the Catholic apologist may insist that the same evidence is conclusive when offered for Catholic miracles and sophistical when offered for others. This is a frank abandonment of rationality in favour of faith. If the non-Catholic then says that he too has faith, and that if faith sanctions exceeding the evidence in one communion it should do so also in others, the Catholic would presumably answer that such sanction could be given not by all faiths, but by the true faith alone. The answer is not calculated to convince those outside the fold. Thirdly, in revulsion against both these views, one may decline to accept any miracle at all except as required by a rational balancing of probabilities. But this is in effect a capitulation to science. It does not mean that one has ruled out miracles absolutely. A given vision or a given cure may conceivably be a break-through of a supernatural will into the order of nature. But it will be so regarded only if this is felt to be more probable than that the event should be the product of any kind of natural causation. And it is to be doubted whether there is any case in human history where scientists would generally admit that the facts point that way.

15 We have been exploring Sir Arnold Lunn's conception of a miracle as a supersession of natural by supernatural law. But there is an alternative conception according to which a miracle, though a suspension of natural law, is not itself an instance of any law at all. The question suggested by such a view is whether a miracle then is a pure accident in the sense of an event that exploded into being causelessly. 'No,' is the reply, 'for God is the cause; he interposes; he sets aside natural law; but neither the volition in his mind nor its action upon the natural world exemplifies any law whatever'. It may be questioned whether this position makes sense. To say that b is caused by a is to say that it follows a in accordance with a law. If an event b followed a today, and tomorrow, in the absence of a, followed with equal readiness from anything else, it would be meaningless to speak of *the* cause of b. In science the rule of causality is interpreted by the uniformity of nature, which assumes not only that all events have causes, but 'same cause, same effect'. Cause and effect are connected through their characters; if a produces b, it is in virtue of its character as a; in short, where there is causality there is law. To assert of a given miracle that it was caused, though in accordance with no law, is thus self-contradictory. Some existentialists of the day have maintained indeed that even ordinary events are eruptions of pure inexplicable spontaneity. But no theist so far as I know has attempted to deal with miracles in these terms.

16   It is time to sum up. The thesis under discussion in this chapter has been the Roman contention that between truths of the natural and of the supernatural order there can be no conflict. We have found all too many evidences of an irrepressible conflict of just this kind. Assuming that science supplies our best illustrations of truths of the natural order, we saw that in astronomy, biology, and psychology— to go no further—Rome has committed itself to positions inconsistent with major theses of modern science. Furthermore in its encourage- ment of popular belief that natural law is continually being set aside by the miraculous interposition of saints, angels, and demons, the efficacy of relics and scapulars, and not infrequent visitations from the Virgin herself, we found an intellectual attitude incompatible with that of science. Revelation as Rome conceives it not only may conflict with natural knowledge; at many points it unhappily does.

CHAPTER IV

CATHOLICISM ON THE MARKS
OF THE CHURCH

'MOTIVES' AND 'MARKS'

1 Of the three points in the Catholic view of faith and reason that we set out to study,[1] we have examined two. (I) The first was that there is accessible to us a body of revealed truth which, though transcending reason, is still in accordance with reason. We have seen that if 'accordance with reason' includes consistency, the body of doctrine accepted as revealed does not appear to fulfil the church's claim for it. (II) The second thesis is that between revealed and natural knowledge there can be no conflict. Our study disclosed, however, that in astronomy, biology, and psychology, the church has formally taken positions not reconcilable with generally accepted scientific conclusions. (III) The third thesis is that the fact of revelation itself can be established rationally by considerations decisive for any open mind. It is this last contention that we shall examine in this chapter.

The question is indeed forced upon us by the results of the first two inquiries. Anyone who found that the content of an alleged revelation was both incoherent in itself and inconsistent with the postulates and conclusions of science would be bound to raise the question whether the revelation had occurred at all. May not the body of doctrine supposed to be revealed be no more than the attempts of earnest and thoughtful but all too human minds to give such account as they could of first and last things? This conclusion, natural enough to modernist or humanist, is firmly resisted by Catholicism. Whatever difficulties there may be in catching the true accents of the supernatural voice, there can be no doubt that it has in fact spoken and that it has spoken through one particular church. This can be amply attested by evidence open to all men. What sort of evidence is this? It is primarily a set of facts about the Scriptures, the church, and its history which are believed to place Christianity in a unique position. They are facts that are unaccountable on any other supposition than that the church has been divinely commissioned and directed. 'Reason declares', says Leo XIII in

Aeterni Patris, 'that from the very outset the Gospel teaching was rendered conspicuous by signs and wonders which gave, as it were, definite proof of a definite truth.'

What are these 'signs and wonders'? They are of very diverse kinds. Catholic apologists commonly divide them into two classes, 'motives of credibility' and 'notes' or 'marks' of the true church. The motives of credibility are a large and miscellaneous set of 'facts' regarded as inexplicable by natural causes, such as miracles, the fulfilment of prophecy, the intrinsic impressiveness of Old and New Testaments, and the growth of a small and feeble community into the main church of the Western world. These are considerations that to many reflective minds have seemed compelling, and it would be interesting and instructive to canvass them in detail. Unfortunately this would require a volume of its own, and we have neither time nor space to attempt it.

The omission is less disastrous to the argument than it might seem. There is no sharp line between the 'motives' and the 'marks'; indeed some members of the two classes have at times been interchanged; and one can conjecture from a critic's dealing with one class how he would deal with the other. Furthermore, the marks are logically the more fundamental. For if the evidence put forward as fact under the head of motives of credibility is called in question, for example the occurrence of miracles or the actual fulfilment of prophecy, the apologist commonly falls back on the authority of the church, and if this in turn is questioned, appeal is taken to those notes or marks which authenticate it as the divinely chosen channel of revelation. Hence in confining ourselves to the marks, we are at least dealing with the considerations felt to be most important in rationally validating this authority.

These authenticating or identifying notes have varied in number from the two recognised by Thomas Stapleton—universality in space and permanence in time—to the fourteen enumerated by Cardinal Bellarmine. But for some centuries they have been fixed at four. These were given official sanction at Trent, and have been incorporated into the Mass Creed.[2] A church, it is argued, that is (1) one, (2) holy, (3) universal, and (4) apostolic establishes by these marks its claim to more than natural origin and guidance.

I   THE UNITY OF THE CHURCH

2   The unity of the church, if this is to be clearly distinguished from its universality, means its identity in time. For nearly two thousand years its faith, worship, and organisation are held to have stood substantially unchanged. As Macaulay wrote in a famous paragraph:

'No other institution is left standing which carries the mind back to the times when the smoke of sacrifice rose from the Pantheon, and when camelopards and tigers abounded in the Flavian Amphi-theatre. . . . She was great and respected before the Saxon had set foot on Britain, before the Frank had passed the Rhine, when Grecian eloquence still flourished in Antioch, when idols were still worshipped in the temple of Mecca.'³ And it is contended that through all the centuries of her existence, while the cultures around her were falling into decay, while numberless sects and systems were having their day and ceasing to be, the church alone remained, with her deposit of faith intact. Not only her manner of worship and the form of her organisation, but also those ideal structures that are so hard to preserve against tarnishing by an inhospitable atmosphere, her creeds, she has kept as bright as they were when she received them from the founders. 'We believe', said Cardinal Wiseman, 'that no new doctrine can be introduced into the Church, but that every doctrine which we hold, has existed, and been taught in it ever since the time of the apostles; having been handed down by them to their successors . . .'.⁴ According to *The Teaching of the Catholic Church*, 'the revelation made to the Apostles, by Christ and by the Holy Spirit when he sent them to teach *all truth*, was final, definitive. To that body of revealed truth nothing has been, or ever will be, added.'⁵ Wherever else the ideas of progress and evolution may apply, they do not apply to true religion. Two popes have spoken their mind on this in identical language: 'These enemies of divine revelation extol human progress to the skies, and with rash and sacrilegious daring would have it introduced into the Catholic religion as if this religion were not the work of God but of man, or some kind of philosophical discovery susceptible of perfection by human efforts.'⁶ To be sure, some articles of the creed have been formulated more exactly as time went on; new languages in which to express them have come into being, and new techniques for propagating them. But the church's teaching itself has remained one stable body of doctrine, without loss and without addition.

If we were invited to estimate this stability, regarded as a human achievement, we should have much that was admiring to say. But the record is not offered us in that light. It is offered as evidence of an identity so complete as to be humanly inexplicable and to point to supernatural and infallible guidance. Such a claim invites examination of the facts.

INCONSISTENCIES IN TEACHING

3(a)   The alleged identity of faith has in fact failed in various ways.

It has failed in the first place through *inconsistency*. We have seen already in the case of Pope Vigilius that official belief may be reversed and re-reversed within the term of a single reign. The precious deposit is in still greater danger when it is passed along from hand to hand, and we may cite an illustrative case or two. Just before he died in 417, Pope Innocent I excommunicated the well known theologian Pelagius and all who accepted his doctrine. In the course of the same year his successor, Pope Zosimus, a Greek, reversed this judgement, declaring for the orthodoxy of the Pelagian doctrines.⁷ In 1279 Nicholas III issued a bull in which 'he declared the Franciscan Rule to be inspired by the Holy Ghost, and the absolute renunciation of property, practised by the Spiritual Franciscans, to have been practised by Christ and His Apostles, and taught by them to their disciples. Yet, in 1323, John XXII published a bull flatly contradicting his predecessor; it was (he said) a perversion of Scripture to assert the absolute poverty of Christ and His Apostles, and henceforth the doctrine must be condemned as erroneous and heretical.'⁸ Anyone moved by a malicious interest to study the integrity of doctrine over two hundred and fifty popes instead of one or two would reap a richer crop of inconsistency than such an attitude would deserve.

ADDITIONS TO THE TEACHING

4(b)   The body of teaching has changed through *additions*. If the changelessness of faith is essential, such additions should not occur, and we have seen that the official attitude of the church regarding dogma is that expressed by Vincent of Lerins: 'to teach anything to Catholic Christians besides what they have received has never been allowed, is nowhere allowed, never will be allowed.' For all that, it has certainly occurred. 'In the Roman Church', said Dean Salmon, 'the idea seems to be now abandoned of handing down the Faith "once for all . . . delivered to the saints". It is a vast manufactory of beliefs, to which addition is being yearly made.'⁹

5   The doctrine of Papal infallibility itself is such an addition, as we shall shortly see. But we shall take as our present example the doctrine of purgatory. This must of course be distinguished from the doctrine of hell, on which we may be permitted a few preliminary words. The Catholic is apparently right that the doctrine of hell, namely that those who die in mortal sin will suffer the agony of eternal fire, has been held by the church from the beginning; he would point out that the same gospel of Matthew which narrates the investiture of Peter with the power of the keys lays down this doctrine also; 'depart from me, ye cursed, into everlasting fire, prepared for the devil and his angels'.[10] Here the crucial phrase is εἰς τὸ πῦρ τὸ αἰώνιον, and what does that αἰώνιον mean? Dean Farrar thought it meant not everlasting but age-long, and wrote a book in passionate advocacy of this view.

'I call God to witness that so far from regretting the possible loss of some billions of aeons of bliss by attaching to the word αἰώνιος a sense in which scores of times it is undeniably found, I would here, and now, and kneeling on my knees, ask Him that I might die as the beasts that perish, and for ever cease to be, rather than that my worst enemy should endure the hell described by Tertullian . . . or Dr Pusey. . . .'[11]

Dr Pusey replied in a volume of remorseless scholarship that in his own opinion and that of 'the best Greek Oxford Scholar of his day, my friend, the Rev J. Riddell,' 'the word was used strictly of eternity, an eternal existence, such as shall be, when time shall be no more';[12] and he proceeded to supply an overwhelming body of testimony to prove that the fathers believed in the same eternity of hell fire for the damned as they did of blessedness for the saved. A doctrine thus taught by both the Scriptures and the fathers must, he held, be accepted, whatever one may think of its morality; one cannot in strict logic deny a doctrine so firmly based without going the whole dark distance to rationalism.

The good doctor may be right. At any rate the Catholic church has been on his side. When Origen advanced a more compassionate doctrine to the effect that the torture of hell might be limited in time, he was condemned by at least three synods and apparently also by the fifth ecumenical council of 553. Augustine argued that since every child is born in original sin, it must, if it dies unbaptised, be punished in the eternal fire of hell, though it would somehow be granted a 'mitissima poena' there. Aquinas held that the majority of men are doomed to an eternity of torment every moment of which exceeds the worst that ever has been or can be endured on earth; and though he believed in a milder region of hell set apart for infants, he discouraged mothers from praying for children who died while unbaptised. The Council of Trent followed this up by insisting in its Roman Catechism that the eternal punishment in store for wrongdoers is the sort of agony felt by the senses of the physical body.[13] Who are to suffer these pains? The answer, given with the authority of both a Pope, Eugene IV, and an ecumenical council, that of Florence, is as follows:

'The holy Roman church firmly believes, professes and preaches that no persons who are not within the Catholic church, which means not pagans only, but also Jews, heretics, and schismatics, can become sharers in eternal life, but will go into eternal fire, which has been prepared for the devil and his angels, unless they are gathered into this church before the end of their life.'[14]

Dante finds in hell a generous population who were denied the immortality of the soul. 'Chrysostom declares his free opinion that the number of bishops who might be saved bore a very small proportion to those who would be damned.'[15] In the Syllabus of Errors of Pope Pius IX (1864), one of the propositions expressly condemned is: 'Men may at least hope for the eternal salvation of those who do not live in the bosom of the true church of Christ'. An Italian priest refused absolution and the sacraments to a parishioner on the grounds that he had professed disbelief in the material fire of hell; the case was taken in 1892 to the Holy Inquisition, presided over by Leo XIII, and the priest's action was formally approved. That the later developments of the doctrine embroider and embellish the original teaching in some degree may well be true, but it is hard to avoid the Catholic conclusion that the stark fact of eternal punishment was taught by both the New Testament and the church fathers.[16]

PURGATORY

6 Of the doctrine of purgatory the same cannot be said. As Dr Salmon points out,

'For hundreds of years the Church seems to have known little or nothing on the subject . . . the chief source of Western information is a Latin book, the dialogues of Gregory the Great, a work of which the genuineness has been denied by some merely because it seemed to them incredible that so sensible a man should have written so silly a book. . . . Gregory, believing twelve or thirteen centuries ago that the end of the world was then near at hand, and that the men of his age, by reason of their nearness to the next world, could see things in it which had been invisible to their predecessors, collected a number of tales of apparitions which, being received on his authority, have been the real foundation of the Western belief in Purgatory.'[17]

Gregory was Pope from 590 to 604. If the doctrine is to be exhibited as the primitive teaching of the church, the evidence must be drawn from an earlier time. Newman tried to produce such evidence. But he found so little to his purpose that he was driven to include the most shadowy of circumstances. There exists an account of a certain St Perpetua, reported to have been martyred in Carthage in the year 203.

'In the course of the narrative, St Perpetua prays for her brother Dinocrates, who had died at the age of seven; and has a vision of a dark place, and next of a pool of water, which he was not tall enough to reach. She goes on praying; and in a second vision the water descended to him, and he was able to drink, and went to play as children use. "Then I knew," she says, "that he was translated from his place of punishment." '18

Newman was apparently ready to accept tales of this kind as evidence for both the currency of the doctrine of purgatory and its truth; and once convinced of its truth, he was able to detect intimations of it in the Psalms, Job, and Lamentations. It takes a great deal of credulity to find any substantial identity between these faint suggestions and the full-blown doctrine of today.

That doctrine is in fact rather complicated. (1) Souls at death are in one of three states, in mortal sin, in venial sin, or free from sin.19 The latter class 'pass straight to behold God in heaven'.20 But it is limited in number, including only (a) Christ, (b) Mary, and (c) children who have been baptised but have died before having a chance to do wrong. If they have not been baptised, they are guilty of original sin, that is, the sin brought upon them by their ancestor Adam when he committed the first sin; such infants go to limbo, which is a part of hell, but without the pain of fire. Pius VI in 1794 formally condemned the disbelief in this doctrine.21 Those who die in unforgiven mortal sin go to hell. But there is a large remaining class, including all whose mortal sins are forgiven in this life but have some punishment still due them, and all who die in merely venial sin. Such persons go to purgatory. (2) This is not a place of probation and continued trial, but of punishment; 'these souls are more helpless than we; they can do nothing whatever for their sins but suffer. . . .'22 (3) The period of their suffering varies. For some it will be concluded only by the last judgement: 'all the souls that are to go to heaven will at that judgment be reunited with their bodies and enter into their everlasting reward.'23 Others will serve terms varying with the depth of their sin and with the number and kind of steps taken to get them out. The theory of their escape is again somewhat complicated. It implies the existence of a large reservoir of grace which has been accumulated by the suffering of certain persons beyond their deserts.

'Thus Christ's atonement being infinite is inexhaustible, and all the sins of the world can be expiated by it. Moreover, the saints have often made satisfaction in excess of what they require for their own sins. This satisfactory value of their acts, not being used for themselves, remains in existence and can be used for others.'[24]

The church has been granted the keys to this reservoir, and may draw upon it for indulgences, that is, formal remissions of temporal punishment. Such indulgences secure the release from the treasury of limited quantities of grace, which are placed to the credit of the soul suffering in purgatory and reduce by so much the duration of his sentence.

Indulgences are usually granted for a consideration of some kind, though the consideration includes a right spirit on the part of the petitioner. Thus the popes used indulgences extensively to secure men for the Crusades, and money for the building of St Peter's; their sale by the Papal emissary Tetzel was a precipitating cause of the Reformation. The price paid for the remission and the amount of punishment remitted have been equated at times with singular exactness. There is at Rome a set of twenty-eight stone steps, now roofed and enclosed, which have been believed for centuries to be the steps of Pilate's palace at Jerusalem, up which Jesus walked to his trial.

'A notice at the foot of them informs the public that Pius VII (1800–1823) has granted the Christian worshipper a release of nine years from Purgatory for every step ascended by him on his knees in prayer. In 1908 Pius X granted a plenary indulgence for every devout ascent.'[25]

Indulgences of varying value may be secured also for the souls of friends or relatives suffering in purgatory. The government of this supernatural region and the state of its inhabitants were made the object of a special study in England by Father Frederick W. Faber, the hymn-writer, who followed Newman to Rome, and in France by the Abbé Louvet. Dr Salmon, in reviewing the latter's work, reports its curiously precise conclusion that

'a Christian of more than usual sanctity, who has never committed a mortal sin, who has carefully avoided all the graver venial sins, and has satisfied by penance for three-fourths of the lighter sins into which frailty has led him, must expect to spend in Purgatory 123 years, 3 months, and 15 days.'[26]

Why recite these details? Merely to show how implausible is the claim that the church teaches nothing but the faith as first delivered. Whether one takes the doctrine of Purgatory as accepted by uncritical devotees or as officially taught by Pope and councils, one will find nothing of the kind in the New Testament or in any apostolic teaching. That teaching, as we have seen, was not free from its own dark imaginings. But this particular province in the geography of Hades, with its graduated penalties and its bizarre eschatological banking system, in which drafts drawn by a living person on a supernatural fund may be used to shorten proportionally the agonies of being burnt, imposed by a Deity who is also represented as infinitely loving, was not derived from the mind of Jesus or Peter or Paul. It was an addition imposed by the superstition, terror, and inhumanity of the Dark Ages.

NEW DOCTRINES REGARDING THE VIRGIN

7 How hard it is to find present dogma in primitive thought is illustrated again by two dogmas regarding the Virgin that the church added to prescribed belief in a little less than a century: that of her immaculate conception (1854) and that of her bodily translation into heaven (1950). The first doctrine means that Mary was from her conception free from original sin. It is true that this doctrine had a history that goes back beyond 1854; Pius X reported that 'the Hebrew patriarchs were familiar with the doctrine of the Immaculate Conception, and found consolation in the thought of Mary in the solemn moments of their life'.[27] It would be interesting to have Newman's comment on this flight of historical imagination, for, as Dr Salmon has pointed out,

'His own inclinations had not favoured any extravagant cult of the Virgin Mary, and he was too well acquainted with Church History not to know that the doctrine of her Immaculate Conception was a complete novelty, unknown to early times, and, when first put forward, condemned by some of the most esteemed teachers of the Church.'[28]

Though present in the deposit of faith from the beginning, it was somehow missed by eyes as sharp as St Anselm's, and St Bonaventura's, and St Thomas's, and St Bernard's (who thought it a preposterous notion); indeed the Papacy did not feel safe in promoting it to a place among dogmas necessary for salvation until the idea had been debated for some four hundred years. As for the most recent addition to the creed, the bodily assumption of the Virgin into heaven,

'There is not a particle of Scripture proof for it. It was not recognised by the great teachers of the Church for almost six

centuries, and then narrated by a credulous French bishop whose
compilations of miraculous stories are unworthy of serious consideration. In the Breviary until 1570 there was incorporated a
lection discountenancing the story, and Pope Benedict XIV in the
18th century declared the tradition was not of a kind sufficient to
rank as an Article of Faith. Yet in 1950 Pope Pius XII announces
it is a truth revealed to the Church by the Holy Ghost; and the
millions of his spiritual subjects receive his decree as final, unquestionable, divinely authorised. It is his prerogative to add to
the original Gospel.'[29]

The apologetics by which such dogmas are found in Christian
beginnings will persuade no one who does not wish to be persuaded.
When an issue like that of the immaculate conception, the number
of the sacraments, or the Trinity, has been the subject of debate for
centuries, and the outcome has depended, so far as human eye can
see, on historical contingencies that might well have been otherwise,
to say that the victorious doctrine is only a freshly discovered component of what the fathers had held from the beginning is all too
plainly a rationalisation.

THE THEORY OF DEVELOPMENT

8 Apologists sometimes maintain that when such doctrines have at
last been defined they represent not an addition to the creed but
merely a 'development' of it. Revealed truth was not at first understood, and hence lay unrecognised for generations before the interpreters gathered its true sense. 'Finally scrutinizing with fresh care
the deposit of revelation, they there discovered the pious opinion,
hitherto concealed, as far as they were concerned, in the more
general formula, and, not satisfied to hold it as true, they declared
it revealed.'[30] The best known defence of this theory is Newman's
Essay on the Development of Christian Doctrine. Newman wanted to
believe that all the teachings now held by the church to be essential
were included in the deposit of faith given to the Apostles and
espoused by the fathers. When he came to examine the writings of
these persons, however, it became plain to him that over and over
again—on purgatory, on the adoration of the Virgin, on transubstantiation, on the books to be accepted as inspired, even on the
Trinity—the convictions of the early writers were not those of the
present church. 'There are three great theological authors of the
Ante-nicene centuries,' he noted, 'Tertullian, Origen, and, we may
add, Eusebius, though he lived some way into the fourth. Tertullian
is heterodox on the doctrine of our Lord's divinity, and, indeed,

ultimately fell altogether into heresy or schism; Origen is, at the very least, suspected, and must be defended and explained rather than cited as a witness of orthodoxy; and Eusebius was a Semi-Arian.'[31] Such discoveries were deeply disturbing. The question of immediate importance, however, was not whether the fathers agreed among themselves—they did not—but whether the dogmas now held by the church had been held by the fathers at all. Here the idea of development seemed to provide a saving bridge. The oak is not identical with the acorn, yet as a development of it is in some sense the same. The green shoot and the ripened wheat, the child and the man, are not the same, yet we do call them the same. May we not continue to say that the present creed of the church, different as it is from that of the primitive church, is still the same in the sense of being a continuous development from it?

Between the two Vatican Councils there has been a singular change in the Catholic estimation of the essay and its author. At the first Council he was considered by Monsignor Talbot, the English private secretary to the Pope, as 'the most dangerous man in England'. At the second, his theory was appealed to as a valuable support by 'the new theologians'; indeed his spirit, according to one observer, Christopher Hollis, seemed to dominate the proceedings. But the famous essay does not give a very firm base for the doctrine of the unity of the church.

For (1) what it does is not so much to explain that unity as to explain it away. If all we mean, for example, by asserting a recognition of the Pope's authority from the first is that the gradual concentration of power in his hands was a natural development from the position and organisation of the early church, then the original meaning of 'unity' has disappeared. Such unity would not preclude our holding that neither the authority nor the belief in it was present in the early church at all. As C. D. Broad has said: 'You have no right whatever to say that the end is just the beginning in disguise if, on inspecting the end as carefully and fairly as you can, you *do not* detect the characteristics of the beginning in it and *do* detect characteristics which were not present in the beginning'.

(2) The theory therefore tends to nullify the dogma of infallibility. How can one hold that any doctrine warranted by the church at a given time is true until one sees the riper form into which it will develop? If the primacy of Peter was potentially present and infallibly true in the minds of persons who did not suspect its being there and even supposed they meant the opposite; and if, when the church now promulgates an infallible truth, its real meaning is as remote from our present sense of it as the present meaning of Roman primacy is from that of the primitive church, then *what* exactly is

it that at a given time is to be taken as infallible? We cannot certainly know, and what we accept as infallible truth may be a mistake.

(3) The theory is bound to end in question-begging or self-refutation. If, for example, only those dogmas are selected as true developments that belong to the Catholic branch of the church, as opposed to those of the Greek and Anglican branches, which have grown from the same trunk, one will hardly convince these other branches that no *parti pris* has entered in. On the other hand, if the teachings of these other branches are also accepted as true 'developments', some of them, e.g. the denial of Roman primacy, will cancel those of the Catholic line, and then a genuine 'development' of the primitive creed may be false. The theory is unsatisfactory in either case.

SUBTRACTIONS FROM THE TEACHING

9(c)   The faith has changed by *loss* as well as by addition. It is hardly to be expected, of course, that doctrines known to have been formally adopted in early times should be formally rescinded later; but the church's deposit of faith is not confined to formal pronouncements. It includes much that has been handed down in oral tradition, such as the keeping of Sunday rather than Saturday, the importance 'of infant baptism, and the legitimacy of taking oaths. Now to suppose that *all* the elements in patristic tradition have survived in the faith of today requires a very hardy power of belief. To take but one example, the church of the early centuries recognised masses of saints and martyrs, whose figures are adorned in early records with glittering prodigies and miracles. Some of these persons are remembered in the calendar; some of them have left fragmentary bones or garments which are alleged to have a mysterious medical potency and still attract flocks of the credulous. But many of them have simply faded out, even from the embalmments of ecclesiastical memory, and their miracles, if recalled at all, are told as legend rather than as history. Who, for example, was St Bettelin? Newman, full of fervour about the fathers even in his Anglican days, gave to the young James Anthony Froude the task of writing the life of this saint. Froude did so, and the investigation that it required helped to engender the revolt of that great historian against the church. In the sardonic last sentence of his study he wrote that 'this is all that is known, and more than all', of St Bettelin; the saint was so encrusted with legend that genuine history was out of the question. These legends were once accepted in all good faith. No critical mind of the present, not even that of the best disposed Catholic theologian can swallow this mythology whole. The St Bettelins rest in peace.[32]

2   THE SANCTITY OF THE CHURCH

10   The second note by which the church may be distinguished from all merely human bodies is its sanctity. 'The Church has ever claimed', says the Jesuit writer G. H. Joyce, 'that she, as a society, is holy in a transcendent degree'. 'It is further manifest', says the article on sanctity as a mark of the church in the *Catholic Encyclopedia*, 'that the Church's holiness must be of an entirely supernatural character—something altogether beyond the power of unassisted human nature'. Good men may and do exist outside the Catholic fold, but their goodness is of that relatively flat kind that is un-leavened by supernatural grace. The goodness of the saints is unique. 'Outside the Catholic Church the world has nothing to show which can in any degree compare with them.' The virtues that are fundamental in the Christian ethic—charity, humility, chastity, the 'love of suffering'—are held to be foreign to any secular morality, both in conception and exemplification.

Now the last thing in the world which any responsible critic would wish to do is to belittle goodness, under whatever creed or sky it may appear. Francis of Assisi and Francis Xavier and Father Damien are flowers of mankind; and thousands of others have proved magnificently the power of faith to extract greatness out of what looked like ordinary clay. There has been no St Francis outside Catholicism. Granted all this and much more, the truth remains (a) that goodness in full measure does occur without supernatural sanctions, and (b) that the morality which claims such sanctions may be wanting in principle as well as in practice.

MORALITY NOT BASED ON AUTHORITY

11(a)   Religious belief often stimulates and strengthens moral purpose; true. The thought of a divine person commanding us to do right, feeling pleasure when we obey and grief or anger when we do not, certainly provides an additional motive for right-doing. Still, such belief is not the true ground for morality, and, when so accepted, may obstruct the passage to moral maturity. The man who is morally mature prefers love to hate, happiness to misery, and knowledge to ignorance, not because God wills that he should so choose, or because he will be rewarded or punished for his choice. Indeed if he wills something merely because God wills it, he is in strictness failing to follow the divine example, since God presumably wills it not because he wills it—a hardly intelligible suggestion—but because it is good. And so far as one prefers good for the sake of a prospective reward, one is like the child whose 'goodness' is bought with chocolates.

From this sort of confusion, at any rate, the man whose guide is rational insight is free. The ends of his life are set neither by dictation nor by an eschatological bait, but by such discernment as he has of good and evil. If his ethics are a poor thing, they are at least his own. There is a depth of moral responsibility and seriousness in the religious liberal that among devotees of authority is too uncommon. Conduct controlled by such authentic vision has a purity and authority about it superior to those even of the saint in the Catholic enclosure. In the mind of the saint, theology and morals are intertwined. The fall of the theological trellis upon which his ethical convictions are trained would carry down everything with it in limp collapse. Cut out from the mind of St Francis what he owed to his childlike faith in a Providence that watched the sparrows fall, and what would become of the gay nonchalance toward fate and pain that makes him the lyric figure that he is? Now the rationalist is not a lyric figure. If he tried to see the world as St Francis saw it, he would seem to himself not childlike but childish. To attempt it would be to do what he had taught himself that he must not do, namely harden poetry into fact, mix value and existence, and as Santayana puts it, 'fuse his physics with his visions'. He sees that much of the world in which St Francis lived—small, intimate, domestic, supervised by paternal loves and mandates—is, to speak plainly, such stuff as dreams are made of. To accept that fact would have put out the sun for St Francis. The rationalist can look a bleak truth in the face and know that, in spite of it, life may be good. His *summum bonum* is not the rider to a precarious creed. His morals are self-subsistent. To be sure, they have taken a sober colouring from the facts of man's place in nature; they do not show the prodigal courage that can throw a life away, certain that in the end it will be restored with interest, or the kind of equanimity that can afford to ignore its losses in the knowledge that they will all be made good in the end. Such courage and equanimity are enviable. Perhaps there is only one thing more enviable, namely the courage and equanimity that persist when such assurance has been withdrawn.

A FLAWED IDEAL

12(b)   Indeed when the claim of a unique sanctity is put forward for ecclesiastical morality, one is constrained to point out that the claim is hardly justified either by the ideal of that morality or by the way in which it has been put into effect. The reader may have noticed that among the virtues cited as specifically Catholic, or as un-recognised outside the pale, is 'the love of suffering'. Here is a point at which a theological ethics will differ sharply from a merely rational ethics. St Paul and many of the fathers believed that it would be imputed to us for righteousness both here and hereafter if we met the seductions of 'the flesh' more than half way and planted an occasional thorn in it before nature did so for us. The lives of the saints are full of self-mortification, whose strange refinements have been described in a well known chapter by Lecky; and though the faithful are not now encouraged to go to the former extremes, these lives are still held up as exemplary, and many survivals of the original attitude are still to be found—for example, the teaching that the celibate life is essentially superior to the non-celibate. Of course the capacity to endure privation is a good thing, and there is no doubt that this capacity can be increased by exercise; William James thought we should all be better for doing daily something that we disliked.

But it is difficult to see that 'the *love* of suffering' has any sound basis at all, nor is it likely that anyone should have supposed so apart from theological prepossessions. Suffering is intrinsically evil. Its gratuitous infliction on anybody, oneself or others, is irrational, and is not made rational by being done for theological reasons. The objection to handing over to theology the decision in such matters is that there are no scales in which theological values can be weighed against human values, and hence that merciful men may find their humanity cancelled by vague, vast mandates that admit of no question. It is only too easy to find historical illustrations. Those who followed the advice of the mediaeval *Witches' Hammer* and broke the bodies of eccentric old women probably believed that they were acting mercifully; for was it not well that such a one should suffer acutely for a limited time if she could be saved thereby from unlimited suffering hereafter? Indeed it was suggested in the handbook just named, which was issued with Papal approval to the examiners, that before they put their victim on the rack to extort a confession from her they should petition an angel to release her from the Devil's control, since otherwise he might save her from the full agony of the torture and so cheat them of their confession. There is no answer to that logic if you grant the examiners their theological premise. The only way to meet them is to deny their right to hold such premises at all. It is far more certain that their victim's suffer-ing was hellish than that there is a hell to save her from. To say that the theological apparatus of heaven, hell, and purgatory on which they based their torture equalled in certainty the evil of her suffering reveals a tragic failure either of humanity, of intellectual responsibility, or more probably of both.

Happily this form of cruelty belongs to the past; the pressures of secular ethics and the church's own teaching of love have mellowed a barbaric theology. But they have not mellowed it enough. One contemporary example must suffice. Until 1973 the laws of New York and New Jersey permitted abortion only to save the life of the mother. Even when a pregnancy was due to incest or rape, or there was a virtual certainty that the child would be born deformed, the mother was bound to carry the foetus to term and accept the consequences in misery. Let us be quite specific. Mrs Irwin Gleitman of North Arlington, New Jersey, contracted German measles in the early days of a pregnancy. She would have much preferred a medically competent abortion to running the grave risk of bearing a deformed and defective child. She consulted two obstetricians who, she reported, gave her no warning of the danger and no help in averting it. Her son Jeffrey was born blind, deaf, dumb, and mentally retarded. When he was seven years old the parents, in their sorrow and frustration, brought suit against the two doctors for neglect of medical duty. The state supreme court, by a vote of four to three, decided that under the law the doctors had neither the duty nor the right to terminate her pregnancy, whatever her desire or whatever the likelihood of a defective child.[33]

Repeated efforts were made to liberalise such state laws against abortion, and in 1973 the Supreme Court stepped in and struck them down. But the efforts were uniformly met by determined and organised Catholic opposition. When Assemblyman Albert Blumenthal introduced a measure of relaxation in 1967, the eight Catholic bishops of the state of New York organised a state-wide campaign against the measure, issuing a pastoral letter that urged all Catholics to fight against it with 'all their power'.[34] What is the ground of such opposition? It is not really humanitarian. If it were, it could not have held out against the facts that 85 per cent of the state's gynaecologists and 90 per cent of its psychiatrists had, in polls, favoured reforming the law, along with the New York Academy of Medicine, the New York county and state medical societies, and the state obstetrical and gynaecological societies. No, the ground of the opposition was theological. Catholic doctrine holds that the foetus, from the moment of conception, is an immortal soul, that to remove it is murder, that such murder, even of a foetus the size of a thimble, is a mortal sin which could condemn the mother to hell, and that if the foetus dies unbaptised, it goes to limbo rather than heaven. Of course, if these doctrines are true, the interventions of the church in medicine are more than justified, and the doctor is only doing his

duty in steeling himself against the temporal misery of a patient in
the interest of her eternal safety. But if, as we shall maintain, there
is an ethics of belief, then it is also the doctor's duty to consider
whether his certainty of the Roman eschatology equals the certainty
of his patient's suffering.

The problem arises again with respect to animals. Just as a
human foetus, even below the conscious level, has an immortal soul
and must be treated accordingly, so, in a theological ethic, an
animal has no soul and may be treated accordingly. And just as the
result is a factitious solicitude on the one hand, so it is an inhumane
callousness on the other. Northern travellers in the Catholic countries
of southern Europe have often noted the comparatively unfeeling
treatment of animals. 'The Church has always taught,' writes
Bertrand Russell, 'and still teaches, that man has no duties towards
the lower animals; on this ground Pope Pius IX regarded the
Society for the Prevention of Cruelty to Animals as ethically
heretical, and forbade the establishment of a branch in Rome.'[35]

So far, then, as the Catholic ideal of right conduct depends on
speculative notions that are unverified and unverifiable, it is a
flawed ideal. We may admit that if that ideal, flawed as it is, had
been adhered to in practice, the world would be a better place to
live in. Unfortunately, it has not been adhered to, even at the
highest levels. The College of Cardinals that elects the head of the
church seeks, and is supposed to receive, divine guidance, but, in
view of some of its elections, one can only conclude that its line of
communications has at times been broken. If Alexander VI were
the citizen of a civilised country today and maintained the level of
conduct he did as Pope, he could not have remained out of prison.
It would be utterly unjust to generalise from such cases, nor do I
have any intention of doing so. A historical generalisation requires
much evidence; the refutation of one requires little. Against the
contention that Catholic faith has radiated so intense and general
a sanctity among those who have held it as to afford proof of supernatural guidance, it is perhaps enough to record without enlargement a comment of the Catholic historian Lord Acton: 'If a man
accepts the Papacy with confidence, admiration and unconditional
obedience, he must have made terms with murder.'[36]

3   THE UNIVERSALITY OF THE CHURCH

13 'The third mark of the Church', says a sixteenth-century
catechism, 'is that she is Catholic, that is, universal; and justly is
she called Catholic, because, as St Augustine says, "she is diffused
by the splendour of one faith from the rising to the setting sun".'

Her founder left instructions: 'Go ye therefore and teach all nations'; 'ye shall be witnesses to me . . . even to the uttermost parts of the earth'. These instructions have been followed. The Catholic church has gone everywhere. It had reached America long before the Pilgrim fathers; it was in India long before the East India Company; it was carried by Francis Xavier to Japan, China, and the South Pacific, and by a devoted host of other missionaries to every country of South America. It draws no colour line. It admits no one because he is rich, excludes no one because he is poor, nor does it, like Marxism, split the world into social classes. Of all institutions it is the most international and cosmopolitan. Yet through all this diversity, so the argument runs, the faith is absolutely the same. There are Indian Catholics, but there is no Indian Catholicism. Although, in diffusing itself through the world, the faith has been filtered through innumerable differing temperaments, races, and cultures, the same product has emerged everywhere. If Catholicism were a merely human creation, the differences of culture in which it has lived would inevitably have made of it one thing here and a different thing there. They have conspicuously not done so. How is this to be explained except by saying that the faith is a donation from without, given to all from the same source?

14 Now unity in diversity may be a powerful argument. If a hundred men at random are asked independently who is the best candidate for an office, and they all respond with the same name, their agreement would be a weighty testimony for the candidate. If a hundred physicists from as many countries were asked to appraise the evidence on which a new theory was advanced, and they all reported that it was demonstrative, the theory would be placed virtually beyond doubt. But if such testimony is to carry weight, one condition is essential, namely that the verdict of each judge be given independently. What makes the final unanimity significant is that since each opinion was free to move in a different direction, the final convergence must be due to the force of the evidence. If it were discovered, on our first instance, that among the qualifications for voting was a prior pledge to support one candidate, or in our second case that no physicist was regarded as qualified to pass judgement unless he had already approved the theory, the consilience of opinion would be worthless.

Unfortunately the argument from universality is very like this. If Catholics from the four quarters of the compass all speak with the same voice on fundamentals, it is because one who spoke with a heretical voice would forthwith cease to be a Catholic. There is comparative peace within the fold because those who would most ably disturb it have been excluded. In regard to this mark of universality, the Catholic thus faces an alternative. If the testimony is admitted only of those who will give the right answer, the argument so obviously begs the question as to be valueless. If the suffrage is widened enough to ensure such value, the argument gives the opposite result from what was intended. A poll of all who had examined the body of Catholic dogma with some approach to objectivity would reveal the widest diversity of result. Even if it were confined to those who claimed the Catholic name, the result would hardly be different, since there has been controversy within the church from the beginning. Indeed when the dissidents have not been cut off promptly, they have sometimes swelled into a majority and threatened the enthronement of heresy. 'When Athanasius was "contra mundum", the Church was to all appearances virtually unanimous in her Arianism; but no Catholic would admit that Arianism was therefore true.'[37] As a rule, Papal decrees have been promulgated precisely to put an end to such controversy. Hence 'it is not too much to say, that every council has been called, every Papal edict issued, because *Catholicity had already been lost*'.[38] The unity that the church now exhibits has been achieved by a process, continued through many centuries, of cutting off angular dissidents on the right and awkward protestant prominences on the left till the body that remained was a nicely rounded whole. Such unity attests nothing but the efficiency of the Holy Office.[39]

4   THE APOSTOLICITY OF THE CHURCH

15   The fourth mark of the church is its apostolicity. This means two things; first, that there is an unbroken 'apostolic succession' by which the authority given to Peter has been conveyed through the long chain of his successors to the present Pope; second, that in all the stages of that succession the faith, worship, and organisation of the apostolic church have been reproduced. Great store is placed upon the first consideration, for the authority of all bishops and priests is derived ultimately from Christ himself through his vicar in Rome, and the invalid election of a Pope would invalidate all the orders consecrated by him. The second consideration sums up and gives point to the first and third notes of the church; it reminds us that the faith and practice already described as single and universal are also those which had the warrant of direct approval by Christ and his Apostles. What are we to say of this double mark?

THE FIRST LINK IN THE CHAIN

16   As for the claim to an unbroken chain, its strength cannot

exceed that of the weakest link in the chain. Unhappily the weak
links are many, and they grow weaker as we follow the chain backward into the mists of antiquity. 'The lists of early Popes and bishops
have no value' wrote Dean Inge. 'In all probability there was,
properly speaking, no bishop of Rome before the reign of Hadrian.'[40]
If any link is the most important, it is the first, since all others
depend upon it; so we shall do well to examine it with some care.
What reason is there to believe that the Catholic church was
instituted by Christ himself? The church rests the case chiefly on
some well known verses in the sixteenth chapter of Matthew. Jesus
asked the disciples, 'Whom do men say that I the Son of man am?'
and they replied that some took him for John the Baptist, some for
Elijah, some for Jeremiah. When he persisted, 'But whom say ye
that I am?' Peter answered 'Thou art the Christ, the Son of the
living God'. Then came the momentous reply:

17   And Jesus answered and said unto him, Blessed art thou,
Simon Bar-Jona: for flesh and blood hath not revealed it unto thee,
but my Father which is in heaven.
18   And I say unto thee that thou art Peter, and upon this rock
I will build my church; and the gates of hell shall not prevail
against it.
19   And I will give unto thee keys of the kingdom of heaven: and
whatsoever thou shalt bind on earth shall be bound in heaven:
and whatsoever thou shalt loose on earth shall be loosed in heaven.

The central words of this passage are inscribed in gigantic golden
letters around the interior of the dome of St Peter's. It is no wonder
that those who take the passage at face value should regard it as
conclusive. The more closely it is examined, however, the clearer it
becomes how unfirm a foundation it affords for the structure the
church has built upon it. We may well remind ourselves of some of
the reasons that have led non-Catholic scholars to think it a foundation of sand.[41]

WAS 'THOU ART PETER' EVER UTTERED?

17(1)   There is grave doubt whether the words were ever uttered
by Jesus at all. None of the other three gospels reports them, which
is an astonishing fact if they are really the Magna Carta of the
Christian church. The passage is not recorded even in the gospel of
Mark, which is the specially Petrine gospel, described by Justin
Martyr as 'the memoirs of Peter', supposed to be largely based on
Peter's own recollections and written by his intimate friend and
travelling companion. Is it credible that, in this gospel above all, the

most important incident of Peter's life, namely the conferring upon him of the headship of the Christian church, should, if it actually occurred, have passed unnoticed? The incidents before and after it are reported by both Mark and Luke very much as they are in Matthew, but this particular passage appears in neither. Furthermore, its failure to appear in Luke suggests that it also failed to appear in Q, the collection of the sayings of Jesus which, together with Mark, was the chief source upon which Matthew and Luke relied, and hence that it had no place in either of the two chief sources of the synoptic gospels. Once more, the language of the passage is uncharacteristic, so much so as to raise further question of its genuineness. Jesus speaks continually of 'the kingdom of God' and 'the kingdom of heaven'; he almost never speaks, as here, of 'the church' (ekklesia), and in the only other place in which he does so, he uses the term in a different sense. The famous passage is thus an anomaly. 'It makes its appearance sixty years after the death of Jesus, in the last redaction of our Gospel of Matthew, which is a compilation of the diverse elements,'[42] and 'It is probable that the passage is an interpolation made in the interests of the rapidly developing official ministry, the origin of which it was desired to throw back into the first age.'[43]

This conclusion receives further support from the context. Immediately after the passage in which Peter is alleged to have been made the head of the church and granted the keys to heaven itself, it is recorded that he received a direct and unsparing censure from his Master. Jesus predicted his own death and resurrection; Peter declared that he disbelieved the prediction; whereupon Jesus 'turned and said unto Peter, Get thee behind me, Satan: thou art an offence unto me: for thou savourest not the things that be of God, but those that be of men' (Matt. 16 : 23). Mark faithfully reports this rebuke (8 : 33) with no mention of the accolade which in Matthew just precedes it. That a friend and biographer of Peter should thus record the rebuke without the honour clearly increases the probability of the first and diminishes that of the second. And the second is rendered still more improbable by the incongruity of its tone with what immediately follows. We are told that a person has been made the head of the church and the vicar of Christ, only to hear Christ himself describing him within four verses as 'Satan' and 'an offence unto me'—surely singular words to stand as the first recorded greeting to the first of the popes.

To be sure, there is evidence enough that Peter was a leading figure among the disciples and was held by his Master in special esteem. But there is no evidence whatever that his Master treated him as his spokesman, mediator, and vicar-general. Indeed the very powers which are supposed to have been reserved for Peter and his successors he expressly delegated to the Apostles generally. 'And when he had said this, he breathed on them and saith unto them, Receive ye the Holy Ghost; whosesoever sins ye forgive, they are forgiven unto them; whosesoever sins ye retain, they are retained.' It was to the Apostles as a group that he said this, not to one alone.

THE ATTITUDE OF THE APOSTLES

18(2) These fellow Apostles were strangely unaware of Peter's primacy. They argued among themselves as to who was the greatest among them, just as if this had not already been settled; and James and John requested the seats at his right and left hand in the kingdom, giving no intimation in their request, nor their Master in his answer, that Peter stood first. When the group of Apostles at Jerusalem, whose recognised head, by the way, was not Peter but James, the brother of Jesus, wished to give moral support to some new Christians in Samaria, they 'sent forth to them Peter and John' (Acts 8 : 14). Such a report, entirely natural if Peter held a rough equality with his fellows, is strangely casual if one of the emissaries sent on the errand was the head of the whole Christian church. Peter was soundly rebuked by Paul for a wrong conception of what Christian conduct implied ('I withstood him to the face, because he was to be blamed' [Galatians 2 : 11]), which is oddly irreverent treatment of the supreme judge on earth of what Christian conduct meant. In the same chapter Paul mentions that on his visit to Jerusalem he found there 'James, Cephas [i.e. Peter], and John, who seemed to be pillars,' without any indication that even among these local 'pillars' Peter stood out; indeed Paul speaks of him as the special agent to the 'circumcision', the Jews, while he was himself the special agent to the 'uncircumcision', which was the larger part of the world. Even Peter himself does not seem to have been aware of his pre-eminence. The New Testament contains two letters accepted by the church as unquestionably his. There is no suggestion in these letters that he is the head of the church, and far from speaking as the prince of a permanent organisation, he tells his correspondents that 'the end of all things is at hand' (1 Peter 4 : 7). This itself is a singular pronouncement to come from one endowed with infallibility, for it was a presently exposed mistake.

THE ATTITUDE OF THE FATHERS

19(3) The picture remains much the same if we widen the context from the Apostles to the church fathers. They too seem to have lived in ignorance of Peter's unique role. 'I believe indeed', writes Bishop Gore after careful study of the matter, 'that none of the Greek Fathers of the first six centuries connects the position of the Bishop of Rome with the promise to St Peter'; the papal interpretation 'cannot show in its favour anything approaching to a consent of the fathers—indeed there is something much nearer consent in a view which excludes it . . .'.⁴⁴ Irenaeus, who died about 202, speaks of Peter and Paul as founders jointly of the church at Rome;⁴⁵ and when a bishop of that church, Victor, tried to 'excommunicate' certain persons for celebrating Easter on the wrong day, Irenaeus, far from accepting the verdict, openly rebuked the alleged head of the church for his attitude. Tertullian (about 150–230), who was perhaps the first to state the monarchical theory of Peter's position, himself rejected it.⁴⁶ Origen (about 185–253) argues that the foundation of the church was not Peter alone, but the Apostles generally. The most distinguished theologian of the next century, St Hippolytus, denounced the then bishop of Rome as a dangerous heresiarch—an impossible position for anyone who believed that bishop to be the final judge of heresy. During the controversy over the Nicene creed, the bishop of Rome, Liberius (of whom, by the way, St Jerome remarked that he had 'subscribed to heretical depravity'), notified St Athanasius that he had excommunicated him. If Liberius had been accepted as Pope in the modern sense, Athanasius would have felt blasted and crushed; as a matter of fact he expresses only sorrow that another good man (he classes the bishop of Rome with the bishop of Cordova) should have shown weakness. In the next century, the fifth, St Cyril of Alexandria still refers to St James as of 'equal honour' with Peter. The fathers were not even agreed as to the interpretation of the famous passage about the rock, and St Chrysostom and St Augustine both gave more than one interpretation of it within their own writings. Chrysostom thought, furthermore, that the statement about Peter of which Catholic apologists have made so much, that Christ 'prayed for him that his strength fail not', far from being a testimony to Peter's pre-eminence, was an indication of his special need for help; he had recently betrayed his Master.

But one may go further. Was Peter ever bishop of Rome at all? It is far from certain. Sabatier writes: 'The most mythical part of the legend is the supposed episcopate of Peter. No writer of the early centuries speaks of any such episcopate. . . . It is not until much later, with intent to articulate the episcopate more closely with the aposto- late, that Peter was admitted to the series of bishops as the first link in the mystic chain on which all the other links depended.'⁴⁷ And 'there are discrepancies in the earliest lists of Roman Bishops which seem quite unaccountable on the assumption that this office, and the question of its first occupant, were originally recognised as matters of unique importance.'[48]

THE ATTITUDE OF THE COUNCILS

20(4)   The position ascribed to Peter is inconsistent with the attitude of the early councils. There were many and bitter disputes over doctrine that could have been cleared up promptly if the members had known that there was an infallible voice among them; yet even at the great Council of Nicaea (325), where the divinity of Christ itself was at issue, it seems not to have occurred to them to let the Roman bishop decide; indeed he was not present at the Council at all. For that matter, when the issue of infallibility was raised for final decision in 1870, the church's leading scholars, men of such stature as Döllinger, Hefele, Dupanloup, and Acton, thought the contention almost absurd that early Christians had accepted an infallible Roman pontiff; Newman agreed; and at the council called to define the dogma, more than two hundred bishops expressed themselves as dissatisfied or avoided voting.[49] They may have reflected that it hardly became them to be certain when primitive councils themselves were so very far from certain. The Council of Chalcedon of 451, while allowing a precedence in prestige to the bishop of Rome 'because it was the imperial city', 'assigned an equal precedence to the most holy throne of new Rome,' that is, Constantinople.[50] We have already noted that at the Sixth General Council, that of Constantinople in 680, a step was taken that would have been out of the question if even then the successor of Peter had possessed the powers now ascribed to him; the Council anathematised the bishop of Rome and cast him out of the church for heresy.[51] The testimony of the ecumenical councils may thus be added to that of the Apostles and the fathers against the Catholic view of Peter's position.

THE EXPECTED SECOND COMING

21(5)   A consideration of another kind tends to the same result. Is it credible, in view of Jesus' expectations regarding the impending end of the world, that he should have inaugurated an ecclesiastical government designed for permanency? Over and over again he says unequivocally that human history is to reach its final pageant in his own generation.[52] If this was his belief, how could he also have sought to found an enduring church on the 'rock' of Peter, and to secure the transmission of the power of the keys to a series of his successors? In so acting, he would have been going counter to his own express and repeated statements about his early return.

The Catholic church believes that Jesus not only made Peter its first head but also ordained its enduring constitution, dogmas, and rites. He instituted its hierarchical order; he prescribed its seven sacraments; he gave directions regarding its membership and its conduct of affairs; he set up a class of church officials with special powers and privileges; he arranged for the transmission of an infallible deposit of faith; he identified the kingdom of heaven on earth, as Augustine did the 'city of God', with the Catholic church. How strange this all becomes if at the same time he was looking forward to the final catastrophe in a few years! Catholic scholarship has, of course, felt the difficulty. It has dealt with it through trying to suppress it by decree. Pope Pius X in his bull *Lamentabili* (1907) outlawed the proposition: 'it was foreign to the mind of Christ to establish on earth a church destined to last through a long series of centuries, but rather that in his mind the kingdom of heaven was to come shortly, together with the end of the world.'[53] The Biblical Commission of the Papacy laid it down in 1915 that even the Apostles did not regard the coming of the kingdom as imminent. Such measures suggest that in view of Scriptural history, the church's position needed vigorous shoring up. There is virtually nothing in the New Testament that can be construed as an attempt either to constitute or to legislate for an ecclesiastical organisation, and popes themselves have been driven to such imaginative flights as that of Innocent III, who claimed that when Peter leaped into the sea, this sea meant the world as a whole, over which he—and Innocent—were to rule. But the church is committed to taking the words of Scripture seriously. And the evidence that Jesus accepted and announced the earthly end of human history is so unequivocal that if a humble layman had denied it instead of the head of the church one would expect him to be anathematised. The prediction is reiterated with a passionate emphasis. If we have to choose between accepting this prediction as authentic and accepting the hypothesis that Jesus was laying down the law for a permanent ecclesiastical hierarchy, it is the hierarchy that must go.

THE RISE OF THE PAPACY

22(6)   One more consideration: it is commonly argued by Catholic apologists that unless the first link in the chain were unbreakable, the whole could not have held; the fact that it has in fact held is therefore proof of the soundness of this first link. The meteoric ascension of an obscure and feeble sect, in the course of a few centuries, to the dominant religious force in the Western world is inexplicable except on the supposition that it was launched from a rock of more than human firmness and that its course was charted by a supernatural hand. That course is indeed most impressive, and this is one conceivable account of it. But there are difficulties. The church has not invariably conducted itself in such a manner as to make this explanation inevitable. Great councils have made decisions after acrimonious debate and by narrow margins; human ambitions and personal animosities have competed with genuine humility and piety for the control of the church's policy; it has produced saints on the one hand and Borgias and Torquemadas on the other in confusing numbers; and for an institution with supernatural support, its halt by the Reformation and its overturn in Russia raise obvious questions.

Is there any plausible alternative to the Roman account of its origin and growth? The materials for such an alternative are far richer than they used to be. To the factors discussed by Gibbon in his famous fifteenth and sixteenth chapters—such factors as the austere morality of the early Christians as compared with the depravity and soddenness of the life around them, the power of their gospel of simplicity, humility, and love to cross the barriers of race and class, and their firm assurance of immortality—there must now be added all the evidence laid bare by historians like Cumont of the unsatisfactory rival religions in the early empire, by anthropologists like Frazer of pagan preparation for Christianity in such dogmas as those of the dying god and the virgin goddess, by psychologists like Freud of the overmastering tendency of desire to generate congenial beliefs. The cogency of such an account would depend on its power to cover the complex details of a long historical development, and we cannot undertake it. Happily that is not necessary for our present purpose. The immediate point is whether the Roman bishops could have made their rapid ascent from impotence to dominion unless the succession had been launched and guided by supernatural power.

There is one fact that by itself goes far toward explaining this ascent on a natural basis. It is simply that Rome was in those years the capital of the civilised world. 'Rome was the centre of the world's movements. Everybody came thither. She was the world's "microcosm". It followed necessarily that she stood, as regards her Church, in a unique freedom of communication with the Churches of the rest of the world. Christians from all parts necessarily gravitated thither.'54 This concentration of influence is surely not without parallel. The lawyers, actors, and doctors of England look to those who lead the profession in London as leaders of the profession generally; the artists, professors, and clerics of France look to those at the top in Paris as outstanding among Frenchmen; the seat of commercial and political power tends to become the centre also of science, scholarship, and religion. Rome was to the civilised world in the first centuries what London is to England and Paris to France. Its emperor, its courts, its wealth and trade, its military dominance, its liberal policy of citizenship and its physical splendour made it easily first among the cities of the world. It was therefore merely natural that its bishop should gravitate toward the primacy among his colleagues from the provinces; indeed the Council of Chalcedon explicitly gave this as the reason for his primacy; it was 'on account of the predominant position of that city'. One may even be surprised that the ascendancy was not achieved and recognised earlier than it was. The first bishop of Rome to assert the later prerogatives with popular acceptance was Leo the Great, who rose to the throne in the year 440, and whose power was accentuated by his success in persuading Attila the Hun to turn back from his march on Rome. Here the Rome of the popes was visibly accepting the leadership that was being lost by the Rome of the Caesars.

THE SECOND MEANING OF APOSTOLICITY

23 We have been considering the apostolicity of the church in its first meaning. According to that meaning, the church can trace its present authority backward along a power-line of transmission beginning with the investiture of Peter, a supernatural line without whose potent current the rise and maintenance of the church would be inexplicable. We have seen that there is room for question about this line, most notably perhaps as to the firmness of its first attachment. But apostolicity has a second meaning. It implies that the church of today is linked with its original founder not only by continuity in its headship but also by its reproduction of the structure and spirit of the primitive Christian community, that in the faith, worship, and organisation of the present-day church we find a true reflection across the centuries of the church apostolic. Is the church of Rome apostolic in this second sense?

24 Unfortunately there is no one of the 'notes' that breaks down quite so tragically. Modern Catholicism a replica of primitive Christianity, a reproduction of the mind and spirit of Jesus of Nazareth! Certainly the claim does not wear on its face any high plausibility. It recalls the question of Sully Prudhomme when he looked over the row of volumes of the *Summa Theologica*, 'How is it that this which is so complicated has proceeded from what was so simple?' In no one of the three respects—organisation, worship, faith—in which the church is supposed to offer a faithful portrait is there any satisfactory likeness. The early churches were simple democratic communities, to whom Jesus had 'proclaimed a kingdom which was shortly to come down from heaven. Nothing was more contrary to his conception of the Kingdom of God than the idea of a monarchical Church modelled upon the laws of the empire of the Caesars, with a similar hierarchy and the same capital.'[55]

Nor does the likeness seem to be greater in ritual and worship.

'He did not love tradition, did not believe in the sanctity of formularies, in the holiness of fasts, the sin and apostasy of all who refused to conform to the priestly law or order. . . . His ideal of worship was filial love expressed in filial speech and conduct; and this love made all places sacred, all times holy, all service religious, all actions duties done to the Father in heaven.'[56]

The question has often been asked, and with point, whether the prophet of Nazareth, if he were conducted into a modern cathedral, would have any conception of what was going on. He would be met with an elaborate ministry to the senses. He would see priests in vestments moving about in candlelight before a richly covered altar; would hear the singing of robed choirs and the chanting of a mass in a strange language; and he would smell the heavy odour of incense. Would he know, one wonders, where to come in with a response, when to kneel, and when to stand?

If he inquired what the figure at the altar was doing, he would receive an extraordinary answer. He would be told that, by reason of supernatural aid, invoked by a potent formula, the priest was converting bread and wine into flesh and blood, which would forthwith be eaten. Why this rite? Because, in the remote past an angry Deity had been appeased by the bloody and excruciating but voluntary sacrifice of his only son. Since the son was sinless, this act had created a vast reservoir of grace or merit, and by partaking of this flesh and blood, worshippers not only paid honour to Father and Son, but averted some part of the Father's anger against themselves. Anger for what? Partly for their own wickedness, but partly also for the sins of their remote ancestors, for which he had determined to hold them responsible. But whose body is being thus eaten? To which there could only come the reply: 'It is your body we are eating; it is you that have appeased your wrathful Father for us; it is by your orders that the censers are swinging, the organ pealing, the mass being celebrated in these vestments.' Would he recognise in all this his own mind and will? We can answer only with another question: How can any student of the simple, poetic, prophetic, unworldly mind of Jesus believe for a moment that this was its natural expression? Dean Inge is probably right that the simple

worship of the Society of Friends, that group which of all Christian
sects stands farthest from Catholicism, is closer to the upper room
than the most orthodox of masses sung under the dome of St Peter's.

The same conclusion seems inevitable about the creed of Catholicism in relation to the faith of Jesus. What the faith of Jesus really
was no one knows with certainty; it must be divined between lines
of uncertain authorship, uncertain date, and at times contradictory
import. But his origin and education were humble, and though he
probably knew some Greek, he seems to have been quite untouched
by Greek science and philosophy. There is surely something grotesque
in the thought of the Galilean prophet's being confronted by the
twenty-two portentous volumes in which, armed with all the sharp
cutlery of the Aristotelian logic, Aquinas dissected, expounded, and
systematised the Christian creed. What would Jesus have made of
the metaphysics of the eucharist, with its play of substance and
accident? Where would he have stood on the *filioque* clause? Could
he, or would he, thread the mazes of Thomistic demonology and
angelology? Was he clear about the length of service in purgatory
required for the expiation of the various classes of sin? To the good
Catholic there is nothing grotesque in these questions, nothing about
which the mind of Christ, carrying, as it must have done, the whole
Catholic scheme of salvation, would have hesitated for a moment.
Others, including myself, can only think that such questions would
have seemed to Jesus, as they do to most of ourselves, artificial and
unreal.

Our survey of the four 'notes' has yielded little. They were
supposed to provide firm foundations for belief in a supernaturally
ordered church. But they seem to dissolve almost at a touch. Where
does this leave the Catholic apologist?

THE DIALECTIC OF AUTHORITY

25 If he means what he sometimes says, it leaves him in an
unhappy place. He sometimes claims to be a thoroughgoing
rationalist, ready to stake the case for the occurrence of revelation
on straightforward argument. For the man of faith, this is questionable strategy. It assumes, for one thing, that the argument he has to
offer will turn out to be conclusive, as the one we have just examined
was supposed to be. But it may turn out to be far from conclusive,
and the apologist will then be empty-handed. But secondly, to base
the claim of an authority supposed to be ultimate on the validity of a
supporting argument is an even more radical error, for it implies a
surrender in principle of the case being argued. If one accepts the
authority because of the reasons, and is ready to abandon it if these

reasons prove invalid, then one is shifting one's ultimate appeal from authority to reason, which is now the power behind the throne, establishing the authority or dismissing it. The more responsible Catholic apologists have seen this, and have taken care to say that while the existence of a supernatural authority can be proved, such proof is not the ground on which faith really rests. That ground is the testimony of Deity himself, the voice of authority speaking directly and infallibly to certain chosen minds.

Now for all one can see, this direct disclosure may occur. Since it owes nothing of its authority to reason, it cannot be discredited by reason, and since it comes only from a supernatural source to a mind supernaturally prepared, no one who has received it can communicate it to anyone who has not. If a man claims to have had a disclosure, those who have not received it must accept its occurrence on the strength of his assertion, without any genuine understanding of what it is that he is asserting; and if one of them denied that such revelation occurred, he would literally not know what he was talking about. Nevertheless, outsiders can and must say this: that when the favoured person retreats in this way behind hedges impenetrable to other men's understanding or verification, he cannot complain if a doubt continues to haunt them as to the authority of the disclosure. It is extremely easy to be mistaken about such revelations, as is shown by the many persons who have been sure they have had them and come later to doubt their genuineness.

Furthermore, in consistency, a person who claims the privilege of accepting as absolute an incommunicable and unevidenced authority, must grant the same privilege to others. But the results, if he does, are disturbing. For among those who claim similar privileges are many whose private disclosures, so far as any inkling of them can be gathered, are in contradiction to his own. The mere assurance, therefore, that one has received such a disclosure is not a certification, since one or other of the contradictory parties must be mistaken, and may not he be the one? If he is a non-Catholic, he may reply, 'I am quite ready to accept them all, and to believe that the contradictory world which they disclose is the real world'. That way madness lies. But this is not the way of the Catholic. He would not dream of abandoning the law of contradiction. Hence to him the dilemma is a serious one: if you rest your appeal to authority on reason, you are making reason, not authority, your court of last resort; if you do not, but insist on the right to accept a revelation on no rational grounds, you should grant the same right to others, and then you will find yourself faced with many contradictory 'revelations'. One can guess the answer that will be made by the scholastic apologist. It is that he possesses the right himself because his revelation is genuine, but that others do not because theirs is illusory. Speaking strictly, there is no breach of logic in this reply. Unfortunately it will convince no one but himself.

BELIEF AND DESIRE

26 Most philosophers and scientists of our day would regard the fabric of revealed doctrine in which the Catholic has traditionally lived as at once impressive and unreal. They would be indifferent whether our criticism was effective or ineffective, for they would take it in either case as a battling with shadows. Why attempt to storm a castle point by point when one can see with a little reflection that it is a castle in the clouds, its towers and turrets steadily dissolving in the breezes of modern thought? What is of interest is not the crevices of error or the loopholes of fallacy that keen eyes may discern in it, but why anyone should have taken such a fabric as truth at all.

That has not been our own question about Catholicism. While unable to accept it, we have paid it the respect of taking its claim to truth seriously. Still the question why, if not true, it has been so widely taken as true is also of interest. The general answer is not far to seek. What sustains a system of this kind is a combination of factors, of which two are outstanding, the satisfaction of desire on the one hand and the congeniality of the intellectual climate on the other.

The importance of desire is surely obvious. Man is a waif in the universe. He is pushed into existence without his consent; he is inevitably pushed out of it before long by forces beyond his understanding. His body is a sort of candle carrying about a flickering flame of consciousness in which everything of value in his universe resides. He knows to a certainty that the candle will not long support the flame, and he does his best to keep its wavering tongue alive against the winds that threaten it from all sides. When he thinks about his prospects, as all men do occasionally, he realises that he is helpless, that the infinite universe has him in its grip, that it can crush him at any moment, and that it eventually will. There is only one hope for him. Might the universe itself be controlled by a power that could be enlisted on his side? Catholicism assures him that this last hope is an actual, joyful fact. Behind the vast indifferent machine is a person more or less like himself, just, solicitous, even loving, who cares enough for his creatures to have paid the mysterious sacrifice of his very self to give them a chance of escape. And this escape is more than a release from extinction; it is the promise of translation into a world without end of security, fulfilment, and happiness, the things men long for most. Is it a matter for surprise that when feeble and fearful persons are offered such a gift they should stretch out their hands for it? Is it likely that before accepting it they should examine meticulously the credentials of the donation? It is true that when first offered it was a strange alloy of fact and myth, but then the means of smelting fact loose from the encasement of myth hardly existed. Enough that their religion answered a tremendous need, and that the intellectual climate of the time lent that answer credibility.

BELIEF AND THE INTELLECTUAL CLIMATE

27 Indeed the intellectual climate has supported the church during most of Christian history, if only because through long stretches of time the church has supplied that climate itself. For more than a thousand years there was little to be found of scholarship, science, or philosophy outside the cloister; and within the cloister a rigorous control was imposed on untoward doubts and inquiries. The Catholic view of the world was the only one available; it was accepted by the body of learned men, most of whom were themselves within the church; and the general opinion was that the church had received it directly from Deity. This view of the world seemed so firm of outline, so persuasive, so harmonious, that disbelief in it was branded as not only stupidity but sin, justly punishable by excommunication if not by thumbscrew, rack, and stake. Since the production of contrary evidence was impermissible, all the evidence at hand pointed in one direction. For those in the Catholic world, Catholicism *was* the world.

To men of today, the mind of mediaeval man seems remote and strangely naïve. How gullible can one be? To believe in witches riding broomsticks against the moon, a devil who, even in Luther's time, could be heard of nights in the courtyard, the magically efficacious knucklebones of saints, the continuing interposition of the Virgin to heal disease and temper the weather—all this seems childish to the man brought up in a world of science. If he rejects such claims, it is not because he could disprove any of them, but because in a world of scientific daylight the monsters and demons that once flourished in shady places find the light too much for them and gradually fade away.

But it must be remembered that for mediaeval man and for some of his modern successors there was no larger world of law by whose light his structure of dogma could be examined and judged; his religion with its foundation in Scripture and its pillars of dogma was the house he lived in; it supplied the solid reality against which other claims were measured. Within it, all the parts seemed coherent and necessary to each other, and in their union they gave the whole an overwhelming credibility. Science could find no means of entrance, for the approach from the side of nature was specially guarded by church teaching. This teaching was that the cardinal points of revealed truth were firmer certainties than anything science could supply, and therefore that in any conflict with natural knowledge revelation must take precedence.

If a devotee takes up his residence in this roomy house of faith, allows no light to enter except through windows stained with the colours and figures of that faith, and stays there resolutely, his eyes become so accustomed after a time to the light of tapers and rose windows that it becomes for him the daylight. Doctrines that to the secular mind seem too bizarre for consideration begin to appear first natural and then necessary. If one has accepted the greatest of all miracles, the incarnation, why quibble about minor ones like the walking on the water or the feeding of the five thousand? If the second member of the Paraclete was born of woman, was she not in fact the mother of God? And if she was thus honoured by Deity, why not pray to her for intercession with Deity? Why not admit that she was free from original sin, as Pius IX asked (and answered) in 1854? Why not take the short further step of accepting her bodily assumption into heaven, as Pius XII asked (and answered) in 1950? Indeed why should one not applaud the Primate of Poland as he begged the assembled bishops at Vatican II 'not to disband before solemnly consecrating the world to Mary'? Each dogma in the system leads to others, and as each is seen to have its place in the elaborately reticulated webwork of doctrine, its plausibility rises. Beliefs like that in the real presence, the sin in the garden, the flood, the stone rolled away, paradise with its flights of angels, hell and purgatory with their flights of devils—beliefs that standing alone would seem incredible—come to seem natural enough to a mind that lives within the system. Start with a body of revelation beyond the criticism of one's natural faculties; develop it, if this should be possible, with the thoroughness of an Aquinas, the logic of a Pascal, and the subtlety of a Newman; scorn as they did to measure its fixities by the changing fashions of science; live as they did in the haunting fear that their inquiring minds might carry them over the brink into heresy and hell; and you have a way of life that virtually guarantees loyalty to the faith.

28 The guarantee will hold, however, on one condition only: intellectual intercourse between the tenants of the house of faith and the world outside must be jealously controlled. For the records disclose that once they have wandered afield and exposed themselves to secular science and philosophy, they have a way of not coming back and, worse, of complaining that the structure in which they had lived, imposing as it was in its interior, seems as they look back at it strangely rickety and insecure. This has always been a problem for the church, and it has become more acute with the rise of science. Vatican II faced it in the form of a dilemma, neither horn of which seemed acceptable, the dilemma between the way of thinking of Cardinal Ottaviani and that of Cardinal Suenens. The redoubtable old head of the Holy Office hewed to the line of traditional dogma; the church had never pretended to be of this world; it had scored its successes by setting itself against that world in belief, in spirit, and in practice; why should it compromise now? To the majority of bishops, however, that seemed like the sort of rigidity from which the good Pope John was seeking to deliver the church. The liberal Archbishop of Brussels took another line. The church should try to understand the modern age, and so far as it consistently could, accommodate itself to the world of science, not fight a losing battle against it; 'I beg of you, Fathers, not to repeat the trial of Galileo. One is enough in the Church.'

That was sage counsel from a brave man, but it was more dangerous, perhaps, than Cardinal Suenens realised. For Catholicism is especially vulnerable to science by reason of the very integration of its theory. If its body of dogma were merely a litter of unrelated theses, each of which could stand or fall alone, the church could lose an occasional dogma to the attrition of science without alarm for the whole. But its body of belief is not such a litter. It has its contradictions, as we have seen, but in the main it is an organism whose parts are so interdependent that the amputation of a dogma is a shock felt at all its extremities. The Virgin birth is an example. Suppose that the youth who accepts it without question becomes a student of biology. In any case but this, he would scout the suggestion of human parthenogenesis. Biological doubts arising, he begins to have textual doubts. He looks more critically at the record, and finds the evidence more tenuous than he would have believed possible; two of the gospels, for example, make no mention of such a birth, and the other two give human genealogies either of which, though inconsistent with each other, would, if true, preclude it. Does he find the evidence such as to demonstrate that the Virgin birth was *not* a fact? No, not that either. Like most others in the theological system, this dogma is incapable of conclusive disproof. It has such credibility as is lent to it by its coherence with the theological system. But how is that system itself to be appraised?

CATHOLIC DOGMA IN THE MODERN WORLD

29 To that question there is only one tenable answer. The truth
of the system must be judged by its coherence with human experience as a whole. It may be said that this is to appeal arbitrarily
from one authority to another, that if two coherent systems of
thought collide, neither should be preferred to the other. But this is
untrue. For the truth of a system must be judged, not by internal
consistency alone, but also by its breadth of inclusiveness; and the
most inclusive available system is that which includes human
experience as extended and interpreted by the sciences. The world
of the Forsyte Saga may be extraordinarily consistent internally,
but that is no guarantee that Soames and Jolyon Forsyte lived and
moved on earth; we cannot fit their world, however consistent in
itself, into the world we actually live in, for that would conflict at
innumerable points with our knowledge of Victorian England and
the facts of Galsworthy's biography. The Greek mythology may
make an astonishingly consistent whole of story, but no one doubts
that it *is* only story, for that hypothesis fits far more consistently into
the body of historic fact and anthropological law than any account
of an actual Zeus meeting with an actual council on the summit of
Olympus.

There is nothing arbitrary in taking reflectively interpreted
experience as the court of last appeal. In the end, it is this or nothing.
The sensations with which experience starts are compulsory; our
interpretation of them in perception is compulsory; the laws of
inference by which we develop and relate our perceptions are
compulsory; and once we are launched on the enterprise of science,
we find that the order of our experience is inexplicable except
through a nature governed by law. The system of thought thus
developed is a natural one, and the ideal of explanation through a
system whose parts are intelligibly related is immanent at every
stage of the development. It is idle for any authority, religious or
secular, to take its stand against this natural order of thought.
Religious systems and scientific theories without number have set
their lances in rest against it only to break themselves on it and disappear. Nor can there be pluralism where truth is concerned; to
say that the bodily assumption is true for the Catholic, though untrue
for Buddhist or Protestant, is only to say that one party *thinks* it
true and the other not; it could hardly mean that the dogma itself
is *both* true and false. One or the other party *must* be mistaken.

In the appraisal of Catholicism as of any other system of beliefs,
we come then in the end to the question whether it can maintain
itself in the light of human experience when this is itself systematised

by the logical ideals implicit in it. The unavoidable answer seems to be No.

30 The world of modern science is one of law. If a new and strange event occurs and the scientist is asked what were the chances of its having a natural cause, as against its having no such cause and being an intrusion of the supernatural into nature, he would probably not rate them as infinity to zero; the profession of absolute certainties does not come easily to him. Instead he would probably rate them as millions or billions to one, which is a fairly close approximation to certainty after all. Now the Catholic system of dogma does not fit into this modern intellectual world. It holds not only that suspensions of law have occurred, and occurred more than once, but that there have been untold thousands of them, from the delivery to Moses of the tablets of stone through the walking on the water and the raising of Lazarus to the myriad interpositions of saints, the miracles connected with relics, the supernatural cures of Lourdes and Fatima, and the continuing transubstantiations of the mass. One cannot hold at once that the world is governed by natural law and also that its laws are continually and massively set aside by powers of which no natural account can be given. The major assumption of science, the law of causality, is thus in conflict with a major Catholic assumption, namely that suspensions of causal law are of daily and hourly occurrence. It may be replied that the law of causality—the law that all events are governed by causal laws—is itself as truly empirical as any particular law; there is hence no necessity about it, and exceptions to it may be admitted without contradiction. Most philosophers of science would so far agree with this as to hold the law of causality to be neither self-evident nor an inductive conclusion (which would inevitably be circular), but rather a postulate progressively verified as science advances. And this means that the Catholic assumption does remain a theoretic possibility in the sense that it is not *demonstrably* false. Nevertheless, in view of the support that has been given to the postulate in an immense variety of fields by the advance of science, this possibility provides somewhat cold comfort. While it vetoes the verdict of demonstrable falsity, it leaves standing so overwhelming an improbability as to give no plausible ground for positive belief.

31 It is not merely over the continuing suspension of law, however, that Catholic dogma conflicts with modern thought. Its two-world theory implies that there are two orders of truth, reaching us from different sources, verifiable by different standards, and carrying different degrees of assurance. Truths of the first order come to us, not through our natural faculties, but from an absolute authority; truths of the second order come to us from human experience, which is finite and fallible; and if truths of the two orders conflict, the first has the right of way. Modern thought finds it increasingly difficult to accept these two orders. If, whenever authority has taken sides against science, it has had to trim and retreat, the claim to a separate and superior order of knowledge becomes steadily less credible, and the conviction that truth is to be achieved only through the exercise of our natural faculties becomes more assured.

Indeed the notion of a double standard seems bound to end in incoherence. Sooner or later a case will arise in which a belief warranted by one standard will be disallowed by the other; what then? The consequences will be far-reaching. If we are told by an authority that something is true which our natural insight tells us is untrue, it is not only this particular belief that is at issue, but the standards of our ordinary thought; these are being set aside as unreliable; and if they are really thus unreliable, the infection spreads through the whole natural field. Furthermore, our insights in ethics are placed in jeopardy as well as those in the natural sciences. If we are instructed, for example, that the delivery of the gospel to one people and one time, to the exclusion of all others, is perfectly just, then our own conception of justice must be distorted. If we are told that perfect goodness presides over nature and history, then the influenza epidemic of 1918 must be a manifestation of it. And if that is really goodness, then our own ethics can no longer stand. It is conceivable, to be sure, that there should be a continuing revelation which at each step was in advance of our own thought, but never so far that we could not on reflection assimilate and grow up to it. But that is not the case or the claim of the revelation here dealt with. That revelation has been given once for all, and between its content, both factual and ethical, and our own standards, there are gaps that seem unbridgeable.

32 If what we have said is true, the ultimate verdict on Catholic dogma is a verdict on a contracted system of thought passed by a more inclusive one. To the mind that lives in the Catholic world, each dogma seems reasonable enough; it has its appointed place in the traditional system and takes its credibility from the mutual sustenance that the members of the system give to each other. But the system is itself a limited one. The block of doctrine of which it is composed was, in the main, hewn out before modern logic, science, or history had been born, and for much of its existence there was no more inclusive system by which it could be judged; it supplied the horizons of the world. But the growth of science has flung back those horizons to an unimaginable distance—in space, in time, and in the complexity and wealth of human knowledge. And wherever that knowledge has penetrated, it has found law. Even in the realm of the submicroscopic it has found at least statistical law. Is it likely that a tiny enclave consisting of one religious community on one minute planet in a universe apparently governed throughout by natural law should be the scene of continual suspensions of that law, made on no discernible plan? No one can be surprised if this claim is greeted with a steadily mounting scepticism.

Science has not proved its major assumption; granted. In the fields of psychical research and mental healing there are occurrences which have baffled every attempt to bring them under known law and which suggest that some widely accepted postulates of science may have to be revised. But three points are to be remarked about such cases. First, the most competent researchers regard them as attestations, not of a supernatural order, but at most of a nature richer in content than the traditional one, perhaps requiring 'extra-sensory perception' for contact with it. Secondly, the relations of these unexplored regions to the familiar world are still regarded as governed by law, even where the law remains to be discovered. Thirdly, the burden of proof must always be assumed by the claim to a suspension of law, from whatever region that suspension is alleged to come. Explanation normally *means* bringing an instance under a natural law, and to hold that there is no law governing the case is considered acceptable only as a last and desperate resort.

Upon such convictions as these the modern scientific mind has been formed. When presented with a system of dogma alleged to be revealed from outside nature and above it, and claiming that interpositions continually occur, contemporary man is sceptical. His scepticism is not primarily of this or that dogma, and if he tried to argue transubstantition or the bodily assumption with a practised Jesuit apologist, he would probably not cut a distinguished figure. Out of his element in scholastic dialectic and confused by the citation of imposing authorities, he would still protest that the over-world of heaven and hell, angels and demons, transcendental cures and ecclesiastically induced changes in the weather seemed to him unreal. Why? He might shrug his shoulders and say he felt in his bones that they were. Inarticulate as his 'intuition' may be, it is not simply to be brushed aside. It may be the voice of a much larger volume of thought and experience than his own; indeed it may sum up the attitude of the 'modern mind', formed and penetrated as this is by the spirit of science. There are those who would find in it the verdict of an older, more experienced, more sceptical world ('*we* are the true ancients,' said Bacon) on a younger and more imaginative but far less critical one.

33 Such a judgement, when made reflectively, would not of course dismiss unheard the claim that there are two world orders. We have tried ourselves to listen to what is said, and to discover whether these two orders can be put together into a coherent whole. The assumption that the world is such a whole, that the two sides of an inconsistency cannot both be true or real, is the basis on which we build. When we have found the two orders in conflict, we have tried to explain as groping hypothesis, imagination, or myth the side that most resisted assimilation into a coherent system. What other road can a responsible thinker take? This attempt to avoid compartmentalisation, to see particular claims in the light of the whole, and to order one's beliefs into consistency and interconnection is for us what philosophy means. If we should need a plea for this reflective ideal, finely and temperately stated, we should turn to no other than Cardinal Newman.

'That only is true enlargement of mind which is the power of viewing many things at once as one whole, of referring them severally to their true place in the universal system, of understanding their respective values, and determining their mutual dependence. . . . Possessed of this real illumination, the mind never views any part of the extended subject-matter of Knowledge without recollecting that it is but a part. . . . It makes every thing in some sort lead to every thing else. . . . To have even a portion of this illuminative reason and true philosophy is the highest state to which nature can aspire, in the way of intellect. . . .'[57]

PART II

REASON AND FAITH:
THE LUTHERAN SUCCESSION

CHAPTER V

REASON AND FAITH IN LUTHER

1   There is no such thing as *the* Protestant view of the relation between reason and faith. That there is a Catholic view we have had ample occasion to see. Catholic philosophers and theologians, to be sure, have presented briefs for many conflicting doctrines, but councils have winnowed these out, and popes have declared heretical those who refused assent to the doctrine finally decreed. Among Protestants there is no such authority, and the debate continues. There is a wide spectrum of theories, extending from high-church Anglicanism on the right, which would accept practically everything in the Roman account except Papal infallibility, to liberal Unitarianism on the left, which is essentially rationalism tinged with emotion, and would reject any belief that exceeds the rational evidence. In reviewing the Protestant position, we are thus in trouble at the outset. If we try to examine all the Protestant views, we are lost in a forest of subtly varying theologies. If we fix our eye on any one doctrine or set of doctrines, we shall be accused of being narrow and arbitrary.

This risk is one that we must take; nor is there any necessary injustice in selecting some positions for discussion and ignoring others. It is absurd to place all Protestant sects on a level, to put Anglicanism and Anabaptism on a par in historical importance, or Calvin and Fox on a par in intellectual grasp. Nor is it fair to say that the many branches of Protestantism make a mere litter. They are all growths from one trunk. What is commonly meant by Protestantism is a movement started at a definite time with the proclamation of definite convictions. These convictions have indeed proliferated in all directions. We shall not enter on the unprofitable question which is *the* main stream of Protestantism, but there is no doubt where its fountainhead lies, or that some of the streams have carried the water of the source with greater purity than others. The fountainhead was Martin Luther. And the Lutheran stream that runs down from the source through Kierkegaard and such eminent theologians of our time as Emil Brunner and Karl Barth surely has as much right as any other to be called the main stream. At any rate this is the one we are to examine. To do so in detail is of course out of the question. All these men were minds of inexhaustible energy, which overflowed into acres of pages. From those pages we must limit ourselves to a single issue, the relation of reason and faith.

WHAT LUTHER INHERITED

2   The Reformation was so decisive a turning-point in history that we are likely to over-estimate the change it achieved in the way of belief; the fact is that Luther, at his most Protestant extreme, agreed with the Catholic outlook far more than he differed from it. The sceptical modern mind has moved so far from the world in which he lived that, before considering what he denied, it may be well to remind ourselves of what he continued to accept throughout his life.

In spirit he still lived in the Middle Ages. When he was born, Gutenberg had been dead only fifteen years, and books as we now know them were just beginning to circulate. Modern science was still in its dawn, or rather in the flush before its dawn, for at the time of Luther's death the birth of Galileo was eighteen years in the future. Word did indeed come to Luther in his old age that a Pole named Copernicus had published a book purporting to show that the earth moved round the sun. Luther was not impressed: 'the fool wishes to revolutionise the whole science of astronomy,' he exclaimed. 'But as the Holy Scriptures show, Joshua commanded the sun to stand still, not the earth.' Luther's world was pre-Copernican in another and more important sense. Its intellectual centre was not experience, as on the whole it is for the modern world, but Scripture, round which everything else revolved, to which everything else came back for its test of truth and importance. Because of this, the mediaeval house of intellect differed as deeply from that of modern scientific intelligence as a mediaeval chapel, with its candles and chants and swinging censers and oriel windows, differs from a modern laboratory. For Luther, both as monk and as reformer, what was important to know was not the constitution of nature or the course of secular history—these things were vanity—but the prophecies of Isaiah and Daniel, the clues to the divine will that might be gleaned from the Psalms, Proverbs, and gospels, and Paul's instructions to the Galatians about the meaning of saving faith.

From first to last Luther looked at the world through these theological spectacles. As Lecky says, 'a theological atmosphere was formed about his mind, and became the medium through which every event was contemplated'.[1] Miracles were common. The devil was a familiar trouble-maker who could sometimes be heard at night clattering about in the courtyard. Half-wits, hunchbacks, the blind and the dumb were probably possessed by the devil or his minions, and Luther's own manifold infirmities were freely assigned to Satan. Good and evil spirits were battling for the control not only of men's minds and bodies but also of the winds and the tides, of hail, thunder, and rain.

If Luther's theological prepossessions could make him see demons peeping from behind cloister pillars and from the eyes of children, still more did they determine what he saw when he contemplated the world in the large. It was a place of probation. God had fashioned it as a home and garden for man. He had made man as an image of himself, clear of mind and pure of conscience, and had placed him in this garden with instructions how to live and with freedom to obey or not to obey. To his anger, man chose disobedience. The taint of this disobedience infected all man's faculties, corrupting his conscience, confusing his intelligence and distorting his will; and, what was worse, it communicated its contagion to his descendants. They became hateful in the sight of their Creator, who not only doomed them to labour and suffering in this life but, refusing them the charity of annihilation, reserved for them an eternity of unspeakable torment in a life to come. In the tables of the divine reckoning, this was no more than just, since an infinite wrong deserved an infinite expiation.

Was there any way in which man could be relieved of this unending punishment? One only; and that was the appearance of a substitute who could offer infinite goodness as a cancellation of infinite guilt. It was obvious that such an offer could come from only one source. The second person of the Trinity, in whom all the powers and perfections of Deity were lodged, elected to be embodied in human form, to be despised and rejected of men, and be put to an excruciating death in order to rescue man from his doom. But even after this sacrifice, man remained under sentence. Though a store of grace had been created by it, this grace was not placed automatically to the credit of the malefactors, but was portioned out by Deity according to an inscrutable preference. In those who received it, it took the form of a faith that could discern truths hidden from secular eyes and a love for their kind that radiated out in effortless good works. This saving grace was all that truly mattered. Nothing else— no loftiness of spirit or purity of aim or even devotion to goodness —could avert the impending doom, for these goods of the natural man were only specious counterfeits of the supernatural realities. Without faith there is no health in us, and no hope; it would have been better if we had not been born. Life for both saved and unsaved is a battle, since the powers of darkness—somehow allowed to operate by an omnipotent Deity—are around us on all sides, tempting us into avarice, ambition, and pride, and the even blacker sins of heresy and blasphemy. In our strength we cannot prevail against these seductions. But God is a mighty fortress in which, with his favour, we may find asylum. And the battle will not be forever. Luther saw many signs that the end was approaching, when the God who came as a bloody sacrifice would come again in clouds of glory as the judge of the quick and the dead. Those whom he had elected to salvation would then be gathered to an eternity of rejoicing in their father's house, and those against whom he had set his face would be cast into a pit of endless, unimaginable torture.

This was the world of thought into which Luther was born, and in which he lived and died. To the eye of a modern philosopher or scientist, the changes he introduced seem tiny when compared with the vast structure of belief he left standing. He denied the inerrancy of popes and councils; he denied the miraculous character of some of the sacraments; he made the Bible rather than the church or tradition the ultimate authority; he disbelieved in mendicant orders and in the requirement of clerical celibacy; above all, he insisted that what justified man in the sight of God was not works, or the performance of outward rites or exercises, but an inward faith. These, no doubt, were points of importance. But there were many devoted Catholics who agreed with Luther about all of them, who were reluctant, as he was himself for long, to desert the old church, and who thought, again as he did, that it would be strengthened, not wrecked, by their adoption. Why should such ideas have rocked Europe? What was there in Luther's thought that aroused in a succession of popes the passionate desire to see him on a pile of faggots?

The answer is not quite simple. It cannot be fully understood without taking into account, first, the extraordinary personality of the man, and then his conceptions of reason and faith.

THE CHARACTER OF LUTHER

3 Many have thought, and with good ground, that apart from the peculiar personality of Luther the Reformation would have taken a very different course. Suppose that the frail child, who was not expected to live, had never reached maturity, and that the leadership had remained in the hands of Erasmus; would the Reformation have taken place at all? Probably, but as a gradual house-cleaning in which the church's teaching was slowly enlightened, its tolerance broadened, and its morality mellowed, by the new humanism, a development that in Goethe's opinion would have been much better for the world than the cataclysm that in fact occurred. But Erasmus and Luther were made from different moulds. The great scholar was the fastidious thin-lipped intellectual we see in the portrait by Holbein; the reformer was the big-boned, bull-necked peasant we see in the portraits by his friend and neighbour Cranach. Erasmus was complaisant, diplomatic, and timid; Luther was impulsive, outspoken, pugnacious, a hater of compromise, and infinitely courageous. To be courageous is not necessarily to be fearless. Luther admitted that when summoned to Worms, where the prospect was that he would be seized and transported to Rome and the stake, he trembled; but he went—went on foot with his pack on his back, saying to his protesting friends, 'I will go if there are as many devils in Worms as there are tiles upon the roofs of the houses'. And devils, for Luther, were real.

He enjoyed a battle, like the scriptural war-horse that 'sayeth among the spears "Ha ha!" '. 'I pray better and I preach better when I am angry', he confessed. An eminent Lutheran scholar describes him as 'a theologian who combined the finesse of Gene Tunney with the violence of Jack Dempsey. . . .'[2] The Pope sent envoys; the Archduke Frederick pleaded with him for moderation, but when Luther conceived that a principle was involved, neither moderation nor compromise was possible. If the church was wrong, it should admit that it was wrong, and if it did not, its motives were of the worst. In this he was only taking a leaf out of the church's own book, for Catholicism has always tended to interpret religious error as sin; but Luther could give lessons to his practised mentors in the art of invective. Because Erasmus, who was in general on his side, would not commit himself unequivocally, he was 'the worst enemy that the church has had for a thousand years'. Of Zwingli and his associates who also had much in common with him, he wrote, 'they are not only liars, but falsehood, deceit, and hypocrisy itself, as Carlstadt and Zwingli show both in deeds and words'.[3] (One of these 'hypocritical' deeds of Zwingli, done soon afterward, was to give his life for his cause.) Nor were these imprecations merely 'the occasional explosions of a capricious volcano', as R. H. Tawney suggested; they belonged to his habitual way of thinking about those who opposed him. Of his enemies 'the papists' he wrote in 1531:

'because they are obdurate and have determined to do nothing good, but only evil, so that there is no longer any hope, I will hereafter heap curses and maledictions upon the villains until I go to my grave, and no good word shall they hear from me again. I will toll them to their tombs with my thunder and lightning. For I cannot pray without at the same time cursing. If I say,"Hallowed be Thy name," I have to add, "Cursed, damned, reviled be the name of the papists and of all who blaspheme Thy name". . . . If I say, "Thy will be done," I have to add, "Cursed, damned, reviled and destroyed be all the thoughts and plans of the papists and of every one who strives against Thy will and counsel. . . ." Nevertheless I have a kind, friendly, peaceable, and Christian heart toward every one, as even my worst enemies know.'[4]

It is not surprising that many thoughtful persons have found Luther unendurable. The historian Heinrich Denifle sets him down as a 'crass ignoramus'. For Jacques Maritain, he was a man 'wholly and systematically ruled by his affective and appetitive faculties'. These are Catholics. Protestants have said the same or worse. To Goethe he was an unintelligent rabble-rouser. To Arnold he was a Philistine. Dean Inge of St Paul's described him as 'the spiritual father of Nazism' and wrote: 'There is very little to be said for this coarse and foul-mouthed leader of a revolution. It is a real misfortune for humanity that he appeared just at this crisis in the Christian World.' To Sir Richard Livingstone also he seemed 'like a fouler-mouthed Hitler'. 'Lutherism in its historical manifestations is for me, I can't deny it, the horror of horrors,' said Max Weber. Whitehead, like many other reflective minds, wished that Erasmus rather than Luther had taken the leadership of the Reformation. 'But he lacked the force; and the matter fell into the hands of Luther and Calvin, who made a fearful botch of it.'[5]

4 Nevertheless the very flaws in Luther's character made him formidable. Erasmus spoke to intellectuals only; Luther had the ear of the people. In a Germany seething with discontent at the foreign hierarchy, the sight of this miner's son shaking his fist and shouting defiance at the hated Italian potentate brought bursts of laughter and cheers from his delighted fellow-countrymen. Among them he had the advantage of the underdog; he knew it, and by instinct exploited it. He was intemperate, unreasonable, violent, and unfair. But it is one of the tragic facts of history that rational causes are sometimes most effectively served by unreasonable agents. A Solomon, nicely dividing truth from error, could not have done Luther's work. The Reformation was a movement of the common people, and if popular opinion was to be aroused, what was needed was a man of passion, without doubts or hesitations, who could wield the vernacular as a whiplash, and satisfy the popular adulation for the man who would stand up and fight. For such a demand Luther was made to order.

5 Even so, he would not have achieved what he did without another striking trait. This was a curious union of humility with towering pretensions, a combination we shall meet again in Kierkegaard. Luther professed to be a very humble man, and in this he may well have been sincere, for if he was ambitious, it was not for the things that commonly lure ambitious minds. He might have become a man of means; as a powerful preacher and natural leader, he might, if he had been willing to pay the price for it, have had a mitre or even a cardinal's hat. Instead he lived in frugal austerity, remaining to the end a simple pastor in a small German town. But along with this worldly humility went extraordinary other-worldly presumptions. 'From the beginning profoundly convinced of his own divine call,' as a discerning biographer says, 'he identified his cause with God's and always attributed the hostility of his enemies to the promptings of Satan, who filled their hearts with hatred for God and all His works'.[6] His insignificance hardly mattered if he could face his opponents in the serene conviction that he was a spokesman of the Almighty. 'If I am not a prophet I am at any rate sure the word of God is with me and not with them, for I always have the Bible on my side, they only their own doctrine. It is on this account I have the courage to fear them so little, much as they despise and persecute me.'[7] 'Whoever obtrudes his doctrine on me and refuses to yield, must inevitably be lost; for I must be right, my cause being not mine, but God's, Whose Word it also is. Hence those who are against it must go under . . . whoever sets himself against me must be ruined if a God exists at all.'[8] This sense that the divine hand was leading him, that what seemed to him true was God's truth and what seemed to him right was God's will, grew on him with the years. To be sure, he was not quick to concede such claims if made by others. When members of the Zwickau school claimed an immediate illumination that took them off on a course of their own, he curtly rejected their claim; 'For I have as yet heard of nothing said or done by them which Satan cannot do or imitate'.[9] But if anyone had suggested that his own passionate intuitions might have been insinuated by Satan or by the machinations of his own complicated mind, Luther would have buried him beneath an avalanche of eloquent invective.

6 The Luther so far sketched is obviously not the Luther of Froude or Carlyle or Protestant tradition. For Carlyle, the close of the speech at Worms, the famous 'Here I stand; I can do no other; God help me,' is

'the greatest moment in the modern history of men. English

Puritanism, England and its Parliaments, Americas, and the vast work of these two centuries; French Revolution, Europe and its work everywhere at present: the germ of it all lay there: had Luther in that moment done other, it had all been otherwise! The European world was asking him: Am I to sink ever lower into falsehood, stagnant putrescence, loathsome accursed death; or, with whatever paroxysm, to cast the falsehoods out of me, and be cured and live?'[10]

This is the Luther of Protestant story, and there is certainly much truth in it. For all his coarseness, arrogance and superstition, Luther had a conscience that was tormentingly alive, the sense of a deep abyss between right and wrong, and a feeling for duty as a divine mandate that gave no rest to himself or others.

7   The religion he saw around him, and above all at Rome, was corrupt almost past belief. The Pope who reigned through his earlier years was Alexander VI, who secured his post by bribery, turned the Vatican into an arena for indescribable orgies, and made a cardinal of one of his numerous illegitimate children, the multiple murderer, Caesar Borgia. The degradation at the top of the church was spreading through its lower orders.

'The high prelates, the cardinals, the great abbots, were occupied chiefly in maintaining their splendour and luxury. The friars and the secular clergy, following their superiors with shorter steps, indulged themselves in grosser pleasures; while their spiritual powers, their supposed authority in this world and the next, were turned to account to obtain from the laity the means for their self-indulgence. . . . There were toll-gates for the priests at every halting-place on the road of life—fees at weddings, fees at funerals, fees whenever an excuse could be found to fasten them. Even when a man was dead he was not safe from plunder, for a mortuary or death present was exacted of his family.'[11]

This buying and selling within the temple was the match that set off the great explosion. When the Papal agent, Tetzel, neared Wittenberg with his load of indulgences for sale, Luther could stand it no longer and nailed his theses of condemnation to the door of the local church. An indulgence is a remission of the punishment due to sin; the theory behind it is that there is a great reservoir of grace accumulated by Christ, the saints, and the martyrs, that the head of the church has the key to this reserve, and that he can deal it out in measurable quantities by way of cancelling the suffering which God's justice would otherwise exact. Luther was not wholly opposed to this theory. He believed, like the Catholic priest he was, that the sacrifice of Christ and the grace accruing to it were the only hope of averting the divine wrath. Why then the torrent of anger with which he overwhelmed the unhappy Tetzel? Because he saw that sin and guilt and repentance and amendment and forgiveness belong to the inner man, and that the state of the inner man in the sight of God is not to be determined by payments, nor by the acts of human officials. The church could reply, indeed, that the effect of the indulgence was conditional upon inner repentance. But the people overlooked the condition, and the church, in sore need of funds, winked at the oversight. The indulgences were widely taken as a chance to compound for immorality by the payment of a fee.

Nor was Luther's anger lessened by the expertness of the Papal emissaries in milking money from devotion and anxiety. Tetzel's black-frocked salesmen stood in the pulpits and painted lurid pictures of a father and mother in purgatory, begging from the flames for the payment of some miserable sum that would release them from years of agony. Luther was revolted. This was making the divine forgiveness something to be bought and sold like merchandise; it debased morality; it prostituted religion. The needle of that restless conscience was here pointing straight at the pole. He had a keen eye for hypocrisy and he noisily branded the mark of Cain not on Tetzel's forehead only, but come what might, on that of Tetzel's commanding officer. He became 'God's angry man,' whom powers and principalities could not shut up.

REASON AS THE ENEMY OF FAITH

8 The Reformation, then, depended in no small measure upon Luther's sensitive, emotional, bellicose, egotistic character. But our chief concern is of course with his thought, and particularly with his views on faith and reason. We have seen that in the Catholic tradition as represented by such minds as Aquinas, reason, if regarded broadly as the sum total of our powers of natural knowledge, was given a long tether in religion. It is true that there were some doctrines of the first importance that reason could never discover or prove, but these were the exception rather than the rule. The forty or fifty portentous volumes of the *Summa Theologica* and the *Summa Contra Gentiles* are a continuous revelry of the intellect, in which an extraordinary intelligence seeks to lay out in order the whole Christian view of the world. Theology was not a region off bounds to our natural faculties; reason pushed confidently on into the citadels of theology—the existence and attributes of Deity, the plan of salvation, the will of God for man and its justification. As

Leo XIII remarked with legitimate pride, 'Reason, borne on the wings of St Thomas, could hardly fly higher.'

Luther's attitude was deeply different. His writing is so punctuated with disparagements of reason as to suggest not merely a conviction of its religious unimportance, but also an emotional antipathy toward it. Reason was 'that smart woman, Madame Jezebel'; it was 'Frau Hulda', a bumbling and officious nuisance, shallow, conceited and myopic; it was 'the Devil's whore'. Whereas Aquinas had placed Aristotle on a pinnacle of respect, commonly calling him '*the* philosopher' and deferring to him as 'the master of those who know', Luther went out of his way to pour contempt on him. Aristotle was 'a blind heathen' and, strangely enough, 'a lazy ass'.

'My advice would be that the books of Aristotle, the "Physics", the "Metaphysics", "Of the Soul", "Ethics", which have hitherto been considered the best, be altogether abolished, with all others that profess to treat of nature, though nothing can be learned from them, either of natural or of spiritual things. Besides, no one has been able to understand his meaning, and much time has been wasted, and many noble souls vexed, with much useless labour, study, and expense. I venture to say that any potter has more knowledge of natural things than is to be found in these books. My heart is grieved to see how many of the best Christians this accursed, proud, knavish heathen has fooled and led astray with his false words. . . . Does not the wretched man in his best book, "Of the Soul," teach that the soul dies with the body. . . . Yet this dead heathen has conquered, and has hindered and almost suppressed the books of the living God; so that, when I see all this misery, I cannot but think that the evil spirit has introduced this study. . . . Oh, that such books could be kept out of the reach of all Christians! Let no one object that I say too much, or speak without knowledge. My friend, I know of what I speak. I know Aristotle as well as you or men like you. I have read him with more understanding than St Thomas or Scotus. . . .'[12]

Luther ranked Aristotle below Cicero not only in rhetoric but also in philosophy and in general learning. As for philosophy itself, it was 'an old woman that stinks of Greece', and he regretted the time he had wasted on it in his youth.

'How sorry I am that I did not read more poetry and history and that they were not taught me! Instead of them, I had to spend my time on devil's filth, the philosophers and sophists, with great labor and damage, so that I had enough to get rid of.'[13]

All this sounds uncomfortably like raving. But Luther had his defence for it. He conceived that there were two realms in the universe, the realm of the flesh and the realm of the spirit, the secular and the religious, the *regnum mundi* and the *regnum Christi*, the things of the world and the things of God. The realm of the flesh included not only physical nature but also the fields of philosophy, mathematics, law, history, and what we should call the social sciences, indeed the whole man and the whole world 'apart from Christ'. In this realm reason is our appointed guide; indeed Luther can even praise it as a '*maximum et inaestimabile donum Dei*'. We have been endowed with a set of knowing processes such as perception, memory, and inference to enable us to find our way about in this lower realm, to get a sufficient mastery of its facts and laws to stay alive in it and adjust ourselves to it. These processes, when so used, serve their modest purpose well. But 'Speculation as such, science as an end in itself, truth for truth's sake,' as Dr McGiffert says, 'never appealed to him; only matters immediately bearing on life and character he felt to be worthy the attention of a serious man'.14 Luther's lack of interest in speculation had a further root: he was convinced that all man's faculties had been corrupted and distorted by his original fall. Just how great his corruption is, and at what points it enters in, we have no safe means of judging, but it is clearly prudent to keep our speculations within bounds if we know them to be vitiated without knowing how deeply or how generally.

Yet to keep reason within bounds is something no secular philosopher can be trusted to do. Philosophy runs into theology in all directions. If we let our thoughts move back along the line of cause and effect, they are bound, sooner or later, to confront the problem of creation; we find order and beauty in nature, and our thoughts leap inevitably to a Designer; we look within at our ideas and feelings, and seem constrained to accept a soul that owns them; we reflect on our conduct, and deplore our sin. But in all these cases we have already crossed the danger line. God, the soul, and sin are matters for theology, not for natural reason. We have been told by moralists and schoolmen that we should 'do the best that is in us', *facere quod in se est*. This Luther granted, but only in its own place, which is in the kingdom of the body. When reason takes it upon itself to move across the line into the kingdom of the spirit, it is exhibiting not a praiseworthy desire to understand, but presumption and impiety. 'No one shall see God and live.'

9 Why did Luther impose this stern curb on reason? Partly, no doubt, because of the intensity of his religious experience. He was a man of the strongest feelings, who had had moments of extreme exaltation as well as others of the darkest depression, and when he

was on the heights he felt that he had been raised into direct communion with the glory of God. But these soarings of the spirit were not rational insights. They were experiences that resisted analysis by reason, whose prosy, plodding detachment seemed utterly alien to them. They were neither conclusions from premises nor self-evident intuitions like $2 + 2 = 4$, but experiences of a non-rational kind.

Secondly, Luther was sure that in curbing reason he was following Scripture. The good news brought by the gospel was not that of salvation by intellect. The apostles chosen to convey the Word to the world were not doctors of philosophy, but ignorant fishermen and the like; Nicodemus, the 'master in Israel', was told that what he needed was to humble himself and be born again of the spirit. St Paul, who was a favourite of Luther, had put the matter uncompromisingly. He was acquainted with the Greek manner of argumentation and was himself a man of some learning, but he had a very low opinion of the wisdom of this world, and thought we were safer on the whole if we remained babes and sucklings in it. Human learning and understanding belong, after all, to the realm of *sarx*, of the flesh, and therefore to that which can reap only corruption; its methods and standards are at best a glass through which we see darkly, and see divine truth not at all. To achieve such truth, it must make a clean sweep of its standards and its pride, and be brought into captivity to Christ.

Thirdly, and for us most significantly, Luther thought that between the structure of divine and human truth there was a fundamental difference, which made any bridging of the gap by human effort impossible. It will be well to illustrate this gap, first from theology and then from ethics.

THE CREED AS FOOLISHNESS TO REASON

10 In Luther's commentary on Galatians, which is at least fifty times the length of the epistle itself, he writes:

'And what saith God? Impossible things, lies, foolish, weak, absurd, abominable, heretical, and devilish things, if ye believe reason. . . . So, if we follow the judgment of reason, God setteth forth absurd and impossible things, when he setteth out unto us the articles of the Christian faith. Indeed, it seemeth to reason an absurd and a foolish thing, that in the Lord's supper is offered unto us the body and blood of Christ; that baptism is the laver of the new birth, and of the renewing of the Holy Ghost; that the dead shall rise in the last day; that Christ the Son of God was conceived and carried in the womb of the Virgin Mary; that he was born; that he suffered the most reproachful death of the cross; that he was raised up again; that he now sitteth at the right hand of God the Father; and that he hath all power both in heaven and earth. . . . But faith killeth reason. . . . So all the godly entering with Abraham into the darkness of faith, do kill reason, saying: reason, thou art foolish; thou dost not savour those things which belong unto God: therefore speak not against me, but hold thy peace: judge not, but hear the word of God and believe it.'[15]

Here is a list of eight or nine of the leading doctrines of the Christian faith, all of them declared to be absurd and impossible to reason. The Sorbonne had maintained that if a proposition was true in philosophy, it was true in theology also. This Luther denied. The proposition 'The word was made flesh' is true in theology but false and foolish in philosophy. The doctrine of the Trinity seems pre-posterous to the mathematician; does this prove it to be untrue? Not in the least; it proves only the inapplicability of mathematics in theology.[16] So different is truth in the two realms that one may start from theological premises that are true, reason with impeccable logic, and still end with a conclusion that in theology is false.[17] Luther's was a highly argumentative mind, and if he had adhered to this view in practice, his works would have been greatly reduced in bulk. He did at times try to adhere to it. 'When Luther, in 1529, met Zwingli at Marburg in order to discuss with him the question of the Eucharist, it is reported that with chalk he wrote upon a table these words, *Hoc est corpus meum*. He then added, "I have not come here to discuss with Zwingli the merits of the dogma of consub-stantiation, I shall limit myself to contradicting him if he happens to differ from me".'[18] On his assumptions this was obviously the right course. If 'all God's works and words are against reason', why argue about them?

REASON UNSAFE IN MORALS

11   This clash between the religious and the rational comes out even more strikingly when he turns his attention to morals. He concedes that reason can tell us how to act in the ordinary business of life, in earning a living, in dealing tactfully with others, in running a household or even a state; it can lay down rules of conduct that we shall certainly profit by following. But he adds that to depend on reason as a guide to genuine goodness, in the world as it is, is like trying to remain chaste in a brothel. It is not merely that the eye of reason has been so dimmed by original sin that it can no longer see clearly; the defect is more radical; reason is simply blind to the only goodness that in God's sight is goodness at all. Such reliance on reason in morals as we find in the Greek philosophers is therefore more than dangerous; 'almost the whole of Aristotle's *Ethics* is the worst enemy of grace'. The Christian must not blink the fact, indeed he must keep it in the forefront of his mind, that God's ways are not our ways.

But what exactly does this mean? If it means merely that any mind with a fuller understanding than ours of the motives and consequences of conduct will judge it more or less differently, that is intelligible enough. But it might mean something more. It might mean that the very standards by which God judges conduct are different from ours. For example, that conduct on our part which we should all regard as good is viewed by him as bad, that some even of his own conduct would be branded by our standard as evil. Now this is precisely what Luther says, and says so often and emphatically that there is no mistaking it. Holding as he did that Scripture is the inspired and ultimate authority, he thought we must accept at face value the statements that God commanded a man to kill his son, that he hardened Pharaoh's heart against the innocent, that he sent plagues and pestilences upon his people. In one of his sermons, Luther paints a vivid picture of Abraham binding and preparing to kill his son at God's command. His biographer Roland Bainton reports that 'Luther once read this story for family devotions. When he had finished, Katie [his wife] said, "I do not believe it. God would not have treated his son like that." "But, Katie," answered Luther, "he did".'19

GOD AND EVIL

12 Indeed Luther went much further. He held that God is ultimately responsible for all the evil that has ever occurred. Man's nature is now so corrupt that he does evil automatically; even when he is trying to do right, he is doing wrong in God's sight; he is completely determined by his inherited infection of sin to go on choosing evil. Where did this infection start? The standard answer is, 'at the fall,' and this is supposed to relieve the Creator of responsibility for moral evil; since man could have chosen obedience, the fault is his own. But Luther saw that this would not do. For one thing, God is omniscient, and must therefore have known every choice beforehand, evil as well as good, and what God foreknew, Luther argued, he must have foreordained. Furthermore, when man does go right, it is only through a grant of grace, which God can always offer and which happily he does frequently offer; and he could as clearly have granted this grace to Adam as to ourselves.

If man at first went wrong, then, it was because he was temporarily deserted by God and left to himself (*desertus a Deo ac sibi relictus*); God *permitted* him to fall (*permisit ruere*). Now if the fall gave rise to a long train of evil consequences, and God permitted this fall, then in effect he gave rise to these consequences. Luther saw no escape from this conclusion. Commenting on the strange statement, 'Wherefore God also gave them up to uncleanness' (Rom. 1 : 24), he says expressly, 'This giving up is not merely by God's permission, but by His will and command, as we see clearly from 1 Kings 22 : 22–23, where we are told that God commanded the lying spirit to persuade Ahab to act against His will . . . when God deals with transgressors according to His stern justice, He permits the perverse sinner to break His commandments all the more viciously in order that He might punish him the more severely.'[20] In his debate with Erasmus on freedom of the will, Luther takes an event that it would seem crucially important to dissociate from God's will, and carries the argument through. Erasmus had pointed out that if God foreordains all, then he must have prompted Judas to betray his Lord, which is outrageous. The conclusion, Luther replies, is unavoidable nevertheless. Judas acted by his own determination, but 'it was certain that this determination of his would be formed, since God foreknew it. His determination was his work, which God, however, by His omnipotence caused to be done, just as He brings all other things to pass.'[21]

Most readers will perhaps share Erasmus's view that this *is* outrageous. Has Luther anything to say that would ease the shock? Very little. He tells us repeatedly that in such matters we must bow to an ultimate mystery. To apply our own standards to the actions of Deity is impious pride; his maxim for such cases was *Quod supra nos, nihil ad nos*, what is above us does not concern us. We cannot even say of God that he does things because they are right, since that seems to mean that he is laid under obligation by some law other than his own will. What God does is right because he does it, and hence it is right whatever it is.[22] It might be objected that, on Luther's account, we are not even free to accept this account as true, since our act of acceptance or rejection is itself determined; how, then, can God command us to do it? Luther answers that he may well be treating us in the manner of the parent who tells the child to come to him before it can walk, by way of bringing home to the child how helpless it is, though there are persons who would probably consider the cat and the mouse a better analogy for such treatment. Sometimes the line is taken that there are in a sense two Gods, the manifest one incarnated in Galilee, who weeps over sinners and pities them, and a dark and hidden one, whose in-

scrutable will is to create men doomed to eternal damnation. If
Luther is asked why God should hide himself from his creatures, he
replies that if all were made clear to us, there would be no room for
faith.

'In order that faith may have an existence, everything believed
must be hidden. But it cannot be more deeply hidden than when the
exact contrary is presented and experienced. Thus, God makes
alive by killing. Thus, He conceals His eternal mercy under eternal
wrath, His righteousness under injustice. This is the highest stage
of faith, to believe Him to be merciful, who saves so few and
condemns so many; to believe Him to be just, who by *His own will
makes us subject, of necessity, to damnation*, so that He appears, as
Erasmus reminds us, to delight in the miseries of the wretched
and to be worthy of hatred rather than of love.'23

Thus, so far as we can see, God's treatment of us has no relation to
what we deserve. If he grants us grace, we never merit it, for however
saintly by human standards, we are all festering with sin. If he refuses
us grace, as he apparently does to most men, he is condemning us
for what we cannot help and for what he himself has made us. If we
rebel against him for treating us in this manner, he will damn us for
calling unjust what our moral perception reveals to be so. It is
evidently safer in these matters not to use one's reason at all. For
whatever God does to us, whether he elects us, on no discoverable
grounds, to an eternity of glory, or consigns us to an eternity of
horror and pain, our attitude must be the same. We must bow our
heads in acceptance, sing his praises, and adore.

THE MEANING OF FAITH

13   The appeal to reason thus repudiated, what did Luther put in
its place? The answer, of course, is faith. 'Justification by faith'—
it is the position with which his name is everywhere linked. What did
he mean by 'faith'? One often longs, in reading him, for precision
and sharpness of thought, above all at points like this which are
obviously crucial. His mind, however, was not primarily that of the
thinker but that of the prophet, of the religious and moral reformer;
and even on such cardinal topics as faith his ideas must be distilled
from floods of passionate disquisition in the form of sermons,
Biblical commentaries, and tracts for the times. What emerges from
such distillation of his wide-ranging comments on faith is something
like the following.

   (1) Faith is belief. In spite of all Luther's disparagement of reason,
he still insists that faith is cognitive; it is a kind of knowledge. To

most religiously minded persons, this is not what the term first suggests; it connotes, rather, emotional attitudes of confidence and trust, perhaps also humility, repentance, and love. Luther did not admit these elements into his idea of faith, thereby breaking with an old tradition. St Paul had spoken of 'faith working by love'; St Augustine and many other theologians, in accordance with this suggestion, had distinguished between the faith that was mere belief, an 'unformed faith' as they called it, and faith that was fully formed because its belief was bathed in love; only the latter was considered as saving faith. This teaching, said Luther, was a blasphemous abomination.[24] There was no comparison between the importance of such things as love and justice on the one hand and correct belief on the other. 'One little point of doctrine is of more value than heaven and earth; and therefore we cannot abide to have the least jot thereof to be corrupted; but we can very well wink at the offences and errors of life. . . .'[25] Errors in the kind of belief of which faith consisted were winked at only at the risk of eternal condemnation; and since many in the Christian church, not excluding bishops, cardinals, and popes, were unsound on essential points, they were presumably destined for perdition, along with the whole non-Christian world.

14(2) Granting that faith is belief, what is it that must be believed? Luther is in difficulty here, because he holds, as we have seen, that the object or content of faith is both above reason and opposed to it; and if so, it will be inexpressible. At times he admits this; 'God setteth forth himself otherwise than reason is able either to judge or conceive.'[26] At other times, he insists that through faith we are assured of a rather wide variety of essential doctrines. But what he steadfastly holds to be the core of faith is *the belief or awareness that we are forgiven*. We do not know why forgiveness should be granted to us rather than to others, or at this time rather than that, but we do know that without it we are doomed, and that if the general doom is sometimes lifted, it is for one reason only: God has extended pardon to certain sinners in virtue of the sacrifice made by Christ. Faith is the assurance that because of this sacrifice our sin is not to be held against us, that the divine wrath has been appeased, and that with omnipotence on our side, we are now and forever safe. To achieve faith is not in essence a coming to admire or reverence Christ as a model of living; anyone may do that; nor is it merely an acceptance of him as divine; it is an awareness that we have been delivered by him from sin and its penalty. It is not a knowledge of what we must do to be saved, but a sure sense that we are saved already. Others who want this security also but have been denied it may raise questions about the justice of an apparently discriminatory salvation and even about its possibility; how can the sacrifice of one person affect the guilt of another or God's judgement of that guilt? With such questioning Luther has no patience: 'Kill reason and believe in Christ'.[27] 'For unless He himself teach us inwardly this wisdom hidden in a mystery, nature cannot but condemn it and judge it to be heretical. She takes offence at it and it seems folly to her.'[28] Indeed he goes so far at times as to say that if reason did understand a religious statement, that in itself would show it to be false.[29] But the fact of which faith assures us remains certain, whether reason can make sense of it or not.

15(3)   Is it only the fact grasped by faith that is above nature, or also the fact of our grasping it? By what organ do we apprehend it? Not by reason, clearly. Is it then by one of our other faculties? Luther thinks not. He is inclined rather to deny that *we* grasp it at all, and to insist that a supernatural fact must be apprehended by a supernatural agency working in and through us. 'The real faith, of which we are speaking, cannot be brought into being by our own thoughts. On the contrary, it is entirely God's work in us, without any co-operation on our part.'[30] Not that he holds to this view consistently. Sometimes he talks as if faith were an act of natural thought or belief; it is *recte cogitare de Deo*. Sometimes it is an exercise of reason assisted by grace to exceed its normal limits. But he prefers to make it the sort of miracle in which Christ himself descends into the soul and does what for man would have been impossible. As God embodied himself in his son in the incarnation, so Christ embodies himself in us in faith. He becomes 'one flesh with us' as his own body and blood in some mysterious manner become ours through the sacramental bread and wine. Faith, then, is not an achievement from which we can draw merit or satisfaction; we neither acquire it nor deserve it. The assurance, as truly as what it assures us of, is supernatural; it is an act of Deity working through us.

FAITH AND WORKS

16(4)   With this doctrine in mind, we can better understand Luther's famous insistence that we are never justified by works. To the unsophisticated mind, it is natural to suppose that we can acquire some merit in God's sight by goodness, by our own efforts to find and do what is right; and Luther's Catholic teachers had so taught him. He later poured upon such teachings a torrent of denunciation; they were 'abominations and execrable lies', 'mere deceits of Satan'.[31] What led him to such heated extremes? It was evidently his doctrine of original sin. Natural man with all his faculties belonged to the realm of the flesh, and the flesh was a mass of corruption. Flesh, 'according to Paul, signifieth all the righteousness, wisdom, devotion, religion, understanding and will, that is possible to be in a natural man . . .' and 'the flesh cannot think, speak, or do any thing, but that which is devilish and altogether against God'.[32] 'Every good deed of the just man is a damnable and mortal sin when judged by the judgment of God.'[33] If this is true, the very struggle to live a godly life would seem to lose its main point. Luther sees this, and says it. 'A most lively sighing goes on throughout the whole length of life: "I would so like to be godly". To overcome this natural desire is a theological virtue.' Indeed, if Christ died for sinners and not the righteous, do we not need a supply of sin to qualify us for salvation? Luther thought we did. 'Unless you are found in the number of those who say: "For our sins" . . . there is no salvation for you.' This was apparently the ground of his advice to Melanchthon to 'sin boldly'.[34]

In this insistent depreciation of outward works, is Luther seeking to exalt instead the value of inward good will? Kant called this the only thing in the world that is good without qualification. But Kant meant by it devotion to duty as revealed to us by our reason; and for Luther such devotion, like ordinary goodness of heart, belongs to the natural man, and hence is without religious value. He rejected 'the vain imaginations of reason, which teacheth that a right judgment, and a good will or a good intent is true righteousness.'[35] What justifies us is neither good action nor good will, but simply and solely the presence of faith, divinely implanted, unachieved, unpredictable, unmerited, perhaps even unsought for. It is what is done for us, not by us, that counts. 'Hearing, not doing, makes a Christian,' 'Mary sits, and she does nothing,' but her passive faith counts for more than Martha's service. Cornelius and his friends sit and do nothing, but the Holy Ghost is upon them nevertheless. Luther took much satisfaction in the efficacy of infant baptism; in this sacrament grace was at work, though we could suppose no contribution whatever from the human side; the faith required and present was a supernatural impartation. It is the main theme of the massive commentary on Galatians that what alone can save is the 'passive righteousness' of faith.

17(5) Though good works are not essential to faith, they are admitted as its natural consequences. Before the fruit can be good, the tree must be good, but if the tree is really good, the fruit will infallibly be good too. To be sure, we must have a care not to be taken in by appearances. The goodness that springs from faith is a

different kind of goodness from any that issues from human reasonableness, kindliness, or love. To the outward eye they may be the
same. To the eye of omniscience they differ as heaven from earth;
one is the sure sign of the working in us of God himself, while
the other is the product of corruption. People who try by themselves to live saintly lives are particularly dangerous: Satan loves
them; the world at its best is really at its worst; [36] they are whited
sepulchres because they present the deceitful appearance of a goodness they do not have. Whether the cup of water given to the thirsty
stands for genuine goodness or not depends on whether the love
from which it issues has the divine or the human quality. To
question that the former is superior is something like blasphemy,
since when faith descends into the soul it is Christ himself who lives
and acts in it.

18 This is not an easy view to maintain, or even to state clearly,
and Luther found himself unable to keep to it consistently. It ought
to mean that the new man, since Christ himself is now in possession,
is morally perfect. Could anyone be pointed to as an example of such
perfection? Around Luther, at any rate, there seemed to be a
singular shortage of these saints, and he did not, at least explicitly,
claim to be one himself. Again, one would expect the descent of
faith on this theory to be not only complete but abrupt, so that the
replacement of sin by grace would occur in a flash, as it apparently
did for St Paul. But things did not commonly work that way, and
Luther urged that men should strive to advance in holiness by
degree (though he also denied, as we have seen, that such striving
could be effective). The thought, however, that even with the help
of grace man could become truly holy was an uncomfortable bed-
fellow of his pessimism about human nature, and at times he insisted
that this holiness was not real, but only imputed to man in virtue of
the sacrifice that had been made for him; though he was not really
good, a merciful Deity would consider him so and treat him accordingly. But it was difficult to see how omniscience could consider and
treat someone as what he was not, and Luther fell back on another
theory. This was to the effect that even the Christ who lived and
worked in us was himself evil. In becoming man, he took our flesh,
and with it all the depravities of the flesh. He was, as the prophets
foresaw, a murderer, an adulterer, and a blasphemer; indeed he was
the greatest sinner the world has known. [37]

Luther's theory, put in simple terms, is thus as follows. The faith
that saves us is not our own, but a divine gift. This gift is the presence
in the soul of Christ himself. Since this presence is perfect, the works
that proceed from it must be perfect. But if the Christ who dwelt

in man were really perfect, he could not have been really man, nor could he have borne our iniquities or atoned for them. He must, therefore, be a sinner and, if a sinner at all, the chief of sinners, since he took upon himself all our sins. A mere moral monster, however, would have nothing to offer that would balance and atone for man's infinite guilt. The solution of the problem, then, must be to accept him as *both* the greatest of sinners and *also* morally perfect. This Luther triumphantly did. He admits that the conclusion is something short of clear; 'Yes, even unto us which have received the first fruits of the Spirit, it is impossible to understand these things perfectly, for they fight mightily against reason.'[38] But the man of faith can rest in the security that here reason is irrelevant.

SCRIPTURE

19 We have now seen where Luther stood on the claims of reason and faith. There is another question that must be answered if we are to understand his central position. What was the ultimate authority to which he appealed in judging these claims? It was not, of course, reason, for reason, like all our faculties, was vitiated by the fall. And if it was the illumination of his own private faith, was it not presumptuous to impose his peculiar convictions as certainties upon a dubious and resistant world? Certainly the Catholics would contend that in putting his private judgement against the vast and ancient authority of the church he was playing the cat that looked at a king, and was only adding to his offensiveness by being self-righteous about it. Did he have anything but his personal judgement to offer against this massive authority?

Yes, he said, he had. Indeed he had an ally that could put to rout single-handed all the popes, cardinals, and councils that might be arrayed against him. This was Scripture. The authority of the Bible was final and infallible. This the church in fact admitted; it rested its own authority upon such passages as the statement to Peter, 'Upon this rock will I build my church.' Where then did Luther differ? He differed in holding that the Bible and the church might conflict, and did in fact conflict, while the church held that this was impossible. It was impossible because the church reserved to itself the right of interpreting the Bible; what the Bible meant could be only what the church said it meant. This Luther denied. He knew that there had been bitter battles within the church as to what the Bible taught, even on the cardinal points of the faith, that Arian doctrine had prevailed at one time and Athanasian at another, and that in attempting to construe the teaching of Scripture councils and popes had disagreed with each other and with themselves. But even with complete agreement, their claim to final authority in interpreting Scripture would still be false; for it rested upon the same foundation of dubious history and apologetics as the claim of the Roman bishop to be the infallible Vicar of Christ. We shall not follow the laborious operations of sapping and mining that Luther directed against that foundation. We have already examined it for ourselves, and have seen that his conclusion about its infirmity, whatever the value of his particular arguments, was in substance sound.

The Bible need no longer be read, then, through ecclesiastical spectacles. Each of us is at liberty to go to it himself and to make of it what he can. On the whole it has a plain story to tell; we could hardly suppose that Deity should will to communicate to us something of the first importance and yet deliberately confuse and mislead us. Does this mean that we are all equally qualified to act as interpreters? Clearly not. Luther, who had been at much pains to master Hebrew and Greek, and who translated the entire Bible, prized Biblical scholarship greatly. Nevertheless the prime qualification for understanding Scripture was not mastery of the original tongues, or historical knowledge, or philosophical acumen, but something wholly different—the same thing, indeed, that was needed for salvation, namely faith. The gospel was good news from a supernatural source. This news, as we have seen, was imperceptible by the human ear or eye; both the news and the means of receiving it had to be supplied from above. With this tremendous aid, a wayfaring man though a fool could read the text and see an unearthly light shining out between the lines; without it, the scholar or the philosopher could wrestle with the text for a lifetime and still only succeed in losing the spirit in the letter.

20 Furthermore, the Bible was a library of uneven books. For all his bibliolatry, Luther was less of a fundamentalist in his attitude toward Scripture than were his Catholic critics. Their attitude was formally expressed by the Council of Trent, in session when Luther died, which laid it down that the Bible with all its parts must be taken as inspired by the Holy Ghost. On the other hand, Luther held some of these parts in so low an esteem that he would have excluded them from the canon if he could. The central message of Scripture was that of man's redemption through the cross, and the importance of the various parts could be measured by their relevance to this nuclear revelation. The heart of the Bible, for Luther, was Romans, followed closely by Galatians, for in these two books, on which he wrote extensive commentaries, the great message came through with the brightest purity. Strangely enough, the synoptic gospels were less important, for the details of Christ's life are of less moment to us than his sacrificial death. Much further out toward the periphery are such books as Jude and Revelation, while the book of James was steadfastly put down as 'an epistle of straw'. The reason for this animadversion is plain and revealing: James stresses works rather than faith; it even says: 'pure religion and undefiled before God and the Father is this, to visit the fatherless and widows in their affliction, and to keep himself unspotted from the world' (1 : 27). Luther felt this to be clearly at odds with the all-important teaching of Romans, and could account for it only by supposing that inspiration was here muted and distorted by a very imperfect instrument.

One might expect that, by applying the same standard, he would find little of significance in the Old Testament. It is true that he made small use of its historical books and would have excluded Esther altogether. On the other hand he gave a central place to the Psalms. This was in part, no doubt, because he found in them, as have countless others, some rare devotional literature. But there was another reason. He thought he saw in them what few modern critics have been able to verify—continued references to, and fore-shadowings of, Christ. 'He finds the death and resurrection of Christ so clearly foretold in the Psalter, and the condition and essential nature of Christ's kingdom and of the whole Christian world so distinctly prefigured, that the Psalter might well be called a little Bible.'[39] The Old Testament prophets, and particularly Moses, who was the greatest of them, were also important as forerunners. As regards Genesis, Luther had no doubt that its ultimate author was the Holy Spirit, though he thought that the actual placing in Moses' hands of the tables of the law was done by angels rather than by the Deity himself. The Old Testament was not the work of men, except as they served as more or less faithful secretaries. It is valuable not only for the poems, prayers, reflections, and stories that have proved so great an aid in the expression of religious feeling, but above all for the thousand adumbrations, prophecies, and foretastes that make it a preface to the gospel.

Both Testaments could thus be read and understood by the religiously qualified layman. Luther often protested Augustine's remark that he would be unable to believe the Bible unless assured of its truth by church authority. The man of faith has an inner light that enables him to appropriate Biblical truth, and even to separate the grain from the admitted chaff in the sacred text. 'You see how the words of the Gospel explain themselves, and have their own glosses, so that it is not at all necessary that other and human words be mixed with them.'[40] This was part of the new priesthood of the believer.

IS SCRIPTURE THE FINAL AUTHORITY?

21 There were two difficulties in this view which Luther never resolved. For one thing, the line of defence moves in a circle. What warrants our so reading Scripture that the death of Christ means more than his life, and the teaching of Romans more than the teaching of James? It is the possession of faith. What warrants us in making such faith the avenue to truth? It is the teaching of Romans rightly interpreted. Faith is our warrant for the meaning of Scripture; that meaning is our warrant for the primacy of faith. Thus Luther was defending the authority of faith by an argument that assumed that authority, and defending the authority of Scripture by an argument that rested on Scripture itself.

He might reply that in special circumstances an argument may be circular and still be valid. In this he would be right, and it is worth pausing to see why. Suppose you attempt to argue that some criterion of validity is the right one; how are you to appraise the arguments offered for it? If you appraise them by some other criterion than the one you are defending, you implicitly surrender your case; if you appraise them by the criterion for which you are arguing, you are going round in a circle. Still, if this criterion for which you are arguing happens to be the true one, the arguments it thus warrants will after all be valid, and your case, though circular, will not be vicious. Sooner or later, every criterion of validity must rest upon itself. Descartes saw that even the force of reason must come back in the end to its own clearness and distinctness of insight.

Luther might, so far, be right in contending that the meaning of Scripture is visible only to faith while faith must turn for its authority to the meaning of Scripture. How are we to tell whether he is or not? The normal way to proceed for a theologian or anyone else who has a case to make is to state it as clearly as possible and to ask whether the case, so stated, commends itself to his hearers when they look at it without bias. And the trouble is that when Luther does so state his case it does *not* commend itself to the majority of his hearers. To him, as he reads his Genesis, it seems self-evident that a human being could not have written it, and as he reads Romans, that the Pauline doctrine of the atonement is true without qualification. Most of us, when we consider these doctrines, have to confess that they are far from self-evident. Luther replies that this is because we are looking at them with eyes made myopic by sin, and that if these were replaced by the eyes of faith, we should see that what before was not even plausible is really irresistible truth. We ask him how we too can get this faith and its attendant vision. He answers that there is nothing we can do to get it, that it is a gift granted to some and denied to others on no assignable ground. We ask whether, even though there is no way to get it, there is not some way to identify people who have it. He answers that people who have it will display in their lives a unique superhuman love. We ask him for examples; does he himself have it in greater measure than, say, the Pope? He answers with confidence that he does. If we agree, we shall presumably end as Lutherans. And if we disagree? He would then tell us, with an embroidery of eloquent invective, that we do so through stubborn perversity. We explain that we did not mean to be perverse; we meant only to report faithfully how the matter appeared to us. To which Luther would answer that such fidelity to appearances is a peculiarly serious sin, the idolatry of our own reason. We ask him how we can avoid it. He answers: we cannot avoid it; we are predestined to it by the God who made us. But is not the God who made us a loving God? Yes, comes the menacing answer, but not so loving that if you continue in this line of questioning he will not commit you to an eternity of pain.

Most modern inquirers would perhaps turn away at this point in aversion, and suggest that what we have here is merely a saddling on Scripture of private prejudice, together with a projection on the universe of a sadism that is more effectively dealt with by Freud than by argument. This may be true. One can hardly read Luther's life in detail without recognising in his violent rages, his alternations of exalted ecstasy and black depression, his seizures and convulsions, his encounters with the devil, and his world-defying self-confidence, the marks of an abnormal mind; and the inference is at least plausible that this abnormality had its influence on his religion and his theology. But I do not propose to pursue this inquiry, because even if we could show, as we cannot with certainty, how far his convictions were linked to psychological causes, we should not thereby show them wrong; a belief may be held on irrelevant grounds and because of non-rational pressures, and still be true. Thus the possibility so far remains—a possibility grim and terrible—that Luther may be right. For all we have seen, the world may in fact be governed by implacable injustice that has doomed the majority of men to something worse than destruction. Whether Luther is right or not can be determined only by placing the circle of argument within which he moved in a wider context than his own. Is it true, as he maintains, that the world is divided into hostile realms of faith and reason, and that history is the drama of their rivalry? It is a question we cannot evade.

IS SCRIPTURE COHERENT?

22 We said, however, that there were two difficulties with Luther's view of Scripture, and we must turn for a moment to the second. This is the familiar difficulty that the Bible, though the product of inspiration, seems to contain contradictions and errors of fact. The Bible, Luther says, is 'alone the fount of all wisdom'; it is 'the book given by God, the Holy Spirit, to His Church'. Yet we have found him admitting that if he had his way he would throw out of it both Esther and James; he had no hesitation in recognising errors of fact in both the Old Testament and the New, and he points out himself that at times they contradict each other. For example, Moses says in the Old Testament that Abraham received the call to go to Canaan while he still lived in Haran; Stephen, recounting the event in the New Testament, says he received the call *before* he arrived in Haran.[41] Stephen seems to make a second mistake in the same chapter: he says that when Jacob's kindred were called about him they numbered three score and fifteen souls, whereas the number as reported in Genesis is three score and ten.[42] Here either the New Testament or the Old, or both, must be in error. How was Luther to reconcile his view of the Bible as divinely inspired with his frank admission that it contained many palpable mistakes?

His answer was in substance as follows. We must recognise in the Scripture two orders or levels of truth. On the higher level are those teachings of transcendent importance that are necessary to salvation; on the lower level are teachings that are not thus necessary, such as biographical and historical details. There is no avoiding the admission that on the latter level many errors have crept in. But there is nothing disastrous about this. The Holy Spirit must, after all, breathe through human instruments that are sometimes tired, sometimes inattentive, sometimes, like the unfortunate James, a little stupid. They do not keep themselves always alert as the dictation flows in upon them, and the dictating Spirit has been tolerant of this remissness. So devoted heads have occasionally nodded, and quills with the best of intentions have set down very strange things. But one does not impeach an earthly author for the distractedness of his secretary, and still less should one lay impious charges against the Author of Scripture because of defects in human reception. When Luther turned to inspiration on the higher level, however, his attitude abruptly changed. That the Bible, whose prime purpose was to convey to man the means of salvation, should have distorted and perverted its chief message was a totally inadmissible suggestion. In its central teachings we have the pure and unadulterated milk of the divine word.

This expedient of distinguishing central from peripheral truths is often used in defending Biblical inspiration, and we have already considered the use made of it by Catholic theologians. It proved to be inadequate there. On grounds of merely human probability, it is unlikely that minds prone to frequent errors of fact should, when they come to matters of higher significance, become incapable of error, and one finds on closer inspection that what this probability suggests did happen in fact. For it is certainly not true that on all those points which either Luther or the church would regard as essential to salvation the report of the Bible as we have it presents a harmonious picture. Luther implicitly admitted this in his attitude toward James. For him the most essential doctrine of all was that of salvation by faith as opposed to works. On that point Paul and James disagree. Luther's method of dealing with this is to pronounce Paul (and himself) right, and, because James disagreed, to question the right of his epistle to a place in Scripture at all.

No doubt for some purposes this is an effective method; one could establish the consistency of Scripture on any doctrine at choice by excluding as uncanonical passages that opposed it. We saw that the Roman church has very effectively preserved its unity of belief by cutting off as heretical those who have disbelieved. But in the one case as in the other, a test conducted judicially will produce a result opposite of the one desired. Take any set of Biblical books accepted by reputable authorities, Catholic or Protestant, but not selected *for* their espousal of certain doctrines, and it is probably fair to say that they will contain divergencies of teaching even on such cardinal points as the idea of God, the relation of the divine and the human, the moral ideal, and the means of salvation. The Protestant appeal to the authority of Scripture ends in difficulties as insuperable as the Catholic appeal to the authority of the church.

THE ARROGANCE OF PHILOSOPHY

23 We now have before us Luther's essential convictions on reason, faith, and Scripture. What are we to say of them? Considering that he remains a towering figure in the history of religious thought, it is curious how little the truth or falsity of his teaching is now discussed. To be sure, teachings similar to his have been put forward by neo-orthodox theologians and canvassed in the seminaries, but the discussion has been theological rather than philosophical; and even those who are styled Lutherans seem to accept him unreflectingly as part of their religious heritage. Contemporary philosophers, preoccupied with other problems, regard him with indifference as beyond the pale of their interest. He would be dismissed by most Catholics, not with indifference but with aversion, as the man who wilfully destroyed the unity of the church. Still another attitude appears in Erik Erikson's *Young Man Luther*, which takes him as a psychological case-study and undertakes to show, for example, how Luther's early hatred of his father projected itself in his conception of a fearful and vengeful God. My own interest differs from all of these. It is that of the speculative inquirer who, aware of the historic influence of Luther's teaching, wishes to raise the one question whether it is true. If it is, its acceptance, as he maintained, is important to the last degree. If it is not true, the business of the philosopher is to say so, and to say why.

This Luther would deny. It is *not* the business of philosophy, he insisted, to pry into these matters; and to assume its right to do so is to assume him wrong at the outset. But it is worth pointing out that he is here asking of us something with which it is hard to comply. Luther's is only one of many forms of faith that have proclaimed themselves to lie beyond rational criticism. Approaching them from the outside, the inquirer does not know beforehand which of them is sound, or whether any of them is. If he accepts Luther's warning that there is one of them upon which the use of reason will probably lead to damnation, his only safe course will be to refrain from using his reason on any of them at all. And this, while it may pave the way of some to an acceptance of Luther's message, will expose them and many more to exploitation by charlatanism; it will remove their one shield of defence. For the defence that lies in faith is not open to them; it is not to be won by effort or thought; it is something conferred from above according to no discernible pattern. We may wait, hope, and pray for it, but without any assurance of a result. To declare us thus impotent in securing the insight of faith and at the same time in peril of perdition if we try to secure it through the exercise of such faculties as we have is surely to beat intelligence down into cowering helplessness. The only road to safety lies in an obscurantism in regard to one's own faith that leaves one defenceless against other and false faiths.

But of course one does not prove a belief untrue by the undesirability of its results in practice. It may be, for all we have seen, that there is in fact such a Deity as Luther believed in, ready to inflict upon us unending and terrible suffering for the attempt to follow reason in these matters. On the other hand, it would be hard to forgive Luther and theologians like him if they were found to have leaped to this conclusion irresponsibly. For then they would have done far more than make an avoidable error on a particular point; they would have sinned against the very light of the mind. They would have sought to invest the free exercise of thought with a vague, vast, crippling, gratuitous fear. Nor is this the sort of fear that troubles superstitious minds alone; it is a sort that tells with especially numbing effect on those who are sensitive and imaginative. Pascal, for example, was an intelligence of remarkable power, and behind his famous 'wager' was the clear perception that while to believe against the evidence was an evil, it was a smaller evil than an eternity of torture, and that it was therefore better to drug and beat a recalcitrant intellect into submission than to give it a freedom that would bring destruction. This kind of theology, through appeal to an overmastering fear, puts a premium on deliberate ignorance and even on intellectual dishonesty. There is no doubt that it has acted in countless cases to repress and discourage inquiry. Luther's denunciation of reason in religion was so confident and forcible, and his audience so vast, that if he was wrong he was catastrophically wrong, retarding for centuries the advance of intelligence in the West.

24 His reply would presumably be that what he was really retarding was the indulgence of human pride. And we must agree once more that he is right if his account of the relation of faith and reason is the correct one. For then any attempt by reason to determine or criticise the content of faith will indeed be presumption. But it must be pointed out that to those who are not in the fold and who have comprised then as now the majority of mankind, charges of pride are stones thrown from a glass house. There is nothing on the face of it impertinent or presumptuous in using those powers which have proved our best and only reliance in understanding nature for the further attempt to understand our origin, duty, and destiny; such inquiry implies an awareness that light is lacking, and a desire for more. Further, as Goldwin Smith remarked, 'Not every doctrine is humility in the preacher which is humiliating to man.'[43] Luther, while insisting that inquiry into these matters was a work of sinful pride, held that true humility was displayed by the person who claimed personal and infallible assurance from on high that his own interpretation of Scripture was right, even when it differed from the whole Catholic tradition; who held that his own view of the limits of reason was right, even if it involved correcting Aristotle and Aquinas. That philosophers have been guilty at times of undue pride in scaling speculative heights is no doubt true, though they would perhaps also agree with Bradley's remark that 'there is no sin, however prone to it the philosopher may be, which philosophy can justify so little as spiritual pride'. Indeed the founder of Western philosophy insisted that if he philosophised at all, it was because he was so acutely aware of his ignorance. When philosophers in this tradition are met with the accusation of pride by one who claims that his accusing accents are not those of pride but merely of omniscience, they are likely to have their own views as to where the charge is most appropriately laid.

The reflective inquirer need not be deterred, then, either by threats or by charges of arrogance from raising the question whether Luther's account of reason and faith is true. The essential points in that account are that man has been vitiated by original sin, that reason is incompetent in the sphere of religious truth, and that faith as distinct from works is the key to salvation. We must consider these points in order.

THE MEANING OF ORIGINAL SIN

25 Original sin was an indispensable part of Luther's system. It explained man's disfavour in the sight of his maker, his helplessness to redeem himself, the feebleness of his intellect and the distortion of his conscience, the necessity of grace from the outside, the need for the sacrament of baptism, and the justification of eternal punishment. Its outlines were firm and definite. Adam and Eve were historical figures; Eve's temptation by the Devil and Adam's by Eve were historical events. The first pair had been placed in the garden morally pure; their yielding to temptation corrupted not only their own minds and wills but also the seed they carried within them; all the descendants that sprang from their loins were there potentially when their sin was committed, and hence effectively shared in it. Sinfulness is a hereditary taint and merits reprobation even before any action has been willed. It is for this reason that infant baptism, cancelling the inherited taint, is so essential. Those who are not baptised, whether children or adults, and whether they have heard of the Christian dispensation or not, are exposed to the divine wrath.

This was the doctrine believed and taught by Luther. It is not dead. In substance it is still the official teaching of the Catholic church, as laid down at Trent,[44] and not since then abjured; it appears among the thirty-nine articles of the Church of England;[45] and the revival of Lutheran theology has given it renewed currency in other churches. One occasionally hears it remarked with a knowing air that *of course* the doctrine of original sin is true. Many persons suppose that modern sophistication has here rallied to the ancient wisdom of the church, that the Freudian exposure of man's irrationality and the revelation in two world wars of his unlimited capacity for wickedness have somehow confirmed the dogma. One needs to walk warily here, for the dogma has been treated like a piece of putty and has been moulded by imaginative hands into very diverse shapes. Sometimes it is taken to say that when the fathers eat sour grapes the children's teeth are set on edge, which may mean only the truism that the sins of the fathers are likely to injure the children, that if the father is an alcoholic, for example, the children will suffer for it. Sometimes it means that the wicked traits developed by the father are transmitted to the son biologically, a proposition that biologists would emphatically deny. Sometimes society replaces the parents; we have inherited from our forbears a defective social order, which warps and deforms us morally; Schleiermacher tried to read the doctrine thus. Sometimes it is supposed to say only that all men are gross sinners and will continue to be, and then any evidence of widespread perversity will be taken to confirm it. Now there is no dogma of any religion that could not be validated with ease, or refuted with equal ease, if treated in this way. Assume that those who formulated it had no definite meaning in mind and were content to speak in riddles and metaphors, and one may safely report onself as either orthodox or heretical as the mood of the moment prompts.

But to Luther and traditional Christianity, the dogma of original sin had a definite meaning, and we have seen what that meaning was. Our present question is where we should stand about it. To that question only one answer seems to me possible. The dogma is false. It is worse than that; in the context of Christianity it is a moral outrage. Such charges may seem extreme. They will seem less so, I suspect, if we pause a moment and reflect on the doctrine.

A DOCTRINE WITHOUT BASIS IN HISTORY, SCRIPTURE, OR SCIENCE

26(1) Luther believed that there was an actual Adam and Eve who were tempted in an actual Eden by an actual devil by whom he had actually been tempted himself. It is idle to say that for him these historical figures and events were mere symbols of an abstract theological truth which would remain unaffected, whatever criticism might do to the historical details. The history was an indispensable part of the truth. If there was no garden of Eden, no first pair created in it, no divine command given or disobeyed, no devil to tempt into wrongdoing, no curse upon the sinners, and no taint transmitted to offspring, then what Luther meant by the doctrine of original sin can only be false. And of course it *is* false. These figures never existed. These events never occurred. Competent biologists are divided as to where and when the first figure appeared that could be rightly described as a man, but they would agree that, whoever he was, he was an emergent from millenniums of animality, perhaps like the Java man, perhaps more like Neanderthal or Peking man, but certainly not like Adam. Need one argue the point? It is probably enough to remark that there was a man named Darwin and that there are accredited sciences of biology and archaeology.

We can see now more clearly than we once could why such a doctrine should arise. The notion that man and society are naturally progressive is a comparatively recent one. Before it came into ascendancy, men were inclined to project their dreams of a perfect order backward rather than forward, to think of the Golden Age not as a promised land to which they were pressing on but as a primeval Eden from which they had fallen away. If their lot was unhappy, as it usually was, at least it had not always been so, for they were descended from a mighty race who had consorted with Thor and Odin, or fought with godlike prowess at Troy, or walked the palaces of the lost Atlantis. Eden was the earthly paradise of the Judaeo-Christian tradition, supposed to surpass anything the Greeks had known; as Bishop South put it, 'an Aristotle was but the rubbish of an Adam, and Athens but the rudiments of Paradise'. The commonness of these visions, brought to light by the anthropologists, and their inevitableness, made clear by the psychologists, have put them in their proper mythical perspective. We know now that Edens, if there are any, lie in the future, and that even the life of 'the noble savage' was less likely to be noble than—as Hobbes allowed—'solitary, poor, nasty, brutish and short'. Bacon, who tried in his *New Atlantis* to turn the current of interest from past to future, was right in insisting the 'we are the true ancients', with far more wisdom at our disposal, however foolishly we may misuse it, than those who lived in the idealised youth of the world. The paradise that was lost and the fall that took place in it are plainly vestigial ideas hanging over from a time when history was naturally and pathetically read backwards.

27(2)   More surprising to many than the fact that the doctrine of original sin has no basis in history is the fact that it has no adequate basis in the Bible. Genesis says nothing of it. No withdrawal from man of his power of mind or conscience is reported, no hint of a hereditary corruption of his nature, no intimation that sin is inevitable. The sin of murder committed by Adam's son Cain is recounted without any suggestion that it is connected with the sin of his father. Indeed one will look for the doctrine in vain in any book of the Old Testament. Even in the New Testament there is only one passage in which the sinful state of mankind is explicitly connected with the sin of Adam:

'Wherefore, as by one man sin entered into the world, and death by sin; and so death passed upon all men, for that all have sinned.

... Therefore, as by the offence of one, judgment came upon all men to condemnation; even so by the righteousness of one, the free gift came upon all men unto the justification of life. For as by one man's disobedience many were made sinners, so by the obedience of one shall many be made righteous.'[46]

Irenaeus, who lived in the second century, worked into a conception of original sin from reflecting on salvation; if men could be saved by participation in the goodness of Christ, perhaps they had been damned in a similar way by participation in the sin of Adam. The parallel is at least rhetorically effective, and it does not seem fanciful to find it already at work in the above passage from St Paul. Paul did not draw the doctrine from the Old Testament or from the teaching of his Master; he seems to have found it floating in the Jewish thought of his time; perhaps he adopted it because it balanced so naturally his theory of redemption. But even by St Paul the doctrine is stated so vaguely that to find in it a transmission of hereditary guilt is somewhat arbitrary. As Dr Tennant says, 'It is easy to read into St Paul's statement each of the later ecclesiatical theories as to the nature of this connexion, just because that statement is so indefinite and colourless as to be capable of accommodating them all. . . .'[47]

28(3) However vague Paul may have been on the transmissibility of sin, Luther committed himself to it in definite terms. Adam's wrongdoing introduced into the race a corruption that, because inherited, became universal, what Luther called a *universa corruptio naturae*. 'Already in the *Sermon on St Stephen's Day* we read of an incapacity of the entire will for love of the good as well as of an incapacity of the reason for knowledge of the right and true.'[48] The incapacity to obey God's commandments was itself morally culpable and incurred the divine anger. It is hardly necessary to remark that this sort of inheritance is unknown to critical or scientific thought. Sin is a kind of activity, and activities are not inherited; it would be meaningless to say that one inherited from forbears the actual process of breaking promises or telling lies. What must be meant is that the power or propensity is inherited; the parents' acting in a certain way specifically affected their genes, and through them produced in the offspring the power or propensity to act likewise. Now it is possible that parental behaviour, if sufficiently dissolute, can depress the general vitality of the reproductive cells, but this suggestion that moral practices can so mould them that similar moral practices will crop up in the offspring is one to which no responsible biologist would subscribe; the evidence against it is overwhelming. We have here a clear case of the conflict of science with theology, and one in which theology is beating a somewhat disorderly retreat.

A DOCTRINE THAT IS MORALLY INDEFENSIBLE

29(4)   It is time the doctrine did retreat and take itself off permanently, if only for the sake of the theology that it has smirched and compromised. The doctrine is, if possible, even more untenable morally than factually. We may begin with the obvious: to make one person responsible and condemnable for the sin of another, and especially of another who died before he was born, can be justified by nothing but sophistry. If someone advanced the thesis that when a man kills another in Iraq a man in Detroit should be jailed for it, he would be regarded as scarcely sane. Still the man in Detroit is at least a contemporary of the murderer and might conceivably have contributed by some unconscious negligence to what happened in Iraq. But to say that he is justly punishable for what someone did in Iraq millenniums ago is to empty the idea of justice of all meaning. Yet that is what the Lutheran doctrine says.

30(5)   It would be unfortunate enough if the sin of our first parent reproduced itself only in a propensity to go and do likewise, but according to the doctrine of original sin, the situation is far worse. Adam's disobedience opened a cosmic Pandora's box, releasing all manner of imps and bats. The Stoics had an all-or-nothing doctrine about keeping the moral law; to keep it was perfection, but any breach of it was as bad as any other, since all alike would cause one to lose one's footing in the heaven of righteousness. Most moralists have felt this doctrine to be intemperate and extreme. One may surely break an engagement for lunch without incurring the criminality of starting a world war, or totally undermining one's power to be truthful or decent. But the doctrine of original sin will have no middle ground. Adam disobeyed; and because he disobeyed, every faculty in his nature was vitiated, every desire was infected with evil, the struggle for goodness itself was perverted into something sinful. The Holy Ghost was withdrawn, and 'man without the Holy Ghost and God's Grace', said Luther in his *Table Talk*, 'can do nothing but sin. This is my absolute opinion. . . .' It is no doubt true that the repercussions of one sin, even a small one, may be far-reaching. But to make it the inevitable source of total moral corruption in the individual and the race is to throw it out of perspective. Why should anyone distort in this way the facts of the moral life? Luther testified that he was utterly terror-stricken at the thought of Christ the Judge, and it is as if his terror had led him not only to abase himself before the Judge, but to make all humanity beat its breast and lament its worthlessness in company with him. Whatever moved him to the belief, there is no proportion in it between the misdeed and its consequences.

31(6) Furthermore, so far as these consequences take the form of original sin, they are not really sins at all. Sin involves an act of will. It is the choice of what is known to be worse over what is known to be better. A mere susceptibility to temptation, a mere potency or capacity for wrongdoing, is not in itself sin. Animals do not sin, for they have not reached the level of moral choice. An infant—even an infant that is destined to become a gangster—has not launched himself on a career of sin while still in the womb or the cradle; like his unfortunate ancestor, he must taste the fruit of a famous tree, that of the knowledge of good and evil, before he can get that career under way. To condemn him morally before he has in the proper sense acted at all is inept; it is to represent him as sinning before the conditions that make sin possible are present; it is indeed to assert a self-contradiction. As Dr Tennant says, 'what is original cannot be sin, and sin cannot be original'.

32(7) It is characteristic not only of Luther but also of Augustine and the grim church fathers who framed the doctrine, to make wickedness heritable, but not goodness. We have seen that, strictly speaking, man inherits neither, but if he inherits either, he must obviously inherit both. As Professor R. L. Patterson has said, 'it is one thing to call him a sinner when he has actually sinned, and another thing to call him a sinner because he is capable of sinning. For man is capable also of noble deeds, of self-sacrifice and heroism; yet one would not call him a saint or a hero until his deeds have actually merited such an appellation. There is no reason why this moral plasticity of man . . . should be equated with sin rather than with virtue.'[49] Luther indeed might reply that there was no goodness in man to be transmitted or inherited. But that would only repeat the denigration of human nature that we have been deprecating.

33(8) It must be remembered that as regards the acts as well as the state of the natural man, Luther was a determinist. He believed that even such actions as Judas's betrayal of his master, given the outer and inner circumstances, are unavoidable. What he is therefore saying in his doctrine of original sin is that man is sinful and guilty for actions he could not help. To be sure, this is not so absurd a view as might at first be supposed. Determinism does not render meaningless all judgements of good and evil; one may quite consistently judge that pleasure is better than pain, even while recognising that these experiences are caused; indeed one may consistently go further and say that actions are right as they tend to produce the former and wrong as they tend to produce the latter, even though the actions are necessitated. But one can hardly say that the notions of sin and guilt themselves are unaffected by determinism. These notions imply not only a choosing of what is believed to be worse, but the possibility of avoiding that choice. If we knew that Judas did only what he could not help doing, that there was no alternative open to him, we could hardly say that he was guilty of wilful sin. And yet Luther seems to be saying both things at once. Man is guilty in the profound and terrible sense in which his sin merits eternal retribution, even while he is doing what he is doomed to do and could not have avoided. This surely is incoherence.

GOD AND ORIGINAL SIN

34(9)   The picture of Deity conveyed by the original-sin dogma is also incoherent. What is most distinctive of the Christian teaching regarding God is his love and forgiveness. The doctrine of original sin, seen in its implications, represents him as a being of implacable cruelty who could have stemmed the flood of evil but chose not to do so. He must have acquiesced in the temptation of Adam; he must have brought Satan himself into being. As omniscient, he knew beforehand what Adam would do when tempted; as all-powerful he fixed the law by which Adam's sin was multiplied through the length and breadth of humanity. Could not Omniscience and Omnipotence have arranged these matters otherwise? It might be replied that there are restrictions even here, that God himself could not have granted freedom to man without the liberty to misuse it, and that its value outweighs any ills that spring from that misuse.

The reply is not convincing. The larger part of human behaviour is governed by causal law, as things are, and to suppose that a limited freedom from such law is worth purchasing at the price of almost unlimited suffering is far from clear. The world, so far as a mere human eye can see, would be a better and happier place if man had been ordained from the beginning to act more prudently and wisely, or, again, if virtue had been made hereditary rather than vice. In any case, there is a vast amount of suffering in the world that has no connection with human mis-doing and appears to be quite pointless. The suffering of the child with cancer, or of the mouse trying to escape the cat, or of the millions swept off by earthquake, cyclone, and pestilence, has nothing to do with moral delinquency, and it produces no known goods that would compensate for it. The standard move of the apologist at this point is to admit a mystery, but to add that if we saw farther we should see that all these things are consistent with the boundless love of the Creator for his creatures; the right recourse is to faith. But the philosopher cannot cut short the inquiry in this fashion; his question is what, in the light of the available evidence, it is most reasonable to believe, and that question is not answered by a resolution to go beyond the evidence and even to flout it if it seems to point in an undesired direction. Perhaps men are happier when, as so many Catholics do, they turn these matters over to the church and stop worrying about them. Unfortunately a faith that may be justified practically and emotionally may be less than justified rationally. For the philosopher at least the inquiry must go on.

Professor A. E. Taylor, an able apologist for Christian theology, wrote in his Gifford Lectures: 'The traditional Christian dogma of original sin, its consequences and the mode of its transmission, as shaped in the West by St Augustine, has always seemed to me, even in the moderated form in which it persists in the Thomist theology, manifestly the most vulnerable part of the whole Christian account of the relations of God and man, and to call more imperatively than any other part of the theological system for reconstruction in the light of philosophy and history.'[50] And Bertrand Russell reminds us that 'Professor Giles, the eminent Chinese scholar, at the end of his Gifford Lectures on "Confucianism and its Rivals", maintains that the chief obstacle to the success of Christian missions in China has been the doctrine of original sin. . . . Confucius taught that men are born good, and that if they become wicked, that is through the force of evil example or corrupting manners.'[51] And F. L. Lucas comments: 'This idea that God should bid man forgive his brother unto seventy times seven, but should consider Himself at liberty to punish His children infinitely and unendingly for a single offence, or even for an offence committed by others, seems to me the strangest, perhaps, of all human manias.'[52] The dogma of original sin strikes an alien and jarring note in Christian theology. A God who is loving and forgiving cannot at the same time be consummately cruel and unjust. It is strange to consider that some deeply religious men, such as Luther and Jonathan Edwards, have been able to unite a tender affection for their own children with an ascription to one whom they described as a heavenly father of shocking inhumanity to children generally. Edwards, whose work on *Original Sin* is described by Lecky as 'one of the most revolting books that have ever proceeded from the pen of man', illustrated the attitude of this father toward his children, says Lecky, from 'those scenes of massacre when the streets

of Canaan were choked with the multitude of the slain, and when
the sword of the Israelite was for ever bathed in the infant's blood'.[53]
Luther seems to have been more reluctant to draw out the consequences of his doctrine. He was clear that the natural man must
receive at God's hands what he variously called 'damnation' and
'death and hell'; and clearly children, before they were baptised,
must be classed as natural men. Furthermore, it was one of his main
theses that the mere reception of sacraments was of no avail, since
they must be accompanied by a state of faith in the receiver; 'Faith
must be present before, or at least in, baptism; otherwise, the child
is not released from the devil and sin'.[54] But how could infants have
such faith? Their prospect looked dark indeed. Luther did his best
for them by arguing that if the parents earnestly interceded for them
the divine mercy would grant a miraculous and precocious faith
sufficient for the purpose. As for the unbaptised child, 'what prevents
children unbaptised from being condemned to all eternity?' he
asked. He was compelled to answer: Nothing but an unstipulated
mercy which, while assuring us through Scripture that they merited
damnation, would somehow find a way to suspend the appalling
sentence.

Still, the quality of that mercy is disquieting. The vast majority of
mankind, past and presumably future, remain under condemnation.
All those who lived before the Christian era must be condemned,
for the grace later made available was not available then. 'If the
choice were given me, I would pick the work of a Christian farmer
or maid, even if it were very coarse and boorish, in preference to all
the victories and triumphs of Alexander the Great, Julius Caesar,
and other heathen. Why? Because here is God; there, the devil'.[55]
Luther is willing to admit that Socrates, Themistocles, and Regulus
exhibited virtues of truthfulness and fidelity, and God does not
entirely overlook such virtues; it was in consequence of them that
he granted to the Romans their great empire. But these were outward forms of righteousness. In their hidden parts the heathen were
corrupt, driven by pride and the desire for glory. Theologically
speaking, their virtues counted for nothing, and Luther denounced
as pernicious error Zwingli's teaching that some of them might be
saved.[56] Again, even in the period since the incarnation most men
have remained in darkness about the opportunity open to them;
they too are under sentence. Nor does it seem certain, in spite of all
the efforts to carry enlightenment into lands of alien faiths, that
heathen pride will capitulate; so the millions who continue to follow
Buddha, Confucius, and Mohammed must join the vast procession
of the doomed.

No doubt Luther, who nominated the Pope for a conspicuous

position among the lost, and the Pope, who consigned Luther to perdition, would agree that such teaching promoted morality by frightening many into the straight and narrow way. As a matter of fact, it instituted a painful divorce between theology and morality. For a Creator to bring into being millions of people who could be saved only by a certain kind of light, then to withhold from them that light, and finally to condemn them eternally for not having it, was a policy that in a human being would have been regarded as extreme cruelty, and yet men were called on to pay it reverence in the person and conduct of Deity. Such a demand was calculated to develop religious schizophrenia in the minds of persons like Pascal and Kierkegaard, torn between logic and terror. In others, like Leslie Stephen and W. K. Clifford, it drove the thinker into permanent antagonism to the whole framework of Christian theology;[57] Clifford's indictment of the dogma voiced the opinion of many thoughtful men:

'to condemn all mankind for the sin of Adam and Eve; to let the innocent suffer for the guilty; to keep anyone alive in torture for ever and ever; these actions are simply magnified copies of what bad men do. No juggling with "divine justice and mercy" can make them anything else. This must be said to all kinds and conditions of men: that if God holds all mankind guilty for the sin of Adam, if he has visited upon the innocent the punishment of the guilty, if he is to torture any single soul for ever, then it is wrong to worship him.'[58]

It has been necessary to look carefully at the doctrine of original sin, since it is perhaps the chief ground for Luther's disparagement of reason. His argument was: man's intelligence belongs to the realm of the flesh; this realm is a mass of corruption owing to man's continual sinfulness; his intelligence somehow shared in this corruption; therefore it is a broken reed. This strange and repellent doctrine is untrue. Reason is not to be disqualified on mythological grounds. But of course it may fail on other grounds, and we must now turn to Luther's account of how it actually fares when it enters the lists of theology.

THE FAILURE OF REASON IN RELIGION

35 He assumes that its failure here is absolute. 'And what saith God? Impossible things, lies, foolish, weak, absurd, abominable, heretical, and devilish things, if ye believe reason.'[59] What is true in theology may, in the eyes of reason, be false. It is therefore necessary to lay down sharp boundaries between the kind of truth apprehended in natural knowledge on the one hand, such as the facts of history, the laws of nature, and the principles of logic, and, on the other the truths, unintelligible to such knowledge, that are supplied by revelation. We shall never understand by mere reflection why the Word was made flesh, or how the Deity can be three persons in one, or why those who are innocent by our standards should be eternally punished. But if the Bible reports these things to be true, they *are* true; that is the end of the matter; and if our reason says they are not, that only shows that reason breaks down when it tries to fly without wings.

We must look more closely into this teaching that a proposition false in philosophy may be true in theology. It may mean two quite different things. First, it may mean what it says, namely that the very same proposition which is false when asserted in philosophy is true when asserted in theology; or, secondly, it may mean that the verbal form which conveys one proposition to the philosopher conveys a different one to the theologian, and that of these one may be true and the other false. It will be worth while to look at each interpretation.

36   The first would be disastrous. It would make reason unreliable everywhere. Suppose a philosopher is told that a historical figure embodied an omniscient mind which, nevertheless, grew in knowledge from year to year; or suppose he is told that to condemn to eternal suffering a person who has committed no voluntary sin is perfect justice. The philosopher contemplates these propositions and reports that he can only find them self-evidently untrue. And suppose he is then told by the theologian that they are true none the less, and moreover that to refuse to admit this is a serious moral offence. What is he to do? He cannot merely admit to a casual error, thank the theologian for setting him right, and abjure what his reason tells him. It is not as if he had made a mistake about the number of peas in a pod, which could be rectified by counting again. It is rather as if he had been told that counting itself was irrelevant in ascertaining number, and that the clearness with which something approves itself to his natural faculties signifies nothing. But if self-evidence itself is to be rejected as a witness to truth, what ground is there for supposing that our reason is reliable anywhere? Nor is the trouble merely with our thought; reality itself is declared to be incoherent. For what is being alleged is that the same proposition is both true and false; the addendum that it is true for the theologian and false for the philosopher does not alter that fact; the real world is X but also not X. But then nothing is secure. If knowledge may be both complete and incomplete, why may not matter both gravitate and not gravitate? It is not only our thought that becomes on this theory a sort of nightmare, but the world itself which thought is trying to construe.

THE WALL BETWEEN THE REALMS

37 Let us then try the other interpretation, which Luther at times expressly favoured. This is that when the theologian uses forms of speech common to the philosopher and himself, he means by them different things. This interpretation does clearly remove the necessity of conflict. If, when the theologian says that eternal punishment for involuntary sin is justice, he means by 'eternal punishment' the loss of divine favour, and by 'justice' accordance with an inscrutable divine will, he is saying something so different from what the philosopher is saying that both assertions might be true.

Unfortunately this conciliatory proposal is not as helpful as it sounds. For one thing, to have two different sets of meanings for common terms produces needless misunderstanding. There are current and standard meanings for the words 'just' and 'punishment'; these are surely the senses in which they should normally be used; and if one wishes to convey a quite different sense, it is reasonable to ask that it be differently expressed.

There is a more important difficulty. It is hard to resist the impression that this resort to double senses is an unconscious evasion. The reader comes upon the Scriptural statement, 'by the offence of one, judgement came upon all men to condemnation'. This statement, since it is in Scripture, must be true, and the judgement referred to, since an act of Deity, must be just. But it is obviously not just in the ordinary sense; it must therefore be just in some exceptional sense; what can this be? The inquirer does not know. He hazards that it means 'in accordance with an inscrutable divine will', and his consistency seems to be saved. But has he done more than push the inconsistency one step further away? He surely assumed the divine will to be righteous, and how could such a will sanction what is self-evidently wrong? To apply the term in its standard meaning leads to incoherence, and the change of meaning is an attempt to avoid this incoherence. If the change is a relatively slight one, as in the case just cited, the contradiction is so thinly veiled as to remain disturbingly alive. On the other hand, if the change is large enough to give genuine relief, one is likely to find that one's idea of God is all but lost in the mist.

This is the experience of many today. They have been brought up to believe that God is good. Little by little they become aware, through grim experience or by report, of the horror in the world,

not only that of the callousness and cruelty of men, which might be
set down to a perverse use of their freedom, but also of 'acts of
God', as the insurance companies call them—accidents that kill or
maim, epidemics that sweep away a Hegel or a Schubert as readily
as they do a drunken profligate, Indian famines and Vesuvian
eruptions and Japanese earthquakes. Confronted by these things,
the believer in the divine goodness is likely to have a divided mind.
These are events in nature, which must therefore have been sanctioned by the Author of nature. They produce unspeakable misery,
and so far as the eye can see, no equivalent good. A human being
who perpetrated such things would be condemned unsparingly. But
from such a judgement upon Deity, religious minds shrink back.
Though they cannot honestly call these horrors good, neither can
they, without emptying their idea of God of all ground for reverence,
call God evil. They must manage to keep both the badness of the
events, which is required for moral integrity, and also the goodness of
God, which is required for emotional peace. They do it by involving
the idea of God in veils of mist so thick that anything can be
reconciled with it. How deep the obscurity is has been brought out
by writers on theology who have invited these persons to say *what*
evils in human experience would serve to shake their confidence in
God's goodness. The reply has come: None whatever; the suffering
of the world might be tenfold what it is and our faith would be
unchanged; though he slay us, yet will we trust him. Unfortunately
this leaves the intellectual problem where it was. What is at work
here is not so much *thought* which has won its way out of incoherence
as a *commitment* of will and feeling which has brushed the intellectual
problem aside.

38   The suspicion is inevitable that Luther's architecture of two
realms, in which the truths of the realm of grace are unintelligible
to the lower realm of reason, is at bottom another case of this well-
meaning evasion. What Luther wanted was reform, the reform of
individual lives and of the church, and he was impatient of anything
that stood in the way of his drive for reformation. He conceived that
reason did stand in the way. It was cold, critical, and inhibiting.
'If anyone summons reason to the council, assent to our articles of
faith is impossible.'[60] His theology was a means of by-passing reason
and getting back to the matter of importance. 'Theology ought to be,
from the beginning to the end, practical. It is by living, yea, by
dying, that one becomes a theologian, and not by knowing, reading
and speculating.'[61] Here theology is presented, not as a means of
clearing up the bafflement of reason, but as a means of ignoring it
and going about one's business in despite of it. In all this Luther

sounds like an impatient and puzzled mind of our own day who, faced by a contradiction between his experience and his theology, elects to commit himself to both and let the pieces fall where they may.

But as a professor of theology he could not rest in such a position. Theology was in its own way a science. It had as its ample data the books of the Bible, and its business was to interpret, defend, harmonise, and explain the manifold truths delivered there. Often these truths made nonsense to reason; 'when God speaks, reason judges his word to be heresy and the word of the devil, for it seems to it absurd and foolish'.[62] But with a strict discipline we can keep reason under. 'The evening sacrifice is to kill reason; the morning sacrifice is to glorify God.'[63] Beliefs that reason tells us are false to the point of absurdity faith assures us to be true, and since the authority and certainty of faith outstrip those of reason, theology is still the queen of the sciences.

THE CRUMBLING OF THE WALL

39 Luther's demand that faith should 'kill reason', however, made the sciences that followed reason not subjects merely, but enemies. And if there is to be peace between enemies, the line between their provinces must be clearly and firmly drawn. Such a line Luther never succeeded in laying down. Tireless and vehement as he was in denouncing reason, he allowed its advance guards to swarm across the theological frontier almost at will. Indeed he found himself forced to co-operate with them. In order to formulate the very interdicts by which he proscribed reason in the realm of faith, he had to borrow scribes from across the line.

We have just mentioned the problem of evil; consider Luther's language about it. We can see clearly enough with our natural faculties that human suffering is evil; we seem to see also, as a necessary inference from this, that whoever inflicts such evil needlessly is himself doing evil. Luther is bound to say, however, that the inference is invalid. Why? Because we know by revelation that God is good. Good in what sense? Is it in some sense that has no relation to common meaning? Then it has no interest for us, since our problem is precisely whether we can still apply the common meaning in the light of bitter experience. And Luther is alive to this, for he is not content to regard God as good merely in some transcendental and unintelligible sense. He is good as a father is good; he is tender and solicitous and forgiving, slow to anger but formidable in wrath and terrible in vengeance, as some human fathers are. In these respects Luther was intensely human himself, and in his passionate fears and prayers he was wrestling with another Person conceived very much in his own image. That was what made his struggles so poignant and his down-to-earth preaching so pungent.

But surely all this goes ill with his theory. According to that theory God was unknowable to human faculty. 'No man shall see God and live'; a man can approach him only if he leaves his reason with his shoes at the temple door.

> 'Even the very particulars which fall within the range of the natural knowledge of God are so far from being thus apprehended in their real character, that Luther says in regard to them, and thus in regard to the entire sphere of religious truth, that reason understands nothing at all about them: "It is not possible to understand even the smallest article of faith by human reason. . . ." In matters of faith, reason is stone blind, and cannot understand a single letter of divine wisdom.'[64]

This is the official doctrine. But when we turn to Luther's actual preaching and writing, we find him pursuing a contrary course with the same confidence and vehemence. The conception of God he there uses is so shot through with ideas drawn from secular experience, and so entangled with relations supplied by natural reason, that it would have collapsed into a sort of jelly without them. When he exhorts men to respond to the love of God or to flee from his wrath; when he refers to the suffering on the cross, or to the malice of the devil who pursued him so remorselessly, or to the Christian virtues of forgiveness, hope, and charity; when he reasons freely about these things, arguing from guilt to the justification of punishment, from the agonies of eternal fire to the prudence of avoiding it, from the need of a greater sacrifice to atone for a greater sin, he is plainly talking theology. Is he talking intelligibly or not? If not, why speak in riddles except to those who, as already in grace, hold the divinely vouchsafed key to them? But if in so speaking he *could* be understood by the many, as he clearly assumed that he could, what becomes of his exclusion of reason from the religious realm? With one hand he pushes it contemptuously away. At the same time he is deftly using it with the other as his main means of interpretation, his chief weapon of argument, and indeed as an indispensable armoury of concepts and relations for the conduct of religious thought.

Luther's insistence on talking intelligibly, even in theology, was thus at odds with his theory of what theology should be. Unfortunately his teaching in this field shows a further inconsistency: it was inconsistent with itself. Some minds, as we have seen, save their coherence by a timely retreat into obscurity; if the evil in the world prevents their saying that God is good in the ordinary sense, then he is good in some extraordinary sense. But one who refuses thus to take refuge in a fog and, like J. S. Mill, 'writes clearly enough to be found out,' may pay for his clarity with painfully definite contradictions. Luther's determinism led him to hold that God was the cause of all things, of Judas's act of betrayal as well as of droughts and epidemics; and for a being who was all-powerful and could have avoided such evils to create them deliberately was plainly not good in the ordinary sense. But unless Luther's language about God's fatherly tenderness and care was to lose its meaning, God *was* good in the straightforward sense. And to combine this with Luther's brand of determinism was clearly inconsistent.

THE ATTACK ON REASON SELF-DEFEATING

40 Indeed if his language is read straightforwardly, as he meant it to be, his theology is riddled with contradictions. 'God is not able to deny His nature, that is, He is not able not to hate sin and sinners', yet 'There is in God no wrath or disfavour; His heart and thoughts are nothing but pure love.'[65] We must believe both that 'the salvation of all men is the earnest will of God'[66] and that he has predestined the majority of them to be damned. If a certain man is lost, it is because he has been thus predestined to be lost, though it is also true that his doom is entirely his own fault.[67] Though God has vouchsafed his grace to only a limited number of men, it is impious to say this or believe it.[68] Since God knows how every deed will work out, he can have nothing to repent; but we must accept the repeated Scriptural report that he 'repented him' of his actions. God commands men to believe, yet often withholds the grace they need to comply with this command. If a human court condemns a man for something done by his father, that is unjust; if God condemns a man for something done by his remotest ancestors, this is perfect justice. Christ was sinless, but as a man he was a sinner. 'Let no one hope to be saved through another's faith or work',[69] though our only hope of salvation is through the faith and work of Christ. It is needless to lengthen the ungrateful list.

Luther could not fail to note the presence of such contradictions. What is remarkable is his boldness in dealing with them. Instead of saying, 'So much the worse for my theology; I must see that it does not fall apart in this way,' he said, 'So much the worse for reason; its criticism is arrogance'. Such a line took courage, a quality in which Luther was never wanting. But it was a policy that neither he nor probably anyone else has ever been able to honour except in the perpetual breach. He made no question that our natural faculties, however corrupted, were competent to guide us in the affairs of business or politics, of science or secular history. That the faculties which had thus sustained the life and progress of the race would take us one inch across the line into theology he emphatically denied. But we have seen that he could not hold the line against them. If one removes from his theology all the propositions thus placed under the ban, what is left? A Deity to whom no attributes of the kind we know can be ascribed, a being without morality in our sense, a being not even consistent with itself. Such a being cannot be made the object of thought, for thought is bound by logic. A more serious consideration for Luther, and one that stirred in him uneasily at times, was that neither could such a being be made the object of Christian reverence, adoration, or worship. For if one could not call it 'good', 'just', 'noble', or 'wise' in the natural meaning of these terms, what was there to adore?

We are compelled to say, then, that Luther's attack on reason, for all its vehemence and scorn, was incoherent. He was not a stupid man, and in his own field of Biblical studies he was a considerable scholar. But he was too impatient and impulsive to be a good philosopher, and his conviction that in the theology of Romans and Galatians he had laid hold on ultimate truth was too much for a somewhat feeble power of self-criticism. This part of the Pauline teaching encouraged him to think that, once grace had descended upon him, he could speak with the accents of Deity, and that if spiritual pretenders like the Pope, or secular pretenders like the philosophers, stood in his way, he could blast them out of it with the lightnings of divine anathema. He did not feel this to be egotism, for on the essential points it was the Deity that was speaking rather than he. He had a new criterion of truth, namely conformity to Paul on salvation, and since this criterion was absolute and certain, he was in a position to brush aside any scientific fact or philosophic demonstration or scholarly conclusion that did not accord with it. Copernicus was a 'fool', Aristotle a 'blind heathen'; Erasmus, 'like Judas, betrayed the Son of Man with a kiss'. If one were to protest that these were not the proper descriptions of men who were trying to be reasonable, Luther would reply that to try to be reasonable is wickedness where faith is at stake. In appraising this position, it has always been difficult to take middle ground. If Luther was right, it is hardly enough to regard him as one of the highest mountain peaks in human history, for on that peak he was receiving from a still loftier region the tables of a new law. If he was wrong, it is hardly too much to call him a fanatic with a touch of paranoia. Men will line up on both sides for centuries to come.

'JUSTIFICATION BY FAITH': WHO IS JUSTIFIED?

41 One more of Luther's teachings, though a most important one, remains for estimation: we are justified by faith alone. Faith is a belief or conviction, the conviction that our sins are forgiven because of the sacrifice made on the cross; and this return to divine acceptance is what is meant by 'justification'. Faith is not an achievement but a gift, to which no merit on our part attaches. Such faith is the absolute good for man. Without it, good will, good works, intelligence, genius count for nothing. If one has it, good will and good works will follow, but they will avail nothing in the final reckoning. Compared with anything else that may happen to us in our short time on earth, the salvation of the soul is uniquely important, for upon it depends our status through eternity. The one thing needful for that salvation is faith.

Luther held this doctrine because he believed that it was the teaching of the Bible, appearing most clearly in his favourite part of Scripture, the epistles of St Paul. Fortunately we are not concerned with the correctness of his Pauline exegesis. Our question is whether his teaching on faith, regardless of its source, and regardless too of its vast historical influence, is acceptable today. We have already stated its meaning. We must now look at some of the difficulties it holds for the modern mind.

42 One difficulty is that in the complex drama of his fate man himself is considered as having little or no part. He is the pawn of the supernatural. In some versions of the drama he did play a part; he used his free will long ago to disobey his Creator, and thus 'brought sin into the world and all our woe'. But in Luther's version, even this part is virtually denied him, for his disobedience was not that of a free agent but that of a puppet. And no rung of the ladder by which he may rise to favour is formed by any act attributable to the natural man. He may repent, implore, refine his conscience, purify his thoughts, amend his ways; but since these actions spring from a corrupted heart and are therefore without merit, they have no influence in averting condemnation or securing grace. Faith, if it comes, is a gift from without, given independently of merit and on inscrutable grounds. The person who lays hold of it is not strictly the 'I' who has done evil, but another I, divinely implanted, 'not I but Christ,' for only faculties divinely supplied can apprehend divine truth. It is this new self, not the sinful old one, that is approved or justified—Deity within me being approved by Deity above. Again, if I succeed in doing right, it is not the I who did wrong that thus succeeds, for that self is incapable of anything good; the agent is the new supernatural self that has dethroned the natural one and taken over the government of my actions. Finally, it is not the old corrupt I who is saved, but the new and heaven-born self. Man's only part in 'this strange eventful history' is to supply the stage on which it happens. The gift of faith, the laying hold of it, the translation of it into act, the receipt of forgiveness, the assumption into heaven, the living out of an eternal life, are all supernatural proceedings, unconditioned at any point by the actions of the natural man. Putting it crudely but not perhaps unfairly, God implants himself in man, forgives himself, approves himself, elects himself, and saves himself.

In such an account the notion that man is on probation, that he is being given an opportunity to show by throwing off his shackles that he merits some divine approval, has been abandoned. He merits nothing but punishment. Nor will he gain anything by his efforts to merit something better, for the natural man is helpless to improve his status before the bar of judgement. Though his own soul—if one may call it his own—is at stake in the drama, he remains a spectator of the proceedings, not an actor. This is the consequence of Luther's sharp separation of the realms of nature and grace. He is so insistent that the natural man can do nothing good that he ends by removing the whole process of man's salvation out of the natural world. And then man as we commonly know him is never saved at all. What we ordinarily mean by moral and spiritual ascent is a process of growth in such faculties as we have—a clearer apprehension of the ends of life and a firmer devotion to them, a completer ordering of thought, feeling, and habit by a set of warranted ideals. In this process the self, while advancing, remains the same, and we can trace the working within that advance of reflection, regret, admiration, and criticism. Luther will not admit that this sort of advance is advance at all in God's sight. What is exclusively of importance is what God does himself. Hence the process of salvation, instead of being a development and refinement of those powers that constitute the self we know, is rather a replacement of them by agencies different in kind.

LUTHER'S DOCTRINE A MORAL DEPRESSANT

43 Such a view, if taken seriously, is a depressant to the moral life. In order to count, we are told, good works must proceed from grace, and grace is beyond the reach of effort. Sometimes it is granted, sometimes not, and the principles governing its bestowal, if principles there are, remain hidden from us. Of course we may rise in the scale of a merely natural morality. It is well to have Luther's words on the value of such morality.

'In Scripture God concludes . . . that all persons who are still in their natural or first state are unjust and evil, as it is said Ps. 116:11: "All men are liars," and Gen. 6 : 5: ". . . every imagination of the thoughts of his heart was only evil continually". Therefore natural man cannot perform any good works, and whatever he attempts in this direction is nothing more than a work such as Cain produced. Here Dame Hulda with the scornful nose, that is, corrupt human nature, comes to the fore, has the audacity to bark at her God and charge Him with falsehood. She puts on her tinseled and tawdry finery, her straw armor, natural light, reason, free will, and natural powers. . . . Aristotle taught that whoever does much good will thereby become good. To this view Dame Hulda firmly clings. Thus she subverts Scripture. . . .'[70]

One may ask Luther whether he can really mean this. Are works that express kindness, affection, the sense of honour or truth or justice, really *sins*? Luther answers: 'No one should doubt that all our good works are mortal sins if they are evaluated by God's strict judgment. . . .'[71] But suppose a man, convinced that mere natural goodness is not enough, tries to take the supernatural into account and acts from the fear of divine punishment; what then? Luther answers,

'he who does a good work because he fears death or hell does it not for the honor of God but on behalf of death and hell, and his act is a work of death and hell. . . . Therefore he remains a slave and servant of death and hell with all such works. But if he remains a servant of death and hell, he must also die and be damned, and the fate of the proverb must overtake him: He who fears hell goes to hell. . . .'[72]

Under such a system it is hard to see why anyone should try to be moral. His conviction that justice is really right and happiness really good is an illusion, for God who sees them as they are brands them as sinful. No matter how hard he tries to act justly and wisely, and no matter how largely he succeeds, he still stands under the curse; he still merits only damnation; and unless God intervenes with a pardon that he is helpless to secure, he is sliding down the incline toward an abyss of eternal torment. With his whole scale of natural values thus denied, why should he not say, 'Let us eat, drink and be merry for tomorrow we die, whatever we do'? It is not a noble course, but then neither is any other that is open to him, and at least he likes it. If nothing he can do will avert the unspeakable evil in store for him, why should he devote himself to anything so hard, so valueless, and so futile as a moral struggle?

It has been replied that he still has a special reason for doing good works, even if their goodness is meretricious. The reason is that though such works are not the condition of salvation they are signs of it, and therefore if he succeeds in doing them, he will at least have comforting evidence that he is among the elect. Good works in Luther's teaching do not guarantee salvation; they are not necessary to it; but they do follow from it. Hence if we produce them, we may infer that however little we merit it, salvation has been mercifully granted us.

Unhappily the inference is invalid. We cannot argue from good works to faith as their source because there are other sources of good works besides faith. If faith produces them, so also do affection and dutifulness and reasonableness and honour. Hence the fact that a certain man has behaved well for a certain time enables us to infer nothing as to the presence in him of faith. Furthermore, just as good acts may be done without faith, so men of faith often do acts that are vicious. Not that faith directly issues in vicious acts, but that in actual operation it is so entangled with human motives that it may seldom express itself with purity. Judging merely by achieved good works, then, a man of faith may rank lower in the scale than a dutiful man who lacks it. To be sure, Luther sometimes teaches that the works of faith so differ from other good works that they wear their heavenly origin on their face. So far as this is true, the man we are considering has no problem; he can look at his life and read off from it whether he is saved or not. But this is surely not the position of the common man. He is genuinely uncertain where he stands. And for such a person to devote himself to good works in the hope that he may catch some dependable clue from them as to where he stands in the great accounting is a course of pathetic desperation.

There is another way in which Luther's doctrine of faith is a moral depressant. It shifts the centre of gravity from conduct to belief. If deeds count at all in one's salvation, it is not one's own deeds but the sacrificial deeds of another, and what makes these efficacious in the present is a state of faith passively received; 'this alone He works within us and without our co-operation'.[73] Luther never tires of deprecating good works in comparison with faith as what truly justifies. 'Hearing, not doing, makes a Christian.' The thought of the Christian will thus be fastened primarily not on what he is to do, not even on a state of mind to be acquired by doing, but on what has been done for him in the past; and his appropriation of the legacy is itself a matter of believing rather than doing. The effect of such teaching is inevitably to turn the direction of his interest away from activity among his fellows to his own inner stage as the thing of importance, to exalt the receptive Marys of the world as having chosen the better part and the one thing needful, in comparison with the shallow and busy Marthas. The 'proper work and merit by which God wishes to be glorified' is the 'passive righteousness' of faith. Whether this stress on passive acceptance as opposed to conduct was sound or not, it certainly marks a shift from both church tradition and common conviction. Luther knew this and intended it. He was demoting morality to second place and giving the primacy to belief.

BELIEF AS THE ESSENCE OF FAITH

44 What now of the belief itself? Is Luther's account of it acceptable?

We have seen that for Luther belief, and above all belief in the atonement, is the effective component of faith. Now belief is a form of thought, and thought is an activity of natural reason. To make belief the very core of a process that is also represented as supernatural and transcendent of human faculty is a paradox. Luther espoused both sides of the paradox with characteristic confidence. Faith *is* Christ in the soul and a 'holiness from without' (*extrinseca sanctitate*), and the victory it effects over the world and the devil— 'a single devil is stronger and wiser than all men'—is 'completely beyond the grasp of human reason and is perceived only by faith, with closed eyes'.[74]

'For human wisdom and reason can rise no higher and get no farther than to judge and conclude as they see before their eyes and as they feel or apprehend with their senses. But faith must conclude above and against such feeling and understanding and must cling to what is placed before it by the Word. Faith cannot do this in the power of reason and human ability. This is the work of the Holy Spirit in the heart.'[75]

Again,

'Faith can see in the dark, where nothing whatever is visible; it feels where nothing is to be felt.'[76]

If the belief that is active in faith is really of this kind, a seeing in the dark, an acceptance 'with closed eyes' of something 'completely beyond the grasp of human reason', it is clearly not belief as we know it. Such a description suggests rather a mystical absorption in that which is ineffable because above the realm of concepts and distinctions in which thought moves. We shall not go into the difficult question whether the notion of such a realm has any meaning. What does seem clear is that this is not a realm with which belief as we commonly know it has any concern. Such belief always has an object of the form 'that x is y'; this object has distinguishable terms with some relation between them; and both the terms and their relation are laid hold of, though not always with full explicitness, by the believing mind. For a person to say that he believes, and in reply to the question *what* he believes to say that he is asserting nothing in particular about anything, is equivalent to saying that he is not believing at all. And Luther's prescription that we *ought* to believe, even when the object is 'in the dark where nothing whatever is visible', is itself a very dark saying.

But faith does not move exclusively at these giddy heights. Luther admits, at some cost of consistency, that it includes the belief of many propositions that are as definite and intelligible as those of science, for example, the statement that Christ 'was born of the Virgin, suffered, was crucified, rose, ascended to heaven'.[77] Indeed there are hundreds of equally definite propositions that may and should be believed as part of the content of faith. The Bible is full of statements not independently known to be true, but it is the duty of faith to accept them nevertheless. Why? Because they are inspired. How do we know this? What assures us, regarding a life lived long ago, that it began with a Virgin birth and that its tragic end expiated man's sin? It is hardly enough to answer that these beliefs have been pronounced true by divine authority, for the question then at once arises, how do we know *that*? Luther answers both questions in essentially the same way. We know by means of the 'heart'. 'Faith is the yes of the heart. . . .' 'Every man is only to believe the Gospel because it is God's Word and because he is convinced in his heart that it is the truth, although an angel from heaven and all the world were to preach against it.'[78] Luther is firm that such faith is knowledge, and in evidence he quotes Peter to the effect that we can 'grow in the *knowledge* of our Lord Jesus Christ' (2 Peter 3 : 18). But he adds that this is not the sort of knowledge that heretics have, and goes on to explain rather quaintly:

'This word "knowing" means as much as; "Adam knew his wife" (Gen. 4 : 1), that is, he "knew" her by the sense of feeling, and he found her to be his wife, not in a speculative or historical way, but by experience. . . . A merely historical faith does not act in this way. It does not add the experience of feeling and the knowledge that it is a personal experience. To be sure, it says: I believe that Christ died and that He did so also for me; but it does not come to this personal feeling, this experimental knowledge.'[79]

With such knowledge reason has nothing to do. It should merely be hushed up. We should not, 'on the basis of reason, argue about how these sublime matters can happen'; we 'must close our eyes, take captive our reason, look at Christ on the cross, and believe the word: he who believes in Me shall not perish but have eternal life'. 80

KNOWLEDGE OF 'THE HEART'

45 What are we to say of this claim that there is a knowledge of the heart, more certain than any gained by our faculties? There are many who would dismiss it contemptuously without examination. This surely is arbitrary. The claim to such knowledge has been made, it is true, by mountebanks without number, but it has also been made by some minds of a different order, such as Pascal: 'the heart has its reasons that the reason does not know.' How is the claim to be appraised? Perhaps the method most likely to be convincing is to ask whether beliefs to which 'the heart' has given an unequivocal warrant have, or have not, stood up in the light of man's experience as a whole. To such an inquiry it might be objected that it really begs the question in advance against any supernatural claim, since in 'experience as a whole' is included that of our natural faculties. But this line of defence is self-defeating. A type of knowledge so out of touch with the rest of our experience that such experience is not even relevant to it can hardly have any meaning for us either. At any rate for Luther, in spite of all his protests against reason, it clearly had both relevance and meaning.

We know by faith, he says, that Christ was crucified and suffered. There would no doubt be overwhelming agreement among historians that these beliefs are true. We also know by faith, he says in the same context, that Christ was born of a virgin and that he rose bodily from the dead. About these beliefs there would be the greatest difference of opinion, all Catholic and many Protestant theologians affirming both views, the majority of scientists probably rejecting both, and others in both camps accepting one and rejecting the other. Those who reject the beliefs presumably do so, not on the ground that the occurrence of these particular events can be disproved, but that both are miracles, and that miracles do not happen. But if called upon to prove this sweeping negation, they could not do so. They might reply that outside the formal sciences proof is difficult if not impossible, that in regard to historical events we must rely on probability, and that probability is against the miraculous in any form. There is force in this old argument of Hume's, but the supernaturalist can reply that however great the force may be, it never amounts to one against zero, and therefore he may still hold consistently that a particular miracle did occur. Besides, if you press the issue, what is the antecedent probability of a world that is lawful over one that is not? Could you prove to a supernaturalist who denied any such probability that he was wrong?

A man who alleges that he has seen by faith that a virgin birth or a bodily resurrection occurred may actually have done so; there seems to be no way of *proving* him in error, either as to the fact or as to his mode of apprehending it. But this is not the only way to test his claim. We may ask whether all the beliefs that have received the full authentication of faith have maintained their position over the years. Have some of them, in spite of this warrant, had to be abandoned by the fideist himself? If there are such cases, he must make the painful choice between renewing his subscription to a belief he holds untrue and admitting that his faith may mislead.

FAITH MAY MISLEAD

46 Now the fact is that many beliefs which according to Luther were authenticated by faith as certainly true have been abandoned as false by fideists themselves. Let us look at a few instances from a field that may be broadly called scientific. Luther felt that on the issue between Copernicus and Scripture, Copernicus was plainly wrong; 'the fool wishes to revolutionise the whole science of astronomy. But, as the Holy Scriptures show, Joshua commanded the sun to stand still, not the earth.' On this ground it was needless to study the wilful astronomer further. Again, Luther had an absolute assurance of the existence and wiles of the devil, not only from Scripture but also from experience; 'By good experience, I know the devil's craft and subtilty. . . .'[81] Sixty-eight sections of his *Table Talk* are devoted to the forms, the depredations, and the most effective methods of foiling 'the father of lies'. 'St Peter speaks of Christ as healing all that are oppressed of the devil'; 'I maintain that Satan produces all the maladies which afflict mankind, for he is the prince of death'.[82] Luther seems to have had the same sort of assurance, both Biblical and personal, about witches. 'We read in the old law, that the priests threw the first stone at such malefactors,' which seemed to him a sound proceeding; indeed 'I should have no compassion on these witches; I would burn all of them'.[83] 'As for Luther,' wrote Charles Kingsley, 'I am very sorry to seem disrespectful to him, but the outcome of his demonology was, that many a poor woman died in shame and torture in Protestant Germany, just because Luther had given his sanction to the old *lie.* . . .'[84]

Take again the sort of assurances Luther drew from his faith about right and wrong. Along with much that was admirable, he was constrained to believe that if God allowed Pharaoh's heart to grow harder, there was nothing wrong in it, though 'Why God did not hinder or restrain him, we ought not to inquire.'[85] Abraham was ready through faith to violate a mere 'law of nature' and kill his son, and Luther through faith to approve such readiness; 'That example of Abraham exceeds all human natural reason, who, overcoming the paternal love he bore towards his only son, Isaac, was all obedient to God, and against the law of nature, would have sacrificed that son.'[86] Toward the end of his life, Luther came out with what a kindly biographer can only call 'a vulgar blast' against the Jews, adding, 'One could wish that Luther had died before ever this tract was written'. What makes his anti-Semitism of interest here is that 'his position was entirely religious and in no respect racial'.[87] According to Scripture, the Jews were guilty of the supreme sin of rejecting Christ, and in this sin they have persisted ever since. One 'can have no patience or fellowship with the blasphemers and profaners of the dear Saviour'.[88] Luther says to them: 'You have been, above fifteen hundred years, a race rejected of God, without government, without laws, without prophets, without temple . . . ye can show no other reason for your condition than your sins'.[89] He would burn their synagogues, confiscate their books, and send them back to their own land; if that were impracticable, he would force them to become tillers of the soil. If Luther were offering these views as mere personal opinions, it could be said in extenuation that he was only echoing prejudices current in his time. But the ill desert of the Jews was not for him a personal opinion; it was a truth doubly guaranteed by faith and Scripture.

What he says about the Jews, however, is clemency itself compared with what he says about papists and the Papacy. And he is careful to point out that he is not speaking as an individual merely; in attacking the Papacy he is trying 'to put Christ's Word in execution'; 'Our dealing and proceeding against the pope is altogether ex-communication, which is simply the public declaration that a person is disobedient to Christ's Word. Now we affirm in public, that the pope and his retinue believe not; therefore we conclude that he shall not be saved, but be damned.'[90]

'Seeing the pope is antichrist, I believe him to be a devil incarnate.' 'Truly, the pope's kingdom is a horrible outrage against the power of God and against mankind; an abomination of desolation, which stands in the holy place.' 'The pope is the last blaze in the lamp, which will go out, and ere long be extinguished, the last instrument of the devil . . . [and a] shameless strumpet. . . .'[91]
'If this sin of antichrist be not a sin against the Holy Ghost, then I do not know how to define and distinguish sins. They sin herein

wilfully against the revealed truth of God's Word. . . . I pray, who would not, in this case, resist these devilish and shameless lying lips?'[92]

'In the day of the last judgment I will denounce the pope and his tyrants, who scorn and assail the Word of God. . . .'[93]

Now, that Luther did expose much ignorance and corruption in the church is well attested fact. But one will hardly be charged with undue tenderness toward the Papacy if one remarks that to 'ex-communicate' the Pope as 'antichrist' and a 'devil incarnate', to accuse him of the sort of 'sin against the Holy Ghost' that must bring damnation with it, was to assert what neither he nor anyone else, as a merely human being, could presume to know. Luther seems to have asserted these things with full confidence that he was hurling divinely sanctioned anathemas.

There may be fideists who still believe that these anathemas expressed inspired and certain truth. If so, they might well consider some of the contradictions pointed out earlier in the content of Luther's faith, and ask themselves whether they would also accept both sides as equally inspired. Surely few if any would be prepared to do so. With the best of will toward Luther, they would find it impracticable to go down the line with him in his long list of vehement claims to certainty. Even fideists, if they are candid, can hardly avoid the conclusion that faith, as he conceived it, is no guarantee of truth.

CONFUSIONS OF 'THE HEART'

47 Where did he go wrong regarding the relation of faith and belief? He was confused, we suggest, in his notion of 'the heart'. In theological usage, the term is a dangerously ambiguous metaphor. Just as the heart is the most important organ in the body, so it is assumed that there is a 'heart' which is the most important organ of the soul, and a long tradition of Biblical and literary practice has confirmed the assumption. 'Let thine heart keep my commandments', 'write them upon the table of thine heart'; 'as a man thinketh in his heart, so is he', 'because of the blindness of their heart' men do not 'see or understand with their heart'; 'their hearts are far from me'; 'did not your heart burn within while he talked with us by the way?'; 'blessed are the pure in heart'; 'let not your hearts be troubled'. The 'heart' in these typical passages has no one meaning; the supposed organ has two entirely different functions. One of them is cognitive; the heart thinks, understands, and may become blind. The other is emotional and conative; the heart is devoted to a way of life or averse to it, is exalted or depressed, indifferent or involved.

Of the two meanings the latter or emotional meaning is primary. One's heart is in a cause when one is surrendered to it, when one's will and feeling are absorbed by it, and it is thus important emotionally.

Now it has been notorious since Freud's day that if something is important emotionally reasons are sought and usually found to justify this importance. Luther's religious emotions were of an almost pathological intensity. He was terror-stricken about his soul's safety; he was fighting a precarious fight for it against a devil so real that he could throw curses and ink-bottles at him. His concern was intensified by his explorations of the Bible, which he read without those curbs on belief that are now imposed by science, critical history, the higher and lower criticism, comparative religion, and depth psychology. The notion that his religion, which was virtually his whole life, should hang on the verdict of a thin, detached, and arid intellect seemed to him intolerable. Faith must be self-evidencing. Surrender to it, kill the devil-prompted doubts of reason, and you will achieve a certainty beyond anything reason can supply, even in its own special province. 'When this Word enters the heart by true faith, it makes the heart as firm, sure, and certain as it is itself, so that the heart is unmoved, stubborn, and hard in the face of every temptation, the devil, death, and anything whatever, boldly and proudly despising and mocking everything that spells doubt, fear, evil, and wrath.'[94] Reflection can only bog down in its attempt to see how the world is governed, but 'through faith the heart sees it as surely as if it were looking at it with bodily eyes.'[95]

A faith so imperious as this has often bowled criticism over and flattened it out. To argue with Luther was like reasoning with a hurricane. But if one can keep one's feet long enough to look the hurricane in the eye, one sees a confusion taking shape at its very centre. It is a confusion between two kinds of certainty. One is the certainty of feeling, what Joseph Jastrow called 'the emotion of conviction'. It is the sort of assurance that patriots often have of their country's being right, or that lovers have of the goodness of those they love. There is no doubt of its reality, and its intensity may be overwhelming; but that intensity bears no relation to the truth of what is believed. This kind of connection may attach itself to the noblest causes and beliefs, but it may attach itself also, as history has tragically shown, to the teaching of some lunatic dervish or 'bloodthirsty guttersnipe'. The other kind of certainty is that of knowledge proper, in which there may be no discernible emotion at all, and yet intellectual insight may be clear and firm—the certainty of the mathematician who has demonstrated a theorem or of the physiologist who has isolated by experiment the cause of disease.

Nothing is easier, even for a sincere mind, than to confuse these certainties. A person with a strong emotion of conviction tends to believe what this emotion requires for its justification, and if it is extremely strong, to suppose that he *knows* this. The patriot, for example, 'knows' his country to be right, and the lover 'knows' his beloved to be beautiful and good in rare degree. In the same way the man of strong religious feeling tends to believe that the framework of dogma which has served since childhood as the great firm trellis of his emotional life must be true. That life would hang in a void if the dogmas were untrue; therefore they are and must be true. If a weaseling intellect brings in a verdict of not proven, then it must be denied that in the realm of truth the intellect has exclusive rights. The heart too must be heard. The depth of the heart's longing is itself evidence in the case. Faith, says Luther, 'always stays in the stage of a wishing and a sighing of the spirit, too deep for a man to express. Then the heart says: Oh, that it were true! Again: Ah, if only one could believe it!'[96] and if one's desire is strong enough, faith and insight follow.

For all Luther's force and eloquence, one can only suspect that he is here sliding over from conviction as feeling to conviction as knowledge, and supposing that if the first is massive and powerful enough it can actually convert itself into the second. Two dubious assumptions seem to be at work, which deserve to be singled out.

48 One is that feeling can know. Of course it is common enough to say 'I feel that a storm is brewing', or 'I feel that John is untrustworthy,' but this may mean only 'I have good grounds for believing thus, though I am not clear what these grounds are.' But if by 'feeling' one means either an emotion, such as love or anger, or an 'affection', such as pleasantness or unpleasantness, it is clear that the phrase 'I feel that—' cannot be correct. One may assert a proposition, or deny it, or opine it, or suppose it, or doubt it, but how could one feel it? One may, to be sure, have a profound 'knowledge of the heart' in the sense of knowing the shades and causes and ways of working of human emotion, but this is knowledge *of* the heart and not *by* it.

49 The other dubious assumption is that if a belief satisfies a massive demand of feeling, that is evidence for its truth. There would be some force in this assumption if one could start with the assurance that the world is governed by a power committed to satisfying our desires, for such a being would presumably so order events as to fulfil our desires where possible rather than frustrate them. But when the existence of such a being is itself at issue, one plainly cannot use the assurance that he exists as part of one's argument for his existence. And without this assurance there is no reason to think that our desires, however powerful, carry with them any guarantee of fulfilment. Men have passionately desired innumerable things—that their children or their business should succeed, that their faith or party or country should prevail—and not only have many of these desires failed of fulfilment; one can see that they had to fail, since they were so often for incompatible ends. All men, or nearly all, want passionately to live rather than die, yet this most universal of desires is universally frustrated. One cannot, even in religion, argue that the depth and generality of men's desire that a belief should be true has any relation to its being in fact true.

FATE AS DEPENDENT ON FAITH

50 There is another point of importance that we must note about Luther's teaching on faith. It makes belief a moral act, and indeed the most important of all such acts, for our fate depends upon it. The most essential items of belief are given in the Apostles' Creed. 'If one item of this creed is lacking, all items must fall. Faith must be complete. . . . To be weak in the faith does not do the damage, but to be wrong—that is eternal death.'[97]

It is hard to see how any reflective and humane person can acquiesce in such a theology. It represents the Christian Deity as a sort of Moloch. For the faith that makes belief possible is not something we can achieve, but something given or withheld at divine discretion, and therefore if we do not possess it, the Deity is represented as first withholding it from us and then punishing us remorselessly for a failure attributable to his own act. Of course if the Deity lies beyond all regard for right or reason, he may very well do what, by our standards, is cruel and vindictive. But to call such action good is to throw these standards to the winds. Luther evidently thought that a Deity capable of such action might also be capable of condemning him for not praising it, and so, terrified of what such a Deity might inflict upon him, could not get himself to call a spade a spade. And given his irrationalist theology, who can blame him? Nevertheless, that a courageous and intelligent man should be driven to such cowering incoherence is sorry testimony to the influence of irrationalism in religion.

But while affirming that belief was beyond attainment by effort, Luther also affirmed the opposite, and it remains to see whether he fared better when he was in this second mood. He obviously thought that if we held reason firmly in check and immersed ourselves in Scripture, if we refused to sully our minds with heretical thoughts and treated doubts as temptations of the devil, we could go far, after all, toward attaining that belief which was the one thing needful.

Now we admit that belief is in some measure under the control of the will. We may confine ourselves to one side of the evidence about a belief; we may associate only with persons who hold it; we may cultivate admiration for those who believe it and dislike for those who do not; we may dwell on the advantages of believing it and the unfortunate plight of unbelievers. It has been seen too, in considering Catholicism, that certainty in advance of critical inquiry tends to inhibit such inquiry. Independent reflection is needless as a means to the discovery or confirmation of the truth, since we have that truth already, and inquiry carries with it the risk, to be avoided at all costs, of undermining our belief and thereby endangering our salvation. The course of safety thus lies in a prudent limitation of our intellectual exposures and a circumspect watch over vagrant thoughts. It was Luther's conviction, shared with his Catholic opponents, that he had an extensive knowledge which was neither derived from rational inquiry nor responsible to it. If reason dealt with these problems at all, which it had better not, it must come out in a preappointed place, the place appointed by faith and Scripture.

AN IMMORAL ETHICS OF BELIEF

51 From the supernaturalist point of view, one can hardly cavil at such restrictions on thought. But from the point of view of the ordinary man attempting to be reasonable, they are inconsistent with fact and strain intellectual integrity.

They are inconsistent with fact because belief is represented as far more dependent on the will than it actually is. Everyone recognises that if a New Englander believes summers to be warm and winters cold, that is not a matter of the will; his assent follows the evidence as helplessly as a needle follows the pole; it would be absurd to praise him for the admirable achievement of believing; and as for disbelieving, he could not do it if he tried. Speculative beliefs are less automatic, but even they will be found to follow local evidence and pressures rather closely. In Islamic countries, most devotees are Moslems; a youth brought up in a Unitarian family in Boston may be found, to no one's surprise, a Unitarian. For something he has thus breathed in with the local air, he would seem to deserve little in the way of either praise or blame. Not so on Luther's theory. In the sight of his maker, this youth in being a Unitarian has committed a serious sin, indeed a sin that merits eternal condemnation.[98] It would be difficult to take this view seriously if so many people had not followed Luther in doing so. To a person of any humanity or common sense, it must surely seem a distortion of moral perspective as gross as it is grotesque. The youth's belief may at no point have involved a voluntary act, except an occasional direction of attention to one fact or book or speaker rather than another, and the belief of his maturity may well have come as the involuntary resultant of such exposures. To treat this belief as a sin comparable with murder is to turn our scale of values upside down.[99]

52 Luther's view also strains intellectual integrity. It does so because it involves appeal to two different standards with over-lapping provinces. The traits of mind that in science and history are intellectual virtues are transformed into intellectual vices as one moves over into religion, and vices become virtues. It would be absurd for a scientist or historian to try to confirm a hypothesis by an appeal to the heart, but when his hypothesis conflicts with a statement in Scripture, the resort to feeling ceases to be an offence, and becomes a duty. It was thus admirable for Copernicus to follow his evidence rather than his heart till he collided with the book of Joshua, but thereafter he must follow his heart and reject the evidence. Luther would no doubt explain to the critic that the feeling which may be trusted to guide religious belief is something quite different from the feeling which is dangerous to secular belief, for the first is divinely prompted and the second a mere natural feeling. But how one is to distinguish the first from the second is not made clear. Nor is one helped in drawing the distinction by Luther's own intellectual practice. To the critical reader, the feeling that often dominates his thought, even on religious issues, seems to be of a kind that honourable secular minds have tried to repress. 'As a rule,' says Dr McGiffert, 'he saw only one side of a question';[100] he was only too likely to take his own feelings and convictions as expressing the divine will, and qualitatively similar ones in his opponents as delusions of Satan; according to merely secular standards, his writing about such rivals as Zwingli and Erasmus, in which he mixed his ink with prussic acid, went beyond the pale of fair controversy, even for a violent time. If his practice reflected at all faithfully his views on the morality of the intellect, rationalists will prefer their own more exacting code.

53 Just as the appeal to feeling, discouraged in secular thinking, was admitted in religious thinking, so the love of truth, exalted to a high place in secular thought, was depreciated in Luther's theology. There is no adequate introspective measure of the love of truth. But most persons will probably agree that it is revealed in certain distinctive attitudes, of which the respect for fact, the respect for relevance, and the respect for consistency are perhaps the most notable. It prefers accuracy to looseness of statement everywhere, and particularly in the statement of an opponent's position, since justice—the most intellectual of virtues—is there involved as well as correctness. Again, the love of truth means care in interpreting facts, that is, in inferring what they imply, a care that resists irrelevant solicitations from one's own desires, from casual associations, and from social pressures. And if one's attempt to interpret facts runs out into inconsistency, the seeker of truth will draw back and admit having gone astray. There is nothing arbitrary in selecting these marks of the love of truth, for they are prescriptions laid down by the nature of thought itself as conditions for reaching its end. Fidelity to fact, care in inference, respect for consistency—these are indispensable if thought is to do its work. Of course one may refuse— for a time—to play the game of thought at all, but if one sits down to it, there is only one way to play it.

FAITH AND INTELLECTUAL INTEGRITY

54 We have heard a biographer, Dr McGiffert, admitting of Luther that 'truth for truth's sake never appealed to him,' and certainly in his theological thought he declined to be bound by any of the prescriptions just named. Even the facts of his own experience were seen through such thick theological lenses that it is hard to gather from his report of them what actually happened. Encounters with the devil were common:

'The devil has often raised a racket in the house and has tried to scare me. . . .'[101]
'In the monastery of Wittenberg, he constantly heard the Devil making a noise in the cloisters; and became at last so accustomed to the fact, that he related that, on one occasion, having been awakened by the sound, he perceived that it was *only* the Devil, and accordingly went to sleep again.'[102]

He claimed to have seen the devil in the forms of a sow and a burning wisp of straw.[103] 'Prussia is full of them [devils]' he said, 'and Lapland of witches.'[104]

'Every form of disease might be produced by Satan, or by his agents, the witches; and none of the infirmities to which Luther was liable were natural, but his ear-ache was peculiarly diabolical. . . . The Devil . . . could beget children, and Luther had himself come in contact with one of them. An intense love of children was one of the most amiable characteristics of the great Reformer;

but, on this occasion, he most earnestly recommended the reputed
relatives to throw the child into a river, in order to free their house
from the presence of a devil.'[105]

Presumably he would have testified against a witch as confidently
as he here did against a child. In such cases his theology made it
impossible to look at the facts directly.

It had a like influence on his inferences from, and interpretation of,
fact. Take, for example, his interpretation of Scripture. It is vivid,
imaginative, colourful, and full of eloquent and moving suggestions
for the pulpit. But it is an interpretation dominated by a special
theology, and above all by his own theories of the atonement and
justification. The gospel of John, which present-day theologians
regard as the least reliable of the gospels historically, is put first
among them by Luther because of its stress on the dogmas he thought
central. For him the really authoritative books of the New Testament
as we have noted, were first Romans, then Galatians, then Ephesians,
because in these the central dogmas were given the place they
deserved. How was the truth of the central dogmas themselves to be
attested? The answer was that, aided by faith, we can see their truth
directly. Having laid firm hold of these, we can then apply them as
touchstones to find which portions of Scripture are essential, which
peripheral, and which dispensable altogether. Since the touchstones
glowed with a divine fire, the interpretation they imposed was
regarded as virtually inspired itself.

Unfortunately this interpretation led to mistakes all along the line.
Impartial critics cannot accept the prefigurings of Christ that
Luther found in Genesis and the Psalms, or his comparative ratings
of the Biblical books in authority and authenticity, or his doctrine
that 'God is truthful, however absurd the things which He declares
in His Word may appear to reason,' or even his special version of the
atonement and justification. Not only his facts but also his inferences
from fact were far too largely determined by theological preconceptions.

Such distortion would have been less dangerous if it had been
checked in the end by an appeal to the canons of logic. But even the
appeal to consistency Luther managed to denounce as a foreign
imposition upon theology. He held that one could start from sound
theological premises, reason from them logically, and yet arrive at
false conclusions; and his way of dealing with such paradoxes was to
say that the canons of reason were not applicable to theology.[106]
But this was rather a device to save himself *in extremis* than a rule of
his theological thinking. He was a formidable controversialist who
was ready enough to employ reason in defending his position until it

landed him in difficulties, when he could protest that reason was not for him authoritative and insist that with the aid of faith one could go so far beyond it as to see that both sides of a contradiction were somehow true. Thus, we should strive for faith, though it is futile to do so; our endeavour must never slacken, though 'to sleep and do nothing is the work of Christians'; the whole creed is essential, though the only essential dogma is the atonement; no one is sinless, but 'he who believes has no sin and does nothing but good works'; the Deity owes man nothing, though man's desperate plight is traced back to the Deity's own making.

Is it possible to maintain intellectual integrity while thus playing fast and loose with the requirements of rational thought, using them when it advances one's case, brushing them aside when they stand in the way? Such an attitude creates a perpetual internal strain. Follow the argument, and faith protests that one is holding sacred things lightly. Follow faith, and reason protests that one is being intellectually dishonest. Are the two sides evenly matched? If so, the prospect for peace of mind is dim. But the fact is that they are not matched evenly, for to abandon reason is not even a possibility. One can affirm that one is doing so, as Luther incessantly did, but to see something to be really true which violates logical law is something else, which was beyond even his considerable powers. It *is* possible for faith to adjust itself to reason. It is *not* possible for reason to adjust itself to faith if this implies abandoning the canons implicit in any attempt to think, for then the power to assert or deny intelligibly, and therefore to say anything at all, is cut off at the root. Religious leaders less headstrong than Luther have seen that one cannot, on entering the religious sphere, put off the natural man like an old coat. John Wesley, after reading Luther on Galatians, remarked:

'How does he . . . decry *reason*, right or wrong, as an irreconcilable enemy to the Gospel of Christ! Whereas, what is *reason* (the Faculty so called) but the power of apprehending, judging, and discoursing? Which power is no more to be condemned in the gross, than seeing, hearing, or feeling.'[107]

55 We have completed our examination of Luther. We have fixed our eyes on three of his cardinal teachings—the dogma of original sin, the inadequacy of reason in theology, and the doctrine of justification by faith. None of them has turned out plausible. The only way to make them plausible is to surrender to a kind of theology that respects neither logic nor ethics. And if rational standards are invalid in theology, it is hard to see how they can be valid anywhere else. Luther found the philosophers erecting a temple of reason on sacred ground. He would have none of it. He marched into their temple resolved to wreck it, and set himself with the resolution and strength of a Samson to pull its columns down. Practically, the adventure may have been a success. Theoretically he pulled the columns down on his own head. 'Kill reason' is a highly treacherous slogan.

To be sure, it has often led to short-run success. Most men would rather feel than think, and Luther gave them the welcome news that in matters of religion it was wiser, better, and safer to feel than to think. 'The world may be divided by temperament, it might be said, into those who like it warm, and those who like it cool; into those who naturally sympathise with Luther and those who naturally sympathise with Erasmus.'[108] The Lutherans are in the vast majority. And 'Luther's heavy peasant fist destroyed at one blow all that Erasmus's delicate penmanship had so onerously and tenderly put together.'[109] It would be churlish to deny that one who could speak with such power to so many was a great man. Luther *was* a great man. Religion in Europe was dying away into an affair of rites and exercises, of reciting creeds and hearing masses without understanding them, of buying insurance policies on the next life, of compounding for one's sins with a venal church, and generally of keeping on the right side of ecclesiastical officialdom. Luther prodded religion awake. His own faith, whatever else may be said of it, was alive, a matter of passionate over-riding concern, not something that could be delegated even to the most powerful of churches, but something that had to be lived anew in the mind of each individual man. When he had finished his lusty and brawling attacks on the establishment, for which a succession of popes would have sent him with relief to the stake, religion had been fanned into flame again throughout central Europe.

56 But though he was more effective immediately than Erasmus, it is the Erasmian coolness that will probably have the last word. The Lutheran temperament is its own worst enemy. Luther could free himself from Rome more easily than he could from his own tempestuous impulses. 'Men of intemperate minds cannot be free,' said Burke; 'their passions forge their fetters.' Luther 'thought with his blood'; for good and evil he was a seething pot of passion— hatred for the papacy, courage and the love of a fight, tenderness for children, an almost sadistic fury toward his enemies and those of the state ('the civil sword shall and must be red and bloody'), terror and abjectness before an angry God, a towering egotism ready to call the Pope himself contemptuously to order, a red-blooded sexuality, a deep and haunting sense of his own sinfulness, sympathy for plain men in their suffering, and finally a frank, withering, philistine scorn for 'the harlot reason'.

Now one can hardly be possessed at once by this sort of scorn and also by the love of truth, or live in a dust-bowl of passion and also manage to see the shapes of things with clearness and perspective. And Luther was deficient in mere loyalty to truth. 'Thought makes the whole dignity of man,' Pascal once said; 'therefore endeavour to think well; that is the only morality.' Luther would have scoffed. The belief and the morality that stood to one's credit on the final ledger were not to be attained by 'thinking well', but by following 'the heart' in defiance of anything thought might say. There was something dramatic in thus thrusting out one's jaw at the 'intellectuals' of the world, and it has had its massive response from the romantic, the impulsive, the frightened, and vast numbers also of simple, earnest, unspeculative people, ready to be swept away by a confident leader. But there is one great weakness in such leadership; it has lost its compass for truth; it has therefore thrown itself open to delusion, and is too likely to end by raising the banner of fanaticism. The doctrine of original sin, which fixed the status of man in Luther's world, is not true; it is a libel based on a myth. Luther's estimate of reason is not true, nor is it even coherent, since it attacked reason with reason's own weapons. The doctrine of a faith that is at once achievable and unachievable, a feeling yet above reason in its cognitive authority, is not true, and it led a powerful and generous mind into absurdity and even cruelty.

The Catholic view on faith and reason we found unsatisfactory in many ways. Unhappily we have found the Protestant view, as represented in its first great reformer, not less unsatisfactory. It remains to be seen whether later figures in Luther's tradition have conceived the relation in a more acceptable way.

CHAPTER VI

REASON AND FAITH IN
KIERKEGAARD

1   In the long line of Lutheran theologians stretching from Luther himself to Brunner, Barth, and Bultmann, Kierkegaard holds a unique place. He holds it in virtue of being the first to state, in extended and more or less modern form, the case against rationalism in religion. Luther had stated it before him, but the rationalism Luther opposed was the comparatively modest rationalism of the schoolmen and Erasmus. What Kierkegaard had to contend with was the most radical and fully elaborated rationalism in history, that of Hegel.

Nevertheless, Kierkegaard's elevation to the place he now holds is a curious fact that calls for explanation. He died in 1855, after a short life of forty-two years, and by the end of the 1800s he was forgotten. In the *Century Dictionary of Names*, published about 1900, one will look in vain for any mention of him. He was rediscovered in the thirties, owing largely to the devoted work of Walter Lowrie in telling his story and translating his books. Since then his name has become familiar in every seminary and every department of philosophy in this country. Why was it that this forgotten figure, who wrote at excessive length in a baffling style and in a minor tongue, should have become, a century later, so bright a star in the theological sky?

He was a forerunner of existentialism; true. So was Nietzsche, but that has hardly served to place him on a theological pedestal. The reason for Kierkegaard's revival, I suggest, is his relevance to the position of religion in our time. Not that he is needed to cope with any danger from Hegel, for to most present-day theologians Hegel is scarcely more than a name. What is formidable today is not the rationalism of Hegel but the rationalism of science. Theologians have discovered that the strange Dane had forged so potent a weapon against rationalism that they could use it against science as effectively as he had used it against Hegel. The weapon was no blunderbuss or fowling-piece, designed to slow the enemy's advance while beating a retreat; Kierkegaard would have no half-measures with an enemy he so cordially hated. The weapon was a bomb designed for whole-sale retaliation. It lay in the thesis that religion was not a rational affair at all, and that reason was therefore incompetent, irrelevant, and impertinent in sitting in judgement upon it. The forces of faith were foolish to take the forlorn liberal line of throwing piece after piece of their creed as sops to the enemy; let them turn on the foe boldly, take the offensive and oust him from their territory, where he had no right to be. This was essentially the line of the neo-orthodox theologians of the twentieth century, of Brunner, Barth, and Reinhold Niebuhr; and Kierkegaard was its pioneer. How exhilarating the new strategy was to beleaguered defenders of the faith will be clearer if we recall some of the incursions made by rationalism into religious territory between the death of Luther and Kierkegaard's timely resurrection.

THE ADVANCE OF RATIONALISM

2   Luther died in 1546; Galileo was born in 1564: and the name of Galileo has come to be a symbol of the scientific challenge to the Biblical view of nature. It was a limited challenge, which seemed at first to affect only some passages in the Old Testament. If the sun really stood still over Gibeon, that must have meant that the earth stopped revolving; but if the earth had suddenly stopped revolving, we should all have been pitched eastward at a thousand miles an hour and blotted out. Since we were not, the record was presumably in error. Such reflections proved, after some centuries, to have been the beginning of the end for the older conception of nature, which has been crumbling slowly away under the attrition of newly discovered fact. If the flood occurred in historic times, how did the sloth manage to cross the ocean from Ararat to Brazil? If the genealogies of the Old Testament are to be accepted, with their patriarchal lengths of life, there were no animals or men on earth earlier than six thousand years ago. But prying palaeontologists kept bringing to light human relics whose period, as reliably dated, was of fifty or sixty times that age. In the Yale museum I have often looked speculatively at the skeleton of a giant turtle, almost per-fectly preserved, whose lowest plausible age is six hundred thousand centuries. It is hopeless to patch the older theory of nature to meet facts like these; that might be done with two or three of them, but hardly with ten thousand. They flowed through its loose-woven mythical texture as through a sieve.

3   After the orthodox theory of nature went the orthodox view of

Scripture. The Church of Rome had committed itself with all the authority of popes and councils to the view that the entire Bible was inspired and therefore true. Most Protestant theologians have long seen that no one can continue to hold such a belief without canons of textual criticism that are naïvely elastic. There is now, I take it, agreement among disinterested scholars that, for example, the order of Old Testament Books bears no relation to the order of their composition, that in a given book conflicting narratives from different hands and different times are often pieced together, as in the early chapters of Genesis, that many of the books of both Testaments are not by the authors traditionally accepted, that none of the gospels, as we now have them, were written until a generation or two after the death of Christ, and that these at many points give conflicting accounts of fact and doctrine. Some of the central dogmas of the faith, such as those of the Trinity and the incarnation, have disclosed under further study so large an admixture of Greek thought as to render an origin in unique revelation hardly credible. Regarding others, for example the Virgin birth and the atonement, such an amazing mass of parallels has been brought to light by Frazer and others from the folklore of kindred peoples and of those at a like stage of advancement as to render quite implausible the theory that they were delivered whole from on high, unspotted by the primitive culture of their time and place of origin. With every passing decade more and still more of the provinces long supposed to be inviolable, because delivered once for all to the saints, have been annexed by 'the new conquering empire of light and reason'.

4 Protestant theologians struggled heroically to remain loyal at once to their religion and to their intellectual conscience. They were unwilling to turn their faith into what they conceived Catholicism to have become, an island of intellectual anachronism safeguarded against invasion by walls of censorship and sophistical apologetic. Why, they asked, in a world where everything else that was human seemed to evolve, should not religion too evolve? Granting that revelation occurred, must it not have been filtered through the all-too-human minds that first received it, and must we not suppose that as the initial message is placed in a wider setting of knowledge and discernment it will receive an increasingly rational interpretation? If the Christian doctrine is true, they argued, it has nothing to fear from advancing knowledge; if at any points untruth has entered in, the best way to purge it out is surely to give free play to critical reason. We shall have to pay a price undoubtedly. We shall have to part with many cherished Biblical stories and many old beliefs, with all the prized associations, comforting assurances and high hopes that

went with them, but we shall at least have kept our integrity of mind. Besides, not everything we have accepted can be dissolved, even by the acids of modernity. Suppose the entire supernatural component of the faith is eaten away, we still have in the record of the founder the outline of an ideal human life, and if our religion must scale itself down to being nothing but a way of living, we have saved after all what is practically most important.

But even here the invading forces would not halt. Though recognising the nobility and beauty of the Christian ideal of life, they went on to question this too. They asked whether its relative silence about the values of knowledge, art, and play, and its strong insistence on those of poverty and non-resistance, conformed to the demands of modern life or were acceptable even in principle to reflective reason. To these questions no answers are agreed upon by twentieth-century moralists. But that is not at the moment the important point. The point is that if not only the theology but also the ethics of Christianity are to be surrendered to the arbitrament of reason, then religion as an ark of the covenant, a deposit of faith, an indefectible revealed truth about anything whatever, must simply vanish, and though one may still talk about a nucleus of revelation which is to be construed and interpreted by advancing knowledge, the very content of this nucleus, all that it means and implies, will now have to be defined, tested, and criticised, by the methods of secular knowledge. And, plainly put, that means that nothing certain will be left to cling to. There will be nothing in one's creed, nothing even in one's moral ideal, that under rational criticism may not have to be revised or abandoned. The religion of revelation will have disappeared.

THE EXISTENTIALIST STRATEGY

5 Now the hold on the contemporary mind of the theology pioneered by Kierkegaard lies in its clear perception of where rationalism tends, and its strategy in meeting the invasion. The tactics of liberals have been the tactics of appeasement. Over and over again they have retreated to what they thought a tenable entrenchment, only to be forced ignominiously back, and still further back. The Kierkegaardians have seen that this will not serve. What you have been doing, they say to the liberal theologians, is meeting reason with reason's weapons, and in that contest you cannot win. Once admit that a dogma or a moral prescription is to be accepted not on faith or revelation but on rational evidence, and no position you ever take will be safe. In the game of argument, the dice are loaded on the side of the rationalist, and if you are to avoid bank-

ruptcy, there is only one way out, namely to decline the game
altogether. This you can do with perfect right. Your true line is to
say that religious belief, far from being an intellectual asset, is a
non-rational decision made possible by a descent of divine grace,
as inexplicable as it is certain. To try to explain it or defend it
rationally is to play into the hands of the enemy. And we must
recognise as the great enemy, says Karl Barth,

> 'the emancipation of reason, the self-sufficiency of rational man.
> If once this magic spell were broken, there would be room for the
> Gospel . . . *the* theological problem as well as *the* Church problem
> is this—to deliver modern man and the modernized Church and
> theology from the illegitimate self-sufficiency of reason and the
> spirit of autonomy.'[1]

And Emil Brunner writes:

> 'What can be proved is *eo ipso* unimportant. . . . Faith only can
> prove the reality of God, because God cannot be known by
> theoretical reason but must be comprehended by an act of
> decision.'[2]

That is the Kierkegaard line precisely.

To countless persons who were trying to combine religious belief
with intellectual honesty such announcements sounded as the guns
of Havelock must have sounded to the defenders of Lucknow. The
long retreat and the desperate defence seemed at last to be over,
and the old roles were to be reversed. The believer was not, after all,
an intellectual Colonel Blimp living in the generation before last,
nor was he clinging pitifully to the old faith because he was un-
adjusted to modern thought and frightened of it; it was he who saw
things clearly and as they were; it was the rationalist who was
deluded. To many tired liberals this call for no compromise, this
summons to turn a retreat into an all-out offensive against the
presumptions of reason, seemed as inspired as it was inspiring.

It is Kierkegaard's part as a staff officer in the anti-rationalist
campaign that we are to study. No doubt the utility of his strategy
in this campaign is not the only cause of his posthumous revival.
His stress on vehement commitment, his disrespect for ecclesiastical
and secular authority, his insistence on will and feeling, and his
scepticism of received values have combined with his distrust of
reason to strike a chord unexpectedly congenial to twentieth-century
youth. But since his importance for our interest lies in his account
of reason and faith, we must confine our attention to this part of his
theory except so far as may be necessary to set it in the light of his
philosophy generally. And that is perhaps just as well, since our

estimate of this strange genius, whether as theologian, philosopher, or man, is far from the popular one.

THE 'STAGES ON LIFE'S WAY'

6   At the centre of Kierkegaard's thought is his idea of human life as lived on various plateaux, each with its special characteristics. The idea probably came to him from Hegel. Just as Hegel recognised three main stages on the way to the Absolute—being, essence, and the notion—so Kierkegaard distinguishes three 'stages on life's way', the aesthetic, the ethical, and the religious. He prefers not to describe these stages in systematic fashion, but to suggest their characteristics through the journals or dialogues of fictitious persons. Thus, for his account of the aesthetic life, we must go to the diary of one Johannes the Seducer, or to the speakers at an imaginary dinner where no one is permitted to hold forth until he is mildly drunk. The advantages of this method are literary rather than philosophical; it is not always easy to make out through the convivial oratory of *In Vino Veritas* what the speakers are trying to say, though one is encouraged to renew one's efforts by the assurances of Kierkegaard enthusiasts that the work deserves a place beside the *Symposium* of Plato. An account of the final stage is given in a more straightforward way in a 'postscript', as the author calls it, of a quarter of a million words. However, the reader who proceeds from the oratory to the philosophy in the expectation that here he will reach clarity and incisiveness will come away with the discovery that between Philip drunk and Philip sober the difference is disconcertingly small.

THE AESTHETIC STAGE

7   Our concern will naturally be with the third or religious level, but the first two should be noticed briefly. The aesthetic life is not, as current usage would suggest, a life devoted to beauty, but is rather, in line with the Greek origin of the word 'aesthetic', a life devoted to the goods of the senses. Kierkegaard's notion of it, as Höffding reminds us,[3] is somewhat like the ideal of Aristippus of Greece, who held that one should follow the impulse of the moment; it suggests, again, the early Pater, who urged that it was unseemly, in this short day of frost and sun, to sleep before evening, and that the ideal is to burn as continuously as one can with 'a hard gem-like flame' of enjoyment. Since music is the most emotional and 'immediate' of the arts, it is discussed at length; since sex is suffused with so much passion and pleasure, it is discussed at still greater length; and since Mozart's *Don Juan* so adroitly combines the two, it is made the subject of an encomium. Johannes the Seducer contributes the observation that 'woman is only the moment', and this suggests to Kierkegaard 'the essential aesthetic principle, namely that the moment is everything'. The aesthetic life is lived for the here and now; it surrenders itself to passion and desire; it refuses to take long views or to look before or after.

Like most moralists, though in more roundabout fashion, Kierkegaard points out that such a life is self-defeating. Though the aestheticist prides himself on his closeness to reality, he is in fact living among abstractions, as Hegel said of the man of mere common sense; for the self is a complex affair, and casual desires, even when they reach their ends, do not satisfy more than a fragment of it. Furthermore, one cannot count on their reaching their ends. The pleasure seeker is soon bored if he tries to squeeze repeated pleasure out of the same things; so he is always trying something new, and often getting burnt for his pains. He tires of his friends, behaves with fickleness toward them, and finds them turning on their heel as he approaches. He tires of one woman, exploits many in the Don Juan manner, and finds himself at last in isolation, with no affection given or received. And he is at the mercy of circumstance. It is part of his strategy of life to have no forelaid strategy; his days have no more unity than those of Plato's democratic man, for what he desired yesterday repels him today; 'All the plans I make fly right back upon myself; when I would spit, I even spit into my own face.'[4] Kierkegaard sums up on the aesthetic life as follows:

'If you marry, you will regret it; if you do not marry, you will also regret it. . . . Laugh at the world's follies, you will regret it; weep over them, you will also regret that. . . . Believe a woman, you will regret it, believe her not, you will also regret that. . . . Hang yourself, you will regret it [this does not seem quite self-evident]; do not hang yourself, and you will also regret that. . . . This, gentlemen, is the sum and substance of all philosophy.'[5]

8 How is one to escape from this dreary round of servitude to impulse? Mere doubt, mere intellectual conviction that these goods are tinsel, will not do; one must resort to something that plays the part in real life that doubt plays in reflection, namely despair. 'So, then, despair with all your soul and with all your mind,' says Judge William.[6] Only through such despair can one ever make that choice which Kierkegaard described as a choice of oneself, in which the essential man, as opposed to a bundle of wayward impulses, declares itself and rises above them. When it does so, it ascends to the second or ethical level.

Whether it will do so or not is the choice before us in Kierkegaard's famous 'either-or'. Although he distinguished three levels on which life might be lived, the upper two lay so close together that, in contrast to the aesthetic level, he often took them as one under the name of the ethico-religious plane. It was impossible, he held, to live at once on the aesthetic plane and on this higher one; we are confronted with a stern either-or, the demand for a total commitment to the one side or the other. The choice between planes is a very different matter from choice *upon* either plane. The problem for the aestheticist is what he wants to do. The problem for the ethical man is what he ought to do. The problem of the either-or is the fundamental one whether by a leap of resolution one will move up to the level where 'ought' and 'ought not' have meaning.[7] To make the leap is to enter a new world and to become a moral being. Kierkegaard here seems to be taking his cue from Kant. Holding, in Kantian fashion, that only the self that makes moral choices is free, and seeing that the rise of the impulsive self to rationality and freedom is a somewhat mysterious process, he describes this as a choosing of oneself. Of course it cannot be really that; it is self-contradiction to talk of a choice which brings one up to the level where for the first time choice is possible. There is a problem here of importance, which deserves an analysis it does not receive. It is not solved by such phrases as 'choosing the absolute', or 'choosing myself in my eternal validity', still less by excursions into the psychology of sex.

THE ETHICAL STAGE

9 On the second or ethical level, what governs is not impulse, but principle. Kierkegaard takes as his example a happy marriage, setting off Judge William's defence of it in *Stages on Life's Way* against the picture of Don Juan in *Either/Or*. In such marriage the impulse and desire that were present in the aesthetic stage are not lost, but they are no longer isolated ends in themselves; they are taken up into another order; they are kept in check or given rein as the good of a life may dictate. And just as an impulse must be kept in place if it is to serve the interests of the whole self, so a self must be kept in place if it is to play its part in society. The ethical man does not claim for himself what he refuses to others; the rule of right is no respecter of persons, for a rule is impersonal and universal. His interest is no longer engrossed in himself; he shares the interests of his wife and children and awakes in them a concern for his own good. He adopts a calling which is, or ought to be, at once an expression of his powers and a way of playing a useful role in his community.

In short he has ceased to be a moth fluttering after every candle and become a rational self ordering his life on principle.

Anyone who reached this stage, Kierkegaard thought, was already on the borders of the third stage, the religious. As a philosopher, he followed Hegel in thinking God was immanent. Hegel believed that when we think or act rationally, a mind to which all our fragmentary minds belong is finding expression through us. If two mathematicians see the same equation written on a blackboard, they no doubt have two different sense experiences of the chalk marks; A's sensations are never B's. But what of the equation they think of? Is this really two different equations that happen to be very much alike, or is it the same equation, presenting itself to both minds at once? When they go on to develop what the equation implies, are they under the constraint of numerical systems that are different, only very much alike, or of the same objective system? Hegel would have said, the same, and he conceived this system in its completion as the Absolute. So far as we succeed in being rational beings, it is because this massive and rational system is having its way with us. Kierkegaard found this striking conception hard to resist. With all his suspicion of Hegel, he too conceived of God as immanent, and as already at work in our minds when we reach the ethical plane of guidance by principle. Hence the lack of any sharp line between his ethical and religious levels.

Granting that we have attained the ethical level, what do its principles demand of us? Nothing short of the transformation of our whole life in accordance with them, down to the last detail. They require not merely that we should be generous, but that whenever we give we should give just the right amount, no more and no less. But that is to ask perfection, and we know that this is beyond us. Perfection in practice is as unattainable as perfection in knowledge; to demand it is like asking of abstract reason that it should know completely the event of our having breakfasted yesterday, or know exhaustively this desk that is now before us. No matter how many qualities and relations of a concrete thing or event we come to know, our knowledge will never exhaust its object; it will always be an approximation merely; there will always be something about the fact that will elude us; thought always falls short of existence. So of the attempt to catch a life in the net of ethical rules. There will always be something in our actual life, indeed much in it, that slips through the meshes and escapes control. It is not that you in particular are a failure; you may indeed be the nearest thing to a saint that the race has produced; no matter; you too have failed, and must go on failing. 'Be ye therefore perfect' is what ethics tells us. And measured by this imperative, the interval between the best and the worst of us is far less than the interval between the best of us and the goal we are jointly seeking.

In these circumstances, what are we to do? No ethical struggle will carry us to the goal. We may multiply our principles, qualify them, and conform to them always more closely; we shall still never be wholly good. All we can do, then, says Kierkegaard, is to bow our heads and concede that before God we are always and infinitely in the wrong. If we cannot do what is right, we can at least recognise that we cannot; we can confess that we are miserable sinners deserving of the divine anger and castigation. It is this breakdown of all morality in confession and repentance that takes us on to the third stage, that of religion.

10   In all this there is no doubt some plausibility. It is true that one can never make action ethically perfect or wholly rational. But most of us will feel that between this and Kierkegaard's conclusion that we are infinitely guilty moral lepers with no health in us there is some sort of gap in the reasoning. The argument seems to be this: We all have a duty to be perfect; whoever fails in his duty is guilty; we all fail abysmally in this duty to be perfect; hence we are all abysmally guilty.

Now this is not so much profound as confused. The first premise is ambiguous. When anyone says that it is our duty to be perfect, does he mean that we ought to *be* perfect or that we ought to do our best to be perfect? If he really means the first, he is asking the impossible. We ought to be perfectly just; yes, of course, in a sense, but in what sense? Is it our duty to be just in the same degree as a man who knows ten times as much about the facts of the case, and is free from our fears and prejudices? Surely to require that of us would be itself as unjust as to ask someone who could barely add and subtract to correct the mathematics of Gauss or Gödel. To blame us for failure here would be wholly unreasonable; we are not at fault for what we cannot help. No doubt we should take perfection as our goal, both intellectually and morally, but that means that we should do our best to reach it. To demand that we should reach it in fact is to demand that we should do more than our best, which is nonsense. Kierkegaard's insistence that moral imperfection entails infinite guilt seems to have been largely based on this elementary confusion.

But it was based also on something more. Kierkegaard believed, with Luther, in original sin. Every man, he said, 'is born in sin and as a sinner'. 'By coming into existence . . . he becomes a sinner.'[8] He did not accept the Lutheran machinery of a literal inheritance of Adam's sin.[9] The doctrine seems, nevertheless, to have had a strong hold on him, and the thought of it was made harder to bear by the suspicion that his own father bore an exceptional load of sin. Had not this man, by his own confession, stood up as a boy of eleven on a Jutland hillside and cursed his Maker? And is it not written that he who does this will not be forgiven either in this world or the next? In the diary of Quidam, who is virtually Kierkegaard himself, there is an entry called 'Solomon's dream'. It describes how the young Solomon, sleeping one night in his father's palace, hears a sound in the royal room. Tiptoeing nearer, he hears his father moaning and groaning in an agony of despair. He returns troubled and fearful to his bed, only to dream that the purple robes of the King are the badge of God's punishment and condemnation. He wakes to the horror of realising what his father really is, and goes on to waste his life in the attempt to forget and escape it. Over and over again Kierkegaard comes back to this identification with his father and to the sense that he is living under the blight of another's wrong-doing.

We have said our say regarding the doctrine of original sin and need not discuss it again. It is a doctrine without basis in biology or ethics, a doctrine, moreover, that is linked, both as cause and effect, to something pathological in human nature—to irrational fear, to a morbid sense of guilt, and not improbably to stirrings of sadism. To say seriously, as so many in the Lutheran tradition did, that we not only inherit immoral promptings from our forbears but are somehow guilty of the misuses they made of them, wicked with the wickedness of men long dead, is not to express a profound moral insight but to darken both moral and religious counsel. If men who are doing their best to live up to such light as is in them are to be condemned for wrongs they never heard of, good has become evil, and evil may as well be called good. If sin is everywhere, then it is nowhere in particular. By making everything sinful, the dogma in effect makes sin trivial.

THE RELIGIOUS STAGE (A)

11 Let us return to 'the stages on life's way'. The second stage, it will be recalled, was the ethical, in which impulse was replaced by law or principle in the guidance of conduct. But laws and principles are worked out by human reason, which by virtue of man's corruption is a fallible guide. If we are to escape this corruption and have any security that we are doing right, the control of both belief and conduct must be placed in more reliable hands than those of reason. What can these be? Only one kind of control can carry us out of despair to full security, and that is the guidance of God himself. We reach the third or religious level when we see that the duty that governs our life is not some merely human rule of reason or advantage but a divine imperative, and when we feel that our failure to do it is an affront to God. But this religious stage is not so much a plateau as a rugged mountain top, and within it Kierkegaard distinguishes two sub-stages which he describes as 'religiousness A and religiousness B'.

The distinction between these is not very clearly drawn.[10] The main difference seems to be that in stage A God is thought of as immanent, as somehow continuous with our own minds and open to some degree of understanding by reason, whereas in stage B, which Kierkegaard sometimes calls simply 'Christianity', we realise that God stands over against us as infinitely different, as quite incomprehensible, and indeed as absurd. The religion of stage A may be achieved by the better pagans or by persons of non-Christian religions, but that of stage B, in which man achieves 'an absolute relation to the absolute' and bows to the absurd with his whole heart and mind, is the possession of Christianity alone. The chief marks that show one's escape from the merely ethical level to the first religious level are resignation, suffering, guilt and—interestingly enough—humour. Let us turn to these in order.

RESIGNATION

12 The resignation must be total. 'By resignation I renounce everything. . . .'[11] The religious man cannot at once serve God and Mammon; he must detach himself from all temporal desires, renouncing without exception all that his heart has been set on. The lover will secretly renounce his loved one; the rich young man will account as nothing his well appointed house, his books, the account at the bank that has meant safety for him, his profession itself. If he is a married man, he will unhappily recognise that he has chosen the worse part.

'It is an abominable lie to say that marriage is pleasing to God. From the Christian point of view it is a crime, and what is odious about it is that by this very crime the innocent individual is introduced into that community of criminals which is human life.'[12]

Such renunciation of human desires, drastic as it is, belongs to the lower stage of religiousness because it can be achieved by a sufficiently heroic effort of the will.

'With my own strength I can renounce everything, and find peace and rest in suffering; I can bear everything, and . . . I can still save my soul, so long as it is of more consequence to me that my love for God should conquer in me, rather than my earthly happiness. . . . The man whose soul has not this sense of the romantic has indeed sold his soul. . . .'[13]

One must be resigned to going anywhere or doing anything, however deeply it may wound one's feelings or flout one's hopes or affront one's reason and common sense, if it presents itself as God's will.

SUFFERING

13 A second religious requirement, insisted upon with strong emphasis, is suffering. Kierkegaard holds that 'the distinguishing mark of religious action is suffering';[14] 'to be without suffering means to be without religion';[15] 'the more the suffering, the more the religious existence—and the suffering persists'.[16] This suffering has nothing to do with outward causes, such as the loss of wealth or health or popularity; the religious man 'requires and has suffering even in the absence of external misfortune. . . .'[17] Nor is Kierkegaard's point about suffering that of the moralist who stresses the value of suffering in mellowing and maturing a character; he often speaks contemptuously of such teaching as the sort of thing that is talked in pulpits. The suffering he has in mind is more fundamental and inescapable, a darkness that remains within even while the outward sun is shining, and belongs to the very essence of religion; 'the religious man believes that it is precisely in suffering that life is to be found'.[18]

Why this insistent, unqualified demand that the religious man should suffer and that his suffering should grow more intense as his religion advances? Kierkegaard explains it as follows:

'This suffering has its ground in the fact that the individual is in his immediacy absolutely committed to relative ends; its significance lies in the transposition of the relationship, the dying away from immediacy, or in the expression existentially of the principle that the individual can do absolutely nothing of himself, but is as nothing before God; for here again the negative is the mark by which the God-relationship is recognised, and self-annihilation is the essential form for the God-relationship.'[19]

This may perhaps be translated as follows. In ordinary life, there are things that we very much want; when we become religious, what we want above all is to do God's will. We then see the worthlessness of our old ends, but find ourselves unable by any effort to achieve our new one; hence we are bound to be miserable.

It is obvious that Kierkegaard is falling back here on the theology of Luther and of his father. God stands over us like a stern taskmaster, insisting on obedience, demanding of us moral perfection. But since we are utterly corrupt by nature, we are unable to do anything that will please him. We are like a person in a nightmare who, with some dreadful form pursuing him, tries to run, only to find that his legs have turned to lead. From the terror and suffering of such an experience the normal man soon wakes up. For the religious man there is no waking up while life lasts. The more perceptively religious he becomes, the wider becomes the felt abyss between what God demands of him and what he can do. And any man who takes seriously the Deity of Kierkegaard's later writings has ample reason for a nightmare life. 'Christianity exists,' he writes, 'because there is hatred between God and men.' 'God hates all existence.'

'To be a Christian means that you will be tortured in every way. The best thing is that you should have an inexhaustible fund of inventions for torturing yourself; but if you are not strong enough, you can always hope that God will have pity on you and help you to reach the state of suffering.' 'It is a frightful thing, the moment when God gets out his instruments for the operation no human strength can carry out: cutting away from a man his desire to live, killing him so that he can live like a dead man. The object of this life is to give us the highest possible degree of distaste for living. Like a man who would be ready to travel anywhere in the world to hear a singer with a perfect voice, so does God listen in heaven; and whenever He hears rising up to Him the worship of a man He has led to the uttermost point of disgust with life, God says quietly to Himself: That is the note.'[20]

It would be unfair to suggest that the only picture of Deity that Kierkegaard carried in his mind was the picture of a celestial ogre. He often said that God was pure love. But he never succeeded, nor could anyone succeed, in fitting the two pictures together. A Deity of pure love who brought into existence millions of creatures only to throw the vast majority into endless unimaginable misery for wrongs they did not commit is a self-contradiction. If there were any sort of reasoning by which this misery could be shown to be necessary to the greater good of mankind, a rational mind might accept this theology. But it was no part of Kierkegaard's programme to render theology rational. How a God of pure love could also be a Moloch was indeed past understanding, but then what right had we to ask that God act intelligibly? The religious man will keep his intelligence firmly enough in its place to accept both pictures. What this meant in practice was an alternate stress on each side of the contradiction, or an acceptance as primary of the picture that best accorded with the devotee's prepossessions. To the man of sunny temperament God would be the loving father; to the man who was gloomy and apprehensive God would be the hard taskmaster. There could be little doubt which picture would be most vivid to a mind like Kierkegaard's. His preference for excluding the sunlight and working behind drawn blinds was symbolic of his inward climate, which was one of an almost pathological gloom. He can write of joy and love, but these are not his native element. Dread, suffering, guilt, and—toward the end—bitterness, scorn, and hatred are his characteristic emotions. And if God is a self-contradictory being, no one can prove you are wrong if you conceive him in your own image.

To the charge that this emphasis on suffering is arbitrary and smells of the hospital, Kierkegaard would no doubt reply that it has an objective and 'existential' ground. It rests on the real pathos of existence. We are sin-infested worms lying at the feet of infinite wisdom, justice, and goodness. The more genuinely religious we become, the more keenly we are aware of the distance by which we fall short. But this argument is double-edged. If we have a long way to go, we have come a long way also, and it is irrational to fix our eyes on one aspect only of the facts, to despair over the failure while refusing to take any satisfaction in the success. But the rationality of healthy-mindedness had no appeal for Kierkegaard. Our success is nothing; it is our helplessness and failure that must be kept in the forefront of our minds. 'Religiously it is the task of the individual to understand that he is nothing before God, or to become wholly nothing and to exist thus before God; this consciousness of impotence he requires constantly to have before him, and when it vanishes the religiosity also vanishes';[21] 'suffering is precisely the expression for the God-relationship'.[22]

THE CLOUD OF MORBIDITY

14 If Kierkegaard did not derive this stress on suffering from the facts, where did it come from? In part, we have suggested, from his own clouded and morbid mind. But we must remember also that the theology he inherited was the Lutheran theology of a human nature so deeply sunk in corruption as to be salvable only by an interposition from on high, an interposition as unpredictable before it happened as it was inexplicable afterward. This view of the relation of God and man was accepted by Luther because he believed it to be the sense of the New Testament, and it was accepted by Kierkegaard on the same ground. On the question whether this theology can maintain itself under reflective criticism, we have said something in the last chapter. The decisive question for Kierkegaard, however, was not whether it was acceptable to a rational mind but whether God had said it. It is therefore worth asking whether his insistence that 'the distinguishing mark of religious action is suffering' does have a Scriptural basis. He admitted that 'little is said in the New Testament' about it; his doctrine of the central importance of such suffering seems to have presented itself as an implication of the teaching of St Paul. The Lutheran theology rested, by Luther's own avowal, on Pauline teaching, and this, as we have seen, had its grim side. But even in Paul's epistles one will look in vain for anything corresponding to Kierkegaard's exaltation of suffering. Paul speaks, to be sure, of the thorn in his flesh, of the struggle to keep the body under, of the warring against each other of two selves in his nature; and these things could not occur without suffering. But surely the dominant tone of his extraordinary letters is not one of suffering, dread, and despair, but very much on the contrary, of invincible courage, of an exhilarating confidence and hope. 'Rejoice in the Lord always, and again I say, rejoice.' One suspects that the exuberant apostle would have been repelled by his successor's gospel of sedulous suffering and despair.

Nor is Kierkegaard's case better if the appeal is carried back to the gospels. Suffering is indeed represented there as an element in the religious life; Christians have a cross to carry; they must be penitent for their wrongdoing and ready to bear the burdens of others; they must turn the other cheek to a persecution thought to be inevitable. That is an important part of the teaching. But of course there is another side to it, what may be called the St Francis side. The yoke is still there, but to the St Francises of the world it is so easy and the burden so light that it is carried with grace and even gaiety. Neither the record of Jesus' own teaching nor the impression he made on those around him suggests an atmosphere of intense and cultivated suffering. Kierkegaard's pronouncement that 'God hates all existence' has a very different sound from 'I came that ye might have life and have it more abundantly'. Nor does his stress on suffering seem consistent with itself. He repeats with a curious suggestion of hedonism that the main object of life is to secure 'eternal happiness' and holds that this happiness is to be secured by compliance with God's will. One would expect, therefore, that an advance in goodness would bring some advance in happiness with it. Yet he also insists that 'the more the suffering, the more the religious existence'. It was as if he was reluctant to accept even the measure of happiness that was open to him, as if he suffered from a congenital colour blindness and saw vividly all the greys, browns, and blacks of the world while having to squint and strain to make out the golds or blues.

GUILT

15 Closely related to the second requirement of the religious stage, namely suffering, is the third, the sense of guilt for sin. It might seem that this belongs properly to the ethical stage, at which the sense of right and wrong, and remorse for wrongdoing, are already at work. But sin and wrongdoing are not the same for Kierkegaard. A pagan or an atheist can do wrong and know it; the sinner is a man who lives 'before God' and sees that his wrongdoing is an offence against God's will. His sin, therefore, is a personal betrayal, an alienation from Deity, which can be set right by no acts of repentance or amendment, but only by a grant of divine grace. To do wrong on a merely ethical level is to break a rule laid down by our reason; to sin is to relate oneself to the ultimate power in the world in a way that bears on one's eternal destiny. Kierkegaard sometimes speaks of the sense of sin as appearing only at stage B of the religious life; guilt at stage A is at most the guilt of violating rules laid down by a Hegelian God, an immanent God of reason, while the full blackness of sin first appears from the altitude of stage B and against the background of a transcendent Deity. It is perhaps needless to settle the precise places of guilt and sin in Kierkegaard's somewhat fluid classification. Suffice it to say that the guilt that is an awareness of sin always involves this new dimension of wrongdoing, a conception of it as no longer mere human waywardness but as a divine affront.

The guilt of the Christian, like his suffering, is inevitable, enduring, and total. As Kierkegaard puts it,

'the decisive expression for the consciousness of guilt is in turn the essential maintenance of this consciousness, or the eternal recollection of guilt. . . . So here there can be no question of the childish thing of making a fresh start, of being a good child again . . . human justice pronounces a life sentence only for the third offense, but eternity pronounces sentence the first time forever. He is caught forever, harnessed with the yoke of guilt, and never gets out of the harness. . . .'[23]

We commonly think of ourselves as on the whole decent and upright persons; we have little lapses from time to time and are duly ashamed of them, but we soon bounce back again to our complacent self-respect. This self-satisfaction shows how fully we have surrendered ourselves to the undemanding standards of our time and place. But 'what is the hour and a half I have to live with men, what but a brief instant compared with eternity?'[24] And living in the light of eternity does not mean the intellectual culture that sees things steadily and whole; it has nothing to do with the philosopher's 'contemplation of all time and all existence'; these are comparative frivolities. Indeed the attempt to understand may be one of the sins that keep us down. 'woe unto me if the Deity were to condemn me in my most inward man for the fact that I wanted mendaciously to be systematic and world-historical, and to forget what it is to be a man, and therewith forget what it means that He is the Deity. Woe unto me. Woe unto me in time, and still more dreadfully when He gets hold of me in eternity! His sentence is the last, is the only one, from His congizance none can flee. . . .'[25]

The present writer is not one of those philosophers who can read such statements in unperturbed serenity. It is part of the business of the philosopher to realise how easily he may be mistaken, and he must feel a certain chill in his marrow when he hears such a judgement pronounced with prophetic confidence by a man hailed by discerning persons as a religious genius. Certainly the ordinary thoughtful man does not go about feeling 'harnessed with the yoke of guilt', weighed down with its 'fetters', and voicing terror at what God will do 'when He gets hold of me in eternity'. According to Kierkegaard he must have these feelings if he is to call himself in the true sense religious, and if he is not religious, he stands in even greater jeopardy. What are we to say about this exaltation of the sense of guilt to a prime place in religion?

16   We must agree that it has its elements of truth. A religion lacking the sense of sin is plainly defective. There is force in the charge against the Greeks, for example, that as compared with the Hebrews they are hardly in earnest about their religion, precisely because of this absence of any effective sense of sin; even Socrates has been accused of being 'too much at ease in Zion'. Again, if religion is to express, in Tillich's words, 'an ultimate concern,' it should have the power of controlling the impulses of the natural man. Those impulses will never be restrained from a wrong act by the merely intellectual perception of its wrongness. This does not mean that morality is impossible without religion, for that can be shown to be historically untrue. It does mean that the vast horsepower at the disposal of human egoism will be kept in check only if the sort of emotion involved in the sense of sin can be enlisted against wrongdoing. It is not enough to have a good eye for ethical distinctions and values; many moral philosophers of Laodicean record have had that. Above and beyond such perception there must be a strain of the Hebrew feeling of something leprous and unclean in moral evil, a stain on one's person that must be washed away in contrition if one is to be healthy again.

We must concede to Kierkegaard, once more, that there is some sense in what he says about the finite facing the infinite. The phrase is apt to produce a block in the modern mind by raising the suspicion that the word 'infinite' is a cover for the lack of any clear meaning. It is probably so in Kierkegaard's case, for he threw such words around recklessly. But if by facing the infinite he means that morality is an endless quest, that one no sooner reaches a given plateau than one sees a further ascent lying beyond it, that the road winds uphill to the end, and indeed beyond any end that we see or may hope to see, he is surely right. Here is another contrast between the Greek and the Hebrew or Christian. Aristotelian morality was a matter of 'my station and its duties', and the modest perfection of the 'golden mean' seemed quite attainable. But to forgive seventy times seven—that is, indefinitely—to love others, even one's enemies, as oneself, to be perfect even as God is perfect, that is another matter. If it is not one's duty to be perfect—and we have seen that it cannot be—it is at least a duty to try to be so, and that means that our reach will always exceed our grasp. Now religion is concerned with man's relation to the ultimate. To conceive morality as a quest, not for an immediate or visible goal but for one that is ultimate and infinitely distant, is thus in a sense to conceive it religiously; the religious man will naturally look at it in this light. If he conceives of it merely as Aristotle conceived it, as in essence a matter of propriety, if he cannot feel the pull of an ideal beyond all ideals, in the sense of something that works in and through them to amend them without limit, then in his moral life he has fallen short of the religious spirit. So far as Kierkegaard means this by insisting that a sense of imperfection and sin belongs to the religious life, we must agree.

But he meant far more than this. He would have regarded our agreement, based as it is on actual experience, as a milk-and-water support, which missed his main point. For the sin he was talking about was more than the continued failure that we can verify daily, and the infinite that condemned us was not a mere ideal, however exalted, but an existent being, powerful and terrible. It is not simply that 'before God we are always in the wrong' in the way just indicated; it is rather that, because God and man are 'absolutely unlike', we are condemned by a standard we cannot hope to understand. God's face is averted from us not only for our conscious misdeeds but for a vast volume of misdoing of which we know nothing, and we must bow to this condemnation, keeping it always in the forefront of our minds. ' "*Original sin*" *is guilt*'; 'that is the real paradox . . . that something is inherited which by definition cannot be inherited. It must be believed. The paradox in Christian truth is invariably due to the fact that it is truth as it exists for God. The standard of measure and the end is superhuman; and there is only one relationship possible: faith.'[26]

GUILT AND IRRATIONALITY

17 Now the requirement of guilt in this sense as a condition of religion we clearly cannot accept. It is not a true exaltation of morality; it is a refusal to take morality seriously; it undermines and confounds the sense of sin. By morality here we mean what everyone normally means by it, the attempt to guide one's life by an authentic perception that some things are right and others wrong. Among the things that we see clearly to be wrong is the condemning of anyone for acts that he did not do. We have just heard Kierkegaard saying that this is what God does; and we are required to acquiesce and approve. The natural protests of our moral sense are overruled by a 'standard of measure' that we are assured is superhuman. But if on a cardinal point like this the human standard is unreliable, it can be relied on nowhere. This conclusion Kierkegaard is apparently willing to draw. If we try to do right and seem to succeed, we must remember that 'before God we are nothing' and that by the superhuman standard we are sinning still. If we do what we know to be wrong, one would think that the superhuman court, so different from our own, might give us an occasional acquittal, but of this there is apparently no hope. And if we do nothing at all, we are still condemned for the depravity we have inherited and which continues to vitiate us even in passivity. We obviously cannot win. We are moral lepers whatever we do.

To ask a reflective man to carry about with him a sense of infinite guilt on grounds like these is to ask what is impossible. The sin for which his overwhelming guilt must be felt he cannot verify in his deeds or his intentions. The towering structure of guilt that is based on it is the creation of a theology whose credentials he cannot verify by his reason, and Kierkegaard would call him a fool as well as a sinner for attempting so to verify them. Ordinary good sense, the ordinary appeals to conscience, the attempt to think things out and get them clear—pathetic expedients to put a lighter complexion on one's guilt—must be firmly put aside. In favour of what? Authority. '. . . Christianity's paradoxical difference from every other doctrine, from a scientific point of view, is that it posits: authority. A philosopher with authority is nonsense.'[27] We are thus invited to accept an authority which overrides both reason and conscience, and which, in defiance of both alike, sets us down as unrighteous altogether. Now authority may demand that a man accept this, and tell him that if he demurs that is the worst sin of all. And he may give in, as many have done, through diffidence about his own insight and sheer terror of the unknown. But a mind that is morally and intellectually sane can hardly divest itself of its sanity on order.

Am I implying that in respect to this sense of guilt Kierkegaard himself was not quite sane? I am implying precisely that. His pattern of profound depression followed by states of exaltation was studied by the Danish psychiatrist Helweg, who found it symptomatic of a disordered mind, and there is much to confirm such a diagnosis. His own conviction that he had often stood on the brink of insanity, his repeated dallyings with suicide, his retreat from the world into his darkened rooms, his alienation from his friends, his family, and even his mother, the paranoiac claims to genius and comparisons of himself to Christ, the perpetual feverish anatomising of his own tortured mind, maintained until, exhausted and prematurely old, he died in his early forties—one wonders whether there is any psychiatrist of our time who would not at once recognise in such symptoms the syndrome of mental illness.

But this is matter for the pathologist, and what I am thinking of here is sanity in a less technical sense, the kind of intellectual health that one looks for in a matured and reflective mind. Intelligence is healthy so long as it adjusts its beliefs to the evidence and succeeds in maintaining harmony among them. It loses this sanity so far as it allows any belief to form a cyst, resistant to evidence, or allows its world of belief to fall apart into incoherence. There is such a thing as the sanity of the judicial mind, which we all recognise by its contrast with the temper of the fanatic, the crackpot, the bigot, and the doctrinaire.

Now whatever Kierkegaard's place may be on the medical chart, he lacked this kind of sanity. He fixed his eye on one part of the evidence, and did not and could not see it in perspective. Sin *is* of course a fact in human nature, and a most important fact. But it is not the all-important fact, to be carried by habit around one's neck like an albatross of doom. By his insistence on so carrying it, Kierkegaard has placed himself among the 'sick souls' in William James's familiar classification. Normal experience or impartial reflection would never suggest this view of sin; it comes straight from a special brand of theology. And this theology itself needs sanity in exceptional degree for its appraisal, for its claims and its confidence are enormous. Unhappily Kierkegaard was peculiarly unqualified to pass judgement on it. He had lived in its midst from infancy like a hothouse plant; his father was absorbed in it with the morbid fascination of one who feared he had committed the unpardonable sin. From the range of critical and scientific knowledge that might have made a fair appraisal possible, Kierkegaard was cut off by accidents of time and place. He died four years before *The Origin of Species* cast its grenade among the fundamentalist theologians. The remarkable movement of 'higher criticism' did begin in his lifetime, but the thought of both of its leaders, Strauss and Baur, had been deeply affected by Hegel, who was a *bête noire* to Kierkegaard throughout his later years. Indeed this hostile reaction to Hegel was one of the chief intellectual facts of his life. He had read that arch-rationalist early, but by the age of twenty-two had concluded that philosophy and Christianity were hopelessly at odds with each other, and that he must take the Christian side. Thereafter rationalism became anathema to him, and the very attempt to apply rational standards to religion came to seem an irrelevance and an offence. Now the truly judicial mind is one which, with a broad apperception-mass of experience and ideas, is able to bring it freely to bear on each point as it arises. On the facts of moral evil Kierkegaard lacked both the breadth and the freedom needed for a fair judgement. He saw these facts, not directly, but through the mist of his inherited theology; and this theology itself he could not appraise, partly because he lacked the required range of ideas, partly because an inveterate suspicion of reason itself deterred him from using freely such ideas as he had.

18   Another circumstance must be mentioned if we are to understand his thought about moral evil. This is the fixation on morality that belongs to Hebraic religion. In both the Old Testament and the New, the approach to the divine is almost exclusively moral. The emphasis in the Old Testament is on the law and the prophets —in the earlier days obedience to the law of Moses, in the later days the acquirement of a clean heart; the emphasis of the New Testament is on the service of God through the love of man. Now man is not merely a pursuer of morals; he is also, for example, a pursuer of beauty and truth. There is no antecedent reason why he should not approach his Deity, and find a revelation of him, through his aesthetic and intellectual faculties as truly as through his conscience. The Hebrew tradition discouraged such notions. It carried suggestions, to be sure, that we should consider the heavens, the work of God's hands, and consider the lilies how they grow, but these whispers are all but lost among the trumpet-calls to morality. There is likewise some recognition that with our other gettings we should get understanding and should love God with our minds as well as with our hearts. But these again are incidental counsels. There is nothing in the Hebrew tradition to compare with that intellectual passion, that love of the play of reason for its own splendid sake, that surged through the great Greek thinkers, nothing to suggest that 'with certain persons', as Bradley puts it, 'the intellectual effort to understand the universe is a principal way of experiencing the Deity'. Here Kierkegaard was surrendered to the Hebraic tradition. He had some knowledge of the Greeks, and even held Socrates in a kind of hero-worship, but art and philosophy were not religion; the very notion that we could apprehend God by reason carried for him a touch of impiety. The umbilical cord from God to man was moral; we were sinners before a righteous Deity who was taking moral account of us. That was the great fact of our relation to him. One might be the first poet or the first philosopher of the world; that was nothing in God's sight. What was important was our moral status; we had sinned, all of us and morally; some of us had had our sins washed away, and would therefore be saved; where we stood in this transcendent reckoning was the only thing that really mattered. To the Greek lover of beauty and reason this would have seemed a strange contraction of divine interest and manifestation into a single channel. But in religion it is Hebraism, not Hellenism, that has won the allegiance of the West. Luther despised the Greeks and exalted St Paul. Kierkegaard looked at Socrates wistfully, fought an internal battle with him and with Hegel, and then in fear and trembling for his immortal soul crept back to his father, Galatians, and original sin.

HUMOUR

19 The final condition of entering the religious level of life is a surprising one, humour. 'Humor is the last stage of existential inwardness before faith.'[28] It has often been noted that the commonest kind of humour rests on the perception of incongruity; a man in a top-hat slips on a banana peel; the butler is mistaken for his lordship and decides to play out the part; the praying mantis, the emperor without clothes, the duchess who has mislaid her teeth—these are comic characters because of the clash between appearance and reality. Now a person to whom the exalted status of the man with the top-hat or the emperor or the duchess conveyed no meaning would see nothing comic in their abject condition; the cream of the jest lies precisely in the deflation of high pretensions by humble fact. The enjoyment of the contrast need not be cruel; there may be sympathy for the fallen estate of the man with pretensions; indeed the main distinction between humour and irony, which appears a little lower in the scale, is that humour has sympathy, while irony lacks it. This, Kierkegaard remarks sagely, is why one never finds irony in a woman.[29] To the person who can look with detachment upon the activity of ordinary mortals, they seem grotesque—puppets strutting about with turkey-cock importance. The loftier the position from which one can look down upon them, the wider will be the range of comic characters included in one's purview. The loftiest of all such positions is the religious. Hence the religious man has an unparalleled opportunity for humour; he holds a position by contrast with which every walk of life, from peasant to king, takes on the aspect of a puppet show. 'Thus if Napoleon had been a genuinely religious individual, he would have had a rare opportunity to enjoy the most divine of amusements; for to have the power apparently to accomplish everything, and then to understand this divinely as an illusion: verily, this is jesting in real earnest!'[30]

There is nothing in principle new in this conception of humour, though Kierkegaard was perhaps the first to show its connection with religion and metaphysics. 'What lies at the root of both the comic and the tragic in this connection, is the discrepancy, the contradiction, between the infinite and the finite, the eternal and that which becomes.'[31] What is 'essential for humour' is 'the retirement out of the temporal into the eternal by way of recollection',[32] a requirement that some humorists of one's acquaintance might have difficulty in meeting. Nevertheless one can see as soon as Kierkegaard points it out that to the person who contemplates life with detachment, who looks at it, as Carlyle occasionally did, against the background of 'the eternities and immensities', a peculiarly rich kind of humour is open. It is a humour, as Kierkegaard noted, that is very close to tragedy. Its note is often sounded by the greater poets.

> Life's but a walking shadow, a poor player
> That struts and frets his hour upon the stage,
> And then is heard no more: it is a tale
> Told by an idiot, full of sound and fury,
> Signifying nothing.

Is the picture comic or tragic? It is clearly both. And what makes it significant is that it holds up to us so vividly the little mouthing puppet that man is against the splendid background of what he thought he was. It is the tragic humour of a brooding disillusionment.

THE HUMOROUS AND THE INHUMAN

20   That such humour exists is plain enough. But in two important respects Kierkegaard's account of it is puzzling. For one thing, the background against which human vanities are to present themselves as comic is so characterless that it is hard to see how contrast with it could render anything comic. When Carlyle called men forked radishes, or Shakespeare saw them as strutting players, the background of aspiration against which they appeared as comic was not difficult to see. What is the standpoint from which the religious man sees them? It is the standpoint of eternity; in looking down on human nature, he is occupying for a time the position of Deity itself. How is that position to be characterised? Kierkegaard tells us that it is beyond characterisation. We know that God's thoughts are not as our thoughts; his ethics contravenes our ethics; he is not even bound by our logic, so that he can do and think contradictory things. Now if men's actions become comic through incongruity, there must be something more or less definite with which they can be incongruous. But according to Kierkegaard, the divine nature has for the religious man no definite character at all; it is paradoxical, unintelligible, even absurd. The ground on which we are to regard human life as absurd is that it seems absurd when viewed from the standpoint of the transcendentally absurd. This is not very illuminating. We take God as absurd because he is so different from ourselves, though how, we do not know, and he takes us as absurd because we are so different from him, though what makes us absurd we again do not know, since his nature is utterly beyond us. Thus Kierkegaard's attempt to connect humour with religion ends in denying that such humour has any intelligible ground.

But theology, like nature, abhors a vacuum. Though Kierkegaard was emphatic in protesting that the divine nature was inscrutable, he was not indisposed to fill in the blank, and the picture that formed itself bore a striking resemblance to the theologian himself. The things that the religious man ought to laugh at were somehow the things that Kierkegaard found comical. He had a high regard for his powers as a humorist, even describing himself as 'solely a humorist'.[33] 'If there is anything I have studied from the ground up, and pursued into its farthest ramifications, it is the comic.'[34] At one point in his most philosophical work he explains a point somewhat obscurely and adds, 'Whoever cannot understand this is stupid; and if anyone dares to contradict me, I propose to make him ridiculous, by virtue of the power I happen this moment to have in comic characterisation.'[35] Since he set so much store by his keenness of humorous perception, it may be instructive to give instances of the sort of thing that he regarded as laughable. He writes:

'when I was older, I opened my eyes and beheld reality, at which I began to laugh, and since then I have not stopped laughing. I saw that the meaning of life was to secure a livelihood, and that its goal was to secure a high position; that love's rich dream was marriage with an heiress; that friendship's blessing was help in financial difficulties; that wisdom was what the majority assumed it to be; that enthusiasm consisted in making a speech; that it was courage to risk the loss of ten dollars; that kindness consisted in saying, "You are welcome," at the dinner table; that piety consisted in going to communion once a year. This I saw, and I laughed.'36

Probably few persons will share Kierkegaard's feeling of the funniness of these things; the tone is that of a cynic rather than of a humorist. Still it is typically Kierkegaardian. His humour expresses a comprehensive scorn, seemingly unmellowed by tenderness. Human beings were comic to him because they were vain and pompous creatures who, he tells us, kept falling flat and bumping their noses, and when such a creature is splashed with mud or killed by a tile from a roof, 'I laugh from the bottom of my heart'.37 Indeed there was something irresistibly comic to him about persons confident of the future being killed by tiles from roofs. He repeats a story from Lucian: Charon tells how a man invited a friend to dinner; the friend said, 'You can count on me quite definitely,' and as he walked away, the inevitable tile fell and killed him; upon which Charon remarks, 'Is not that something to laugh yourself to death over?'38 Of course in the sense in which this is laughable, we are all more laughable than we know; 'the speech of daily life makes us as humoristic as funeral sermons generally, according to which every moment sees the burial of a hero'.39 A man with these genial feelings about his fellows will have an ample field for humour, and Kierke-gaard, as he tells us, never stopped laughing.

THE RELIGIOUS STAGE (B)

21 The four conditions we have now considered—resignation, suffering, guilt, and humour—are requisites for the first stage of religion, called by Kierkegaard stage A. It is the second stage, however, referred to as stage B, that is the goal of the Christian pilgrimage, and in describing it he gives his final answer to the question that preoccupied his mature life: 'How am I to become a Christian?' His answer is somewhat difficult, and it is made more so by his preference for stating his position not in a straightforward way but in scores of fragmentary discussions scattered through thousands of pages in a dozen volumes, and contributed by characters that sometimes speak with his voice and sometimes not. The sub-stance of this answer, so far as I have been able to sift it out, may be

given in three statements: one becomes a Christian in the full sense
only (1) by overcoming objectivity, (2) by achieving subjectivity,
and (3) by a leap of faith from a subjective base. On each of these
points Kierkegaard had arresting things to say.

OBJECTIVITY: THE FAILURE OF PHILOSOPHY

22 To most scientists or philosophers the remark that they had
achieved objectivity regarding their subject would seem high praise.
But if made with truth about any man who was trying to understand Christianity, it would be, according to Kierkegaard, an
evidence of failure. The objectivity aimed at in philosophy and
science he held to be a mistaken ideal in theology, 'for an objective
knowledge of the truth of Christianity, or of its truths, is precisely
untruth.'[40] What led him to adopt so paradoxical a view? He had
several grounds for it.

23 The most important was that thought—the kind of thought at
work in philosophy and science—can deal only with abstractions,
not with existence, and that since being a Christian is a way of
existing, it is beyond the scope of such thought. He put the point
variously. 'A logical system is possible; an existential system is
impossible.'[41] When we attempt 'interpretations of existence', we
find that

> 'speculative philosophy has of course no part to play here, since,
> being objective and abstract, it is indifferent to the concretion of the
> existing subject and at most has to do with the pure idea of man-
> kind. . . .'[42] 'Because abstract thought is *sub specie aeterni* it ignores
> the concrete and the temporal, the existential process, the predica-
> ment of the existing individual arising from his being a synthesis
> of the temporal and the eternal situated in existence.'[43]

Kierkegaard has clearly been reading Plato and Hegel, and here
he is offering one of the stock objections against any thoroughgoing
rationalism. The objection is that reason can deal only with universals, and that therefore particulars, which plainly exist, are bound
to slip through its meshes and get away. Philosophy, for example,
deals not with this or that particular thing or man, but with 'as
suches'—with the nature of matter as such, or with man as such, or
with mind or cause or time as such. Kierkegaard would say that
the same holds of science. It may be that a particular apple fell at a
particular moment on the particular head of Isaac Newton, but if it
did, that is no part of science, for science is concerned only with law,
for example the law that matter as such obeys the gravitational

formula. Now to understand anything by the use of reason, Kierkegaard suggests, is to reduce it to a set of as suches or universals, and then to connect these with others by laws which are themselves universals. In these laws there is no reference to any particular event or to any individual thing or man. They are timeless, like the statements of logic and mathematics. But the occurrence of a particular event is *not* timeless, and the existence of an individual man, oneself for instance, is *not* to be resolved away into any set of assuches. The particular occurrent and the individual thing or person therefore defy explanation by any process of thought, however extended.

INDIVIDUALS AND ABSTRACTIONS

24 There is something in this objection, and since Kierkegaard places great store by it, we shall do well to try to see what this is. In one use of the term 'universal', it is plainly true that an individual thing cannot be reduced to universals. Suppose we say of Socrates that he is human and has a certain height, weight, and colour. These words, it is often said, connote universals; 'human' means the range of properties owned in common by all human beings, 'height' the common property of all particular heights, and so of the others. Now it is obvious that an indiviual thing or man, say Socrates, is not made up of universals like these. He is not a composite of humanity as such, plus height that is no height in particular, plus weight with no definite poundage, plus colour of no specifiable shade. One could assemble as many of these pale abstractions as one wished and still fall immeasurably short of the actual flesh-and-blood Socrates, who possesses these characters, not as abstractions, but in specific forms—a height of five feet ten, a weight of 180 pounds. If Kierkegaard means that an individual cannot be resolved into universals of this type, he is right, even if it is hard to think of any rationalist who could serve as a culprit.

His point, however, may be different. He may be maintaining that even if we take the characters of an individual in their completely specific form, their totality is not enough to constitute the man. This position, unlike the preceding one, is actually advanced by some rationalists. The traditional concept of a universal is that of a character that may occur in varying contexts. Suppose Socrates is five feet ten and weighs 180 pounds. Are these characters universals? Clearly they are by this definition, for other persons besides Socrates may also have this specific weight or height. Now the nature of Socrates does seem to be made up of specific characters like these. Each is a universal because each could in principle be repeated, nor can one place any limit on the number of them that might be repeated together. And thought can obviously deal with universals of this kind, both singly and in groups. It can note that this wholly specific shade is brighter than that. It can note that John Doe's wholly specific weight is greater than Richard Roe's. If thought can deal with such characters, both singly and in sets, and the individual is made of them, why should Kierkegaard say that intelligence is helpless in dealing with the individual?

Two answers are possible. Intelligence may fall short because it cannot exhaust the characters of the individual, or because in this individual there is something that can be set over against its characters as not a character at all. The first answer is that of the thoroughgoing rationalist, who would say that Socrates *is* a set of characters and relations. He admits that we cannot deal with an individual, even a broomstick, if this means that we can apprehend *all* its properties; they are presumably infinite, and we shall never wholly exhaust them. But this is merely because our intelligence is limited. And it would be absurd to say that we cannot think of Socrates at all because we cannot exhaust the millions of attributes that an infinite knowledge would find in him.

But this is not Kierkegaard's answer. For him there is something in the individual that lies beyond all its characters and is therefore beyond the grasp of thought, however far extended; 'the particular cannot be thought, but only the universal'. 'The only thing-in-itself which cannot be thought is existence, and this does not come within the province of thought to think.'[44] This view has some plausibility. For consider: a character may either exist or not exist. I may clearly conceive a character; I may conceive your height for example; but can I in the same way conceive its existence? If so, what sort of entity is it that I am conceiving? Is it some further attribute possessed by this height, so that when I say it exists, I am asserting some predicate of it? No, existence is not an attribute; it is not a predicate; it is not a character or quality; it is not a 'what' of any kind. Even to *ask* what I am asserting when I say that something exists is subtly to beg the question, since it assumes that existence *is* a content or character which I can conceive as I do roundness or the colour blue; and it is nothing of the sort. Thus the inference seems clear that if thought can deal only with characters, and existence is not a character, thought cannot deal with it. Rationalism is therefore doomed to inevitable defeat, not in a minor skirmish, but on an issue of major moment. The most important thing about any character or essence or universal is whether it exists, for on this depends whether it will be a cipher in the world of change or a dynamic agent that affects the course of events. Yet before existence thought stands

helpless. Its explanations move among universals. It can note that
with a certain fall of temperature water becomes ice, but this law
is still a connection between as-suches. In short, since reason moves
among universals only, it can neither explain existence nor conceive
it.

THOUGHT AND EXISTENCE

25 Here Kierkegaard has plainly gone too far. If he were saying
only that relective thought *may* abstract from existence in the sense
of temporarily directing attention away from individuals to the
abstract connections they exemplify, no one could take exception to
what he says. But it would not be very interesting, for it would
amount to saying that abstract thought is abstract. He clearly means
to say something more important. He means to say that objective
thought by its very nature is unable to deal with existence. And this
seems to be false to fact. There is no discontinuity between thought
in philosophy and science and that of ordinary life, in which we
find ourselves dealing constantly and successfully with existence. If
Kierkegaard looked at us in puzzlement as to what we could possibly
mean by saying that elephants exist but mammoths do not, or that
King Alfred existed while King Arthur did not, he would suddenly
find us intelligible enough if we said that three cases of smallpox
existed in Copenhagen or that his particular house was on fire.
We manage to think such thoughts without feeling the slightest
obscurity about them. Why then should a sane man say that thought
cannot deal with existence?

Some confusion is evidently at work. It may be that the speaker is
confusing connotation and denotation, or Frege's *Sinn* and *Bedeutung*.
Convinced that the *Sinn* or sense of an assertion consists of characters,
he may have assumed that this exhausted the meaning, and that
we could not refer to anything beyond it. But the fact that we do
refer to existence is surely more obvious than any antecedent
generalisation about what thought can or cannot do, and Kierkegaard would have done better to engage in a little sharp analysis
than to indulge in a priori pronouncements about thought and
existence. Again, one might start with the assumption that the
objects of thought must be somehow embraced in the thought itself,
which seems plausible enough when we think such abstractions as
that $2 + 2 = 4$, whereas when we say that Gibraltar exists it is not at
all plausible to suppose that the rock exists bodily in our consciousness. But it is an illusion to suppose that in order to refer to an
object thought must contain it; the end of that road is solipsism.
It is surely clear that if I talk of a Gibraltar across the sea or of an

event that happened before I was born, I am not talking merely of my own state of mind.

Indeed if the thought of the philosopher or scientist could not move among existent individuals, it is hard to see how it could ever have arrived at its abstractions, 'Because abstract thought is *sub specie aeterni*,' says Kierkegaard, 'it ignores the concrete and the temporal, the existential process, the predicament of the existing individual. . . .'[45] But how could it deal with the eternal except by contrast with the temporal, and how could it deal with time as such if it had never apprehended particular lapses of time? How could it reach the abstract idea of humanity except by experiencing individual men and marking off in thought what they had in common? How should we ever have known that billiard balls roll or that water congeals into ice at 0^0 centrigrade except by finding the connection exemplified in particular cases? For that matter, even a truth as 'timeless' as $2 + 2 = 4$ is learned with the help of marbles or matches, and except through the counting of such individual things would never be learned at all. Thought does of course have the power of isolating characters and dealing with them and their relations in abstraction from the individuals in which they appear. But to make thought a contemplation of nothing but unchanging and eternal essences is to make that achievement itself unintelligible. The road to the universal lies through the individual.

26 A logical system is possible, says Kierkegaard; an existential system is impossible.[46] His reason for saying this is, as we have seen, that a system is a set of related concepts or universals, and that existence necessarily falls outside it. But no sooner has he pronounced the above judgement than he throws us off balance about it. 'Does this mean,' he continues, 'that no such system exists? By no means; nor is this implied in our assertion. Reality itself is a system—for God. . . .' But if what prevents the existent from entering into a system is that it is not the sort of being that can so enter in, then it is idle to tell us it does so in the thought of God, for this is to say at once that it does and that it cannot. Kierkegaard might of course reply, as he does in some other cases, that contradiction presents no difficulties to Deity. But what that means is in effect that reality is self-contradictory and then it is meaningless for him to say, as we have just heard him saying, that for God reality is a system. A system that is incoherent violates the very notion of system.

Furthermore, is it true that finite beings have failed so utterly in the attempt to make existence intelligible? Kierkegaard speaks of philosophy as if it were a system of concepts hanging in air. But what of the philosophy of history? Here is a clearly philosophical discipline whose avowed and special subject-matter is actual historical events. 'Yes', Kierkegaard would reply, 'and what a pretentious and egregious failure it is! Only look at Hegel.' Very well, look at Hegel; a glance will suffice to show whether he is an appropriate object for such derision. Of course if one approaches Hegel expecting a deduction of history in its infinite detail, one will not get it, nor did Hegel ever pretend to offer it. But neither did his thought move solely among abstractions. He discussed the rise and fall of particular civilisations, such as the Chinese and the Greek; he discussed particular movements, like the crusades and the Reformation; he even discussed individuals, like Caesar and Charlemagne. Many inquirers have thought they drew from him a flood of light on the historical process—a fuller insight, for example, into the causal importance of the rise of Athens and the barbarian invasions of Rome, and a better understanding of the cultural importance of feudalism and the enlightenment. A philosophy that many critics have found so illuminating seems hardly an appropriate butt for Kierkegaard's mockery. But did it render the events of history completely intelligible? Can any 'miniscule professor', working with imperfect records and limited powers, understand them fully? Obviously not, as Hegel would have agreed. But to suggest that because thought cannot understand the historical process fully it can render it in no degree intelligible is both a non sequitur and contrary to fact.

How jaundiced Kierkegaard was in his attack on Hegel will become plainer from another consideration. Suppose we grant him that in every event there is an 'existence' inaccessible to reason, and that in the absence of this element the 'what' or character would be an 'airy nothing', powerless to make any difference in the actual course of events. It would remain true nevertheless that the only way we can deal with such events, either in theory or in practice, is by recourse to their character; we must control existence through essence. To be sure, the mere general statement that the *type* of disease called malaria is caused by a certain *type* of virus carried by a certain *type* of mosquito says nothing about little Susy, whose health may be at the moment of prime concern to us. But if in the light of this generalisation we can prevent the disease in her particular case, or if, when she gets it, we can predict and halt its course, that is not a negligible achievement in the understanding and control of existence. It is made possible by the assumption, now verified on a vast scale, that an event is causally linked *through its character* with that of some preceding event which is *such as* to produce it. Because men have assumed this linkage of events through their characters, they have achieved that mastery of nature, theoretical and practical, which is called modern civilisation. To depreciate such 'objective' and generalised thought as somehow failing to deal with existence is singularly inept.

THE FAILURE OF OBJECTIVE THOUGHT TO GIVE CERTAINTY

27 Kierkegaard's contention that 'objective' thinking cannot deal with existence has been discussed at some length because it has often been regarded as a profound insight of existentialism. But he had other grounds for his protest, which can be dealt with more briefly. A second ground was that in religion we need certainty, and 'objective' thinking can never achieve it. If Christian doctrine is true, a gift of infinite value is offered to us, a gift of eternal happiness, but it is offered on the condition of our belief. Suppose we try by thinking to determine whether the doctrine is true. It tells us that in certain places of what is now Israel and Jordan there lived and died some two thousand years ago a person who embodied Deity, performed miracles, and spoke with the voice of absolute authority. Is there any process of thought, philosophic, scientific, or historical, by which we can prove these things to be true? Plainly philosophy is not enough; we must concede to Kierkegaard at once that no process of speculation can prove the occurrence of a single past event. Can science do it? No, again. The major assumption of science is the reign of law, which would rule out miracles at the outset, including the central one of the appearance on the planet of a being unaccountable by human antecedents. Can history do it? No, once more. We may grant that historical research, by seeking independent confirmation of the report of a given gospel may lend a given event a higher probability, but certainty is beyond our grasp.

And certainty we must have.

'There has been said much that is strange, much that is deplorable, much that is revolting about Christianity; but the most stupid thing ever said about it is, that it is to a certain degree true.'[47]

Unfortunately reason can say no more. We are thus left with a hopeless disparity between the value of the prize and our power to appropriate it. On our acceptance of Christianity depends nothing less than a future of infinite happiness, but if this acceptance turns on rational calculation, it is beyond our reach. We must remember, says Kierkegaard,

'that even with the most stupendous learning and persistence in research, and even if all the brains of all the critics were concentrated in one, it would still be impossible to obtain anything more than an approximation; and that an approximation is essentially incommensurable with an infinite personal interest in eternal happiness.'[48]

On the question whether we can reach by objective thinking the sort of certainty desired, we must grant that Kierkegaard is right. Theologians as different as St Thomas and Luther have agreed that some of the cardinal doctrines of the faith are indemonstrable, and however strong the confirmation may be for events in the synoptic gospels, it will always fall short of certainty. If our eternal happiness does indeed depend on our certainty about them, the situation is tragic. Nor is it enough to reply to Kierkegaard that a kindly Deity would not dangle so great a prize before mankind while endowing us with natural faculties unable to embrace it. For the Deity accepted by Kierkegaard was not governed by human standards of justice or goodness and was capable of demanding what, by those standards, was impossible or wrong.

28 But does not this very consideration blunt the point of the present argument? Kierkegaard tells us that a prize of infinite value is before us, and that if we depend on objective thinking to secure it we are bound to fail. There must, therefore, be some other means to the certainty which we so passionately desire, one that he finds in a non-rational 'leap of faith'. But the argument is not very convincing. For if the divine justice is so very different from our own, why should it *not* leave the pearl of great price dangling permanently beyond our grasp? In a world governed by justice in our sense of the term, it would certainly be strange if an acceptance of Christianity were exacted from us while the powers with which we were endowed would not allow us to do more than 'approximate' to it. But then we are expressly told that the world is not of this kind, and indeed that it is impious to ascribe to Deity a logic and ethics like our own. In that case why suppose that the impotence of our reason has any remedy at all? The circumstance that our plight would then be shocking to us would not disprove or remove the fact. Kierkegaard, like Kant, thought that in depreciating reason he was clearing the way for faith. In Kierkegaard's case, at least, the argument was a boomerang. For if the world is really irrational, how can we argue from the irrationality of a certain ordering of things to the conclusion that it is unreal? It may be that reason, with all its imperfections on its head, is the best means to certainty we have, and that we shall always fall short of the goal.

BELIEF AS COMMITMENT OF THE WILL

29 Sometimes Kierkegaard puts forward a third ground for his distrust of objective thinking. The belief that is required from the Christian is not an intellectual affair at all, but a matter of action, and to try to prove or disprove an action would be meaningless. Christianity is a way of living; even the acceptance of it is a decision, a commitment of the will, an instance of doing or becoming, not of contemplating. By action Kierkegaard was careful to explain that he did not mean overt behaviour; Luther's great action, for example, was not his appearance in the flesh before the Diet of Worms, but the inward decision from which that behaviour flowed.[49] It might be supposed that if action is thus made an inward affair thought and will would blend with each other indistinguishably. But this would be an example of the old mistake that existence is a content.

'Between the action as represented in thought on the one hand, and the real action on the other, between the possibility and the reality, there may in respect of content be no difference at all. But in respect of form, the difference is essential. Reality is the interest in action, in existence.'[50]

The passage from thought to decision is not like a transition from one idea to another, but an unpredictable, inexplicable break from one order of being into another, from the realm of thought to the realm of existence. 'The transition thus reveals itself clearly as a breach of continuity . . .';[51] 'the category of transition is itself a breach of immanence, a *leap*'.[52]

That there is something in willing or deciding that goes beyond the mere thought of the willed behaviour seems clear enough, though what exactly this is has often puzzled introspective inquirers. Some have said, with James, that if the thought occupied itself exclusively with the action proposed, and did not divide attention with anything else, the thought *was* the volition; others have found that a special 'feeling of innervation' was necessary. Kierkegaard's habits of thinking did not lend themselves to precise analysis and such pronouncements as 'reality is the interest in action' and 'the category of transition is itself a breach of immanence' are not very helpful. But he does appear to be saying that what is important for religion is not belief or understanding in any cognitive sense, but on the contrary a sheer act of will, which, as an element of existence or process, falls outside the realm of ideas and is beyond the support or confutation of reason.

30   Now this sort of division between thinking and willing cannot be maintained. All thinking involves willing, and all willing involves thought. Taking the former point first: a process of thought is itself a process of willing; to hold attention to a certain course and to resist the solicitation of irrelevancies may be voluntary action of a peculiarly resolute kind; indeed James considered the control of attention the essential factor in willing. On the other hand, Kierkegaard speaks of philosophers as if they had opted out of the world of volition and existence. 'It is only systematists and objective philosophers who have ceased to be human beings, and have become speculative philosophy in the abstract. . . .'[53] Curiously enough the life that for Aristotle was the fullest and best realisation of human nature was for Kierkegaard a desertion of one's humanity for a flight into the unreal. We need not go the whole way with Aristotle to perceive how artificial is this contrary view. With all respect to the religious devotee, it is not very convincing to say that the life of an Aristotle himself or a Kant or a Hegel lacks commitment and therefore reality as compared with that of a Salvation Army worker untroubled by a doubt. There are many opportunities from which the life of thought cuts one off, but that of voluntary effort is not one of them.

If will enters into the process of thinking, it is equally true that thought enters into volition. Two types of volition are of particular interest here, the will to believe and the will to behave. Consider first the act of believing or assenting. If to reflect is an act of will, as we have seen that it is, then the judgement that concludes reflection is also an act of will. But is this act therefore a breaking out of the order of thought into an alien order of existence where thought cannot follow with its canons of relevance and validity? This seems to be Kierkegaard's meaning in such pronouncements as that 'the category of transition is itself a breach of immanence'. But no act of judgement does or can break out of this 'immanence' in the sense suggested, for the act *is* an assertion of content, and is so bound up with that content that it could neither be nor be conceived without it. As such an act, it remains within the province of logical thought. It makes a claim that is true or false, a claim that can be appraised by thought alone. If Kierkegaard supposes that by making belief an act he is putting it off cognitive bounds where it is no longer responsible to logic, he is fabricating a psychology to fit his irrationalism. An act of belief or assent is truly an act; agreed, but it is an act done in the service and under the implicit criticism of a rational ideal.

But there is another kind of action which answers more nearly to ordinary usage: the inwardly taken decision which initiates outward behaviour; and it is no doubt this that Kierkegaard usually has in mind when he insists that Christianity is action, not thought. To put it with his characteristic obscurity, 'The only reality that exists for an existing individual is his own ethical reality';[54] which seems to mean that one really exists only when one is choosing between right and wrong. And what counts here, he insists, is the decision or choice, not the thought. Does this view make sense? I do not think it does. The attempt to place decision or commitment beyond the jurisdiction of thought backfires here again. For what one elects or chooses in a choice of this kind is a course represented in thought, and presumably represented as right. This rightness is always assumed in ordinary life to be something open to debate and reflection, something that can be supported or impugned by reason; we have no doubt that some choices are reasonable and others not. Our ways of showing this reasonableness may indeed differ. Perhaps most commonly we bring the course envisaged under the head of some rule accepted as self-evident, like 'Keep your promises', or argue that the action is a necessary means to goods valuable in themselves, like happiness or fulfilment. But whatever form the defence may take—the appeal to principle, to consequences, to conscience, to authority, to 'inner light'—thought, implicit or explicit, is always involved. If we doubt the rightness of an act, thought is the only way out.[55]

We find this here denied. 'The ethical lays hold of each individual and demands that he refrain from all contemplation, especially of humanity and the world. . . .'[56] 'In all his writings Kierkegaard maintains that doubt is not checked by means of reflection but by an act of will.'[57] Will may rightly terminate reflection, but in ethical choice reflection must not impose itself upon will. We are warned that so far as thought is in control we are falling short of the vividness and tang of real existence. But surely this is to make action irresponsible. The way to achieve reality is now to assert ourselves in independence of any appraisal by thought of the wisdom or rightness of our action. Indeed no such appraisal can be given. As Thomte says, Kierkegaard 'presents no objective ethical values, the only value being the inwardness of the existing individual as he faces crises and makes his choices.'[58] It is thus impossible to give rational guidance in advance of choice; it is impossible for the person choosing to choose on a rational basis; it is impossible for the critic reviewing the conduct to judge it by any rational standard. What is described as 'ethical reality' looks under scrutiny like an apotheosis of thoughtlessness.

SUBJECTIVITY: ITS MEANING

31 We have seen that in 'the task of becoming a Christian' Kierkegaard finds 'objective thinking' unnecessary. Indeed, 'the greater a man's equipment of knowledge and culture, the more

difficult it is for him to become a Christian.'[59] Objective thought
cannot deal with existence; it cannot give certainty; it falls short
of the action in which religious living consists. What is to replace it
in Kierkegaard's scheme of things?

The replacement is subjectivity;

> 'becoming subjective is the task proposed to every human being,
> and his highest task. . . .'[60] 'Only in subjectivity is there decisive-
> ness, to seek objectivity is to be in error';[61] 'since all decisiveness
> . . . inheres in subjectivity, it is essential that every trace of an
> objective issue should be eliminated';[62] 'the subjective acceptance
> is precisely the decisive factor; and an objective acceptance of
> Christianity . . . is paganism or thoughtlessness. . . . It is subjectivity
> that Christianity is concerned with, and it is only in subjectivity
> that its truth exists, if it exists at all; objectively, Christianity has
> absolutely no existence.'[63]

What did Kierkegaard mean by these cryptic pronouncements?

He meant of course to deny that one could be religious in virtue
of mere intellectual assent, going so far as to hold that it is better
to worship an idol with the right subjective attitude than to worship
a God truly but objectively conceived, if this attitude is lacking.
He meant also to deny that the religious life was a matter of outward conformity to any pattern of behaviour. The true religious
attitude lay in 'subjectivity'. We must try to penetrate the meaning
of this very important term.

32 We may note, first, that in subjectivity one's self is felt as
active. In perception and even in thought it is comparatively passive.
The philosopher 'contemplates all time and all existence' much as a
spectator looks at a landscape; he does not create the objects before
him; they are there to see if he opens the eyes of his mind. But in
active decision or choice we feel the self creatively at work. More
surprisingly, so far as we are subjective the self is not only the
operator but also the object of the operation. '. . . Christianity
protests every form of objectivity; it desires that the subject should
be infinitely concerned about himself.'[64] 'Kierkegaard regarded
"the individual" as his own peculiar category so wedded to his name
that it would be a fitting inscription upon his grave.'[65] Just as it is
through individual action that we first really exist, so it is with our
own individual life that we are, and indeed ought to be, chiefly
concerned. Kierkegaard speaks on occasion of the interest in others
as if it were possible only for the man whose faith has given him an
assurance, unattainable by reason, that there are other persons at all.

His ethics are curiously egoistic; 'the sole ethical interest is the interest in one's own reality'.[66]

Secondly, to be subjective is to be passionate. 'Christianity wishes to intensify passion to its highest pitch.'[67] 'the scribbling modern philosophy holds passion in contempt; and yet passion is the culmination of existence for an existing individual';[68] it is 'the highest expression of subjectivity'.[69] One can assent to theological dogmas with the cool impersonal neutrality of a geometer, but to be religious is to take a stand on a matter of life and death, and neutrality on such an issue is indifference or blindness. We must feel 'the infinite passion of inwardness,' and pray with 'the entire passion of the infinite'. To contemplate Christianity, to doubt about it, to weigh it in rational scales, to compare it favourably or not with other religions, even to assent to its doctrines, is to stand off from it and look at it from the outside, not to engage oneself in it. Engagement requires commitment of the will; commitment is to action and existence, not thought; and since in this action one's 'eternal happiness' is at stake, it is interested, concerned, emotional action. 'There is only one interest, the interest in existence; disinterestedness is therefore an expression for indifference to reality.'[70] The man who is truly engaged will be in a consuming passion; 'the absolute consciousness of God consumes him as the burning heat of the summer sun when it will not go down, as the burning heat of the summer sun when it will not abate.'[71]

Thirdly, our subjective experience is incommunicable. The Christian lives alone. Such external things as propositions he can no doubt share with other people; for when two persons say that $3 + 3$ are equal to 6, they are grasping the same equation. But neither can communicate to the other his emotion. I may try to evoke in you an emotion similar to mine; I may describe my feeling, or make gestures, or write a poem, but I can no more transfer my feeling into your mind than I can transfer a toothache. Subjectivity is existence, and existence is always particular and unique, never shared or shareable; 'existential reality is incommunicable'.[72]

SUBJECTIVITY AS TRUTH

33 There is another and fourth fact about subjectivity that is momentous, though it is hard to grasp. Kierkegaard holds that subjectivity is *truth*. At first this seems quite meaningless. How could a commitment of the will, however passionate, be true or false? Is it not precisely as we lay aside subjective desires, purposes, and prejudices and look at things objectively that we can hope to see things as they are? Kierkegaard does not oppose such objectivity in science, but he holds that in religion it is irrelevant or worse; 'an objective knowledge of the truth of Christianity, or of its truths, is precisely untruth'.[73] The belief or acceptance of Christianity is for Kierkegaard, as we have seen, a decision of the will, and he is quite prepared to say that this decision is not a cognitive act at all. But though neither true nor false in the conventional sense, he felt that the word 'true' could still be applied to it significantly. As so applied, it was really an adverb rather than an adjective, for its application was now to an act. What was important in Christian assent was not any content assented to but the manner of the acceptance, not the what but the how. 'At its maximum this inward "how" is the passion of the infinite, and the passion of the infinite is the truth.'[74] 'The truth is precisely the venture which chooses an objective uncertainty with the passion of the infinite.'[75] 'Subjectivity is the truth.'[76] Kierkegaard was fond of repeating 'only truth that edifies is truth for me'. Since Christianity is not a set of doctrines but a way of living, the truth that it possesses is a quality of the act of accepting it; we accept it 'truly' if we commit ourselves to it whole-heartedly, unreservedly, and passionately. It was in this sense that for Kierkegaard subjectivity was truth.

Such teaching was revolutionary. It abruptly altered the theological tactics for the defence of Christianity against all forms of rationalism. Instead of answering the critics point by point, Kierkegaard shifted ground and held that their criticism required no answer because it was irrelevant. They had tried to equate Christianity with a set of dogmas that were to be approached in the same manner as Newton's theory of gravitation or Locke's theory of matter, by a rational appraisal of evidence. Kierkegaard denied that Christianity had anything in common with such theories. It did not consist of doctrines; its acceptance was not an affair of cognition; and in trying to refute it the critics were therefore beating the air. Christianity was true, indeed, but not in their sense. Its truth lay not in the conformity of statement to fact but in the sincerity, the completeness, the passionateness, with which one committed oneself to it as a life.

With countless persons this strategy has proved effective. It appeals to the widespread conviction that any attack upon religion as a set of dogmas is an attack upon a straw man. The sense that Kierkegaard is right against intellectualism in religion is the main reason for his extraordinary revival. Furthermore, in his insistence that religion is not a merely intellectual affair we can only agree with him. A Catholic who believed every clause in the Nicene, the Athanasian, and the Apostles' creed, or an Anglican who subscribed without demur to all the thirty-nine articles but who hated and exploited his neighbours, would certainly not be regarded as a Christian. Christianity *is* a way of life. And a way of life can hardly be brushed aside as speculative cobwebs can, by the flourish of a dialectical broom.

THE FAILURE OF SUBJECTIVITY

34 But there is more to be said. To reject intellectualism in religion is one thing; to embrace subjectivity in Kierkegaard's sense is quite another. If we absorb the what into the how, if we reduce the acceptance of Christianity to a passionate commitment of the will in divorce from any attempt at objective thought, we are banishing the intellect from religion altogether. And is one extreme not as objectionable as the other? Certainly Christianity as historically accepted has never been a matter of will and action only. Besides having a committed will, a Christian has certain beliefs. Even though he lives whole-heartedly for the good of his community, if he has no belief in a God, rejects the divinity of Christ, finds the atonement meaningless, and denies a future life, he will hardly be regarded as a Christian. The intellectual element, though it does not stand alone, is and must be there. Kierkegaard, in his endeavour to make Christianity 'existential' rather than 'objective', distorts and depreciates this element beyond recognition. When he says that the truth of Christianity consists in a passionate decision to act, he is not only eviscerating Christian beliefs of their meaning but also denying that belief, in its ordinary sense, has any part in religion at all. This is a most unconvincing position, which Kierkegaard was unable to maintain consistently.

Consider his way of dealing with the doctrine of immortality. No doubt this doctrine has meant different things to different minds, but for the great majority of believers it has had one simple and central meaning, namely that they will continue as persons after death. This is a belief about their future, and whether it is true or false clearly depends on its relation to future fact. Not, however, for Kierkegaard. His way of posing the question of immortality is as follows:

'Objectively the question cannot be answered, because objectively it cannot be put, since immortality precisely is the potentiation and highest development of the developed subjectivity. Only by really willing to become subjective can the question properly emerge, therefore how could it be answered objectively? . . . people will not understand that viewed systematically the whole question is nonsense, so that instead of seeking outward proofs, one had better seek to become a little subjective. Immortality is the most passionate interest of subjectivity; precisely in the interest lies the proof.'[77]

That is, the way to gain assurance that one will survive in the future is to take a passionate interest in it now; if the interest is strong enough, that will attest that the belief is true. On the assumption that immortality carries its ordinary meaning, this is plainly nonsense, since it is absurd to attest the truth of propositions about the future by going into a passion about them. It makes sense only on the assumption that Kierkegaard is not talking about immortality in its common meaning at all, but about something else to which he has chosen to attach the word. Not that he takes the word consistently in its new sense, whatever that is, for then his discussion would lack even apparent relevance to the traditional question. He understands well enough what the traditional meaning is, both of this and of other religious questions; in converting them into the sort of issue that can be settled by an eruption of feeling and will, he is merely 'changing the subject'.

35   Why did he insist on replacing objective truth with this curious subjectivity? Partly, no doubt, because he had convinced himself that the general propositions of science and philosophy dealt only with universals, not with particular things or persons; 'all men are mortal' stated a connection between humanity and immortality but said nothing about *me*. We have seen that there is no good ground for this strange interpretation. The statement *is* about me, for if it is true, I shall die, and if I do not, that will render the statement false. Again, Kierkegaard seems to have held that belief in the ordinary sense was not something that could enlist one's passion, whereas one could be fully engaged emotionally about a decision to act. On this, T. S. Eliot's remark is pertinent that 'it is by no means self-evident that human beings are most real when most violently excited'. Nor is it self-evident that the person who feels most strongly about death realises its nature most fully, that the kind of criminal, for example, who is soddenly indifferent until impending execution jars his torpid feeling into life, and is then dragged shrieking to the chair, has necessarily seen the meaning of death more clearly than the man who has reflected about it long and quietly. Sometimes again, Kierkegaard's ground for exalting subjectivity seems to be the conviction that thought must be pale and cold. This too is untrue. There are persons, as Sir Thomas Browne observed, who love to 'pursue their reason to an "O Altitudo" ', and indeed follow philosophy, as Spinoza and Bradley did, as 'a way of experiencing Deity'.

Occasionally the reader, casting about for reasons why this strange doctrine should have commended itself, is driven to the suspicion that other and plainer confusions are at work. Kierkegaard holds that 'the entire essential content of subjective thought is essentially secret, because it cannot be directly communicated'; all one can do is to help another grasp it by an act of his own. But strictly speaking, all thought is of this kind, even $2 + 2 = 4$. If I want to communicate this to you, I can make noises or write symbols, but you can gather what I am thinking only by rethinking it for yourself. Thus the fact that a thought can be communicated only indirectly does not, as Kierkegaard supposed, distinguish a subjective from an objective form of thinking. Perhaps because of a perception of this, he seems at times to identify subjective thought with the act of judgement itself as a bare psychological event, distinct from anything judged. This act is really subjective in the sense that your act can never be mine, nor mine yours. But then it becomes meaningless to speak of the judgement as true or false, for a mere event can be neither. Furthermore the whole campaign against the 'objective' thought of the philosopher would become pointless, since acts of thought are as truly subjective in this sense as the most passionate acts of the devotee.

SUBJECTIVITY AS PASSION

36 All these confusions may have contributed to Kierkegaard's insistence on subjectivity. But the main reason for it was his obsession with immediacy as what brought him closest to existence. His attitude at this highest level reminds one, as did his attitude on the lowest level, of the hedonism of Aristippus, for whom what was all-important was the feeling of the moment; and it was anticipatory of Bergson, for whom reality lay only in the immediate. Kierkegaard wanted to sink himself in immediacy. All ideas, all speculation, all reference beyond the experience of the instant were unreal, and even the experience of that instant was tainted with unreality unless it could be reduced to the immediate without remainder. One can see that the contention is not wholly without point. The thought of a distant thing or person is only a thought; it is *not* the thing or person, and it cannot bring them into existence; it is only a shadow, a suggestion, a foretaste of its object. Banish it then. Get down to the really real—pure action, pure passion, unalloyed and unvitiated by thought.

It was an impossible enterprise. We never do or can reach pure immediacy, as has been seen; we leave it behind in infancy, if indeed we ever experience it; by the time the child recognises a ball or a milk-bottle, he has lost his innocence and eaten of the tree of knowledge. The attempt to strip experience of thought while retaining its immediacies is radically mistaken, for if the ideal elements of our experience were removed the immediate ones would go too, or at least would lose their character. Consider emotion, for example. Emotion was for Kierkegaard an immediate experience, and therefore subjective and real. Thus the fear one feels if one hears a tiger roar in the jungle is intensely real, though the thought of the tiger is not. Or to take the sort of case that Kierkegaard prefers—for he was preoccupied with the erotic—the love of Dante for Beatrice was real, though a vast gulf separated the thought of her from the existent woman of flesh and blood. But what would be left of the 'real' emotion in either of these cases if the 'unreal' thought were taken away? Nothing. It is the interpretation imposed by thought on the roar in the jungle that arouses the emotion and gives it its tone of fearfulness. It is the thought of Dante about Beatrice as a person of grace and goodness that appoints his complex feelings about her. In the same way, it is the religious man's thought of God as a person concerned about the fall of a sparrow, or as a ferocious Moloch demanding the first-born, that fixes and colours his feeling about Deity. Without religious thought, religious feeling would be without form and void, and religious commitment would be *to* nothing. Kierkegaard wants to keep the immediacy of religious experience —its passion and practical devotion—without those intellectual elements that involve it in doubt and strife. It was a vain attempt. He might as well have tried to keep the colour of the rose while doing away with its form.

37 The doctrine that truth lies in subjectivity is self-defeating in another way. It makes truth relative to the passions and preferences of the individual mind, no matter how anarchic or conflicting these may be. One would say unhesitatingly that it would justify both sides of a contradiction except for Kierkegaard's insistence that truth belongs to pure acts or decisions, which, not being true or false in the ordinary sense, cannot contradict each other in that sense. But though he does insist on this, he also, with his customary generosity, talks continually as if it were not the case, and draws freely on examples that would be meaningless unless truth *were* taken in the ordinary sense. We may therefore follow him as he does so. He takes the case of Pilate, called upon to judge whether the prisoner before him had committed a capital offence, and maintains that Pilate erred because he tried to deal with the issue objectively.

'But whoever is neither cold nor hot is nauseating. . . . Had not

Pilate asked objectively what truth is, he would never have condemned Christ to be crucified. Had he asked subjectively, the passion of his inwardness respecting what in the decision facing him he had *in truth to do*, would have prevented him from doing wrong.'[78]

This is singularly unconvincing. The roles of intelligence and feeling have somehow got reversed. So long as Pilate allowed himself to be governed by the evidence objectively considered, his stand was for acquittal. 'Ye have brought this man unto me, as one that perverteth the people: and, behold, I, having examined him before you, have found no fault in this man touching those things whereof ye accuse him.'[79] It was only when Pilate, against his objective judgement, capitulated to the passion of the accusers that he gave the tragic sentence. 'And they were instant with loud voices, requiring that he might be crucified. And the voices of them and of the chief priests prevailed. And Pilate gave sentence that it should be as they required.'[80] Kierkegaard says that if subjectivity had been allowed to settle the issue, the right verdict would have been given. He fails to note that it was precisely subjectivity that did give the verdict— the passionate, unreflecting, unquestioning, moral condemnation of the priestly accusers. He denounces the attitude that 'found no fault in this man' and exalts the attitude of non-objective and passionate self-righteousness that led to his conviction.

It may be replied that the attitude of the accusers was not genuine subjectivity, and could be regarded as such only if it gave the right verdict. But we must remember that no objective method is now left us by which we can find what *is* the right verdict. If Kierkegaard is to present the product of his own subjectivity as truth and that of others as error, he must be prepared to show how to distinguish a real subjectivity from a fraudulent one. This he cannot do. His description of the state as active, passionate, and incommunicable applies as well to the accusers' state of mind as to the defenders'; the high priests were vehemently sure of themselves. If subjectivity as described is the only test available, the conclusion seems clear: you can justify anything by it. A man has a sincere, unquestioning, unreflecting, passionate conviction that something is right; therefore it *is* right.

This conclusion will plainly not do. It has provided through many centuries a charter for those who have burned witches, supported slavery, and put down heresy by force, and it further simplifies their task by enabling them to dismiss appeals to reason as irrelevant. If the peculiar quality of a man's 'subjectivity' happens to be hatred, as it frequently was with Kierkegaard, what is dictated by this hatred assumes the vesture of certain truth, and its presentation to the public with a suitable show of reluctance attests at once devotion to truth and devotion to duty. Kierkegaard found the equation of truth with subjectivity a great convenience. With an apparently untroubled conscience, for example, he could seek to destroy the growing reputation of so harmless a friend as Hans Christian Andersen through an anonymous manuscript 'published against his will by S. Kierkegaard', and could subject another friend, the kindly Bishop Mynster, to public vilification after his death. If people pointed out that this was not fair, if they protested, as they did, that it was less than accurate to describe priests as 'cannibals' and fellow-Christians as 'whoremongers', Kierkegaard could reply that 'there still remains One that I take with me in my disrepute, God in Heaven. . . .' For anyone who regards his passions, and particularly his malevolent passions, as 'the truth', it is prudent to secure unimpeachable references.

THE LEAP OF FAITH

38   It will be recalled that to reach the highest level of the religious life three things were necessary: first, the abandonment of the search for certainty through objective thought; second, the falling back on subjectivity as a passionate, non-rational act of will; third, the leap of faith. We have examined the first two, with results that do not raise expectations as we turn to the third. Still, this leap of faith demands scrutiny. It is the last step in the ascent which takes us to the highest summit of religious knowledge that man can achieve.

What is it that distinguishes an act of faith from other subjective acts, such as making a moral decision? It is that faith is concerned with a special type of problem. Christianity requires a commitment to certain beliefs. Among these the central one is the belief in the incarnation, namely that at a certain point in past time God actually became man. 'The object of faith is thus God's reality in existence as a particular individual, the fact that God has existed as an individual human being.'[81] This is the distinctive fact of Christianity, which marks it out from all other religions. And we have seen that, according to Kierkegaard, it is a fact incapable of establishment by any process of objective thought. You can never *prove* the existence of any past fact. It might seem, then, that the proper attitude is one of doubt and suspended judgement, just as it would be if we were asked to accept the existence of King Arthur. The two facts, however, are not comparable. For the unique Christian fact, if a fact at all, is one of overwhelming moment, upon whose acceptance our eternal happiness depends, and if there is any chance of its reality, an attitude of reserve and detachment would be flippancy. So, 'while objective knowledge rambles comfortably on by way of the long road of approximation without being impelled by the urge of passion, subjective knowledge counts every delay a deadly peril, and the decision so infinitely important and so instantly pressing that it is as if the opportunity had already passed.'[82] The decision is what James called a 'forced option'; we cannot evade it, since with so high a prize at stake to evade decision is in effect to reject the offer as illusory.

39 The man who attempts to make this decision on the ground of evidence is in an even worse position than we have suggested. For the incarnation is not a fact of more or less probability; to our reason it is bound to look like an impossibility. To say that Deity became an individual human being is to say that the eternal or timeless became temporal, that the infinite became finite, that omnipotence became limited in its power, that omniscience grew in knowledge as a man does, that moral perfection was tempted and therefore attracted by evil. These things are not mere probabilities, low or high; to our intelligence they are absurdities. What, then, are we to do? If we appeal to our intellect for guidance, it conducts us to a blank wall, for 'the contradiction that God has existed in human form'[83] is not knowable or even thinkable.

'To speculate upon it is a misunderstanding, and the farther one goes in this direction the greater is the misunderstanding. When one finally reaches the stage of not only speculating about it, but of understanding it speculatively, one has reached the highest pitch of misunderstanding.'[84]

The attempt to know religious truth by the intellect is thus fundamentally misguided because destined to defeat by the nature of its object. 'For the absurd is the object of faith, and the only object that can be believed.'[85]

Fortunately this defeat of intelligence does not leave us without recourse, for faith remains. But there must be no looking back, no longing for the unprofitable old fleshpots of rational understanding and certainty. One must recognise the sophisticated intellect for the dangerous thing it is, and be content to become a child again. 'When faith requires of a man to give up his reason, it becomes equally difficult for the cleverest and the most stupid person to believe, or it becomes in a sense more difficult for the clever.'[86] The difficulty must be overcome, not by thinking more critically, which is futile, but by a resolute act of will. The leap of faith is a daring, passionate, non-rational commitment to the paradoxical and the unintelligible.

'Faith begins where thought leaves off.'[87] 'Without risk there is no faith.' 'The truth is precisely the venture which chooses an objective uncertainty with the passion of the infinite . . . the above definition of truth is an equivalent expression for faith. . . . Faith is precisely the contradiction between the infinite passion of the individual's inwardness and the objective uncertainty.'[88] 'Faith is what the Greeks termed divine madness.'[89]

Kierkegaard's best known illustration of the meaning of faith is drawn not from theology but from morals. The ultimate source of right and wrong is the will of God, and 'the knight of faith', like the knights of the Round Table, will at every moment of life be in the service of his royal Master. Not that he needs to renew the appeal to this will at every moment consciously; for the lower-level guidance of his own ethical faculties will normally suffice. The ethical level, says Kierkegaard, is the level of 'the universal'. By this cryptic pronouncement he seems to mean one or the other of two things; that the moral man will either, in Kantian fashion, ask what conduct could in principle be consistently adopted by everybody, or, in Hegelian fashion, ask what the community generally would approve. Most modern moralists would regard either of these appeals as hopelessly inadequate, but Kierkegaard had little grasp of ethical theory. His chief contribution to it is to say that at times it breaks down, and that when it does, our resort must be to a 'teleological suspension of the ethical' at divine behest. The nature of this behest can be ascertained only by faith.

THE CRUCIAL CASE OF ABRAHAM AND ISAAC

40 How is he to show that our natural faculties do break down in morals? The most effective way would be to show that our clearest moral judgement may stand in radical conflict with the divine will. Can any case of such conflict be cited? Yes; we find it in Scripture itself. The most revolting act of which a human being is capable is to destroy his own flesh and blood. In the book of Genesis we find Abraham commanded by God to do just this, to take his only son, the son of his old age on whom the joy and hope of his life were concentrated, to the summit of Mount Moriah, to bind him, cut his throat, and use his body as a burnt offering. Anthropologists who have studied this legend have considered that it is probably a relic of the custom of human sacrifice which once held in many parts of the world, and apparently even in the prehistoric past of the Hebrew people. However that may be, Kierkegaard takes it in all historic and symbolic seriousness. Is it not the point of this story, which is clearly inspired, that it was Abraham's duty, and may at any moment be ours, to trample down the affections of the natural man and all his nicely calculated goods and evils? Kierkegaard's answer is an emphatic Yes.

In his essay on *Fear and Trembling* he goes into the matter with gusto and in detail. After a 'Preliminary Expectoration', as he calls it, in which he spews philosophy, ethics, and even reflective theology out of his mouth as incompetent to deal with the case, he goes on to consider what is implied in the command to Abraham. There have been cases in history and literature in which a father's killing of a child may in some degree be reconciled with our moral sense. Brutus ordered the execution of his sons, but they were, after all, guilty of treason, and does not a general's duty to the state take precedence of his own affections? Jephthah made a grateful vow to Heaven to offer as a sacrifice the first person he met on his return from victory, and if this happened to be his daughter, he would nonetheless be breaking a sacred oath by sparing her. If Agamemnon kills Iphigenia, it is to appease the wrath of Artemis, who holds the power of destruction over his fleet and army. These are not, therefore, pure cases of 'the teleological suspension of the ethical'; in all of them the killing of the child is dreadful, but it is not entirely pointless. The great thing about the act demanded of Abraham was that it was pointless absolutely. Isaac was wholly innocent; Abraham loved him beyond anyone else in the world; no conceivable good to anyone could be anticipated from killing him. It was an act in which every human consideration was lined up on one side and on the other nothing at all but the command from on high to kill. Abraham bowed to it and drew his knife. The fact that at the last moment he was relieved of the need to strike is irrelevant in appraising him. Whether he actually killed or not, he showed that he possessed the one thing needful, namely the readiness to kill.

For Kierkegaard this makes him the perfect knight of faith. 'Venerable Father Abraham! Second Father of the human race! . . . thou who first didst know that highest passion, the holy, pure and humble expression of the divine madness. . . .'[90] Abraham is 'great by reason of his wisdom whose secret is foolishness, great by reason of his hope whose form is madness, great by reason of the love which is hatred of oneself.'[91] He surrendered himself to the 'paradox which is capable of transforming a murder into a holy act well-pleasing to God.'[92] '. . . Abraham believed and did not doubt, he believed the preposterous.'[93] 'He believed by virtue of the absurd;

for all human reckoning had long since ceased to function.'⁹⁴ He
was called upon to renounce the moral for the religious, the finite
for the infinite. 'This is . . . clear to the knight of faith, so the only
thing that can save him is the absurd, and this he grasps by faith.'⁹⁵
Here is the meaning of that most deceptive phrase, 'the teleological
suspension of the ethical'. 'Teleological' means 'for an end', but
what Kierkegaard is praising here is the abandonment of all thought
of ends and the doing of something that from every human point
of view is productive of nothing but evil. 'As soon as the will begins
to look right and left for results, the individual begins to become
immoral.'⁹⁶

KIERKEGAARD AS A MORAL NIHILIST

41 What are we to say of a rhapsody (in forty thousand words) in
praise of pure and holy murder, of a defence of the humanly immoral
on the ground that it is religious duty? Kierkegaard, in choosing
such ground, believes that he has cut off the possibility of rational
criticism. And clearly if an appeal is taken to the unintelligible and
the irrational, it is begging the question to protest against it on any
grounds of sense or reason. Sense and reason have been deliberately
left behind. But we can at least point out that the irrationalist
defence is double-edged. If it undercuts its opponents, it also undercuts itself, in the sense that it has foregone all right to the rational
criticism of others. If opponents claim a divine warrant for the
opposite of what Kierkegaard proclaims, all he can do is denounce
them as impostors.

Of course there have been countless claims of this sort. There were
Jewish leaders who claimed a divine imperative to destroy the
Amalekites, man, woman, and child. There were Christians—St
Louis described himself as one—who thought the proper Christian
reply to an argumentative Jew was to bury one's sword in him to the
hilt. John Woolman felt a divine interdict against his preparing
papers as a magistrate for the sale of a slave; but John Newton, the
hymn-writer, reported that some of his sweetest hours of communion
with the divine were spent while he was the captain of a slave-ship,
separated by a few planks from a weltering mass of human misery.
Joseph Smith claimed to know that the divine will approved of plural
wives; Mohammed made a like claim, but limited the divine
approval to four; the Christian fathers limited it still further to one;
and St Paul construed it as favouring those who did not marry at all.
St Basil, St Gregory of Nyssa, and St Ambrose thought it a divine
imperative that one should not accept interest on loans. St Abraham
the Hermit appears to have thought it the divine will that, beginning

with the day of his conversion and continuing for fifty years, he should wash neither his face nor his feet. There are few practices too trivial or too eccentric to have been included among actions enjoined or prohibited by divine will. If claims to such guidance are to be above rational criticism, what we have is a chaos of voices, each announcing itself as authoritative, each denouncing its opponents as deceivers, and none of them able to defend themselves against the others.

Such chaos raises suspicion of all the claimants. Nevertheless, it supplies nothing decisive against the objective rightness of any of them. To suppose that it does is a common error in these days, particularly among 'cultural relativists'. They have succeeded in showing by diligent investigation that virtually every practice regarded as wrong at one time and place is accepted as right at some other, and have often concluded from this that 'the mores can make anything right', that all claims to objective truth for moral judgements must be equally thrown out. The conclusion does not follow. If Pericles differs from the Polynesians, it is not necessarily dogmatism to say that he speaks for a higher culture and is more likely to be right. If it were, one could by a parallel argument call Newton and Einstein in question because John Alexander Dowie disagreed with them and insisted that the earth was flat. No such argument will be offered here. We must in fairness agree that among the chaos of claimants to supernatural direction Kierkegaard might be right and all who differ from him wrong. The issue can be decided only by scrutinising his particular claim. The questions to be asked about it are of two kinds, intrinsic and extrinsic. The intrinsic question is whether the content of faith, the beliefs disclosed to it, are meaningful and credible; the extrinsic question is whether their credibility is affected for better or worse by the sort of mind through which they are disclosed. It will pay us to look briefly at each of these.

42 Abraham was enabled by faith to see what ordinary men were unable to see. What exactly was this? It was that an act which, so far as the human mind could judge, was productive only of evil was nevertheless right—a duty because the will of God. For the person who possesses the insight, the principles and consequences involved in the act are held to be irrelevant; its character as seen by faith is its true character, which takes precedence of any judgement of our merely human faculties. Faith thus revealed to Abraham in the most dramatic and decisive way that it may be duty to reduce rather than to increase, to destroy rather than to create, the values recognised by reason and conscience.

Now when 'the knight of faith' claims that he has had this kind of insight, can we credit what he says? It is hard to take the claim seriously. A person may *say* that it is really better that the powers of youth should be frustrated than fulfilled, that excruciating pain is better than pleasure, that sorrow and anguish are better than happiness, but can we believe that he has in fact seen these things to be true? The question is not, of course, whether pain, misery, and the destruction of life may be *means* leading to later goods; this is true enough, but is irrelevant here; for we are expressly forbidden to try to justify the divine command by any such considerations. What was presented as Abraham's duty, what he was honoured for accepting, was the production of these evils without any thought of compensating goods.

When the question is thus clearly put, one must take leave to doubt not only whether such insight occurs in fact but whether it could possibly occur. For what the insight amounts to is that there is no such thing as good or evil, right or wrong, better or worse. If the killing of innocent youth without regard to consequences may be right, then anything may be right, since our moral sense has proved delusive at the very point of its greatest confidence. If pleasure is intrinsically evil and pain intrinsically good, if misery is in truth more desirable than happiness, then the clearest and surest judgements about values are worthless, and it is no longer possible to hold that anything is really better than anything else. The entire realm of values, including moral values, becomes a mirage. Now one may talk as if it were, but one cannot live or think accordingly. Daily and hourly we make choices implying judgements that it is better to be happy or enlightened or at peace than it is to be the opposite; indeed the person who chooses to affirm that nothing is better than anything else presumably assumes that it is better so to affirm than not to do so. The Kierkegaardian 'knight of faith', in electing the 'absurd', is divesting himself of the shackles of all such insights. But to do that is to be not a saint but a moral nihilist.

RATIONAL MORALS REPUDIATED

43 Those who accept Kierkegaard's knight of faith as the true saint may well pause over this conclusion. The popularity of his religious ethics in our schools of theology is a genuine anomaly. The Christian saint, we must admit, has at times been a strange character whose asceticism and other-worldliness have set him apart from the run of men and caused him to be regarded with uncomprehending wonder. Still, in the main he has accepted and exemplified the values most prized by his fellows and has been honoured by them accordingly; he has believed in the superiority of love to hate, in the relief of human misery, in refusing to count his own good as more important than that of others. These are virtues that we can see to be virtues with our unaided human faculties. But for Kierkegaard as for Luther, these faculties are corrupt; all the principles laid down by them are open to a 'teleological suspension of the ethical' imposed from above; they are subject at any moment to cancellation by 'the absurd'; and if in the face of such a suspension we retain our old adherence to love or loyalty or even conscience in its natural sense, the charge of immorality is compounded with a charge of impiety. Furthermore, the saint or knight of faith, according to Kierkegaard, is a man whose leading concern is not the welfare of others but his own 'eternal happiness', a description incidentally that applied to himself. 'If ever a person was self-centred,' says Professor Paton, 'it was Kierkegaard; he hardly ever thinks of anyone but himself.'[97] What we have in this strange version of Christianity is thus an insistence on the selfish character of the religious motive combined with an insistence that the values of the Christian life, so far as these can be understood, are provisional only and may at any time be overridden. Kierkegaard revelled in paradox; 'if anyone has ever used the slogan *credo quia absurdum*,' says Emil Brunner, 'it was Kierkegaard'.[98] Those who love daylight, even in religion, will greet the absurd with less acclaim. To them it will still seem odd that one should have to become immoral in order to be religious. They may recall Halevy's remark that 'virtue is more dangerous than vice, because its excesses are not subject to the restraints of conscience'.

The knight of faith sometimes startles us as much by his banality as by his transcendence of moral claims. Kierkegaard assures us that if he were to meet such a man, who was living on the religious summit, he might find nothing about him that distinguished him from anyone else. He imagines himself meeting such a person:

'Good Lord, is this the man? Is it really he? Why, he looks like a tax-collector! However, it is the man after all. I draw closer to him, watching his least movements to see whether there might not be visible a little heterogeneous fractional telegraphic message from the infinite, a glance, a look, a gesture, a note of sadness, a smile, which betrayed the infinite in its heterogeneity with the finite. No! I examine his figure from tip to toe to see if there might not be a cranny through which the infinite was peeping. No! . . . when one looks at him one might suppose that he was a clerk who had lost his soul in an intricate system of book-keeping. . . . He goes to church. No heavenly glance or any other token of the incommensurable betrays him; if one did not know him, it would be impossible to distinguish him from the rest of the congregation, for his healthy and vigorous hymn-singing proves at the most that he has a good chest. . . . On his way he reflects that his wife has surely a special little warm dish prepared for him, e.g. a calf's head roasted, garnished with vegetables . . . his appetite is greater than Esau's. His wife hasn't it—strangely enough, it is quite the same to him. . . . In the evening he smokes his pipe; to look at him one would swear that it was the grocer over the way vegetating in the twilight. . . . And yet, and yet—actually I could become furious over it, for envy if for no other reason—this man has made and every moment is making the movements of infinity. With infinite resignation he has drained the cup of life's profound sadness, he knows the bliss of the infinite . . . the whole earthly form he exhibits is a new creation by virtue of the absurd. He resigned everything infinitely, and then he grasped everything again by virtue of the absurd.'[99]

There is thus no telling what life in the absurd may require of us. It may summon us to something dramatic and unconventional, such as murder on a mountain top; 'men will continue to commit atrocities,' said Voltaire, 'as long as they continue to believe absurdities'. On the other hand, it may affect our conduct so little that even our friends may never detect that we are among the chosen of mankind. We may achieve full religious absurdity with so little trace in our conduct of any new mellowness or affection or unselfishness or refinement of feeling that we are undistinguishable from our brother grocers and tax-collectors. The discontinuity is so great between the inner man, occupying his stratosphere of absurdity, and his natural interests and activities that the two may coexist in the same person without visibly affecting each other. The notion of the Christian spirit as permeating natural attitudes and transforming selfish conduct seems to have been supplanted by a different kind of picture. And it is a somewhat odd picture to hang in a gallery of 'saints' alongside those of St Francis and Thomas à Kempis, of John Woolman and Albert Schweitzer.

RATIONAL THEOLOGY REPUDIATED

44 We have been dealing with the absurdity apprehended by faith in the field of morals. But it will be remembered that the central dogmas of the creed are also apprehended by faith, and are regarded as equally absurd. Sometimes the absurd is presented as the merely improbable. 'Faith has in fact two tasks: to take care in every moment to discover the improbable, the paradox; and then to hold it fast with the passion of inwardness.'[100] Sometimes, as we have seen, the paradox that must be held fast is more than improbable; it is impossible. The central fact of Christianity, Kierkegaard holds, is the incarnation. 'The object of faith is hence the reality of the God-man in the sense of his existence . . . the fact that God has existed as an individual human being.'[101] But he admits that by rational standards this fact is inconceivable and inconsistent with itself. A being who is eternal or out of time cannot have measured out his life in human years. A being who is omnipresent could not be confined in his movements to a small area in the eastern Mediterranean. A being who is omniscient cannot grow in knowledge, or a being who is perfect grow in grace. A son who is a separate person from his father cannot also be one with that father; still less can three persons be one. So speaks logic. But faith requires us to put logic aside and accept what Kierkegaard flatly calls 'the contradiction that God has existed in human form'.[102] 'In my God-relationship I have to learn precisely to give up my finite understanding, and therewith the custom of discrimination which is natural to me. . . .'[103] A man must somehow learn 'to relinquish his understanding and his thinking, and to keep his soul fixed upon the absurd. . . .'[104] He must achieve a 'crucifixion of the understanding',[105] and by a leap of faith embrace the improbable and even impossible as nevertheless certain.

The difficulty with this claim is to attach any definite meaning to it. If we were told that though a certain belief was improbable we should try to make ourselves believe it, that would be intelligible, whether ethical or not. If we were told that a belief, though beyond our present understanding, was vouched for by others who did understand it, and that through provisionally accepting this assurance we might come to understand it ourselves, that too would make sense. But if we are told that although a belief is both un-intelligible and self-contradictory we shall see that it is absolutely true and certain if we commit ourselves to it passionately enough, we can only question whether the proposer knows what he is asking of us. The law of contradiction is not a principle that is valid in some cases and not in others; if it is invalid in any case, it is invalid *as such* and therefore in every case. But if it is thus universally invalid, then in no case does the assertion of something as true exclude the truth of its denial, and *nothing* is true rather than untrue. And that makes assertion meaningless, for *what* could one be asserting? Just as Kierkegaard's ethics implies the denial of a realm of value, so his trans-logical truth undermines truth as we know it. Not that he saw this implication or held to it. If he had, he would not have argued at all. He was in fact proud of his prowess as a dialectician, and took pleasure in pitting himself against Hegel. But his philosophy terminates in a rejection of those very principles of logic on which he proceeded as a philosopher. He can hardly have it both ways. If the logic he assumes in his philosophy is valid, then the faith which stands at the summit of 'the stages on life's way' is meaningless. If that irrational faith is accepted, the principles on which reflection conducts itself are everywhere impugned. In that case, Kierkegaard should merely smile like Buddha and remain silent.

What would he reply to all this? Probably that he was not concerned with the truth of doctrines at all; 'Christianity is not a doctrine but an existential communication expressing an existential contradiction.'[106] He would fall back on his notion of subjectivity; 'the passion of the infinite is the truth. But the passion of the infinite is precisely subjectivity, and thus subjectivity becomes the truth.'[107] (This looks like both an undistributed middle and an illicit minor, if logic still has any importance.) He would renew his attack on the attempt to understand, insisting that the 'objective acceptance of Christianity . . . is paganism or thoughtlessness'.[108] He would remind us that religion is a commitment of the will, that 'Christianity wishes to intensify passion to its highest pitch,'[109] not to induce in us belief of comprehension.

We have seen long ago that this will not do. Christianity does include beliefs, and it insists rightly or wrongly that these beliefs are true in the common and ancient sense. To adopt Kierkegaard's new sense, peculiar to himself, which reduces truth to a passionate commitment of feeling and will, would not save Christianity; on the contrary, it would largely destroy it. For it implies that there are no common truths for Christians to accept, no common principles by which their lives may be guided, indeed no common Deity for them to contemplate and worship. The Kierkegaardian subjectivity would dissolve these things away into a set of processes in individual minds where there would be as many Christianities as there were persons to exercise their 'inwardness' and their passion.

THE THINKER AND HIS THOUGHT

45 In this review of Kierkegaard on faith and reason, we have been examining the thought, not the man. Ad hominem reasoning, besides being distasteful, is never conclusive and is often self-defeating. But I do not wish to conceal my own belief that psychological causes as distinct from logical reasons had much to do with his conclusions. I cannot think that a psychopathologist would have much trouble in connecting the irrationalism of his thought with the irrationality of his temper. He said himself that his thought must be understood through his personality; and that personality was profoundly abnormal—so abnormal as to have cut him off from his fellows, his friends, and his own family. His alternations of exaltation and depression, his temptations to suicide, the feverish activity of an over-pressed brain in darkened rooms, the hysterical-sounding claims to being 'a genius in a market town' and his comparison of himself to Christ, the frenzied excoriations of church and clergy in his later years, his own report that he had stood on the verge of insanity—it would be a mistake to pass over these things as if they were wholly irrelevant. They suggest, though with a force difficult to assess, that Kierkegaard's singularities of thought were less the product of judicial reflection than the by-product of a sick spirit.

I will take two examples that may serve to make clear what I mean. First, his overwhelming, persistent, and surely morbid sense of guilt. This was partly, as we have seen, an infection from his father, who lived in terror of having committed the unpardonable sin, partly the reaction to youthful irregularities on the part of an excessively introspective mind brought up in a theological hothouse. Georg Brandes reminds us that 'he lived his life through in an atmosphere saturated with theology and theological discussion; at least three fourths of his near acquaintances appear to have been theologians, chaplains, ministers, bishops, clerics of every rank.' This atmosphere kept alive and flourishing in Kierkegaard's anxious mind a conviction which, if exposed to the air and light of free secular discussion, would probably have been dissipated, the inherited Lutheran conviction that we were born in sin, utterly corrupted by it, and doomed by it to condemnation unless faith could somehow be won. Kierkegaard, like his father, lived in fear. 'The whole of existencé frightens me, from the smallest fly to the mystery of the Incarnation; everything is unintelligible to me, most of all myself; the whole of existence is poisoned in my sight, particularly myself.'[110] The cure for this fear was faith, and Kierkegaard was terrified that, by losing his faith, he might also lose his 'eternal happiness'; he must therefore keep it at all costs. He saw clearly the tendency of 'objective thinking' to undermine and disintegrate this faith. Is there any wonder that an imaginative mind, living in a 'sickness unto death' of fear, despair, and dread, should come to conceive of philosophy as the enemy? If one wished to preserve one's faith, it was safer not to play the philosophical game at all. 'The ungodly calmness with which the irresolute man would begin in the case of God (for he would begin with doubt), precisely this is insubordination; for thereby God is deposed from the throne, from being the Lord. And when one has done this, one really has already chosen another master, wilfulness. . . .'[111] To argue the case with the philosopher is to risk defeat on an issue too important by far to be dealt with by a match of wits. It is better to ignore him, to insist that faith is one thing and reason quite another, and to settle the issue decisively by a leap of faith. That is the only escape from despair.

46 For the other example of how Kierkegaard's thought is rooted in his life, we may refer to his too celebrated love affair. Much in his philosophy seems to have been a rationalisation, in the Freudian sense, of his conduct in this affair. He had long contemplated with growing passion a neighbour's daughter, a girl in her teens named Regine Olsen. He at last declared himself, led her on to a whole-hearted reciprocating passion, then threw her abruptly over and went off to Berlin, where he wrote up his experience in *The Diary of a Seducer* and other edifying discourses. By merely secular standards his behaviour was that of a cad, and he seems to have realised this, for running through much of his work from this time on, there is a veiled attempt to justify himself. To his credit, he has occasional doubts. 'Had I had faith I should have remained with Regine,' he once confided to his diary.[112] But the line he more commonly took was that he threw her over because he did have faith, or at least because renouncing her would give exaltation to his spiritual life. He prefers to write about it in parables, but the reference is unmistakable.

'Love for that princess became for him the expression for an eternal love, assumed a religious character, was transfigured into a love for the Eternal Being, which did to be sure deny him the fulfilment of his love, yet reconciled him again by the eternal consciousness of its validity in the form of eternity, which no reality can take from him.'[113]

In this treatment of her, the simple Regine was unable to share 'the eternal consciousness of its validity in the form of eternity', and was broken-hearted. Kierkegaard probably realised that, as mentally and sexually abnormal, he was no fit person to marry at all, and if he had rested his desertion on such ground, one could understand it, though wondering why the discovery came so late. But such an explanation was not satisfactory to a mind in which a messianic egotism was mixed in unwholesome fashion with his eroticism and piety. He had done wrong; he knew it; and if he was to retain his picture of himself as genius and saint, he must explain his action by lofty motives. He chose the loftiest. As Buber suggested, God was Regine's successful rival. The desertion was in obedience to a secret imperative from on high, which, like the hero of *Fear and Trembling*, he was ready to obey, whatever the cost in renunciation.

Regarding this book, Professor Paton has passed judgement in terms with which, severe as they are, it is hard to disagree.

'. . . what makes it nauseating as a professedly religious work is that, as he himself has said, it is a "mystification" which reproduces his own life. In other words, it is an account of his unhappy love affair with Regina Olsen, an account in which his own deplorable behaviour is supposed to be similar to that of Abraham. We may pity his unhappy and diseased temperament, but neurosis is a poor qualification for setting up as a religious guide. . . . Self-centredness is the very antithesis of religion; and if the paradox of faith is—as he says—a willingness "to do the terrible and to do it for its own sake" (as well as for God's sake), then the less of this kind of faith we have the better.'[114]

CONCLUDING UNHAPPY POSTSCRIPT

47   This is a grim note on which to end our study of Kierkegaard. He is a figure who of late years has received almost lyrical praise for the depth of his thought and the penetration of his psychological insight. We have been assured that he 'belongs to all time and to all humanity, just as surely as do Plato and Aristotle, Spinoza and Hume and Kant and Hegel.'[115] We have been assured over and over of how profound he is. 'Kierkegaard's explanation of the dialectical relation of freedom and fate in sin is one of the profoundest in Christian thought'; and similarly 'Kierkegaard's analysis of the relation of anxiety to sin is the profoundest in Christian thought.'[116] Georg Brandes in a letter to Nietzsche says that Kierkegaard 'is in my view one of the most profound psychologists of all time. . . .'[117] '. . . Harnack's once celebrated essay on *The Essence of Christianity* seems incredibly trivial,' remarks a disciple, 'when one has read S.K.'[118]

I recall that, stimulated by such fair words, I approached his books with high expectations. My experience was like that of John Laird, who wrote, after a determined attempt on *Either/Or*: 'By the time I had finished the first enormous volume I was sadly disconsolate. Even on a wide literary interpretation of "philosophy"—and no other could be appropriate—I found very little that seemed to be worth stating in any formal way.'[119] One reads a few puzzling pages with the feeling that the writer must be catching his breath and getting slowly under way; some definite point will soon emerge. It does not. One reads on with gathering disillusionment, coming in the end to realise that Kierkegaard, if a philosopher at all, is a distinct species of philosopher, and that it is useless to look for clearly stated theses, still less for ordered arguments in support of them. He combined an undisciplined intellect with a remorseless, facile, unchecked, limitless, compulsive loquacity; he was, as Disraeli said of Gladstone, 'inebriated with the exuberance of his own verbosity'. He is said to have written twenty-two books by the time he was thirty-five; and since they have no firm construction, no obvious beginning or ending, and no internal reason why they should ever end, one can read them only by allowing one's critical sense to be lulled into drowsiness and one's mind to be floated along on the tide of words. Unfortunately, no sooner has one made one's peace with the indiscipline of thought and style than one must begin the battle over again with the man himself. The self-absorption, the strange blend of piety and contempt (his two dominant emotions, according to Brandes), the dogmatism, the proclamations of un-appreciated genius, the imprecations on church and clergy, the gospel of universal guilt and despair, the homilies on love from a mind that was simmering with hatreds, the scorn for those who, in religion, try to understand—these things have an effect that the reader must manage to suppress if he is to go on. He must remind himself that though this is a sick and twisted mind, such minds have, on occasion, shown a sharp eye for truth.

48 What was the truth that Kierkegaard saw? The great insight claimed for him is that in religion objective thinking breaks down and that the insight it seeks is obtainable by faith. As for the in-adequacy of thought, a case can certainly be made for it, and such a case was actually presented with a force of statement and argument beyond Kierkegaard's range by an English contemporary, Dean Mansel of St Paul's. Kierkegaard's own case is unimpressive. His contention that thought cannot deal with existence is put so obscurely that there is difficulty in extracting from it a meaning definite enough to refute. Furthermore, he seems never to have worked out what was involved for the normal exercise of reason by its breakdown at crucial points—for ethics by the suspension of its clearest rules, and for logic by the admission of contradictions to the status of higher truths. As a philosopher he employed with scornful confidence the reason which, as a theologian, he dismissed with equal scorn. He was too impatient to get on with his writing to declare a moratorium on it while he achieved coherence in his theory of knowledge.

What of the second half of the great insight attributed to him—that where reason fails faith succeeds? Unfortunately this is more obscure than the first. Perhaps it is inevitably so. Where one has bid good-bye to reason and made the prodigious non-rational leap into the rarefied air of paradox, one should presumably say nothing, since anything one did say would have to be said in the distorting accents of the reason one has left behind. The silence, nevertheless, is a pity. Men struggle onward and upward through the stages on life's way; a hardy few reach the summit; and when they descend, the many waiting below ask a report on the splendid vision from the top. Kierkegaard, so voluble elsewhere, here finds his tongue at last tied. The stage that was supposed to cast illumination downward on all the others turns out to be strangely dark and empty. Practically, indeed, it is rather worse than empty. Kierkegaard insists that the love felt by the knight of faith is not mere human love, and if one can make any inference from his own practice, he was right, since the love displayed in that practice permitted a selfishness and harshness toward others—toward Hans Andersen and Regine and his mother and brother and Bishop Mynster and the unfortunate 'Christians' about him—which the lower love would have rendered impossible. Nor is the insight of faith into truth comparable with a merely human knowledge. Just as it gave Luther the power to see through and around Aristotle, so it gave Kierkegaard the power to see how superficial were all the systems of philosophy, and to see of science, without the need to study it, that if it differed from faith at any point it was wrong.

In the end Kierkegaard stands, in his thought as in his life, a defeated figure. He was like a business man who builds up a commercial empire by condemning and buying up the businesses of all his competitors on the strength of promissory notes which he cannot redeem. He indicts reason; he indicts rational ethics; he indicts love and justice of the merely human variety; he indicts with eloquent contempt the Christianity that is practised around him. He invites them all to accept subordination to one directing head in return for grandiose, even infinite, promises. But when they present their claims, they find the bank vaults empty. The large promises of a new directorate are never fulfilled. Just how reason is to be rectified or ethics reformed, just what the new golden affections are that are to replace the old leaden ones, just what we are to believe or do or feel—these all-important directions never transpire. Faith has leaped so high that it has shot up beyond the earth's atmosphere to where thought and conscience can no longer breathe. These may be poor things, but we know them, and know that they have served us not badly. We shall do well to keep them, even when notes are flourished before us that are stamped in infinite denominations, unless we can be sure that the issuing bank is solvent. That assurance Kierkegaard never supplies.

CHAPTER VII

REASON AND REVELATION FOR EMIL BRUNNER

THE REVOLT AGAINST LIBERALISM

1 The last half-century in theology has been remarkable for its reversal of expectations, its sudden turning of a tide that had seemed irreversible. For centuries liberal theology had been slowly gaining ground. It recognised that the dominance of science was the chief intellectual fact of the modern world, and that if theology too was to be a science, it must accommodate itself to this fact. And it *was* a science, the liberals insisted. It was a rational discipline which should not only adjust itself to the advances of science generally but should borrow and use for its own purposes the intellectual methods that had proved so successful in other fields. Kierkegaard, a century before, had protested the use of these methods in theology, but Kierkegaard's was a voice in the wilderness whose very echoes had died away. The alternative before Western Protestantism seemed clear: it could cling to the Lutheran tradition with its opposition of faith to reason, refuse to accommodate itself to the demands of secular knowledge, and slowly die of maladjustment to the modern world. Or it could appropriate to its own use the methods of secular research, join the march of science, and look forward to some share in its triumphs. Many liberals had misgivings, to be sure. Might not the old faith be engulfed and lost in the rising tide of rationalism? Still, to oppose oneself stubbornly to that tide was to take the hopeless line of a theological Canute. If theology had a future at all, it surely lay with liberalism.

Then a strange thing happened. A new generation of able theologians appeared who, instead of marching forward under the liberal banner, left the ranks and repudiated the movement as essentially a mistake. They did not act in ignorance of liberalism: they had been brought up under its wing; several of them had been students of Adolf Harnack. But they came to think that the tendency of liberalism was not toward the better grounding of the Christian faith but toward its distintegration, and that the faith must at all costs be preserved. Emil Brunner, Karl Barth, Friedrich Gogarten, Rudolf Bultmann, Anders Nygren, Paul Tillich, Reinhold Niebuhr —all were men of strong individuality who went their own ways, but in this at least they agreed, that the Christian faith was not a product of man's culture but a gift from beyond his horizon, that man cannot fit revelation into the rickety crates of human faculty, and that it is impious for him to try. What is important is that God came to man, not that man should grope his way in darkness up a stairway that ended in mid-air. 'I look up, and put myself in the attitude of reception,' Emerson once said, 'but from some alien energy the visions come.' That is the right attitude. The business of theology is not to examine our epistemological apparatus in the hope of finding cracks and crevices through which light might filter in from a supernatural source, but boldly to affirm that we stand in the blaze of such a light, and let the philosophers make of it what they will. It was a stunning reversal of attitude: a worm had not only turned but boldly taken the offensive. Harnack, contemplating the phenomenon of Karl Barth, said he would not have thought it possible that in the course of his lifetime a theology would emerge which was incomprehensible to him because of the lack of any organ through which he could tune in to it.

The new view was variously called 'dialectical theology', 'the theology of crisis', and 'neo-orthodoxy'. None was a good name for it, but 'neo-orthodoxy' did point to an important fact about it, since it was essentially a return to Martin Luther. As Wilhelm Pauck has said:

'There are large passages in Barth's *Dogmatics* which are nothing other than reverberations of Luther's faith. Brunner calls upon Luther again and again as his chief ally, especially insofar as he understands the Christian faith and life as a personal encounter with the gospel of the forgiveness of faith. Bultmann's existentialism is Lutheran through and through. Niebuhr's basic teaching is nothing but a modern version of Luther's view of men as *simul iustus ac peccator*. And it is characteristic even of Tillich that the most powerful and persuasive passages of his book *The Courage to Be* are directly inspired by Martin Luther.'[1]

2   Of the leaders of this theology, the two that stand most directly in the Lutheran line are Brunner and Barth. To many laymen they are all but indistinguishable, a pair of theological twins. Both came from German Switzerland; both served their apprenticeships as pastors in Swiss villages; both held chairs of theology in Swiss

universities, Barth in Basel, Brunner in Zürich; both wrote volu-
minous works on *Dogmatik*, Brunner in three volumes, Barth in
about fourteen; both courageously denounced the Nazis; both were
Gifford lecturers in Scotland; both, after an early exposure to
liberal teaching, became leaders in the reaction against it. It is
true that there were differences which to the two men themselves
seemed considerable. Brunner was more interested than Barth in
ethics and social movements. Brunner was a steadfast opponent of
communism, while Barth, to the indignation of political thinkers like
Reinhold Niebuhr, was strangely complaisant toward it. Brunner
was a world traveller who lectured in many countries of Europe,
besides America, Korea, India and Pakistan, and spent two missionary years in Japan, while Barth remained for the most part in
his study. As one might expect from this record, Brunner communi-
cates better. Though often obscure underneath, he commands a
style that is crisp and easy, while Barth writes in the tradition of
Teutonic philosophy, with (to fall into its style) ponderous and
crepuscular prolixity. In the thirties there was a brief flare-up
between the two when Brunner published a pamphlet on *Nature
and Grace*, in which he argued that man's knowing faculties had not
been so completely corrupted by the fall as to prevent their gaining
some slight glimpse of the nature of Deity; to which Barth replied
in a thunderous essay entitled *Nein!*, virtually excommunicating his
colleague for so gross a compromise with Catholicism and rationalism. To the layman the difference as compared to the common
ground seemed miniscule.

In this chapter on Brunner and the one that follows on Barth,
most of what is said, either in exposition or in criticism, will apply to
either man. But the emphasis will be different, corresponding to their
major interests, Brunner's in ethics, Barth's in the kind of knowledge
that is possible of Deity.

Ethics, for Brunner, is inseparable from theology. This position
is not unknown to textbooks on ethics; it was held, for example, by
William Paley, who defined rightness of conduct as conformity with
the will of God. But Paley thought that the will of God could be
ascertained by reason, either from nature or through a rational
interpretation of Scripture. Brunner's ethics is more deeply embedded in theology. He holds that the natural man can neither
know good nor do it, that genuine goodness can be achieved only
through a descent of divine grace. This plainly calls for exploration.
We shall understand Brunner's meaning better if we dwell for a
little on his ideas of (1) the natural man, (2) faith, (3) the sort of
guidance provided by faith, and (4) the relation between revealed
and natural knowledge.

BRUNNER ON HUMAN NATURE

3(1) For Brunner human nature, like much else in the world, is a paradox. His view of it comes not from philosophy or psychology or anthropology but the epistles of St Paul. Man is a double creature, *in* the world but not *of* it. A great deal can be learned about him from the sciences; he has a body that obeys the laws of physics as fully as a boulder does, a digestive system that has been explored and explained by chemistry, ways of growing, ageing, and dying that are common to him with other biological organisms, ways of thinking and acting that are being illuminated in depth by psychology. To the scientist he is one kind of object among others, highly complex, to be sure, and not yet wholly understood, but quite obviously a product of nature, evolved from it, continuous with it, and part of it.

This, Brunner holds, is half the story, but not the whole. For besides being an object, man is a subject—a subject that is not itself a part of nature and is beyond scientific grasp or understanding. He is a self, a free agent, who can look before and after, accept responsibility for his decisions, and feel guilt about them. Such a self is not an object or thing among other things, nor are its decisions predictable by the fullest knowledge of psychology. So far the theory is not unique, for other thinkers—Kant, for example—have held similar views of the self. But Brunner is notable for his insistence that it can be understood only through a Pauline type of theology. We must 'start from the centre, from the revelation of God in Jesus Christ, and ask ourselves in what light man is there revealed. Then we may go on to the various anthropological utterances of the Old and New Testaments, interpreting them in the light of this central knowledge. . . .'[2] This 'central knowledge' is gained only through revelation, a revelation that was made first in Christ but may be renewed through grace in chosen individual souls. Only by means of this revelation, and never by scientific or other inquiry, do we know what we really are, namely immortal spirits made by God and responsible to him; 'it is one and the same thing to know of the holy, loving God, and of this human nature of mine as it is moulded by its Creator.'[3]

Now this spiritual part of us has itself two parts. We are informed in Scripture that God created us in his own image. But it would be impious to say that sinful man with all his imperfections on his head is the image or replica of God. There must, then, be two sides to the image, one of which reflects its Creator, and the other not; these two Brunner describes as the formal and the material image. The formal image, which retains traces of the nature of its maker, is very much of an abstraction; it is our *capacity* for thought, speech, and responsible decision. 'This formal structure of man's being . . . is identical with his humanity . . . and only disappears where humanity itself disappears, at the frontiers of idiocy or insanity.'⁴ Being the point where human nature is likest God's, it supplies a 'point of contact' which makes it possible for the maker to communicate with us. If man were like the beasts of the field, there would be nothing in his nature that could respond to the demands for obedience from above.

The material image, as distinct from the formal, is the concrete self that we have built up through the use of our freedom. This image would reflect its Creator only if man had used his freedom as he was meant to use it, and this use is really made only when one can say with the apostle, 'not I, but Christ who liveth in me'. The Christian is the man who can use 'I' with this transmuted meaning. And the new material self, according to Brunner, is the true fulfilment of the formal self. It was over this point that the stormy controversy of the thirties developed between Brunner and Barth. Barth refused to recognise the formal-material distinction. He held that man is in no sense or degree an image of God, who is wholly other; by his sin, man lost all remnants of the image in which he was created. If God now chooses to grant his grace, he needs no 'point of contact' through which to work his will on us, and the new man he creates is not a fulfilment of the old but a new, divinely created, discontinuous replacement of the old. This question whether it is a replacement or a fulfilment we shall leave to the theologians. What is more important for our purpose is that Barth and Brunner are in agreement on the concrete condition of man, which determines his status in God's eyes. He is utterly sinful—corrupted, alienated and lost; there is no health in him.

4   How has this unhappy state of things come about? Barth and Brunner attribute it to the fall of man, an event not known to us through history but revealed to us in Scripture. Neither theologian is a fundamentalist in the sense of accepting the story of Genesis as literally true; like Luther, they rely chiefly on St Paul. And the revelation that comes through St Paul tells us that man was not always so corrupt, that at the time of his creation he was a being of perfect purity, without a trace of evil impulse or desire. Nevertheless, when tempted, he chose evil rather than good. That a person wholly pure should thus choose evil is admitted to be a paradox, but then man's state, as presented to us in revelation, swarms with paradoxes, and to boggle at them shows that one is putting reason above revealed truth. Man's first sin alienated him from God, and since

'his relation to God is identical with his essence,'[5] the infection spread through all his thoughts, feelings, and acts. And not only this; all his progeny became infected also; 'hostility to God now forms part of the very nature of man'.[6] Why one man should be regarded as sinful because some other man has sinned is admitted to be a further mystery. How a God who would condemn one man for the sins of another could also be a God of pure love is again a mystery. But the mind that has got past the initial difficulty of accepting one paradox will find little added difficulty in accepting many.

The depth of corruption of the natural man can hardly be over-stated. His wickedness shows itself not merely in the occasional flights of vice which we can all see to be sure, for 'sin is not a dark spot somewhere but is the total character of our personal existence, the character of all our personal acts'.[7] Even when man wills what he takes to be good, he is always deluded, for no end of the natural man is really good, and in seeking such deceitful ends his will is always evil. If he takes moral satisfaction in attaining them, that is apparently the worst sin of all. Brunner speaks of '*the sin par excellence,* the desire of man to live his own life in his own way, apart from God'.[8] This attempt on men's part to be something of themselves is the blight of non-religious morality. In their struggle with evil, they fail to recognise 'the main factor, the human will, as it is: sin-bound and egoistic. They are blind to the real enemy who must be fought. Nay, this failure to recognize the enemy *is* the real enemy, the fontal source of evil in the world: from it flow self-reliance, self-confidence, the illusion of freedom and good-will upon which all idealism is based—the inability to realize the helpless condition of man.'[9] If this condition of deep depravity is not clear to us, that is because the depravity has destroyed our power to see ourselves as we are. With the eye of faith we could recover this sight, and what we should see would appal us. Most of us think, for example, that if we have not committed adultery we have obeyed at least the seventh commandment. The person who sees with the eye of faith, however, sees that this is not so; 'he knows, since he understands this commandment in a radical way, that he is an adulterer, and that in his honourable civil state of marriage he stands before God as a sinner who can only exist because of the forgiveness of God'.[10] The practice of religion itself by the man to whom grace has not yet been dispensed is sinful: 'Even in your religion, in so far as it is your experience, you do not cease to be sinner and liar.'[11]

5   It might be thought that if man is doomed to sin by the very nature he was born with, he could not be blamed for it as his

ancestors were who elected it freely. This appears to be a humanitarian illusion. Man 'remains a responsible person, in spite of the
fact that through sin the true personality, the state of freedom in
dependence, has been destroyed, so that his freedom has become
alienation and his connexion bondage.'[12] He cannot help his
wickedness, but he is none the less responsible, guilty, and condemned because of it. This is another paradox or contradiction.
But it is revealed to us by one who we are assured is a God of love
and we must therefore accept it.

'With all his striving man will never attain. This is the tragedy of
the ethics of self-righteousness.'[13] All men are sunk in the same
slough, and for anyone to try to make himself better than others is,
if possible, to make himself worse; Brunner speaks of 'the worst
enemy of true community, the Pharisaism of "wishing to be
better". . . .'[14] He admits, indeed, that the divine command requires
that we should do as well as we can the duties of our station, and
from this point of view 'the relative distinctions between "better"
and "worse" become extremely important'. But it is hard to see
why this should be so, since from the truer point of view of faith 'the
difference between "above" and "below" loses all significance'.[15]
Nor is there any hope for mankind through evolution or moral progress. There is really no such thing, whether this means the self-
improvement of the individual or that of the race. Religious persons
have sometimes claimed, it is true, to find in the Bible the record of
such an advance among the Hebrews, fostered by prophets who were
'religious geniuses'. This Brunner regards as a dangerous distortion
of Scripture; 'there is no question of development or evolution'; it
is rather a matter of 'ingression, a breaking into the world of something beyond, something foreign and transcendent. It is not a
continuous growth on the horizontal plane of history but a vertical
disruption of the historical process by forces interposed from beneath
or above. . . .'[16] And just as man, by his own efforts, has achieved no
genuine moral progress in the past, so he can hope to achieve none
in the future, and it is idle to try; one will end by falling into the
'hopeless resignation of the reformer'.[17] Brunner would presumably
say with Yeats that saints and drunkards are never Whigs. Many
interpreters have thought of the gospel as a programme for gradually
introducing the Kingdom of God by the purification of man's
ideals and the deepening of his loyalty to them. This, says Brunner,
is a perversion of New Testament teaching; 'the teaching of the
gospel and the theory of progress are irreconcilable opposites'.[18]
'The New Testament does not expect that things on earth are changing more and more for the good. The opposite is true; the last times
shall be the most terrible. . . . No such evolution is hoped for;

indeed, the directly opposite prospect is held out, namely, that the
forces of evil must increase until the last day . . . neither sin nor
death can be overcome step by step. . . . It is this conception of
totality that makes it impossible for the writers of the New Testament
and for anyone who sees this totality to believe in evolution.'[19]

6   Once we have seen the futility of the effort to make ourselves
better, our natural state, as Kierkegaard held, is despair. The more
earnest and anxious we are about moral matters, the deeper and
more inevitable this despair becomes. We try to walk outwardly in
accord with all the commandments; it is of no avail; outward
observance will not remove the rottenness at the core. 'Hence all
this kind of morality, whether it takes a secular or religious form,
carries with it a bad conscience, as a sign of its deceitful character.'[20]
So we attempt through meditation and religious exercises to purify
our inward thought, feeling, and will. Still to no avail. However far
we go, conscience dogs us with its accusing finger. Conscience for
Brunner is not a protest against this or that yielding to temptation;
it is 'something far more sinister', the voice of our whole lost, restless,
unhappy nature, welling up 'like the inarticulate groaning of a
prisoner in his dungeon'.[21] It is not to be quieted, therefore, by
occasional convulsive efforts at amendment. Nor can it give us any
reliable guidance. It prompts us to go on groping, 'but it so distorts
the way back to God that the soul can see nothing clearly'.[22] Thus
we are without hope altogether. There is no therapeutic within the
range of man's fallen faculties that can purge his cancerous corruption. All the roads he can take converge upon defeat. The road of
obedience to the moral law, the road of inward purification, the
road of more conscientious refinement and intensified devotion all
lead to despair. Nor is it the despair of mere discouragement or
depression. It is the rayless, black despair of the man who stands
guilty and condemned before a judge of infinite power, without a
word he can say in his defence and unable to lift a finger to avert
his doom.

BRUNNER ON FAITH

7(2)   Here enters the second main element in Brunner's teaching,
his doctrine of faith. Faith is our way of escape. So far as we ourselves are concerned, there is no way. But though there is no road
from man to God, there is a road from God to man, and God has
seen fit to make man's extremity his own opportunity. A release that
could never be won or merited is made available by direct dispensation from on high. 'Man assumes that he can help himself by means

of his philosophy or his religion. The Gospel is the end of these efforts.'[23] 'The new birth' is not a growth nor is it an acquisition of one fresh power after another, but a sudden and total release of the soul as a whole from darkness into light, effected by a deliverer from outside. If a man bears in mind that 'autonomy is equivalent to sin',[24] that 'faith is through and through heteronomous',[25] and that 'He who relies on himself is a dreamer of dreams',[26] he will be more ready for that complete surrender which must precede being born anew. Such a man 'looks to God for all his help'.

The transmutation that takes place at this new birth is indescribable to anyone who has not undergone it. It is not in the ordinary sense an experience. It is the creation of a new self which appears in the midst of the old one, and its arrival is so discontinuous with all that precedes it that it is both unpredictable before it comes and inexplicable afterward. It is 'the Ego's independence of all its inner conditions'. 'In faith man becomes certain that he has his self not in himself, but in God's Word. That is the reason why faith cannot be understood psychologically: it is the speaking of the Holy Spirit in the *psyche* (the soul), therefore it is not itself psychic.'[27] Though Brunner does not profess to convey what the new self is or sees, he is emphatic about this discontinuity with what goes on in the natural man.

'Faith is neither a psychological function nor a combination of such functions; it is the life-utterance of the total self in its unanalysable unity.'[28]

This transformation of man at the centre, indescribable as it is, suffuses or irradiates his entire nature; Brunner uses the striking figure of a wheel with many spokes but with a hollow at the centre of its hub. All man's thoughts, feelings, and actions acquire a new quality. His belief has a new certainty, which is not arrived at through evidence; 'In the act of believing you *do* nothing, you merely *get* something.'[29] His old feeling for mankind is supplanted by a new love. This again is quite different from the merely natural love of David for Jonathan or Darby for Joan: 'Love in the sense in which the New Testament uses the word, is not a human possibility at all, but it is exclusively possible to God,'[30] who in some sense takes possession of us at the rebirth and manifests this love through us. Similarly our moral will is radically though inexplicably transformed.

'The "Good" which issues from effort is, for that very reason, not really good; the Good must descend from above, not be striven for from below, otherwise it lacks genuineness and depth.'[31] 'For before the Good can be done the agent must be good. But the only Doer of good deeds is God. Man, therefore, can only do good deeds in so far as God does them in him. . . .'[32]

8   This insistence that in the new birth God is the agent and man a relatively passive vessel raises an obvious question. If the initiative must come so completely from the divine side, what can man do to secure the boon? It is his one hope: he must secure it if he can; is there nothing he can do himself to bring it about? We have seen that the answer is No. To be sure, 'Good will is identical with the surrender of self-will,' but this, it is instantly added, is 'an act of which we are not capable, but which is done by God for us and in us, and which we accept in faith as having been done'.[33] 'Without any complementary human effort man receives, purely as a gift, that justification which he seeks in vain to attain for himself.'[34] This seems decisive. But the contrary answer is also given. Man *can* do something to secure his release. Brunner writes that 'what is got or begotten is the decision of the will of man for God, the one and only act in which man is really free and which is wholly his own.'[35] 'In this act of God which is unthinkable without a *responsive* act of man, that is, in this *responsibility*, man has his being.' 'Faith does not consist simply in passive acceptance; it always means, at the same time, an act of "pulling oneself together". . . .'[36] The conclusion would seem to be that in this encounter man is wholly a recipient though he is also an agent, that he is completely determined yet also free, that he cannot surrender his own will, though he is intensely guilty if he does not, that the gift of grace is unconditional but that it is also conditioned on our readiness to receive it. How does Brunner remove this paradox, or nest of paradoxes? The answer is that he does not attempt to remove it. That it is there he freely recognises. But 'To attempt to resolve it into something which we could conceive with our minds would mean turning the personal into the impersonal.' 'We have no right to attempt to remove this final paradox.'[37]

BRUNNER ON THE GOOD LIFE

9(3)   Assuming now that faith has been granted, what way of life does it prescribe? How do one's duties after the new birth differ from what they were before?

Outwardly they may remain largely the same. We are all members, for example, of many 'natural orders'; members of a particular sex, citizens of a particular community, parents or children, grocers, farmers, or teachers. We do not cease to be

members of these orders when our inward life is transformed; and it
will be part of our new 'calling' to go on with such duties of our
station as are appointed by our work, our age, our means, and our
powers. Divine law prescribes these duties for regenerate and unregenerate alike. But on the inward side, duty is an entirely different
thing in the two cases. Acts that are outwardly the same, when done
by the regenerate, spring from a new source; the inward man has
been made over. Indeed in a sense it is not he who is willing and
acting at all; 'the miracle of faith happens *only* where Jesus Christ
is no more object of my knowledge, but He Himself has become
subject within me.'[38] And within this new subject the spring of
action is love. 'The ethical impulse is now no longer that of self-
respect, but of love.'[39] Love is 'the way of life of those who have
been born again. . . .'[40] It is henceforth love that appoints all one
does.

'It is love which does not steal, does not kill, does not lie, does
not commit adultery, but does its best for its neighbour.'[41] 'Love
is not only the fulfilment of the law, but also its end, and thus the
end of all ethics.'[42]

Once this love is achieved, or rather is vouchsafed, some most
important consequences follow. Most of the struggle and all the
self-reproach that belonged to the regime of duty are now done
away. Obedience given from love is unconstrained. If his faith is
complete, the new man finds himself equal to all occasions. 'God is
—as it were—always behind him, not in front of him as the legalist
believes. This it is which constitutes the joy and the peace of the
new state of life.'[43] Again, the man of faith is free. He has been bound
by a sense of obligation, bound by his own selfishness, bound by
natural law. Now he breaks through them all. 'To be free means to
be that for which God created us,'[44] namely for complete absorption
into his own purpose and use as instruments of his will. Once more,
since we are acting freely, what we shall do cannot be anticipated.
This does not mean merely that psychological law is repeatedly and
miraculously suspended, though as a matter of fact that is true. It
means also that the agent is no longer acting under the direction of
rule or law. 'Love is "occasionalist" ';[45] 'the will of God cannot be
summed up under any principle. . . .'[46] Man's 'obedience is rendered
not to a law or a principle which can be known beforehand, but only
to the free, sovereign will of God. The Good consists in always doing
what God wills at any particular moment.'[47]

But how are we to know what God wills? John Stuart Mill, in a
well known passage, says that the Christian need not object to
utilitarianism, since if God exists we may be sure that he wills the

happiness of his creatures, and this is precisely what the utilitarian wills. Brunner undercuts this argument. Mill was assuming that what was self-evidently good to us must be likewise so to God, and this Brunner denies. We cannot argue to what God wills from anything that we value as natural men. '. . . God's standards are very different from ours.'[48] 'The ways of God are quite different from the ways which we can construct by means of our own moral reason.'[49] 'There are no Ends, Ideas, Goods, Values, no abstract entities, neither Culture, nor the State, nor "sphere of Spirit" to which the human personal life can be subordinated.'[50] 'Hence there are no "intrinsic values".'[51] In the view of many religious moralists, Thomas Aquinas for example, acts are not right because God wills them; He wills them because, like ourselves, he sees that they are right objectively. Brunner apparently rejects this view. 'The Good is simply what *God* wills that we should do, not that which we would do on the basis of a principle of love.'[52] 'There is no Good save to obey God, and there is no evil save in disobedience to God. The End, "to serve God," makes everything holy, and the lack of this End makes everything unholy.'[53] 'Only religious ethics is really ethical,'[54] and the duties of the religious man all resolve themselves into one: 'There is nothing in the whole wide world which we are bound to do save this: to glorify God, and this means: to believe.'[55]

Does this still seem too exalted and general an answer to the question how one goes about it in a specific case, to discover what to do? Let us press Brunner a little further. He insists that '"duties" as such do not exist,' and that law, civil, moral, or customary, 'never tells me what the will of God is'. To which it is natural to reply: But we do seem at times to have obligations that conflict, and if there is no sort of rule to give us guidance, just how does the new man go about it to resolve such conflicts? He answers: 'In a situation of this kind I must proceed as follows: with the help of my "schedule of duties" and in the light of the various claims which clamour for my attention and constantly overlap—all of them apparently justifiable and necessary—in the spirit of faith (and this means, too, in view of the actual situation) I must listen to the Divine Command in order that I may be able to do what I am really bidden to do, that is, my real duty. Then, however, I shall find that *one* thing and *one only* is really commanded, is really my duty, and that the "conflict of duties" is only apparent, and does not really exist at all.'[56]

Practically minded readers are likely to grow impatient here. They ask Brunner how to find what they ought to do, and he answers that if they put their reliance on an unpredictable, non-rational, and unearthly guidance, they will be told what to do. Still, this is not quite fair to him. What they are asking of him is some principle by which competing claims can be adjudicated and competing values appraised. But this assumes that there is such a principle, and he has expressly said that there is not. He is not saying, of course, that claims and values are to be ignored. They are a part, and an indispensable part, of the data for the decision. Indeed, he would insist that it is only in a Christian ethics that all the relevant data ever do come into the picture, for here alone we take account, not merely of the claim of the claimant, but of the whole concrete man. The data for an ethics of principle consist of abstractions. The data for an ethics of love consist of persons. The only possible rule, therefore, is to contemplate the persons affected by any proposed act and then do what love, divinely granted, prompts one to do. What it prompts may seem irrational and queer; that cannot be helped. We may do it, nevertheless, in the confidence that it is right. For in acting from love we have done the will of God, and doing the will of God is what right means.

'God takes over all responsibility for our action . . . if we, on our part, will only do here and now that which the present situation demands from one who loves God and his neighbour.'[57]

BRUNNER ON REVELATION AND REASON

10(4) It will now be evident why Brunner calls his ethics 'theological' (the subtitle of *The Divine Imperative* in German is *Entwurf einer protestantisch-theologischen Ethik*). All the main points we have considered—that natural man is fallen and corrupt, that faith is a transformation divinely effected, that such faith, acting through love, appoints man's duties—these are all theological assertions. And the question that many persons will now want to put to Brunner is, How do you make these assertions out? You say that everything depends on them, but, so far, you have assumed that minds in the right state will accept them without question. How are you going to validate them to those who have not attained the right state and find them hard to believe? Assertions put forward as true usually admit of rational support. What support of this kind can you offer?

To this Brunner would reply: You are speaking like a rationalist, and to be a rationalist in these matters is to beg the question. You are assuming that if we are to know we must know rationally. And that is false. Not only is there knowledge other than that of reason, but this other knowledge is far better than anything reason can give us. The truths of which we have been speaking are examples of this other and higher knowledge. To offer a rational defence for them would betray a fundamental confusion.

We must try to see how these types of knowledge differ. Rational knowledge is achieved by an activity of our own minds. Whether we are interpreting sense-impressions, grasping the self-evident, or following the track of inference, to know rationally is to think. But to know what is revealed is not to think. Revelation is given; it is as truly presented to us from the outside, as unconnected with any grounds that may have been in our minds before, as truly un-summoned by any premises, as the sensations that are forced upon us by the outer world. Further, just as the two kinds of knowledge differ in their mode of attainment, so do they differ in the character of what is known. Rational knowledge is always of the impersonal. This is obviously true of science. Brunner thinks it also true of history and even of our knowledge of each other. I may hear sounds which I call the sounds of your voice and see motions which I say are the movements of your body, but these sense-data of mine are not *you*. Do such poor tags and oddments represent my closest approach to another self? Yes, if it must depend on merely rational knowledge. Fortunately, says Brunner, we do not have to depend on that alone. A second sight is open to us, by which we can look right across the 'salt estranging sea' of this isolationist rationalism. This comes to us first as a knowledge of God. When God reveals himself to us, it is not as a system of propositions, but as an I to a Thou. He 'imparts Himself to me', he says 'I am the Truth and the Life'; and 'This truth,' says Brunner, 'is personal encounter'.[58] The critic may protest that this identifies the new knowledge with the new life generally, and makes knowledge indistinguishable from a variety of other things, such as (a) faith, (b) the descent of the divine into one's own mind, (c) the act of personal decision and surrender, and (d) the awakening of the new love. So far as I can see, Brunner would calmly accept this general merger. Regeneration is a total affair. The new vision a man acquires is so blended with the new faith, love, and moral will that the lines between them are lost. His faith in God is his love for him and his acceptance of him, and in these very things lies the knowledge of him also.

REVELATION AND REASON IN CONFLICT

11   How are the two kinds of knowledge related? Brunner's answer in brief is this: Each has its own sphere, and so long as it keeps in that sphere, it is consistent with the other and supplements it. Un-fortunately each has sought to invade the sphere of the other. When they have done so, we have had theology ignorantly obstructing science, or, more commonly, science and philosophy smashing what they ignorantly take to be idols. These points must be drawn out a little.

As to the separateness of the two spheres, Brunner is most emphatic. 'Revealed knowledge is poles apart from rational knowledge. These two forms of knowledge are as far from each other as heaven is from earth.'⁵⁹ The province of rational knowledge is the world. Most philosophers and scientists would accept this, and add, 'After all, what else is there to know?' To which Brunner would answer, God remains. God is other than the world and transcends it; and it is the nature and relations of God that form the province of revealed knowledge. 'The Living God is not known through thought, nor through conclusions drawn from the structure of the universe, nor through profound meditation on the nature of Spirit; He is known through revelation alone.'⁶⁰ If those who pursue the two kinds of knowledge—and that should include us all—would only keep them firmly in their appointed spheres, there would be no trouble; 'good fences make good neighbours'. But what we have actually had, century after century, is an endless, needless clamour and din of conflict between religion and science. How has this come about?

It has come about because of confusion on the one side and arrogance on the other. The confusion is on the side of theology. The faith that was taught in the New Testament Brunner believes to be precisely the faith he is expounding; it has nothing to do with intellectual belief; it is non-rational trust, love, and obedience given to a divine person, and made possible by a divine unsealing of one's eyes. Early in Christian history this view became confounded with another. Partly through the influence of the Greeks, with their sharp stress on the intellect, partly through the insistence of the Catholic church on the acceptance of a creed, faith came to mean belief in doctrine. This, says Brunner, is 'the greatest tragedy in Church history'.⁶¹ It started Christendom down a path of division and confusion two thousand years long, a path from which even the clear call of Luther could not bring it back into the highway. It has made of revelation, not a personal encounter renewable indefinitely, but the proffering from on high of a body of abstract, infallible doctrine to which men must subscribe, no matter what the evidence.

So for centuries feckless theologians have been rushing in where scientists themselves hardly dared to tread. They have launched irresponsible invasions of scientific ground, and tried to lay down the law to the laboratory and the observatory. Of course the result was ignominious rout. When they proclaimed that the earth was the physical centre of things, they were proved wrong by Copernicus and Galileo. When they insisted, through Vice-Chancellor Lightfoot of Cambridge, that the world was created on Friday 23 October 4004 BC at 9 a.m., science had only to point to certain stars from which the light must have started before the universe, on this theory, had begun to be. Having denounced evolution, they were shortly presented with cratefulls of half-human fossils hundreds of thousands of years old, and pterodactyls and archaeopteryxes a hundred million years old. Then, having retired in disorder along the whole scientific front, they had to retreat again from their inner lines of historical and Biblical criticism. They are now everywhere on the defensive, so that one could almost apply to them generally the ironic description of fundamentalists as 'besieged Christians trying to dictate the terms of surrender to science'.

All this, says Brunner, was needless. It all sprang from the original blunder of thinking that revelation had something to do with intellectual belief. That made conflict with science inevitable. In virtue of the line they have taken, theologians only show themselves disingenuous when they try to deny this conflict. 'It is both ridiculous and disgraceful,' Brunner writes, 'when the theological apologetic which for two hundred years fought against Copernicus, Galileo, Kepler, and Newton, in the name of the Bible, now that the matter has been decided against it, maintains that there is no conflict at all. There is no doubt that there is one. . . .'[62] In this conflict he himself, theological conservative as he supposedly is, stands firmly with science. He is ready, for example, to reject the Virgin birth and to support 'the higher criticism' in its exposure of myth, inaccuracy, and contradiction in the texts of both Old and New Testaments. He would say that theologians who try to extract science from revelation deserve what they generally get.

Still, it is not theology, Brunner thinks, that has been chiefly at fault in this dreary conflict, nor the sort of natural science that knows its bounds. The real villain of the tragi-comedy is a temper of mind that has unhappily come to dominate both science and philosophy, the spirit of rationalism. This is the sort of temper in which Benjamin Jowett, according to undergraduate doggerel, allowed that he was the Master of Balliol College and that what he knew not was not knowledge. It is a rationality whose success has gone to its head and now appears as intellectualism. It thinks that because methods of rational explanation have been applied with such effect to the natural world, they supply the means and the standard for knowing the supernatural also. Now the attempt to know the transcendent with methods suitable only to nature is bound to fail. 'Reason is not given us to know God, but to know the world.'[63] '*The* theological problem as well as *the* Church problem is this—to deliver modern man and the modernized Church and theology from the illegitimate self-sufficiency of reason and the spirit of autonomy.'[64] In revelation 'God gives the world something absolutely new and at the same time

final from outside of all that is historical, ideal, and human; something therefore which cannot be verified, pronounced upon, or
pigeon-holed, but only believed. . . .'[65] Not only is the attempt to
possess the supernatural by reason a mistake; it is sin, and apparently
the fundamental sin. 'This autonomy of man, this attempt of the
Ego to understand itself out of itself, is the lie concerning man which
we call sin.' 'Autonomy is equivalent to sin.'[66]

THE FAILURE OF REASON

12 Why is it that reason fares so badly in its attempt to understand what is revealed? Is it merely because the supernatural,
though fully rational, cannot be mapped with the feeble powers we
now bring to the undertaking? This, as we have seen, is the line
taken by Catholic apologists. True faith and morals, they say, have
nothing to fear from reason, for they are completely in accord with
it, and if reason seems at times to be at odds with them, that is only
because it has become confused as to what its own standards demand.
To the rationalist this defence is exasperating. He points out in
alleged revelation what appear to be flat contradictions, and is
smilingly told that the church believes in reason as much as he does,
that since these things are revealed they must be true and reasonable,
whether they seem to be or not, and that if he cannot see this, what
that shows is not that the church belittles reason but that he does not
know what reason is. This theory does at least lip service to reason.
It never explains the failure of thought to penetrate to the mysteries
by saying that in these mysteries there is something hopelessly and
forever irrational. Faith is wholly rational in the end. Man is but
imperfectly rational. The difference, however great, remains one of
degree. Is this also what Brunner holds?

Clearly not. With him the conflict is irreconcilable; the chasm is
beyond bridging by any extension of reason. To be sure, he sometimes denies this, or seems to, and many of his followers are eager
to deny it for him. 'The truth of revelation,' he writes, 'is not in
opposition to any truth of reason, nor to any fact that has been
discovered by the use of reason. Genuine truths of faith are never in
conflict with logic or with the sciences; they conflict only with the
rationalistic or positivistic metaphysics, that is, with a reason that
arrogates to itself the right to define the whole range of truth from the
standpoint of *man*.'[67] But this last clause is vague. What is this that
distinguishes the arrogance that must be rejected from the responsible use of reason that is approved? If 'to define the whole
range of truth from the standpoint of man' means to claim that we
can achieve all truth with our present powers, we may agree that this

is an arrogance which is properly rebuffed. But is reason also to be rejected if it insists on adhering, wherever it goes, to its own standard? If we begin with the facts of experience, interpret these as logic requires, and reject what is incoherent with the system of thought thus formed, is that also to be put down as arrogance?

This is the ultimate issue, and when he is brought face to face with it, Brunner does not mince his words. Reason is utterly without right to appeal to its own standards in dealing with the supernatural; these standards do not apply there; what is false and self-contradictory to reason may nevertheless be true for faith. 'Of the truth of God it must ever be said, since it is God's truth, that it is foolishness unto human reason. . . .'[68] 'God, therefore, can reveal himself only as One who is in contradiction to the present world and breaks through its immanent order or law,'[69] and what we gain when he thus breaks through is 'the one paradoxical non-rational message of the living God. . . .'[70] 'Paradox is the essence of the Gospel';[71] 'Biblical and natural theology will never agree; they are bitterly and fundamentally opposed.'[72] Indeed Biblical theology does not wholly agree with itself, 'For at some points the variety of the Apostolic doctrine, regarded purely from the theological and intellectual point of view, is an irreconcilable contradiction.'[73] We must believe it, notwithstanding, since the intellectual point of view is not to be carried into these regions, and 'doubt is a form of sin'.[74] In laying hold of the truths of faith, the philosophers who believe in reason and follow it are no better off than the sceptics: 'From the Christian point of view Freud, or, if you like, Hume, has just as much relative justification as Plato or Aristotle.'[75] All this applies equally to Christian ethics. In speaking of secular ethics Brunner says that 'the universal validity and universal intelligibility or rationality of its principle . . . must be absolutely rejected by the Christian ethic.'[76] 'The rationalism of the philosophical ethic can never be combined with the recognition of a divine self-revelation.'[77] Such statements, which could be many times multiplied from Brunner's writings, make it clear that what he objects to is not the tendency of philosophers to dash out on occasional sorties beyond what the evidence warrants, but the attempt of reason as such to apply standards of coherence and intelligibility to the content of revelation. Here Barth is more uncompromising still.

REASON AS UNAVOIDABLE

13 We have concerned ourselves primarily with Brunner's ethics. But we have also had to consider his view of the relation of reason and revelation because his ethics depends upon it and one must take account of it in any appraisal of the ethics. Yet how is any rational estimate to be made of it? We seem to be faced with a simple dilemma. Either we have been granted the revelation that is central in Brunner's thought or we have not. If we have, no argument is necessary, for we possess the truth already. If we have not, no argument is possible, for we cannot understand what is being said to us, let alone pass judgement upon it. The neo-orthodox theologian appears to have ensconced himself upon his summit beyond the range of any artillery that the rationalist may bring to bear on him. He has seen—simply, securely, and finally—that he has the truth about God in his relation to man, and any argument against him will only beg the question. For it will assume the validity of the rationalist logic, and that validity he denies.

Now some of us must admit that we have never had the overpowering visitation that for Brunner brings the solution to all these problems. If the gift he has received is the pearl of great price that he says it is, we all need it desperately, and it would be foolish as well as wicked to turn our backs on it. What are we to do? He insists that we cannot gain it by any efforts of our own, for it is vouchsafed only through the inscrutable operations of grace. The conclusion would seem to be that each of us should go his own road, with a hope akin to despair that a Deity whose ways are not our ways should note us and take pity on us. Reason and desire may protest over their helplessness, but in ultimate matters they have no standing.

I own that I am not content. It is probably the moral rather than the intellectual complexion of Brunner's world that most gives me pause. Many philosophers have held that nature is neutral to our values; many have held that these values are transcended but not wholly lost in an Absolute. But the view that the ruler of the universe holds before our eyes a pearl of incomparable price, tells us that we shall be condemned everlastingly if we do not secure it, and adds that there is nothing we can do to secure it, that he grants or withholds it for no discoverable reasons, that he chooses to give it to the few and withhold it from the many, and yet that all are bound to acclaim his justice and goodness as perfect—this view is so repellent in its conception of Deity and so melancholy as to the hopes of mankind that one can accept it only if one has to. *Does* one have to?

14 I do not think so. I do not think that even the neat logical dilemma in which the position was stated a moment ago will stand inspection. We are told that if we are in receipt of revelation no criticism of it will be needful, and that if we are not, none is possible. We deny the second horn. Criticism *is* possible. It is possible because the reason which Brunner tries to exclude from the province of revelation is there in spite of him, and where reason is being employed, its standards are being admitted as relevant, willy nilly. We have found this half-conscious intrusion of reason already in Luther and Kierkegaard; it is beginning to appear inevitable, and we shall see it again in Barth. Brunner of course denies that the kind of beatific vision granted to the man of faith is expressible in conceptual terms or bound by logical rules. Does he therefore refrain from discussing it in these terms or employing this logic in doing so?

Look at any of his books for the answer. All of them have this vision at their centre. He says in his striking simile that life is like a wheel whose spokes all radiate from a certain centre, but that where the hub should be there is for the natural man a blank and a mystery. But on his own showing, the hub is neither a blank nor altogether a mystery. It is filled with manifold attributes—love, mercy, justice, truth, forgiveness, repentance, happiness, submission, aspiration, and many more. Sometimes, to be sure, in accordance with his doctrine that the divine nature is unintelligible, he tells us that these attributes are indistinguishable from each other, that in God love, justice, and truth are all the same. But he does not adhere to this. If any inferences are made as to God's love, justice, or truth, those terms must bear distinguishable meanings, and those meanings must be within measurable distance from their standard meanings. We do not find Brunner arguing that it is the special characteristic of God's love to send men to eternal perdition, or of his forgiveness to make two and two equal four. In explaining revealed truth as it presented itself to Paul, or as it appears obscurely in the Old Testament, or more explicitly in the Sermon on the Mount, Brunner brings to bear his rich endowment for discrimination, generalisation, analysis, and inference. If these powers are being legitimately applied, if the concepts and connections he points to are there to be pointed out, then the web of relations that Brunner disclaims as irrelevant to revealed truth must be present in it after all.

Furthermore, how can one maintain consistently that the laws of logic are valid in chemistry or biology and invalid in the central area of human life? The laws of identity and contradiction, of excluded middle and sufficient reason, the law of causality, the principles of probability and inductive reasoning, are not put forward as sometimes valid and sometimes not, as holding in physics but not in anthropology; they are accepted as holding alike in all fields or in none. If an event were known to have no cause at all, or to vary regularly with some other event without any causal connection between them, the discovery would not be an oddity merely but the violation of a principle of reasoning accepted as valid irrespective of the field of its application. If such a principle is found invalid anywhere, doubt is inevitably aroused about its validity everywhere.

THEOLOGY VS PSYCHOLOGY

15 Brunner was disturbed by such criticism. He disliked being regarded as an enemy of reason, and sometimes when science seemed to conflict with theology, as in the case of the Virgin birth, he was found on the scientific side. How was he to reconcile the validity of natural reason in one province with its invalidity in another?

At times he made the difference a matter of degree. This is the meaning of his 'law of contiguity': 'inasmuch as an assertion of reason approaches the center it loses its validity, and the assertion of faith steps into its place.'[78] Or, put a little more fully:

'The nearer anything lies to that center of existence where we are concerned with the whole, that is, with man's relation to God and the being of the person, the greater is the disturbance of rational knowledge by sin; the farther away anything lies from this center, the less is the disturbance felt, and the less difference is there between knowing as a believer or as an unbeliever.'[79]

Physics and astronomy, being remote from the personal centre, are common ground for the man of science and the man of faith, but as the centre is approached, the methods of reason are less and less applicable, and the man of faith must take over. We can agree with Brunner that the methods of mechanistic science require supplementation as one moves up the ladder of being from matter to life and mind; new concepts must be added; purposive causation, for example, is as essential in human conduct as it is superfluous among sticks and stones. But this introduction of new concepts is not an abandonment of reason; it is a requirement of reason for the understanding of new types of behaviour. It is otherwise with the 'law of contiguity', which requires the abjuring of reason as one approaches the central fact.

16 Consider what the 'law' would imply for the science of psychology. Here we are dealing with the behaviour of persons. If a person is without religion, or has only a non-Christian religion, no incursions from the supernatural may be expected to interrupt the even tenor of his way, and his behaviour will be a fit subject for psychological study. But suppose he is a Christian in Brunner's sense. Then whenever his true self is engaged in thinking, feeling, or willing, his behaviour will be beyond the range of such study. For the psychologist, his behaviour will issue out of nothing; to inquire as to its cause or its motive, its moral character, or its consistency with his other decisions will be asking illegitimate questions. To be sure, there is much in the man's behaviour that will still be explicable psychologically; it seems unlikely that his choice of Quaker oats for breakfast or a brown tie to go with his brown suit calls for a transcendental explanation. But one may be mistaken even here. Thinkers in the Kierkegaardian tradition insist that in becoming a Christian the whole man is replaced by a new one, inaccessible to the secular mind, and hence that acts outwardly the same as before issue from an entirely different source.

I cannot accept this kind of transcendentalism. In criticising it, I wish to make clear, however, that I am not doing so from the point of view of a reductionist or behaviouristic psychology. It ill becomes anyone who rejects fundamentalism in religion to accept a fundamentalism in science which denies the most important fact in the world, namely consciousness, because it cannot fit this fact into its preconceived notions of scientific method. But the acceptance of consciousness is one thing; the acceptance in man of a core of impenetrable irrationality is another. For neo-orthodox theology, it is not only God who is a 'wholly other'; it is also man himself when he enters into the Christian status. His old self is replaced by a new one; this new one is no part of the natural and rational order in which he has been living, and it is impious to study it as if it were. Its descent into a human mind is inexplicable; its nature is inexplicable; it works through the natural man not by intelligible law but by recurrent miracle. We shall not try to work out in detail the plight in which this would leave the study of human nature, but the general difficulty is clear. If the new self takes over completely, any rational understanding of its behaviour is admitted to be impossible. If the replacement is partial, if habits already acquired can be explained, but fresh decisions spring from the new non-natural self, what part of my action in reading this morning's editorial in *The Times*, or in inviting John and Mary to come for the week-end, has an intelligible cause or reason, and what has not? Again the question seems unanswerable. Human nature becomes an immense twisted cable in which continuous strands of causation are joined with strands that terminate abruptly in miracle.

The neo-orthodox theologian may reply: 'You do not refute a doctrine by showing its inconvenience, however enormous.' True. But this is not a matter of inconvenience merely. It is a matter of conflict between what theology tells us and what science tells us. There are numerous sciences dealing with man. There is psychology, with its many subdivisions of psychoanalysis, psychiatry, group psychology, the psychology of religion, of motivation, of adolescence (which Starbuck showed so significant for religion); there is sociology, with such specialised departments as criminology and the sociology of religion; there is anthropology, with its studies of racial, cultural, and sex differences; and of course many more. The investigators in these fields have not carried on their inquiries under the assumption that some members of the race are a race apart, only partly human, and presenting an impenetrable wall to their research. They have never stumbled on this wall and are unaware of its existence. Yet they have produced illuminating results about men of different religions and men with none. Are these researchers into human nature now to be told that their studies, legitimate enough for the mass of mankind, are illegitimate for the Christian minority? Would they not reply with some justice that if an alleged wall has been invisible everywhere along the extended front of their researches, this raises a fair presumption that the wall is a myth?

THEOLOGY VS HISTORY

17 Consider, again, what this theology entails for history. History consists for the most part of a record of human behaviour with a running attempt at explanation through cause and effect. Suppose the historian accepts the neo-orthodox account of man. All will be well so long as he confines himself to the record of non-Christian peoples; he will not differ greatly from the secular historian in his account of Pericles or Caesar, or in his explanation of the French, the Russian, or the Chinese revolution. In none of these, probably, will his lines of causation be cut off at critical points by non-natural interventions. But what will he do with St Francis? Francis was a Roman Catholic whose mind was infected with Romanist error; did this, or did it not, affect his receipt of grace? The question would have to be settled before any attempt was made to explain the phenomenon of Francis. For if he was really in a state of grace, no historical explanation of him is possible; the self from which his actions issued was a vertical ingression into the historical order from a realm outside it and unintelligible to it, and at the point of such an ingression history must stop. Or what of George Fox? Macaulay deals with him in a few severe pages, explaining his convictions and actions as the joint product of abysmal ignorance and an abnormality approaching madness. Was he right? That depends on whether Fox had true faith or not. If he did not, Macaulay's account will retain a high verisimilitude. If he did, no human account, Macaulay's or any other, can possibly be correct. For Fox then represented an abrupt discontinuity in the human order of things, in which, as we trace the line of causation backward, it runs up into the empyrean where no human eye can follow it. Fox was expressing and enacting a Deity lodged within him, whose ways are not as our ways.

Or suppose the historian comes to the Reformation. Among the outstanding causes of the Reformation, by universal agreement, was Martin Luther. Very well, what were the forces that produced Luther? Professor Erikson, in *Young Man Luther*, links his struggle against the Pope with his early struggles against the authority of his father. James Anthony Froude gives an account of him that differs greatly in its respect for the man from that of Catholic critics, but all agree in dealing with him as if he were a historically explicable figure. A neo-orthodox theologian could not accept these views. If there was any one man, he would say, in the history of Christendom who could claim to be a man of faith and a recipient of grace, it was Martin Luther. His decisions and actions must therefore have sprung from a source inaccessible alike to psychology and to secular history. When he nailed the theses to the church door, when he derided Tetzel, when he defied the Pope, these were presumably actions unaccountable by anything in his human past, because they issued not from the man Luther but from the transformed and transcendental Luther planted within the same human form. This is a startling way to account—or not to account—for the Reformation. Its root cause is now an inexplicable bolt from the blue, establishing in Luther the supernatural self from which his later actions sprang. The theory has, of course, some difficulties of detail. Not all of Luther's decisions look to the secular eye like acts of indwelling divinity. His advice to certain parents to throw their son into the river because a demon possessed him, and to the German princes to settle the peasants' war by slaughtering the peasants, seem to require a discrimination between those acts that were wholly due to the indwelling spirit and those that were a mixed product of divinity and human caprice. And how is this distinction to be made? We are told that acts done from the spirit may look exactly like those done from natural causes. The recognition, then, of what acts of Luther, or what portions of those acts, were done by Luther the vessel of grace and what by Luther the natural man cannot be made by any human discernment, but only by sympathetic intuition on the part of a historian who, himself in a state of grace, can recognise grace in others. It is not easy to think at the moment of any history of the Reformation that would qualify under these requirements.

THE RELATION OF THE TWO ORDERS

18 Brunner's efforts to show how his two realms are related fall short so uniformly that one suspects he is attempting an insoluble problem. Sometimes he begins with points of identity between the two realms, but it soon transpires that those identities are really differences masked by identical names. Sometimes he begins with the differences, but then the differences prove so great that the chasm between them is unbridgeable. It will be worth while to look at examples of each approach.

Brunner holds that the supernatural man, like the natural man, is an agent in the human scene; he acts causally with important results to himself and others. Now when a cause acts in the natural order, it produces the effect it does in virtue of having properties of one kind rather than another; a bullet penetrates because of its mass and velocity; a helium balloon rises in air because it is lighter than air. But the divinity that acts in man has no distinguishable properties; to find them within it is the specious work of the analytic intellect, which cannot operate in this area. When the spiritual self acts, it acts as a whole, the same cause producing a wide variety of effects; and any attempt to connect the effects differentially with parts or aspects of the cause is misguided. That implies that there is and can be no causal law governing the process, which implies, again, that the 'causality' alleged as common to the two realms must mean very different things.

Or consider this: 'Revelation and reason possess one common element: they both claim truth'; and 'we would reject the very notion of a double truth. . . .'[80] Brunner is here denying that anything true for revelation can be false for reason, and vice versa. But he achieves this peace between the two realms only by making 'truth' mean utterly different things. Truth in ordinary discourse means a relation between proposition and fact, a relation most commonly conceived as coherence or correspondence. This is not what it means in Brunner's non-natural realm. In the spiritual or supernatural province of man's mind, everything is blended with everything else, and hence truth becomes the same as encounter, existence, faith, and love; it is something incapable of analysis or even discussion.

'. . . I understand encounter only as the truth which comes to us in faith in the self-communication of God. This truth creates a knowledge which rises above the subject-object distinction. We cannot make it an object of epistemological discussion, except by referring it back to its own source, God's self-communication.'[81]

It is safe to say that a 'truth' that cannot be made the object of epistemological discussion is not the truth that has embroiled philosophers in discussion for the past twenty centuries. There seems to be nothing in common between the two 'truths' but the name.

Usually, however, when Brunner discusses the two realms, he stresses the difference rather than the likeness between them. 'In the person of Jesus God tells us what no man can know, what is in no kind of continuity with our human ideas, no, not even with the best and highest we possess.'[82] But if the supernatural realm really has 'no kind of continuity with our human ideas,' how is 'encounter' with it possible? We are told that our supreme duty is to believe, and also that if we are ordinary human beings, what we are to believe will be unintelligible to us. Is the demand for such a belief a practicable one? We are to give complete obedience to the divine will; but to men in our status, the divine will is and must be a closed book. We are to accept as true something that we are also told cannot be verified as true, and to pronounce absolutely certain something that cannot be pronounced upon at all. We do not get nearer to God as our philosophic insight deepens; indeed Brunner says that as we approach the divine, intelligence is more and more misleading. We do not approximate the goodness demanded of us by Deity as we rise in the ladder of human goodness, for the ladder of human goodness does not connect, even at its top, with the lowest rungs of the divine goodness. It would seem as if Brunner, in stressing the breadth of the chasm between man and God had made it unintelligible how either could reach the other.

19   That precisely is what he has done. God does come to man and dwell in man, but only by a continuing miracle which it is futile to attempt to understand. Eternity breaks into time; that is a contradiction, but it happens. Omniscience is embodied in a growing mind; that is a contradiction, but it happened, and we must believe it. Common sense tells us that our discernment of what is true and right depends on our level of intelligence and moral sensitivity; but the insight of faith plays free of natural capacities. 'Faith cannot be understood psychologically: it is the speaking of the Holy Spirit in the *psyche* (the soul), therefore it is not itself psychic.'[83] Can we do anything to lift ourselves into faith? With his unshakable serenity, Brunner provides contradictory answers. In gaining faith, 'what is got or begotten is the decision of the will of man for God, the one and only act in which man is really free and which is wholly his own'.[84] That sounds unequivocal. But it should be remembered that the man who is to make this decision is the natural man whom the decision will release from his chains; and we are expressly told that the natural man cannot make such a decision; he is too far gone in corruption. Hence the man who decides must be the spiritual man.

But this implies that in order to make the decision by which one becomes a spiritual man one must be a spiritual man already. This is not very helpful. Is there anything the natural man can do to facilitate his escape to the higher status? Can he better his case by watching or praying, by self-instruction or discipline? Brunner answers No; he can do nothing. If the new self is achieved, it is due altogether to an inscrutable descent of grace. On this matter 'religion', with which Brunner contrasts his own type of faith, has generally been mistaken.

'All religion, in the final analysis, bases salvation on an activity of man, either on his cognition, his cult, or his mystical meditations. All religion and philosophy—as Luther saw it clearly in his day —seek righteousness by works, by human self-assertion. Man assumes that he can help himself by means of his philosophy or his religion. The Gospel is the end of these efforts.'[85]

In sum, the freedom that Brunner began by asserting is an illusion. Natural man is not free to rise into the realm of faith, for his will is in total bondage to sin. If he does decide for faith, it is not he that has made the decision but a miraculously created divine self that has replaced his own; and if this replacement has occurred, it has occurred through a grant of grace with which he has had nothing to do. Why grace should be granted to so few is of course unintelligible, and when it comes, its coming is unintelligible.

TENSION BETWEEN THE ORDERS

20 The disparity Brunner finds between the two realms makes conflict between them in his opinion needless: 'All conflicts between "faith and reason",' he says, 'are sham conflicts. . . .'[86] If theology confines itself to presenting and interpreting revelation, and natural reason to understanding its own world, neither will suffer from the intrusion or dictation of the other. (He also takes the opposite view: 'Biblical and natural theology will never agree; they are utterly and fundamentally opposed.'[87]) If we ask him what the hands-off policy of theology toward philosophy means in practice, we receive a curious answer. His favourite philosophy is the critical philosophy of Kant, because Kant insisted that reason can operate only within the sphere of phenomena and exceeds its bounds when it attempts to know the reality beyond phenomena—a doctrine that accords happily with Brunner's own view. He gives it, therefore, the warrant of his approval and withholds his warrant from all others: 'only the Christian can think truly critically, and truly realistically, and only the critical philosopher can be a Christian.'[88] The argument thus comes to this: there can be no conflict between faith and philosophy because only that kind of philosophy which avoids conflict with faith is to be recognised as truly philosophy. Theology does not interfere with philosophy; it only reserves the right to say which are valid philosophies and which are not. Kant was a genuine philosopher because he held that God was unknowable by reason. Spinoza, Leibniz, Hegel, Bradley, and Royce, not being Christians in Brunner's sense, were so unable to 'think truly critically and truly realistically' that they supposed themselves to possess some rational knowledge of God and must, so far, have been incompetent philosophically.

Now of course there can be no objection to a theologian's preferring a philosopher who agrees with him to others who do not. But there are very obvious objections to his saying (a) that theology has no business to interfere with the work of reason, and (b) that since it speaks in the name of a higher truth, it can give its warrant to some philosophies and impose its veto on others. The objections to such a position are (1) that it is plainly inconsistent with itself, and (2) that it denies the autonomy of reason even within its own realm; it claims the right, on non-rational grounds, to prescribe what conclusions reason shall arrive at. It says to the philosopher: 'You may go your own way and I will not interfere; only you must come out at the destination I set for you.'

21 There will be those who regard such criticism as unfair. 'You object,' they say, 'to dictation by faith to reason; but are you not proposing a similar dictation by reason to faith? You hold that the authority of logic is absolute; Brunner holds that the authority of faith is absolute, and his authority seems as overwhelming to him as yours does to you. Neither authority can excommunicate the other without begging the question, since each, in supporting its case, must appeal to its own authority again. In such circumstances, is it not the fairest course to respect both sovereignties equally and draw boundaries in as conciliatory a way as we can? If "live and let live" has proved so useful a maxim in practice, why not try it also in theory?'

The answer is that what is feasible in practice is often not possible in theory. One may decline to press a practical claim because, though convinced of its justice, one can also see that more will be lost than gained by insisting on it; compromise is clearly possible and is demanded by prudence. But in a case like our present one, compromise is *not* possible. For what we are confronted with is two ultimately different standards for determining what is true, and we saw in dealing with Catholicism that where there are two such standards they are bound sooner or later to come into conflict. One of them will warrant as true something that the other will exclude as false; and there can be no compromise between the sides of a contradiction. That there is such contradiction Brunner has reluctantly to admit; and hence unless inquiry is abandoned a choice has to be made. The question before us is: Do these two authorities have equal claims upon us, or is there something in the conditions of the choice that gives one of the two greater strength?

THE PRIMACY OF REASON

22   To me it seems clear that the stronger claim lies with reason, and I will give two grounds for thinking so. It may be objected that I am begging the question even in offering such grounds. This is true. I am defending the appeal to reason by giving reasons for it, when the question at issue is whether reason in any form is ultimately valid. The first ground will supply the answer to this objection.

(1) The answer is that the acceptance of reason in the sense here relevant, namely the authority of logical law, is not a matter of option or opinion; it is the condition of any action or belief whatever. This is not true of faith. Brunner admits that most men are without it and that, however miserable their lot and prospect, they somehow manage without it. But without logic they could not take a step or make a remark. When they take a step, it is in reliance on their belief, implicit in their perception, that what is before them is solid ground, and that being solid ground excludes *not* being solid ground and being instead such stuff as dreams are made of. When Brunner denies the authority of logic in the sphere of revelation, his very denial takes its significance from the logic he is questioning; for unless this logic is valid, the denial of its validity would not exclude that validity, and he would be saying nothing. In short, conformity to logic is the indispensable condition of experience, the opposite of which is strictly unthinkable. In order to deny its claim, Brunner feels forced to say that the 'experience' of faith is not an experience at all, but a form of existence inconceivable to the natural man, alien to his ways of thought and action and vouchsafed to only a small fraction of the race. To say that the standards of such an existence have a claim upon us greater than those of the logic which forms the basis of human life is surely not plausible.

'There you go again,' it may be said; ' "plausible" means reasonable, does it not? So you are moving in the old circle and defending reason by the appeal to reason.' But the objection is pointless by now; indeed it is one more nail in the irrationalist coffin, for it is further evidence that the appeal to reason is beyond escape if one thinks at all. Any argument on the ultimate test of truth that was *not* circular in this sense would invalidate itself by its own canons. We conclude that when the natural man has to choose between two claims to truth, one admitted to be meaningless to him, the other the implicit basis of all his experience, one answer only is responsible. We cannot ask him to lay his reason, and with it his common sense, his science, and his philosophy, upon the altar of a God admitted to be un-unknown and unknowable to him.

23(2)   The second ground for granting priority to reason is that the very election of faith as an authority is, if the choice is responsible, itself an act of reason. We have been told, of course, that we do not elect to receive revelation; it elects us as its recipients if we are fortunate. But then there is no problem of choice at all; we stand and wait till the lightning strikes or passes us by. But suppose, as Brunner does, however inconsistently, that man has some choice in the matter; consider what he must choose from. He finds himself confronted by a plurality of proffered revelations. The one offered by the Lutheran tradition is an important one, but far from the only one; there are many others that present themselves with impressive guarantees for both present and future. The Roman revelation through the church is one such, and if we go a little further afield, the candidates are legion, from *The Book of Mormon* and Mrs Eddy's *Science and Health* to Zen and Yoga and the luxuriant visions unlocked by Oriental poppies and Mexican weeds. These are not all on a level, to be sure. But how does one know this? It is not very practicable to try all of them in succession, and even if it were, on what basis should the choice be made? Having exposed oneself to them, one would have to stand apart and view them comparatively, and by what standard would one prefer any one to any other? All one could do would be to review them by the light of common day, and conclude, for example, that Brunner's essentially Pauline illumination was richer and truer than that of Zen or Joseph Smith or Mrs Eddy. But when one speaks of one illumination as richer or truer than another, what could one mean except that it is judged so by standards implicit in the judging mind? And what could these be except the standards of that common reason which presides over all reflective choice? One could, of course, throw dice, or follow vagrant impulse, but I assume that a serious choice is called for. What one could *not* do is to make the non-rational decision called for by Brunner and Kierkegaard, for that decision is impossible to the natural man. He must, even in choosing between the revelations offered him, fall back on his own reason. What else could he possibly do?

THE DIVINE IMPERATIVE

24 We have been exploring some of the difficulties in getting Brunner's two realms together. But we may recall that his special achievement in his own eyes and those of others is in ethics, and we must now briefly consider this achievement.

The central idea of his ethics is 'the divine imperative'. Right conduct consists in doing the will of God; obedience to this will is impossible to the natural man because he cannot grasp it, but is possible and even effortless for the new man who is the product of grace. The two selves, the natural man and the spiritual, are two thoroughly different egos, and just as there is a discontinuity between natural and spiritual knowledge, so there is discontinuity between natural and spiritual standards of goodness.

Much that might be said about this view has been said already. Readers will recall that it is essentially the position of Kierkegaard, with its puzzling double standard. Brunner's debt to Kierkegaard is explicitly avowed: 'Today I, in contrast to Karl Barth, still profess allegiance to this great Christian thinker to whom present-day theology, Catholic no less than Protestant, owes more than to any-one since Martin Luther.'[89] The picture drawn by Brunner of the Christian life, with all its actions proceeding from a centre consisting of love—the love of God and the love of man—is more attractive than that of Kierkegaard, in whom the milk of Christian kindness was soured, as it was for Swift, by a *saeva indignatio* toward all mankind. The temper of Brunner's morality is softer and gentler. The love he exalts to so high a place looks enough like simple human affection to make his picture of the good life in some degree sympathetic and intelligible.

He would receive such praise wryly. For whatever his temper and practice, his insistence in exposition is on the complete discontinuity between divine and human goodness. Man's goodness is so corrupt that even the attempt to better himself morally is put down as egotism. Man 'can only do good deeds in so far as God does them in him. . . .'[90] As for his own efforts, 'sin is . . . the total character of our personal existence, the character of all our personal acts'.[91] 'Even in your religion, in so far as it is your experience, you do not cease to be sinner and liar.'[92] Not only is natural man a sinner; his very 'autonomy is equivalent to sin' and his conscience is 'deeply involved in sin'.[93] 'The rationalism of the philosophical ethic can never be combined with the recognition of a divine self-revelation,'[94] since it must be prepared to be countermanded at any moment from on high. 'The science of good conduct, of ethics, is only possible within that other science which speaks of the Divine act of revelation, that is, within dogmatics.'95 The characteristic terms of ethics, like 'good', 'right', 'ought', 'value', 'love', 'aspiration', have different meanings in the context of faith, so that the characteristic virtues of the natural man are themselves part of his corruption; Brunner can speak of 'the Pharisaism of "wishing to be better",'96 of aspiration as something that ceases for the Christian,97 and of the conception of value as useless in solving ethical problems.98 The goodness of the natural man at his highest is still evil if compared with the daily round of the man of faith.

MORAL NIHILISM AGAIN

25 This discontinuity of the two moral orders we considered and had to reject when we met it in Kierkegaard, and we must reject it as unequivocally now. One can no more dismiss man's natural sense of what is good and bad and still leave ethics standing than one can dismiss the laws of logic and leave human knowledge standing. Brunner is prepared, as Kierkegaard was, and according to the legend, Abraham was, to accept as a divine imperative a command that overrides his clearest rational insight into duty. What that implies is not only that such insights are untrustworthy but that the whole hierarchy of values bound up with them is untrustworthy. If the will of God is so alien to those values as to require the readiness to murder a son with no discernible good in sight, then between the divine standard and our own there is little or nothing in common; God's good may be our evil, and his evil our good. If pointless murder may be right, anything may be right, whatever reason or conscience says to the contrary.

This is not a religious exaltation of goodness, but in effect moral nihilism. We have seen that the natural man who is told these things is not able by any effort to achieve the faith that would make true goodness possible for him; he is assured that the reason and conscience which are his only available guides are blind leaders of the blind. He must believe that his faculties are so deeply perverted that his right may be really wrong, and his wrong, right. But then why try to be moral? Where all is rotten, and the very organ by which one might discern comparative rottenness is a broken reed, why accept anything as better than anything else? The natural conclusion from Brunner's two-tiered ethics is thus moral scepticism. You have (1) natural man whose morality is a sink of corruption, (2) a divine will that condemns that morality while withholding from men the only light by which they could correct it. Why should they not be moral agnostics?

If natural man has the courage of his own insights, the conclusion will be worse still, for then the inference appears irresistible that God must be evil rather than good. God made man free, with the knowledge, since he is omniscient, that man would misuse it to his perdition. This is not, in human reckoning, an expression of love. God has sentenced to condemnation millions of persons for the sins of others now dead. This is not, in human reckoning, an expression of justice. God has endowed these persons with a reason, conscience, and moral aspiration that have led them to hope and struggle for a truly good life, and has also assured them that their hope is vain and their struggle itself somehow sinful. Such action, if done by a human being, would be called inhuman. God chooses some persons, for no ascertainable reason, as recipients of a grace that gives them light, security, and peace, while denying it, again for no discoverable reason, to the great majority of mankind, including many who in the world's view are saints. By merely human reckoning this is unfair to the point of cruelty. These are the actions of a being to whom Brunner ascribes love and justice in perfection; and it is the imperatives of this being that are the ultimate directives of the moral of life. What is to be the attitude of the man who follows his own conscience and reason toward this sort of religious teaching? Surely he will be revolted or torn in two. For he is being asked to revere, worship, imitate, and obey a God whose morality, as explicitly set before him, is not above his human standard but below it.

MORAL SANITY

26   It is obvious that Brunner's two spheres of morality are out of harmony with each other. As in the conflict between revelation and logic, one cannot accept both. One must ask, as before, whether either of the two claimants has a stronger initial title to respect.

By this time there will be no doubt what our answer must be. Just as common sense, science, and philosophy have a set of logical principles that are at work in all inference and proof and can be discarded only at the cost of total disaster to the life of thought, so in the moral life there is a set of values that lie behind all responsible choice and whose fall would carry morality as a whole down with them. We cannot attempt an inventory of them here, or examine our mode of knowing them, and fortunately it is unnecessary. We do somehow know that happiness is intrinsically better or more worth having than extreme misery, that wisdom is better than ignorance, that justice is better than injustice. These are assumptions implicit in our ordinary choices; our approvals and disapprovals turn on them, and their falsity would spread chaos through the moral life. We can of course deny them in words, but we cannot make ourselves accept as true what such words mean. If a man were to appear with a new ethic in which he proclaimed his right to torture another for his amusement, or recommended the death penalty for the wickedness of knowing the multiplication table, we should be less likely to regard him as a genius than as morally insane. This does not mean that our ordinary moral judgements are infallible; they are continually refined, clarified, and amended in the course of moral growth. But unless there were this accepted stock of common standards, life as we know it would be unlivable. It would be what it was in Hobbes's celebrated state of nature, 'solitary, poor, nasty, brutish, and short'.

There is such a thing as moral sanity, and acceptance of the scale of values and the set of rules that make society possible is an essential part of it. Our moral judgements, like our scientific judgements, must, if valid, be consistent with each other, and they are knit together into a web whose parts are all interconnected. If it is wrong to inflict needless pain on another, then by the same principle it is wrong to take his purse, his house, or his reputation. Our moral world is thus a system, never fully integrated or complete, but providing the only ground we have for appraising the new and morally questionable. To ask a man to accept a proposal which would wreck that system is to ask him to pull his house about his ears, and unless he is ready for both inward and outward anarchy, he will find it impossible to take the proposal seriously. Mere moral sanity will forbid it.

27 Now it is this moral sanity that Brunner is challenging with his two-storied morality. Natural affection, the judgements of natural reason as to what is fair and unfair, the protests of natural conscience against cruelty or disloyalty, the obligation to improve one's mind or morals, these are all imperatives that from the transcendental point of view are 'sinful' and may at any moment be overridden by a command to disregard them, issued by an authority so incommensurable with the natural one that any attempt to appraise it, any attempt to assimilate it into a rational system of morals, anything indeed but total uncritical surrender is wrong and impious. I doubt whether Brunner or Kierkegaard or anyone else who accepts it can have thought out what this means. We have seen that if Abraham's readiness to kill his son is to be taken as evidence of a higher goodness, what is being renounced is not merely an isolated rule of paternal duty but human morality as a whole. To the ordinary man, such renunciation will be nonsense. Brunner agrees that it is nonsense, and serenely quotes Scripture for its being so: we can only expect that the word of God will be foolishness to human reason. But then human reason is all that natural man has to go by. If he looks at an imperative calmly and steadily, if the moral system that speaks through him—the system that he and the race have developed in their long slow groping toward rationality—pronounces that imperative to be wrong, if he realises that acceptance of it would wreck his moral world, and if nothing intelligible to him is offered in its place, then there is only one responsible course that he can take. He must decline obedience. To expect a kindly and reasonable man to rub his hands over sacred murder, as Kierkegaard does, or, as Brunner would have him do, make over a check for his life's accumulation of wisdom to an account labelled 'foolishness', is to invite him to give up also his moral sanity.

THE DANGERS OF MISPLACED DIVINITY

28 Furthermore, in minds where this sanity has less than secure control, the new morality is attended with genuine danger; a horse with no bridle may take its rider in any direction. Such a charge, it may be said, exaggerates the difference between natural and transcendental morals; ordinary morality would not be scattered to the winds, and ordinary life would only be changed for the better, in a regime dominated by Christian love. Try an experiment in idea. Imagine a society in which, by some turn of fortune's wheel, a man of Brunner's outlook were placed at the head of church and state and given dictatorial powers; would there be anything really disquieting in such a prospect? We may agree that if he were, like Brunner himself even by the standards he depreciates, a good and just man, he would be a vast improvement over other dictators one might mention. But the point is not so much what the divine imperatives might be in a mind like Brunner's, but what his theory would justify to minds less moulded than his own by reflective and civilised standards. These standards, he tells us, lose their control both de facto and de jure when the new sovereignty takes over; all causal lines from past habit, education, and reflection to the new command-centre are cut; hence no prediction on their basis is possible and no judgement they might pass on the new order is legitimate. Is there not ground for apprehension as to where such freedom from rational standards might lead?

'He who has taken the inner fortress of your soul, i.e., your Ego,' Brunner writes, 'will not stop there but will take you with him to conquer the world. The eschatological substance of faith works itself out in supremely aggressive action in the world.'[99] What form would this 'aggressive action' take? A dictator appears with the conviction of Luther that witches should be burned and rebellious peasants slaughtered, or with the firm conviction of another German leader of some influence as to 'the final solution of the Jewish question'. What ground have we for protesting against the demands of such persons? We may object that their 'intuitions' are utterly unreasonable, but they reply that they are not under the judgement of reason and are acting from a higher source. What line would Brunner himself take regarding them? Presumably he would hold that his own illumination was clearly contrary to theirs, and hence that both directives could not be divine. He would, of course, be introducing into the super-rational realm those standards of rational consistency that are supposed to be there transcended. But let that pass. He would be making another admission more germane to our present purpose. He would be implying that two men, both in receipt of genuine grace, can firmly believe that they are receiving from a higher than rational source imperatives that are in fact contradictory of each other. I am not thinking so much of his difference with Hitler (a difference courageously pressed by Brunner), though how in theory one is to decide between two such disparate non-rational claims is not clear. But what about Luther? Luther believed, when he made his most important pronouncements, that he was speaking with divine direction, and he would presumably say this about the two judgements just reported. Brunner would add that if any man ever spoke from the inspiration of a genuine faith it was Martin Luther. But Brunner surely did not accept it as a divine imperative that all witches should be burned, or that rebellious peasants should be slaughtered. And if he did not, he would seem to be committed to one or other of two conclusions. One is that since God is not rational in our sense he may indeed have planted contrary insights in Luther and in himself. I think he would have drawn back from that, for all his insistence that God is not accountable to reason. And the alternative is to admit that even a genuine recipient of grace may be deceived as to whether an imperative that presents itself as divine is in truth divine.

ERROR IN HIGH PLACES

29 Such an admission would have important consequences. For it is not only half-mad fanatics like Hitler who may be deceived in their non-rational intuitions, nor imperfectly Christian men of action like Cromwell, Stonewall Jackson, and Chinese Gordon, but men acclaimed as religious geniuses—men like Martin Luther, Francis of Assisi, and George Fox. Presumably when Luther prescribed his cruel remedies for witchcraft or devil-possession, when St Francis called on people in plague-ridden places to gather in church and pray, thereby spreading the disease more widely, and when Fox 'spoke out' against music, they felt confident that they were voicing a divine imperative—as confident as at other times when their judgement was more defensible. They thought they were being divinely led and they were not. In the light of such errors, it is plainly all-important to have a criterion by which divine imperatives can be distinguished from the promptings of ignorance, prejudice, and paranoia; and that necessary criterion is not here provided. It is not merely dervishes who lack it; everyone seems to lack it, once he has lost the compass of reason. Even the towering lighthouses of religious humanity lack it, men to whom divine openings have presented themselves with the most undoubted certainty and who have announced them with the calm authority of a 'thus saith the Lord'.

30 The fact that such errors have occurred, and occurred frequently, in religious history is significant for our final estimate of Brunner's theology. For these errors have natural explanations, and if natural explanations can be found for convictions wholly indistinguishable, for those who make them, from convictions due to supernatural agency, then the suggestion is irresistible that these last convictions too may have natural explanations. Modern research has thrown a flood of light on the unconscious causes of conscious belief. Brunner insists, of course, that faith has no natural causes at all, though it has momentous natural effects. Its convictions, insights, and imperatives 'fall as the gentle rain from heaven upon the place beneath'. The man of faith is a Melchizedek, without human parentage and without roots in nature; his beliefs are not mental occurrences, nor his volitions human acts, nor his feelings, if he can be said to have them, experiences at all; he is a supernatural avatar, a light shining in darkness, which the darkness cannot comprehend, a mysterious meteor that darts down from remote and unknown regions to burn brilliantly for a time in the fetid atmosphere of earth.

Now the fact and frequency of error in these manifestations make it impossible to maintain plausibly the partition between the two realms. If Luther thought he was speaking with a divine accent in urging that witches be burnt and peasants slaughtered and the Pope branded as Antichrist, he was an honest but very human and mistaken man whose mistakes were explicable by the facts of his time, his place, and himself. He believed in witches because the people around him did, because his supreme authority, the Bible, underwrote that belief, because the evidence of hearsay and even of perception was twisted into conformity with his religious preconceptions in ways of which he was unaware but which are familiar to modern students of the workings of the mind. His violent views about peasants and the Pope may be understood in similar fashion. One cannot consistently take them as openings from on high, and they are plainly not rigorous deductions from impartially gathered evidence; it is far more plausible to take them as conclusions of an able, impulsive, self-confident, vehement mind that was enmeshed in the religious and political prejudices of the time, and buffeted about by personal fears, ambitions, and dislikes. No one can profess a complete understanding of Luther, but it is safe to say that a man who thought of his mind as an arena of incessant combat between God and the devil, and who would have rejected as impossible and impious any science of the mind, must have been moved by many factors of whose working he was unaware.

Now the question that must be put to Brunner is this: is it reasonable to believe that those elements of an alleged revelation that happen to be exposed as erroneous should admit of a natural explanation, while other elements qualitatively indiscernible from them should belong to a different order of being and remain wholly inexplicable? To any modern mind with a tincture of science, such a view is improbable. But that does not disprove it. Is there any empirical evidence that would help us to appraise it?

THE ANALOGY TO MYSTICISM

31   Brunner excludes such evidence as irrelevant by his denial that the revelation he proclaims has any empirical content; the knowledge, love, and happiness of the man of faith are not what these terms mean in ordinary usage, and the unity in which they appear in the new state of grace is beyond analysis or description. But this high hedge against trespassers does not prevent Brunner himself from speaking more or less freely about the content of the new state, and what he does say about it sounds very much like what has been said by other religious writers who were less averse to description. In James's *Varieties of Religious Experience* there are many accounts of the state of mind of the mystic and of the converted man that are strikingly like the state of faith as sketched by Brunner. And regarding mystical experiences Brunner argues that they are perfectly natural products of perfectly natural causes.

Some of the main characteristics of the mystic experience are its implicit claim to insight or knowledge, its passivity, its transcendence of ordinary ways of thinking, and its discontinuity with what went before, all of which are characteristics likewise of Brunner's state of faith. Mystics have often reported insights into the heart of things which came to them as absolutely certain. They have seen—or thought they saw—that God exists and is good, that evil is unreal, that the human spirit is deathless, that time is an illusion. These insights, far from being the conclusions of reflection or the achievements of effort, seemed rather to come as a munificent, uncovenanted bounty from above. The visions, when they do come, cannot be caught in words or concepts, the mystics tell us, though the conviction and exaltation they carry with them have glowed through many memorable pages of prose and verse. That such insights have sometimes been true we are not concerned to deny. Our question is only whether these experiences are discontinuous with the lives of those who have them, so that they are wholly inexplicable.

The evidence is against it. Consider one point only: the way in which mystical insights follow the teaching in which the mystics have been brought up. Evelyn Underhill writes that history

'shows us, over and over again, the great mystics as faithful sons of the great religions. . . . Thus St Teresa interprets her ecstatic apprehension of the Godhead in strictly Catholic terms. Thus Boehme believed to the last that his explorations of eternity were consistent with the teachings of the Lutheran Church. Thus the Sūfis were good Mohammedans, Philo and the Kabalists were orthodox Jews.'[100]

The insights of all these mystics came as self-authenticating and independent of prior teaching. Yet the Brahman mystics loyally report an impersonal, pantheistic Deity, while St Teresa and St Ignatius report that they have seen God to be three persons in one. It is hard to believe that this coincidence between their past teaching and what was revealed to them was merely an accident, or—since the insights were not consistent with each other—that an identical revelation was being offered in different forms. It is far more likely that their visions welled up out of the depths of their own minds, which had themselves been filled by the streams of their respective traditions. And if this is true, the illumination is not nearly so discontinuous with the rest of their life as it appeared to be. It is no coincidence that the man converted to Christianity in a Christian community should be aware in moments of exaltation of Christ as his redeemer while a man converted to Islam will have no such intimation.

Brunner sees that this line of thought, if applied to the illumination of faith, will tend to domesticate it within the sphere of the natural. How does he avoid this? He contends that in other faiths the state of religious exaltation is a natural phenomenon and therefore admits of the sort of explanation that psychologists might supply, while if a

Christian reports in similar words what seems like a similar experience, it belongs to a different world. It is not really an experience at all; it cannot be accounted for by any past teaching, by any instruction in thought or discipline of feeling, or by anything whatever in the life or environment of the subject; it is a direct, inexplicable, errorless descent of divinity into the man's soul. Between the Christian's assurance in his convictions and that of every other worshipper there is an absolute difference in kind. Brunner writes that such an 'uncompromising, absolute attitude toward the world religions is the natural and inevitable consequence of the Christian faith itself.'[101] Christianity is not one of the religions of the world at all, if that means that it is a species of the same genus as the others; and accordingly Brunner often speaks of religion in surprisingly disparaging terms.

Such considerations do not prove Brunner wrong in making faith unassimilable to human experience or Christianity unassimilable to the religions of the world. But they surely raise a strong presumption against his view. When experiences which seem to mirror the state of faith at many important points are admitted to be continuous with the rest of life, how can one plausibly maintain that the faith state itself is absolutely discontinuous with it? Everywhere else, when confronted by similar phenomena, we look for similar causes. To be told that in this case it is a mistake not only to look for such causes but to look for causes at all, that faith is a state so remote from every other that no laws apply to it, no principles are to be extracted from it, no concepts are applicable to it, no analysis of it is possible, no grounds are needed for its truths, and no certainties can compare with its own ineffable ones—we can only say that all this runs so counter to the principles by which the rest of life is ordered as to be improbable in the extreme. Brunner does not, like Butler, accept probability as the guide of life, because he thinks that something infinitely superior to the reason that employs probability has been granted to some fortunate persons. Whether in fact they possess it seems on closer inspection to be itself a matter of probability. And unhappily the probability is not high. It looks increasingly as if reason, which in Brunner's picturesque universe figures only as a broken reed, may have to be reconceived as the head of the corner.

CHAPTER VIII

REASON AND REVELATION FOR
KARL BARTH

THE NEO-ORTHODOX POSITION

1 In Karl Barth we reach the culmination of the course of Protestant thought that began with Luther and advanced through Kierkegaard and Brunner. He developed this type of theology with a thoroughness and massiveness that seem unlikely to be surpassed by any later theologian. His many-volumed *Dogmatik* is one of the most intimidating of theological works, and if his own comment is true that no critic should presume to criticise him without reading him in his entirety, I can only admit the presumptuousness of the pages that follow. I shall not be concerned, however, with the details of his Scriptural interpretation or with the slight modifications of view that took place over the years; my interest will be confined to his teaching on the relation of reason to revelation. This central teaching reappears in all his works, but it will be studied chiefly as it is presented in his Gifford Lectures at Aberdeen on *The Knowledge of God and the Service of God*.

That Barth should have been invited or should have consented to give these lectures is something of an anomaly. He began by citing the specification in Lord Gifford's will that the lectures were designed for the 'promoting, advancing, teaching and diffusing' of natural theology, 'without reference to or reliance upon any supposed special exceptional or so-called miraculous revelation'. Regarding such natural theology Barth said at once, and with disarming candour, 'I do not see how it is possible for it to exist. I am convinced that so far as it has existed and still exists, it owes its existence to a radical error.' The service he proposed to render to natural theology was to stimulate such life as might be left in it by stating the case for its mortal enemy, 'that totally different theology by which "natural theology" lives, in so far as it must affirm what the other denies and deny what the other affirms'. In the face of all the projectionists who, like Freud and Feuerbach, would make religious 'knowledge' an imaginative fulfilling of need, of all the pragmatists who, like Dewey, would make it merely a means to human betterment, of all the rationalists who, like Hegel, would make it philosophy, half grown up, of all the psychologists, who, with Schleiermacher and Ritschl, would make it essentially a matter of feeling, Barth proclaimed a full-fledged return to the theology of the Reformation, in which God is set over against the world as 'wholly other', known indeed to faith, but unknowable, unapproachable, and unimaginable by any natural faculties.

It is this doctrine of God as the 'wholly other', and discontinuous with us in nature, as closed to our thoughts and alien even to our ideals, that is the arresting note in Barth's teaching; and we shall turn to it in a moment for special attention. But first let us see its place in the wider setting of his theology.

2   That theology has been rightly described as neo-orthodox. Orthodoxy for Barth, as for the Roman Catholic, is a serious matter; to him the notion is frivolous that each of us can go to the Bible and pick out from it what happens to suit his own taste or temperament. In his early days he saw this happening among German liberals. Even Harnack, who was his teacher and who made so much of objectivity, looked at the gospel through his own glasses; he saw Jesus as a social reformer in advance of his time, not as incarnate Deity. Now if Jesus is not incarnate Deity, no doubt the liberal approach to him is right. He will then present the tragic figure of a poet and prophet trying to make the world over by gentleness, and subject to many illusions. If this is what he was, the long 'quest of the historical Jesus' by researchers bent on describing, interpreting, and amending him will be in order.

But this is not the orthodox view of Jesus. The orthodox view is that he spoke as never man spoke because he was more than man, because he was the embodiment on earth of an eternal, all-knowing, all powerful, infinite Creator. This Creator made man and enjoined him to obey and glorify his maker. The first man broke this command. In doing so he brought sin into the world. This sin corrupted not only his own nature but also the whole race of his descendants, who therefore stand utterly condemned in God's sight. Only an infinite sacrifice could atone for their guilt. This sacrifice was in fact made when the second person of the Trinity, himself infinite in power and goodness, offered himself as a ransom to the first person, and though living a sinless life on earth, subjected himself to a cruel death. Because of this sacrifice, God has made available to certain men, not through any effort or merit on their part but through his mercy alone, the gift of grace, which both averts from them the wrath which is their due, and transforms them inwardly so that they become capable again of faith and righteousness.

To ears accustomed to liberal scepticism or rationalistic philosophising, Barth admitted that such language sounded archaic. But
it is more important to note, he thought, that according to the
Reformation, according to the church, and according to the Bible,
it happens to be true. And if it is true, the work of the Christian
is clearly appointed. It is not to hammer out a theology with the
crude tools of his own reason, or to exalt the whisperings of his own
conscience into the laws of the good life. It is his business, if God has
really spoken, to be silent and listen. And the business of the church
is not to wrangle with the philosophers or to compete with politicians
and economists in social reform. In so doing it would be taking a
feeble and febrile stand; it would be throwing away Excalibur and
doing battle with an absurd tin sword. The true line for the church
is to stand up and say, as the prophets did, 'Thus saith the Lord'.
This bugle note of uncompromising confidence and courage rallied
behind Barth's leadership many thousands of persons who were
feeling faint of heart about the Christian prospect in the modern
world.

For Barth, then, there is one fact that stands out in monolithic
majesty on the plain of human history: God spoke to man in
Christ. Of that revelation we have a witness in the Bible and a
further witness whenever God in his mercy gives us grace to believe.
It is upon this fact of revelation, therefore, that we must fix our eye.
How does Barth know when it is occurring and what it says?

WHAT REVELATION IS NOT

3 He gives us his answer through a series of denials. Revelation
has been thought to occur in many areas of experience. Many poets,
scientists, and philosophers have professed to find it in nature.
Wordsworth found it in the light of setting suns; Kepler held that
in his astronomy he was 'thinking God's thoughts after him', and the
evolutionist John Fiske wrote a book charting the passage *Through
Nature to God*. But when Emil Brunner ventured to suggest that there
was some truth in this idea, Barth answered, 'Nein'; natural
theology 'can only be becoming to the theology and church of
Antichrist'.[1] 'Except in His Word, God is never for us in the world,
that is to say in our space and time.' There is no road from science to
faith.

Is there any road from philosophy to faith? Many of Barth's
distinuished predecessors in the Gifford lectureship, for example the
brothers Caird, held that there was, and that our thought of the
world, so far as it becomes coherent and comprehensive, is in rapport
with a reason immanent in nature; reason rightly used is indeed one

with revelation. Barth will have none of this. God is and must remain the unknowable 'wholly other'. As Gogarten puts it, he is 'the Unknown by our knowing, the Unconceived by our concepts, the Measureless for our measures, the Inexperienceable for our experience'.[2] This does not mean that we have no knowledge of God of any kind, for faith is itself the highest knowledge. But having said this, Barth adds at once that this knowledge 'differs completely from anything else which man calls knowledge, not only in its content, but in its mode of origin and form as well'.[3] 'Further, it is forced down my throat that the Dogmatic theologian is under the obligation to "justify" himself in his utterances before philosophy. To that my answer is likewise, No. . . . It cannot be otherwise than that Dogmatics runs counter to every philosophy no matter what form it may have assumed.'[4] The very attempt to know God by thought is impiety, since it is an attempt to catch the infinite in the net of our own categories. Though Barth dislikes and distrusts philosophy, he did in his youth study Kant's first critique. For his own position it was a happy choice, since Kant confirmed him in the view that reason is made for nature and cannot penetrate beyond it.

4 Kant thought, however, that in the experience of duty we did manage to go beyond it, and moralists of such different stripe as Butler, Newman, and Martineau have agreed that in some sense the voice of God is to be heard in the voice of conscience. Would Barth agree? His answer again is an emphatic No. For there is really no health in us, and conscience, as an organ in the natural man, is infected by his disease.

Barth is scornful of 'poor present-day man with his utilitarian notions'[5] and the 'happy gentleman of culture who today drives up so briskly in his little car of progress and so cheerfully displays the pennants of his various ideals. . . .'[6] He praises the Scottish confession because it 'is opposed, and rightly so, to all talk about the goodness of the Christian life'.[7] There is something startling about a theologian belittling goodness itself, but Barth does not flinch from it if the goodness is merely human goodness. 'In the Christian life we are not concerned with our becoming Christian personalities. . . . All that . . . can be very fine, but yet it looks as if there were already in process here another instance of the idolatry in which man wishes really to make his own achievements the basis of his confidence,'[8] and, for Barth, man's attempt to justify himself by works is a sin against the Holy Spirit. Between God's goodness and man's there is a deep gulf, and it is misleading to say of the sinlessness of Christ that it is an example of what we mean by moral goodness. Canon Quick complains of Barth's speaking 'as though it were treason to

the Christian faith to seek to commend the truth of the Christian
revelation to non-Christians on the ground that the character of
Jesus is surpassingly good and beautiful, and that His life reveals
thereby the beauty and goodness of the Godhead.'9 One would
expect Barth to reject the social interpretation of the gospel, but he
seems at times to go further and to disparage the very idea of service;
'speaking generally,' he says, 'the Church has not to be at the service
of mankind'. It has higher work to do.

REVELATION VS THE BIBLE

5 If we are not to look for revelation in any of these quarters, shall
we find it perhaps in the Bible? No again, if that means that we can
hope to find it by analysis or interpretation or any other process of
sifting meanings. God does speak through the Ten Commandments
of the Old Testament, but their meaning is not what a moralist
could arrive at from reflection on natural rights or through listening
to his own conscience.10 Revelation comes also and comes indeed
supremely, through the Christ portrayed in the New Testament. But
Barth is quite ready, as Catholic and Protestant fundamentalists
are not, to let the critics go ahead with their work of dissecting and
reconstructing this portrait, since it is idle in any case to look for
revelation in it. God is not revealed to us in the character or mind
of Jesus, in anything he did or said or was, so far as this is apprehended with our natural gifts; the Jesus of history is not the Christ;
God dwelt in him only incognito. 'The Bible is God's Word . . .'
says Barth, 'so far as God speaks through it'. But we shall never find
the points at which he is speaking through it by raising questions
of authenticity or reasonableness. This is merely one more attempt
to appraise divinity by human tests.

6 Baffled in the search for revelation in any of these quarters,
suppose we take the last step open to us. If we look in vain for
revelation in nature, in thought, in conscience, in the Bible, in the
Jesus of history, may we not find it in immediate religious experience?
There is of course a vast volume of Christian tradition to the effect
that we may. The mystical vision, the Quaker inner light, the
Methodist's conversion, the common experiences of faith and prayer
have been felt by millions of persons, both simple and sophisticated,
to give them contact at first hand with the divine. May we agree with
any of them? Barth's answer is not only uncompromising but
startling. He would ask first whether these experiences are genuinely
human experiences, the sort, for example, that James described in
the *Varieties*, that psychologists are able to connect causally with

adolescence or sex or emotional need, that are reported in other religions as well as the Christian. If the answer is, Yes, they *are* experiences of this kind, then Barth replies that to take them as revelations is impious. The mystic's claim to union with God is blasphemous. God is never present in the human heart, and it is idolatrous to suppose that he is.[11] Prayer, if a seeking for God's presence, is presumptuous and separates us from him; Barth notes 'How profane a world this world of prayer is. . . .'[12] Religion as such is not spared; 'the Church does not take the slightest interest in religion . . .';[13] religion is a 'misfortune which takes fatal hold upon some men';[14] 'the vast pandemonium of human piety' is dangerous to the God-seeking soul.[15] 'Religion must die. In God we are rid of it.'[16] Thus natural religion in its most intimate experiences of piety, prayer, and mystical exaltation is set down as dangerous delusion.

7   Now if revelation is not to be found in any of these areas or experiences, what sort of message does it have for us, and how are we to recognise this when it comes?

WHAT REVELATION IS

To the first question, what does it say? Barth replies that no answer is possible of the kind that presumably is wanted. If one is asking for a set of commands, ideas, or propositions that can be understood, put into words, and communicated to other people, one is asking for an impossible translation of the 'wholly other' into human terms. A faithful interpreter writes: 'When one has stated what Father, Son, and Spirit in God mean, says Barth, one must continue and add that one has said nothing. The *mysterium trinitatis* remains a mystery.'[17] 'To know this God in His dealings . . . means necessarily to know God's free *mercy*, the most incomprehensible of all *miracles*.'[18] To call him wise or good or powerful or just or even gracious, in our senses of these words, to say that he has qualities analogous to these in any sense that we can understand, to draw inferences about him that are based on these concepts, all these are alike and in principle illegitimate. In talking about revelation, we are using a denotation without any clear connotation. Barth felt free to call it by many names, since none of them is descriptive; in referring to revelation, the terms 'God', 'Christ', 'grace', 'faith', 'the Son', 'the Father', the 'mercy' or 'love' or 'justice' of God all mean the same thing; even 'the service of God' and 'the knowledge of God', since both mean simply the indwelling God himself, again mean the same thing. To the quesion what is revealed? Barth's answer is as succinct as one could wish: 'Gott selbst, Gott allein!'

To the other question, how we recognise revelation when it comes, Barth again admits that he has no answer that will satisfy. What is wanted, no doubt, is a criterion or set of marks by which an authentic revelation can be distinguished from a pseudo-revelation. And there are no such marks. How then is my groping search to proceed? How am I to recognise the boon when it presents itself? The truth is, says Barth, that *I* cannot recognise it. To say that I could would be equivalent to saying that the finite can recognise the infinite, that the temporal, while still sunk in time, can view eternity, that corruption as such can put on incorruption. No, man as he is cannot respond to or even identify revelation. It is only God in him that can rise to so high an occasion and interpret what the testimony for revelation really means. 'How could revelation ever be recognised as the divine content of that testimony except through revelation? But so to recognise revelation through revelation means to recognise it by revelation awakening one's faith.'[19] 'It is faith which knows God as a child knows its father,'[20] and faith is an exercise of no human faculty; 'the man who really has faith will never consider his faith as a realisation or manifestation of his religious life, but will on the contrary admit that his capacity for religion would in itself have led him to the gods and idols, but by no means to Jesus Christ.'[21] Deep can speak only to deep. In this respect the achievement of an understanding faith is like the achievement of genuine goodness; neither is really an achievement. We must admit that 'what we wish, will and strive after to-day, i.e. what we are to-day, is simply our sin . . .';[22] on the other hand, 'all our works which proceed from faith will be good works,' and only these.[23] The faith that sees and the goodness that embodies that faith are alike the work of Deity, who in his inscrutable grace descends at times into human life.

Barth's view of revelation, though developed through many thousand pages, is thus in essence simple. There is no road from man to God, no way of gaining knowledge or union with God through human experience or through reflection on that experience. There *is* a road from God to man. That road was taken in the incarnation. It is taken now in unpredictable times and places by divine grace, but since the revelation comes from a 'wholly other', discontinuous and incommensurable with all our powers, both that which speaks in us and that which hears it transcend the human level.

BARTH'S ACHIEVEMENT

8 What are we to say of this teaching? Two things we must grant to it without reservation. First, it achieved a dramatic and unexpected turning of the tables on rationalism and liberalism. In the first two decades of the century, as noted in the last chapter, liberalism seemed secure in its ascendancy. I recall hearing an eminent theologian say, 'One thing is now clear: liberalism is dead.' I suspect that he was mistaken, but there can be no doubt that an astonishing change of theological climate occurred in the first half of the century, and that this change was due to Barth more than to any other man.

I think too that, whether we are persuaded by it or not, we must admire the adroitness of Barth's strategy. He chose his own ground, and for the most part refused to meet his critics on ground where he would be at a disadvantage. He was not a philosopher and he knew it. If he had attempted a systematic argumentative defence of his position, he might have been manoeuvred into logical disaster by rationalist tacticians; it is obviously dangerous for anyone advancing an irrationalist thesis to defend his case with rationalist weapons. Barth may have learned this from considering the way in which conservatives met the great upsurge of liberal rationalism under Hegel and Strauss in the last century. Kierkegaard met it with a shrewd denial that religious faith was a rational matter at all, and Kierkegaard's voluble ghost is still very much alive in our divinity school quadrangles. Mansel, with a greater logical skill than that of either Kierkegaard or Barth, attempted to defend a similar view of revelation by argument. His book had the misfortune to fall under the eye of John Stuart Mill, and for once a book got reviewed. Mansel was crushed, apparently beyond revival. Barth has prudently reverted to the line of Kierkegaard. He says to the philosophers bluntly: I decline to recognise your jurisdiction; my appeal is to a court in which your logic-chopping has no standing.

IN WHAT SENSE IS REASON UNTRUSTWORTHY?

9 Our first step in examining him may well be to ask whether he is entitled to this appeal. Philosophers can admit an appeal from logic-chopping, but not from logic, and when Barth declines to be judged by the standards they employ, we must ask rather more precisely what he means. He might mean any one of three things. He might mean, first, that the ultimate truth about God and the world is so far beyond us that any conceptions of it arrived at with our present powers are bound to fall short. Or he might go beyond this and mean, secondly, that in the picture of the world which we are now bound to accept, taking both revealed and natural knowledge into account, there are genuine contradictions, but that these are rather incident to the process of search than indicative of irrationality in the world. Or he might mean, thirdly, that they do indicate just this, and that we must therefore say that the very attempt to grasp ultimate truth by reason is misguided, since it is bound to be flouted in the end by the object it is trying to understand. Which of these things is Barth saying?

He is obviously saying at least the first, and here we may surely agree with him. The ideas we form of the world always grow out of our experience; that experience is severely limited by the range of our senses, by our flickering attention and vagrant reflection, and indeed on every side by our imperfectly evolved powers of mind. If rationalism implies the claim that our present ideas, even at their best, on the nature of matter, time, life, mind, personality, or value, or on the place of any of these in the universe as a whole, are adequate and final, then we may agree with Barth that rationalism is absurd. Unfortunately, the agreement is not very significant, since this is not a kind of rationalism that any responsible rationalist would avow.

KNOWLEDGE AS INCOHERENT

10 Does Barth then also take the second position, that there are contradictions in our knowledge, though not in reality? He has not discussed, so far as I know, the antinomies in natural knowledge alleged by Zeno, Kant, and Russell. But he has held that revelation presents us with insights which, when placed side by side with those of natural knowledge, result in contradictions from which we cannot escape. That revelation is to be considered a kind of knowledge is attested by his entitling one of his books *The Knowledge of God*. And he would not deny that science at its best is knowledge. But when we try to put these into one whole, it breaks into contradictory pieces. Barth perhaps takes less delight in dwelling on these contradictions, which he would rather call paradoxes, than Tertullian and Kierkegaard did, and he has never, so far as I know, set them out in formal fashion. But they are there in plenty. For the sake of clearness, I will list a few of them.

First there are the contradictions about original sin. No man can be justly condemned for the deeds of another, but nevertheless man stands under just condemnation for the sin of Adam. Sin is distorted or perverted will; but original sin somehow infects us before we can use our wills.

Secondly, there are the contradictions about God's justice. God is perfectly just; yet we have to ascribe to him acts that appear plainly to be unjust. He has withheld his revelation from some persons and nations and granted it to others in a manner that, for all we can see, is arbitrary; he has remitted punishment that is due to certain men because he is appeased by the sacrifice of another, and has inflicted his punishment or displeasure on persons who, to the best of our knowledge, are innocent.

Thirdly, there is the great nest of contradictions about the incarnation. God really became man. But an omniscient mind cannot also be a mind that is limited and growing. A mind with no evil in it cannot be tempted as we are. A mind that is really eternal cannot be temporal for thirty-three years. A mind that is absolute, in the sense that it is free from finite conditions, cannot be personal, in the sense that it knows, feels, and wills what is other than itself. A God who is pure goodness cannot also, in becoming man, share man's corruptness and sinfulness. But Barth insists that he does: 'The completeness of God's humiliation . . . lies in His taking upon Himself as man *everything* which man's rebellion against Him has made inevitable—suffering and death but also perdition and hell. . . .'[24] To this passage Barth adds in a characteristic note: 'I have received a letter, the writer of which maintains that it is both impossible and incomprehensible that God should suffer death and perdition. To this I would reply that this is the sacrifice of which the Bible speaks.' The person of Jesus Christ is to Barth what it was to Kierkegaard, who regarded it as something logically incredible against which 'reason beats her brow till the blood comes'.

Fourthly, our attainment of goodness is unintelligible. We meditate, pray, resolve, and struggle, all to no avail; we are still in God's sight repellent. We are helpless to secure his grace; Barth insists that we cannot even co-operate with him in securing it; such efforts are tainted with evil. When we do attain to goodness, it is not we who attain it but God in us, who, for no reason that our minds can hope to understand, has chosen to descend into us and act through us.

Fifthly, we are told that with God all things are possible. If so, it was possible for him to create a world in which the vast mass of suffering that is morally pointless—the pain and misery of animals, the cancer and blindness of little children, the humiliations of senility and insanity—were avoided. These are not the products of free will; they are inflictions from without, and apparently therefore inflictions of the Creator himself. If you admit that, you deny his goodness; if you say he could not have done otherwise, you deny that with him all things are possible.

THE ABANDONMENT OF NATURAL REASON DISASTROUS

11   Here is a long series of contradictions which it would be easy to extend. Barth would say that in some sense we know both sides of each. What can he mean by this? Does he mean that they are temporary confusions that will be cleared up as knowledge increases, or does he mean that the world is really like this, a place of ultimate chaos and incoherence?

Some readers have taken him in the former and less radical sense. Let us see what this would involve. When a contradiction is at issue, there is only one way in which consistency can be saved: if both propositions are to be retained as true, the meaning of one or other (if not both) must be altered; both cannot be taken as true in their contradictory senses. Now the contradictions we have listed are, without exception, cases in which on the one side stands an insight of the natural man and on the other an insight alleged to have come by revelation. If reconciliation is to be achieved, either the revealed or the natural meaning must, as it stands, be given up.

Suppose first that we give up the revealed meaning. This is the line that naturalists would take. But since it would amount to denying revealed truth, Barth would not consider it for a moment. The main point of his thinking and writing is to insist that revealed knowledge is final, that it takes precedence over everything that is or can be set against it, that it is beyond amendment or appeal.

Very well; let us try the other alternative, and say that what must be given up are those affirmations of our natural knowledge that stand in contradiction to revealed truth; these illusions are the growing pains of knowledge and will disappear as humanity matures. I have more sympathy with this suggestion than some of my philosophic colleagues, for, holding as I do to the theory of internal relations, I would go so far as to say that none of our so-called knowledge is wholly true just as it stands. But this dependence of our concepts and insights upon the changing context of knowledge is itself a matter of degree. To say that the proposition 'colds are produced by a virus' is not true with its present meaning would be a minor shock, but its repercussions would not be nearly so destructive as those of denying that two and two are four. Our question then is, How serious would be the consequences of denying the sort of propositions to which Barth is opposing revelation?

I can only think they would be disastrous. For among the propositions that would have to be given up are some of the central insights of ethics and cosmology. Is there anything clearer in ethics than that a man cannot be condemned as morally evil because his great-grandfather sinned, or that to inflict extreme and gratuitous pain on a child or an animal is wrong? Is there anything clearer in cosmology than that if a mind knows all there is to know it cannot grow in knowledge; that if it is not in time it cannot grow older in time; that if it is omnipresent there is nothing outside itself to know or love? These are the kinds of insight which, in Barth's theology, conflict with revealed truth. They cannot be reconciled with that truth unless their present meaning is revised out of recognition or set down as false. And that would quite simply destroy both ethics and speculative thought. If it were now to be called right to condemn the living for the deeds of the dead and to inflict gratuitous suffering, then anything could be right; the distinction between right and wrong as we know it would have ceased to exist. If a mind could at once grow and not grow in knowledge, grow older and yet not grow older, love others without there being others to love, then anything could be true, and the distinction between truth and falsehood has been blurred irreparably. Natural knowledge would be so confounded that both sides of a contradiction might be true.

Let us see where we are. We have been considering what Barth can mean by denying the jurisdiction of philosophy or natural reason over theology. If it means merely that reason as now exercised falls short of ultimate truth, we can only agree. If it means that the conflicts between revealed and natural insights are such as may be removed by expanding knowledge and are only a temporary veil for a coherent world beyond them, the question is on which side the revision is to take place. That revealed knowledge can be revised Barth would of course deny. What must be given up as it stands is therefore natural knowledge. But we have seen that the required revision of natural knowledge would revise it out of existence by denying the truth of insights that are clear and crucial. It would even compel us to accept as true what presents itself as self-contradictory. But to say that a statement, though self-contradictory, is still true is to say that reality itself is incoherent. This second interpretation of Barth's meaning, if thought out, thus carries us on to the third.

BARTH'S IRRATIONALISM

12 The third interpretation is that the conflict is genuine and beyond remedy. Revelation tells us what is not only unintelligible to natural reason but a challenge and offence to it, and before a challenge from an absolute authority reason can only surrender. This, I think, is what Barth was really saying. In spite of the attempt by some of his followers to tone down his conflict with philosophy and to deny any disparagement of reason, he was surely saying this: revelation is not subject to rational tests, and even if it requires, as it does, that we should abandon some of the most certain of our ethical and speculative insights, or the law of contradiction itself, it is ours not to reason why, but to obey.

There are those who would say that even with this interpretation

Barth is no enemy of reason rightly conceived. When in a lecture at St Andrews I ventured to describe him as an irrationalist, an eminent Scottish theologian took me to task in the Edinburgh *Scotsman*, insisting to my astonishment that 'Barth stands out in Europe as the great protagonist *against* irrationalism'. His case, as I recall, was this: the task of thought is to conform to its object. If its object happens to be one that does not obey the rules we have set up for the conduct of reason, then the truly rational course is to conform to the object and override the rules. What is really irrational is to try to force reality itself into the rickety procrustean bed of our own logic.

That seems at first sight rather sensible. It has often been suggested that the laws of logic are laws of our thought but not of reality. But consider what that means. Take for example the best known law of logic, the law of contradiction. When we say that although thought must conform to this law things need not, what we must mean, for instance, is that there may be a surface that in the same sense and in the same place is both black and not black. Now we can either understand this proposition or not. If we claim that we can, we have contradicted ourselves, for by saying that the law of contradiction is a law of thought, we mean that we cannot escape from it, that we cannot see two contradictory things to be true. On the other hand, if a thing's having and also not having a certain character is inconceivable, then our thesis—that reality may be self-contradictory —is itself inconceivable. One may protest that this is logical hocus pocus. But to philosophers logic is not unimportant, and a predicament from which it is impossible to conceive what an escape could mean is not a predicament in which it is very tragic to be caught.

13 When Barth says that, illumined by revelation, we must accept things as true which mere reason would call false, he is implying that the standards of reason are invalid. This view, as just suggested, seems incapable of clear statement. We may add that no one, Barth included, can live up to it in practice. He prefers, as we have seen, not to rest his case on argument; he appeals straight to absolute authority. Still he does write theology indefatigably, and just what is theology? As practised by Barth, it seems to consist of statements written in German or English and professing to be true statements of historical fact, of the meaning of Biblical passages, of the relation of rational to revealed knowledge, of conjectures and conclusions innumerable about nature, grace, sin, miracle, creation, judgement, life and death. Barth plainly expects us to accept his statements as true, his exposition as relevant, and his conclusions as valid. He expects us to accept all this while accepting at the same time his indictment of natural reason as unreliable, while believing that some of its clearest and most certain insights are false, while questioning even its simplest and most universal demands. Are we not justified in saying to him: You cannot have it both ways? If reason at its best and clearest is an unsafe guide, then your theology, dependent at every step on the exercise of that reason, is itself a journey over quicksands. On the other hand, if the guide that has taken you over the vast theological mileage you have travelled is as reliable as you plainly assume, then you can hardly turn, at the threshold of revelation, and dismiss it as a blind leader of the blind.

Barthians would no doubt reply: We have every right to do that. We are not denying the validity of reason generally; we are admitting its competence in its own field, which is that of nature, and denying its jurisdiction only beyond that field, in the region of the supernatural. Surely that gives you philosophers room enough. Why are you not content?

THE EXPROPRIATION OF PHILOSOPHY

14 We are not content because in the area thus forbidden to us lie many of the problems which a deep concern and an old tradition have made specially our own. Philosophers for some thousands of years have been searching into creation, immortality, God, freedom, evil. They have not, perhaps, been notably successful, but they have closed many misleading trails and achieved, as they thought, some glimpses of the summit toward which they have been struggling. You now tell them that, with supernatural aid, you have been privileged to see the summit, that it is not in their world at all, that there is no road to it from where they stand, that all the trails they have been exploring wind up in swamps or deserts, and that they had therefore better give up their misguided effort.

Now it is not very likely that on receipt of such instructions philosophers will cease and desist from their efforts. Except in authoritarian communities, ecclesiastical or political, they lack practice in such obedience, and besides they have much at stake. If their occupation is to be so largely gone, they will want to know what precisely Barth has seen during his sojourn on the hilltop which vetoes their attempt on the summit from another side. When they ask this question, they receive, as we have seen, a most disconcerting answer.

The answer is that there is no answer they could understand. Even in his revealed essence, says Barth, God is 'unenthüllbar'; even as *Deus revelatus* he is *Deus absconditus*; he is the absolutely other; he is 'pure negation'; he cannot be described in any terms available to our human faculties. 'Revelation', says Kraemer, 'is by its nature inaccessible and remains so, even when it is revealed'. Brunner agrees: 'in the person of Jesus God tells us what no man can know, what is in no kind of continuity with our human ideas, no, not even with the best and highest we possess.' The content of this revelation cannot even be recognised as such by human faculty; if I do recognise it, it is not I but God in me that does so; if I converse with you about it, it is not you but God in you that understands. Now surely the appropriate mode of expression for such a revelation is silence. What has been seen is more ineffable than the mystic's vision. When the mystic comes down from his hilltop, he comes as a rule with a smile, but a smile means that something in our sense good has been experienced, and the transcendentalism of Barth and Brunner outsoars all human good. The life of the religious man, in Brunner's striking image, is a wheel whose spokes all radiate from a hub— only the hub is hollow. Man's highest hopes and efforts are bent toward reaching a shrine whose doors are at last flung open only to reveal to his straining sight that it is empty.

But if it is thus empty, what are those thousands of pages about? Barth says that though the content of revelation is wholly beyond us there are *witnesses* in the way of Scriptural texts, the words and acts of Jesus, the history, liturgies and sacraments of the church, that are relevant to this revelation. I do not see how they could be. To say that they are relevant to the truth, or a witness to it, in the sense of offering evidence for it, is to bring this truth within the field of rational thought, where one belief confirms or disconfirms another. To say that in the character of Jesus we have a suggestion or an adumbration of the divine character is to say, if anything at all, that the character of Jesus is more or less like the divine character, and then the contention that God is wholly other has been abandoned. Sometimes Barth qualifies his agnosticism by admitting that we can make the acts or deeds of Deity the objects of our thought, but not Deity himself, since he is a subject. Now it is true that I shall never know you or make you my object if that means that I shall sense or directly perceive you. But that does not imply that I cannot know you in another and perfectly relevant sense. Even if, in order to reach each other, we must cross a bridge of inference, we may know each other very well indeed. Of course Barth may mean by 'subject' something wholly different from what the term commonly means. If he does, the argument ceases to be invalid and is merely unintelligible.

UNINTELLIGIBILITY RAMPANT

15 There is a certain advantage in asserting the existence of the unintelligible. For you can then say unintelligible things about it, and to any objection you can reply that it is unreasonable to insist that the unintelligible should appear out of character. We have already found suggestions of this procedure in Barth. In endeavouring to communicate the incommunicable, he uses many descriptive terms as somehow appropriate to revelation. It is a message or a word; it is also the person of Christ himself; it is a state of faith; it is a state of knowledge; it is a decision or act, though also an influx received passively; it is truth; it is the service of God; though this is the same as the knowledge of God, and the same again as the justice, mercy, and grace of God. What is Barth trying to tell us by all these characterisations? If revelation is utterly discontinuous with all we know, they can mean nothing, and why mislead us by using them? If they are really descriptive of revelation, even by metaphor or analogy, then God is not discontinuous with us after all. And since in that case they bear meanings that we can make sense of, should not some regard be paid to those meanings when the words are put together? To say, as Brunner does, that 'only by this act does man become a person' and then to add that faith is a free gift in which man does not act at all; to say, as Barth does, that revelation is truth (that is, a relation between proposition and fact) but also somehow a person, though it is really also a state of knowledge which somehow is also a decision—to say these things is to offer for our belief an incoherent patchwork. If a philosopher were to say them, he would be dismissed as gabbling, since they cancel each other out. And he is disposed to wonder, perhaps naïvely, why that which would be gibberish in his own mouth should be profundity in another's.

Barth calls his theology dialectical. To the philospher dialectical thinking means thinking that takes us slowly nearer to the goal through a series of zigzag steps. We are now told that this is just what thinking cannot do. The thinker can no longer take a 'position over against God so that from this he may form thoughts about God, which are in varying degrees true, beautiful and good.'[25] 'The value of what theology has to say is measured by no standard except that of its object,' and that object is separated by an impassable chasm from even our highest thought. The thinker is thus compelled to relinquish a powerful means of persuasion, the value of a felt approximation to an immanent ideal. Though there is much in Hegel's reasoning that seems to me invalid, there is something most impressive in the widening sweep of vision as he climbs the ladder of his categories toward the absolute idea; it is not hard to feel, as one follows him, something of the excitement that Spinoza felt as he approached his third kind of knowledge, that Newton felt as he found himself drawing nearer to the supreme law of the physical universe. The steps of the intellectual dialectician may be halting and his progress slow, but his quest itself is not misguided; indeed it is the inevitable expression of 'the intellectual love of God'. But if the theologian disclaims what is so natural and inevitable, if he insists that progress toward the end of knowledge brings us no nearer to God at all, then in emancipating himself from human nature he is also emancipating himself right out of human interest. When the dialectical pursuit of truth can promise no better knowledge of ultimate things, even at the end, than irremovable illusion, why travel the stony road at all?

NON-ETHICAL ETHICS

16 Something similar must be said about ethical thinking. The character of Jesus is for me, as for so many millions of others, a source of recurring wonder and fascination. When it is put forward as the flawless ideal to which all human conduct should try to approximate, I take the claim seriously, though I cannot simply shut my eyes and swallow it. I try to understand it; I try to test its claim in the only way open to me, namely by noting whether, as my moral insight matures, I find myself closer to it, and whether, as I read expositions of it by preachers and theologians, I can say, 'Yes, on this point and on this, I now see that he is right.' The most powerful plea for a moral authority is one that, forgoing all appeal to authority, asks only the ratification of reflective conscience; does the ideal, if it is lifted up, draw to it all honest and thoughtful minds? Some expositors make a powerful case by revealing, perhaps unconsciously, what life in that personal presence has done to them. To take a few examples that may mean less to others than to me: when one comes in touch with the singular moral grace of Dean Church, or the inexhaustible affection for his fellow men of Scott Holland or Charles F. Andrews, or the sunny serenity of Phillips Brooks, or the ethical sensitiveness of James Martineau, or Schweitzer's sense of fellowship with even the humblest life, one may feel a little like Adams and Leverrier when they marked the aberrations of Uranus from its orbit; they were sure that there was a great unseen body farther out that was pulling the planet toward it.

Perhaps by reason of my own obtuseness, when I read Barth I feel nothing of all this. I hear the bleak strident voice repeating that the Wholly Other is over all, that we have no claim on his mercy, that though he has made us he finds us hateful, that he commands absolute acceptance, unquestioning obedience, unconditional abject surrender. It is as if the harsh voice were determined, in demanding this surrender, to beat us down still further by insisting that there is and can be no earthly reason for it. If one is attracted by the kindness or courage or tenderness of the Jesus who loved children and would break the Sabbath for an ox in distress, one is attracted by the wrong things, the kind of virtues that mere natural man can respond to and hope to attain, whereas the Jesus to whom surrender should be made is the incognito Jesus who was wearing these virtues as a disguise. One of the most persuasive arguments in the old theological armory was that in Christianity we find life and find it more abundantly, and that its way of life alone can satisfy our native moral sense. To Barth this argument is without force.

Indeed we may wonder whether Barth, in his eagerness to save the *Deus absconditus* in the life of Christ, has not overshot the mark and compromised much that is essential in Christ's own teaching. One is often made uneasy in reading Barth by the sense that his guide in interpreting the New Testament is not the Jesus of the synoptic gospels but the Paul of Romans and Galatians, in short that he is more Pauline than Christian. As Dr McGiffert pointed out, Jesus

recognized virtue as a natural achievement, not a supernatural gift. He had an uncommonly high estimate of man's moral powers. In spite of all the wickedness he saw about him, and the disobedience to the divine will, he could summon his hearers to be perfect even as their Father in heaven was perfect without ever suggesting that divine aid was needed or that they would have to be made over by divine power if they were to measure up to such a standard. Of the pessimism so widely prevalent in the Hellenistic world, the pessimism that counted man wholly incapable of good without the influx of the divine, there is no trace in the Jesus of the Synoptic Gospels. . . .[26]

In dealing with the character of Christ, interpreters have often gone to one or other of two extremes. Those like Luther or Calvin who have stressed his identity with Deity have often exalted him out of human understanding, while thinkers like Renan, concerned wholly with his humanity, have found in him a soft-hearted and romantic visionary. It seems probable that the worship of the Virgin, whose human tenderness there was no reason to explain away, was in part a reaction against an exaltation of Jesus that made him unapproachably remote. Needless to say, the Jesus that appears in Barth's pages is astronomically far from that of Renan; some will think him also far from the gentle and often intensely human figure of the biographical gospels.

STRANGE AFFINITIES

17   Because of this uncompromising distrust of the thought and conscience of the natural man, Barth has strange philosophic affiliations. In the theory of knowledge he shares important convictions with the positivists. He holds, with Ayer and Carnap, that the attempt by rational thought to go beyond nature to the supernatural is inevitably defeated, though of course he draws a different inference from the defeat. He concludes that since we cannot reach a knowledge of God through rational means we must do so through non-natural means; the positivists conclude from the same premise that the attempt itself is meaningless. But as to the futility of metaphysics, the two schools join hands.

In ethics, Barth has a striking affinity with Stoicism, though at one of its weakest points. The Stoics taught that virtue and vice were not matters of degree; if you were guilty of one peccadillo, you had broken the moral law as truly as if you had murdered your mother, and there was no health in you. Barth talks at times in a curiously similar vein. 'Either we love God and our neighbour or we hate them both. Either we are obedient or we are not. There is no possibility here of a third, middle course, consisting in some sort of approximation. . . . Man with all his outward and inward achievements . . . stands in the presence of that Law as one who is unthankful and impenitent, and who, since he does not love God or his neighbour, must hate them . . .'[27] There is much that is admirable in Stoicism, but its black-and-white notion of goodness is surely inhuman. It seems likewise inhuman in Barth. If anything can be said with confidence about human nature, one would have supposed it to be that we are neither saints nor satans, that we are all blends of aspiration and sordidness, in short that we all fall in that third class which to Barth is a null class. To say that if we lack his kind of faith our attitude toward our fellow men must be one of hatred suggests that he is adjusting his facts to his theology rather than his theology to the facts.

THE MORALITY OF THE SPHINX

18 Because of this alienation from humanity in both senses of 'humanity' Barth's ethics seems to me strangely sterile. It is hard to deduce anything helpful from a conceptual blank. At first one is impressed by the high line taken. To the question, How should I live? Barth gives the same answer as to the question, What is revealed?—simply 'Jesus Christ'. 'The Law, the rule and the first principles underlying all service of God are—*Jesus Christ*.'[28] 'Was sollen wir denn tun?' he asks in the *Römerbrief*, and answers: 'We can, indeed, do one thing, not many. . . . For what can a Christian do in society other than follow attentively the doing of God?' No one wants to be put in the position of criticising action from such a source, but one does need more than a name. One wants guidance; one wants to know how Jesus would deal with a communist, whether he would approve the professional artist, soldier, or athlete, what he would say to a confused youth about sex. To all such questions Barth's answer seems to be the same: Act out the indwelling Christ. But since the Christ who may dwell in us is discontinuous with us, both psychologically and ethically, it is hard to see how any inference can be drawn from his presence as to what a human being in a given position would or should do. If, in our eagerness for some cue, we were to look at Barth's own life, with its curious mixture of courage toward the Nazis, complaisance toward the Communists (he was silent throughout the Hungarian crisis), kindliness to the men in Basel jails, and arrogance toward critics (anyone who ventures to criticise 'should have read me completely'), the light gained is flickering.

Brunner takes the same puzzling line. 'We never know what is right for us,' he says, 'nor what is best for the other person. We go astray when we think we can deduce this from some principle or other, or from some experience. . . .'[29] Both men are clear enough about what non-Christian living means; it means everything that in our own persons we do, from holding up a bank to rescuing a drowning child. But genuinely Christian living is far more difficult to detect, since it is apparently beyond identification by the natural man. Christian action springs from love, but this is not the sinful love felt by unregenerate man for his fellows. How we are to recognise a Christian when we meet him, I do not know. We can be fairly confident, I suppose, that if he is as much of a Hindu as Gandhi or as much of a humanist as Schweitzer, he is not a good man in the true sense; one must be a Christian in Barth's sense in order to be that. But is the man who robs a bank also beyond the pale, along with the Gandhis and the Schweitzers? How can one tell? If human virtues may disguise sinners, may not human vices disguise saints? If the centre from which a man's actions proceed and the standard employed in those actions are discontinuous with our natural ones, it is hard to see how any judgement is possible. The courts indeed might have something to say, but they are administering mere human justice, which we are assured is corrupt. If Barth means what he repeatedly says, it seems to follow that our jails may be filled with Christians under aliases, just as our churches and humane societies are filled with people suffering from sinful human kindness.

I do not suppose that Barth actually thinks in this way. The absolute wall of separation between natural and supernatural is like

the 'absolute' American wall of separation between church and state,
or the 'iron curtain' between East and West; there is a continual
osmosis through it. Does Barth really feel natural love and selfless-
ness to be as little irradiated by the divine presence as hatred or
malice? That is hard to believe. His transcendence tends, in spite
of itself, to melt into moral immanence. There is a similar welcome
inconsistency in his account of the approach from below. He is
constantly using terms in his theology that seem to bear more
meaning than they ought to bear if his theory is true. He remarked
in the first of his Princeton lectures: 'the God of the Gospel has a
genuine interest in human existence;' 'the God of Schleiermacher
cannot show mercy. The God of the Gospel can and does'; 'God is
father, brother and friend'. If such statements do not imply that
our thought of God as a person is justified, that we are right in
ascribing to him the sort of interest, mercy, and kindness that we
know, their meaning is lost on me. In most of his writings Barth
repudiates the applicability of such concepts to God. In one of
his Princeton lectures he seemed to acknowledge the harshness of
this position by making a distinction, not developed, between
'theanthropology,' which he considered permissible, and 'anthropo-
theology,' which he did not. This distinction I have failed to grasp.

BARTHIANISM AND THE NON-CHRISTIAN WORLD

19 Still, discontinuity has been his main insistence. It is on this,
not on his lapses from it, that we must fix attention. And I should
like now to say something about the relevance and opportuneness
of this teaching in our present situation. I cannot think that the
future is on its side. Not that this would disprove it; truth and
success are different things, and the truth of a speculative doctrine
is not to be tested either by the range of its acceptance or by the
good or ill effects of accepting it. But Christianity is more than a
speculative doctrine; it is also a way of life; and in appraising a way
of life, we cannot be indifferent to its working in society. Christianity,
as Barth interprets it, involves an attitude toward thought and action
that impinges on the culture of our time in significant ways.

Consider first its impact on the non-Christian world. Our mastery
of space is crowding us so closely together that we are now less than
twenty-four hours away from great centres of Hindu, Islamic, and
Buddhist population. Since our ties with these cultures are bound to
grow closer, the need of understanding and friendship is also growing. Scholars are discovering in the faiths of the world many areas
of resemblance and finding the same sense of dependence on the
unknown, the same universal yearnings for light, security, and

guidance. These other religions are the product of many centuries of what we may call religious experimentation in the way of thought, ritual, and practice; they have the deep respect and allegiance of their followers; indeed the people of India are disposed to think that, whatever the advantage of the West in material wealth, they themselves have been more sensitised by their religion to things of the spirit than we have by ours. What is the neo-orthodox attitude toward these faiths?

'The God of Mohammed', Barth answers, 'is an idol like all other idols, and it is an optical illusion to characterise Christianity along with Islam as a "monotheistic" religion'.[30] All other religions are the product of the natural man, the sort of religion, one gathers, of which he says that 'the Church does not take the slightest interest in religion' and 'religion must die'. With such faiths the true faith cannot compromise. Revelation has been given through one man only, Jesus of Nazareth, and through him only to the eyes of the elect; to say that it was in this sense present in any degree in the Buddha, for example, is blasphemy. If the people who follow Buddha do not see this, it is because God has withheld from them that power to do so with which he has favoured many people in the West, and there is no effort on their part that can hope to open their eyes or secure a similar blessing.

What is the likelihood that Christianity, so interpreted, will be heard gladly or with conviction by the people of other faiths? Surely not very great. They will suspect, and with some reason, a hidden link to that Western arrogance of which they carry long memories. They are invited to accept, without argument and in scorn of argument, a Deity who has focused his favours on a fraction of the race—and not their fraction. They do not see why revelation should come through one Scripture only, or one life only, or why the miracles of one faith should be true miracles and those of all others fraudulent, even when equally well attested, or why religious experiences that seem qualitatively very much alike should be revelatory in Basel and illusory in Bombay. The Christianity that is a gospel of love, overflowing boundaries of race, class, and colour, they understand, and their Gandhis and Tagores and Suzukis have listened to it and gratefully borrowed from it. But when offered this exclusive transcendentalism with the take-it-or-leave-it postscript, they may be expected to return it to the sender with the endorsement, 'Thank you very much; on the whole, we prefer to leave it'.

THE FUTILITY OF MORAL AND RELIGIOUS EFFORT

20 Consider, secondly, how the temper of this teaching suits that of our newly emerging world. The new atmosphere is one of hope, based on effort plus the increasing mastery of nature. Since the United Nations was founded, scores of new nations have been added to its membership, most of them exultant over their freshly won freedom. These peoples are trying to absorb the ambition, energy, and self-reliance that have made the more advanced nations what they are. The Russian experience in particular seems relevant to them, because, as they see it, the Russians lifted themselves by their own rough boots in a single generation from poverty and ignorance to some degree of prosperity, and to impatient eyes that means hope. The fact that Russia has chosen to make its effort without benefit of clergy is not lost on these observers. They are not indifferent to the things of the spirit; they long for them. But they hold increasingly to a conviction, now orthodox among the Russians, that the spirit has long roots in the body, and that if it is to produce its proper flowers, those roots must be studied and watered and nourished. The precipitate progress of the last few decades has come through a new mastery over natural processes, including that mastery over the body that has added so many years to men's lives. There is a restless and urgent hope in the air, the hope of emergence into a larger life through the control of its natural conditions.

On this sort of hope neo-orthodoxy throws a douche of cold water. Through its doctrine of discontinuity it declines to admit that the spirit, in its true sense, has its roots in the body at all. The goods that are so rooted and that may therefore be gained by cultivation are constantly disparaged. Barth has been particularly critical of American 'materialism' and its goals. Brunner depreciates all merely natural morality. Of the morality in which we judge conduct by the natural goods it produces he says: 'this whole moral gradation which for us is absolutely necessary, simply does not count ultimately, that is, in the sight of God . . .';[31] indeed he goes so far as to say, 'in the last resort it is precisely morality which *is* evil.'[32] And beyond all this is the iteration that, valueless and sinful as man's whole natural life is, there is nothing, absolutely nothing, he can do to lift himself out of it. 'We have as little share in our rebirth,' says Barth, 'as we have in our being created . . .'[33] 'Man's salvation is the work of God *exclusively*, and to say anything else is to blaspheme against Jesus Christ. . . .'[34] Is this not a somewhat chilling gospel for a world of rising hope in what man can make of man?

Its bleakness has repelled many even of those brought up in the Christian tradition. Professor Marion Bradshaw has written of it with feeling: 'when I find a theology advocated by its adherents because it makes men feel their helplessness and the worthlessness of even the best that men can think and do, it is simply impossible for me to regard it as "more desirable and profounder". Reading much more of it could easily have led me into a measure of sympathy with Whitehead's dictum that Christian theology is one of the great disasters of the human race.'[35]

Barth would probably deny that his theology is incongruous with the time, and would like to think it equally relevant to all times and places. But it is hard for an energetic American or an aspiring African of the present day to feel its relevance or to forget that it is the product of a very different moral climate from his own.

'we cannot understand Barth's teaching,' says Cave 'unless we remember the mood of reaction from which it sprang. In his youth he had shared the generous enthusiasms of the labour movement, and had looked to it to secure the peace of Europe. The War shattered all hope in man and man's achievement. Henceforth it must be utter despair or else reliance upon God alone.'

Of Barth's *Romans* the same writer adds: 'Everything human is in it scorned and condemned, and, not least, religion, man's approach to God.'[36] 'A religion', says John Baillie, 'that refuses to exhibit its own reasonableness is fellow to a political régime that refuses to submit to a free referendum, and it is no accident that the two are products of the same age.'[37] But that age is not our age. Authoritarianism no longer commends itself to free minds in any field. Trust in man's power to shape himself and his future is returning, and a wave of awakened life is rolling over people who fifty years ago would have seemed buried centuries deep from civilisation. For such people, the Barthian theology is an anachronism. To faces turned toward us in hope it preaches despair of all human aspiration or effort.

NEO-ORTHODOXY AND SCIENCE

21 Consider, thirdly, the attitude of this theology toward science. There is no need in our day to stress the importance of science, which has been done to the point of weariness; if one wants some measure of its improved position one need only compare a college catalogue of the 1870s with one of the 1970s on the relative places of science and the classics.

When I speak of science, I mean both the results and the methods of scientific study. As for the first, the results of science, the neo-orthodox attitude seems to vary. Sometimes it takes the line that revealed and natural knowledge are in hopeless conflict, but that this does not really matter, since the supernatural is beyond our logic. We have dealt with that line already. Sometimes it insists rather that between revealed and natural knowledge there can be no conflict because the realms are different. Barthians are not fundamentalists. They can read Darwin, Freud, and Einstein without alarm; they have no aversion even to the criticism of the Scriptural record by linguists, anthropologists, and archaeologists. Still, their readiness to approve such criticism is not based on any sense of its importance for their own province. On the contrary, their tolerance springs from a serene conviction that the results of such criticism are irrelevant to anything of real importance in religion. The human body, even the human mind, may have evolved from the inorganic; a new gospel of St Thomas and new scrolls from the Dead Sea may revise our records of the life and times of Jesus; such discoveries matter little. For the planes on which faith and science move are discontinuous with each other. Nothing central to the Christian position could possibly be touched by these researches. With this insight, the theologian remains above 'the conflict between science and religion,' which is only an illusion anyhow; what has occurred is a tiresome clash of zealots, ignorant on both sides of where the real boundaries lie.

This is an attitude that wears on its face a certain respect for science. But is it really more respectful than that of the fundamentalists? The fundamentalists fought Darwin at Dayton, Tennessee, because they saw, or thought they saw, that he was saying something important for faith as well as for science; Genesis and *The Origin of Species* could not both be true, and if they were forced to choose, they were going to stay with Genesis. Astronomy was important, for if it succeeded in proving that on a certain day in the first century darkness did not cover the earth, then the New Testament was at one point (Luke 23 : 44) unreliable, and it might be so in others. Science is thus paid the respect due to a formidable foe. To neo-orthodoxy in one of its standard moods, science is not sufficiently relevant even to be an enemy. The evolution of body and mind may be a fact; the received history in the New Testament may be through and through inaccurate; but the truth that God exists, that he created the human soul, and that he revealed himself to this soul is untouched by these or any other scientific theses. And the liberals are just as wrong as the fundamentalists. For the liberals, also frightened by the alleged conflict, try to make peace not by adjusting science to dogma but by adjusting dogma to science. What is called for is neither war with science nor surrender to it. Rightly conceived, science is no menace at all. It never penetrates beyond the purlieus of the temple; it deals with accidents, not with essence, at best with mere external witnesses to the faith, not faith itself. As neutrals, we should allow it to go its own way, without either fright or provocation.

22 I do not think this high line will stand examination; there are too many holes in the fence that Barth and Brunner have tried to erect between faith and science. The liberals, I think, have been right in their sense of the importance of scientific advance for theology. If one ignores the rising tide of science, one is only too likely to be drowned in it. To say that the evidence for man's ascent from the inorganic or for the dependence of mind on body has no relevance to the nature or destiny of the soul seems to me plainly untrue. That evidence may be indecisive, but if so, it will be shown to be so by further evidence, conceivably brought to light, for example, by psychical researchers, who are fighting their own courageous battle with the fundamentalists of science. Dean Inge was surely right in thinking that the second law of thermodynamics is a serious threat to the belief in a God who loves mankind, and in writing a book to consider gravely whether there is any way out for the theologian. [38] The anthropologists of religion like Frazer and the psychologists of religion like James and Freud, who have offered naturalistic explanations for religious beliefs and experiences, can be met if at all only by a more thorough criticism than any they have yet received from neo-orthodoxy.

And it is not only science but the philosophy of science that needs consideration. Barth can afford to be disinterested about this or that miracle because he is so certain that the Christian revelation is one great miracle, and he could conceivably be right, that those who have eyes to see will simply see this to be true without aid from evidence or argument. But for those who doubt it or deny it or think it a partial truth, some clear discussion of the meaning and probability of miracle in a world of science is surely called for. Barth's way of dealing with such questions, I take it, is to say that the certitude possessed by the man of faith about the occurrence of this great miracle is supreme and not really comparable with the confidence of the scientist that it does not occur; that if one has the insight of faith, argument is unnecessary, and that if one lacks this, it is unprofitable. One can understand the persuasiveness of such an attitude for anyone in the inner circle. But it leaves those outside of it singularly cold.

23 Science, however, means more than a set of conclusions; it means also a set of methods and intellectual habits. The most important of these habits is adherence to a rule that is felt to be at once intellectual and moral, the rule of adjusting one's assent to the evidence. This rule is not a restriction on intellectual freedom. It says nothing against our entertaining the wildest of hypotheses; one of the heroes of science, Darwin, admitted that he had taken seriously many hypotheses that he would not care to report. But on the assumption that we are interested above all in truth, the rule does forbid us to commit ourselves intellectually without grounds, or to withhold assent where sufficient grounds are present. The wild hypothesis may be entertained, but must not be believed before we have evidence for it, and if the evidence makes both ways, we should accept such probability as the evidence warrants; desire or fear that something should be true is no basis for assenting to it. This principle of intellectual rectitude is spreading steadily into other areas and is making itself felt increasingly in religious and political discussion.

The Barthian would reject this principle at the outset. To chain belief to the evidence in the field of religion would seem to him an absurd restriction, in that it doubly begs the question. It assumes, for one thing that religious belief is the kind of belief that rests on empirical or rational evidence, and this he denies. Secondly it assumes that such belief is an intellectual act, which can be willed or inhibited, and it is one of his main points that it is no act of ours at all but an uncovenanted, uncontrollable descent of grace. These are large issues which cannot be dealt with in passing. Suffice it to make two further remarks.

First, we must frankly admit that when the Barthian takes this attitude it is unfair to charge him with the irresponsibility that a scientist would exhibit by a like attitude in his own province. The Barthian is not denying that the principle of mental rectitude is sound for inquiries into nature, and if confronted by persons who stubbornly adhered to the flatness of the earth or flew to a belief in centaurs and leprechauns for which they could produce no evidence, he would no doubt feel as the rest of us do. But he insists that if a belief is such that scientific evidence can have no bearing on its truth, one way or another, then to charge him with illicitly exceeding the evidence in the same fashion is false and unjust. There is nothing wrong in ignoring evidence known to be irrelevant. And of course if it is known to be irrelevant, he is right.

But here we must add our second remark. In spite of his protestations of neutrality toward science, he is clearly hostile to its own conception of its work. He is claiming a knowledge of objects that it cannot see, by means of faculties that it does not recognise. He would no doubt reply that for science to question the existence of objects and faculties merely on the ground that it has failed to observe them is the sort of arrogance that appears in Russell's calm remark that what is knowledge is science, and what is not science is not knowledge. And if it is true that science is only a set of statements about what is or may be given in sense, as some positivists have maintained, there is force in this reply. But science need not be identified with myopia. It is a systematic attempt to explore and understand every kind of fact. It does not object to anyone's announcing the discovery of a new kind of fact or faculty; what it does insist on is that there should be some means of checking or verifying the alleged discovery. Not that the new object must be a public and physical thing like the sun and moon, but at least that if it is private, like a pain or an emotion, it must have some sort of continuity with the experiences of other persons, or some sort of generic resemblance to them, so that reports about it will carry meaning. I do not think that science would deny the possibility of an insight so exceptional that it could not be communicated to others, but it would deny that the occurrence of such an insight imposed any obligation on others to accept it so long as it remained for them without content.

Science does not consider this attitude dogmatic or negative. It is at least hospitable to any belief that can show itself in any degree probable to normal minds. Of the major beliefs of neo-orthodoxy, however, it seems to be admitted and even insisted that no such account can be rendered and that they remain nevertheless the most luminously certain and overwhelmingly important of all beliefs. And we are called on to honour this certainty and importance even though we have never had the sort of experience out of which they arise. To be sure we cannot have faith, for with that our wills have nothing to do. But Barth does not speak only to be converted, and when he announces to scholars and scientists what the Scripture really means, he seems to be asking them to lay aside that intellectual pride which asks for evidence in advance; they should rather follow the principle he quoted from Calvin in his Princeton lectures, 'omnis recta cognitio Dei ab oboedientia nascitur'. This makes a demand of the scientist to which he finds it very hard to accede. For implied in the demand is the rejection of that very principle of intellectual rectitude by which he has lived, through which he has gained his successes, and through which he justifies himself in his own eyes. He is assured that from time to time there are lodged in men a set of faculties so discontinuous with their other faculties as to be undiscoverable by observation or introspection, by means of which they can apprehend truths beyond the range of merely human verification. The majority of men, even of educated men, though they bent their attention assiduously to what was being said to them, could not understand it, nor could they hope to do so by any earnestness of research, reflection, or sympathy, though something might at any moment be done to them from outside nature, for no reason that they could discover, which would flood the hitherto unintelligible with supernatural light. I have said already that I do not think this view can be worked out in detail without conflicting with the conclusions of science at many points. But even if such collisions could be avoided, the Barthian would still be asking of the scientist an ethics of belief, an attitude toward the use of evidence, and a conception of what evidence consists in that would require him to set aside his scientific way of thinking.

PRIDE

24 What if the scientist declines to bow at the altar of an unknown God? What if he asks for reasons why he should worship where he cannot see? That, he is told, is pride, and pride is a very great sin. At the accusation of pride from this particular source, he will perhaps blink a little. If his bedside reading includes theology, he may recall a letter of Newman's to Cardinal Manning: 'I do not know whether I am on my head or my heels when I have active relations with you. . . . Meanwhile I propose to say seven masses for your intention. . . .' Consider what is being said to the scientist. It is not pride for a man to dismiss the scientific view of the world and the entire succession of rationalist philosophers from Plato to Whitehead, and to report that he has received a revelation from Omniscience which is true beyond all possibility of criticism from either science or philosophy. That is quite consistent with modesty; 'evangelical theology,' Barth told his Princeton audience, 'is *modest* theology'. On the other hand, to look before one leaps and ask for light before committing oneself, to display the kind of integrity that tries to hold its belief strictly to the evidence, to adhere to what philosopher and scientist alike regard as a primary virtue, that is pride and sin. Is there not here some lapse of humour? I am tempted to call in aid two honoured teachers of mine. 'Humour and humility,' said C. C. J. Webb, 'are qualities apt to go together; and one misses both when called upon, with no hint that the invitation has about it anything strange which might require apology or explanation, to express a certain truth not "in the language of our experience" but "from God's standpoint".' If that is humility, one wonders what higher standpoint is left for pride to occupy. 'A very little modesty', says H. J. Paton, 'might suggest to the prophet that to question the truth of his message is not the same thing as to sit in judgement upon God. Theological arrogance can also be a form of sinful pride.'[39]

THE TEMPTATION OF IRRATIONALISM

25 It must be admitted that the appeal to reason is not an exciting appeal, and that when some short-cut to absolute truth has been offered in tones of authority men have often shown a delighted alacrity in throwing down the laborious tools of reflection and trooping after the prophet. Our own generation has seen millions of people following political leaders who refused ostentatiously to be judged or guided by reason. Such irrationalism is perhaps easier still in religion, since its dogmas are so little susceptible of familiar kinds of check. And so Tertullian and Luther and Pascal and Kierkegaard and Barth each gain a fervid following when they raise their voices against the presumptions of reason. Even in a communion as comparatively generous to reason as Catholicism, the tendency has often been manifested. We have just mentioned the fascinating Newman. Many commentators have pointed out that Newman's appeal, subtle as his intellect was, was not essentially to reason.

'Dissenting altogether from Bishop Butler's view that reason is the only faculty by which we can judge even of revelation, he set religion apart, outside reason altogether. From the pulpit of St Mary's he told his congregation that Hume's argument against miracles was logically sound. It really was more probable that the witnesses should be mistaken than that Lazarus should have been raised from the dead. But, all the same, Lazarus was raised from the dead: we were required by faith to believe it, and logic had nothing to do with the matter.'[40]

And even the young intellectuals of Oxford, we are told, began to go about murmuring 'credo in Newmannum'. We have something similar in today's outbreak of theological irrationalism. As Anders Nygren puts it, 'There is coming to be a regular cult of the paradoxical and irrational, as though irrationality and lack of clearness were a hall-mark of Christian truth'. Reinhold Niebuhr, whose politics were as much the admiration as his theology was the despair of some liberals, could write: 'The canons of logic and rationality are transcended when reason attempts to comprehend the final irrationality of things.' And Niebuhr and Barth had voices that were heard in the land; they even achieved the popular canonisation of appearance on the cover of *Time*, as mere philosophers like Whitehead and Russell never did.

What is the person to do who has had respect for reason bred into his bone? He does not want to be *der Geist der stets verneint*. He knows that science and philosophy too have their dogmatisms, and he may recall the remark of Bradley that 'there is no sin, however prone to it the philosopher may be, which philosophy can justify so little as spiritual pride'. He knows that even logic has had its history, indeed that it has shown extraordinary changes in his own lifetime. And if he is the son and grandson of the parsonage, as the writer happens to be, he will have too many memories of the power and attraction of the religious life to wish to line up with its enemies, even if much that was credible to his parents is no longer credible to him. The humility, the capacity for reverence, the high concern for ends neither material nor selfish, the morality touched with emotion, which religion has stood for over the centuries, are still invaluable, and are deeply needed in our troubled time.

26 On the other hand when invited to let all holds go by which he has clung to his standards of reasonableness and to commit himself to a world discontinuous with everything he knows, in which paradoxes are absolute truth, ethics prides itself on leaving reason behind, and all activities of the natural man, including religion itself, are set down as sinful, he feels bound to reflect before accepting the invitation. If he is told that what to his reason is contradictory may still be true he will see and say at once that this is nonsense which cannot even be clearly thought. On the other claims of the new theology he will judge more tentatively. He knows that many of its claims, like those of miracle and revelation itself, are incapable of conclusive disproof and must be dealt with by considering their probability in the light of systematic knowledge and reflection. If he is told that such tests are invalid, he will reply that they are the best he has, and that according to his theological advisers themselves he cannot hope by any effort to gain higher ones. When the theology offered him is thus set in the common daylight, its appearance is less imposing. The experiences reported as unique and ineffable take on a family resemblance to others that are intense and exalted indeed but still natural. The inconceivable dogmas begin to look less like flashes from the super-rational than like the vaguely formulated beliefs of natural minds, suffused with passionate conviction. The central experience, instead of being an inexplicable, vertical descent into the natural order from an utterly foreign realm, begins to seem like many another supposed visitation which appeared on retrospect to be explicable after all by the dark forces of man's own mind, not the least of which is his desperate desire to escape from them and gain a foothold on a firmer shore.

It has been said that in religion men tend to divide by nature into the children of Luther and the children of Erasmus. I belong to the tribe of Erasmus. I am content to take my stand with those un-romantic liberals who, before they give assent to a doctrine, ask what it means. One of these was my honoured colleague Douglas Clyde Macintosh, who, though no lover of Hegel, loved still less that Hegelianism in reverse to which neo-orthodoxy tends, in which the real is the irrational and the irrational is the real. Another was

H. J. Paton, who has rightly warned us: 'To declare war upon reason is to alienate all who care for truth and to hold open the door for the impostor and the zealot.'[41] Still another is Professor C. A. Campbell, who has used words that I should be happy to make my own: 'The philosopher *must* claim, I think, that wherever the question of objective truth arises, whether it be the truth of religion or of anything else, it is for reason, and for reason *alone*, to carry out the assessment of the evidence, and to make the final adjudication upon it . . . what is there save *reason*, the philosopher asks, to perform this office?'[42] To that question liberals would answer, None. Some of them would go further and hoist a danger signal. A lifelong student of religion, James Bissett Pratt, wrote:

'The position taken up in certain passages of Kierkegaard and in some of the Barthian writings is sheer defeatism. It is a notification to the enemy and to the world at large that Christianity is no longer logically defensible, that it is frankly unreasonable, and that no one who respects human intelligence can consistently or conscientiously remain within the Christian fold.'[43]

These are strong words from an exceptionally sane critic. They call for a better answer than they have yet received.

PART III

ETHICS AND BELIEF

CHAPTER IX

RATIONALISM AND CHRISTIAN
ETHICS (I)

1 We have been discussing the tensions between reason and faith. Revelation and church authority have frequently said one thing while secular reflection has demanded another. The tensions that have concerned us have arisen for the most part over theological dogmas. But the discussion will be incomplete unless we go on to deal with similar tensions over the precepts of Christian morality.

Between the dogma and the ethics of traditional Christianity no sharp line can be drawn. The teaching that the morality taught and exemplified by Christ is a perfect one is as truly a part of the Christian system of belief as any clause of the Nicaean or Apostles' Creed; and hence it would be strange if the tension between reason and belief extended only to the factual parts of the creed and stopped short of its moral injunctions. Furthermore, in Christianity creed and conduct, theology and morals, are inextricably bound up with each other in their meaning. The two main commandments, love God and love man, have always been taken as interdependent. God is conceived as a father, loving and brooding over the children he has brought into being; loving him entails seeking to know his will for man and doing it; and this means treating mankind as brothers. Similarly, to love man is to love God, for he is the source from which the beloved community sprang, and his will supplies the ideal end which the love of man seeks to embody. In the original Christian teaching, morality and religion were thus inseparable. If one considers, for example, the Sermon on the Mount, and that essential kernel of it, the Lord's Prayer, it would be grotesque to find in it a conscious passage from one field, theology, to another field, morals. 'Our Father which art in heaven, hallowed be Thy name. Thy kingdom come, Thy will be done in earth as it is in heaven.' In such a passage religious belief and its attendant morality form one seamless whole. For anyone who takes these words as they were plainly meant to be taken, to be religious entails being moral, and to be moral implies being religious.

Any tension, then, that develops between reason and the more fundamental Christian beliefs is bound to extend itself to Christian ethics. Many questions at once arise here. Is ethics logically dependent on religious truth? What is the proper place of the appeal to authority in ethics? Is morality dependent on religious belief for its practical motivation? What in fact has been the influence of such belief on moral practice? These are important inquiries, and our proposed answers to them will appear as we proceed. But the question that must now concern us is this: Is Christian ethics also a rational ethics?

The question is in a sense unfair. We have just admitted that, as traditionally understood, Christian morals and Christian belief are interdependent, and if so, any attempt to examine the ethics by itself will do violence to the way it works in living minds. We shall attempt the examination nevertheless, and for more than one reason. Though moral and theological teachings have always in fact been closely combined in Christian teaching, it is still possible in thought to distinguish theory from precept, and to consider each in the light of the criteria appropriate to it. We have already done this for some dogmas of the creed, considering how they would fare if removed from the shelter of revelation and placed intellectually in the open. A similar inspection should be possible for the moral components of the creed. For such examination there is another and more immediate reason. It lies in Lord Gifford's famous injunction to his lecturers, already quoted: 'I wish the lecturers to treat their subject as a strictly natural science . . . without reference to or reliance upon any supposed special exceptional or so-called miraculous revelation.' The kind of examination here proposed, however inadequate, will at least be of the kind Lord Gifford seems to have desired.

There are many persons, of course, who will still think such an examination inappropriate and even obnoxious, since to inquire into the justifiability of the Christian ethic implies that it might *not* be justifiable, and in view of the importance the Christian ideal has in the lives of millions of people, it is thought better not to raise such questions at all. Here I can only dissent, though not without respect for the objectors' uneasiness. I have already agreed that it is odious manners, even if nothing worse, to be flip and glib with positions that, for many, lie at the centre of their hope and faith. There is more to life than logic, and a great deal more to ethics than logic-chopping. On the other hand, for the person who is trying to see things for himself and as they are, there is no forbidden question. And for the philosopher, the more central a question, the plainer it is that he ought to raise it; that is his business. Of course rights, here as always, involve duties. The right to examine either Christian theology or Christian morals implies the obligation to do so with consideration for the very deep feelings involved and with such objectivity as one can command. The present writer feels the same dislike for the emotional attacks on the Christian ideal by Nietzsche as for the irrational defence of it by Kierkegaard.

2 There is another difficulty we face at the outset. We have been told by some contemporary theologians, of whom the leader was none other than Albert Schweitzer, that Jesus himself did not offer his ethics as a pattern for the future of mankind because he did not believe that mankind had a future. He thought that the current chapter of human history was about to close with a tremendous pageant, in which sun and moon would be darkened, the stars would fall from the sky, and the Son of Man would be seen coming in judgement in clouds of glory. This was no far-off divine event; 'this generation shall not pass till all these things be done'. For a time there was a tendency among theologians to take the passages about the coming kingdom to mean a spiritual kingdom, the reign of Christ in the hearts of men, and to dismiss these statements about the imminent end of things as poetry or metaphor. Schweitzer rightly objected to this. After all, these predictions of the early end of the world are given unequivocally in all three of the synoptic gospels. We cannot overlook them or explain them away. In his exposition of Christian ethics, Dean Inge has to admit that

'a strange blindness about the future pervades all the Ethics of the New Testament, including the Gospels . . . in many of our social problems we cannot find the help in the Gospels which we should have welcomed, because the early Christians never thought about an earthly future for the human race.'[1]

There seems to be no denying that Jesus did expect the end to come within a few years, and that in this expectation he was mistaken.

How does this affect the validity of his ethical teachings? It does show that he was susceptible to error on matters of importance in theology and science, and hence that his pronouncements are not those of omniscience. This does not prove his moral judgements to have been faulty, but it does pose a question about them: if he believed that the end of the world was imminent, would not his teaching be an *Interimsethik* as Schweitzer says, a set of rules to live by in the brief interim before the heavens finally opened? Some of the rules offered do suggest this, for example, 'Take no thought for the morrow' and 'Sell all thou hast and give to the poor'. These would be easier to accept if the morrows we had to provide for were known to be few. Men's lives neither would nor should be the same if they knew that this year or the next would be the last in human history. Who, for instance, would found a college or start an encyclopaedia? It has sometimes been replied that while the belief in an imminent end of things would affect one's long-range plans, it would not affect the order of priority among one's intrinsic values; that wisdom and beauty, for example, would still retain exalted places among the values most worth seeking. But this is true only with qualifications. Wisdom and beauty require for their realisation the sort of discerning eye that can be achieved only by long cultivation, and their value would certainly be less if only so much of them counted as could be achieved in a week or a year. Again, Jesus' values were bound to be affected by the sort of final judgement believed to be imminent. This judgement was exclusively moral and religious. Men's election to an eternity of bliss or pain would not depend on the extent of their knowledge or their aesthetic responsiveness, but on whether they were righteous or unrighteous. And it is idle to say that the expectation of such a judgement would not affect profoundly the goods one would consider it best to pursue in the brief and precious time at one's disposal. How much the eschatology of Jesus did influence his views of the good life it is now impossible to determine; it was probably decisive at some points and all but irrelevant at others. What is important for us in any case is not the origin of his teachings in his own state of mind but their degree of permanent validity, and this can be made out only by applying to each that test of reasonableness which throughout this study has been our court of final appeal.

CENTRAL STRESSES IN CHRISTIAN ETHICS

3 Very well, what was his ethical teaching? In detail, we shall never know. Jesus wrote nothing, and he spoke in a language, Aramaic, that is now almost extinct. The reports of what he did and said were translated after his death into Greek, and translated again for our use into beautiful but archaic Elizabethan English. No contemporary record of him remains. Mark, the earliest gospel, was probably written about a quarter century after his death, Matthew and Luke a half century, John three-quarters of a century. Our chief sources are Mark and a lost document called Q (for the German *Quelle* or source) which was drawn on for much of their material by Matthew and Luke. This material consists in sayings, stories, fragments of sermons, reports of miraculous events, which were current in the early Christian community and transmitted by word of mouth. This community was a simple one, with no notion of science in our sense, and very little of history or critical biography.

Each compiler of fragments had his own special interest: Matthew in Jesus' relation to the Jews, Mark in his messianic sonship, Luke, who was a gentile, in the wider outreach of the new gospel, John in rethinking the message in a way acceptable to the Greeks. These men, of whose very identity scholars are uncertain, often disagree. Furthermore, the Jesus that comes through to us from their writings had no interest in philosophic argument or in putting his teaching in systematic form; his mind was not Greek but Oriental in its preference for teaching by poetry and parable. His principles have to be extracted precariously from his reported sayings and character, and when we have extracted them we do not find them always consistent. One teaching about divorce, for example, is given in Matthew, another in Mark and Luke; Jesus came to bring peace on earth and good will among men, but he also said that he came to bring not peace but a sword.

4 Still we can discern clearly enough where his main emphases lay. There was a negative emphasis and a positive one. On the negative side was a strong reaction against the official teaching of his own people. The good man had come to be thought of as the man who kept the commandments, and the commandments had been ravelled out into a set of regulations governing conduct in minute detail. These regulations told people what they should wear, what they should eat, what kind of dishes it should be eaten from, when they should work and not work, how they should say their prayers, and how they should treat friends, women, strangers, and enemies. For the Pharisees particularly, who were leaders in scholarship and piety, the Mosaic law had become a complicated straitjacket of requirements. Jesus broke this straitjacket deliberately and publicly. He broke the rules about the Sabbath, saying that the Sabbath was made for man, not man for the Sabbath. He broke the rules about ceremonial cleanliness, about eating and drinking and fasting and praying, and about association with social outcasts. He had his hatreds, and one of them was for hypocrisy. He saw that it was possible to achieve high standing in this ethics of conformity and still be a hollow man, and he launched at the very people who were proclaiming their own piety some of the most scorching denunciations on record: 'Ye whited sepulchres, full of dead men's bones and all uncleanliness, how can ye escape the damnation of hell?'

5 When he rejected the ethics of conformity, what did he put in its place? Strangely enough, one will find no statement or discussion of the Christian ethics in the ordinary ethical textbook, often indeed no mention of the moral teaching that has had most influence on

Western civilisation. Why is this? Chiefly, no doubt, because philosophers are analysts and reasoners, not prophets or practical counsellors. They belong to the tradition of Greece, not of Judaea; they are interested in a precise and reasoned account of what makes an action right, and this they do not find in the New Testament. Still, it is not impossible to assign the approximate place of Christian teaching in the framework of traditional ethics, and it will tend to clarity if we try to do so at once.

Moralists have commonly distinguished three components of an action: the motive, the behaviour, and the consequences. And the main types of ethical thought differ from each other chiefly as to which of these components is made the principal element in right conduct. Consequences are stressed by the schools of teleological ethics, the ethics of ends or goals to which action is instrumental, though the kind of consequences chosen as intrinsic goals vary greatly, from pleasure and power to wisdom and self-realisation. Some form of teleological ethics is held by the majority of modern moral philosophers. In common sense ethics the stress is rather on behaviour, and rightness consists in conformity to such rules as 'Pay your debts', 'Tell the truth', 'Keep your promises'. A minority of moral philosphers, of whom Kant is the most distinguished, have placed their stress on the motive. It is in this last class that Christian ethics falls.

But between Kantian and Christian ethics there is a profound difference in how the motive is conceived. Kant held that only those actions are right which spring from a good will, and this has, indeed, a Christian sound. But what Kant meant by a good will had little in common with the New Testament meaning. Kant was a rationalist; Jesus certainly was not. For Kant good will was loyalty to reason. In deciding how to act, one must first see what the principle was that a proposed action would embody, and then ask whether one could will consistently that everyone should act in accordance with it. The good will was thus for Kant respect for rational consistency. Such a conception would certainly have repelled the unintellectual fishermen who were the first apostles of the Christian evangel, and probably their Master also.

It is true that the Christian ethics, like that of Kant, was an ethics of inwardness or of motive; both stood at the opposite pole from Marx, who taught that the outward circumstances determined the inward. Jesus taught the contrary view: cleanse the inside of the cup, and the outside could be left to itself. But between the Kantian and the Christian there was a difference, so to speak, in the seat of the motive; for Kant it was in the head, for the Christian in the heart. 'For from within, out of the heart of man' proceed all moral goods and evils. 'Be this' was the typical Christian teaching, rather than 'Do this'. What man needed was new feelings and dispositions. If we could free ourselves from anger and hatred—that is, hatred of persons, for hatred of some attitudes Jesus entertained himself—we should get rid of violence; if we could exclude undue pride, we should be slow to take offence; if we would rid ourselves of adultery and theft and cruelty, we must uproot the lasciviousness and covetousness and hard-heartedness out of which these actions spring.

6 Jesus' programme, then, was the reconstruction of the attitudes of the inner man. He was reluctant to lay down rules of behaviour; if one had the right inward attitudes, one could be left to make one's own rules. What, then, were the new inward attitudes that were to supplant the old evil ones? They were laid down in the Beatitudes, which form the opening words of the Sermon on the Mount. These have a strange sound to modern ears and need some interpretation. Blessed are the poor in spirit, that is, the humble, the teachable, those of open mind, as opposed to the conceited and the self-righteous. One is reminded of Santayana's remark: "There is hope for a libertine; there is no hope for a prig." Blessed are they that mourn, which does not mean to praise the lugubrious, but in the context seems to mean, Blessed are they that mourn their defects, who are aware of their moral shortcomings and are repentant of them. Blessed are the meek, those who know how to bear and to forbear as opposed to the aggressive and the irascible. Blessed are they that hunger and thirst after righteousness, not as a means to success or approval in men's eyes, but as an end in itself. Blessed are the merciful, that is, the compassionate and understanding as opposed to the hard and the indifferent. Blessed are the pure in heart, those who are single-minded and not devious and divided in their devotion to goodness. Blessed are the peacemakers, as opposed to the makers of suspicion, enmity, and strife. Blessed are they that have been persecuted for righteousness' sake, those who are ready to persist and pay the price of loyalty to duty. Notice that these are qualities of character rather than prescriptions of behaviour.

When Jesus was asked by a lawyer to put the gist of his teaching in a nutshell, his answer was: love God and love man. If we were concerned here with the religious as distinct from the ethical outlook of Christianity, we should have to say much about the first of these, but our concern is with the second. What did he mean by the love of man? Not an emotion merely, for it is not in our power to have a feeling on command; we cannot say, I will love Jones, blackguard as he is, beginning tomorrow at seven. Love was, rather, a settled good will, a permanent concern for the good of other people. That kind of love was already enjoined by the prophets toward one's family and one's own people; the originality of Jesus lay in universalising it, in saying that if it was called for toward friends it was also called for toward enemies, toward men as men, without regard to race or sex, and whether they were Jews or Gentiles.

THE CLAIM TO FINALITY

7   This, I take it, is the essence of the Christian morality. In the churches of the West, it has been presented as the final morality from which nothing can be taken away and to which nothing can be added. A much respected moralist, Dean Rashdall, writes: 'the ideal alike of human life and of the divine Nature actually to be found in the critically sifted records of the life and teaching of Jesus Christ is, in its essential principles, the ideal which the moral consciousness of Humanity still accepts and proclaims.'[2] Goethe spoke for millions when he said: 'Let intellectual and spiritual culture progess, and the human mind expand as much as it will; beyond the grandeur and moral elevation of Christianity, as it sparkles and shines in the Gospels, the human mind will not advance.' What is a rationalist in morals to say about this claim?

The first thing he would want to say is that he has felt, like those millions of others, of every intellectual hue, the fascination of this moral genius, so familiar and yet so remote. The figure of Jesus is unique. There has been only one Christian, said Nietzsche, and he died on the cross. He tried the impossibly beautiful and touching experiment of trying to love everyone, in the trust that they would respond in kind. He seems at the end to have regarded the great venture as a failure, but the world has not been willing to let it die. From a tiny point of light in an obscure corner of the Roman Empire, his influence has risen like the sun and changed the aspect of the entire Western world. If Tacitus or Pliny, who dismissed him in a few words, or Marcus Aurelius, who regarded him as a seditious fanatic, were to be told that he would have a place in history that none of the Caesars could rival, they would have thought the idea absurd. But so it has been. No other figure in human record has approached him in the veneration and devotion he has aroused. Most of us can at least understand what Charles Lamb meant when he said that if any of the heroes of literature or history should enter the room, he would rise; if this Galilean workman entered, he would kneel. Even those who have deplored what he stood for have had to admit his supremacy, as the reluctant Swinburne did: 'Thou hast conquered, O pale Galilean, The world is grown gray with thy breath.'

But having acknowledged the immense attraction that the figure of Christ has exerted on the imagination and aspiration of mankind, the rational moralist must return to his appraisal. He would perhaps agree that the core of the Christian ethics was sound and not likely to be invalidated by criticism. At least, if love may be taken as implying benevolence, that is, being habitually solicitous for others' good as having an importance as great as one's own, it is an attitude hard to challenge on rational grounds, and in making it central to the moral life the ethics of Jesus may well be an ultimate ethics. Certainly the ideal it proposes is exacting in the extreme. Some contemporary theologians think that no intensification of strength and no widening in the area of natural affection could ever carry men up to the level of Christian love; such love, they hold, is different in kind from anything in the natural man; the *eros* of Plato has an element of self-seeking in it, while the *agape* of the New Testament is self-giving, and is to be achieved only by an ingress into the soul of a divine insight and power. We have looked at various forms of this transcendentalism in Protestant thought between Luther and Barth, and seen how difficult it is to draw any line between the human and the superhuman that does not run into insupportable paradox. But it is not necessary to take Christian love as a miracle in order to see how exalted is the standard it proposes. We may have met a few persons who exemplified it in brief spells, but certainly no one whose life as a whole did so; and we can see that if men in general took it seriously their lives would be radically transformed.

8 I have said that the attitude of Christian love is hard to challenge on rational grounds. It may be asked how any attitude can be either challenged or defended on rational grounds; love and hatred are not true or false; only propositions are; and hence only they can be disproved or established by evidence. I agree. If Christian love is to be shown by reason to be a valid component in the good life, it must be in virtue of some principle implicit in it which is itself capable of rational support. I have ventured to conceive this as the principle of benevolence. It has been recognised by many moralists as self-evidently true. What is this principle? It has been put by Sidgwick as follows: 'one is morally bound to regard the good of any other individual as much as one's own, except in so far as it is less, or less certainly knowable or attainable.'[3] Sidgwick considers this and certain other highly abstract propositions of ethics as self-evident; he says of them: 'I regard the apprehension, with more or less distinctness, of these abstract truths as the permanent basis of the common conviction that the fundamental precepts of morality are essentially reasonable.'4

Questions are bound to arise here. Is love necessarily benevolent, in the sense that the lover seeks the good of the person beloved? There are kinds of love—sexual love, for example—that seem to provide exceptions to the rule, but a love that sought the harm of the beloved, or was indifferent to his good or ill, would not be accepted as Christian. Is the good sought for the beloved person that which is really his good, or what the lover thinks is his good? The answer is: inevitably the latter, but, unless the lover is mistaken, the former too. Is the good of one man really as important as the good of another? No; equalitarianism of that kind is sentimentality. Both intrinsically and as a means to the general good, it is more important that Shakespeare or Beethoven should exist and achieve what is in them to achieve than that an idiot or moron should do so. But the principle of benevolence does not deny this; what it says is that if the intrinsic good of one man is the same in amount as that of another, the two persons must be treated accordingly; if they are treated differently, as is sometimes necessary, it must not be done arbitrarily, but on reasonable grounds. A parent is not unchristian, for example, who concerns himself more with the good of his own children than with others; there are obvious reasons why he should. This suggests the answer to another common question: How can one love *all* men, particularly if that means actively concerning oneself about their good? The answer, once again, is that love need not exclude common sense. There is no inconsistency between a genuine regard for the good of all men and a recognition that this good is most effectively furthered by each man's concerning himself most with those whom he can best serve. No one but Mrs Jollyby would feel bound equally to her own family and to the natives of Borrioboola-Gha.

Christianity is widely believed to provide an ultimate morality. So far as it founds itself on the principle of benevolence, I see no grounds for disputing the claim, since that principle itself seems to be a dictate of reason. There is, of course, no school of morals that can claim exclusively to represent what reason would say in ethics; but many of the modern moralists who have applied rational methods most rigorously to the problems of morality would accept the rule of benevolence as fundamental—such utilitarians as Mill and Sidgwick, such 'ideal utilitarians' as Moore and Rashdall, such self-realisationists as Paulsen and Bradley. Mill, for example, who rejected Christian belief unequivocally, says of Christian morality: 'I believe that the sayings of Christ are all that I can see any evidence of their having been intended to be; that they are irreconcilable with nothing which a comprehensive morality requires. . . .'5

9 At the same time Mill did not think that the original Christian teaching provided a comprehensive morality itself; excellent in its leading principle, it was incomplete and fragmentary. To criticise an ethics for what it is not, rather than for what it is, may seem unfair. And so it would be in any ordinary case. But Christian ethics is not an ordinary case. It has been presented, if not by its founder, at least by authoritative church teaching, as the guide to a perfect life, offered by one who exemplified perfection in his own life. The 'imitation of Christ' has been enjoined in numberless religious manuals, whose burden is that in the degree to which anyone approaches the life of Jesus he is approaching the ideal, that so far as his motives and values embody those of the Sermon on the Mount, he is achieving the best life possible for man. It is believed, furthermore, that this moral teaching is guaranteed errorless by nothing less than Deity, whose will it reveals, and who, as perfectly good and wise, cannot mislead his creatures. Many scholars have thought that Jesus himself made no claim that his teaching was an ultimate or errorless or even adequate guide to the good life. Fortunately we need not enter the controverted territory. Suffice it to say that the claim has been continually made for him, and by high authority. It is that claim that we must try to appraise.

The strongest emphasis in his ethics was on love, and we have seen that the natural tendency of love is to seek the good of the persons beloved. But *what* goods should love promote? Sooner or later, that question must have an answer. One may say that the good of *A* lies in promoting the good of *B*, and that of *B* in promoting the good of *C*, but sooner or later there must be some indication of *what* the good of these persons consists in. The point of the service of others is that it enables them to realise the intrinsic goods of life, and the business of ethics is less to exhort us to service than to enlighten us about the ends toward which that service should be directed. Though the Greeks had a great deal to say on this matter, the Christian ethics said comparatively little. As it stands, it must therefore be admitted to be a truncated ethics requiring large supplementation. Insistent, and rightly so, on the importance of the springs of action, it all but ignores some of the great goods of human life.

CHRISTIANITY AND THE GOOD OF KNOWLEDGE

10 Consider one intrinsic good that the Greek thinkers were inclined to put at the head of all goods, that of knowledge or understanding. There is one point in Aristotle's writings, and apparently only one, at which that sober thinker breaks out into something like a paean of praise, and that is when he comes to the joy of the philo-

sopher in looking before and after, and seeing in intellectual vision
the eternal why of things. Modern science and philosophy are largely
the product of the Greeks. We are justly proud of such theoreticians
as Newton and Einstein, Russell and Whitehead, and it seldom
occurs to us to ask whether the quest to which these men were
committed has the sanction of Christian ethics. Does it? There seems
to be no good ground for saying so. The record discloses no interest
on the part of Jesus in the pursuit of knowledge for its own sake,
or in anything that we should now call science or philosophy. It
may be replied that he had no occasion to express judgements on
this kind of pursuit, and that one cannot argue from his silence to his
indifference or disapproval. These demurrers may be true. On the
other hand, one can hardly hold at the same time that Jesus' ethics
provides an adequate guide to life and also that it is confined to the
issues that would arise in a relatively primitive Eastern community.
Furthermore, as a matter of fact the Greek language and influence
did swirl around him; in his own Galilee there were two Greek cities,
one of them, Tiberius, not many miles from Nazareth, and the values
of Hellenistic culture were hotly debated among his Jewish contemporaries. He seems to have remained untouched by it nevertheless. If a dialogue between Jesus and a Socratic defender of the life of
reason could be unearthed in some Dead Sea scroll, it would be a
priceless addition to our understanding of him. There is a bare
possibility that it would justify the exclamation of Erasmus, 'Saint
Socrates, pray for me'.

But the nearest thing we have to an early Christian estimate of the
Greek love of reason is the attitude of St Paul, who knew Greek and
who visited Athens. Paul's attitude is not one of praise or even of
indifference, but one of outspoken contempt. 'Where is the wise?
Where is the scribe? Where is the disputer of this world? Hath not
God made foolish the wisdom of this world?' In accordance with
this attitude, the church for many centuries regarded faith as a
duty and doubt as a sin. Some magnificent intellects have been
placed at the service of the church, above all that of Aquinas, but
St Thomas found his philosophical warrant and model not in the
gospels but in Aristotle; and too often when the intellectual in the
church attempted to follow the argument where it led, as Descartes
for example did, he found himself on the Index. To those who
thought that with every passing day their eternal destiny was at
stake, the pursuit of knowledge for its own sake was bound to seem
of small importance. When John Wesley visited the British Museum,
he wrote:

'Seven huge apartments are filled with curious books, five with manuscripts, two with fossils of all sorts, and the rest with various animals. But what account will a man give to the Judge of quick and dead for a life spent in collecting all these?'

The pursuit of truth for its own sake, however, is not the only business of intelligence. Many moralists would consider that its main use falls in the middle ground between motives on the one hand and remote goals on the other; it is the means of implementing desire in such a way that its ends may be achieved. Here foresight and inference are called for, and many kinds of special knowledge. We should feel sympathy for the sick, but if that sympathy is to be fully effective, it must be guided by medical expertise. We should feel charity for the poor, but if they are to be efficiently relieved, we must call in aid the knowledge of the economist, the sociologist, the psychologist, and the large-scale organiser. An admirer of Whistler's pictures once asked the painter what he mixed his paints with, to which Whistler replied, 'With brains, sir'. This is not the reply one would expect from an early Christian if asked about his morals. The sympathy Jesus showed and taught was personal and immediate; he was the tactician, not the strategist of charity, dealing with each case as it arose, and—according to the record—resorting in emergencies not to the expert but to miracle. This stress on love and this understress on knowledge remained characteristic of his followers for centuries. Bertrand Russell writes:

'Neither love without knowledge nor knowledge without love can produce a good life. In the Middle Ages, when pestilence appeared in a country, holy men advised the population to assemble in churches and pray for deliverance; the result was that the infection spread with extraordinary rapidity among the crowded masses of supplicants.'[6]

The secular moralist of today finds this lack of interest in knowledge as end or means a defect in the plan of life sketched in the gospels.

CHRISTIANITY AND THE NATURAL MAN

11 To the Greeks, the play of intellect was a great good because it was the satisfaction of a deep hunger in human nature. The Greek was a naturalist, in the sense that he thought human goods to be appointed by human nature; they were all fulfilments of instincts, needs, drives of the natural man, and the ideal life was one in which these drives were fulfilled harmoniously. And they must be fulfilled in this life or not at all, for the Greeks did not look forward to any other. The Christians, however, did, and to them it mattered little how high a price they paid in the good things of this world if the sacrifice helped to secure salvation in the deathless world that was to follow. The goods of the natural man were therefore not so much evil in themselves as irrelevant—tempting rivals of true goodness, which it was best to ignore. Sometimes Jesus put it more strongly; 'He that hateth his life in this world shall keep it unto life eternal'. What were these goods of the natural man that the Greeks prized and the gospels prized so little?

First, there were the obvious goods of eating and drinking, good clothing and comfortable living. We all value them now, and think it part of our duty to diffuse them. How were they valued in the Christian ethics? There are some very unqualified statements about them. 'Seek not what ye shall eat, or what ye shall drink'; 'Take no thought for your life, what ye shall eat; neither for the body, what ye shall put on'. How far these injunctions rested on the expectation of an imminent end to the present order, it is impossible to say. In any case, on the ground of such sayings, of which there are many, Jesus has often been charged with teaching asceticism. This has been indignantly denied by able interpreters of his ethics, such as Dean Inge and Dean Rashdall. And it is true that by his own report he was accused by enemies of being gluttonous and a winebibber. He was certainly far from the asceticism of the second century, when many who called themselves Christians chose to live in caves or in the desert, half-starved and verminous.[7] Nevertheless, by the standards of modern man his attitude toward these simpler goods was very severe. He appears to have had no home of his own; he commanded his disciples on their journey to take no bread and no money; he was poor himself; he repeatedly denounced wealth. His attitude toward the creature comforts of life was one of indifference, and many of his early followers took it as negative. On the other hand, the attitude of the modern moralist toward these goods is certainly positive. The satisfactions of good food, good clothing, and a comfortable house he would take as intrinsic goods of real though subordinate value, and instrumental goods of high order. He would say, furthermore, that if, by honest labour, a man can have round him books to dip into with pleasure, and some art and music to refresh him, he is the gainer, not the loser, by such possessions. Is he the less Christian? Many modernisers of the Christian ethics would deny this, but it is hard to see how they could reconcile the denial with the text of the New Testament.

The Greeks, I have said, were naturalists. So too is modern science, which tends to dominate modern thinking about everything it touches. Consider how it has affected our view of body and mind. It holds that the roots of the mind are in the body, and that only as those roots are well tended, only as the body is kept healthy and vigorous, will the mind be healthy and vigorous. *Mens sena in corpore sano.* That was the Greek ideal, and modern man is taking it over. He has revived the Olympic games; Americans in particular glorify physical prowess, and give more of their substance to their athletic heroes than they do to their foremost judges and scientists. The question was proposed a moment ago what Jesus would have made of such lives as Einstein's or Whitehead's, and if we can ask that, we can also ask what he would have said if confronted by such phenomena of modern America as Babe Ruth or Willie Mays. Would he have approved them or been repelled by them? Who knows? What one suspects is that with his quick and large sympathy he would have found something admirable in these splendidly embodied souls. But does not the very oddity of the question suggest that they are outside the orbit of the kind of life he contemplated? His interest in the body seems to have gone scarcely beyond the relief of the sick. Indeed he told men, as we have seen, to take no thought for their bodies, and it is not clear how Olympic games or Greek statues, American gymnasiums or fitness programmes are to be forced into accord with that advice. While the gospels do not decry bodily achievement, the seeds are there which quickly sprouted into that warfare of flesh and spirit which came out openly in St Paul, with his struggle to keep the body under. Here again the modern estimate has drifted far from this sort of anchorage. That estimate is not expressed in St Paul's 'in my flesh dwelleth no good thing'. It is much closer to Browning:

> 'Let us not always say
> "Spite of this flesh to-day
> I strove, made head, gained ground upon the whole!"
> To man propose this test—
> Thy body at its best,
> How far can that project thy soul on its lone way?'

CHRISTIANITY AND WEALTH

12 Indifference toward food, drink, and comfort are not the same as indifference toward wealth, but they do tend to go together, and they did in the life and thought of Jesus. Here he is clearly opposed to the values of modern man. Most of the world's peoples are struggling for a higher standard of living, of which greater wealth is a condition. Those who have already achieved the higher standards, and Americans in particular, are often accused of being materialists, in the sense that they want money only as a means to material possessions or for the sake of the money itself. I doubt whether either charge could be made out. There is perhaps no country in the world where the tradition of substantial giving to non-materialist causes such as education, religion, and art is so ingrained. Nor does the quest of money in itself, as distinct from the comfort, power, and security that it can buy, seem at all common. Where it does exist, it is undoubtedly irrational. On the other side, the glorification of poverty as such seems as irrational as that of wealth. 'But it remains true, nevertheless, that this glorification—the word is scarcely too strong—of poverty, or at least of the freedom from material possessions, as in itself a state of blessedness, is a note not only of all the Gospels, but of most of the other great religious books that have moved the world.'8

The emphasis is strongest in the gospel of Luke. In its first chapter is the song of Mary, described by Bernard Shaw as the most revolutionary of songs: 'he hath put down the mighty from their seats, and exalted them of low degree. He hath filled the hungry with good things; and the rich he hath sent empty away.' Again, 'Blessed be ye poor, for yours is the kingdom of God'. 'Woe unto you that are rich!' (6:20,24). In the same book, 'a certain rich man, which was clothed in purple and fine linen, and fared sumptuously every day,' had at his gate a beggar named Lazarus, 'full of sores'. At their death, Lazarus went to heaven and the rich man to hell, where his pleas to Abraham for release from the fire and a warning to his relatives were disregarded. There is no explanation of the disparity of treatment except that the one is rich and the other poor (Luke 16:19–31). In some other cases the explanation is added that one cannot serve God and Mammon, as it was when the young man of 'great possessions' was sent away and told to sell all he had and give the proceeds to the poor (Matt. 19:16–22). But the comment that follows, 'It is easier for a camel to go through the eye of a needle, than for a rich man to enter into the kingdom of God,' suggests that it is not only difficult but impossible for the rich man to reach the kingdom. Wealth is repeatedly denounced as such, and poverty as such exalted.

At the same time the rewards held out for avoiding the one and espousing the other are surprising. When Peter heard the denunciation of wealth, he reminded his Master in the name of the disciples that 'we have forsaken all and followed thee; what shall we have therefore?' Two somewhat different answers are given. In Mark the answer is that everyone who has forsaken all for the Master's sake 'shall receive an hundredfold now in this time, houses, and brethren, and sisters, and mothers, and children, and lands, with persecutions; and in the world to come eternal life' (10:30). In Matthew the

hundredfold return is also promised, but with the further promise
to the disciples that when the kingdom comes they 'shall sit upon
twelve thrones, judging the twelve tribes of Israel' (19 : 28). This
leaves the waters less than clear. It encourages the cultivation of
poverty less for itself or as a means to spiritual purification than as a
step to preferment, enrichment, and power.

A rational moralist can hardly endorse any of these motives for
avoiding wealth and embracing poverty. Wealth does, beyond
doubt, increase the temptation to indolence, self-indulgence, and
arrogance, but it does not by itself produce them, and in the free-
doms it offers—freedom to educate oneself, freedom to choose one's
own course of life, freedom from gnawing want and worry—its
opportunities surely outweigh its disadvantages. There are those
who would deny this and praise poverty, among them, strangely
enough, the economist and moralist Adam Smith. 'In case of body
and peace of mind,' he wrote, 'all the different ranks of life are
nearly upon a level, and the beggar who suns himself by the side of
the highway possesses that security which kings are fighting for.'9
His defence is unconvincing. Security is, above all, what poverty
lacks. There can be no certainty about health where there is uncertainty about food and medical care; and it is sentimentality rather
than experience that considers it an advantage to be without the
means of travel, leisure, a library, an adequate diet, insurance
against accident and sickness, and an assured future for one's family.
The New Testament acclaim of poverty seems irrational unless made
in the expectancy of an early end to the existing order, and in that
case it sprang from an outlook so far from accordance with fact as
to reflect doubt about other injunctions as well.

Modern man can hardly accept, then, the Christian teaching
about poverty as a means to the enrichment of the spirit. Still less
can he accept this so far as it appeals to the other two motives we
have mentioned. Poverty in itself, like wealth in itself, is morally
neutral; its values and disvalues are instrumental; and it is a mistake
to seek either of them for itself. As for the end envisioned by Peter
and the other disciples, namely a hundredfold windfall in the satisfaction of very earthly desires, it added to error a touch of ignobility.

We should add, in fairness to the first Christian teaching, that
along with its theoretical exaltation of poverty went a noble practical
effort to relieve it. Jesus was in the straight line of those Hebrew
prophets who insisted on the duty of mercy to the poor and the
suffering. 'Is not this the fast that I have chosen?' said Isaiah, 'to
loose the bands of wickedness, to undo the heavy burdens, and to let
the oppressed go free, and that ye break every yoke? Is it not to deal
thy bread to the hungry, and that thou bring the poor that are

cast out to thy house? when thou seest the naked, that thou cover him . . .?' (58 : 6, 7). Nothing like this sympathy for the poor is to be found among the moralists of Greece; the charity of Aristotle's 'high-minded' man was a mere feeling of noblesse oblige, with an eye on the figure cut by the giver rather than on the needs of the recipients. Jesus inherited to the full the prophetic feeling of duty to relieve poverty while maintaining, with no apparent sense of inconsistency, that the poor were better off spiritually than the rich.

CHRISTIANITY AND ART

13 In contrasting Greek naturalism with Christian otherworldliness, we mentioned the Greek stress on art and music, and it is appropriate at this point to ask whether Christian and secular views agree on the place of these things in the good life. It must be admitted that there is almost as sharp a conflict here between the Greek and the Judaic strain in our civilisation as there is on the place of intellect. The Greeks were of course lovers of beauty. Where would one look, even today, for things more perfect in their kind than the Milonian Venus or the Victory of Samothrace, the plays of Sophocles or the architecture of the Acropolis? What would Jesus have said of these things, or of the artists who gave their lives to creating them? We do not certainly know. He was, presumably, never exposed to them. He was not, indeed, insensitive to things of beauty. He considered the lilies of the field, was familiar with the poetry of the Old Testament, and told parables that had a simple beauty of their own. But it seems not unfair to say that, in his teaching, that side of life which finds its flowering in the art and sculpture, the literature, music, and architecture of the world was left almost a blank. His immediate followers, indeed, read his attitude toward these things as negative; 'the lust of the eye,' construed by man as the love of visual beauty, as well as 'the lust of the flesh,' was condemned as 'not of the Father, but of the world'. It is perfectly true, of course, that we owe to the Christian church the patronage of some of the most magnificent art in history, notably the great mediaeval cathedrals and the paintings that grace the walls of Italian churches. But these were hybrid products, due to the crossing of Christianity with the Renaissance, the Gothic spirit, and much else. In the early church no paintings were allowed except of plants and animals, and even in the years of the church's great power the leaders who remained closest to the pure and primitive teaching—St Francis, St Bruno, St Bernard, Savonarola—were puritans about the fine arts.

CHRISTIANITY AND CIVIC DUTY

14 Any comparison of Greek with Christian ethics is bound to touch on their contrasting notions in another area, civic duty. Aristotle defined a state as 'an association of similar persons for the attainment of the best life possible,' holding that the individual man could achieve this life only in and through his service to the state. Plato also made the good life rest on one's station and its duties within the state. It cannot be said that the Greeks were very successful either in the theory or the practice of politics; even Athens, the most enlightened and democratic of their states, was far from democratic in the modern sense. At the end of the fourth century BC it had about four times as many slaves as citizens; 'the slave,' said Aristotle, 'is a tool with life in it, and the tool a lifeless slave'. Women also were excluded from public life. Nevertheless, the role of persons fortunate enough to be citizens was dignified and exacting, and included the duty of serving on occasion as soldier, public speaker, political leader, and judge of the arts. According to Aristotle the business of a man lay in performing his function in the social organism just as the business of a hand is to serve as an organ of the physical body, and neither the hand nor the man would be what it is if amputated from the whole.

What was the Christian view of civic duty? It was certainly not a blank, for the comprehensive duty of good will toward one's fellows dictated the temper in which all political activities should be carried on. But it is notorious that men of good will may turn up on the political battlefield as enemies, and if one looks beyond the rule of good will for definite guidance from the teaching of Jesus, one will look in vain. 'It never seems to have occurred to him that his moral principles could have any political application,'[10] says James Seth; 'It is impossible in the Gospels,' says Percy Gardner, 'to find any statement of men's duties to the organised state'.[11] Dean Inge remarks that Jesus 'never showed any interest in economic questions,'[12] and laments that 'the original Gospel leaves us with no clear guidance or encouragement in what for many men and women to-day is the purest and most disinterested of their aspirations—the desire to help in making human life in this world a better thing in the future than it is now'.[13] Some thoughtful men have been outspokenly critical of Christianity for this lack of concern. Whitehead remarks that 'a sense of responsibility for the continuance of a social system is basic to any morality. Now this form of responsibility is almost entirely absent from Christianity. Jesus hardly mentions it, except for one or two remarks.' Christianity, Whitehead goes on, 'held that the externals of life are not worth caring about and at the same time insisted on types of moral conduct which cannot be observed—without perishing—unless the externals of life are sufficiently well organised. A society run on strictly Christian principles could not survive at all.'[14] And Ernest Renan, discussing this political detachment, goes so far as to say that 'Christianity, in this sense, has contributed much to weaken the sense of duty of the citizen, and to deliver the world into the absolute power of existing circumstances'.[15]

This is obviously not the whole truth, since it would be equally easy to show that Christianity has done much to deliver the world *from* existing circumstances. But the vagueness of gospel teaching here is undeniable. 'Render unto Caesar the things that are Caesar's.' But what things are Caesar's? The state commonly claims the right to dip deep into its citizens' pockets and use the money thus gained to make war, to give or withhold education, to lay down and enforce the rules of marriage, of property, of freedom or restriction in speech, activity, and art, of justice between man and man, of the punishment of offenders, of the treatment of one race or sex or class by another. The state has the power to make or break any of its citizens. Do we owe loyalty to it or not? 'Render unto Caesar' sounds as if we did. And this is the interpretation placed on it by the early church. Indeed Paul went further and put divine patronage behind the state. 'The powers that be are ordained of God. Whosoever therefore resisteth the power resisteth the ordinance of God; and they that resist shall receive to themselves damnation' (Romans 13 : 1, 2). 'The teaching of the Early Fathers on the subject,' says Lecky, 'is perfectly unanimous and unequivocal. Without a single exception, all who touched upon the subject pronounced active resistance to the established authorities to be under all circumstances sinful. If the law enjoined what was wrong it should be disobeyed, but no vice and no tyranny could justify revolt.'[16] Disobedience permissible, but not resistance! This is perilously close to self-contradiction, since disobeying a law and resisting it are commonly supposed to be the same thing. What is apparently meant is that one owes obedience to the law except where disobedience is required by conscience at the behest of a divine command. And even then violence is to be eschewed.

CHRISTIANITY AND NON-RESISTANCE

15 Here one comes to the most definite crystallisation of the law of love in the sphere of civic duty. Whether in dealing with the demands of the state or the malevolence of other persons, one is never to resort to violence, however unreasonable the demand may be. Resist not evil; give the soft answer; if a man strikes you on one cheek, turn to him the other; forgive seventy times seven, that is, indefinitely. The assumption is that if the person offended is able to meet his offender with a wholly genuine good will, the good that is in the offender, as it is in all men, will be stirred into life and his malevolence be disarmed. This was a new element in moral teaching. Good will to one's neighbour, even the love of one's neighbour as oneself, was an old injunction of the Mosaic law, but to love your enemies, to do good to those that despitefully use you and persecute you, this was an immense extension by Jesus of the older morality. That it does in numberless cases have the effect of shaming the offender and turning him to reason again is in no need of argument here.

Non-violence was so firmly taught in the early church that soldiers were excluded from membership and were admitted only three years after their discharge. 'When the Lord deprived Peter of the sword,' said Tertullian, 'he disarmed all'. Firm as this teaching was, however, it must be added that neither the personal example of Jesus nor the later teaching of the church was wholly consistent with it. Jesus overturned the tables of the money-changers and drove them out of the temple with a whip. The attitude of most churches, Catholic and Protestant, is probably expressed in the 37th article of the Church of England: 'It is lawful for Christian men, at the commandment of the Magistrate, to wear weapons, and to serve in the wars.'[17] In the course of time Christianity drifted far from its original moorings. St Louis and St Joan of Arc were sainted in spite of, or because of, being military heroes; Oliver Cromwell and 'Chinese Gordon' and Stonewall Jackson were formidable Christian warriors. But they were certainly not Christians in the New Testament sense.[18] The Hindu Gandhi was nearer to the spirit of Christ than any of them.

16 Our interest, however, is not in historical changes but in how the teaching of Jesus stands in the eyes of philosophical moralists. It is clear that such moralists, while deprecating in most cases the resort to violence, would not do so universally. They would depart from a thoroughgoing pacifism, I suspect, in at least three respects. The first has to do with the relation of person to person, the second with the relation of the group to the individual, the third with that of groups to each other.

(1) It was with the first of these, the relation of man to man, with which Jesus was exclusively concerned. An attitude of good will toward one's brother man seemed to him incompatible with a readiness to harm him. The secular moralist, while agreeing that gentleness is normally the right approach, points out that there are

some men in any society who take such gentleness as an invitation to exploit it to their own advantage—the bullies, the sadists, the moral morons, persons who are mentally and morally diseased—and that reasonable men are not called upon to capitulate to these outlaws. Gandhi could use moral suasion on such an 'enemy' as Lord Halifax because Lord Halifax was also a man of good will, who invited Gandhi to come and pray with him for joint guidance; but what did non-resistance gain for the Jews as against Hitler and his thugs? When one is faced with a 'mugger' in the streets or a gunman invading one's home, it is no doubt often the part of prudence to offer no resistance and comply with his demands, but is it one's duty to do so if resistance is feasible? Popular judgement would not say so, nor would the judgement of the secular moralist. The case becomes stronger if the attack is made not on oneself but (say) on a member of one's family; for here the very principle of love for others may dictate the stronger line. Passive surrender to thieves and thugs is more likely to enlarge their ranks than to win them over to reasonableness.

COURAGE

'Christianity, faithfully presented,' says Dean Inge, 'is a creed for heroes';[19] and so it has often proved, if the heroism called for is that required for facing persecution or even martyrdom. How then can it have attracted such jibes as Mencken's about its 'weakness for weakness,' or Nietzsche's compendious insult to 'cows, women, sheep, Christians, dogs, Englishmen, and other democrats'? The answer is that while the standards of Jesus regarding the courage of endurance and sacrifice were lofty and exacting, he seems to have had no use for the kind of courage that the world most admires. 'For him', says Warner Fite, 'the all-important thing was that the impulse to self-assertion be completely rooted out.'[20] And this takes a great deal with it. The courage of the Greeks at Marathon, which saved the civilisation of the West, the courage of chivalry, with its strange blend of Christian charity and Gothic combativeness, the courage that sprang, in Burke's panegyric, from 'that chastity of honour which felt a stain like a wound,' the courage that carried Lindbergh across the Atlantic, the courage of the athlete, the astronaut, the pioneer, the soldier—courage of all these kinds fell outside the interest and attention of the gospels. The courage they inculcated was not that of the natural man, standing on his own honour and intelligence, but one that rested on faith in a super-natural power; not one that bent nature and human nature to its ends, but one that seemed to imbue frail men and women with a will not their own, through which they could keep the world, the flesh, and the devil at bay. It was the courage of a double passivity; by being passive to the divine influences, they achieved the power to meet passively temptations of the flesh and the affronts of the world. Indeed there was little point in any other kind of courage if the end of all things was imminent; and some have thought that Jesus' coolness toward worldly courage reflected his views on the impending fate of all things worldly.

However that may be, the rational moralist would not depreciate natural courage. He would admit that it is a dangerous quality, which may intensify vice as well as virtue, and has been displayed in generous measure by criminals and brigands. Nevertheless, it has held a central place in men's admiration, as is suggested by its very names; the Greeks called it andreia, manliness, the quality of being a man; the English name, 'courage', comes from the Latin cor, the heart. It connotes self-respect and self-reliance, trust in one's own values, seriousness in a cause while not taking onself too seriously to incur risks in its behalf. 'Courage,' said Emerson, 'is that virtue without which one cannot be sure of retaining any other'. Courage of this kind is more closely akin to pride, which Christianity would put low, than to humility, which it places high. The low estimate of this secular courage is part of that general transvaluation of worldly values which makes the Christian ethics at once so challenging and so difficult of acceptance.[21]

17(2) The second point at which Christian pacifism runs counter to modern thought is the relation of state to individual. Most political philosophers have thought that a chief aim of the state is to protect the life, liberty, and property of its citizens. One outlaw at large in a community can terrorise all the rest, and the only practicable means by which such persons can be restrained is a police force, acting on behalf of the citizens generally. And if it is to deal with criminal behaviour, such a force must be prepared to use coercion, sometimes in violent form. How is a Christian to act who is a member of this force? As a Christian, he must follow the injunction to resist not evil; as an officer of the law, he is committed to resisting it to the limit. The two duties cannot be reconciled. Most theologians would now agree that the prime Christian duty of loving one's fellows requires protective action on the community's part; the restraint of malefactors by force is an indispensable means to the general good.[22] (That is why the attempt of extremists to brand the police generally as 'pigs' is an affront to the community whose agents they are.) The argument is so irresistible that one can hardly conceive that Jesus would reject it. He could accept it, however, only by abandoning his sweeping mandate against violence. Is there any way of saving Christian consistency here? Only, one suspects, by holding that Jesus did not envisage his followers in political office at all. In his own time, there was no call on them to enter it, and the vast complex of modern government, with its public servants in tens of thousands, was wholly beyond his horizon. But to say this is to admit that his ethics was a prescription for a simpler age, which does not necessarily apply under the conditions of modern society. That conclusion seems beyond escape.

18(3)   The third field where the injunction against violence might apply, the relations between groups, is even farther from the sort of situation Jesus had in mind. Deeply concerned as he was about the conduct of individuals toward each other, he had nothing to say about the conduct of states toward each other, and hence nothing about war. He might very naturally have expressed himself on it, for in the Old Testament, with which he was familiar, there was much on the glories and atrocities of war. He never mentions them, and we can only arrive by inference at his judgement on making or participating in war. His disciple Peter once had an interview with the centurion Cornelius, who commanded a cohort in the Roman army, but there is no hint in the record of any disapproval of the soldier's calling. There can be little real doubt, however, of Jesus' teaching on this matter. War involved the killing of human beings, often of innocent and helpless human beings; and the firm mandate against violence to the individual would hold with multiplied force against the mass slaughter of war.

Whoever realises what an elementary modern bomb did to Hiroshima and what a war on a modern scale could do to New York or Moscow must look with sympathy on any sort of proposal for preventing such a conflict. Even if war is admitted to have made sense at Marathon and Tours, it does not follow that it would make sense now; in a war between America and the only power that could threaten it, victory would be hardly distinguishable from devastating defeat. But an argument straight from this to the primitive Christian conclusion of complete non-resistance and the acceptance of dictation by an enemy is not convincing either. The logic of the case is the same as that of conflict between individuals. There are nations, as there are men, who trample upon the rights of others, usually proclaiming that they are acting in self-defence; the longest war in American history was fought in 'self-defence' against a small power on the other side of the earth. When one individual is attacked by another, it is often the part of prudence to capitulate; the same is true when one nation is attacked by another; it would have been futile for Czechoslovakia to try to throw back the Russian tanks. But a general capitulation to ruffians would be intolerable, and on the individual level, reasonable men have solved the problem in an obvious way. They have organised themselves into a community, commissioning certain of their number to draw up equitable rules, and to enforce them with all necessary vigour. Foreseeing the difficulties on occasion of identifying the lawbreaker, they have set up courts to resolve such difficulties. The problem has thus been solved simply and rationally. The same reasoning is applicable to that larger community in which the units are themselves communities. To employ war to settle disputes between nations is as mindless as a resort to mayhem to settle the borders of one's lot with a neighbour; any resemblance to justice that may be secured by either method is purely coincidental.

Can the same be said of war when it is of the very exceptional kind that is waged by an international government against a nation that has taken things into its own hands? Clearly not. The use or threat of force is as legitimate, because as necessary, to restrain national banditry as it is to restrain individual bandits, and if the international anarchy that has hitherto obtained is ever to be replaced, it will be by an organisation of this kind. The difficulties are of course enormous, but they are not difficulties of logic or ethics, where the case is plain, but of psychology. Nations must give up some part of their independence; they must believe in a reason that transcends prejudices and international boundaries; and they must be willing to hand over to a super-national government the control of the major weapons of destruction. That the 130 governments now in the United Nations, and particularly the half dozen most powerful ones, can be induced to take this line before the outbreak of Armageddon does not seem very probable. However that may be, there is only one way out of anarchy, whether individual or national.

Such a way might involve a war of all against one, and therefore consistent Christian pacifists would have to oppose it, just as they would oppose war between individual nations. They would no doubt remind us that war involves killing, and that if every soul is of infinite value in the sight of its Creator, no gain can be worth the price. But unless two souls of infinite value are of no more value than one, the argument proves the opposite of what was intended. If the nations that disapproved of Japan's invasion of Manchuria in 1931, or of Mussolini's invasion of Ethiopia in 1935, or of Hitler's invasion of the Ruhr in 1936, had acted instantly and jointly against the aggressor, the aggression either would not have been carried out or would have been thrown back by overwhelming power. Such action would have halted the wave of aggressions which, because permitted to continue, mounted into the deluge of World War II. It might have cost thousands of lives, but it would have saved millions of lives. And a million lives of infinite value are worth more than a thousand. A thorough-going pacifism seems to me inconsistent with a Christian love that is really directed to the good of mankind.

To summarise what we have said on Christianity and force: Jesus believed that in personal relations good will would disarm malevolence. There was far more truth in this than had ever before been discerned, and his own life gave moving evidence of it. But the truth did not prove to be universal; it did not, indeed, disarm the malevolence of his own enemies. As for the relation of the state to its citizens, or of states to each other, he taught nothing directly, and if one tries to solve the problems of these fields through merely personal good will, there is little or no likelihood of success.

CHRISTIANITY AND NATIONALISM

19 Let us look now at some of the barriers that continue to divide men from each other, and the Christian teaching about them. Christianity, with its doctrine of good will toward all men, has been a potent influence in lowering the ancient fences of nationality, race, and sex. The opposition of Jesus to these barriers has been taken so much as a matter of course that it may be well to remind ourselves of his actual words.

There is a tradition in the church that Peter was the apostle to the Hebrews and Paul the apostle to the Gentiles, and so far as this means that Paul was the first Christian spokesman to give the gospel explicitly a cosmopolitan application, it is true. Perhaps it will be objected that this universal application was implicit from the first in the injunction to love one's fellows, and this too may be true. But Jesus' own words do not consistently yield that interpretation. On one of his journeys, a woman who was 'a Greek, a Syrophenician by nation,' came to him and begged his aid, saying that her daughter was 'grievously vexed with a devil'. Here is the passage that follows:

But he answered her not a word. And his disciples came and besought him, saying, Send her away; for she crieth after us. But he answered and said, I am not sent but unto the lost sheep of the house of Israel. Then came she and worshipped him, saying, Lord, help me. But he answered and said, It is not meet to take the children's bread, and cast it to dogs. And she said, Truth, Lord: yet the dogs eat of the crumbs which fall from their masters' table

(Matt. 15 : 23–27). And he said unto her, For this saying go thy way; the devil is gone out of thy daughter (Mark 7 : 29).

The commentators have not known what to make of this passage. It expressly limits the mission of Jesus to the Jews, and seems to accept the Jewish national feeling of separation from other peoples. Nor does it stand alone. When Jesus sent out the twelve Apostles, he 'commanded them, saying, Go not into the way of the Gentiles, and into any city of the Samaritans enter ye not: but go rather to the lost sheep of the house of Israel' (Matt. 10 : 5, 6). Again, when after the death of Jesus Peter was invited to visit the home of Cornelius, he felt it necessary to explain to his friends that though it was 'an unlawful thing for a man that is a Jew to keep company, or come unto one of another nation,' God had just granted to him a special vision saying that he 'should not call any man common or unclean' (Acts 10 : 28). Would this explanation have been necessary to a Christian group who had already been taught by Jesus that all such barriers were down?

The German Orientalist Reimarus thought the conclusion inescapable that Jesus shared the Jewish nationalism of his time. Passages may be cited on the other side, notably the injunction of the risen Christ, 'Go ye, therefore, and teach all nations, baptizing them in the name of the Father, and of the Son, and of the Holy Ghost'. But Reimarus showed that this was probably an addition to the gospel, made by the church at a later date. The reason is not merely that it commands the baptism of converts, whereas Jesus did not himself baptise anyone;[23] the difficulty is that Jesus is represented as inculcating the dogma of the Trinity, a dogma of which the synoptic gospels knew nothing. How are the universal and the rationalist aspects of his teaching to be reconciled? Probably they cannot be. He may well have accepted both. Nothing is more certain about his teaching than the injunction to love mankind; but love was an inward attitude which, when translated into practice on different occasions and toward different persons took very various forms. Good will would flow most easily into the channels already marked out by the law and custom of his people. If these channels were too narrow, it is not impossible that they should have held back and even tainted the clear waters at the source. There is evidence of struggle in the mind of Jesus to overcome the obstacles imposed by the prejudices of his time. Of course if he was omnipotent Deity, such a struggle would be meaningless. On the other hand, if he was merely a great man, his struggle and imperfect success would be intelligible and natural. It is the lot of mortals, even the best.

CHRISTIANITY AND SLAVERY

20 Did Jesus offer any teaching about race? No, except as implicit in his doctrine of love. Nor did he take any stand on an institution that has often been associated in history with racism, namely slavery. If he had turned his attention to the issue, would he have spoken more clearly about it than he did on nationalism? It is less than certain. Slavery had been a common practice among his own people, and in the Old Testament there were regulations governing it. 'Both thy bondmen, and thy bondmaids, which thou shalt have, shall be of the heathen that are round about you; of them shall ye buy bondmen and bondmaids' (Lev. 25 : 44 and cf. Exod. 21). It is hard to suppose that Jesus would have approved slavery, as Aristotle did, but though he suspended a number of Old Testament teachings, there is no record of his having repudiated this one. Nor does it seem to be challenged elsewhere in the New Testament. Paul in his letter to the Ephesians urged 'servants', a term translated by Ballantine and Goodspeed as 'slaves', to 'be obedient to them that are your masters according to the flesh, with fear and trembling, in singleness of your heart, as unto Christ . . .' (6 : 5); and the brief book of Philemon is a letter of Paul's, transmitted by a runaway slave to his master, in which the apostle returns him to his owner with a plea for generous treatment.

Many persons have been shocked by this acquiescence in a custom so repellent to the modern mind. But it must be remembered that this custom was widespread in both the Greek and Roman empires and that to most of the ancient world it seemed eminently natural. The Christian spirit, though in the long run a principal agency in destroying the custom, took more than a thousand years to achieve this in Europe, and many centuries more to achieve it elsewhere. The attitude of the early Christians was curiously ambiguous. On the one hand, they were committed by the express teaching of their master to sympathy with the poor and the oppressed, and this sympathy was the more genuine because many of them were themselves former slaves or even still in bondage; it has been pointed out that most of the names that Paul salutes in the epistle to the Romans are names borne by the servile classes. The attraction of Christianity for those in servitude was increased by its exaltation of the virtues that a servant class had of necessity to acquire—meekness, obedience, resignation, the patient bearing of ills and affronts. Slaves who became Christians and found their peculiar virtues—so remote from pagan virtues—now a badge of moral distinction felt a new self-respect, and some of them went on to become leaders in the Christian community. By the end of the first century a slave,

Evaristus, had ascended every level of the Christian hierarchy, becoming successively deacon, priest, bishop, and finally Pope of Rome.

On the other hand, these very Christians were so accustomed to the institution of slavery that they found it natural. They conceived their mission as less to destroy it than to humanise it by imbuing the masters with charity and the slaves with loyalty. 'Slavery,' says Lecky, 'was distinctly and formally recognised by Christianity, and no religion ever laboured more to encourage a habit of docility and passive obedience'.²⁴ The church fathers, though they regarded the manumission of slaves as meritorious, remained curiously acquiescent in the institution. As late as the sixth century Gregory the Great, who was the first of the temporal princes of the church and who was elevated to sainthood, was the master of a great number of slaves, though he also freed many as an act of piety. The incongruity with the Christian spirit of buying and selling one's fellows entered more acutely with time into the awareness of the church, and after the twelfth century slavery in Europe was melted down into mediaeval serfdom, which, to be sure, was not always an improvement. The institution lingered for long, even within the boundaries of Christian powers—in the British Empire until 1833, in the United States until 1863, in Brazil until 1888.

CHRISTIANITY AND THE POSITION OF WOMEN

21 A more ineradicable division of mankind than that arising from either nationality or race is that of sex. Here again the account of the Christian attitude must follow a line by now familiar; a teaching on the part of Jesus that is hardly more than a spirit or tendency crystallises itself in course of time into a set of rules that are far more questionable.

The attitude toward women supplied to Jesus by his inheritance was Oriental, not European; and the contemporary Jewish view of woman was not high. Westermarck points out that the Jews 'both permitted and practised polygamy in the beginning of the Christian era'.²⁵ The Old Testament taught that through the agency of woman sin and death had come into the world, and both the Jewish prophets and the church fathers regarded her as a standing source of temptation. The wife was not considered the equal of her husband either in fact or in right; her business was to minister to him, to bear him children, and to attend to the details of the household. Even in the paean of praise in the book of Proverbs to 'the virtuous woman' whose 'price is far above rubies' (31 : 10 ff.), there is no intimation of equal companionship or romantic love: 'She layeth her hands to the spindle, and her hands hold the distaff. . . . She looketh well to the ways of her household, and eateth not the bread of idleness.' Indeed the singer of these praises may have purchased her from her father with hard money. This seems to have been common practice among the ancient Hebrews, though if a man could not produce the purchase price he could offer the girl's father the equivalent in work, as Jacob did in buying Rachel and Leah from their father Laban (Gen. 31). Divorce was, for the husband relatively easy, though for the wife all but impossible. 'When a man hath taken a wife, and married her, and it come to pass that she find no favour in his eyes, because he hath found some uncleanness in her, then let him write her a bill of divorcement, and give it in her hand, and send her out of his house' (Deut. 24 : 1). There is no mention in the Hebrew law of a right of divorce on the woman's part, though it seems to have been occasionally recognised in later times for leprosy or extreme disfigurement in the husband. It was assumed that a woman needed a male guardian; and as Hobhouse points out, if she lost her husband, 'the husband's brother, in fact, had the duty of marrying the widow, and, failing the brother, the obligation fell on the kindred'.[26] In the book of Ruth, often thought of as a Hebrew love story, Ruth, who has lost her husband, becomes the ward of her rich kinsman Boaz, who first offers her to a relative and then, when the offer is not accepted, announces that he has 'purchased' her himself. No doubt the law of a country is not an adequate reflection of what happens among actual men and women, and Hebrew customs mellowed with time. But in the Palestine of Jesus' day, the position of women was still a grimly subordinate one.

What was his own attitude toward this position? It must be gleaned not from his express teaching but from the few scattered anecdotes that touch upon his relations with women. What emerges most notably from such a gleaning is his freedom from convention or stereotype in his dealings with them. The scribes and Pharisees brought to him a woman taken in adultery, obviously with the intention of catching him in a dilemma. The Mosaic law said that a woman so taken should be stoned. If Jesus supported this law, he would be flouting his doctrine of love; if he opposed it, he would be giving his critics grounds for denouncing him as a heretic. He did neither. He said to the accusers, 'He that is without sin among you, let him first cast a stone at her'; and one by one they vanished. When they had gone, and he was left alone with the woman, he said, 'Neither do I condemn thee; go, and sin no more' (John 8 : 7, 11). The implication was not that adultery was sinless but that he forgave her in spite of the sin. Then there is the story of how, when Jesus was dining with a friend, a woman of some notoriety for loose morals came in, impulsively washed his feet, dried them with her hair, and poured upon him an expensive ointment that she had treasured in an 'alabaster box'. The disciples, complaining about her waste of means, apparently wished that he would rebuke her and have her thrown out. He rebuked the disciples instead. As for the woman, he said, 'her sins, which are many, are forgiven, for she loved much . . .' (Luke 7 : 36–50; Matt. 26 : 6–13). In the story of the Samaritan woman, as given in John, he astonished the disciples by talking with her freely, as Jews were forbidden to do. With Mary and Martha, sisters of Lazarus, he was on terms of easy familiarity. What these facts suggest is a freer intimacy with and understanding of women than were common among his people, a special responsiveness, sympathy, and compassion for them. He treated them not as servants or chattels or objects of desire, but as persons, and persons with whom, as having a special gift of affection, he could feel a special affinity.

This affinity in turn throws light on his own nature. If Christianity has always possessed a stronger appeal for women than for men, this is not an accident. The exalted position of the virgin mother has something to do with it, but much also is due to what may be called the feminine characteristics of Jesus himself. This side of his nature has been well brought out by A. E. Garvie.

'It is supremely significant that love, the grace of the home, and not justice, the virtue of the State, is made the first and greatest commandment (Mk xii, 29–31). The child is nearer, means more, to the mother than to the father; and Jesus understood and cared for children (Matt. xi, 16, xviii, 2–3, xix, 13–15). Does not the modesty of the woman appear in His reference to the lustful glance (Matt. v, 28) . . .? His defence of the offering of love shows not only His active but also His receptive affectionateness, His yearning for, as well as bestowal of, the generosities of the heart. He was not only intensely emotional, but quick in expressing His emotions (Jn xi, 33, 38; Mk vii, 34, viii, 12 . . .). His tenderness, gentleness, patience, and forbearance are more distinctively feminine than masculine graces. In His resignation and obedience to His Father's will (Matt. xi, 26, 29) is there not a womanly rather than a manly submissiveness? The prominence He gives in the Beatitudes to the passive graces of endurance rather than the active virtues of endeavour (Matt. v, 3–10) vindicates the distinctive excellence of womanhood. . . . The mind of Jesus was intuitive rather than ratiocinative; His moral judgment was swift and sure; His spiritual discernment direct; and these are characteristic of women rather than of men.'[27]

22 Though Jesus felt a certain comradeship with women, there is no indication of his having felt a sexual interest in them. Of course, one cannot draw any sure conclusion from such silence. It was the almost universal expectation and custom of Hebrew youths to marry before the age at which he began his ministry, and it has been argued with some plausibility that he too had followed the custom of his country. But this is speculation. What is not speculation is that he drew a line between *agape* and *eros*, between the Christian love of a woman as a person and the desire for a person as a woman, and that he exalted the first type of love and depreciated the second. The mere stirring of sexual desire, apart from any action upon it, he seems to have regarded as evil; 'whosoever looketh on a woman to lust after her hath committed adultery with her already in his heart' (Matt. 5 : 28). One must note also the strange declaration: 'there are eunuchs who have made themselves eunuchs for the sake of the realm of heaven. Let anyone practice it for whom it is practicable' (Matt. 19 : 12, Moffatt's trans.). Here one seems to see in the bud that teaching of the separation of flesh and spirit which was to grow under the influence of St Paul into a doctrine of war between two levels of human nature. The very different notion which was adumbrated in Dante, which came into an early bloom in the 'courtly love' of the Renaissance, and which has been familiar to all since Freud, that sex is the root of romance and that the romantic yeast is a leaven permeating the whole life of the spirit, is an idea quite foreign to the New Testament. The Greeks seem not to have developed the sense of sexuality as evil; Socrates acknowledged a debt to the instruction of a courtesan Diotima, and near his death, had a friendly discussion with another, Theodota, as to how she could ply her trade most successfully. But the Greeks did not hold the advantage over Christianity in this field that they held in some others we have considered, for in spite of their exaltation of the natural man, they tolerated sex practices that were notoriously unnatural. It is curious and tragic what a chaos has been made of sex by the chief contributors to Western culture. Greek naturalism was so permissive as to encourage perversions of sex, and Christianity so suspicious as to try to suppress it. In the life and teaching of Jesus himself, little is to be found about it, though that little is negative enough to carry the seeds of later trouble.

23 On one matter, indeed, Jesus forsakes the generality of most of his teaching and lays down a definite rule. This matter is divorce. In both Mark (10 : 11) and Luke (16 : 18) he declares against divorce unconditionally. But in two passages of Matthew (5 : 32 and 19 : 9) he is described as abandoning this sweeping prohibition and allowing an exception for adultery. The inconsistency is so clear as to nullify by itself any claim of the Biblical text to inerrancy. Does it commit us to the view that on this issue the teaching of Jesus was itself contradictory? Not necessarily. Mark is the oldest of the gospels, and a chief source for both Matthew and Luke. On Jesus' teaching about divorce, Luke follows the rigorist line of Mark. The question, then, is whether to accept as authentic the joint teaching of Mark and Luke or the divergent teaching of Matthew. The former course is the more plausible. Matthew was apparently the latest of the synoptic writers; he is known in other cases to have introduced modifications of the original teaching to suit new conditions; in his report of the teaching about divorce he closely follows the passage in Mark except for the clause about adultery; and the most natural explanation of the inconsistency is that this clause was a later insertion, designed to ease the rigour of the original teaching. If this inference is correct, Jesus taught the strictest monogamy. Whether this teaching depended on his belief in an imminent end of the world is presumably beyond knowing.

24   Both the friendliness Jesus felt for women and his rigorist teaching about divorce suggest a respect for them that went beyond the attitudes of his time. There are two circumstances, however, which show that this advance had definite limits. One is that of the twelve Apostles he selected to carry his message to the world none was a woman. The other is of a different and unexpected kind, namely the treatment he accorded his mother. This may be a surprise to Catholics, among whom the adoration of the Virgin amounts almost to worship.[28] The record shows a curious coolness toward her. At the wedding feast in Cana, she reminded her son that the guests had run out of wine. His reply began, 'Woman, what have I to do with thee?' When he was discoursing to a closely packed crowd, word was brought to him that his mother and brothers were on the outskirts of it and wanted to speak to him. 'And he answered them, saying, Who is my mother, or my brethren? And he looked round about on them which sat about him, and said, Behold my mother and my brethren!' (Mark 3 : 32–34). In the same chapter is recorded an attempt, by his 'relatives,' of whom his mother may or may not have been one, to place him under restraint for being out of his mind. On another occasion, a woman in his company pronounced a heart-felt blessing on his mother, on which his evasive comment was, 'Yea rather, blessed are they that hear the word of God, and keep it' (Luke 11 : 28). Even the last words to his mother from the cross are hardly an exception to the general tenor. Mary and the apostle John were present; he said to his mother, 'Woman, behold thy

son!' and to John, 'Behold thy mother!' (John 19 : 26–27). As the
account of a filial relationship, the record seems strangely cold.
Far from supporting the church's exaltation of Mary, it shows
surprisingly little affection on the part of such a son for what we are
told was such a mother. What it rather suggests is coolness of feeling
and lack of understanding between them.

ST PAUL ON THE POSITION OF WOMEN

25 In sum, Jesus' attitude toward women presents itself to the
reflective observer as a set of rather faint pluses and minuses which
scarcely admit of a confident interpretation. What determined the
posture of the church, however, was less the attitude of Jesus than of
Paul. And Paul's position was forthright. Women were inferior
human beings. They were daughters of that Eve who 'brought sin
into the world and all our woe'; and they remained weaker vessels,
prone to sins of the flesh, and an enduring temptation to such sin on
the part of mankind. Intimate relations with them were best avoided.
'It is good for a man not to touch a woman. . . . I say therefore to the
unmarried and widows, It is good for them if they abide even as I.
But if they cannot contain, let them marry; for it is better to marry
than to burn' (1 Cor. 7 : 1, 8–9). Marriage was, for Paul, a second
best, a refuge from fornication: 'to avoid fornication, let every man
have his own wife, and every woman have her own husband'
(ibid. 7 : 2). What was to be their relation within marriage? Paul
answered: 'Wives, submit yourselves unto your own husbands, as
unto the Lord . . . as the church is subject unto Christ, so let the
wives be to their own husbands in every thing' (Ephes. 5 : 22, 24).
Women could be church members, but 'Let your women keep silence
in the churches, for it is not permitted unto them to speak; but they
are commanded to be under obedience. . . . And if they will learn
any thing, let them ask their husbands at home, for it is a shame for
women to speak in the church' (1 Cor. 14 : 34–35). They should
know their place, and stay in it. 'Let the woman learn in silence with
all subjection. But I suffer not a woman to teach, nor to usurp
authority over the man, but to be in silence' (1 Tim. 2 : 11–12).

Silence, submission, subjection, obedience! It was not an in-
spiriting role for women, nor one that a rational ethic could endorse.
How could Paul have approved it? He was a generous man, who
was able to say elsewhere that 'there is neither male nor female, for
ye are all one in Christ Jesus' (Gal. 3 : 28). But he was under a
variety of pressures that forced him to defect from this insight. In
placing women in an inferior position, he was yielding to the general
view of the eastern Mediterranean in his time. Furthermore, he

shared the early Christian expectation that the world was soon to
end, which affected the apparent timeliness of marrying and giving
in marriage. Again, he was swayed by a theology, largely the product
of his own fervid brain, which represented humankind as sunk in
sin and abhorred by its Creator, who nevertheless was offering it a
second chance through a second Adam if it abandoned its wicked
ways and walked in the spirit. Finally, walking in the spirit was
linked in Paul's thought with a dualism stressed by the ascetics and
neo-Platonists of his day, a dualism of spirit and flesh. Plato had
held that man was a twofold being, a participant through his senses
in the world of change and decay, but also a participant through his
mind in an eternal world of ideas. Paul too believed that man was a
twofold creature, whose life was under competing controls, that of
bodily impulse on the one hand, and on the other that of 'the Christ
that liveth in me', the indwelling Holy Spirit. The body was a
temple of this spirit, which should be kept clean and consecrated,
and it suffered pollution if the passions of the flesh were allowed to
have their way with it. Of all these passions, sex was the most wayward and unmanageable. A firm discipline of the will fortified by
religious dedication was required to bring it under control; 'I keep
under my body, and bring it into subjection,' says Paul in a passage
that Moffat translates 'I maul and master my body' (1 Cor. 9 : 27).
That man was safest who did not compromise with sex at all. 'He
that is unmarried careth for the things that belong to the Lord, how
he may please the Lord: But he that is married careth for the things
of the world, how he may please his wife' (1 Cor. 7 : 32–33).

In this suspicion and deprecation of sex, is Paul speaking the
mind of Jesus? Dean Inge thought he was. 'St Paul dwells on these
[sexual offences] more than Christ ever did, but there is no reason
to think that Christ would not have approved of all that he says.'[29]
I cannot think this is true, and if it is, the task of the Christian
apologist in the modern world is certainly made more difficult.
Bernard Shaw was perhaps nearer the truth, in spite of his characteristic exaggeration, when he said, 'There has really never been a
more monstrous imposition perpetrated than the imposition of the
limitations of Paul's soul upon the soul of Jesus'.[30]

26 In any case, Paul's view of sex became the official view of
the church. The early fathers dwelt with fascinated aversion on the
dangers of sex, the wiles of woman, and the impurity of sex relations,
regular or irregular. In his *De Cultu Feminarum* (i, 1) Tertullian spoke
his mind to women:

Do you not know that you are each an Eve? The sentence of God on this sex of yours lives in this age; the guilt must of necessity live too. You are the devil's gateway; you are the unsealer of that [forbidden] tree; you are the first deserter of the divine law; you are she who persuaded him whom the devil was not valiant enough to attack. You destroyed so easily God's image, man. On account of your desert—that is, death—even the Son of God had to die.[31]

Tertullian was not alone in these profound reflections. Lecky reports as follows the views of the church fathers generally:

'Woman was represented as the door of hell, as the mother of all human ills. She should be ashamed at the very thought that she is a woman. She should live in continual penance, on account of the curses she has brought upon the world. She should be ashamed of her dress, for it is the memorial of her fall. She should be especially ashamed of her beauty, for it is the most potent instrument of the daemon. . . . Women were even forbidden by a provincial Council, in the sixth century, on account of their impurity, to receive the Eucharist into their naked hands. Their essentially subordinate position was continually maintained.'[32]

It would be a mistake to say that the ecclesiastical view of sex had no redeeming features. In making marriage a sacrament and likening it to the union of Christ with the church, it gave dignity and stability to the marriage relation; and when, after several centuries, the Virgin Mary began her ascent to a queenly position in the church, her less privileged sisters could feel a greater self-respect. Nevertheless, as Christianity prevailed in the Roman Empire and marriage became a religious sacrament rather than a civil contract, the ecclesiastical view became the standard view, and it prevailed through the Middle Ages. 'In the whole feudal legislation', says Lecky, 'women were placed in a much lower legal position than in the Pagan Empire.'[33] When the duty of submission to the husband's will is combined with a prohibition of divorce, women can scarcely be called free. Under the church's canon law, women's right of inheritance was narrowly limited, and since they were supposed to be weaker of mind as well as body, they received little encouragement to educate themselves or to qualify for a profession. Even within the church, though there were celibate sisterhoods that devoted themselves to admirable works of mercy, the priesthood and higher offices were reserved for men, and for that special class of men who were unsullied by marriage. St Jerome professed as one of his ends 'to cut down by the axe of Virginity the wood of marriage', though what he expected to remain after the wood was finally cleared is not quite plain. The Council of Trent, in its section on the sacrament of matrimony, decreed: 'If anyone saith that the marriage state is to be placed above the state of virginity or of celibacy, and that it is not better and more blessed to remain in virginity or in celibacy than to be united in matrimony, let him be anathema.' This was St Paul in formal dress. But Scriptural views on women were not confined to Paul's epistles, and the church took all Scripture to be inspired. Women were enjoined in Genesis to be fruitful and multiply; so in spite of its depreciation of marriage, the church opposed any artificial means of preventing conception. Genesis also said to women, 'in sorrow thou shalt bring forth children,' and this was enough to induce even some Presbyterians to inveigh against Dr J. Y. Simpson's introduction of chloroform to mitigate the pains of childbirth.

In the light of such attitudes as these, it can hardly be said that the line taken by Christian ethics regarding the relation between the sexes is that of a rational ethics. Some modern critics have been very emphatic about this. Bertrand Russell held that 'Christian ethics inevitably, through the emphasis laid upon sexual virtue, did a great deal to degrade the position of women. . . . It is only in quite modern times that women have regained the degree of freedom which they enjoyed in the Roman Empire.'[34] H. L. Mencken argued that 'The emancipation of women . . . owes nothing to organized Christianity'.[35] Both held that the recognition of women's rights sprang not from any religious vindication of those rights but rather from the free play of secular reason, which broke loose with the French Revolution and found expression in such writers as Mary Wollstonecraft and John Stuart Mill. If this contention is to be admitted, however, its bearing should be made more precise. 'Christian ethics' is a vague term. It commonly includes extraneous matter from three sources outside the teaching of Jesus himself: the Old Testament, which carries a heavy burden of Oriental legend and primitive morality, the teaching of St Paul, which on the issues in question was theologically warped, and the views of many religious leaders over the centuries. These views have varied greatly, but in too many important cases —those of the church fathers and Luther, for example—they were built on unexamined and untenable premises. To saddle the distortions that rose from these sources upon the original Christian ethic is scarcely just. Those distortions were neither produced by, nor consistent with, its central doctrine of loving consideration for all mankind. But then this doctrine, as we shall have further occasion to see, was not taught or applied with full consistency by Jesus himself. Its application to the great issue we have been discussing was vague enough to make misunderstanding inevitable.

CHAPTER X

RATIONALISM AND CHRISTIAN ETHICS (II)

CHRISTIANITY AND JUSTICE

1 In the previous chapter we considered how far the Christian ethics, as presented in the gospels, is in accord with rational standards in its treatment of special groups—of the rich, of the poor, of male-factors, of slaves, of persons differing from ourselves in nationality or sex. We saw that on all of these points the ethics of Jesus differs, in some cases slightly, in others profoundly, from the standards current today, and even from what reflective moralists would conceive as the requirements of reason. To questions of applied justice also his answers were at times surprising and disturbing. They are bound to raise the question whether he gave to justice as important a place as it holds in the thought of most other moralists.

I think the answer must be that he did not. Indeed this conclusion follows from the all-importance he gave to love and from his intensely personal way of conceiving morality. He taught that if one loved God and man unreservedly, all other virtues would take care of themselves since they were all really manifestations of love. 'Justice, self-respect, truth and honor,' says Warner Fite, 'are swallowed up in love. . . .'[1] George F. Thomas points out that in his ethical teaching Jesus, 'always seems to conceive of a moral situation as one in which one person stands in relationship with another *person* or with each of several other persons'.[2] But as Professor Thomas adds, this is not the sort of situation in which reflection on justice most easily arises. Justice is no respecter of persons; it attempts to abstract from the personal; it seeks a rule in accordance with which the peculiarities of the individual case may be disregarded and people may be treated alike. Love with its bent toward partiality, and justice in search of impartiality, at times conflict with each other, as those well know who have to write letters of recommendation or consider their children's advantage in school. But I follow Professor Thomas in thinking that justice, though often at odds with the immediate and personal demands of love, is a necessary instrument of that larger love—really a settled benevolence—which is directed to mankind.

That is the kind of love Jesus advocated. Still, his preoccupation with the personal was so strong as apparently to stand in the way of that abstraction which produces the rules of justice and that reflection on long-range consequences which provides their warrant.

2   The result is a set of teachings that in their general drift are nobly humane but resist reduction to any consistent whole. Classes that were unjustly treated in his own time, and indeed in all subsequent times—slaves, women, children, the poor, the sick, the exploited—have always felt that he was on their side, that if his compassion ever crept into the general mind it would sweep away the injustices from which they suffered. Their intuition is probably right. Nevertheless there is evidence that his insight into the relations of love and justice wavered. His illustrations of what love requires in the way of justice are sometimes puzzling, nor do we always find that reflection removes the difficulty.

Consider the central Christian teaching that God is morally perfect. His love and justice are presumed to be without defect; and we are enjoined to strive to be perfect, even as he is. And yet God is described as holding attitudes which, in those enjoined to imitate him, would be considered unjust in the extreme. It is man's duty, for example, to forgive seventy times seven, that is, indefinitely or without limit. But God is held to have no such obligation. 'Whoever speaketh a word against the Son of man, it shall be forgiven him: but whosoever speaketh against the Holy Ghost it shall not be forgiven him, neither in this world, neither in the world to come' (Matt. 12 : 32). Some persons have wondered whether Jesus could have said anything so incongruous with his teaching that God is love. But the German theologian Schmiedel has argued that this passage is one of the 'foundation pillars' of whose authenticity we can be most certain; it is so obviously at odds with the general drift of his teaching that a worshipful biographer would not have included it unless it were undeniably authentic. Other commentators such as Henry Churchill King, apparently committed to the truth of everything Jesus said, take the passage as a statement about man rather than about God; it is a warning against 'moral suicide', that 'playing fast and loose with one's conscience' which blurs and in the end destroys one's sense of good and evil.[3] But the question is not whether this is a serious sin, which no one doubts, but whether God will ever forgive it, which is here clearly denied. Such absolute unforgiveness seems triply inconsistent. It is inconsistent with the notion that God is love, with the injunction to man to forgive without limit, and with man's own sense of justice.

Similar difficulties arise about Jesus' denunciation of the Pharisees for their hypocrisy and of others for their lack of compassion. No doubt the Pharisees did show varying degrees of hypocrisy. But in the long, sweeping, and bitter arraignment of them ending, 'Ye serpents, ye generation of vipers, how can ye escape the damnation of hell?' (Matt. 23), it is hard to discern the accents of love or justice, to say nothing of mercy. The punishment Jesus promises for certain sins of omission is no less severe. God will say to those who have *not* fed the hungry or clothed the naked, 'Depart from me, ye cursed, into everlasting fire, prepared for the devil and his angels' (Matt. 25 : 41). To inflict the unimaginable suffering of being burnt in an everlasting fire (or even one that is age-long, if one prefers so to translate) for such sins of omission is clearly not in accord with human conceptions of justice.

Such reflections cut deep, for they affect the Christian conception of God and his relations to mankind. They could indeed be carried further. For just as the punishment meted out to sinners is out of accord with what we know as justice, so also is the traditional theory of how that punishment may be averted. The edge of the divine wrath against mankind is turned by the voluntary submission to torture and death of a wholly innocent person. Theologians admit that in a merely human light it is a mystery how such suffering on the part of the innocent could affect the deserts of the wicked, or how a just Deity could either require or allow such substitution. Some critics find in the dogma of the atonement not profound and mysterious truth but the lingering remains of a primitive morality. 'Christianity in its essence', said Albert Camus, 'is a doctrine of injustice. It is founded upon the sacrifice of the innocent and the acceptation of that sacrifice.' We have repeatedly brought to light in both Catholic and Protestant theologians, and above all in the line of thought that runs from Luther through Kierkegaard to Brunner and Barth, a tendency to meet such problems by throwing them into the realm of the unintelligible, of truth that outsoars human reason. This, as we have seen, is an evasion. If the doctrine is unintelligible, in the sense of meaningless, it is not a doctrine at all. If it does say something meaningful about justice, what it says must be appraised by our own moral sense, for we have nothing else to use. If what it says is then rejected by our moral sense, we can only abide by that decision. One is cutting morality at the root if one insists that what to this sense is black is really white. Human reason, as embodied in our moral sense, is a fallible instrument; granted. But one will not get a better by throwing away the best we have.

3 We have been considering Christ's teaching about justice as exhibited in his thought of Deity. Unhappily the difficulty is not much relieved when we turn to his account of justice in individual behaviour. The law of Moses said, 'an eye for an eye, a tooth for a tooth'. As we have already noted in another connection, Jesus repealed this law, and in doing so urged a surprising alternative. 'But I say unto you, that ye resist not evil, but whosoever shall smite thee on thy right cheek, turn to him the other also. And if any man will sue thee at the law, and take away thy coat, let him have thy cloak also. And whosoever shall compel thee to go a mile, go with him twain' (Matt. 5 : 39–41). Of course few of those who consider themselves Christians behave in this way. Even if they restrain the impulse to return blow for blow or take out their anger on the thief or mugger, they would probably see to it, with the aid of the police, that such molestation of themselves and others did not continue. They do not do this with an uneasy conscience. They regard the active prevention of injustice as not only a right but a duty. 'Not to do wrong is one side of justice,' says the eminent moralist Friedrich Paulsen; 'its complement is not to permit wrong to be done, either to self or to others. This is what the Greeks and Romans understood by the duty of justice. . . .' He goes on: 'Primitive Christianity does not recognize justice in this sense as a virtue; it is acquainted with only one side of it, with the duty not to do wrong, not with the duty not to permit wrong.'⁴ Professor Francis W. Newman, the Cardinal's brother, made the same criticism: 'Jesus forbids us to stand up for our rights; we are to surrender them to the first violent claimant.'⁵ Could a society maintain its safety or freedom if its members thus bowed to coercion? The answer is only too certain. The decent many would be terrorised by the unprincipled few, and these few are always present. No community is secure whose individuals are unwilling to stand up for their rights, and for the rights of those others who are unable to stand up for themselves. It is a truism that eternal vigilance is the price of freedom. Christian ethics, with its attention focused on personal attitudes, overlooks this public and preventive side of justice.

4 To such criticism it may be replied that we have the teaching of Jesus only in fragmentary form, and that if we had his applications of it in parable and practice the difficulties would vanish. That is possible. But we do have several parables touching on justice, and they increase rather than remove the difficulties. Consider the parable of the householder. This man owned a vineyard in which work had to be done. He went out early in the morning to hire labourers in the market, offering them a shilling a day. Needing further help, he went out again at nine o'clock and hired more, saying that he would pay them 'whatever is right'. He repeated this process at twelve o'clock, at three in the afternoon, and again at five, when the working day was nearly over. In paying the labourers off at the day's end, he gave exactly the same wage to those who had worked all day and to those who had worked an hour. Not surprisingly, there was grumbling among those who had worked the whole day: ' "These last have only worked a single hour, and yet you have ranked them equal to us who have borne the brunt of the day's work and the heat!" Then he replied to one of them, "My man, I am not wronging you. . . . Take what belongs to you and be off. I choose to give this last man the same as you. Can I not do as I please with what belongs to me?" ' (Matt. 20 : 12–15, Moffatt.) The parable is offered to illustrate the attitude of the king in the kingdom of heaven toward his subjects. The moral it most obviously teaches is that a person of wealth is not called upon to obey the rules of justice in disposing of it; he can do what he will with his own. There is no suggestion that the last shall be first and the first last on any ground of superiority or merit. The persons paid at the higher rate are those who have spent most of the day in idleness, and the persons paid the lower rate are those who are expressly said to have borne the burden and heat of the day; nor is there any intimation that the householder has acted unjustly. As it stands, the parable seems cut to the order of Kierkegaard, suggesting as it does that divine and human justice are incommensurable.

Other parables touching on justice offer similar puzzles. 'The kingdom of heaven is like unto treasure hid in a field; the which when a man hath found, he hideth, and for joy thereof goeth and selleth all that he hath, and buyeth that field' (Matt. 13 : 44). Slightly expanded, the parable seems to be this: a man finds in another man's field a large treasure, worth more than the field itself. He conceals its existence from the owner until he can command the price of the field. He then with 'joy' gets both field and treasure from the man he has kept in ignorance of the value of his property. On this Warner Fite remarks: 'The lesson of the parable is then a recommendation of what I think more honourable men of today would condemn as a piece of sharp practice in dealing with a stranger, and certainly as a gross bit of trickery in dealing with any one with whom one might be on friendly relations. Of this it seems that Jesus is quite unconscious.'[6]

The parable of the talents is also puzzling. A man about to travel 'into a far country' leaves his money in the safekeeping of three servants. To the first he gives about five thousand dollars, to the second two thousand, and to the third one thousand. On his return, the first two report that, by enterprising investment, they have doubled the money left with them, and they receive their master's thanks and praise. The third makes a different report. He says: 'Lord, I knew thee that thou art a hard man, reaping where thou hast not sown, and gathering where thou hast not strawed. And I was afraid, and went and hid thy talent in the earth: lo, there thou hast that is thine' (Matt. 25 : 24–25). Though he returned intact the money entrusted to him, his master's judgement was, 'Thou wicked and slothful servant, thou knewest that I reap where I sowed not, and gather where I have not strawed. Thou oughtest therefore to have put my money to the exchangers, and then at my coming I should have received mine own with usury' (26–27). The parable ends, 'cast ye the unprofitable servant into outer darkness; there shall be weeping and gnashing of teeth'. What is striking about the story is, first, the purely commercial tone of it, and, second, the acceptance by the master of the charge of being a hard man, reaping where he had not sown; this is strange because the master is the symbol of Deity, and therefore of perfect justice. The harsh business tone has been hidden for many by the ambiguity of the word 'talents', and the consequent ease of taking the parable to mean 'Develop your talents', or 'Realise your potentialities'. But the word 'talent' meant in its Greek original, and also for its King James translators, simply a weight or amount of money; its use for a natural gift seems to have stemmed from this interpretation of the parable rather than to have preceded it. In any case the parable leaves the reader with an uneasy sense that justice is being conceived as that of an avaricious and arbitrary employer rather than that of an ideal morality.

   To conclude this brief review on justice: Christian ethics, through its emphasis on love and compassion, rectified many injustices to the poor and the exploited; but its conception of justice, whether as exercised by God or as a pattern for relations among men, was undeveloped and ambiguous.

CHRISTIANITY AND WORK

5   From this mention of the New Testament conception of justice in the rewards of work, we may conveniently turn to the Christian estimate of work itself. On this point, as on many others, there is a curious contrast between Jesus' own teaching and modern Christianity. The teacher who has done most to fix the attitude of the modern Christian toward work is John Calvin, whose view had a profound effect on the Christianity of the new world. He sought to bring the whole of life under religious direction, abolishing the distinction between sacred and secular, and making a man's work as farmer, mechanic, or business man a part of his divine calling. Idleness was a serious sin. The diligent performance of one's work,

without waste of time or money, and without indulgence in pleasure except as contributory to one's work, became a religious duty. 'So we can understand', writes Dean Inge,

> how Calvinism created that curious product, the modern business man, who works like a slave in accumulating money which his tastes and principles forbid him to enjoy, and about the value of which to himself and others he asks no questions. No system was ever devised so effectual in promoting that kind of progress which is measured by statistics. If a nation can be convinced that steady industry in profitable enterprise is eminently pleasing to God, but that almost all unproductive ways of spending superfluous wealth are wrong, that nation will become very rich.[7]

There is no doubt that the strong Calvinistic strain in Puritanism, with its gospel of hard work, has had much to do with the moral ideal of the American business man. The Puritan influence on such business paradigms as Rockefeller, Carnegie, and Ford is plain.

But did Jesus teach this Calvinistic Puritanism? There is small ground for thinking so.

> If the daily toil were so important, Christ Himself would surely have set an example of work, or have praised the sanctity of work; yet there is no evidence of His having toiled at all for a livelihood, and all His teaching is against work, or at least the overshadowing cares of work. Anxiety for bodily needs—food and raiment and shelter—how light He made of them! The lilies in His parable neither toiled nor spun, Martha was rebuked for housewifely care. It was a gospel of simplicity, of peace, of love, never a gospel of work.[8]

'Take no thought for your life, what ye shall eat, or what ye shall drink; nor yet for your body, what ye shall put on' (Matt. 6 : 25); that was the teaching of the Sermon on the Mount. The fowls of the air did not sow or reap, yet they were amply cared for. To be sure, the Gentiles sought security in mammon, but for Christians this was needless, for if they sought 'the kingdom of God and his righteousness,' even the things that mammon could buy would be added to them unasked. And it was idle to think that God and mammon could both be served; one must be chosen and the other left.

Here, as so often, the Oriental custom of speaking in metaphor and parable leaves us at a loss. Jesus seems to be saying that the sort of work men normally have to do to support themselves and their families is superfluous. 'Neither from the practice nor from the precepts of Jesus as we have them, could anyone discover that Industry is a duty.'[9] It may be that during the unreported years of his life he had followed the trade of carpenter, but of those years we know nothing. We do know that in his time manual labour was held in small respect. His own people, the Jews, thought of it as a punishment for sin imposed by God, who said to Adam 'because thou hast eaten of the tree, in the sweat of thy face shalt thou eat bread'. The Greeks thought manual labour the appropriate lot of slaves, not of free men. They seem to have included in their aversion even the manual labour involved in experimental science, and thus, according at least to John Dewey, were prevented from reaching the level in such science which they attained in mathematics and metaphysics. The Romans also turned over to slaves such work as they could, looking with respect on the gentleman farmer and the wealthy patron of sport and the arena, but holding the manual labourer in something like contempt.

Jesus was probably not immune to the influence of these attitudes, particularly that of the Jews. The early Christians are known to have disparaged trade, and to have disapproved the taking of interest on money. Many mediaeval and modern students have thought they found in the Christian ethics an attempt to spiritualise labour, to make toil the expression of humility, fidelity, and worship. The monks were fond of saying *laborare est orare*. 'He doeth much that loveth much,' said Thomas à Kempis. George Herbert wrote 'Who sweeps a room as to thy laws/Makes that and the action fine'; and Browning added in like vein, 'All service ranks the same with God'. But this does not seem to have been the actual teaching of Jesus. Mary and Martha are set over against each other, as are the service of God and the service of mammon; and when the Apostles were called, it was not to continue their old work in a new spirit but to abandon that work for a type of life in which worldly goods and worldly work were left behind. One suspects that Jesus' teaching at this point was tied to his expectation of an imminent end of the world. At any rate, his words and example would have been more helpful to labouring mankind if, instead of sharply contrasting the realms in which he lived, he had shown how they could be joined.

CHRISTIANITY AND FAMILY RELATIONS

6 Work is, of course, the normal means by which the family is supported, and if Jesus placed so little emphasis upon it, it might be expected that his view of family relations would be unconventional in other respects also. And it was. His teaching in this field is important, since the family is the most universal of all social organisations, and on its character and strength depends in large part the moral health of any people. When children are brought up in an atmosphere of parental love and justice, they absorb these attitudes as norms for themselves, and go out into the world as potentially good neighbours and good citizens. Christianity as traditionally interpreted, stressing the permanence of marriage, likening the relation of man and wife to that of Christ and the church, and harbouring memories of Christ's tenderness toward children, has had important civilising influences on family life; and its conception of God as the exacting but loving Father of mankind has made the brotherhood of man an easier and more credible notion.

For many persons, this general benignance toward family life is enough; it gives them a text which they can embroider into their own pattern for family life. But to stop with those generalities would be untrue to the reported facts of Jesus' words and actions. He had more to say, and the more is puzzling. He was an individualist whose ultimate loyalties were to no organisation and whose orders he believed to have come to him directly from on high. These orders showed little regard for family ties. If such ties conflicted with them, they must be ruthlessly broken. Jesus, who remained without wife or family, demanded of his followers a loyalty to himself that should take precedence over any family loyalties of their own. 'He that loveth his father or mother more than me is not worthy of me: and he that loveth son or daughter more than me is not worthy of me' (Matt. 10 : 27). 'For I am come to set a man at variance against his father, and the daughter against her mother, and the daughter-in-law against her mother-in-law' (10 : 35). 'If any man come to me, and hate not his father, and mother, and wife, and children, and brethren, and sisters . . . he cannot be my disciple' (Luke 14 : 26). One person who had decided to follow him begged for a brief delay to perform a pious duty: 'Lord, suffer me first to go and bury my father. But Jesus said unto him, Follow me; and let the dead bury their dead' (Matt. 8 : 21–22). We have already noted the coolness shown to his mother and brothers. And his coolness toward his family seems to have been heartily reciprocated. They once attempted, as we have also remarked, to place him under restraint as out of his mind. His brothers did not believe in him (John 7 : 5), and let him make his crucial trip to Jerusalem alone. His neighbours are reported to have had similar feelings about him. When he returned to his own country, his townspeople were so sceptical of him and 'offended at him' that 'he marvelled because of their unbelief' and could 'do no mighty work' among them. 'A prophet is not without honour,' he lamented, 'but in his own country, and among his own kin, and in his own house' (Mark 6 : 1–6).

What are we to make of such passages? It is idle, in the light of them, to say that Jesus' view of family duty is clear and simple, and if we forget these passages, there are persons who will remind us of them. 'By the Chinese and the Japanese it is regarded as one of the great defects of Christianity that it acts rather as a solvent than as a consecration of family ties.'[10] That the great exponent of love for all men should, without very special reason, have countenanced indifference to one's own kith and kin is incredible, to be sure. The only plausible interpretation would appear to be this: he conceived himself as the bearer of an all-important message whose delivery to mankind could not wait, since the end of the present order was impending; and in his mind the urgency of the situation reversed the ordinary priority of duties. It was precisely men's family loyalties that would stand most obstructively in the way of their giving up everything and following him; hence if his summons was to be heeded at all, the primacy of these loyalties must be denied in the sharpest way. This removes the inconsistency between his teaching of love and his strange disparagement of it within the family circle. But it must be admitted that consistency is bought here with a price. The price is that one can no longer take his teaching about family duties as generally or permanently applicable, since it was offered under a major misapprehension about God's relation to the world and the course of future history. Indeed the Christian is left in a dilemma. If he accepts at its face value Jesus' teaching about the family, he must do violence to his natural feeling and even his conscience; he cannot 'hate' his own family, or leave a beloved father's body to be collected by the sanitation department. On the other hand, if he claims exemption from this teaching on the ground that it was offered under a delusion, how far does that delusion extend? It cannot be confined to the sphere of family relations. It threatens to undermine Jesus' teaching in many other areas as well.

We have made no attempt to explore the influence of this delusion except indirectly, by raising as we went along the question of the rationality of a given teaching. We found in our various confrontations with Christian theology that reasonableness in the light of reflection is the only standard which holds in the end. This standard is harder to apply to feelings than to clearly formulated dogmas, but since Christian ethics chiefly consists in injunctions to inward attitudes, we have had to make the attempt. And there are some attitudes as yet unconsidered that enter essentially into the kind of life enjoined by Jesus. These now call for comment.

CHRISTIANITY AND THE LOVE OF GOD

7   In his own summary of his teaching, the love of God took pre-

cedence of everything else. This is a difficulty for us. Neither the
feeling he entertained toward God nor the ethical importance he
attached to it is easy for the modern mind to understand. The love of
another person who is near and intimately known to us is intelligible
enough; we have so much in common with him that we feel at home
in his presence; his hopes and defeats become our own in the sense
that we follow his successes with pleasure and his sorrows with
anxious sympathy. Can we love God in any such way? It seems very
dubious. In love for him, just what object are we loving? Do we
know, for example, what we mean by calling that object 'he'? There
seems to be no ground for regarding it as father rather than mother.
And what do we own in common with it that supplies a basis for
intimacy? With a human stranger we can easily conceive of finding
enough in common—interests, likes and dislikes—to arouse com-
radeliness and affection. Can we feel anything similar toward the
maker of the Milky Way and the galaxies beyond it? The God of
traditional theology is a being who, as omnipresent, could love only
himself or part of himself; who, as all-powerful, has none of our
weaknesses and none of our unattained ends; who, as all-knowing,
has none of our problems; who, as all-good, has none of our vices,
none of our unsatisfied interests, and none of our temptations. The
profoundest philosophers have been baffled in the attempt to provide
any definite conception of such a being. And how can man love he
knows not what?

Theologians also have floundered desperately when they have
sought to describe the 'love of God'. According to Anders Nygren,
it is not a human possibility at all, but a divine implantation in men;
furthermore, it is irrational in the sense of being unmotivated and
hence is independent of the moral character of its object. This theory
does not make sense. Besides being curiously non-moral, it ends in
self-contradiction. For God's love, which is admitted to provide a
paradigm for man's, is also admitted to be discriminatory; it grants
salvation to some and withholds it from others. Augustine, by a bit
of legerdemain, equates God with good, and thus translates the love
of God into the pursuit of moral perfection. He can then show that
both self-love and the love of others are really the love of God in
disguise; self-love is the pursuit of one's own perfection, i.e. the
realisation of God in one's self, and the love of others is really the
love of God as embodied in those others. This theory has some
interest if offered as the philosopher's own; but it is fantastic as an
account of the meaning of Jesus. He was a Jewish prophet, not a
Greek metaphysician; he thought in images and taught in homely
parables. He talked of God very much as a Palestinian son would
talk of a Palestinian father. His 'father who was in heaven' was

loving but also stern and formidable, concerned about his children's health and comfort but more about their character, a being close at hand for consultation or petition, whose commands were not always intelligible but must be obeyed without question, who was grieved by a child's disobedience, delighted by the return of a prodigal son, and at times driven to terrible anger when treated without due reverence.

8   The Bishop of Woolwich is surely right in saying that the love of God in this sense is not open to the modern mind. Its object is too plainly a product of man's imagination in the service of his need— his need for comfort and assurance in the face of a universe that is too much for him. Religion is largely a cry for help in a world one did not make and cannot control; 'When other helpers fail and comforts flee, Help of the helpless, oh abide with me'. This motive remains at work in modern man's religion, but it found readier play in more primitive times. Nature as we know it had not entered into the mind of the Palestinian of the first century. It was not, as it is for us, a fixed order of law, but an arena where God on the one hand and Satan and his minions on the other did continual battle for the souls of men. The agency of God or his enemies might be witnessed daily in the raising or stilling of storms, in plagues of drought or locusts, in epidemics of disease and sudden inexplicable cures, in strange portents, in the inspired words of prophets, and in old prophecies fulfilled. God had not yet been pushed by science into the dim distance beyond the natural order, for in the modern sense there was no such order; he manifested a somewhat capricious will through individual events; and this will might be deflected by earnest and timely pleas. He was, as Arnold said, 'a magnified non-natural man,' whose co-operation might be obtained by due obeisance, and whose favour was essential if one's future, here or hereafter, was to be secure.

    Love for such a being was in many ways similar to love for another man. God was the father of his people and captain of the host in whose ranks they were serving. He fought and suffered much as they did; he had them under his solicitous care; in his tenderness he numbered the very hairs on their heads. Jesus' converse with him was intimate, constant, and undoubting to the end—or almost to the end. There came a moment, the most tragic in human history, when he too doubted. His doubt was not apparently whether the God he had worshipped was real, but whether that God had not forsaken and repudiated him. To the man of later time the wonder is not that the doubt arose but that it did not arise earlier and more insistently, for the God that Jesus revered could hardly be held in permanent reverence by a deeply reflective mind. If he was tender about the fall of sparrows, he could also order destructive demons into the Gadarene swine; he could strike a man dead in anger for telling an untruth; he could turn his face forever from a certain class of miserable sinners; he could be jealous, vengeful, and exceedingly cruel; he was capable of consigning men, for the missteps of a transitory life, to suffering without mercy and without end. Love as mankind knows it is not offered without regard to the character of its object, nor should it be. Men have tried for many centuries to achieve the love of God as Jesus conceived him; some of them have professed achievement of it and even a readiness, by reason of it, to suffer damnation themselves. The human mind being what it is, one wonders whether the incentive to both professions was not an overmastering fear of what such professions might serve to avert. In any case, with the recession of this fear from the modern mind, the love of God, as either the Old or the New Testament represents him, would seem to be neither rationally nor practically possible.

This does not imply that it is impossible in all its senses. Indeed the love of God may be made the essence of religion, and thus given whatever importance its proponent chooses to assign to religion as such. It is of course capable of profound philosophical interpretation, and that it has received at the hands of some contemporary thinkers. One of the ablest of them, Paul Tillich, conceived it as an ecstatic 'participation' of the finite spirit 'in the transcendent unity of unambiguous life'.[11] Whether this recondite notion is really Christian is debatable, but I doubt whether Professor Tillich would think the answer greatly mattered. He was clear that the Christianity of the first century could not be the standard for the twentieth, and that the conformity to be demanded of the theologian was not conformity to a Biblical text, even that of the New Testament, but conformity to truth as it presented itself to the reflective and rational mind. In this of course we agree. Unfortunately the task of interpreting 'the love of God' rationally, whether in his or in other terms, is not one that can be undertaken in passing.

THE LOVE OF GOD AS A MOTIVE

9 The reason for introducing the idea at all is that Jesus took the love of God to be an essential part of morality. Jointly with the love of man, it was the prime motive of the good life. True Christians were to be childlike in their teachableness and affection, and of such he declared the kingdom of heaven to be composed. Their trust in their divine father was absolute; the good life meant his will for them, and their overriding concern must be to learn that will and do it. The love of man was important too, but Jesus seems not even to have considered the possibility of its standing alone. Human selfishness, lust, and greed would be too much for it. It was only as morality was infused with religion and human souls were seen as children of God that their infinite value could be recognised. And

> 'in asking . . . "What shall it profit a man if he shall gain the whole world and lose his own soul?" he put a man's value as high as it can be put. The man who can say "My Father" to the Being who rules heaven and earth, is thereby raised above heaven and earth, and himself has a value which is higher than all the fabric of this world.' 'A man may know it or not, but a real reverence for humanity follows from the practical recognition of God as the Father of us all.'[12]

It was Christianity, Harnack goes on to contend, that first made men fully aware of the value of human life; and civilisation, as a result, was lifted to a new level. Conduct took on a new seriousness. The decisions of daily life—of getting food and drink, of working or idling or helping one's neighbour—became issues of eternity, not in the sense alone that one's eternal destiny depended on them but in the sense that the lord of the whole universe was concerned about them and might even serve as a partner in making them. Indeed a moral choice, made in a right spirit, could have something of the sweep of luminous vision with which divine decisions themselves were made. The right spirit was a prayerful spirit—if prayer is conceived in Emerson's manner as 'the contemplation of the facts of life from the highest point of view'. In the daily decisions of moral living, one immortal soul was interacting with other immortal souls, with tremendous issues hanging in the balance, and all under the scrutiny of an eye that missed nothing in either motive or consequences.

Morality has never reached, before or since, so lofty a level of seriousness. A rationalist view of morals is likely to seem cold and pinched in comparison with it. And some of its high seriousness may be gratefully accepted by the rationalist. Even the sceptical John Dewey admitted that morality at its best exhibits 'religiousness', by which he meant the attempt to act in the light of the longest and most comprehensive view of the consequences.[13] Any added discernment a man can acquire as to how his action affects other minds, any advance of insight into the values of those minds or their experiences, will reflect itself in action that is more finely ethical. Still, it would be absurd to say that what Dewey called 'religiousness' exhausted what the New Testament meant by the love of God and its place in conduct. When Jesus spoke of God he meant an existing being, as real and near as an earthly father or mother, in whose devoted service religion and morality alike consisted. A morality cut off from religion he would probably have regarded as no morality at all, but a half-blind groping under the guidance—or rather misguidance—of selfish and sensual impulses. Without a constant reference to the divine will, which could be consulted, like that of an earthly father, at any time of need, even he would have felt himself lost. And the question is whether this opening to Deity is essential to the moral life.

10　Clearly it is not. It adds an incentive to right conduct, to be sure. If life is lived as 'under the great taskmaster's eye', both fear of God and the love of God will contribute a motive power not otherwise present. But there are two considerations that show them to be not ethically necessary. First, they are not obviously ethical motives at all. Take fear. So far as a man pays his debts and avoids stealing because he is afraid he will be caught and punished, he is doing what is right for the wrong reason; and if the punishment anticipated happens to be that of 'the great taskmaster', the reason is still the wrong one. As for love, it is no doubt a higher motive than fear; the love for a human father that leads to sacrifice for his welfare or happiness is a noble impulse. Must not the love of a divine father be similarly regarded? Unfortunately the two are not really parallel. To say that human love could advance the welfare of God is hardly an intelligible notion; and to increase his pleasure or happiness, while intelligible enough if he is conceived as a magnified man, becomes all but meaningless if he is conceived in more modern and critical terms—in those, for example, of Tennant, Tillich, or Whitehead. And if the love of God does its work in conduct through the delight in doing his will, this too needs analysis. To do something because one loves the person who commands it is not necessarily to do the right thing or even to act from a high motive; one may kill for the love of a Hitler. If one does something because one knows the person loved to be wiser and better than oneself, the motive is a good one, but still not the best, for it falls short of what moves that wiser person himself. That person presumably does what he does because he sees it to be right, and when we reach moral maturity, that is our own proper motive also. We may put the argument as an alternative. If the love of God moves us because we see that his will is 'true and righteous altogether', the ethical part of our motive is respect for right doing itself, and in this there is nothing necessarily religious. On the other hand, if God is loved regardless of his moral quality, the love remains in a sense religious, but it is now a positive moral danger; it may lead, as it did for Kierkegaard, to the glori-

fication of immorality.[14] From the moralist's point of view, the
love of God thus tends to resolve itself into a purely moral passion,
or else into a worship that is morally ambiguous.

The second reason why such love is not a necessary component
of morals is that moral values may be authenticated and fully potent
without it. The ultimate warrant for a rule of conduct is not deliverance by authority, religious or otherwise, but its self-validating
power when seen as belonging to a form of life which carries certain
intrinsic values with it.[15] Justice, wisdom, and beauty are not good
because God approves them; if he approves them, it is because they
are good. And the mere perception of these values is a powerful
motive to their realisation. Indeed the insight that wisdom is better
than ignorance is so effective a motive to the getting of wisdom that
all three of the great Greek thinkers believed that if the insight was
clear, action in accord with it followed inevitably. And though this
is not quite true, it is very nearly so. Such insight and such a motive
are not themselves religious. The existence of purely secular goodness has often puzzled religious persons, but there is no doubt of its
existence. Take for example what may be done from devotion to the
goods of the intellect, which we have just mentioned. If Benjamin
Franklin gave of his substance to found the University of Pennsyl-
vania, and Jefferson of his means and energy to found the University
of Virginia, if Grote, James Mill, and Bentham did the same for
University College, and Sidgwick for Newnham, it was not out of
Christian motives, for none of them could be called Christian, but
because (no doubt along with other motives) they prized the
educated mind.

The conclusion is that while the love of God, in one or other of
its senses, may be, and often has been, a powerful supplementary
motive, it is not, as the New Testament teaches, indispensable to the
moral life, or on an equality with the other great principle of the
love of man.

CHRISTIAN HUMILITY

11 We turn to another attitude regarded by Jesus as fundamental,
humility. The first and the third Beatitudes are both commonly read
as enjoining this virtue: 'Blessed are the poor in spirit' and 'Blessed
are the meek'. What does humility mean? It is not an easy virtue
either to define or to appraise. We should hesitate to call a man
humble who takes himself at his full worth, and hence humility
seems to involve taking oneself at less than one's true worth. But to
regard that as a virtue seems to be glorifying error. Apparently we
do at times think better of a man morally for being deceived about

himself intellectually, for thinking less of his powers and importance than they deserve; Sidgwick, holding this misprising of oneself to be part of 'the common account of humility', found this account unacceptable.[16] And there is surely something absurd in making a virtue out of a mistake. Still, it is not this mistake, if such there be, that we prize in humility, any more than it is the reverse error that we deplore in Aristotle's unattractive picture of the great-souled man. It is rather an attitude or disposition that readily gives rise to error but does not involve it necessarily. It is a disposition to think *comparatively* low of one's own attainments and deserts, and in the meaning of this 'comparatively' lies the essence of virtue.

The meaning is twofold. First, the standard by which humility measures its attainments and deserts is not the standard of what is, but of what might be and ought to be. One may in fact be cleverer, more sensitive, more hard-working, truthful, and loyal than any of one's neighbours, and there is nothing inconsistent with humility in being aware of these facts. But the humble man knows well enough that, judged by the standards of what ought to be, he is dull, crass indolent, untruthful, and unfaithful, in short a pretty miserable sinner. Humility consists in the habitual measurement of oneself, not by others or by current standards, but by a standard transcending these. Jesus perceived that being humble in this sense provided the soil of teachableness and therefore a moral growth. The Pharisee who proclaimed his virtue in public was hardened against change because he was self-satisfied; the despised publican had the root of the matter in him because he was self-dissatisfied, and hence prompted to reach out for better things. It has indeed been argued that the Beatitudes were a deliberately arranged progression, and that in putting the demand for humility first Jesus was suggesting that it was the gateway to the other virtues.[17]

There is another and more subtle implication of humility, which lies in the difference of attitude taken by the proud man and the humble man toward their fellows. Let us suppose that each of them is in fact more able, honest, and generous than any of those around him. Now the relation of being higher than his fellows is exactly the same relation as their being lower than he. But the same relation may be the object of morally different attitudes. The proud man regards the gap between him and his fellows with satisfaction because he is on the upper side of it. The humble man regards the same gap with less satisfaction or none, because his fellows are on the lower side of it; he cannot take pleasure in contemplating their shortcomings and misfortunes. Pride fixes on one aspect of the relation, humility on the other. One's self is superior to others; pride gloats over that. Others are struggling along on the flats below; that is what impresses humility; and it extends its compassion to them. Pride is thus self-regarding, humility other-regarding. This intimate connection of humility with compassion and consideration is one secret of the charm it has always exercised over men's affections.

12 Jesus raised humility to a new and lofty place among the virtues. But there is a curious rift of consistency in the New Testament picture of it. Consider Luke's parable of the master and his servants:

> 'Which of you, with a servant out ploughing or shepherding, will say to him when he comes in from the field, "Come at once and take your place at table"? Will the man not rather say to him, "Get something ready for my supper; gird yourself and wait on me till I eat and drink; then you can eat and drink yourself"'? (Luke 17:7–8, Moffatt's trans.)

What is arresting about this parable is first its disclosure of the accepted way of treating servants, and, secondly and more surprisingly, Jesus' implied approval of that treatment. The servant has been out labouring in the Palestinian sun; the master wants his supper; and without for a moment considering the servants' hunger, thirst, or weariness, he commands him, 'wait on me till I eat and drink'. Humility is conspicuously absent; the assumption is that we are masters who owe our servants nothing, and further, in the light of the context, that God is a master who owes us nothing. How this is to be reconciled with the doctrine that he is chief among us who is the servant of all is not apparent.

JESUS: GOD OR MAN?

13 A further problem about humility, and one that will take us far, is whether Jesus himself exemplified it consistently. It is true that on one side of his life, where St Francis has been his most notable follower, he was the greatest of all exemplars of this virtue. He had none of the worldly goods that men commonly take pride in, and he pointed out that though the foxes had holes and the birds of the air had nests, he had not where to lay his head. He was as ready to associate with the dregs of humanity as with those in power and place; he talked with disdained Samaritans and Syro-Phoenicians; he washed the feet of his own disciples; he left an image of humility that has attracted the readers of many centuries by its simplicity and beauty. But along with this humility went claims that were not merely exalted but stupefyingly vast. He was that member of the house of David who, according to ancient pro-

phecy, would come as the Messiah to give deliverance and victory to
his people. He could cure diseases instantly through the direct power
of his spirit over other minds and bodies. He could create by a wave
of his hand a supply of loaves and fishes that would feed thousands.
He could turn water into wine, walk on the sea, and calm the winds
and waves. He could raise the dead. He could recognise the presence
of demons and cast them out. As the surrogate of God on earth,
he could forgive men their sins. In the gospel record, his claims
went even further. He *was* God. 'I and my Father are one' (John
10 : 30). 'In the beginning was the Word, and the Word was with
God, and the Word was God' (John 1 : 1). 'Thou lovedst me before
the foundation of the world' (John 17 : 24). He would return
after his death in the clouds of glory as the judge of all the earth.
It cannot be said that his cosmic claims are limited to the gospel of
John, for this latter claim at least appears in all the gospels.

How to bring into harmony the self-abasement of Jesus with this
limitless self-exaltation has been a problem for sixty generations of
theologians. The orthodox answer is that all these claims are true,
and that the humility of Jesus was divine condescension. Suppose,
however, that he was not incarnate Deity but only a human being;
how then account for the appearance in a humble mind of these
cosmic pretensions? Did he know that they were untrue, and make
them nevertheless in order to attract his gullible countrymen who
were expecting the Messiah? This position has actually been taken,
but it seems incredible. For whatever his shortcomings in science or
history, he was a passionate moralist, and to make this side of his
life a deliberate imposture is irresponsible. Were the claims then
sincere, but those of an unbalanced mind? A group of critics trained
in psychopathology have professed to find in him the standard
symptoms of paranoia. Albert Schweitzer, himself a physician,
examined these findings with care, and found them quite inadequate
to the conclusion drawn from them.[18] The only tenable alternative to
these theories would seem to be that he was a moral genius whose
claims were sincere but in part mistaken and in part attributed to
him in error by his very human biographers and interpreters. This is
the conclusion to which I think the evidence points.

The two major hypotheses between which we must choose are,
first, that he was God, second, that he was a great but in part
mistaken man. One's confidence in his moral teaching will vary as
one adopts the first hypothesis or the second. If he was really the
embodiment of omniscience and perfection, no pains could well be
spared to determine what he said and did, and no refusal on the part
of a believer to accept and follow his teaching would be excusable.
On the other hypothesis, one will have to make up one's mind as

best one can as to the soundness of his teachings; their validity will
not follow from his authority, but his authority from the degree of
their validity. It will be evident from the whole tenor of the discussion to which of these two camps I belong. There may be readers
from the first camp who have been deterred from taking the discussion seriously because they have sensed its tendency from the
beginning. This process of picking and choosing among the doctrines
of an inspired text, this rationalistic sniping at a body of teaching
that, in spite of all the difficulties of transmission, has stood for some
twenty centuries as 'the church's one foundation' will seem to them
something like sacrilege.

Over and over again in earlier parts of this study I have en-
countered this attitude, and I have tried to treat it with due respect.
'The feeling of reverence should itself be treated with reverence,' says
Santayana, 'although not at a sacrifice of truth, with which alone,
in the end, reverence is compatible'.[19] Any fair-minded critic will
recognise that the worship of Christ as Deity has been the attitude
of many better, abler, and more learned persons than himself.
James Anthony Froude, the historian, a friend and follower in his
youth of Cardinal Newman, tells how in a sermon in St Mary's,
Oxford, 'Newman described closely some of the incidents of our
Lord's passion; he then paused. For a few moments there was a
breathless silence. Then in a low, clear voice, of which the faintest
vibration was audible in the farthest corner of St Mary's, he said,
"Now, I bid you recollect that He to whom these things were done
was Almighty God". It was as if an electric stroke had gone through
the church, as if every person present understood for the first time
the meaning of what he had all his life been saying.'[20] Between the
Newmans of the world, who believe without reservation that Christ
was God, and the doubting, tentative rest of us, there is a great gulf
fixed. But I do not think that anyone unable to understand that
silence in St Mary's is likely to write about Jesus convincingly to
those on the other side of the gulf.

14   The chasm is not of the sort that is readily bridged by argument.
No one could accuse Newman, still less perhaps Augustine, Aquinas,
or Pascal, of intellectual obtuseness; and yet one can hardly imagine
any of them surrendering his central convictions to the dialectical
sword-play of an unbeliever. Belief or unbelief in these regions is
more likely to turn upon what used to be called the 'apperception-
mass' of accepted ideas and attitudes that one brings to bear on the
issue. In 'the ages of faith' nearly everyone believed; in the age of
science the tendency of most educated men is either to dismiss the
claims of tradition as obviously incredible because beyond assimila-

tion to the world they live in, or, if they accept them, to do so with an unhappy sense of living in two worlds imperfectly joined. We have seen that this latter course is the one that both Catholic and Protestant traditionalists are in fact taking.

We have seen also that none of the minds we have studied has been able to live in both worlds at once without compromising his intellectual integrity. The acceptance of two standards of truth— authority and reason—ends sooner or later in conflict, and there is only one way to resolve the conflict. One cannot discard the standard of reason even if one tries. To do so would be to discard the condition of sanity itself. If two inconsistent things can both be true, one cannot with confidence believe anything whatever. Of course, people do believe irrationally. Newman believed that Hume's argument against miracles was unanswerable; he also believed that the blood of St Januarius was liquefied yearly to the edification of the faithful, that the commandments were actually engraved on tables of stone by God's finger, and that the house of the Virgin at Nazareth had been miraculously translated through the air to Loreto in Italy. We have all achieved the height, such as it is, of believing both sides of a contradiction. What no one has ever done is to make both sides true. At that point the nature of things intervenes and we shall do well to recall Carlyle's remark on hearing that Margaret Fuller had decided to 'accept the Universe': 'Gad, she'd better.'

In view of the multiple causes of religious belief as well as men's gift for believing absurdities, it is perhaps oversanguine to expect anyone's belief on the central issue now facing us to be affected by a mere appeal to consistency. Yet for speculative problems of this kind, it is the most applicable and decisive of tests. The author of the Sermon on the Mount and the founder of Christianity—was he God or only a very remarkable man? That is the issue. No third theory is available. The theory that he was both God and man is not a third theory at all, but a form of the first and exclusive of the second. Other theories are of course conceivable, for example that he was a demon or that he never existed at all; but their degree of plausibility hardly justifies their discussion. Fortunately the two eligible theories are so related that each excludes the other, and the falsity of either would in effect, even if not in strict logic, serve to establish the other.

15   Here, as so often with disjunctions, the easiest course is to go to a conclusion through disposing of its alternative. And there can be little question which of the alternatives is the more vulnerable. It is the first, the identification of Jesus with Deity. The other alternative, that however exceptional he was only a man, is much harder to dispose of. The natural way to attempt it would be to show that some of the things he taught and did were beyond human powers. Was this not true, for example, of his ethical teachings? But how are we to show this? We do not know the range of human powers in this field. Can we say, then, that his miracles were beyond human range? Before we say yes, we must assure ourselves that the miracles occurred. But if one proceeds upon the assumptions that govern historians elsewhere, the hypothesis that the reporters of these wonders were in error is much more credible than the hypothesis that storms were actually stilled or that loaves and fishes were created at command. Supernaturalists may then fall back on Jesus' own claims that he was more than human, that he was one with the Father, that he was the coming judge of all mankind; and they may add, 'You must either accept these claims as true, or else, if you take them as authentic at all, you must set them down as colossal errors. And how can you admit the genius of Jesus and also lay such errors to his charge?'

Many humanists have offered hypotheses to reconcile these things, the more important of them recounted in Schweitzer's *Quest*.[21] They all face the initial difficulty that we do not certainly know what the claims of Jesus were; the gospel of John, in which they took their most exalted form, is of all the gospels the least reliable historically. Furthermore, the genius of Jesus was moral, not scientific or philosophical, and who knows how much depth of moral perception is consistent with great intellectual error? One of the most certain facts about Jesus' teaching, reported in all the gospels, is that he prophesied the speedy coming of the end of the world. On this major point, then, whatever his moral stature, we know that he was in error; and if he erred in this, he was capable of erring in other things. It would be impossible without long research to say which of the humanistic theories covers the known facts most adequately. But to demonstrate beforehand that in the nature of the case none of them *could* cover the facts would be an impossible undertaking.

LIMITATIONS IN KNOWLEDGE

16 Are we in the same position regarding the other hypothesis? I do not think so. The attribution of Deity is commonly taken to imply that the subject has unlimited knowledge, power, and goodness. Now there are two ways of showing that a subject alleged to possess these attributes does not really possess them. One of them is purely logical, is temptingly short and sharp, and has often been used with effect; but it is, I think, irrelevant. The other, though merely inductive, is both relevant and decisive. It is the one I shall employ. But the first deserves mention if only as an illuminating mistake.

It attempts to show that the ascription of Deity to anyone is illegitimate, since the traditional notion of God is self-contradictory. Is God infinitely powerful? In that case, as the Sunday-school boy asked his teacher, could he make a stone so big that he could not lift it? If you say he could, you admit that there is something he cannot do, namely lift that stone. If you say he could not, you are admitting equally that there is something he cannot do, namely make that stone. The same difficulties break out with regard to the other attributes. Is God all-knowing? In that case, could he contrive a puzzle so difficult that he could not solve it? Is he perfectly good? Then he could never be really tempted by evil. But if never tempted, he lacks one kind of goodness, namely resistance to temptation. All these puzzles turn on definitions. If you define 'almighty' in such a way that God can do anything whatever, even to making both sides of a contradiction true, then the very ascription of it is incoherent. And so of the other two attributes. But as Rashdall objected to McTaggart, who had used this sort of argument against theology, no philosophically competent theologian would so define his terms. If 'almighty' is to have an intelligible meaning, it must be defined in some such way as 'capable of doing anything not inconsistent with itself'. And so of the other two terms. If they are so defined, they can no longer be dismissed on purely logical grounds.

Can the attributes of Deity, when ascribed to Jesus, be dismissed, then, on inductive grounds? We shall see that they can. It is surprisingly easy to show that if any reasonable meaning is given to these attributes, the New Testament record itself excludes them all. On such inductive grounds one error would nullify the claim to completeness of knowledge. One clear bit of evidence that the agent was ever frustrated of his aim would reveal limitation of power. One unkind word, one loss of temper, one act of less than full justice, one instance of underrating or overrating any of the intrinsic goods of life, would be inconsistent with a claim to moral perfection. Now, however ungrateful the assignment, we can only report that the recorded life of Jesus does not pass these tests. That he was an extraordinary moral genius, a great teacher and reformer whose life turned the current of history for the better will not be disputed here. The world owes him an incalculable debt, if only for his attempt to substitute good will for violence in the relations of mankind. But he has been transfigured by a partisan theology into something he was not, so that it would now require both immense historical erudition and extraordinary independence of mind to see him as he was. Since the present writer cannot lay claim to either qualification, his conclusion cannot pretend to much weight. But it may be reported for what it is worth. Jesus was a sensitive and discerning moralist, a new kind of personality, in whom an order of unworldly values was embodied with unexampled attractiveness and grace; he was a uniquely great man. But he was not God. The positive parts of this statement hardly need support. The negative one perhaps does.

17 Consider the claim that has been made for Jesus to perfect knowledge. There are three principal forms in which a falling short of such knowledge might be evinced: ignorance, error, and inconsistency.

Is there any reason to believe that Jesus was free from the burden of ignorance? He could hardly have been thus free if he *grew* in knowledge, as it is recorded that he did (Luke 2 : 52), for such growth means ascent from one degree of knowledge to another, and degrees of knowledge are, from the other side, degrees of ignorance. Henry Parry Liddon, the eloquent Victorian Canon of St Paul's, argued 'that since the founder of Christianity, in divinely recorded utterances, alluded to the transformation of Lot's wife into a pillar of salt, to Noah's ark and the Flood, and to the sojourn of Jonah in the whale, the biblical account of these must be accepted as historical, or that Christianity must be given up altogether.'[22] The acceptance of this as a true dilemma would ensure the abandonment of Christianity. However great a figure Jesus was, he was not infallible and not omniscient. Did he know, for example, what the modern biologist knows about the origin of species, or what the geologist knows about the formation of the earth, or what the psychologist knows about conflict and repression? There is no evidence that he did, and a strong presumption that he did not. He knew his Old Testament, with its account of the creation of the earth and the sun (in that incorrect order), of the creation of birds and reptiles (also in that incorrect order), of the creation of man from 'the dust of the ground' and of woman from the man's rib. He read these things in his Scripture, which he regarded as inspired, and presumably accepted them as others did. Diseases that a modern psychiatrist would probably diagnose as epilepsy or schizophrenia he took as demon possession, and believed that he cured them (which he possibly did) by casting the demons out (which he pretty certainly did not). To say that he was somehow in command of modern knowledge in these fields is not only without ground; it is to indict him for indifference to his own people; for if he knew what the modern mind knows without making any effort to impart it, he was deliberately keeping his people in darkness. Since there is no reason

to impute to him such a desire, we can only believe that in these
and many other fields he shared the ignorance of his time.

Did he commit errors of fact? The New Testament records that
he did. There were errors as to the past, the present, and the
future. As for the past, he accepted the content of the Pentateuch
generally as written by Moses, whereas it was not, and ascribed to
David the authorship of the 110th Psalm (Mark 12 : 36), which most
modern critics agree could not have been David's. As for mistakes
about what to him was the present, he mistook the character of
Judas when he was selecting his disciples. As for the future, he told
his disciples that they should not have gone over the cities of Israel
before he returned to earth in judgement (Matt. 10 : 23); they went
over the cities, but his promised return did not come. He predicted
that those who were faithful to him would receive 'now in this time'
a hundredfold in such things as houses and lands (Mark 10 : 30);
they did not receive them. He seems indeed to have held important
misconceptions about himself. Was he the Messiah expected by the
Jews? His own opinion on this point apparently varied. He never
called himself the Son of David, a common way of referring to the
Messiah, and preferred to call himself 'the Son of Man', which was
not so used; indeed in one passage he seems to disavow the Messiahship (Matt. 22 : 41–45). But in another he seems to accept it (Matt.
11 : 2 ff.). It is probable, as Erdmann argues, that his conviction of
being the Messiah came to him gradually, in which case either the
earlier or the later conviction must have been in error. And how are
the final tragic words about having been forsaken to be interpreted?
The only intelligible way to construe them is that he had expected
some form of divine co-operation and that the expectation had not
been realised.

18   The record, then, does not support a claim that he was free
from errors of fact. What of consistency in his reported life and
teaching? Here too theological zeal on his behalf has shot beyond
the mark. We have noted several instances already in which his
teaching, as recorded, was not coherent. There were the two
doctrines about divorce, the universality of his mission combined
with its confinement to the lost sheep of Israel, the exhortation to
honour father and mother combined with the refusal to let a disciple
bury his father; the injunction to non-resistance combined with the
violent clearing of the temple. One inconsistency that we have noted
must be stressed again, since it comes so near to the heart of the
ethical teaching. If there was anything central in that teaching, it was
the stress on love and forgiveness. Yet in both his teaching and his
practice Jesus seems to have departed from the ideal repeatedly

and in perplexing fashion. 'Whosoever shall deny me before men, him will I also deny before my Father which is in heaven' (Matt. 10 : 33). This sounds uncomfortably like the expression of a vengeful spirit. A different kind of vengeance, but one still strangely at variance with the central Christian teaching, is ascribed to God by Paul. He writes of certain persons who 'received not the love of the truth' that 'for this cause God shall send them strong delusion, that they should believe a lie' (2 Thess. 2 : 10–11). To the modern mind this seems more like cat-and-mouse morality than like love or even justice. Along with the injunction of love, the spirit of revenge played a part in early Christian teaching that is explicable only on the assumption that this teaching had imperfectly broken away from the semi-barbarism of the day. In the epistle to the Hebrews, it is taught that even repentance is impossible on the part of a Christian who has been baptised and slipped away (Heb. 6 : 4–6); he will presumably be damned in spite of all efforts to repent.[23]

It may be suggested that though a vengeful spirit may have been displayed on occasion by Paul and some of the other early Christians, it was never approved or exhibited by Christ himself. This is not borne out by the recorded facts. Christ specifically ascribed acts of vengeance to God: 'Shall not God avenge his own elect . . .? I tell you that he will avenge them speedily' (Luke 18 : 7–8); and we have seen that he represented God as inflicting for certain sins a penalty of everlasting agony disproportionate to any finite offence. Furthermore, if his denunciation of the Pharisees as 'full of dead men's bones and all uncleanness', as 'serpents', 'offspring of vipers', and due for 'the damnation of hell' is expressive of love or forgiveness, it is difficult to see what resources of language are left to provide a vehicle for condemnation. It may be answered that he denounced the sin, but loved the sinner. But he seems in some cases to make the sinners blacker than the sins. 'So far as I can make out . . .,' writes Professor Fite, 'the dark picture of the Pharisees presented in the Gospels, often in the words of Jesus himself, stands alone in the history of the sect, unconfirmed by other evidence'.[24] In his parable of the rich man and Lazarus, the rich man, condemned incidentally for no reported reason except his wealth, is denied, even in the flames, the means of wetting his mouth or of warning his brothers of what lay in store for them. Immediately after saying that the stone which the builders rejected would become the head of the corner, Jesus added: 'but on whomsoever it shall fall, it will grind him to powder' (Luke 20 : 18). He is widely believed to have preached and practised unfailing love. But toward certain classes of persons, most notably hypocrites, his attitude as expressed would be more accurately described as an intense and withering detestation.

There were other breaches of consistency. He declared: 'whosoever shall say, Thou fool, shall be in danger of hell fire' (Matt.
5:22), but on more than one occasion he used the forbidden phrase
himself (Matt. 23 : 17; Luke 12 : 20; 24 : 25). He announced that
he came not to destroy but to fulfil, and that not a jot or tittle of the
law was to pass away; but he repeatedly set aside the law with the
remark, 'it has been said . . . but I say unto you'. He promised
that his yoke was easy and his burden light; he also warned that
any man who would follow him must 'deny himself and take up his
cross'. He blessed the peacemakers, and his birth was heralded,
according to tradition, by the proclamation of peace on earth; but
he also said that he came to bring not peace but a sword, and to set
one member of a household against another.

19 The ease with which such inconsistencies, which are certainly
not all verbal, can be found suggests that Jesus' mind belonged to
a different mould from the mind of the West, with that interest in
clearly reasoned positions which it inherited from the Greeks. This
impression is strengthened when we study the replies he gave to the
many who questioned him. Seldom is a quite straightforward answer
given. Sometimes the question is evaded. Was it in accordance with
the law of Moses to give tribute to Caesar? The answer, 'Render to
Caesar the things that are Caesar's' (Mark 12 : 17), was scarcely an
answer at all, since the question was precisely whether such tribute
was to be included among 'the things that are Caesar's'. The evasion
here may, to be sure, have been a justified resort to political ex-
pediency. But it was not always so. The Sadducees, who disbelieved
in personal immortality, asked him regarding a woman who had
been married seven times, whose wife she should be 'in the resurrection' (Mark 12 : 18–27). The reply given, namely that 'when
they shall rise from the dead, they neither marry nor are given in
marriage, but are as the angels which are in heaven,' answers the
question in a sense, but by suggesting a degree of impersonality and
sexlessness in the next life that threatens the notion of personal
survival itself. The Pharisees asked him when the kingdom of God
would come. His reply was that 'the kingdom of God cometh not
with observation', meaning apparently that whenever it did come
it would not be outwardly observable. The evasion is not made
easier to understand by the fact that on another occasion he frankly
stated that he did not know when the kingdom would come (Mark
13:32), and also that men would '*see* the Son of man coming in the
clouds with great power and glory' (Mark 13 : 26; italics mine).
The Pharisees asked him whether divorce was lawful. He replied,
'What . . . God hath joined together, let not man put asunder'.

They pointed out that their lawgiver, Moses, had expressly permitted divorce, which was correct. He replied: 'Moses because of the hardness of your hearts suffered you to put away your wives' (Matt. 19 : 3–8). The reply again is puzzling, both because there seems to be no ground for it in the relevant Mosaic account (Deut. 24), and because it is hard to see why, merely because men were hard-hearted, their hard-heartedness toward their wives should have been legitimised. Sometimes the evasive answer was given with impressive intellectual skill. Certain doubters, noting his confidence that his acts embodied the divine will, asked him by what authority he did these things. He replied that he would tell them if they would first answer a question of his own about the baptism of John: Was it from God or from man? This was a dilemma on whose horns the questioners were neatly impaled, and they found themselves unable to give either answer. Whereupon Jesus said, 'Neither do I tell you by what authority I do these things' (Mark 11 : 33). His disciples seem to have complained to him on one occasion that they were short of bread, to which his response, as reported, was, 'Take heed, beware of the leaven of the Pharisees, and of the leaven of Herod' (Mark 8 : 15). The disciples were puzzled as to the relevance of the remark. So is the modern reader.

Much that puzzles us would no doubt be cleared up if we knew the circumstances of the case and the motives of the questioners. Jesus possessed an extraordinary power of divining what these motives were, and of giving answers that were relevant not so much to the questions asked as to the state of mind of the inquirers. And in spite of the skill he sometimes displayed in intellectual thrust and parry, it was not this kind of activity in which his heart lay, or his power. He was a practical moralist who wanted to regenerate men's feelings about others and about the goods they lived by, and he instinctively adopted the language that would speak to their feelings, the language of parable and poetry. When challenged to formulate his ethical counsels exactly, or to state in express propositions what men were to believe and why, he was still inclined to fall back on metaphor and simile, so that we do not know, and presumably never shall, what precisely he meant by some of the cardinal terms of his teaching: 'the kingdom of God', 'the love of God', 'the fatherhood of God', 'the son of man', 'everlasting life', 'heaven', 'hell', 'peace'. The fathers of the church and Catholic theologians have developed an immense intellectual apparatus to explicate and relate these ideas, all based on the assumption that through the simple language of the sower and his seed, of lost sheep and prodigal sons, houses built on rock or sand, candles hid under bushels and lambs led out to slaughter there is peeping an elaborate and articulated cosmology, with the Trinity, the creation, the incarnation, the atonement, the salvation of the faithful, and the eternities of heaven and hell all taking their precisely defined and rationally appointed places. To anyone who tries to get rid of preconceptions and to read for himself the simple and beautiful language of the gospels, all this seems just the way in which the mind of Jesus did *not* work. He was not an 'intellectual'. A third-rate logician can point out inconsistencies, obscurities, errors, ambiguities, and fallacies almost without number in the record of his life and teaching. This does not show that he was not a great moralist or great man. It does show that the attempt to make of him an embodiment of omniscience does not correspond to fact.

LIMITATIONS IN POWER

20 So does the attempt—on which we may dwell more briefly— to show that he is a being of unlimited power. That he did possess powers not owned by ordinary human beings will seem probable even to those who interpret the 'miracles' of healing as faith-healing, for though this kind of therapy is common enough, few can employ it, and no one fully understands it. There is no compelling ground, however, for classing such cures as miraculous in the sense of transcending natural law, for we have not explored sufficiently the relations of body and mind to be able to say of a particular wonder whether it is a suspension of law or an exemplification of some law unknown. Such performances as the walking on the water and the bringing to life of a body four days dead might well show supernatural power if in fact they occurred, but their occurrence is surely less probable than errors on the part of observers or reporters. With the dismissal of the physical miracles, the ground for attributing to Jesus supernatural power largely disappears. He is recorded indeed to have said: 'All power is given unto me in heaven and in earth,' but the statement appears only in the questionable appendix to Matthew, where he is said to have made it after his death to a group of somewhat sceptical disciples. The vast claims of St John were part of an apologetic tract rather than of a factual history. And in more reliable passages, Jesus admitted his sharp limitation of power. We have seen that when he returned to his own town he could 'do no mighty work' because of the attitude of the towns-folk. He said in a curious passage that when a woman in a crowd around him touched his robe and was healed, he felt power passing from him; and such power as he had was not beyond the need of recurrent periods of restoration. But a more telling kind of evidence for his limitation of power is that if it had not been thus limited he could, and presumably would, have done so much that he did not do. He could have saved his people from the Romans, have carried his message into all the world, and, using only powers attributed to him in the gospels, have saved men without number from famine, deformity, and disease. We cannot suppose that, being what he was, he did not desire these goods. If he did not achieve them, it was because he could not.

21 To all this it may be replied that the uniqueness of Jesus lay in a wholly different direction. Limited in knowledge and power he may have been, but on the ethical side, in his moral teaching and moral character, he was subject to no such limitations. His ethical teaching, it is confidently claimed, showed an originality and penetration as far beyond human authorship as his life—the one stainless life on record—was beyond human imitation.

This view has been so long and widely held that many or most persons in Western lands feel an inner resistance to any criticism of it. They would feel no such resistance to the imputation that there were flaws in the ethical teaching of a Socrates or Marcus Aurelius, a Thomas More or Martin Luther, or even perhaps to the charge that one of these moral heroes had told a lie or done something dubious in business. About Jesus they feel differently. Others abide their question, but not he. The truth of his teaching and the perfection of his life do not seem subject in the same way to the cavils of the moral philosopher or the historian. They belong in the sphere of religion, where they stand under the guarantee of revelation; and even for those who do not hold to revealed truth, they are still surrounded by an aura of sacredness that arouses a vague sense of impiety in those who try to dissipate it. Even minds whose primary loyalty is to reason may be troubled by such a sense, though they may be intellectually clear that no limit should be placed on rational inquiry and that such inquiry would only add strength to claims that were really valid.

For a free mind the question inevitably arises whether the teaching or the character of Jesus provides us with an ethical absolute. As for the teaching, we have already given our answer. In one important respect it has stood the test of time and criticism, and will presumably continue to do so. The law of universal love, or, as we have understood it, the duty of settled good will toward all mankind, seems unassailable. On the other hand, the claim of the Christian ethic to completeness as a guide to the good life, its applicability to the modern social and political scene, and its internal consistency have been shown to fail at many points; and it is needless to pursue the matter further. One fresh question, however, may well be asked.

Part of the claim for the Christian ethic has often been that it is unique in the sense of being original and unprecedented. Is this claim valid?

THE ORIGINALITY OF JESUS

22 Of course originality has nothing to do with truth. Much that is original had better never have been said, and many unoriginal minds have been admirably loyal to truth and reason. But a combination of truth with thoroughgoing originality would place anyone in a category unique among mankind. Does Jesus belong to this category? It is now well known that in many of his cardinal teachings he was anticipated by other moralists to whom in fact he had access. Take a few of these teachings almost at random. On the duty of loving one's neighbour, consider this from Leviticus: 'thou shalt love thy neighbour as thyself' (19 : 18). On the fatherhood of God: 'Have we not all one father?' (Mal. 2 : 10); 'Like as a father pitieth his children, so the Lord pitieth them that fear him' (Psalms, 103 : 13); 'I am a father to Israel' (Jer. 31 : 9); 'the mighty God, the everlasting Father, the Prince of Peace' (Isa. 9 : 6). The Jewish Talmud taught that 'the real and only Pharisee is he who does the will of his Father because he loves him'. 'Every Jew of the period,' says D. C. Simpson, 'could have subscribed to the opening formula of "the Lord's prayer" '.[25] On the duty of charity, Sidgwick writes: 'in laying stress on almsgiving Christianity merely universalised a duty which has always been inculcated and maintained in conspicuous fulness by Judaism, within the limits of the chosen people';[26] and he points out that the teaching of humility also is 'to some extent anticipated in the Rabbinic teaching'. In a remarkable book by an unknown writer, entitled *The Testaments of the Twelve Patriarchs*, and written about a century before the Christian era, there are passages that show the spirit and some of the phraseology of the Sermon on the Mount. Dr R. H. Charles, an eminent scholar in the field, thought that Jesus must have known this book and that St Paul used it as a *vade mecum*. The Mosaic law taught that the Sabbath should be carefully observed; Jesus departed from this by teaching that the Sabbath was made for man and not man for the Sabbath; but it has come to light that there was a rabbinic saying, 'the Sabbath is yours, and you are not for the Sabbath'. Warner Fite writes: 'his praise of the childlike attitude (of the "little ones"), his condemnation of him "who looks upon a woman to lust after her"—both have been included among the marks of a finer morality distinctive of Jesus; yet to both we may find parallels in the *Rabbinic Anthology* of Montefiore and Loewe. Note that, in the passage numbered 1447, "he who sins with the eye is also an adulterer".'[27] The doctrine of non-resistance was taught some five or six centuries before Christ by Lao-Tse and Buddha. The restraint placed by Christian ethics on the natural man was anticipated by many ancient sects: the Egyptian priests of Isis were celibates; the Orphic brotherhoods of Greece practised fasting; the Pythagoreans were ascetics in some respects, and the Cynics in many. Whether Jesus was influenced by reports of these practices is unknown; he may or may not have been; in any case, his curbing of the natural man in a religious interest was not a new thing in the world.

These parallels between the teaching of Jesus and those of his predecessors could be continued, and if they were completed, probably few of his teachings would be left standing as quite new. Does this mean that his ethics as a whole was unoriginal? Certainly not. For he combined the elements as no one else had ever done, and he suffused the whole with a passion of religious devotion that brought these elements to fresh life. The love of God, the love of man, forgiveness, non-resistance, humility, otherworldliness, can all be found in other moralists, but nowhere in their Christian unity and interdependence. He is unique among moralists, and indeed among mankind, for his simple, overwhelming conviction of the reality of the unseen, and for his subjection of all the details of thought, feeling, and action to the control of a will not his own, so that he was a 'God-intoxicated' man. The sense of the reality of the divine was linked in his thought and practice with a sense of the divine in man, and therefore of the value of all men as persons. Like St Francis, in whom he was so largely reincarnated, he had nothing but compassion for the morons and lepers, the prostitutes and untouchables, around him; wherever his message has penetrated, those who are 'despised and rejected of men' have felt themselves befriended in an unfriendly world, and somehow important in spite of their seeming worthlessness. And the form of his teaching, like its substance, uniquely combines convention with novelty. It echoes the phrases of the prophetic preaching and the cadences of traditional poetry, but in the Sermon on the Mount it achieves a succinctness, and in some of the parables, like that of the prodigal son, a vividness and economy, that have given his words a permanent place in the literature of the world. Thus the originality of Jesus, despite all that must in detail be subtracted from it, remains extraordinarily high.

THE CLAIM TO MORAL PERFECTION

23 What of his personal character? The tradition in the church is of course that he was sinless and perfect. But Jesus did not hold this view of himself, and it is not supported by the portrait of him in Scripture. When a follower addressed him as 'Good Master', he rebuked him, saying 'Why callest thou me good? None is good save one, that is, God' (Luke 18 : 19). Zeller thought that he would not have used such phrases as 'Forgive us our sins' and 'Lead us not into temptation' if he had thought of himself as above sin.[28] Nor would he have felt the need of baptism. 'The baptism had a particular symbolic meaning; it implied past sin, present repentance, and preparation for the expected Messiah....'[29] His injunction to his hearers was to follow him, not only in his teaching but also in his example; but his example would hardly have been an example if he knew nothing of the common man's temptations and frailties; as Leslie Stephen insisted, 'you sever the very root of our sympathy when you single out one as divine and raise him to the skies. . . . The ideal becomes meaningless when it is made supernatural.'[30]

This picture of a character with flaws is supported by the portrait supplied by his biographers. The torrents of merciless invective poured upon the Pharisees and the readiness to consign them to endless torment are not only inconsistent with his own teaching of forgiveness, but, it must be candidly said, inconsistent with rational standards of justice and humanity. Bertrand Russell can even write: '. . . He goes on about the wailing and gnashing of teeth. It comes in one verse after another, and it is quite manifest to the reader that there is a certain pleasure in contemplating wailing and gnashing of teeth, or else it would not occur so often.'[31] And what is one to make of the incident of the fig tree?

> 'he was hungry: and seeing a fig tree afar off having leaves, he came, if haply he might find any thing thereon: and when he came to it, he found nothing but leaves; for the time of figs was not yet. And Jesus answered and said unto it, No man eat fruit of thee hereafter for ever. . . . And in the morning . . . Peter calling to remembrance saith unto him, Master, behold, the fig tree which thou cursedst is withered away' (Mark 11 : 12–14, 20–21).

In anyone else this would be regarded as an outburst of petulance, natural enough in hunger and frustration but still unreasonable; and so it probably was in this case. To orthodox interpreters it offers a conundrum hard to solve, since the agent, as sinless, was incapable of anything so petty as losing his temper. In the incident of the Gadarene swine, again, there is no apparent thought of the loss to their owner or of the drowning animals themselves. In some instances he displays a spirit that would, in another, have been set down to inconsiderateness or spite. When he sent out his disciples, he instructed them to take no money with them, but to depend on charity; 'And whosoever shall not receive you, nor hear your words, when ye depart out of that house or city, shake off the dust of your feet. Verily I say unto you, It shall be more tolerable for the land of Sodom and Gomorrha in the day of judgement, than for that city' (Matt. 10 : 14–15). Klausner thought that the saying, 'Whosoever shall deny me before men, him will I also deny before my Father' expressed a spirit of vengeance.

When Jesus' appraisals differ from ours we do not always, on reflection, retreat. We have seen that he sometimes exhibits, as in the case of Lazarus and the rich man, an apparent antipathy to rich men because they are rich and approval of poor men because they are poor. This is not quite easy to justify on ethical grounds. Sometimes, again, he shows a curious disregard for what we should call property rights. On his way to Jerusalem he had need for some means of transport. He told two of his disciples to go to the next village where they would find a colt tethered in the street; they should simply take it and bring it to him. If anyone asked why, they should say 'the Lord hath need of him' (Luke 19 : 29–35). We are not told that it belonged to a friend, or that permission was asked, or thanks returned. And those unfortunate Gadarene pigs inevitably crop up again; they were presumably someone's property; were they paid for? That seems to have been too trifling a detail to find entry in the account.

Once more, in his recurrent crossing of verbal swords with 'the scribes and Pharisees', does he provide a model of controversy, a better model, say, than Socrates? Not on the intellectual side, but what of the moral side? Socrates was not above arguing for victory; Jesus too appears to have taken satisfaction in confounding his opponents by dexterous fencing. Sometimes, as we have seen, he employs what looks like deliberate mystification; and at times he did what the urbanity of Socrates never permitted him to do, namely excoriate the character of his opponents. It may be protested that Socrates was a mere man, without the sure insight into men's hearts that could justify such denunciation. But that consideration is double-edged. If Jesus was indeed an ultimate judge of men who could turn with full knowledge from argument to denunciation, *we* certainly are not, and hence his conduct of discussion could hardly serve as a model for ourselves.

There is another puzzling feature in the moral attitude of Jesus. He takes us aback from time to time by urging that conduct which is outwardly right should be done from motives that seem wrong. The right motive for giving to another is the desire for the good of that other, not the good of oneself. But Jesus says, 'Give, and it shall be given unto you; good measure, pressed down, and shaken together, and running over, shall men give into your bosom' (Luke 6 : 38). This seems unsatisfactory, whether as moral counsel or as statement of fact. Even in his injunction to prayer the motive suggested sounds strange: 'pray to thy Father which is in secret; and thy Father which seeth in secret shall reward thee openly' (Matt. 6 : 6). We do not consider that goodness moved by the desire for reward is a high type of goodness. Neither do the gospels, at least uniformly: 'love ye your enemies, and do good, and lend, hoping for nothing again' (Luke 6 : 35). But even here there comes the immediate addition, 'and your reward shall be great'. The moral values of the different motives that may lead men to right conduct seem never to have been clearly distinguished in Jesus' teaching; actions done from the love of God, the fear of God, the desire for a heavenly reward, the desire for a reward on earth, are all grouped as praiseworthy along with genuine compassion for human suffering, and sometimes treated as on a level with it. The desire for heaven and the fear of hell are represented as among the worthiest of motives.

CHRISTIANITY AND THE REGARD FOR REASON

24 This brings us to our final comment on the ethics of Jesus. Along with much that is noble and appealing, it is deficient in its respect for reason. Its emphasis on good will and its consideration for the intrinsic value of every human life must remain central in any valid ethics. To be sure, the teaching is not consistently presented; and its followers have found in its silences and ambiguities an excuse for much cruelty and injustice. It has served, nevertheless, to redress the ancient imbalance of the natural man, with his bias for the goods of appetite, wealth, and power. By its quiet insistence on the goods of the inward life—on affection, compassion, humility, and clearness of conscience—it has done an incalculable service to mankind.

The great defect remains. It is not a single simple defect, but a set of related ones, which spring from the same root—the failure to take reason seriously, to see how fundamental cognition is among man's faculties, to see how largely reflection can make or unmake a world, and how central it is even in morals. This failure manifested itself in several forms.

25(1) In the first place, Christianity tied its ethics to an unreal world which was bound to dissolve when the winds of criticism began to blow on it. That Jesus should have accepted the outlook of his time and place is no matter for surprise unless one begins by assuming him to be Deity, and then it becomes an insoluble problem. How could he be omniscient if he accepted error; how could he be good if, knowing it is error, he did not disclose it? Ethics and religion were to him inseparable, and at the heart of his religion was the Jewish cosmology of his day. With certain humane changes of emphasis, his God was still the God of Abraham, Isaac, and Jacob, a person like ourselves but older, wiser, and more powerful, loving toward his chosen people but imperious, jealous, and quick to anger. He had made the world not very long ago; every male ancestor of Jesus back to the creation could be named. God had created Adam and Eve as mature beings without youth or ancestry, and his permission to Satan to tempt them in the garden was part of a larger plan for mankind. All the world was a stage on which the creatures made in his image could be tested for more permanent roles under his critical eye; and the ground for judging all of them was the same, namely obedience to his will. The chief motives of their conduct were to be the love of him and the fear of him. The rewards and punishments he dealt out had been conceived by the ancient Jews as coming in this life, and any life beyond the grave was vague and doubtful to them. Jesus added to the older motives, and gave a more definite shape to the older anticipations. Men could play their roles on the world's stage with the certainty that if they did it to their maker's pleasure their lot would be eternal bliss, and if they failed, a torture appalling beyond words or thought. As to the final judgement that would usher in these two eternities, it was almost upon them; it was to come like a thief in the night in his own generation. This was the world framework in which Jesus lived, and to which he bound his ethics with chains as strong as he could make them. Except within its limits, life was vanity.

Now this framework has collapsed. It has disintegrated with the advance of knowledge. Whatever God may be to the modern mind, he is not the God of Abraham, Isaac, and Jacob, a magnified man, siring the human race, championing a chosen people, tender and ferocious by turns, with a reward in one hand and a fiery scourge in the other. The creation, as Jesus must have thought of it, never occurred; there was no Eden, no Adam, no tempting Satan, no fall, no inherited sin. The confidently predicted world catastrophe deferred itself indefinitely. Little by little this entire theological scheme of things came to seem unreal. The idea that a universe stretching billions of years into the past and billions of light-years into space was all fabricated as a stage for the performance of one biological species, appearing transiently on one floating grain of dust, strikes the scientific mind as grotesque. Not that the older framework has ever been conclusively demonstrated to be mythical.

But two things have happened to it. It has been frittered away around the edges by a long series of abrasives, supplied among others by Galileo and Descartes, Lyell and Darwin, Strauss and Freud. Secondly, the structure as a whole has become increasingly unbelievable through its incoherence with the world of natural law. It is true that one cannot decisively disprove a single miracle. Jesus may in fact have walked on water and brought a dead friend to life. But as man's grasp of nature becomes more complete, the crevices through which the supernatural flowed in have become fewer and narrower; and as his understanding deepens of the ease and range of his self-deception, the ratio of fact to myth in the old cosmology grows steadily smaller.

Nevertheless, to that unreal cosmology Jesus tied his ethics. The two, he believed, must stand or fall together. As it turned out, the cosmology failed to stand, and if we were to draw the inference he thought inevitable, we should have to reject the ethics with it. Many have done that, and with a New Testament warrant in their hands. I have declined to follow them. There is too much in Christian ethics with which we cannot afford to part. But the New Testament makes that course difficult by lashing its ethics so firmly to a sinking ship. When we say that Jesus failed to take reason seriously enough, part of what we mean, then, is that he bound what was morally valid to what has proved intellectually untenable.

26(2)   This unhappy liaison affected the ethics itself. The relation of morality to the divine will and the motives for right conduct were both distorted. The will of God was taken as the ultimate authority, which man was to obey without question; whatever God willed was right. But this cannot be the true ground of rightness. If God wills an action, it must be because it is right; it is not right because he wills it. Otherwise his will becomes irrational and whimsical; if he wills that we murder, murder thereby becomes right. That could be accepted by the elastic moral sense of a Kierkegaard, but it is not in this direction that moral sanity lies. One clearer-headed moralist, Paley, did attempt to defend the definition of 'right' as 'willed by God,' but his defence has been too often and decisively dealt with to require reconsideration.

The linkage of ethics to a faulty world view had another morally unfortunate consequence. An important part of that world view was an eschatology that was bound to distort men's motives. Its influence took two forms. In the first form, it worked through the expectation of an early second coming. We have repeatedly seen how hard it is to be sure what lay behind Jesus' injunctions. Was his injunction to take no thought for the morrow or not to lay up treasures on earth a general warning against worldliness, or special advice in view of the shortness of the time? Schweitzer and many others have thought that his mistaken expectation threw its long, obscuring shadow across the whole of his teaching, making it impossible to distinguish with confidence what was the by-product of error and what was independent insight.

In its second form also, the New Testament eschatology has had a large and dubious influence. Jesus saw that if our actions carry with them an everlasting reward or penalty, that consciousness should never be far from our thought. It is plain enough that Christians have not generally taken this prospect very seriously, for if they had they could have thought of little else; the next life, with its overwhelming sanctions, would dominate this life completely. Nevertheless it has had great effects, both historical and moral. It has undoubtedly coerced many to keep their feet outwardly on the straight and narrow way. It has also justified enormous cruelties. It provided a logically impeccable excuse for the gagging of critics and the torture of heretics. The influence of such otherworldly expectations when entertained for some twenty centuries by even feeble imaginations is incalculable. Whether that influence is legitimate depends, of course, on the truth of those expectations, a question we cannot here explore. Suffice it to say that if Jesus' doctrine of a God of love is true, the doctrine of eternal punishment cannot also be true.

The question remains whether the expectation of such rewards and penalties provides morally sound motives. In the form presented in the New Testament, it does not. If the teaching were that we shall 'fare ever there as here', it would be a ground of hope, for the next world would be, like this one, 'a vale of soul-making,' where continued advance would be possible. But this is not the picture painted in the gospels. Heaven and hell are depicted in hedonistic colours, with the good eternally happy and the wicked without hope in a place where 'their worm dieth not and the fire is not quenched'. Such prospects throw all human motivations out of true perspective. If the thief or the killer holds his hand not from consideration for his victims but from fear of his own pain, his 'right conduct' is a hollow shell. If the man who sacrifices himself for another does so as a step to his own happiness, his 'sacrifice' is in reality self-seeking. With so tremendous an egoistic lure hovering always in the offing, no motive is safe from taint.

27(3)   The insufficient respect for reason has shown itself in other ways than by tying morals to a false cosmology and eschatology. It has made escape from these more difficult by a peculiar ethics of belief. Man's intellect, when granted free play, could and eventually did make its escape, but the ethics of belief inculcated in the gospels declined to grant it free play. Instead, contentment with the prescribed world order was made a virtue, and disbelief in it— even doubt of it—was made a sin. Hence the process of correction which should have been made from within by critical reflection was delayed until the correction was battered home from without; and we have seen that resistance to rational battering is still strong in both Catholic and Protestant communions. The strength and weakness of the Christian ethics of belief, however, is a large and important subject, whose fuller consideration is reserved for the chapter that follows.

28(4)   In saying that the Christian ethics did not take reason seriously enough, I have in mind still another meaning. It failed to recognise the place of reason in the moral life itself. It did not perceive the degree in which ethics is autonomous. The principles of ethics are not derived from some authority outside itself, even theology, but from the reason implicitly at work in all morality. Most philosophical moralists have held that the rightness of conduct turns on the intrinsic values it brings into existence. What sort of insight is it which enables us to see that an experience possesses value in itself, or that one intrinsic value is greater than another? The main tradition of Western thought would say that it is a rational insight; and we agree. Even those in this century who have devised the theory that it is nothing but an emotional preference are now saying that it is at least a preference for which valid reasons may be given. In the statement that happiness is better than misery, understanding than ignorance, the experience of a cool drink in a parched throat than a raging toothache, there is something very like self-evidence; no deduction of it from theological or metaphysical premises is as compelling as the statement itself. Anyone who rejected such statements, when offered in unambiguous form, we should probably regard as perverse or not quite sane. This is not to say that moral judgements are incorrigible. It is to assert that, like other judgements, they belong in the province of truth and falsity, and evince a reason that is pressing in and through them toward an ideal of objective truth.

The ethics of the Sermon on the Mount did not flatly reject such a view. If Jesus had been asked such an improbable question as whether it was self-evident to him that love was better than hatred and forgiveness than vengeance, one can only guess that he would have said Yes. But like other great moral reformers, he was more interested in the truth of what he said than in the way of arriving at it. His way was that of the prophets, who were seers, not epistemologists. And when the prophet speaks, it is not his intellect that is chiefly engaged. He would be impatient of distinctions between logical certainty and emotional certitude. There are poor and wretched people around him in whose misery he partakes. He has had a vision of what life might be if mankind were a brotherhood instead of an arena for rivalry and greed; his account of his vision has something of the lyric cry about it; and he lashes out in fury at those who, having ears, refuse to hear. Because his words come from the heart and are the utterance of passionate sympathies, antipathies, and aspirations, they will almost certainly have wings. But they are not likely to express the balanced judgement of the sage.

29 Does this line of reflection apply to the ethics of Jesus? Without undue disparagement of so great a figure, one may venture to think that it does. If his ethics had been the expression of a critical reason, his order of values would surely not have been what it was. For him religion and morality were virtually the whole of life; nothing mattered much except the hunger and thirst after righteousness. He was the last and greatest of the prophets, and the old tradition spoke through him when he focused his teaching on the moral side of life. But morality, though the most important thing in life, is not all of it, and in fixing on it so exclusively he undervalued the other great goods of life. The adequate appreciation of these had to be learned from other sources—of intelligence and beauty from the Greeks, of justice and order from the Romans, of courage from both, as well as from the Goths. The moral philosopher knows that these are goods, and great goods, which should have their part, if possible, in every life. But no Hebrew prophet, even of transcendent genius, was a moral philosopher. They were all passionate purveyors of a single message—the kingdom of God and his righteousness. They are not to be blamed for lacking a range of contemplation that, in their position, was impossible for them. It is otherwise with those who, without their genius, have a command of history, philosophy, and science that was never available to them. Jesus was the supreme prophet, poet, and genius of inward goodness. But we mistake his office and narrow our possibilities if we look to him alone for the architecture of the good life.

CHAPTER XI

THE ETHICS OF BELIEF

1   In the first eight chapters of this study we were concerned with traditional Christian beliefs, Catholic and Protestant, and regarding many of these beliefs we expressed doubts and reservations. In the two chapters just concluded we have been concerned with Christian ethics. But one important question about Christian ethics we did not press. Would it, or could it, approve the sort of treatment, full of doubts, reservations, and criticisms, that we have accorded to Christian beliefs? Is belief, in this region, a duty, whether the evidence justifies it or not? Or is it our duty rather to proportion belief to evidence as nicely as we can? Is there one ethics of belief for science and another for religion, or is there a single ethics of belief that holds alike in every field? These are the questions to which we must now turn.

To some persons the very idea of an ethics of belief will appear bizarre. Morality they regard as concerned exclusively with practice. If a man neglects to pay his rent, or borrows books and keeps them, or helps himself to so much as a collar-button at a department store counter, he is looked upon, and with justice, as behaving immorally. In matters of taste he is comparatively free from such restrictions. If he prefers a banjo to the best of string quartets, or the comic strips to T. S. Eliot, his choice may cause some raising of eyebrows, but hardly the suggestion of a defect in his morals. Similarly in matters of belief. The man who believes that Shakespeare was Bacon or that the woods are haunted by leprechauns may provoke slights to his intelligence, but to infer that his character is in any way questionable would seem to most people mere confusion.

This attitude is held with a curious inconsistency. There is one field, namely religion, where people do very commonly take belief to be a matter of moral concern. They would regard with equanimity the belief on the part of a son or brother that Shakespeare was Bacon, and with a somewhat puzzled amusement his belief in leprechauns. But if they were Catholics whose belief he has exchanged for Methodism, or Methodists whose belief he had abandoned for atheism, they would very probably regard the change as involving a moral lapse.

2 This looks like inconsistency, and I think it is. But the line I am inclined to take about it will be as unpopular, I fear, with the critics of this common position as with its holders. The critics will probably say that belief is a morally neutral affair and should remain as neutral in religion as in the secular field. On the contrary, I think it is neutral in neither field, that everywhere and always belief has an ethical aspect. There is such a thing as a general ethics of the intellect. The main principle of that ethics I hold to be the same inside and outside religion. This principle is simple and sweeping: Equate your assent to the evidence.

To think is to seek to know. In seeking knowledge, we assume that it is something worth having, something intrinsically good, that to miss it through ignorance or error is an evil, and that the more of it we have, the better. To court falsity is wrong, and that is what we do when we allow belief to outrun the evidence. To forgo truth needlessly is also wrong, and that is what we do when, with sufficient evidence before us, we decline to believe. Strangely enough, the rule that we should equate our belief with the evidence seems to have no exceptions. Most maxims of conduct, of course, do have exceptions. The rule that we should keep a promise must at times be broken for the sake of the over-riding good of saving a life. The rule that life should be saved must at times be broken in the interest of the over-riding good of a nation. But it is hard to imagine any circumstances in which it would be right, if we could avoid it, to believe either more or less than the evidence before us warrants.

This is a large claim, and in making it we must guard against other statements that might be confused with it. We are not saying, for example, that the search for truth is one's only, or chief, obligation. Truth is a great good, but it is obviously not the only one, and sometimes it may be our duty to abandon its pursuit in order to fulfil competing obligations of a different kind, for instance, to abandon one's research at the call of national service. Again, in insisting on fidelity to truth, we are not insisting on fidelity to truthfulness. A detective may find that the only way in which he can hope to apprehend a dangerous criminal is to deceive people about his own identity and what he is doing. We are not maintaining that it is never wrong to deceive others, but that it is always wrong to deceive oneself.

When the rule is put in this form, few perhaps will deny it, or even suppose that it conflicts with their own practice. Still, the fact remains that it is not only denied at times by all of us in assuming that belief is not an affair of right and wrong at all; it has also been denied, in one form or another, by some of the most influential writers in history, by Augustine, for example, and St Thomas, and Calvin, and Luther, and Pascal, and Newman, and Kierkegaard, and William James.

IS BELIEF VOLUNTARY?

3 It has been held on two grounds that belief and disbelief are not of moral concern at all. One of these is that believing and dis- believing are beyond our control, and that only what is within our control is ever a duty. The other is that only such actions as affect others for better or worse are matters of obligation, and that the conduct of our own thought is not conduct of this kind.

As for the first of these grounds, we must agree that if a kind of behaviour is beyond the control of our wills, it is idle to approve or blame us for doing it. If a man suffers from an involuntary tic, such as a twitching face, we do not condemn him for it. But another example will show that this is not the end of the story. Suppose a man comes to work some morning with a violent cold, which ex- presses itself in a running nose and uncontrollable sneezes and coughs. We hardly blame him for what his body is so unpleasantly doing; it would be brutal to blame him for what he cannot help; we condole with him and move away. But then suppose we find that he acquired his cold by going to an ice-show the previous evening in summer clothes; is our attitude toward him unchanged? No, it is not; we then tend to lose patience with him, and to say that if he had taken the slightest trouble, he could have avoided being the nuisance he now is to himself and others. He is not *directly* responsible for his sneezes and coughs, for, given his state of body, he cannot prevent them. But he is *indirectly* responsible, nevertheless, for with due precaution he would not have been cursed with this state of body at all.

4 Now, beliefs are rather like tics and sneezes. In some cases they are completely uncontrollable, and then to talk of duty in connection with them is absurd. If a man were offered a million dollars to believe at this moment that three and four made eleven, or that the chair on which he seemed to be sitting was the only living unicorn, he would lose the money. When a proposition is self-evident, or the evidence for it is plain, familiar, and overwhelming, belief is as automatic and inevitable in a normal man as a patellar reflex. To praise or blame anyone for belief of this kind would be silly. But a great many of our beliefs are not of this kind. They are beliefs that must be made out, if at all, by evidence beyond themselves, evidence that is in many cases extensive, conflicting, and difficult to secure. When such beliefs are proposed to us, our acceptance, doubt, or denial, will spring as inevitably out of our state of mind as do the sneezes and coughs from the state of body of the man with a cold. But we may be as truly responsible for this state of mind as he was for his state of body. Though not directly responsible for these beliefs, we may be responsible for them indirectly.

We may exert this indirect control in many ways. We may determine whether in a certain field we shall have any beliefs at all by deciding whether or not to secure the information needed for such belief. Most persons have no convictions, one way or the other, about the economic interpretation of history, or Hinayana Buddhism, or the semantic theory of truth, or the nebular hypothesis, because they have no notion what these things mean. If beliefs of any kind are to be entertained about them, the first step is to inform oneself about their meaning, and that is fortunately within our power. Of course, knowledge is not understanding, and it is understanding that is the ideal of reason. But knowledge is the condition of understanding. Much of the intellectual poverty of the world is due, not to lack of ability or to lack of potential interest, but to the mere ignorance in which minds go to sleep for lack of material to work on and incitements to work on it.

Granting, however, that a man knows enough of a subject to have opinions about it, what determines those opinions? The conviction that leaps into his mind at a given moment is a function not only of the evidence before him but also of a set of habits acquired by past acts of will and therefore modifiable by further acts. He has formed the habit, perhaps, of suspended judgement, of turning over the evidence till his mind is clear before committing himself to a decision, or on the contrary of leaping to a decision impulsively; Descartes suggested that all error sprang from the latter source and hence was in some measure culpable. A reasonable standard of what in practice shall be allowed to pass as clear is itself a slowly won achievement which one may promote, as Mill reports that he did, by deliberate application to logic. Again, opinions are so subject to influence by likes and dislikes that unless one has considered how these affect belief and made some effort to counter them, one's beliefs may be ridden with prejudices. A host of other more or less controllable factors enter in. Can one hold a suggestion quietly in mind while it sprouts its implications? Is one's real interest, when one thinks on a certain subject, the interest in seeing it as it is, or in showing one's independence of common opinion or perhaps in scoring off an opponent? Is one given to analysis and argument, or does one detest such activities? Is one habitually loose in putting thoughts into words? Of course we do not think of these factors when a decision or belief is called for; we simply respond as our state of mind at the moment dictates; our opinion no doubt seems like a simple function of the evidence before us, and therefore the sort of automatic response that has no moral complexion whatever. It does have such a complexion nevertheless. Its clearness, its definiteness, its promptness, its cogency, its fairness, not improbably its very existence, are dependent on processes that spring from our wills.

A man who is disposed to believe in the animal origin of man but would rather not believe in it because he thinks it degrading may show surprising resources in circumventing the evidence. He can fix his mind on the degrading aspects of the belief; he can concentrate on the evidence against it and ignore the evidence for it; he can attend to the frailties and vulgarities of those who have advocated it and the nobility of those who have opposed it, until the mass of factors tending to disbelief outweighs those on the other side and he finds that his automatic response has changed from positive to negative. So far as this is possible, his belief *is* under the control of his will, not directly indeed, but indirectly.

The first objection, then, to an ethics of belief, namely that belief is involuntary, is not very compelling. It does obviously hold of certain classes of belief. It holds of perceptual beliefs such as that this is a table and that is a tree. It holds again of self-evident beliefs such as that a straight line is the shortest one between two points, or perhaps that proposition q follows from proposition p. When such beliefs are proposed to us, acceptance is so automatic that belief and evidence seem to be one. But the farther the belief is removed from the evidence, and the more complicated and divided that evidence becomes, the more fully is the belief determined by habits that are under our control. And the beliefs that fix our positions on major issues are of the latter class—our beliefs about politics, morals, education, economics, religion. To say that we hold no responsibility for our beliefs on these things because they are involuntary is clearly untrue.

ARE OUR BELIEFS OUR OWN CONCERN ONLY?

5   What about the second objection? This was that, since the beliefs we form in the privacy of our own minds make no difference to others either for help or for harm, they are no one's concern but our own, and we may indulge in them or not as we please. There are two distinct questions here, the question of our duty and the question of society's right.

Are our beliefs of enough social importance to make our habits in regard to them a matter of moral concern? If a choice or belief makes no difference to anyone in the way of good or evil, it does not seem to be of moral moment. If there are two paths to one's office of a morning, and the consequences of taking them are exactly the same, no moral choice is involved. Is it not similarly true of beliefs that they tip no balances of good or evil and hence are without moral complexion?

No, it is not. To be sure, when we call to mind some routine act of assent, particularly if it is in agreement with what everyone believes, we may be unable to see that it has made any difference anywhere, and probably it has in fact made little. But one must be wary here. Though the difference made by a belief is often of an impalpable kind, consisting in the confirmation or weakening of general habits of belief, still the fabric of belief in which we live is sustained or dissolved by such acts of acceptance or dissent. This fabric, as a whole, is of vast importance; it determines the cultural level of the community. Every community has a *Weltanschauung*, a system of beliefs which cover all the main problems of life, and constitute the common sense of that community. Many of these beliefs are universal and incorrigible, since experience forces them on all alike—beliefs about the value of food and drink and the care of children, beliefs about the number and the round of the seasons, about the uses of fire and water. But when communities go beyond these elementary beliefs, they tend to fabricate worlds of their own. Socially, the Indian Brahmin lives in a different world from that of the Nebraska farmer; religiously, the Burmese Buddhist lives in a different world from that of the Mussulman in Bagdad or the Catholic in Madrid. Scientifically, an Eskimo village lives in a different world from that of the Massachusetts Institute of Technology. To each of these parties, their own world seems the only real one, to which any fundamental challenge seems merely absurd. Most men live like raisins in what Bagehot called a cake of custom.

Now, some of these intellectual worlds are far more advanced, and more rapidly advancing, than others. It is perhaps dangerous, if there are anthropologists about, to assert that anything is *really* better than anything else, but they might do well to investigate whether this doubt or denial is not part of their own cake of custom. At any rate, I shall be so rash as to suggest that the intellectual world of, say, the London Athenaeum is a better world than that of a head-hunting council in Borneo, in the sense that it is richer in scope and more accurate in its reflection of fact.

How has it come to be so? Part of the answer, certainly, is that whereas among backward people the fabric of belief and custom tends to be so rigid as to keep the individual mind fixed like a fly in amber, in a group that is progressive the medium is kept from solidifying by the constant beating of small individual wings. Indeed, in some remarkable societies, like that of fourth-century Athens or of eighteenth-century Edinburgh, the free and critical exercise of mind has itself almost become one of the mores of the tribe. In such a society every man, as regards some part of his belief, is a member of 'his majesty's loyal opposition' and is not ostracised but respected for his dissent. Not, to be sure, that there is anything creditable in dissent as such. If that is not something to be condemned in itself, as it was among those ancient Locrians who, when a man proposed a change of laws in their assembly, kept a rope round his neck to swing him by if his proposal was rejected, neither is it a virtue, as it is for so many village atheists and for orators in Hyde Park. What is creditable and socially valuable is not the mere belief in this or that but the having arrived at it by a process which, had the evidence been different, would have carried one with equal readiness to a contrary belief.

Now, such a habit of mind is bound to come sooner or later into conflict with communal orthodoxy. Why so bound? Because, unhappily, much of the fabric of belief in which we live is almost certainly false. How do we know this? By reflecting that the intellectual worlds that modern communities live in are inconsistent with each other, and that where there is such disharmony there must be error on one side or the other. Whether the error lies with us, only reflection can reveal. Whether this reflection will go on freely and with common encouragement, or furtively and sluggishly, depends on whether the intellectual climate favours the critical use of one's mind. And in the end that climate depends on the multitude of little people like ourselves.

6　We all count in our various degrees. Some 'quarto and folio editions of mankind' have counted enormously; one need only refer to what Copernicus did to the older astronomy, what Darwin did to the older belief about human origins, or what Gandhi did to untouchability. In these cases, where a conspicuous lead was given, many promptly followed. But many did not, and it is instructive to consider why. The reason was not that the new belief was so difficult to understand, nor merely that vested interests were piled high on the other side; many who failed to follow would have profited by doing so. The root difficulty is the sheer inertia of human thought. It sometimes seems as if the pragmatists were right that men never reflect until there arises some block to their activity which forces them to it. In fact this is not true, for men do think at times from the sheer interest in knowing. Nevertheless, *denken ist schwer*; conformity is easy; even reformers with a clear case and the greatest courage commonly get their case accepted only when they themselves are memories. Beliefs that, attended to in detachment, are obvious, still have to fight their way against mountainous sluggishness, as we may see in the slow recognition of the rights of women and of the cultural irrelevance of one's colour.

Unhappily one cannot, by choosing, be a Darwin or a Gandhi. But one can at least resolve that one will not form part of the automatic resistance movement when some Darwin or Gandhi does appear. If people generally did that, if they reached the point where it was as much a matter of self-respect for them to have reasons for the faith that was in them and to be ashamed of being unreasonable and gullible as it now is to wear clothes that are in fashion and to have acceptable manners, civilisation would be transformed. *What* we believe is less important than its source in intellectual habit. Edward Caird used to say to his students that it was important that a belief should be true, and important that it should be reasoned, but it was more important that it be reasoned than that it be true. Beliefs that spring from reflection, even when false, have behind them the means of their own amendment.

SOCIAL IMPORTANCE AND SOCIAL CONTROL

7 Granting now that my beliefs are of importance to society, does that imply that society has the right to step in and tell me what to believe? Here the answer must be a firm No. On this answer the socialist politics of the Hegelians and the individualist politics of Mill would unite, though for different reasons. Green and Bosanquet, admitting that the character of one's thought did make a difference to others, still held that society should keep its hands off, on the ground that only if we were allowed liberty to make our own mistakes should we ever become responsible minds. This seems to me the sound view. Mill would agree, but he sometimes based his claims to freedom on another ground. Society was justified in interfering with our conduct, he said, when that conduct affected society, but not when it affected only oneself. And our own beliefs and tastes did not, he suggested, affect others in any important way, as our actions did. Hence they were not society's concern, but solely our own. This is dangerous doctrine. It implies that, if the beliefs of the individual *can* be shown to make an important difference to society, society has the right to step in and attempt their regulation. I do not think this follows. We may owe a duty to another which he would be most imprudent to try to extort from us by compulsion,

and for society to attempt compulsion upon our beliefs would be
doubly mistaken. (1) It would be imposing a requirement it could
not properly enforce, since it cannot invade a mind and extirpate its
beliefs; and (2) by trying it would probably kill the goose that lays
its most precious eggs. What we owe to society and society may
rightly ask of us is not passive acceptance but active reflection, the
thought that brings intellectual advance; and this is destroyed if the
right to free questioning is denied.

THE RIGHT TO BELIEVE: A CRUCIAL CASE

8 The two main objections to taking belief as a matter of morals,
namely that it is involuntary and that it affects ourselves alone,
appear to be unsound. But to some the conclusion may still seem
paradoxical. 'People surely are not to be lauded or condemned for
their *beliefs*,' it will be said. 'We may call their *actions* wrong because
they produce evil effects or because they spring from evil motives.
But a belief is not an action. One cannot say that it is *duty* to believe
or disbelieve, or that a certain belief is one that a man has no moral
right to entertain.'

But is this strictly true? Take a famous case. Many years ago in
Spain there was a brilliant but modest and devout young man who,
though the son of a distinguished house, gave up his worldly prospects to live a life of austere service in a Dominican convent. Being
of great ability and earnestness, he was given increasingly large
responsibilities, till at sixty-three he was made inquisitor-general for
Spain and all her possessions. In the remaining years of his life this
earnest and devoted man, whose name was Thomas Torquemada,
put to death by fire some two thousand persons who could not
believe as he did, many of them after prolonged torture. Was this
wrong? Most of us would say that it was hideously and atrociously
wrong.

But why precisely? When an act is set down as wrong, it is usually
because of bad consequences or a bad motive. Suppose that in this
case you fix upon the consequences, which included the excruciating
suffering in mind and body of many good men and women.
Torquemada would have admitted the suffering. But he would have
pointed out that in his view the consequences included very much
more; they included the cleansing from Spain of human plague-
spots from which a pestilence was spreading, a pestilence that
threatened to carry large numbers of persons to perdition and was
averted cheaply by this relatively small number of deaths. So far
as consequences were concerned, the balance was therefore good.
As for motive, the highest of all motives is the sense of duty, and this

Torquemada felt strongly. One may say that a human being should have some humanity as well as a sense of duty. He would probably reply, following Augustine, that he was doing a genuine kindness to the people he sent to the stake. If they continued heretics, they would suffer agonisingly and eternally in hell; so far they had resisted everything that might, by inducing them to recant, have prevented their going there; there was some chance that, if put on the pyre and burnt by a slow fire, as they not infrequently were to give more time to repent,[1] they would renounce their errors; and was not an hour or so of fire in this life a low price at which to purchase exemption from an eternity of fire hereafter?

This is a very strong case. Grant Torquemada his premises, and the conclusion follows irresistibly that torturing and burning people may be a duty and a kindness. You can hardly say he was a wicked man for living up more courageously than others to what he and they believed in common, or for acting sincerely in what he believed to be the interest of his victims. We cling, nevertheless, to our conviction that he did wrong, and atrocious wrong. And the question presses more urgently than before, where does the wrongness lie?

9 I see no escape from the answer that he had no right to *believe* what he did. That his action would cause excruciating suffering and death to many was certain; the belief on the strength of which he caused it no responsible mind has any right to call certain. We commonly say that if a man sincerely believes something he ought to live up to it, and we are following a false scent if we condemn him for loyalty to his convictions. But we may justly insist that if what he believes calls for torture and slaughter he should have excluded all possibility that he might be mistaken before applying the rack and the torch. We may concede that there is small harm in some beliefs, in the belief of a friend of mine, for example, that a minute shoe he once picked up in Ireland was a fairy's shoe. There may be no great harm even in believing, as another and kindly friend of mine did during the war, that all Germans should be exterminated, if the belief is held in the half-whimsical way which makes it inconceivable that it should ever be acted on. But as the evil entailed by holding a belief grows greater, so does the responsibility of holding it, and when that evil is overwhelming and unquestionable, the belief too must be unquestionable or the act is fiendish. 'After all,' as Montaigne said, 'it is rating one's conjectures at a very high price to roast a man alive on the strength of them'.

It is not good enough to plead that one is sincere in one's belief; there are some wrongs to mankind for which mere sincerity is a totally inadequate excuse. Torquemada was very probably sincere in his belief that heretics should be exterminated, just as Hitler may have been sincere in believing that Jews should be exterminated. But that does not make their beliefs the less mistaken or their victims the less dead. Sincerity and dutifulness only make wrong more inevitable when they are the tools of fanaticism; as Grattan said of intolerance, 'conscience, which restrains every other vice, becomes the prompter here'.

No doubt such fanaticism as this is more than merely intellectual error; one would probably find in such natures dark strains of hatred and sadism which predisposed them to their beliefs; and it may be said that their beliefs are the symptoms and rationalisation of evil tendencies which themselves are what we condemn. I am sure there is much truth in this. But there are many persons, after all, who feel such hatreds without acting on them; it was the belief that in these cases raised the floodgates, whereas a contrary belief would have kept the flood in. I am not questioning that the distortion of beliefs from some impulses is worse than from others; I am saying that where great human goods and ills are involved, the distortion of belief from any sort of avoidable cause is immoral, and the more immoral the greater the stakes.

10 We have probably said enough to make clear that belief and disbelief are matters of moral concern. We now turn to the more controverted question: Granting that they are so, what is the rule that should guide us? It may seem at first glance that there is no problem here at all. 'Surely the only possible rule', one may say, 'is to believe what is true and disbelieve what is false'. And of course that would be the rule if we were in a position to know what was true and what false. But the whole difficulty arises from the fact that we do not and often cannot. What is to guide us then? Sometimes what seems to us true conflicts with what authority says is true; sometimes what the evidence suggests as true is something that will make ourselves and others very unhappy; sometimes on pressing issues the evidence is conflicting. In such cases what are we to believe?

SCIENCE AND THE ETHICS OF BELIEF

11 What makes this issue a live one for many persons is that two of the great disciplines of our Western culture, science and theology, have tended to give opposing answers to it. The answer of science is the simpler. It was formulated by T. H. Huxley as follows: 'it is wrong for a man to say that he is certain of the objective truth of any proposition unless he can produce evidence which logically justifies that certainty.'2 It has been put by Bertrand Russell in the form: 'Give to any hypothesis which is worth your while to consider just that degree of credence which the evidence warrants.'3 It was put even more uncompromisingly by another eminent scientist, W. K. Clifford: 'It is wrong always, everywhere, and for anyone, to believe anything on insufficient evidence.'4

The scientist is trained to scepticism. In his own province, he ties his self-respect to his power to tell the difference between an unfounded conjecture, a reasonable hypothesis, an accepted theory, and an established fact, and to give to each the credence that it merits. A young scientist is secretly rather pleased if he is regarded as so hard-headed that, like Charles Lamb in one of his whimsical moods, he would refuse to admit that two and two were four until he knew what use you proposed to put it to. If he is a sociologist, and you remark that the American police and priesthood are recruited chiefly from the Irish, he wants to know whether any statistical studies cover this point, and, if so, what proportions of these two classes are in fact drawn from this national group. If he is a biologist, and you remark that American intelligence has risen as a result of general education, he will point out that, so far as intelligence is an innate character, there is no good evidence that education can improve it as it passes from generation to generation; and if you cite the opposite conclusions of Professor Kammerer, he will not improbably illustrate the present point in two ways at once, by pointing out that Kammerer had been too uncritical in his procedure and that when it was brought home to him that he had allowed one of his students to deceive him systematically, the unfortunate man, unable to face the blast of ridicule, took his own life.

Indeed, as is suggested by this case, the scientist's pride in refusing to go beyond the evidence may easily be carried too far. Sometimes it is carried so far that he falls over backward, and either concludes before examining the evidence that it can prove nothing—a popular attitude of American psychologists toward psychical research—or disqualifies it by preconceived notions of what evidence should be, as witness those positivists who declared it unscientific to believe in other minds. But I think that such extremes would be conceded by most scientists to be inconsistent with the scientific ideal. That ideal is to believe no more, but also no less, than what the evidence warrants.

RELIGION AND THE ETHICS OF BELIEF

12 When we compare this attitude of antiseptic caution with the attitude approved and indeed exacted by the religious teaching of the West, we find a startling difference. Professor D. M. Baillie has pointed out that faith, comprising a double attitude of belief and trust, occupies a place in the Hebrew-Christian tradition that is unique among the religions of the world.[5] What is insisted on is not the withholding of belief till the evidence warrants but, on the contrary, the embracing of belief, whether intelligence is satisfied or not. In the eighth century BC we find Isaiah saying to King Ahaz when Judah was threatened with destruction by the Assyrians, 'If ye will not believe, surely ye shall not be established'.[6] This particular note, sounded then for the first time in the Biblical word, was struck thereafter loudly and insistently; indeed if the fortunes of the people went awry, it was commonly laid to their want of belief; 'they believed not his word, but murmured in their tents . . .'; 'they believed not in God and trusted not in his salvation'.[7] The two attitudes mentioned here, of belief and trust, were not usually distinguished; thinking, as a purely theoretical activity with ends and standards of its own, had none of the attraction for the Jews that it had for the Greeks; what was demanded was the complex attitude later described as faith, in which intellectual assent was blended with other attitudes, notably the trust a child feels in a father, a spirit of obedience, and the courage and hopefulness that come with unquestioning trust.

THE GOSPEL TEACHING

13 The duty of such unquestioning acceptance is stressed even more strongly in the New Testament. The teaching of Jesus himself on this head is less than certain. To be sure, some very unqualified statements about it are attributed to him. 'He that believeth and is baptized shall be saved; but he that believeth not shall be damned.'[8] Again, when Thomas doubted and asked for palpable evidence that it was his Master who was before him, he was rebuked for his unbelief and told, 'Blessed are they that have not seen and yet have believed'. But it has been pointed out that neither of these passages is certainly authentic. The first occurs in a section at the end of Mark which is plainly an addition from another hand, and the second occurs only in the latest of the accounts, and the least reliable historically, the gospel of John. There is no doubt, however, that Jesus stressed the importance of belief. He healed the centurion's servant, saying 'as thou hast believed, so be it done unto thee';[9] to a man who brought a son troubled with a demon he said, 'If thou canst believe, all things are possible to him that believeth,' and when the father replied, 'Lord, I believe; help thou mine unbelief,' he cast the demon out.[10] Repeatedly he said to those whom he healed, 'Thy faith hath made thee whole'.[11] It seems clear that in such passages Jesus was not referring to mere intellectual assent; he was thinking of faith and belief much as the prophets did, as something exercised by the whole man, in which the belief accorded by intellect, the trust accorded by feeling, and the obedience accorded by will were not distinguished. We can only believe that Jesus was not greatly concerned with, or interested in, those processes of observation, analysis, and inference that now pass under the names of science and philosophy, a fact that is the more noteworthy because the Greek language, presumably carrying with it intimations of the theoretical interest so characteristic of the Greeks, must have flowed round him rather freely. How much we should give for some recorded conversation between him and a Greek like Socrates! To be sure, there is something incongruous in picturing him as engaged in dialectical passages-at-arms with speculative opponents; his emphasis on childlike trust suggests rather the prophet and poet than the argumentative rationalist. Still, what he would have said about the intellectual pursuits of an Einstein or a Frazer, or the intellectual scruples of a Huxley or a Clifford, we do not know.

THE PAULINE TEACHING

14 But we do know pretty clearly the attitude of St Paul, and in this particular province it was the teaching of Paul rather than that of Christ himself that proved decisive in the thought of the West. There are two distinct strains of doctrine running through Christian history, one coming from the synoptic gospels and stressing salvation by goodness, the other coming from Paul and stressing salvation by faith. Neither emphasis means to be exclusive, though their difference is important. Paul was a man of some learning who, though a Jew, wrote in Greek and probably read his Old Testament in Greek. His city, Tarsus, had a university in which Hellenistic philosophy flourished. He knew the Greek passion for speculation and argument. And knowing it as few others of the early Christians did, he explicitly repudiated it. The wisdom he stressed was sharply contrasted with 'the wisdom of this world'. 'Let no man deceive himself. If any man among you seemeth to be wise in this world, let him become a fool, that he may be wise. For the wisdom of this world is foolishness with God.'[12]

'For it is written, I will destroy the wisdom of the wise, and will bring to nothing the understanding of the prudent. Where is the wise? Where is the scribe? Where is the disputer of this world?

Hath not God made foolish the wisdom of this world?'[13] 'We walk
by faith, not by sight.'[14]

The road to belief for Paul lay not through the thickets of theological
disputation but around them, by a path open to 'babes and
sucklings'. Indeed if this path had not been open, we should all have
met disaster, for it is by such faith only that we are 'justified' and
'saved from wrath'. Paul's emphasis on faith was not universally
accepted in the early church. As Westermarck points out, the epistle
of James 'looks like a definite polemic against Paul's teaching of
justification by faith only . . .';[15] 'faith without works is dead', it
says; 'the devils also believe, and tremble'.[16] But the Pauline
emphasis is seen again in the classic, though somewhat cryptic,
account of faith in the epistle to the Hebrews as

'the substance of things hoped for, the evidence of things not seen'.
'Through faith we understand that the worlds were framed by the
word of God . . . without faith it is impossible to please him.'[17]
'For whatsoever is not faith is sin.'[18]

15 Little by little, in the hands of imperfectly enlightened writers,
this doctrine was developed into a hard requirement that no matter
what the evidence one might suppose one had, assent must be given
to certain tenets of the creed as a condition of salvation. 'To no
other has Christian orthodoxy owed so much' as to Tertullian, 'a
lawyer by profession and temperament [who] renounced the liberty
of Christ for a tradition in doctrine and morals more rigid than
Pharisaism,' 'a Puritan, whose decent instincts were repressed and
heavily charged with Sadism. . . .'[19] He seems to have exulted in
believing things that his reason outlawed; *credo quia impossibile est.*
Lactantius took a similar view. 'If anyone out of Noah's ark could
escape the deluge,' said Cyprian, 'he who is out of the Church may
also escape'. Fulgentius held that 'without a shadow of doubt all
Jews, heretics, and schismatics will go to eternal fire'. 'In the third
century', says Canon Raven, 'truth was something to be sought;
in the fourth something to be understood; in the fifth something to be
accepted'.[20] Augustine described heresy as not only blasphemy but
murder, the murder of souls, and therefore deserving of the death
penalty. 'What is more deadly to the soul', he asked, 'than the
liberty of error?' To such minds, 'Scepticism,' as Santayana says,
'instead of seeming, what it naturally is, a moral force, a tendency
to sincerity, economy, and fine adjustment of life and mind to
experience—scepticism seemed a temptation and a danger'.[21]

Unfortunately Augustine's view of what Christianity asks of the
intellect became, under his vast influence, the official view of the

Catholic church, and it remains so. Pope Gregory XVI, repeating in a bull of 1832 the words of Augustine we have just quoted about heresy as the murder of souls, took occasion to denounce what he described as a 'most pestilential error,' 'that absurd and erroneous opinion, or rather that form of madness, which declares that liberty of conscience should be asserted and maintained for every one'.[22] Protestantism has granted a greater latitude to thought and conscience than Catholicism, as one would expect of a movement that made so much of private judgement, but its record is most inconsistent. The early reformers were anything but tolerant. 'If, outside of Christ, you wish by your own thoughts to know your relation to God,' said Luther, 'you will break your neck. Thunder strikes him who examines.' When Calvin sent Servetus to the stake for his wrong views about the Trinity, he had the cordial approval of Melanchthon and most other Protestant leaders; and John Knox argued that those who allowed active disbelievers to remain alive were themselves incurring the divine wrath. 'In the seventeenth century the Scotch clergy taught that food or shelter must on no occasion be given to a starving man unless his opinions were orthodox.'[23]

It is needless for our purpose to go into historical detail; what we are interested in is the view of the ethics of religious belief that has prevailed in the West during the greater part of its history. Regarding this we cannot do better than to quote the sentences in which Lecky, in his great work on the rise of rationalism, summarises a long discussion:

'Until the seventeenth century, every mental disposition which philosophy pronounces to be essential to a legitimate research was almost uniformly branded as a sin, and a large proportion of the most deadly intellectual vices were deliberately inculcated as virtues. It was a sin to doubt the opinions that had been instilled in childhood before they had been examined. It was a virtue to hold them with unwavering, unreasoning credulity. It was a sin to notice and develope to its full consequences every objection to those opinions, it was a virtue to stifle every objection as a suggestion of the devil. It was sinful to study with equal attention and with an indifferent mind the writings on both sides, sinful to resolve to follow the light of evidence wherever it might lead, sinful to remain poised in doubt between conflicting opinions, sinful to give only a qualified assent to indecisive arguments, sinful even to recognise the moral or intellectual excellence of opponents. In a word, there is scarcely a disposition that marks the love of abstract truth, and scarcely a rule which reason teaches as essential for its attainment, that theologians did not for centuries stigmatise as offensive to the Almighty.'[24]

16   What broke the hold of this system was the birth of a conviction that there was such a thing as an ethics of the intellect, and that those who followed it should be encouraged, not chastised. This was implicit in the arguments of the reformers, however reluctant they were to recognise it; for unless a man was justified in following such inward light as he had, Protestantism had no ground to stand on. Little by little, and with painful struggle, the principle won its way that when one's own considered insight conflicted with the authority of a great institution or of common belief, one had a right and even a duty to respect that insight. Modern thought began with an insistence on this principle by Descartes, who in his *Rules for the Direction of the Mind* laid down as the justification of belief not authority but one's own 'clear and distinct perception'. Descartes was a Catholic, and tried to remain in the good graces of the church, but his works were put on the Index; M. Maritain regards him as the chief architect of intellectual disaster.[25]

Descartes' independence was re-enacted by two great Englishmen, an earlier and a later contemporary of his own. For Bacon, who was even more suspicious than Descartes of older traditions, 'the very contemplation of things as they are, without superstition or imposture, without error or confusion, is in itself more worthy than all the produce of discoveries'. And the plodding, honest John Locke gave it as his opinion that 'to love truth for truth's sake is the principal part of human perfection in this world, and the seed-plot of all other virtues'. These writers also have found their place on the Index. The eminent Papal apologist De Maistre described Bacon's thought as 'false and dangerous' and wrote that 'in the study of philosophy, the contempt of Locke is the beginning of wisdom'.[26] One may scorn Locke's conclusions if one wishes, but one scorns his spirit at one's peril. His great book is not only a classic of philosophy; it is in a sense a moral classic, by reason of the transparent disinterestedness of his sober and honest mind. It captivated Voltaire, and through his demonic energy helped the French revolutionists to pry up the lid of Pandora's box. Many repellent forms fluttered out of that box. But it was found when they had settled that the hold of authority was conclusively broken.

17   As one looks back over this long struggle of intelligence for freedom, it is hard to deny that there has been a real conflict of principle, that while the scientific mind has on the whole, though with many lapses, held it wrong to exceed the evidence before it, the religious mind has held that there is one great exception, and that in this exceptional case it is not only a right but a duty to give one's belief a freer rein. Indeed Dean Sperry has said that 'nine persons out of ten who profess and call themselves Christians . . . still hold that if some newly discovered or formulated truth is incompatible with statements embedded in religious tradition, it is incumbent upon them to ignore the truth and hold the faith.'[27]

Many defences have been made of this conception of faith. Faith, it is said, is a different state from ordinary belief; it contains its own kind of self-justifying insight; it carries an assurance not based on reasoning nor open to its criticism. This has been a repeated contention of 'existentialist' theologians, and we have examined several forms of it in the theologies of Luther, Kierkegaard, Brunner, and Barth. In none of these forms was a credible account provided of the relations between the insight of faith and the insight achieved by natural faculties. Sometimes the apologetic becomes a defence of mysticism. But mysticism is open, I think, to a similar kind of criticism; a brief indication of my own attitude toward it will appear later in this volume. Sometimes, again, the techniques of current linguistic philosophy are invoked. The language of the religious man is declared to be a natural and legitimate language because it refers to authentic experiences of reverence, prayer, and exaltation, and when he uses such language he is as little open to rational criticism as when he talks of tables and chairs. This sort of apologetics is singularly unconvincing. No one doubts that religious language refers to experiences that actually exist. The question of importance is whether these experiences show the further existence of the Deity which they presuppose. To suggest that the answer to the former question is also an answer to the second is a logical howler.

Whether there is some other way in which the faith experience can attest the reality of its putative object we cannot here inquire. The question that concerns us is that of the right intellectual ethics for those who cannot claim such special illumination. Ought they to believe where they do not see? Many of those who would answer Yes would add that their answer is the one required by Christianity. Since this answer is clearly in conflict with the rule of science, let us ask how those who accept it would justify it. There have been various ways, and it would be idle to try to look at them all. So let us take for closer scrutiny the view of a distinguished thinker who felt with equal force the claims of science and religion, and tried hard to do justice to them both, William James.

JAMES'S REVOLT AGAINST RATIONALISM

18   James was a scientist himself; he knew the rules laid down by Huxley and Clifford to guide the belief of scientists, and he deliberately rejected them. This was partly because, in the light of what he knew of psychology, which was certainly considerable, he thought their rules naïve. They assumed that beliefs were far more largely a matter of reason and far less a function of wish, will, impulse, hope, and fear than they are or can be. Though this theme of James had already been developed by Lord Balfour in his *Foundations of Belief*, it still had at the turn of the century an air of novelty that it would not carry today. In recent years we have perhaps had a surfeit of this doctrine, and the readiness with which some amateur psychoanalysts would now reduce all speculative beliefs to rationalisations would not improbably horrify James.[28] However that may be, he thought the high talk of the intellectualists about the sin of allowing one's belief to be affected by one's desires was unconscious cant. Such talk itself, he thought, was an example of the very thing it protested against. If we look behind 'the snarling logicality' of such men as 'that delicious *enfant terrible*, Clifford,' and his insistence, 'with somewhat too much of robustious pathos in the voice,' that we commit ourselves to no belief of any sort that the universe does not extort from us by irresistible evidence, do we really find the delicate balance of judicial impartiality? Do rationalists hold the beliefs they do about religion because an impartial standard requires them, or are they insisting on a certain standard because that would justify their beliefs? James thought it was the latter. 'When the Cliffords tell us how sinful it is to be Christians on such "insufficient evidence", insufficiency is really the last thing they have in mind. For them the evidence is absolutely sufficient, only it makes the other way.'[29]

This approach is not wholly convincing. It is true that many of our beliefs are determined by causes rather than by reasons, but to show that they *are* so determined is not to show that they *ought* to be, unless indeed we cannot help ourselves and all our beliefs are puppets pulled about by wires of prejudice. Of course, if that is true, to ask that anyone be reasonable is absurd. But James does not hold that view. He holds that within limits it is possible to be reasonable, to suspend one's belief till one has evidence and then to adjust it to the evidence. And if such rational beliefs are possible, James would have been more generous, and perhaps more fair, to his rationalist opponents if he had admitted that their belief and their ethics of belief might fall among these. I see no good ground for thinking that the negative conclusions of such men as Clifford, Huxley, and Russell are examples of the will not to believe rather than to follow the evidence, and it would be hard to prove it if they were. The same holds of their belief about the ethics of belief. To be sure, James seems to think he is scoring at the expense of 'intellectuals' if he shows that the interest in precise and grounded knowledge is itself an emotion or passion, for then the intellectual must admit after all that passion is leading him about by the nose. But this is a hollow sort of victory. The love of truth is no doubt an emotion, but it is the one emotion that takes one toward truth as toward a magnet. And even of this emotion the rationalist would point out that it has no part in justifying or establishing belief; it sustains the search for knowledge, but whether a belief should be accepted or not depends entirely on whether it passes intellectual tests.

JAMES AND THE WILL TO BELIEVE

19 This James denies. That is the point of his famous essay on *The Will to Believe*; evidence is not the only thing that justifies belief. Regarding most problems he would agree that we should suspend belief till the evidence comes in, and in many cases we could quite well suspend it permanently. There would be no sense in labouring for a decision as between sub- and supra-lapsarianism, because neither position is today a live or plausible hypothesis; nor would there be any sense in entertaining a conviction about the number of hairs on one's head, for that is not worth finding out; nor would there be any point in rushing to an opinion about the nebular hypothesis; that can wait.

All this is obvious enough. But now suppose you are confronting an option that unlike the first is a live option, unlike the second is momentous, and unlike the third is forced. Suppose, to take James's example, you are confronted with the option whether to believe in God or not. Then what should you do? People around you draw you both ways; the issue is clearly a live one. It is momentous because, at the least, it means much to your happiness. And it is forced, for you can hardly dodge it; you have to take some attitude; you have to act either as if God existed or he did not; even to decline the choice is to commit yourself, since it is in effect to act as if he did not. What are you to do? You try to look at the evidence, with the result that your head begins to go round; you were not born to be a philosopher. You read a bit of C. S. Lewis and a bit of Bertrand Russell, and find that arguments which to the first are demonstrative are to the second preposterous. Your thought is confused; the evidence conflicts; the doctors disagree. If, in this predicament, you went to James for advice, it is pretty clear what he would do. In his enthusiastic, generous, affectionate way, he would put his hand on your shoulder and say, 'My dear fellow, forget your scruples. Life is more important than certainty, and action than knowledge. Don't be a lily-livered intellectual. Go ahead and believe.'

He would support this advice as follows. If you insist on not exceeding the evidence, you will avoid being taken in, and that, to be sure, is something; but by such a policy you make your life cautious, unadventurous, negative, and thin. On the other hand, if you commit yourself, you do run the risk of error, but you gain all the advantages—the assurance, the hopefulness, the serenity, the indomitableness, the fundamental freedom from care—of the man who is convinced that 'God's in his heaven and all's right with the world'. James felt that the advantage of the man with such a belief is enormous, and for my part I should agree. His point is that to govern your belief in an issue like this by considerations of evidence is to fail to see the problem in perspective; it is to make too much of truth in comparison with the other values of life; it is to fail to see that such a choice of belief is really an investment in which we should be governed by the largest prospective return.

20 There is something extraordinarily persuasive about this view, particularly as urged with James's infectious warmth. And yet even before we have examined it we may feel in it too much of the siren's song. To put it baldly, is not James telling us that we should believe something, that is, accept it as true, on the totally irrelevant ground that it will be to our advantage to do so? And is not that telling us that self-deception is at times a right and a duty? For surely we should be deceiving ourselves if we believed on that ground, as is plain in coarser cases. If a man justified his belief that he had an IQ of 160, or that his motor car was the fastest in the country, on the ground that it gave him the greatest satisfaction to think so, we should suspect a twist in his mind. These beliefs might be true, but we should regard it as fantastic self-deception to believe them for the reasons given. The personal advantage or disadvantage of believing something, we say, has simply nothing to do with its truth. And when we are told to act as if it had, we inevitably shrink back.[30]

James might ask, 'Just why should you shrink back? To be deceived is bad; admitted. But in the first place, there is a chance that you may *not* be deceived; you do not know that your belief is false, and it may turn out true. And in the second place, the personal gains, whether it is true or not, are so enormous as to outweigh the evil of any possible error.' Neither point leaves one content. Even if the belief we accepted on these grounds did turn out to be true, we should still have deceived ourselves, for we told ourselves that we might justifiably take it as true, whereas on the evidence before us we could not.

No doubt James would here fall back on the second contention. The rationalist, he would say, is forgetting that reason is only one of life's activities, and its good only one among many goods. You cannot order the whole of life with reference to just one of its activities, and sacrifice the good of the whole man to the particular good of man as thinker. What you would be doing if you did that would be to make your special rule of intellectual ethics violate your rule for ethics generally; you would exalt a narrower and smaller good over a wider and larger good.

James is here on strong ground. It is right for the artist to pursue beauty; but the artist is also a man, and his duty as a man takes precedence over his duty as an artist; to purchase artistic distinction at the price of moral degeneracy, as Verlaine and Gauguin did, is not to make a good bargain. It is right to pursue truth, but we know that when duties to family or country conflict with it we should sometimes give up that pursuit. At times it would seem to be a duty to leave ignorance and error undisturbed. If an old man or woman is happy in a faith one thinks illusory, it is certainly the kinder and probably the better course to hold one's peace. Henry Sidgwick, when he was no longer able to accept Christian theology, used to withhold his negations from his students unless expressly asked about them, since he thought acceptance of it would probably contribute more to their happiness and indeed their goodness than such grey tidings as he had to tell. The values of the intellect, of understanding and reasonableness, are great goods, but it is possible to overrate them.

THE LOVE OF TRUTH AND ITS REPRESSION

21 Granting this, I think that James was underrating them; and this for three reasons. (1) The first is that happiness bought at the price of illusion is 'a goodly apple rotten at the heart'. That we set a higher value on truth than perhaps we know may be made clear in an imaginary case. Suppose we had to choose between two futures, in one of which we should be very happy, but our happiness, unknown to ourselves, was based on a set of false views about the nature of things; and suppose the alternative was a future in which we were somewhat less happy, but lived in a world of sober belief that we knew to be true. Which would we elect? I do not think it a forgone conclusion that people generally would choose the world of happiness and illusion. Many would say, I suspect, and perhaps to their own surprise, that happiness bought by delusion was not worth the price.[31]

22(2)   James thinks we may legitimately be moved to believe by thought of the advantages of belief. But is this psychologically possible? Certainly a man cannot say to himself, 'I know that the evidence for this belief is inadequate, and that it may therefore be false, but because the advantages of believing are so great, I hereby resolve to believe'; and when the course is thus baldly described, it is hard to suppose that James would think it either possible or desirable. Yet he is saying something painfully like it, and whatever precisely he meant, it will repay us to consider this view.

We have seen that it *is* possible to control belief in some measure if it is done indirectly and over a period of time. Many persons, when they have become aware that they were moving toward an abyss of scepticism, have met the danger not by going forward and exploring it but by retreating into a tent where the thought of it was taboo; and they have found that if they stayed long enough in that close atmosphere the stirrings of conscious questioning gradually ceased. It is dangerous to cite cases, because one is raising questions here of ultimate sincerity on which no one but the man himself, and probably not even he, can speak with certainty. But in reading Newman's account of his religious development, one can hardly miss his sense of how hard it is to achieve rational certainty of anything, how terrible it would be if his belief should crumble, how important it was to guard against influences that might undermine it. One feels the presence in him, as Mill did in F. D. Maurice, of 'that timidity of conscience, combined with original sensitiveness of temperament, which has so often driven highly gifted men into Romanism from the need of a firmer support than they can find in the independent conclusions of their own judgment.'[32] He seems to have acted in accordance with the advice that his friend John Keble gave to Thomas Arnold when Arnold was troubled with doubts about the Trinity, to 'put down the objections by main force whenever they arise'. In a day when French and German scholars were transforming Christian history and criticism, Newman chose to remain in almost total ignorance of their work and to dwell instead on the controversies of Arius and Athanasius. And he apparently did succeed in putting his conscious doubts behind his back.

I recall a conversation with an able Catholic scientist who seemed to take a similar attitude. I asked him what he would do if he found that a Papal pronouncement, declaring itself authoritative, conflicted with something which, as a scientist, he knew to be fact.

He said he could not accept this even as a possibility. If such a conflict seemed to occur, he would know beforehand either that what he took to be a fact was not a fact or that the terms of the pronouncement had been misunderstood, and if properly construed, would be found true. He was prepared to follow the evidence up to the point at which his leading principle was threatened, but if that principle itself was in question, discussion was clearly futile; his commitment to it seemed to be absolute. Science and official theology *could* not conflict, and evidence purporting to show that they did would be trimmed and pared to any extent necessary to keep that principle intact.

Recent studies have brought to light a somewhat similar position in the mind of Robert Browning. A dark discontent seems to have lain not far beneath the surface of that aggressively confident mind. He had one of the best intellects of his generation, which was in ceaseless buzz-saw activity, and if he had not kept it carefully in hand, it would have torn great pieces out of his creed. Instead he put guards around the creed and repeated firmly, 'I believe, I believe, of course I believe'.

> 'Wholly distrust thy knowledge, then, and trust
> As wholly love allied to ignorance.'

23 Those, then, are right who say that a man, convinced that the consequences of a belief would be disastrous, may by skilful engineering, avert that belief. But can he do it without penalty? I cannot think so. Students of the mind now know far more about the subconscious than even James did; they know that the deliberate repression of some impulses, notoriously that of sex, is likely to produce internal strain and conflict, though the subject may have no inkling of the cause. And it is my own surmise that in the somewhat shrill and metallic ring of Browning's 'I believe, I believe, of course I believe', we can hear the overtones of a repression which is connected with that long winter of his discontent. An active and questioning mind can beat down its questionings, as Keble suggested, by main force, but that is not the end of them. Like sex, if they have never been frankly faced, they do not simply die; they maintain a furtive but tormenting existence underground, which shows itself by alternations of over-vehemence and anxiety.

As for Newman, the question of his ultimate sincerity, as we have owned, is beyond settlement. Of the kind of sincerity which consists in scrupulous fidelity of word to thought he was one of the world's great masters, and I confess that when I read him I feel inclined, as Lytton Strachey evidently did, to forgive him practically anything. But did that complex, uneasy, tormented mind, so fearful of unbelief, so anxious about the security of his own soul, show equally that other sincerity which consists in the fearless pursuit of truth, in never putting aside a question because its answer might be alarming, or a relevant inquiry because it might endanger a dear conviction? As to that, I am less sure; indeed I should not be greatly surprised if the unfortunate Kingsley, supposed for so long to have been routed utterly in the famous exchange, turned out to be substantially right. Newman's sudden unbaring of those merciless claws showed how tender a spot had been touched. Leslie Stephen, who as a cleric turned agnostic had a keen eye for intellectual distempers, thought that Newman was 'simply a sceptic who had backed out of it'.[33]

TRUTH OR CONSEQUENCES

24(3) There is a third comment that must be made about James's doctrine of the will to believe—which ought, as he recognised, to have been called the right to believe. It is an uneasy halting-place; one must withdraw from it or go beyond it. What James said in the famous essay was that consequences might be appealed to when logical evidence failed, on the ground that though one might thereby miss truth one would gain other and greater advantages; on the ground of these advantages we were justified in taking the belief as *true*. Now the only evidence that is relevant to the truth of a belief is evidence that is *logically* relevant, and critics were not slow in pointing out that the advantages of a belief, as opposed to its implications, were *not* logically relevant. James was thus left in the uneasy position of saying that we were justified morally in accepting what we were clearly not justified in accepting logically; I say uneasy because if we know that we are not logically justified, to say that we are morally justified is to warrant an attempt at self-deception. James could escape from this position either by retreating or by going forward. If he retreated, and held that we should equate our assent to the evidence, the point of his essay was lost. If he went on and held that the advantages of the belief were really relevant to its truth, he was embracing a full-fledged pragmatism. What he in fact did was to choose the latter course. The tension between logical and moral justification then ceased, for all the logical *and* practical consequences of a belief were thrown into one big basket and considered alike relevant. Philosophically, the result was disaster.[34]

PASCAL'S GAMBLE

25 James spoke from a Protestant tradition. A Catholic justification of exceeding the evidence, in principle similar to James's, was offered by that remarkable compound of intellect and passion, Pascal. He too held that we cannot evade religious belief, since we we must live either as if such belief were true or as if it were not; and yet neither its truth nor its untruth is capable of rational proof. This was a situation that aroused the interest of Pascal as a mathematician. Could it not be regarded as a matter of chances, as a sort of gambler's risk? Suppose that, on the basis of what you know, the chances are even that the God of Christianity exists and that he does not exist. And suppose, first, you vote No. In that case there are two possibilities. If you are right, and God does not exist, you have the advantage, such as it is, of being correct, though you will presumably never know it. If you are wrong and God does exist, you are open to all the punishments of those who disbelieve. Now suppose, on the other hand, that you vote Yes. Again there are two possibilities. If you are wrong and God does not exist, you have made a mistake, but you have lost virtually nothing. But what if you are right? Then there is all infinity to gain, immortal life and immortal bliss. In short, if you vote No, you have little or nothing to gain, whatever the truth may be, and much to lose, while if you vote Yes, you have an even chance of an infinite gain. Would a man not be a fool who threw such a chance away?

Pascal sees that not all men will find this argument convincing, but suggests that if so, the trouble must come from the non-rational part of their nature, since, simply as argument, the case is irresistible. They should, therefore, take steps to bring themselves round emotionally. 'So you want to achieve belief, and don't know the way? Learn from those who have been bound like you, and who are now staking all they have. . . . Follow the path they started upon, that is, of acting in all things as if they believed, of taking holy water, having masses said, and the rest. That, by a quite natural process, will dull you and make you believe.'[35]

Professor Chevalier describes this 'wager' as 'that famous argument around which modern thought ceaselessly flutters like a moth round a candle', and it is true that we see revealed in it with pathetic clearness the struggle that goes on in the religious mind between the heart and the head, the feelings and desires on the one hand that reach out anxiously for security, and on the other the chill grey inhibiting intellect. Pascal, who on the intellectual side was a sceptic, thought he had found a way of checkmating his own doubt.

Yet most people, when presented with the famous argument, hardly take it seriously. Why? For one thing, because it raises again the questions of intellectual honesty that have been troubling us in James. The question whether we shall gain or lose by believing something is wholly different from the question whether or not it is true, and we cannot solve the second by means of an answer to the first. And if we deliberately decide a question on grounds we know to be irrelevant, we are clearly tampering with our honesty; indeed we are asking ourselves to do something that, if done with open eyes, we could not make ourselves do at all. Is there not a thoroughly cynical note about Pascal's final suggestion that if your mind holds out against the wager the issue can be settled by betaking yourself to masses and holy water, and dulling your wits till belief at last sets in? (His word is to make oneself stupid like a beast.)

26   But this is not all that is at fault in the argument. We feel that there is something very wrong with it on the religious side. It assumes that God is a Grand Inquisitor who hovers over us and demands threateningly that we believe in him even for reasons that are no reasons, and who will punish us relentlessly if we do not. Pascal was ready to believe such things; he was capable of believing that God consigned small children with no wills of their own to eternal damnation. Now if you start with this assumption that God, if he exists, is wicked, or at least what we should call wicked if we dared to, you are bound to take the wager seriously. Dishonesty of mind is of course an evil, but it is not the worst of all evils; an eternity of excruciating torment for oneself and perhaps one's family would presumably be worse. And who could blame a man if, convinced that the world is governed by remorseless cruelty, he tried to coerce himself into believing anything whatever that might win him exemption from such horrors? What is so revolting about the wager is not merely the spirit of cold calculation it urges upon us, but the apparently inevitable logic by which, from a conception of God that has been very commonly held, it deduces the duty of intellectual dishonesty.

There is some comfort, perhaps, in seeing that the logic is not so rigorous after all. If God's standards of good and evil are so profoundly different from our own, how do we know what attitude he would favour on our part, and what he would condemn? Is it not just as conceivable that he would prefer independence or a sturdy defiance to credulity? One cannot cogently start with the notion of God as a being who repudiates our standards of justice and goodness, and then argue to what he approves as if he did hold these standards. Thus there appears in this famous argument not only the evidence of a dark agnosticism, the attribution to God of shocking wickedness, and a recommendation of intellectual dishonesty, but also a radical incoherence of thought.

THE STAKES OF RELIGIOUS BELIEF

27 We have looked at only two proposals for justifying a belief that goes beyond the evidence, but I think we should find the others similarly wanting. The natural conclusion from this line of argument is that belief is the same thing everywhere, and does not have one set of conditions in physics and chemistry and a different set in religion, that the ethics of belief, the meaning of intellectual honesty, is everywhere the same. This, I suggest, is the unavoidable conclusion. Belief should follow the evidence, neither stubbornly denying what it establishes nor impulsively running ahead of it and embracing as true what it does not warrant. When put in this way, probably most religious persons would accept the conclusion. They would, at any rate, draw back from the suggestion that the religious conscience is a coarser and less scrupulous organ than the scientific.

Yet it must be admitted that in the practical difficulties that arise the two fields are hardly comparable. There is little talk in scientific circles of an ethics of belief. Most of the issues of science offer small temptation to our feelings to believe in one way rather than another. Of course when a man is offering a new theory to which he has tied his professional hopes, he is only too likely to overrate the evidence in hand and ignore what makes against his theory. It is said that Newton, as he approached the end of his calculations about gravitation and saw the great law coming nearer, could not trust himself in his excitement and turned over the final calculations to another hand. But here was a theory with tremendous implications, in which he as its discoverer had a personal stake. Most scientific problems might be settled in any one of many ways so far as most of us are concerned; we should find it difficult to work up any sort of passion for or against the binomial theorem or Ohm's law.

The situation as regards religion is different. Whether the world is governed or not by love and wisdom is an issue of large concern to us; whether we shall live again after death is an issue to which no one who loves life and cares for others can be indifferent. The achievement of a positive belief on these points alone may alter the complexion of our world and give us a fresh infusion of buoyancy and hope. It is entirely intelligible that persons who have such beliefs should look with something like moral loathing on those who would introduce into these all-important matters the detachment, the cool appraisal of evidence, the reservations and doubts and hesitancies, of the rationalistic mind.

Even for those with the talent and leisure for inquiry such objectivity is difficult. And for the rest of us, the reply will come, it is out of the question. You cannot ask the plain man to sickly his whole life over with the pale cast of thought. He has no time for these ultimate speculations; he must get on with his work; and what he needs from the philosophers and the theologians is an outlook that will enable him to do that work with a heart and a will. Refinements about going beyond the evidence are all very well for the philosopher who can afford such luxuries, but they are lost on men who barely know what evidence means. Professor Dorothy Emmet asks with point, 'Whoever worshipped a tenable hypothesis or a balance of probabilities?'

28 Every person of common sense must feel the force of this. It seems to present us with an unwelcome dilemma: we must give up either serenity or intellectual honesty, either the peace that goes with confident beliefs on ultimate things or else that saving salt of scepticism that is needed for integrity of mind. Is there any way out?

We should be merely deceiving ourselves if we thought that there was any wholly satisfactory way out. Something valuable must go. St Francis was a great and happy man; so was Socrates; and in giving up the hope either of the childlike faith of St Francis or the questioning spirit of Socrates, we should be losing much. But it is idle to say that we can have them both. Plant Socrates' mind in the soul of St Francis, and the pearly gates and jasper towers would come tumbling down in irreparable ruin. Plant the soul of St Francis in the mind of Socrates, and the world of essence and implication and logical distinction would seem insupportably grey and inhuman. A man may try to be either Francis or Socrates, but if he tries to be both he will assuredly be neither.

One cannot have the blessings at once of an uncritical faith and a critical intelligence. 'But then,' it may be said, 'no one in these days wants an uncritical faith, and there is no reason whatever why if the dogmas of one's faith are true at all a critical intelligence should not disclose their truth and thus confirm one's faith. There is no necessary conflict between faith and reason.' But we have seen in the first two parts of this book that between reason and the sort of faith that is found in two important forms of current religion there is a very extensive conflict. And remembering how much in the way both of peace of mind and of moral direction and sanction are bound up with religious belief, the impatient reader may well ask whether such doubt-provoking inquiries are worth the price.

TRUTH THE COMPASS OF THOUGHT

29 In reply there is one thing that must be said unequivocally. To think is to try to get at the truth, and the person who professes to be doing that will be a dupe if he consciously allows any thought of his own or other people's advantage to affect his conclusions. He will be worse if he does this as a professional philosopher, a person maintained and paid to think as straight as he can on problems of difficulty and to make his conclusions known. Everyone has been repelled by the parlour atheist whose spirit of contradiction is obviously belted to a noisy little dynamo of self-importance within, or the lover of paradox who would rather coin a new epigram than see a new truth. 'An ethical sympathy in an artist', said Oscar Wilde, 'is an unpardonable mannerism'. We are not convinced. Neither are we by those books on apologetics or Christian evidences in which the overwhelming importance of reaching the right and edifying conclusion held the writer's mind in a straitjacket. In my youth I thought Mark Hopkins' *Evidences of Christianity* a great book. When I return to it now I see that Mark Hopkins was so good a man, if one may say so, that it is idle to go to him for the truth; when the ark of salvation was at stake, he could afford to treat the evidence cavalierly, because he knew beforehand what it proved and had to prove. I agree that a man is on a higher level if his intellectual compass habitually veers toward human good than if it veers to party or self-esteem. But as a *thinker* he has no business to let it veer toward any pole but one. Truth lost through noble motives is just as truly lost as if one were deceived by some malicious demon.

SCEPTICISM AND MORALITY

30 It may be said that this somewhat self-righteous line may do for a philosopher, but that before he sows his doubts abroad he may well think what they involve for the great majority of people who lack the way and the will to become philosophers. The whole-hearted acceptance of religious conclusions means much, both emotionally and morally, to numberless people; doubt of these conclusions, to say nothing of their rejection, robs them of their efficacy. 'You destroy what these people find precious, and give them nothing in its place.' There are philosophers today who look down on all such objections from a great height. I do not belong to their party. Agreeing that knowledge is a great good, I think that hope and peace and happiness are great goods also, and I can conceive a situation in which it would be better for mankind to remain in permanent error on some matter of belief if this were the price of happiness than to know the truth and be unhappy. Pedantic and cavilling intellectualists in these matters are, as James thought, bores. But several things need to be said.

First the notion that either men's morality or their happiness is bound up with any set of dogmas about ultimate things seems to me untrue. It is unquestionable that religious belief may affect their motives for right doing in various and potent ways, but to say that apart from such beliefs we should have no ground for discriminating good from evil, right from wrong, is irresponsible. Our knowledge that love is better than hatred, happiness than misery, enlightenment than ignorance, is not an inference from theological premises but an independent insight which may be had with equal clearness by Christian, Buddhist, and secularist. It may be replied that this may be correct in theory but that practical morality is so entwined with belief that the two stand or fall together. But practical morality does not rest on so tremulous a base that in order to keep it standing we must surround it with a veil of illusion as to what it really stands on. No doubt if people have supposed their morals to rest on their theology, they will go through a period of bewilderment if that theology totters. But if they are reflective, they will soon see that morality has a much firmer base than any of the speculative dogmas on which it is supposed to be built. If they are not reflective, they may fly about aimlessly, but thoughtful persons can hardly be asked to keep their candle under a bushel for fear that some human butterflies should singe their wings at it.

31   There is a somewhat similar connection between belief and happiness. Religious dogmas may contribute to happiness; indeed, as McTaggart said, they may 'change the whole aspect of heaven and earth for those who believe in them'. Nevertheless they do not seem to be essential to happiness. People of all faiths have been happy; people of all faiths have been unhappy; it is probable that such things as health and temperament have more to do with happiness than any theological belief. The general presumption must surely be that one's happiness is more secure if it is accompanied by a true apprehension of the nature of things. These premises are perhaps enough for us to go on. If no dogma is essential to happiness, and happiness is more likely with the truth than without it, inquiry into truth need not be inhibited by worry about the consequences of what it may uncover.

THE USE OF AUTHORITY

32   It may be held, again, that if religious beliefs are regarded as justifiable only on evidence, we are asking plain men to settle for themselves questions which the experts have found baffling. This would certainly be unreasonable. Tired farmers and preoccupied business men cannot be saddled with the ultimate problems of the universe. But of course we would not urge that they should. When they are confronted with problems that are too hard for them in science or criticism or politics, they appeal to authority for guidance, and everyone agrees that this is a legitimate course. It is also legitimate in religion. The responsibility of the plain man will then be, not to settle ultimate problems by his own unpractised wit, but to appraise the relative weight of authorities. There is no escaping this responsibility in any field. In science it is carried easily enough, since the first scientist one goes to will probably speak for most or all of his colleagues. In politics it is far more onerous, since among experienced men in public life unanimity is so conspicuously lacking. Still, the acceptance of reponsibility for choosing one's leaders is the very heart of democracy, and unless men can do at least this with some discrimination, the democratic process may as well be abandoned. The acceptance of such responsibility in religion is the point of intersection between democracy and Protestantism. The democratic view in religion, as in politics, is that only if plain men are given the privilege of choosing their guides can they come to choose either their guides or their beliefs responsibly. They have made dreadful mistakes. They will no doubt continue to make them, since in religion as in politics the doctors so notoriously disagree. But freedom comes at no cheaper price.

CERTAINTY AND PROBABILITY

33 Anyone who proposes the same test for religious as for other beliefs is bound to face a further difficulty. Such a test would reduce the status of many beliefs from certitude to probability at best, and must not a religious dogma be held as certain if held at all? Men will die for a dogma, Newman thought, but not for a conclusion, for any process of reasoning may conceivably be mistaken. The essential plea of such theologians is for a dissociation of certitude from certainty. Certainty is what attaches to clear and distinct insight; certitude is the emotion of conviction. It is possible to have full certainty with very little of the emotion of certitude, as in the insights of the mathematician. It is possible to have a high degree of certitude when certainty is wholly absent, as the passionate avowals of a cloudy creed by many a communist and fascist have made clear. But it seems to be true, and if true is very important, that what is efficacious in belief is certitude rather than certainty, for certitude is an emotion. Religious leaders, like political leaders, have therefore sought at times to preserve the efficacy of belief by saving its certitude, even when certainty is impossible. This has brought them painful comparisons and insinuations. If they were to accept our proposed principle of adjusting assent to the evidence, could they accept certitude as a substitute for certainty? No, they could not. Would they have to sacrifice in consequence the practical efficacy of belief? In part, yes. It is not only that certainty, as we have said, lacks the emotional power of certitude, but also that if belief is harnessed to evidence it is unlikely that even grey intellectual certainty will be left on any ultimate issue. And is this not equivalent to abandoning religious belief in its traditional sense altogether?

Again we must admit that in a sense it is. Religion in the West has often encouraged us to believe with a confidence that bore a direct ratio to the difficulty of the matters at issue. It did not greatly care what we believed about the efficacy of medals or holy water, which could in a measure be tested, but demanded unquestioning assent to dogmas of such metaphysical profundity that St Thomas and Leibniz themselves groped their way to them with difficulty. It seems clear that on the standard we are proposing even minds like these, to say nothing of our humble selves, would be vain if they professed certainty. We should of course like to know more; it is our duty to go on trying to know more. But if we know little, it can hardly be a duty to profess that we know much.

34 And is it quite clear that a religious dogma which is less than certain is of no value at all? If so, religious thought is very different from thought in other provinces. It was the sober Bishop Butler who said that probability is the guide of life. There is in fact astonishingly little of which we are certain, yet even so we manage to act. The explorations and adventures that have meant most to man were not made under a banner of certainty; it was hypothesis, consciously held as such, that sent Caesar across the Rubicon, Columbus across the Atlantic, and Churchill into the gathering storm. Action is no less courageous, indeed it is more courageous, if not done with the certainty that the powers ordering the universe are on our side. And there is an exhilaration in trying to find our place in the mysterious universe, in trying to throw back by a few feet or inches the mist that surrounds us on all sides, an exhilaration which in the view of many thoughtful men makes it better to travel hopefully than to arrive.

Further, there are theologians who, starting from James's doctrine of the will to believe, have made a modification which in words amounts to little but which transforms the doctrine ethically. James had said that where an option is live, momentous, and forced, and decision on the evidence impossible, we may adopt the belief that promises best in practice. That means believing on irrelevant evidence, and we have protested. But in such a case to adopt the nobler hypothesis *as* a hypothesis which further living may confirm or disallow has nothing dishonest about it, nor necessarily any shadow of self-deception. If the doctrine that Deity was manifested in the mind and morality of Christ is not vetoed by such evidence as one has, there is nothing in our suggestion to discourage one's accepting it in the sense of adopting it as a major working hypothesis, keeping one's mind open as one uses it, to all that would support it or render it doubtful.

I realise how dreary and negative all this must sound to those whose belief is unquestioning, exuberant, and joyful. To go on questioning to the end! To live on hypotheses and probabilities! What sort of answers are these to people who want a creed to live by? Dusty answers, to be sure. And in cases of great suffering or great loss, they may seem dusty beyond all tolerance. To many, belief tied to evidence seems nothing but a fair-weather craft, and they look with an expectant curiosity to see what happens to it when storms blow up. Sometimes it sinks; 'Lord, I believe; help thou mine unbelief'. But what exactly does this show? It shows that if sufficient pressure is applied some people will believe what they need to believe in order to gain comfort and assurance. It does not prove that these people are more sensitive than others, or nobler than others, or that the beliefs they have found so comforting are the more likely to be true.

One's respect indeed is greater for those who do not break, who appreciate to the end that fact does not order itself with reference to our desires, that recognition of it and resignation to it are the true part for a man. When T. H. Huxley lost his eldest son, he was numb with grief, and a friend whose faith was serene and confident wrote to him wondering how his ethics of belief was faring under the blow. He replied:

'My business is to teach my aspirations to conform themselves to fact, not to try and make facts harmonise with my aspirations. Science seems to me to teach in the highest and strongest manner the great truth which is embodied in the Christian conception of entire surrender to the will of God. Sit down before fact as a little child, be prepared to give up every preconceived notion, follow humbly wherever and to whatever abysses nature leads, or you shall learn nothing.'[36]

A confident belief is a great good if one can come by it honourably. If not, so also is this sort of honesty and courage.

CHAPTER XII

MYTH IN RELIGION

RELIGION AS A THREEFOLD RESPONSE

1 Religion is an attempt to adjust one's nature as a whole to ultimate reality. In a sense all human life is that. But whereas the larger part of such life consists of an adjustment to what is immediately around us, religion seeks to go behind the appearance of things to what is self-subsistent, to something which, intellectually and causally, will explain everything else. And it must be conceived as a response of man's nature as a *whole*. The attempt has often been made, but never with success, to conceive religion more narrowly as the function of some part or faculty of human nature. Some have lodged it in the activity of knowing or thinking. E. B. Tylor described it as 'the belief in spiritual beings';[1] Freud said that 'religion consists of certain dogmas . . . which tell one something that one has not oneself discovered and which claim that one should give them credence';[2] many persons would identify it without further ado with the acceptance of their own creed, and would view with honest astonishment the suggestion that persons who would reject that creed *in toto* might still be thought religious. Others have held religion to be a matter of feeling merely. For Paulsen it lay in feelings of humility and trust; for Schleiermacher it was a feeling of absolute dependence; 'it resigns, at once, all claims on anything that belongs either to science or morality'.[3] For others, again, religion has been primarily a matter of practice, either in the form of ritual observance, as with the ancient Pharisees, or in the form of morality generally. Religion for Kant was the acceptance of duty as the command of a God not rationally knowable; for Matthew Arnold it was 'morality touched with emotion'.

2 None of these conceptions will serve. They all break down for the same reason, namely that what we ordinarily mean by religion, vague as that meaning is, is not to be imprisoned in one side of our nature. Make it simply a matter of knowledge or belief, and one is

434

compelled to say that the professor of theology who can recite and give reasons for all the thirty-nine articles, but happens to be both irreverent and dissolute, is a religious man. Make it a matter of pure feeling, and it crumbles away in one's hands. One can hardly fear, and yet fear nothing; if one trusts or loves, one must have somebody or something for an object; this object must be apprehended, and then thought is obviously involved in addition to feeling. As Dean Inge says about Schleiermacher, ' "Mere dependence" is nonsense, unless there is a known object on which to depend'.[4] If we then go on to make religion an affair of morality solely, common thought and usage again rebel. It is not beyond doubt that Luther was a better man morally than John Stuart Mill, but there would be very little doubt that he was a more religious man; and there is certainly something deserving of a separate name that marks off a St Francis or a George Fox from even the purest of secular saints.

If we may take the old trio of cognition, feeling, and emotion, as covering the field of human faculty, we may say that religion employs all these activities at once and hence engages the whole man. On the cognitive side, the religious man is a philosopher ex officio, whether a competent one or not. Since he is trying to adjust himself to the government of the world, he will inevitably feel some interest in knowing the truth about it, and hence be carried on to form some conception of it. This conception, in turn, will evoke toward its object some attitude of reverence, love, indifference, or fear. Again, if he conceives the world to be governed by a personal being who is wise and good, as Christianity does, he will try to bring his practice into line with what he takes to be the divine will. His religion, then, will not be a function of thought *or* feeling *or* will; it will be the joint activity of all three; it will be the response of the man as a whole to what he takes as ultimately true and ultimately good.

3 If all these factors enter into the essence of religion, we may of course go on to say that they have been involved in it at every period of its history. But they have not been at all times equally prominent. Sometimes the rational element has been in the ascendant, sometimes one or other of the non-rational elements. I have noted in an earlier study[5] the long struggle between reason and feeling for the primacy in moral judgement and the moral life. There has been a somewhat similar struggle between rational and non-rational demands running through the history of Western religion, and the position in which religion finds itself in our day marks the most recent stage of that struggle. We shall not understand this stage unless we know something of its predecessors. But before looking at the steps by which we arrived where we are, may I say in a few words what I see when I look back on the journey as a whole?

Religion at the beginning was no doubt chiefly a matter of impulse and feeling. An intellectual element was present, but it had to work within the medium of imagination, and imagination was the puppet of irrational forces. As reflection began to stir uneasily in the religious consciousness, and to achieve some freedom of movement, it slowly transformed the object of worship in the attempt to accommodate it more fully to the contrary claims of fact and desire. For many centuries after the Christian era its main work continued to lie in this internal transformation, in which, while its own standards were pressing their rights more imperatively, it remained, on the whole, the servant of religious need. It touched its highest point in this service in the thirteenth century with the great attempt of St Thomas to articulate and rationalise the religious view of the world. With the coming of Descartes, reason freed itself from the service of faith, and began to judge theology no longer by standards set by religious desire and need but by standards of its own, now isolated and defined. Since then the older world-view has been slowly disintegrating, and has not yet been succeeded by any philosophic or scientific construction that can take its place. I am convinced that religion has reached a stage where it must either vote its own dissolution or reconstruct itself on an altered pattern. These are large assertions. In my limited space I can hardly hope to render them plausible except to those whose experience has supplied them with favouring predispositions. But let us take a rapid survey and begin at the beginning.

THE ANIMISTIC ORIGIN OF RELIGION

4 It seems to me almost certain that religion sprang in the first instance from animism. Animism is the recognition, at first virtually instinctive, of a spiritual or non-rational agency in physical things. Aristotle thought religion was born of wonder, but if wonder means the raising of questions and the deliberate thinking about them, there is no doubt that animism is far older, older indeed than any explicit thought. There are signs of its presence even in the animal mind. It is difficult to interpret otherwise an experiment which Darwin once carried out upon his dog. He tied a fine thread to a bone, and then from a distance, while the dog was looking at the bone, he pulled it about by this invisible thread. The dog, seeing a 'dead' bone apparently come to life and start doing things by itself, almost went into convulsions of fascinated fear. Here already there

seems to have been a sense of something mysterious and dreadful controlling a familiar object to unknown ends. It is not nature generally that the primitive mind takes as animated; souls peep through only in its interstices, when something happens that calls for special explanation. That water wets or fire burns or round things roll is no puzzle; these things behave as they do because that is their habit, and so long as they go on behaving so, primitive curiosity would not worry its feeble head about them. But when a bone gets up and walks, that is something else. Or suppose a child eats an apple that looks like any other apple, only to writhe and die in pain. Suppose a raging wind arises, beyond anything in memory, and sweeps one's house away. These present themselves not as the workings of nature's habits, but as violent breaches of habit that call for something behind the scenes to account for them. What could this be?

There is only one cause that seems adequate to the effect. The one quite natural explanation is a supernatural one. There is malice here, working its malignant will against us. Children and savages live in an intensely personal world. If the child is fed and dressed, or spanked or put to bed, it is by the will of persons stronger than he; all that is most important in his life issues from these personal wills. What more natural, then, than to think that if a door catches his finger, it has hurt him in spite?—and we find him pommeling it vigorously. It would be putting the case far too intellectually to say that he is using a conscious argument from analogy; the extension of the personal account to 'inanimate' things is not felt as really an extension. An angry person struck and hurt me; an angry dog bit me painfully; an angry wind ripped my house down; there was something evil in that apple that struck at me through my child; as one moves along this line, there is no sense of having passed over from fact to theory, or from perception to inference; implicit inference is accepted as fact throughout. We can now see that none of these is a case of mere perceived fact, that all alike are inferences. The child, of course, does not see or feel his father's annoyance in wielding the slipper; he must reach it by interpretation of what he sees and feels. We should now say that the reading of the signs to mean anger in the parent and the dog is, or may be, correct, while it is pretty certainly incorrect in the cases of the wind and the apple. But that is a later refinement. For the primitive mind, the movement of thought is the same throughout. And that simple instinctive movement is the origin of religion. It is hard to resist Tylor's conclusion that 'animism is, in fact, the groundwork of the Philosophy of Religion, from that of savages up to that of civilised man.'[6]

THE PRIMITIVE IDEA OF THE SOUL

5 When the savage makes this leap behind the scenes, what is it that he takes to be there? The question has been pressed upon him times without number by prying inquirers, armed with pads and pencils. Their unhappy victim squirms and twists; sometimes he is in terror about answering their questions; these matters have dark associations for him, which he does not call up willingly. When he forces himself to answer, the result is disappointing, and yet all that one could rightly expect. To take perhaps the least questionable case, he would say that behind the angry look and blow of the person who struck out at him was a self that aimed the blow. This self is not the man's body but what managed his body, as I now manage my own. But of course his body is all that one sees. And how is a groping mind to think of what eye has not seen nor ear heard? If you press the matter, what comes out is the thought of another more subtle and elusive body—a wraith, a mist, a wisp of vapour, a breath, possessing the likeness of the body we see but without its solid substance. This groping venture into metaphysics gains encouragement from the happy way in which it accounts for other experiences as well, and soon the savage mind begins to feel the satisfaction of a coherent theory and of a new territory won for its understanding. In dreams he sees people who were not there bodily; if their bodies have doubles, ghost-souls that can wander afield, these must be what he saw. And he himself wanders afield in dreaming, while his body, so he is assured, never left its corner; evidently his own soul differs from its body, and can make pilgrimages of its own. There is a widespread courtesy among primitive peoples toward a dreaming man, which would deter them from waking him abruptly lest his soul should not have time to return and adjust itself to its familiar lodging again.

If the soul is thus distinct from the body, we have a convenient theory of death, that most shocking of all vicissitudes. My companion is badly hurt. Yesterday he was talking, laughing, planning exploits with me; today, as his blood ebbs away, he becomes something like a log, only more repellent from being so alien to what it once was. Has not something else ebbed away, that which made him laugh and plan? The spirit in him, his animating breath or soul has gone. But it has not ceased to be. It hovers wistfully for a time about its old haunts; hence the bamboo tubes in the grave, that allow it to go freely out and in, and the doll buried in the woman's arms that the wanderer may still think her child is there. Hence, too, the logic of the strange cruelties that often multiplied the terrors of primitive death—the killing of wives and servants and horses that the soul of the master might be less forlorn in its new land through the attend-ance of familiar shades. And what is the new land like? Not un-naturally, primitive thought on this head is as vague as it is reluctant. It is a shadowy land, where shades continue to live, but live the impotent life of shadows. The king of Babylon is assured by the writer of Isaiah that when he arrives in Sheol, 'All they shall speak and say unto thee, Art thou also become weak as we?'[7] and the Preacher exhorts us to do with our might what our hands now find to do, 'for there is no work, nor device, nor knowledge, nor wisdom, in Sheol, whither thou goest'.[8] When one finds Odysseus in Homer visiting a Greek replica of the Hebrew Sheol and conversing with shades that flitted about inconsequently and talked in barely audible voices, we may wonder at the closeness of the parallel in two cultures that hardly touched each other. But the point is that mutual influence, even if it occurred, would not be needed to account for the parallel. The common logic of the primitive mind is enough, and no doubt a diligent searcher could find parallels the world over.

THE BIRTH OF MYTHOLOGY

6 The next step is myth.[9] In mythology, animism escapes into freedom of imaginative play. The animist says that when echoes come across the glen somebody is there and answering; the myth-maker says that the 'somebody' is a tribe of little hill people, merry dwarfs, who find glee in mocking us, and who came there in such and such wise. The animist says that if it thunders and lightens, a mighty being is angry with us. The myth-maker is not content. He accepts the suggestion, but embroiders it imaginatively. He says that this is the heaven-god Indra, who shoots great gleaming arrows with his rainbow and hurls his bolts at the sky-dragons, the clouds; or it is Thor laying about him in a rage with his mighty hammer. The animist thinks vaguely of sun and moon as personal powers. To the weaver of myths they are man and wife, or brother and sister, Apollo driving his blazing chariot across the sky and Artemis keeping state in her silver chair; and then since each must have a character, and ancestors, and designs, and adventures, each becomes the root of an exuberant flowering of legend. The general pattern of these legends bears a striking similarity as one passes from people to people. The most arresting aspects of nature and the most important epochs of experience are largely the same for all men. Sun, moon, and stars, the coming of the mysterious night, the winds that are sometimes wanton and sometimes angry, the new life in the spring, the minds of animals, so near to us and yet so far away, human birth and death, and the crises that, for all alike, lie between them of inexplicable luck, untoward accident, and the blight of sickness and pain—it is inevitable that when men set themselves to muse about these things their fancy should spin webs of similar patterns. The fables on which we have been brought up are drawn from three or four peoples, the Greeks, the Romans, the Hebrews, and perhaps also the Teutons. But there are vast masses of more or less parallel legends awaiting us if we care to explore the records of the red Indians and the Mexicans, the Chinese, the Zulus, and the Persians.

What is important to us about these records is not, of course, their diversities, not even their identities, if that means similarities of story. What we are interested in is their character as exhibiting one stage in the advance of reason in religion. And from this point of view there are three things to note about the making of these myths. (a) Although it is a telling of stories, it is an exercise in reason. (b) At the same time, its satisfactions and its sources of control lie as much in sensibility and desire as in intelligence. The result is (c) that we have in myth an extremely viable hybrid, a weed so hardy that to root it out one would almost have to uproot religion itself.

MYTH AS INCIPIENT SCIENCE

7(a) The reason that was at work in animism extends its operations in myth. We have seen that the child who pummels the door and the savage who cringes before the angry thunder are seizing on the best, and indeed the only, explanation open to an unreflective mind. They are explaining through analogy with the kind of causation they know best, which is that of their own will. But there is nothing like explicit reasoning in the process; they are not theorising; speculation is so firmly captive within perception that the anger and the thunder are taken alike as perceived facts. On the other hand, myth is conscious theory. The explanation is still in personal terms, but there is no pretence that the glorious Apollo and the queenly Artemis are facts before one's eyes; they are rather what the fact requires if we dwell on them wonderingly. They eke out the fragmentariness of nature as we see it, fill in the interstices, supply stage and setting for otherwise disconnected events, and so make them parts of a single intelligible drama. In myth the mind has broken loose from the tied ideas of perception, and, with the achievement of free ideas, can range at will from the creation of drama to the final fall of the curtain.

It is true that free ideas need not be abstract ideas. The notion of law, the conception that each event, or rather each element in each event, is connected with some element in an earlier event by an abstract unchanging thread of causation, is still far in the future;

and if this is science, myth is not. Yet myth quite obviously is incipient science; for it is an attempt, however stumbling and blundering, to construe the constitution of things and to shape, in the mind's eye, the fashion of their coming to be. Incapable as yet of analysis, the primitive mind explains in terms of wholes—not of qualities and relations, but of things, actions, and persons—as children do. And some of its shots in the grey dawn reach their mark. To say that night comes because Apollo plunges with his steeds and his flaming chariot down under the earth and drives them from west to east is, to be sure, to fire a blunderbuss at nature; and, from the point of view of a modern astronomer, most of one's shot has gone wild. But embedded in the legend, after all, is the truth that night *is* caused by the sun's travelling, relatively to us, under the earth and in a direction opposite to its daytime journey. If primitive man has to shoot a whole covey of ducks to get the one he wanted, that is no reason for denying either that he was trying for a particular duck or that he did in fact bring it down.

Of course, to say that myth was aiming explicitly at scientific explanation would be absurd. One cannot aim at what is yet invisible. In the primitive mind there is no clear line between what is perceived and what is read into perception, between the relevant and the irrelevant, between impersonal thinking and the sort of thinking Bacon described as 'drenched in the affection'. Its reasoning is association, its causes are powers, and its powers are ultimately wills. The scientific end has not yet detached and defined itself as against all the other ends that are working in conjunction with it. Nevertheless it is there, confused and distorted often by the imaginative medium in which it has to move, but very much alive. The myth is the first large-scale attempt of an understanding still in fetters to make sense of its world. The fact that it is so plainly the parent of literature and religion should not blind us to the fact that it is only a little less plainly the grandparent of philosophy and science.

THE MANIFOLD OFFICES OF MYTH

8(b)   Still, the impulse that makes myth is not in the main intellectual. It is that, to be sure, but it is a great deal more, and for the primitive mind this 'more' is what chiefly counts. As the joint contrivance of many impulses, the myth must satisfy all its artificers if it is fully to pass muster. And since, when myth emerges, intellect is without discipline and its requirements are loose, the non-rational requirements are the really decisive ones. We have agreed that the tale is a theory; and, as such, it must fit the facts in a way that experience renders plausible; the thunder must genuinely seem like a tremendous hammer pounding on the floors of heaven. To Eskimos who find with atonishment that they can rub sparks from the coat of a reindeer, the notion is not incredible that in the far regions from which the northern lights are rising there is a great herd of celestial reindeer rubbing their furry coats together. But one need only consider such a myth to see how feeble and easily satisfied the intellectual demand must be and how much more important is congeniality to feeling and imagination. Press such a myth ever so gently on the factual side and it collapses ignominiously like a pricked bubble. If it survives, this is not because it has passed intellectual criticism, which is non-existent, but because, again like the bubble, it is pretty to look at, a satisfying picture to dwell on.

So of myths generally. They are less theories than works of primitive art. In this they are like ballads. It is far more important to their survival that they should be dramatically satisfying, that they tell a tale of thrilling prowess like that of Theseus and the Minotaur, or mighty strength like that of Hercules and his twelve labours, or 'capable and wide revenge' like that of Odysseus and the suitors, than that they should be true. What the qualities are that make myths satisfactory will vary with the aesthetic perceptiveness, the cheerful or melancholy temper, and the practical ideals of the people who create them. The gods of sunny Olympus would hardly have been satisfactory deities for the Hebrews in their flight from Egypt or in their Babylonian captivity. The uproarious banquets of Valhalla, with their gargantuan haunches of venison and their undrainable goblets of wine would probably have held small appeal for the people of India, not because they were less true than the tales of Vishnu and Varuna but because they would not answer to the gentler and less boisterous Indian desire. The figures drawn upon the clouds are projections, with suitable amendments, of the self. As Montesquieu put it, 'Si les triangles faisaient un Dieu, ils lui donneraient trois côtés'.

WHAT MAKES A MYTH LIVE

9(c)   Here already within the myth we see the seeds of that conflict between reason and desire that is to run through the later history of religion. All that was needed to produce scepticism in the mind of the myth-maker was an independent theoretical interest. What this means in practice is the appearance of some man who recognises the autonomy of the intellectual life, the distinctness of the desire to know, who goes on asking why, and declines to be put off with congeniality to feeling as an answer to his question. Socrates was a man of this sort. He is alleged to have held that if you looked at the

sun through the glare-proof glasses of fact you would see that it was
not the chariot of Phoebus Apollo but more probably a great hot
stone. His fellows rightly sensed in him a danger to their whole
scheme of things; such a spirit is the death of mythology; and they
saved themselves for a time by doing away with him. The inertia
of the human mind in regard to the system of ideas in which it has
been brought up is notorious, and suggests that the poet was perhaps
right who called the love of truth the faintest of human passions.
Men can continue to live quite placidly in a framework that would
dissolve if touched by the faintest breath of critical reflection. They
can entertain both sides of a contradiction without a qualm. It is
reported that in some parts of China where eclipses have long been
predicted with accuracy there persists side by side with this scientific
knowledge the belief that a great monster is making an attack on the
sun; the announcements of an eclipse serve only to warn the people
to get ready the bells and gongs with which to scare the monster
away.

Nor need we go so far as China to find our illustrations. The peace
is still deeper before science has begun to stir in the womb of myth.
Since there is neither science nor rational history, imagination can
play unhampered. The desire for fact and explanation are there, as
we have seen, but it has developed no secure test for telling fact from
fancy or a coherent hypothesis from a story that imaginatively hangs
together. A man among ourselves who had no sense of the line where
facts end and pleasing fancy begins, who believed quite unsuspect-
ingly that horse-hairs turn into worms and men at times into were-
wolves, that in certain insalubrious places it rained toads, that crops
might be ruined by an evil eye, or favour incurred in heaven by
kissing the toe of a statue, would be thought, and justly, either to be
mentally subnormal or to be living on an island in the modern
world. What is the use, we ask impatiently, of all the techniques
which logic has developed to distinguish proof from guess, which
history has developed to distinguish fact from fiction, which science
has developed to distinguish the probable from the improbable, if
people are to go on swallowing these childish things whole?

Our impatience would be justified. But of a child himself we
cannot ask that he should be other than childish, and we cannot
sensibly ask it of the childhood of the world. To understand the
very young mind we must put ourselves a long way back in individual
or racial life, before prose and poetry parted company. What is
Santa Klaus for a child? Is he fact or fancy? Is he a fat jolly old man
in red who actually comes down the chimney with a pack on his
back, or is he a picture that young eyes can dwell on with delight
and grow large and round in contemplating? There is only one

answer; he is both. For the child, neither part of the answer gets in the way of the other. The world of imagination in which he lives is not poetry, for the poet knows well enough that he is improvising, and that the test of what he makes is whether it satisfies. But neither is it knowledge, for it may be false, which knowledge cannot be. The child's imagination is antecedent to these distinctions. It provides him with fact that is still malleable like poetry, truth that can be pulled about by one's heartstrings like a puppet.

So of myth. It was made by the man as a whole, and it will answer only to the whole of him. Its plausibility, its being a good round tale that appeases our wonder and our admiration, its picturesque and exciting and dramatic satisfactoriness—these *are* its truth for mythology. Robin Hood and his merry men, St George and the dragon, Jonah and the great fish, the siege of Troy, Atlas holding up the world—who is to say that these are false? Did the Creator first make night and day, and then later hang the sun, moon, and stars in their places? Did he make first the waters and then produce the dry land out of the waters? Anyone who knows the rudiments of astronomy or geology knows he did not. Genesis says he did. But when Genesis was written, astronomy and geology were still themselves of the household of myth, and you cannot set a myth to catch a myth. What could history be except mythology when there was no science and no written records? In every part of the world men were musing on how things might have come about, and dozens of accounts were hazarded, two of them in Genesis itself. All of them had their points. None of them could be checked or therefore dismissed. If they told an attractive story and became current, they were forthwith elected as history.

Many factors have been stressed in accounting for myths. Euhemerus stressed their origin from the lives of actual beings, Max Muller from the metaphors that are so plentifully embedded in language, Andrew Lang from abnormal events that would now be given over to the psychical researchers, Robertson Smith from ritual. Myths that some students regard as virtually made out of whole cloth others regard as roughly historical records. We shall not follow these controversies. For however myths came to be, there can be little doubt how they came to be accepted. And because what commended them to general acceptance had very little to do with their truth, the question of their origin is, for our purposes, hardly worth pursuing. Even if originally true, they would be forgotten or revised if they did not suit the taste of those who later rehearsed them, and their falsity would not prevent their retention if they clothed things in desirable guise. The point to insist on is that they were versions of what might have happened, taken in all innocence

as what did happen, that they offer us poetry and reason fused into
an imagination that follows rules of its own.

Is this now all gone, like an insubstantial pageant faded? Not
wholly. Myth is unconscionably long in dying. Millions are trying
to live still among its melting cloud-castles. Perhaps all of us keep
a few sheds and outhouses among the ruins that we like to regard as
of firmer stuff than the structures that proved so nebulous when the
winds set in from scientific regions. But it is obvious that critical
minds could not live permanently among these illusions. How did
they effect their escape?

THE MYTHOLOGY OF THE HEBREWS

10 They did so by various routes. By far the most interesting and
important of these routes for Western religion is the road taken by
the Hebrews, and it will repay us to follow it in some detail. It lay
through the moralisation of mythology. The Hebrews in our first
records of them were very much like the tribes around them. Their
cultural world was constantly being penetrated by the superstitions
and practices of the Moabites and Philistines to the east and west of
them and the Phoenicians and Edomites to the north and south;
since their little land lay at a crossroads between several great
empires, it was successively overrun by the armies, and to some
extent the ideas, of Egypt, Assyria, Babylonia, and Persia. They had
their own tribal god, Yahweh, but they knew that neighbouring
nations, often stronger and more cultivated than themselves, had
other gods, and the heads of their two little kingdoms had to fight
a perpetual battle against the vagrant impulses of the people to bow
down to Baal and'Astarte.

These alien loyalties often went far; some parents adopted a
widespread practice of the early Semites of which gruesome evidence
has been found beneath the ruins of Carthage, and offered their
first-born child as a sacrifice to the god. We have seen that the
legend of Abraham and Isaac, which Kierkegaard dwelt on with
such enthusiasm, was probably a relic of human sacrifice. The
Israelites at times called their own god Baal; one of their kings,
Ahab, after marrying a worshipper of Baal, Jezebel, erected a
separate temple in honour of his wife's god, while retaining his own
worship of Yahweh. There was a general belief in spirits inhabiting
wells, caves, and mountain tops, and after the Hebrews had made
contact during their exile with the hierarchy of spirits worshipped
by the Babylonians, this belief flowered out into the acceptance of
armies of angels. Again, the character of Satan, as known in later

Hebrew and Christian tradition, would seem to be largely the result of absorption, during the captivity, of the Persian notion of Ahriman, the evil spirit who is in perpetual battle with Ormuzd, the god of goodness and light. The belief in a resurrection, with future rewards, and punishment, which was no part of the earlier Hebrew world-view, may have come from the same source.

What the religion of the primitive Hebrews was like it is hard to make out with certainty, for much of it as it presents itself to us in the earlier books of the Old Testament is the retrospective product of those years in Babylon that split the pre-Christian history of Hebraism approximately in half. When Nebuchadnezzar destroyed Jerusalem in 597 BC, he carried off with him to Babylon the flower of the Hebrew people and established them in a separate community. Here their historians, with the help of such records as they could bring with them, set about refashioning in imagination the Hebrew past, and it is to their work that we owe much of that great mass of legend with which Western man is so familiar, such as the stories of Adam and Eve, of Noah and the ark, of Lot and the pillar of salt, of Moses and the pillar of fire; of the mighty Samson and the jaw-bone, of Joshua and his ally, the sun; indeed the whole early history of the Hebrews in its present form seems to be the product of this time of brooding. Piety and patriotism combined to people the great days with a set of figures more intimately human even than those of the Iliad and the Odyssey.

Now this mythology was in many respects extremely crude. Yahweh was a tribal deity, jealous, irascible, and cruel. He demanded incessant sacrifices as the price of his continued favour; he approved and commanded such barbarities as Samuel's hewing of Agag in pieces before his altar, Saul's destruction of the Amalekites, man, woman, and child, and Elijah's slaughter of the four hundred and fifty priests of Baal. The worship accorded by the Hebrews to their savage deity was frankly utilitarian; he had made a covenant with them that he would carry them through to prosperity and victory if they would propitiate him duly, and if they kept the covenant, it was less because they were moral idealists than because they wanted the promised fruits. But, to put it baldly, a tribal deity that undertook to challenge the powerful imperial deities round about was facing fearful odds, and here at least the gods seem to have been on the side of the heavier battalions. The Assyrians under Tiglath-Pileser and Sargon came down like a wolf on the fold and the ten tribes of Israel disappeared forever; a century or so later Nebuchadnezzar at the head of a Babylonian army repeated the performance in Judah and destroyed Jerusalem. What were the devotees of Yahweh to conclude?

MYTH AS EDITED BY MORALITY

11 There were two possible explanations of what had happened, one obvious, the other more subtle. The more obvious was that the tribal deity was himself a broken reed, that the defeat of his people revealed him as no match for the powerful deities that had brought ruin on his chosen people. Many of the Hebrews did in fact draw this conclusion and go over to the gods of their conquerors. The other and more subtle interpretation was offered by the prophets. It was not the weakness of Yahweh, they insisted, that had allowed his people to be overthrown, but rather his anger and desire to punish them. His people had broken their side of the covenant; they had foolishly mistaken his will; they had supposed that what he wanted was the smoke of sacrifice whereas it was really a clean heart and conformity to an appointed way of life. The demand of the Ten Commandments was not primarily for rites and observances but for morality. It seems probable that the delivery of these commandments to Moses on Sinai was itself a tale of the prophetic historians who, in the brooding days of the exile, partly edited and partly fabricated the national history in the interest of two ends that were not then clearly distinguished, edification and truth. Looking back, they could see that while the people had remained loyal and obedient even the might of Egypt had not prevailed against them. It was pride that went before their destruction, a haughty and rebellious spirit that preceded, and no doubt caused, their fall. Let the people only keep the commandments of Yahweh, and he would turn from his anger and still carry them to lordship over the whole earth.

When, after sixty years of exile, those who wanted to return to the homeland—and there were many who did not—were allowed to make the long march back across the desert to the mound of ruins that was Jerusalem, they had to start from the beginning and build anew. They were resolved that this time they would make no mistake. What they did was to build a theocracy, a community dominated by religion from top to bottom. Their high priest was their only king, his associates in the priesthood were the aristocracy, and the life of the people was regulated as completely as practicable by the minute requirements of a code. This was not what the prophets had asked for. But their gospel of individualist inwardness seemed beyond the bounds of ordinary human nature, while a carefully planned programme of prayers and observances could, with due effort, be carried out. Could Yahweh ask for more? Here was a whole community centring its life in his temple, ordering its daily walk in accordance with his code. Surely here was the obedience that would at last bring triumph. Did the triumph come? On the contrary, what followed was disaster, utter and appalling. The brutal Persian soldiery under Artaxerxes III stormed into Jerusalem, ripped off the ornaments of the temple, burnt it to the ground, destroyed the synagogues throughout the country, and strewed the streets of the capital with the bodies of the religious aristocracy.

The official philosophy had again conspicuously failed. The perplexities of the surviving remnant found eloquent expression in the drama of Job. Many gave up once for all the old allegiance to Yahweh. But there was a core of unyielding loyalists whose position was 'Though he slay me, yet will I trust him'. It was still they who were at fault, they confessed, not their god. They had been wrong in seeking victory or strength, wrong in prizing material goods at all. Yahweh could at any time have ushered in the new kingdom in which all men would bow the knee to his chosen people, but he had deliberately seen fit to do otherwise; his will lay elsewhere; only too probably this sort of kingdom would never come. We must not ask him to conform his ways, which are so plainly not our ways, to our uninstructed wants. He will not desert us in the end; we shall receive in his good time a full measure of justice, pressed down and running over, though we may, in his wisdom, have to wait for it till this time of probation is over. For the present we must accept the hard truth that whom he loveth he chasteneth, that his kingdom is a spiritual kingdom, in which the desires of the world and the flesh can have no part, and where his will, not ours, must be done. We must accept our lot and call it good through faith that its giver is good. 'Thus,' says Santayana, 'the prophet's doctrine that not prosperity absolutely and unconditionally, but prosperity merited by virtue, was the portion of God's people changed by insensible gradations to an ascetic belief that prosperity was altogether alien to virtue and that a believer's true happiness would be such as St Francis paints it: upon some blustering winter's night, after a long journey, to have the convent door shut in one's face with many muttered threats and curses.'[10]

In the thousand years or so between the time of Moses and the time of Christ the Hebrews had travelled far. Starting as a horde of nomads with a tribal god for whose protection they bargained their best rams and bullocks, they developed, with the help of their pagan neighbours, a full-fledged mythology, with detailed accounts of the creation of the world and of the origin of their people, and with an extensive pantheon of divinely guided heroes, captains, and law-givers. The chief concern of their god and his earthly lieutenants was to see that Israel prospered and that its enemies were scattered. The actual history of the people was one of almost unendurable hardship and of defeat continually repeated. For a small Oriental tribe there was nothing unusual in such a history. What was unusual about the Hebrews was the way they took it. It led not to the abandonment of their mythical theology but to its progressive moralisation. First there was the message of the prophets that misfortune was the punishment of sin, and that Yahweh was a god of righteousness whose favours would not be given except to the clean of heart. Then there was the message of Job that even the clean of heart cannot present commands to their god to stand and deliver, that his wisdom and justice are beyond the bounds of man's understanding, and that they must utterly humble their pride when they come before him. This development seems to have occurred nowhere else in ancient religion. From our point of view it was supremely important, since it paved the way for Christianity.

CHRISTIANITY AND THE LIBERATION OF MORALITY FROM MYTH

12 Jesus stood in the direct line of the prophets. His great work was to sound the note of inwardness in its purity, to disengage the prophetic teaching from its entanglements with worldly advantage, to free the humility of Job from its humiliation, and to make the spiritual life one of liberty rather than of Pharisaical conformity to law. Much of what he said had been said already by the prophets and psalmists whose words he had by heart. They had insisted, as he now did, on compassion and purity in the inward parts. But as a rule, in the back of their minds was the notion that this was the price demanded by Yahweh for sparing his children the rod and for supporting them in their pursuit of prosperity and pre-eminence. For Jesus it was irrelevant whether these perquisites were attached or not. Love alone really counted. If a man had that, it was of no consequence whether he was as rich as Dives or as poor as Lazarus; indeed if he had a choice, he might better be Lazarus, since it was hard for a rich man not to be over-involved with what he owned. On the other hand, if he did not have a loving spirit, he had really lost his own soul, and for that nothing could compensate, not even the gaining of the whole world. Again, in Jesus' attitude there was nothing of the muted faith of Job. Except for some tragic moments at the end, his attitude seems to have been not that of sad and puzzled submission to an inscrutable will but the happy unquestioning confidence of a child that its love is reciprocated, that every sparrow is cared for and every hair numbered.

Just as his love of man was free from utilitarian design, so his love of God was free from speculative perplexity. It was a lyric and childlike love that felt a response in kind from the heart of the world. Such a love did not need to be regulated by priestly ordinances. It was already the source and the end of such ordinances, and hence could afford to be a law unto itself. Rules about fasts and dress and the Sabbath were useful for keeping us in order so long as we had no inner principle of guidance, but once we had achieved that principle, to go on obeying them mechanically was to put ourselves in a straitjacket; rules were made for man, not man for rules.

13 Here was an amazing approach to morals without mythology. The central positions of the Christian ethics, that love and humility and compassion and forbearance are better than their opposites, and that an outward life that reflected them would be a heaven on earth, are not derived from speculations, verifiable or otherwise, about the ultimate nature of things, nor are they refutable by any theological considerations; they form a set of insights and inductions based directly on experience. They are propositions that could be understood and appraised by any sensitive person, whether he had the theological convictions of a Hebrew, a Greek, or a Hindu, or no theology at all.

This is not to say that as they presented themselves to the mind of Jesus they had no involvements with theology. We have seen that they did. Jesus seems to have accepted unquestioningly most of the local framework of belief. He accepted the existence of a personal devil, and of demons who could get control of men's minds and bodies; he presumably credited as historic truth the generally received stories about the creation and the fall, the flood and the tablets on Sinai; he evidently believed in Jewish prophecies about the coming of a Messiah who would save his people; and there are apparently authentic passages that predict the end of human history, with the coming of a divine judge, before a generation has passed away. How he conceived of his own place in this framework of belief will always remain uncertain. There is no doubt of his having conceived of a 'Father in Heaven' in whom he maintained a filial and unquestioning trust. But the whole cast of his mind was opposed to the precise conceptual elaborations by which a Greek thinker would have attempted to define his relation to God. The probability, as Renan maintained, is that his conviction as to his nature and destiny underwent great change; it seems to have been only gradually that he came to think of himself as the Messiah foretold by the prophets, who would shortly return to deliver and judge his people. That these convictions should affect his teaching about the conduct of life was inevitable. He could hardly give the same counsels about providing for the support of one's children, for example, or about laying political plans, if all human affairs were to be wound up within a generation, as he would if they were to last indefinitely. St Paul seems to have interpreted his teaching against a background of such expectancy: 'the time is short; let those who have wives be as though they had none.' And there have been scholars, as we have seen, who would dismiss the whole ethics of Jesus as an *Interimsethik* whose validity disappears when its theological framework is discarded.

MORALS AS THE SHIFTING BASE OF THEOLOGY

14 This clearly goes too far. It fails to catch the true direction of Jesus' thought. His commendations of brotherliness and humility, his denunciations of cruelty and hypocrisy, were not deductions from a theory of the nature or will of God, or from what God required for one's inclusion among the sheep rather than the goats at an imminent assize. The trend of his thought was probably the other way about. 'The moment Jesus speaks,' says Matthew Arnold, 'the metaphysical apparatus falls away, the simple intuition takes its place; and wherever in the discourse of Jesus the metaphysical apparatus is intruded, it jars with the context. . . .'[11] He was passionately committed to certain great goods—sincerity, sympathy, affection, peaceableness, docility of temper; he was passionately opposed to certain other states of mind as poison of the spirit—anger, hatred, hypocrisy, mammon-worship, fear. Starting from these devotions and antipathies, or, if one prefers, these moral insights, he conceived God in terms of them. That is what all the prophets had done before him. As their own conceptions of good and evil were pruned and purified, they reshaped their notion of Deity in accordance with them.

Where, indeed, but from their own moral experience could they draw the means of such reshaping? One can hardly answer 'from revelation'. For if one accepts the old canonical books as conveying revelation, the character of God there revealed is hopelessly inconsistent with that disclosed by Jesus; the God who ordered the extermination of the Amalekites is remote from the God of the New Testament. On the other hand, if one regards the disclosures of Jesus as alone revealed, one is still in trouble. For the awkward fact remains that while he corrected these earlier revelations he seems to have accepted them as genuine. The natural suggestion of these facts is surely the relativity of revelation to the capacity of the receiver. One of the principal values of the long Scriptural record is the documentary evidence it offers of the way religious advance followed ethical clarification. Take what the Biblical record says of God as inspired throughout, and nothing but palpable sophistry can put its reports together into a coherent whole. Take that record as the projection into the ultimate of men's changing conception of the ideal, and the story makes sense.

THE AUTONOMY OF CHRISTIAN INSIGHT

15 If we are not mistaken, then, the inner movement of Jesus' thought, whatever the outward form of his teaching, was not from God to man but from the assured perception of what was good on earth to the conviction of what must be God's will. His true greatness lay in the greatness of his spirit, not in the fantastic eschatology, the bizaare metaphysics, and the suggestions of thaumaturgy with which tradition has surrounded him, and which, since he shared inevitably the conceptions of his time, did in some measure invade his thought. He caught a glimpse of what human life might be if perfected in its inward temper. It was an exquisite and moving vision and his own embodiment of it in practice greatly strengthened its appeal. This vision constituted an immense moral advance. Its acceptance would have transformed the course of history; indeed it did so, even in the altered form in which it survived.

I have admitted it to be defective. The claim that it presents a rounded, infallible, and final portrait of the ideal life for man will not stand rational scrutiny; the attempt to derive from it the sort of recognition of science, art, philosophy, economic and physical well-being, and legal and ethical justice that, after twenty centuries of experience and rational reflection, we must accord them smacks of special pleading.

But granting all this, granting that the insights of Jesus did not cover all human values, and that they come to us half buried in a primitive Eastern mythology, the ethical gold of his insight was none the less pure gold because embedded in this crude ore. One cannot read the fragmentary accounts of him that remain to us, with their obvious innocence as to where fact ends and fabrication begins in either science or history, and their continual resultant distortions, without astonishment at the figure uncertainly seen through them. The other great founder of Western ethics, Socrates, has been handed down to us by a writer who knew the master intimately, understood him thoroughly and, in all the arts of presentation, was greater than the master himself. The figure and teaching of Jesus come to us through a set of writers whose identity is most doubtful, who may in no case have known him personally, who compiled their work a generation or two after his death from conflicting records and traditions, and who had only rudimentary notions of either scientific or historical fact. Yet all this only increases the fascination that surrounds the person of Jesus. Here, beyond the possibility of creation or concealment by these compilers, was a figure who was not only the supreme poet of the moral life but an ethical teacher whose insights all men could verify as, in the main, true.

THE LOST OPPORTUNITY OF THE WEST

16 Rationality calls for adherence to such verifiable truth, and its separation from the unverifiable. It is not at war with imagination; it has no wish to expel myth or metaphor; it only asks that these things be not confused with truth and substituted for it, and it asks this on the ground that such confusion leads to a superstitious cosmology and a perverted morals. In the generations following the Sermon on the Mount, the Western mind had an extraordinary opportunity. In centres like Antioch and Alexandria, the currents of Christian and Aristotelian teaching flowed together and intermingled. The ethical teaching of Aristotle was sane, naturalistic, and civilised; it had emancipated itself once for all from mythology and achieved the fundamental insight of a rationalist ethic that the good life for society is what fulfils harmoniously the human nature of its members. But it was uninspired and unimaginative, and in its Greek preoccupation with the ends of conduct was unduly insensitive to the springs of action from which conduct emerges. The genius of Christianity, on the other hand, lay precisely in the delicacy with which it discerned those springs of action, and felt their moral import. But Christianity, unlike Greek naturalism, arose in an Oriental setting, where imaginative congeniality was still confused with truth, and where the stream of ethical thought, even at its clearest, carried the debris of centuries of myth.

Each ethic sorely needed the other. The Greek needed the Christian inwardness and sense of sin; the Christian needed the Greek reflectiveness and freedom from illusion. How different the course of history might have been if, in the critical years, some moral genius had arisen to effect the rational junction of the two great streams! There might have been no Catholicism, no Holy Roman Empire, no holocausts for heresy, no wars of religion, no Reformation or Counter-Reformation. Morality, taught as the obvious requirement of sense and sanity, might have been detached altogether from supernatural imperatives and terrors. Whether a morality thus freed from all that was adventitious to it could have secured the allegiance in practice that Romanised Christianity did is a question beyond solution.

RETURN OF THE CHURCH FATHERS TO MYTHOLOGY

17 In any case, what we did in fact get was something extremely different. We got the church fathers. Instead of an eclectic genius who could fuse what was rational on both sides into a stable amalgam, we got St Paul and Origen, Irenaeus and Tertullian, Justin Martyr and Jerome, Arius and Athanasius, and that inexhaustible factory of dogma and fantasy, Augustine. What did they do? Instead of freeing the moral teaching of Jesus from the mythology that had enveloped it, they ossified this mythology in a quasi-rational system. Apologists rather than inquirers, they took over the Hebrew legends *en masse*, accepting without question that the Deity had been hovering over this chosen people since the creation, legislating for them, admonishing them, halting the sun over Gibeon till they completed their massacre of the Amorites, sweeping Elijah to Heaven in a chariot of fire, healing the leprosy of Naaman, stretching the lives of favoured patriarchs into centuries.

Where in this gorgeous tapesty of legend were the fathers to place its culminating figure? What were they to say of Jesus? He had spoken, they were sure, as never man spoke. Contemplating him from within an Oriental tradition, they dealt with him in the way that had become natural to the Oriental mind. If an ethically exalted spirit appeared, no explanation would satisfy that mind but an environment of signs and wonders commensurate with his moral stature. So these devoted weavers and spinners went to work upon their prophet. Anyone who has looked into the history of dogma knows the result. We have the gradual accumulation in stratum after stratum and century after century of what can only be called a new mythology, austerely intellectualised and closely articulated, in which the exquisite figure of Jesus is buried almost irrecoverably in a kind of primitive metaphysics. Even when Greek thought took a hand in the interpretation, as it conspicuously did in the fourth gospel and in Origen, it worked in fetters; John does not offer a rational appraisal of Christian teaching, but the translation of an antecedently accepted theology into terms familiar to Greek readers. When men like the church fathers, ingenious, fertile, and not seldom fanatical, fascinated by the figure of Jesus but unhampered by any canons of science or scientific history, let themselves go about him, the crop of theories was prodigious; and many of these theories hardened rapidly into dogmas.

In the course of a few centuries the prophet of Nazareth, with his gospel that we should become as little children, reappeared as the uncreated and eternal second person in the Trinity, who was mysteriously incarnated without original sin, whose death was a

ransom paid, as some doctors maintained, to Satan, and others to the
first person of the Trinity to forestall the damnation of the race for
the sins of its ancestors. The problem of the union within one person
of an omnipotent, omniscient, and perfect Deity with a struggling
human nature that grew from boyhood to manhood, and that in its
manhood confessed ignorance and was tempted like as we are,
produced a spate of tortured theories; and for centuries the dis-
putants spilled ink and sometimes blood over Ebionism and Docetism,
Sabellianism and Arianism, Nestorianism and Eutychianism, Mono-
physitism and Monothelitism. From these disputes, which seem to
present-day philosophers unreadably unreal because so uncritical
in their premises, the church in time winnowed out a body of
doctrine which it imposed under heavy sanctions on all who would
calls themselves Christians. It did this with the deepening conviction
that the process of winnowing was itself supernaturally guided and
that the doctrine ultimately declared orthodox had lain in the
Christian teaching from the beginning. The process of selection,
definition, and elaboration still goes on.

18 Should this system of dogma be taken seriously by philosophers? It is notorious that many of them think not. 'The idea that
religion contains a literal, not a symbolic, representation of truth
and life,' said Santayana, 'is simply an impossible idea. Whoever
entertains it has not come within the region of profitable philosophising on that subject'.[12]

Though I think, as Santayana did, that most religious dogma
belongs in the sphere of myth, I have tried to show that myth is
more than vain imagining. It is an attempt at explanation on the
part of minds to whom better tools are not available. The church
fathers who elaborated the creeds and the millions who have continued to accept them, including not only the unlettered and
untutored but also the Pascals and Newmans of the world, the
Barths, the D'Arcys, and the Gilsons, would reject as irresponsible
the view that creeds are flights of primitive imagination. For such
persons the only tolerable attitude on the part of a critic is one of
respectful consideration of a dogma as at least a candidate for truth.
That has been my own attitude, and unless I could have taken it,
these pages would not have been written. My chief interest has been
in whether a dogma is true rather than in how it arose.

When the charge of mythical status is made of a particular dogma,
however, the most effective criticism is often genetic. Such criticism
was first offered on a large scale by David Friedrich Strauss in *Das
Leben Jesu*, probably the most influential work of Biblical criticism
that has yet been written. How far Strauss's attempt to show the

mythical character of supernaturalist dogma generally is to be taken as a success is too large an issue to raise here, since his success varied greatly from one dogma to another. But his name reminds us that the dialectical approach to the truth of doctrine is not the only one. The probability or improbability of a belief may be affected profoundly by the circumstances under which it came to be believed. A doctrine springing from careful observation or from self-critical reflection would have a better chance of truth than one springing from fear or popular desire. It will be worth our while, by way of illustrating the possibilities of the historical method, to apply it in some detail to a single case. We shall take as our example the place in Catholic belief of the Virgin Mary.

A SAMPLE: THE MYTH OF THE VIRGIN

19 Surprisingly little is said about Mary in the New Testament. In what is probably the earliest of the gospels, Mark, there is no mention of a Virgin birth, nor does Peter, Paul, or the author of the fourth gospel seem to have heard of it. Matthew and Luke report the story of the miraculous birth, but with inconsistencies which show that at least one of them must be reporting incorrectly. Moreover, both writers cite facts and use language that are inconsistent with their own reports of this birth. Both of them give genealogies for Jesus—themselves conflicting with each other—which trace the descent of Jesus through Joseph, on the assumption that Joseph really was his father. Indeed it is only if Joseph was his father that the claim for his messiahship as the 'son of David' can be made out. Some Catholic apologists, perceiving the difficulty, have entered a claim for Mary as the daughter of David, but this is afterthought and conjecture. 'The birth stories in Matthew, taken as a whole,' says the Anglican Bishop Barnes, 'were built up conscientiously on texts of the Old Testament which could be regarded as prophetic'.[13] Dean Inge agrees: 'The story of the virgin birth turns on a text from Isaiah.' He quotes Loisy's judgement on this part of Matthew: 'rien n'est plus arbitraire comme exégèse, ni plus faible comme narration fictive.'[14] The text of Isaiah 7 : 14, quoted in Matthew 1 : 23, is 'a virgin shall conceive and bear a son'. It is not improbable that much of the weight of legend that has grown up about Mary rests on a mere mistranslation; the Hebrew word for 'young woman' was translated into the Greek παρθένος, meaning virgin, an error corrected in the revised version of 1953.

There is further internal evidence that the story is fictitious. The birth that was attended with so many miraculous manifestations, bringing the Magi from the East to worship, was apparently unknown to Jesus' own fellow villagers, who, when he came among them, asked: 'Is not this the carpenter's son?' (Matt. 13 : 55); 'Is not this Joseph's son?' (Luke 4 : 22); 'Is not this Jesus, the son of Joseph, whose father and mother we know?' (John 6 : 42). Such a reception can only raise doubt about the angelic and political fanfare of his birth. Apparently these townsfolk barely remembered a person whose entrance into the world had been heralded by flights of angels, the visits of wise men from a distance, piloted by a star, and the wholesale massacre of infants by Herod, the king, in order to cut off a rival leader of his people. Could Jesus' neighbours have remained thus indifferent and unknowing if these wonders had occurred when he first came among them?

Nor is the account in the gospels of the relations between mother and son at all what one would expect from such a mother and such a son. The record suggests a relation of coolness and even misunderstanding. A lack of rapport with his mother seems to have manifested itself early. When his parents took him at the age of twelve to Jerusalem and were on their way home, they found that he had disappeared from the caravan, and it took them three days to find him. When they did find him, his mother expostulated with him: 'My son, why have you behaved like this to us? Here have your father and I been looking for you anxiously.' To which the boy's reply was: 'Why did you look for me? Did you not know I had to be at my Father's house? But they did not understand what he said' (Luke 2 : 41–50; Moffatt). This story is full of surprises. Both his behaviour and his reply seem curiously wanting in consideration. And Mary, on her part, certainly does not act like a 'Mother of God'; she reproaches her errant son for his indifference; she speaks to him of 'your father', which she knew Joseph was not; more surprisingly, though she realised that his Father was God himself, she was lost as to what he could mean when he said he must be about his Father's business. Neither his attitude toward his mother nor hers toward him makes sense on the traditional theory.

The references to Mary during the adult life of Jesus are few. We have mentioned these already in discussing his ethical attitude toward women, but we may return to them for a moment, since they bear poignantly on our present topic. If Mary was indeed the Mother of God and the sinless Queen of Heaven, one would expect that a son who had all the ordinary grounds for affection would give evidence in his treatment of her of these further grounds for respect and veneration. This expectation is not fulfilled. Mary was present at the marriage feast in Cana, and appealed to her son to replenish the supply of wine. His answer, 'Woman, what have I to do with thee?' (John 2 : 4) is not the language of veneration. She next appears on the outskirts of a multitude which was surrounding and harassing him. She sent him a message that she and certain of his brothers were there, on which he said, 'Who is my mother and my brethren? And looking round on them that sat round about him, he saith, Behold my mother and my brethren' (Mark 3 : 33–4). Here again we have the same cool note. His strange comment, on hearing his mother blessed by an admirer of hers, was 'Yea rather, blessed are they that hear the word of God, and keep it' (Luke 11 : 28). His last words to his mother were addressed equally to her and to John; to his mother he said, 'Woman, behold thy son!' and to John, 'Behold thy mother!' (John 19 : 25–27). She appears again only when mentioned as having been present at a gathering after the ascension 'with the women, and Mary the mother of Jesus, and with his brethren' (Acts 1 : 14). In view of what Mary was to become, it is an extraordinary fact that in the twenty-one letters from Apostles included in the New Testament her name is never once mentioned.

Here then is the Mary of the New Testament. Apart from the stories of the miraculous birth, whose character and inconsistencies make them quite incredible, she plays a role in the record of Jesus' ministry that was pathetically dim and insignificant. The exalted place she was later to occupy was unsuspected not only by the apostolic writers but also by the early fathers of the church. She was not exempted from original sin, for example, by Irenaeus, Origen, Cyprian, Jerome, or Ambrose.[15] Tertullian and Chrysostom describe her as being rebuked by her son for her presumption.[16] Her perpetual virginity is contradicted in the New Testament itself, which records that she and Joseph had four sons and at least one daughter. No one seems to have thought of addressing prayers or worship to her for more than three hundred years. 'There is further no ancient consent,' writes Bishop Gore, 'even for her actual freedom from venial sins—no evidence at all of any one having held her immaculate conception.'[17] Certain apocryphal writings, indeed, were circulated with picturesque embroideries on the theme of the nativity, but these were pretty clearly exercises in imagination and were not accepted in the canon. The prospect was that Mary would remain the somewhat wistful and shadowy figure that appears in Mark and John.

20 Then began what is surely one of the most extraordinary translations that has ever occurred to a mortal man or woman. A number of forces, some internal to developing Christian dogma, some external, combined to exalt, magnify, and transfigure her into something very like deity. Take one example of the internal agencies.

Augustine asked himself how, if Jesus had been exempted from the taint of original sin inherited by the race from Adam, this exemption had been effected. Was it to be believed that a person wholly without taint was formed in the body of a person who herself was vitiated through and through by this taint, as other human beings were? Augustine was puzzled, and he allowed that the argument seemed to point in the direction of Mary's sinlessness. Had she been miraculously exempted, then, from the taint of the rest of mankind? No. He was prepared to say that she had never in her life committed a sin; but that she had been really freed from this metaphysical burden was too much for him to believe, and his views on this point were shared by the most influential church writers for many centuries.[18] As time wore on, however, and acute minds played over the logic of the matter, theologians arose who maintained a different view. They held it more logical to suppose that if Jesus had been immaculately conceived so had his mother, since otherwise the danger of contamination would not have been wholly escaped. To the layman it is not quite easy to see why the process should have stopped there. If, in order to render the last-born in the line immaculate, it was necessary to render his mother immaculate, one would have thought that to render her thus immaculate, her own mother must be immaculate, and so on back to Eve.

This step was not taken. Indeed the doctrine of an immaculate conception seems not to have been clearly stated and urged before the twelfth century, and then it met with vigorous opposition. It was denied by both St Bernard and St Thomas Aquinas, and became a bone of contention between Franciscans and Dominicans, the former upholding the doctrine and pointing to the visions of St Bridget in support, the latter denying it and citing in support the visions of St Catherine of Sienna.[19] Pope Innocent III in the early thirteenth century denied the immaculate conception of Mary; Pope Sixtus IV in the fifteenth century, convinced that it was a fact, offered indulgences to those who had masses said in its honour. The truth did not finally emerge till 1854. In that year Pius IX, in the bull *Ineffabilis Deus*, announced that 'the blessed Virgin Mary in the first moment of her conception was . . . preserved immune from every stain of original sin,' and that henceforth this 'is to be firmly and constantly believed by all the faithful'. From that time forward, for one of the faithful to believe what St Augustine and St Thomas had believed, and presumably also St Mark and St Paul, was to place his soul in peril.[20]

21 But in explaining the cult of the Virgin, the external influences were more important than the internal. Christianity had to make its way in a Graeco-Roman and pagan world peopled with numberless divinities. Zeus and Jupiter were in a sense presiding deities, but there was a host of lesser figures. The shift from the pagan to the Christian worship would obviously be easier if the new pantheon contained figures that could be substituted for those of the old. Christianity was pressed to accommodate itself to the established habits and felt needs of the people to whom it was appealing. This it did. In place of the old local divinities it gradually provided a rich variety of local and patron saints, whose aid and protection could be invoked very much as the pagan divinities were. How easy it is to effect such a transition is shown by the Catholic worship of today in Mexico, where the old divinities of the countryside have fused with the Christian saints and apostles without producing any sense of incongruity. And among the divinities worshipped by the pagans, goddesses played an important part. Demeter, Persephone, Isis, and many others had their eager devotees. To such persons there would be something lacking in a worship that had nothing corresponding to these figures.

Furthermore, conspicuous among the pagan goddesses were virgins. The finest temple in the world, the Parthenon at Athens, was the shrine of a virgin, Athena Parthenos. Dr Farnell in his Gifford Lectures reminds us of the significant fact that Greek women, in worshipping Hera, thought of her in quite inconsistent ways as suited their special need, young girls praying to 'Hera the girl', married women to 'Hera the married one', widows to 'Hera the widow'.[21] Among the adherents of Mithraism, which was for a time the leading contender with Christianity for the devotion of the West, a heavenly virgin, accepted by the Semites as a form of Astarte, was held to have borne the sun-god Mithra on the twenty-fifth of December. It is most probable, as Frazer has contended, that this is what fixed the date of the Christian Christmas; and so strong was the influence of this Mithraic worship on the early Christian community that both Augustine and Leo the Great found it necessary to remind its members that Christmas did not celebrate the birth of the sun but the birth of Christ.[22]

Now when the worshippers of Mithra went over to Christianity, it was natural enough that for the worship of Mithra they should substitute that of Christ. But for the heavenly goddess who was the mother of Mithra, what substitute was to be found? None was available but Mary, and if Mary was to be available, a place must be accorded her which had no warrant in the gospels themselves. The reasoning by which this difficulty was surmounted was plausible enough. If Jesus was an incarnation of Deity, and she was his mother, then in a sense she was the mother of God, and indeed the only queen of heaven, and must have divine powers in her own right. If so, it was appropriate to pray to her for protection, to place images of her in the churches, and to ask her intercession with the persons of the Trinity; indeed, by the eighth century John of Damascus was placing her just below the Trinity in the Christian hierarchy.

22 This development was furthered by a famous controversy and the church's decision of it. In the fourth century occurred the debate between Athanasius and Arius over the union of the divine and human natures in Christ. Athanasius held that the two were identical in substance, that the Christ who lived and laboured on earth *was* the uncreated and eternal God. Arius held, on the contrary, that to refer to an uncreated and eternal Deity as now three years old and now six was absurd, that the spirit incarnate in Christ, while exalted above all human spirits, was nevertheless created by God in time and subordinate to him. It was to settle this controversy, which threatened to tear the church in two, that Constantine called the Council of Nicaea in 325. This council decided for Athanasius. But the victory proved equivocal. The orthodox party—as they were from now on—expected that the decision would confirm and strengthen the worship of Christ as God himself. But the effect upon many seems to have been to remove him so far from humanity into theological absoluteness that they needed a more human and less formidable being to pray to and confide in. This they found in Mary. They could appeal directly to her understanding heart to intercede for them with her son, who was now enthroned in remote and awful splendour. A century later the worship of the Virgin had become so general that Nestorius, the eloquent preacher and patriarch of Constantinople, not only warned against it but insisted that those in his charge must not refer to Mary as Mother of God. He little knew what was in store for him. His words provoked such a storm that the then emperor felt obliged to call another council at Ephesus in 431 to allay it. The decision went against Nestorius, and he was deposed and exiled.

The result gave free rein to the popular enthusiasm for Mary; pictures and images of her multiplied; she was frankly worshipped as divine. She became so exalted that some people raised the question whether she was not best approached through her own mother, St Anne. The Bible was searched for confirmatory evidence of her greatness and made to yield it plentifully. The salutation in Luke 1 : 28, 'Hail! thou that art highly favoured' or 'much graced', was interpreted to mean that Mary was herself a source of grace. She was the bride of the Song of Solomon; she was the woman in Revelation who was clothed with the sun, and also the woman who was attacked by a dragon with seven heads and seven crowns. She was made the subject of many prophetic passages in the Old Testament without suspicion that later descriptions of her may have been influenced by those passages; 'the bush that was on fire and was not burnt' was Mary who had conceived a son without being burnt by sex; Eve, Sara, Deborah, Judith, and Esther were all symbolic forerunners of the queen of women; the ark of the covenant, carrying in itself something infinitely precious, was, if one looked keenly between the lines, Mary again.

When Christianity spread to the Teutonic tribes, Mariolatry received further support. These peoples held woman in higher regard than the Southern or Eastern peoples, and the same sentiments that made the institution of chivalry attractive to them made it acceptable also to include a woman among the objects of their worship. To this must be added the natural tenderness felt everywhere for a mother and her child, and the security that was given to apprehensive minds, in a world supposed to be peopled with malignant demons, by the consciousness that a mother's solicitude was always open to them when they were in fear or pain. These attractions, again, helped to give Mary and her child the quite extraordinary place in art that they held for many centuries. The great artists of the mediaeval and modern church devoted much of their time and skill to her. The madonnas of Giotto and Leonardo, of Raphael and Titian, of Botticelli, Correggio, and Holbein are among the great paintings of the world.

23   Thus, little by little over the years, a young woman of whom practically nothing is known with certainty became the Morning Star, the Queen of Heaven, the sinless Mother of God.[23] Since the twelfth century countless devoted worshippers have depended on her to present their case at the throne of heaven. The Ave Maria became a regular form of Catholic prayer; St Dominic introduced the string of beads called the rosary to make easier the repetition of 150 Ave Marias along with 15 Pater Nosters; Ignatius Loyola is described as having prayed to Mary daily for hours and having taught that in the eucharist one partakes of the flesh of Mary as well as of Jesus; St Bonaventura describes her as the 'porta caeli, quia nullus potest jam caelum intrare nisi per Mariam transeat tamquam per portam'.[24] Alphonso dei Liguori, who wrote an immensely popular work called *The Glories of Mary* and who was later canonised, taught that God gave no grace except through Mary, a doctrine that was later defended by Cardinal Manning. Innocent III said that 'to a sinner who has lost Divine grace, there is no more sun,' this being the symbol of Jesus, 'but the moon is still on the horizon; let him address himself to Mary'. J. J. Olier, the influential founder of the French seminary of St Sulpice, argued that from the time of the resurrection Jesus was identified with the Father, and hence took the Father's attitude of rejection toward sinners, 'so that the difficulty is to induce Him to exchange the office of Judge for that of advocate. . . . Now this is what the saints effect, and especially the most Blessed Virgin.'[25] Some Catholic writers have gone further still and maintained with Bernardinus de Bustis that 'the blessed Virgin is herself superior to God, and God Himself is subject unto her in respect of the manhood he assumed from her'.[26] Of course this is excess of zeal, not Catholic orthodoxy. But what counts is less the technical definitions of the learned than the practical attitudes of the many, and these attitudes have been permitted and encouraged to outstrip official doctrine. It has been noted that out of the 433 churches and chapels in Rome two are dedicated to the Holy Spirit, two to the sacraments, four to the crucifix, five to the Trinity, fifteen to Jesus, and 121 to Mary.[27]

The glorification of Mary, however, is neither a thing of the past nor a popular movement only. The two dogmas which perhaps come nearest to fulfilling the requirements of infallibility, those of the immaculate conception and the bodily assumption, have both been promulgated since 1850, and both concern the Virgin. In 1854 Pius IX declared it a doctrine 'revealed by God' that Mary, alone among mankind, had come into the world free from all taint of original sin, and added that 'if any presume to think in their heart otherwise . . . they have suffered shipwreck as regards the faith. . . .'[28] Enthusiasm for Mary among the faithful continued to rise. On 23 February 1870, two hundred bishops asked that the Vatican 'expressly and solemnly define that Mary with her spotless soul and virgin body is enthroned in heaven at the right hand of the Son of God, as our most powerful mediatrix. . . .' The suggestion that her *virgin body* is enthroned in heaven' seemed to call for a further dogma. 'It is certain', writes Joseph Duhr, SJ, in his *Glorious Assumption of the Mother of God*, 'that no truly faithful believer will ever accept the idea that the Virgin Mary's body, the august tabernacle of the Word made flesh, could become the prey of worms, or that it remains somewhere shrouded in silence and indifference'.[29] In Pius XII Mary had a follower whose devotion and power enabled him to dispel with authority so repulsive a thought. On 1 November 1950, he had the satisfaction of defining another revealed truth, binding on all the faithful. Mary's body as well as her soul had, at her death, been miraculously translated directly into heaven.[30]

THE RATIONAL APPRAISAL OF DOGMA

24 Now I suggest that the decision whether this complex of beliefs is true lies neither with scholarship nor with dialectic, but with the sort of philosophy, or as I should prefer to say, reasonableness, which consists of refined and extended common sense. There are many glib secularists in these days who dismiss such belief as merely stupid and ignorant. No one can take that view who has exposed himself to the learning and subtlety of the theologians who have dealt with it. Indeed if one is of a speculative turn, and can with good conscience make the initial leap of faith which enables one to accept the collection of Biblical writings as containing a supreme and unique revelation, the fascination of searching this out and piecing it together is wholly intelligible. Put yourself inside the system, accept once and for all the exciting view that hidden in these cryptic prophecies, oriental metaphors, and dramatic narratives, and only waiting to be construed by us, is the truth about the nature and eternal destiny of the race, and there will obviously be nothing more important for scholarship to undertake than the deciphering of the divine code. The 520-page letter that Pusey wrote to Newman about whether the Virgin was freed at her own conception from the burden of original sin will then be a real service to mankind. Pusey believed that the doctrine could be refuted by careful reasoning, starting from the Scriptures and the fathers; Newman believed—at least after the Papal edict on the matter—that it could be established in the same way.

It would be foolish to question the scholarship or acumen of these men, or of their present-day successors. We can and should admit it to the full. And yet what modern reader who is not already committed, heart and mind, to the system within which their thought revolved is moved in the least by this erudition? They and their successors were really ignoring the question which the modern mind wants settled. That question is not whether, given certain doctrines within the system, certain other doctrines follow, but whether the system itself as a whole can any longer be lived in, whether it can be coherently included in a world that also includes, and must include, modern biology and physics, psychology and anthropology, Freud and *The Golden Bough. That* question cannot be answered from within the system, even by the most masterly dialectics. I have made no attempt to consider the pros and cons of the dogma I have fixed on, because I think that for most present-day students that would evade the fundamental issue, and because that issue is more effectively dealt with simply by projecting the story of the dogma against the background of modern knowledge.

What confronts us is two hypotheses, each so complex that neither can be proved, and we must choose between them on the basis of comparative probability. Nearly everything in the chronicle of Mary is logically possible. It is possible that a Jewish girl in about 5 BC did conceive a child in a manner of which there is no other biological example; that she was made to do so by the miraculous intrusion into nature of an omnipotent and omniscient power; that Matthew and Luke were confused when they traced the descent of her son through Joseph; that there is such a thing, not as inherited sin, which is a contradictory notion, but inherited evil, and that Mary was exempted from this by supernatural intervention; that she never in her life did anything wrong; that the magi knew in advance about the miraculous birth and arrived in time to adore and bring gifts, though the townspeople did not learn of it; that Jesus regarded his mother as virtually divine, though some accident has prevented any hint of this from appearing in the record; that the silence of St Paul and the fathers for some four centuries about her true position was again a curious accident in a development that was, on the whole, supernaturally ordered; that her exaltation, when it came, was quite independent of those other contemporary faiths where virgins were worshipped, and was only the belated acknow-ledgement of a truth known all along; finally that her corpse was reanimated and swept intact out of the world of space and time, though her contemporaries, so ready to believe such things, never seem to have heard of it, and the church took eighteen centuries to make up its mind that it had taken place. All this, I repeat, is possible, not in the sense that it would be consistent with physical law, since it would collide with biology and physics at many points, but in the sense that there is nothing obviously self-contradictory in it.

The other hypothesis is simpler. It is that as the figure of Jesus was thought about and talked about over the years by followers who loved and worshipped him but who were as uncritical as children in their attitude toward the marvellous, a set of legends collected around him, and that for such reasons as we have mentioned these legends gradually extended themselves to his mother and were embroidered with time. This hypothesis, like the other, is neither impossible nor demonstrable. The choice between them, I repeat, is one of comparative probability. And if, in estimating this probability, one starts from the only assured basis, that of actual experience and the principles it forces upon us, I do not see how the question can be answered in any way but one. The first hypothesis, if true, would shake the whole fabric of common sense and scientific belief in which modern man lives. The second hypothesis would square with that belief throughout. For minds brought up on scientific method and critical history the choice is hardly a live option. They could not accept the first hypothesis unless they could divest themselves of their own past and secede from the intellectual world they live in.

THE MELTING AWAY OF DOGMA

25 We have glanced at only one dogma, or one small cluster of dogmas, from the immense system that grew up in the first thousand years of our era. I have suggested that this part of the system would almost certainly turn out under scrutiny to be as truly a product of the myth-making faculty, rather than of reason operating freely upon the evidence, as the earlier legends of Samson and Joshua. I do not want to suggest, far less to argue, that all the dogmas in that great system are in similar case. That there is a great deal of truth in the system, important and helpful truth, I should not question for a moment, and still less should I care to question the ability that went to its elaboration. There are few if any enterprises in intellectual history that can compare with that of St Thomas in the skill with which the available knowledge of the time is reduced to coherent order. It is, and will remain, like the *Divine Comedy*, one of the most impressive of human achievements. If it is to be criticised, this must indeed be on the ground that it is too much like the *Divine Comedy*. Let anyone pick up at random a volume of the *Summa* and examine its contents. Along with acute discussions of substance and accident, unpretentious but extensive Biblical learning, and penetrating commentaries on Aristotle, he will find discourses on angels and demons, an undoubting assumption that the entire mass of Hebrew legend from Cain and Abel to Daniel in the lion's den is inspired truth, and a virtually total absence of any reference to the world of observed fact.

It gradually comes home to the reader what an extraordinary phenomenon this is—one of the great intellects of the race struggling within the walls of its cell to elaborate a view of the universe, not from the materials that science and history laid before him, for neither science nor history, as we know them, then existed, but from a set of fragments of the ancient world, a few treatises of Aristotle being the chief source for method and the Scriptural canon for truth. We have seen enough about the Hebrew writings to have some idea of what this meant. It meant that any clear water he might have drawn from his sources was muddied by an infusion of myth as rich and legendary as the siege of Troy. The *Summa* is like a gigantic sponge which shrinks to small proportions when this water is squeezed out of it. The critic who enters the system and tries to argue with Thomas about his particular deductions is probably riding for a fall, since the great doctor is a formidable antagonist in any argumentative lists. The trouble the modern mind finds with him is not with the validity of his deductions but with the truth of his starting-points, and hence with the instability of the whole construction. His belief in the literal truth even of Hebrew chronicle was such as to make him say that if Elkanah was not the father of Samuel then revelation as a whole was placed in jeopardy. The truth of the entire system, with all its intricate and subtle argumentation, depends on a proposition which every objective historical critic would now regard as false, namely that the Bible is to be treated not as literature but as the record of assured historical fact and infallible truth. Grant him that proposition, and you may as well surrender to him first as last. Question it, and the central bastions of the grandiose edifice become a cloud castle.

This suggests what has actually happened to the philosophy of Thomas in modern times. Something similar must be said, no doubt, about the nearest Protestant counterpart of the *Summa*, the *Institutes* of Calvin. These men were both great rationalists in the sense that if you supplied them with premises they could perform prodigies in the way of constructing upon them massive and orderly structures of thought. Neither had the kind of intellectual radicalism required to carry the process downward by continued questioning of these premises till they came to the bedrock of rational certainty. This is what modern thought has attempted for them. It has never, I take it, refuted them, in the sense of showing that they built incompetently with the materials they had. It has refuted them only in the sense of showing that even they could not build structures of enduring truth out of materials that were half myth. The process of separating fact from myth, particularly in an extended system whose branches intertwine with every physical science and which includes a panoramic history of the world from the beginning to the final catastrophe, is no instantaneous process like the perception of a fallacy; it is properly the business of centuries, in which there emerges a new realm of scientific and historic truth, and with it a new sense of how such truth is to be established. The emergence of these things is the birth of the modern intellectual world. The story of this long hard labour has been often told, and need not be repeated. But it may be well to remind ourselves of the main intellectual movements that hastened the process.

26 First there was the renaissance of ancient humanistic culture, which suggested experiences and ways of living quite different from those of the religious tradition, yet apparently self-justifying. Then there was the Reformation, which insisted that the important point was not what a man could get the church or the saints to do for him but what happened in his own mind, a conviction which encouraged the individual to take more responsibility for his beliefs and attitudes. Then came the revolutionary suggestion of Descartes, who, though a loyal churchman himself, has become for such thinkers as Maritain the great source of modern intellectual perversion.[31] For Descartes held that the appeal to reason was the ultimate test of any belief. Was the belief held with the clear and distinct conception of its terms and their relation that we have in mathematics? If so, it must be as true as $2 + 2 = 4$; self-evidence is the test of truth. Descartes tried to make an exception of revealed truth, but the exception was so contrary to the spirit of his system, which was in essence an uncompromising rationalism, that the church put him on the Index.

It did so too late, however, to prevent the seed that he planted from growing. His idea that rational necessity is the bar to which every proposed belief must in the end be brought was accepted and developed by a line of thinkers that form the most distinguished single tradition in modern philosophy, a line that runs through Spinoza, Leibniz, Kant, and Hegel to Bradley, Royce, and McTaggart. This tradition did not conceive itself as, on the whole, hostile to religion. Among the more impressive in the long series of Gifford Lectures are those in which idealistic rationalism has been expounded as the one true basis of religious belief, the lectures of the Cairds, for example, and of Royce, Bosanquet, Watson, and Haldane. Yet no historically minded readers of these lectures can fail to see that they defend Christianity by rewriting it. The theology of Bosanquet is almost as far from that of St Thomas as that of St Thomas is from that of the gospels.

While this new and formidable rationalism was developing on the continent, there appeared in Britain a quite different kind of philosophy, which was to prove in the end even more dangerous to theological tradition, though it was founded, like rationalism, by men who conceived themselves as defending that tradition. This was the empiricism of Locke and Berkeley. The gist of it was that ideas come from sense experience. At first little attention was paid to the contrapositive of this assertion, namely that whatever ideas do not come from sense experience are at best but pseudo-ideas. This consequence was underlined with devastating theological effect by Hume. The influence of his scepticism has fluctuated greatly, but in recent years it has been very strong. When such empiricists as Carnap and Ayer dismiss theology as meaningless, they are standing admittedly on Hume's ground. They argue that to derive from sense experience, or to verify by it, beliefs in the fall, or original sin, or the incarnation, or the eucharist, or the existence of God is impossible, and hence such terms are meaningless. Similar views have been urged by some of the linguistic philosophers. I have examined a number of these theories of meaning in another work, and found them unsatisfactory. Still, empiricism has been the order of the day in recent British and American philosophy, and its temper has been clearly hostile to the traditional forms of religious belief.

27 Influential as philosophy has been among the few, however, its influence among the many has been far outweighed by that of science. In explaining the resurrection of Kierkegaard we listed the main inroads of science on theology and may here be brief. There is no one of the sciences that has not at some point or other trespassed on the domain that once belonged to theology and followed up the trespasses by wresting territory from it. Theological astronomy was replaced, after an acute struggle, by that of Copernicus and Newton. The theological biology that assigned past life on the earth a duration of six thousand years has been snowed under by fossil discoveries. The world of witchcraft, demons, and divine scourges in which Thomas lived was gradually transformed into one in which witches were cured and demons expelled by psychopathologists, and epidemics controlled by scientific medicine. Magic was replaced by chemistry and physics; miracles were either refused credence or domesticated as examples of unfamiliar law. Hebrew mythology, though containing some historical fact, was found by students of anthropology to parallel many other mythologies whose status as such no one could doubt. The inevitableness with which the scientific account of things made its way is symbolised by what happened when Smith's *Dictionary of the Bible* was compiled in Victorian days. The editor wanted a book written by authorities, but nevertheless safe. He assigned the article 'Deluge' to a competent scholar, but got from him an article so heretical that he decided it would never do. So under 'Deluge' he entered 'see Flood', and gave the article to another and, he believed, less dangerous hand. But the second article, when it came in, was more alarming than the first. So, desperately writing under 'Flood' 'see Noah', he appealed to a distinguished Cambridge professor to save the situation. He too turned out to have conceded the case to the new geological science. But he did so with a sufficient depth of professional obscurity to exempt the editor from the need of further struggle.[32]

Darwin's theory has been before the world only since the year in which Dewey, Bergson, and Husserl were born, 1859, but the change in attitude toward it has been an all but complete reversal. It is hard now to believe that the denunciations of his view came

not only from such persons as the Pope[33] and the rather sorry
Wilberforce, who was Bishop of Oxford at that time, but from such
relatively enlightened minds as Carlyle, who described Darwin as
an 'apostle of dirt worship', and even from the eminent historian of
the inductive sciences, Whewell, who refused to permit a copy of
The Origin of Species to be placed in the library of Trinity College,
Cambridge, where he was master. When Mr Bryan attempted to
take a similar view at the Scopes trial of 1925, the world laughed.

28 No doubt the application of reason that for many was hardest
to bear was its criticism of the Scriptural text. This had begun as
early as Spinoza, who showed that the Pentateuch had been compiled
from various sources and long after the time of Moses. But the great
development of this sort of criticism took place in nineteenth-century
Germany, Holland, and France. Kuenen, Wellhausen, and others
showed by irresistible internal evidence that the Old Testament
books had been written in another order, by other hands, at other
times and places, and under other influences than had been supposed,
for example that the Mosaic law and its historical background were
mainly projections into the past from a much later epoch. A succession of scholars from Strauss and Renan to Harnack and Schweitzer
did for the New Testament what these men did for the Old. They
revealed that Matthew and Luke were chiefly compilations from
Mark and one other source, now lost but largely reconstructed by
Harnack; they showed that John differed profoundly in purpose and
doctrine from the other gospels; they brought to light countless
errors and inconsistencies which clearly excluded the character
assigned to any of them by the Roman and the more conservative
Protestant interpreters; they threw a flood of light on the actual life
and teachings of Christ. The resistance to the new results was
determined. But it could not prevent, it only delayed, their general
acceptance.

These results, aided by George Eliot's translation of Strauss and
the literary brilliance of Renan's *Vie de Jésus*, penetrated slowly to
Britain and America. The change in the climate of opinion in the
last century may be brought home by one illustration. The famous
volume of *Essays and Reviews* by Jowett, Mark Pattison, the elder
Temple, and others appeared in 1860. All but one of its authors were
clergymen, and their position was one many churchmen of today
would regard as not only conservative but almost reactionary. They
did try to make use, however, of some of the recent German discoveries. This was the signal for a vigorous attack both on them
and on the attempt to apply scientific and historical method to
Biblical study. The hue and cry was prodigious. Two of the writers

were prosecuted in the clerical courts and suspended from their posts. They appealed to the Queen in Council, who referred the case to a judicial committee headed by the lord chancellor, and including the bishop of London, both archbishops, and a number of distinguished laymen. One of the culprits was charged with having betrayed his office by denying the doctrine of eternal punishment. The lord chancellor and the majority of the committee declined to find him guilty, saying that they did not conceive themselves required 'to punish the expression of a hope by a clergyman that even the ultimate pardon of the wicked who are condemned in the day of judgement may be consistent with the will of Almighty God'. Both archbishops voted against acquittal on this point, and when the decision freeing the essayists was made known, a petition of protest came in, signed by eleven thousand clergymen, and deputations representing great numbers of laymen waited on the archbishops to thank them for their efforts to save the faith. But the lord chancellor stood firm. An epitaph of the time, composed for him by an admirer, ran: 'He dismissed Hell with costs, and took away from orthodox members of the Church of England their last hope of everlasting damnation.'[34] One wonders how many clergymen would sign a petition now insisting on this 'hope'. It is significant of the change that has occurred in the past century that in 1945 a book entitled *The Rise of Christianity*, accepting whole-heartedly the methods of continental 'higher criticism' and incorporating many of its most radical conclusions, was published, not by an obscure cleric, with trial and suspension hanging over him, but by the bishop of Birmingham, who was admonished in consequence by some colleagues but who remained serenely on his episcopal throne.[35]

29 The advance of rationalism had one more step to take, a step which, as we have seen earlier, aroused passionate resistance. So far, though it had insisted on bringing Biblical theology and history to the bar of reason, it had been inclined to leave Christian ethics untouched. There was, of course, the diverting spectacle of Nietzsche beating his breast loudly and proclaiming himself the Antichrist, though his voice, like that of Kierkegaard on the other side, was obviously not the voice of reason, but of something less or more— fanaticism or prophecy as one preferred. If anyone spoke with the voice of reason, however, it was that 'saint of rationalism', as Gladstone called him, John Stuart Mill. Mill offered sober criticism of various points in the Christian ethics as he understood it, for example of the character it ascribed to God in connection with the evil in the world, a character Mill thought immoral, of its condemnation of heresy as carrying a moral taint, and of its lack of due concern for the physical basis of life. Similar doubts were raised, again with the impressiveness that belonged to high character, by John Morley; and in the present century the debate about Christian ethics has become an open one, with such vigorous debaters as Shaw, Russell, and Westermarck on one side and Dean Rashdall, Dean Inge, and Bishop Henson on the other. This marks the high-water line of rationalist criticism. It means that there is nothing whatever in the great structure of belief and faith begun in the first century and virtually completed in the thirteenth that is now considered outside the bounds of rational inquiry and correction.

30 Even in the most authoritative of the Christian churches, scepticism is spreading at surprising speed. When Pius XII in 1950 announced as a necessity for all Catholics the belief that the body of Mary was translated directly into heaven, he threw down the ecclesiastical gauntlet to the modern world. He little knew how quickly that gauntlet was to be picked up, not only by outsiders but by members of his own communion. His successor, the good John, saw that the church could not play the role indefinitely of a Canute defying the tide of secular thought, and began a process of accommodation to it. The concessions were modest, but they proved to be a sowing of the wind, of which his successors have begun to reap the whirlwind. One small bit of evidence: in May 1972 the present writer took part in a dialogue between Catholic and rationalist thinkers in New York, about twenty-five members from each side being present. What was surprising to the rationalists was not so much the amount of difference as the amount of agreement between the two groups. While the Catholic members could hardly have been representative of their church at large, the readiness with which they rejected the traditional dogmas of their church, repudiated the pronouncements of popes and councils, and insisted that they too were essentially rationalists was as astonishing to their critics as it would certainly have been perturbing to the head of their church. The fact is that the appeal to authority among Catholics and the appeal to revelation in both the great Christian communions are steadily losing their credibility.

What is taking their place? The appeal to reason? Perhaps. But reason provides no answers that compare in definiteness or breadth of support with the answers given by revelation and church authority. Reason, to be sure, is the best and indeed the only illumination we have in this field, but it is after all a flickering candle in a universe that stretches out indefinitely on all sides and lies chiefly in shadow. To the questions of the religious man there is no one set of answers that can be offered as *the* answers of reason, but only the speculations of individual men, through whom the voice of reason is never heard in its purity, but always with provincial accents and personal inflections. Certainly the chapters that follow, in which I give some account of my own tentative answers to these questions, do not pretend to be more. But any reader who has lasted through so many chapters of negation will be more than ready for some effort at construction.

PART IV

A RATIONALIST'S OUTLOOK

CHAPTER XIII

COSMOLOGY

1 In the first two books of this study we examined the views of reason and revelation held by Catholics and by one important line of Protestant theologians. Neither of these traditions could be described as passing the examination with honours. In each of them much error and incoherence came to light.

Why have they persisted so long in spite of such defects? In the last two chapters we have had a partial answer to this question. They have persisted because religion is a fundamental activity or attitude, always present in some form and degree, and these two great traditions gave it an expression which, in view of man's limited knowledge, was highly plausible. They persisted, again, because both developed an ethics of belief which made doubt or denial, even when reached by disinterested inquiry, a sin. They persisted, once more, because in both there was a large freightage of the sort of myth that was congenial to men's feeling. With the growth of knowledge, the relaxation of the ethics of belief, and the increasing freedom of intellect in religion, the massive edifice of dogma in which men had lived for centuries crumbled slowly away.

Unfortunately, the dissecting intellect is a better critic than architect. Though most philosophers would probably agree that the traditional theologies are no longer credible, they disagree on what should replace them. This is not, as many would like to think, an indictment of reason itself. Reason, in the present use of the term, means simply the disinterested application of our cognitive faculties to the problems of belief, and though this application has been protested in both the Christian traditions, the protest, as we have had full occasion to see, is not very cogent. If 'reason' pronounces diverse judgements, it is not because the ideal of validity differs from man to man; if it were, they could not be sure there was any point even in arguing with each other, for one man's proof might be another man's irrelevancy. The diversity of men's conclusions is due

477

rather to the fact, admitted by all the great rationalists from Plato down, that man is brokenly and imperfectly rational. His thought is seldom picked up by the logic inherent in the nature of things and carried straight to a conclusion; his nature has long roots in an animal past which distorts his thought continually through his non-rational impulses and desires. How deeply his thought is affected by these sub-rational pushes and pulls is clear from the millennia of struggle it has taken for his reason to break free from myth into some measure of autonomy. The struggle, of course, still goes on.

2 When the proponent of revelation turns on the proponent of reason and says, 'You have done your best to drive me from my ancestral house; now show me the more stately mansion your "reason" has prepared for me,' the rationalist is likely to be embarrassed. There are all too many mansions in his province, many of them obviously disreputable and none of them bearing the plaque of official approval. The revelationist will complain that he is being invited to exchange certainty for confessed uncertainty, and a clearly structured universe, in which his place was clear and important, for a bewildering twilight world in which he is secure of little except his own insecurity. But the rationalist need not apologise. He is not inviting his neighbour to give up any certainty to which either logic or ethics entitles him. The rationalist has seen, or thinks he has seen, that the system of dogma, if accepted as revealed and certain, leads straight to self-contradiction, and therefore cannot be what it claims to be. And he is not offering his twilight world as one that is more comfortable or pleasing to live in than others, though he is personally grateful for having escaped the horror of the Lutheran world, in which most men are predestined to unremitting torment for what they are predestined to do. Whether a world view is pleasing or not has nothing to do with its truth, and it is truth that the rationalist above all wants. He wants to see things as they are. Whoever attempts this must admit that even the men of highest ability who have sought to make sense of the world have differed in their conclusions about it, and also that, considering the complex and shifting evidence, it would be astonishing if they did not. The chance that any one of them, even one as able and as devoted to truth as Spinoza or Hume, should arrive at any ultimate truth about the world which could stand in the form he gives to it is very small, and the chance of a less able inquirer smaller still.

But every negation has a positive base. The long series of negations with which historic dogmas have been greeted in this book could only have sprung from positive convictions of some sort, whether or not they were realised at the time; and it is only fair to opponents that, before taking leave of them, the writer should lay his own cards on the table. To set out these convictions with a proper defence would be to write a system of metaphysics, which is no task for the last pages of an overlong book. But a sketch may be better than nothing. It will at least give to outraged persons who have been involuntary targets a target to aim at in return; and it may give a glimpse to the curious of the sort of world one rationalist lives in.

THE WORLD A COHERENT WHOLE

3 I start with the law of contradiction: a statement and its contradictory cannot both be true. Here at the first step I hold we are committed to a world that is rational to this extent, that nothing in it is either self-contradictory or contradictory of anything else. The real world is a coherent world, in the sense that it is at least self-consistent.

It may be objected, of course, that the world is full of contradictions. Einstein contradicted Newton, Newton contradicted Leibniz, Leibniz contradicted Spinoza, and Spinoza contradicted Descartes. What the Kremlin wants in the Near East is a contradiction of what the White House wants. Even self-contradiction is notoriously common. Did not Russell hold that moral judgements fell outside the province of reason, and at the same time appeal to reason in condemning President Johnson? According to Marxism, progress consists in the constant overcoming of contradictions; the contradiction between the workers and the bourgeoisie, for example, was overcome by the October revolution.

Objections of this kind are mere misunderstandings. The law of contradiction does not say anything so absurd as that no statements are ever contradictory of others. It says only that *if* they are thus contradictory, they cannot both be *true*. And for two persons or nations or classes to have conflicting desires or interests is no contradiction. The fact that John wants Susan is not a denial of the fact that James wants her also, and is quite consistent with it. Conflicts of bodies or wills are common; *inconsistencies* between assertions or beliefs are common; inconsistencies between truths or facts, we should hold, do not and cannot occur.

Among those who have freed themselves from such mistakes, however, there are persons who would interpret the laws of logic in a way that would make a rationalist metaphysic impossible. Something must therefore be said about them, although it may involve a little more technicality than will be to everyone's taste.

4(1) First, there are those who say that the law of contradiction

is merely a linguistic rule, a statement that we propose to use
language in one way rather than another. When we say, for example,
that the same surface cannot at once be black and non-black, what
we are saying is that we propose not to use the term 'non-black' of
any surface we call black. I agree that such a proposal may be
implied, and that no sane person would want to use these words
otherwise. But why? If we are free to use them otherwise, why do
we never take advantage of that freedom and use 'black' and 'non-
black' of the same surface? The answer is clear enough. If we did,
our language would not answer to the facts; we should be applying
two adjectives to the same thing when it was plain that if one applied
the other would not. Linguisticism has recently gone so far as to
suggest that language makes the world in its own image. This has
things the wrong way about. The truth is rather that language is an
attempt to reflect the world. Instead of black being made exclusive
of non-black by our usage, the exclusion is there in nature, and our
usage, if it is sensible, will respect and reflect this fact.

(2) Sometimes the interpretation takes a slightly different turn.
The law of contradiction is not now a convention of language but a
convention of thought. It is true that we normally choose to conform to it, but our conformity is a matter of choice, not of necessity;
the rules of logic, Carnap once maintained, could be chosen 'quite
arbitrarily'.[1] But those who take this position never hold to it in
practice; nor can they. When they have shown by what they take to
be sound reasoning that these rules are arbitrary, they consider that
they have made out their case, and that anyone who, accepting their
evidence, rejects their conclusion is unreasonable. But if the rules of
inference are really arbitrary, why should I not accept the evidence
and reject the conclusion? Indeed, why should I not say, since no
logical rule now binds me, that I both accept the conclusion and
reject it? Since the law of contradiction is a convention only, I
choose to say that the statement 'the law is conventional' does not
exclude the statement 'the law is not conventional', and hence that
my opponent and I, though contradicting each other, are also in
agreement. Of course no conventionalist would accept this nonsense.
He never means that his statement of the arbitrariness of logic, or
his argument for it, is itself merely arbitrary. They at least are really
valid, and anyone who rejects them is missing the truth about logic.
The theory that logic is conventional is not itself a mere convention.
But if so, the theory has been abandoned.

(3) Sometimes still a different tack is taken. The laws of logic are
laws of thought, but not laws of things. They are necessary in the
sense that we cannot escape from them; we cannot think their
opposites; we cannot see, for example, how anything could at once

be *x* and not be *x*. But our inability to *think* this, we are told, is not the same as *x*'s inability to *be* this; it might, in spite of us, both have a quality and lack it. But what precisely does this mean? It means presumably that though we cannot think *x*'s being at once black and not black, it might in fact be both. But a moment's reflection will show this to be meaningless. Remember that according to the theory we cannot think *x*'s being both black and not black. If so, then in asserting that *x* may be both we are saying what has just been admitted to be unthinkable and therefore without meaning. On the other hand, if the statement is accepted as meaningful, if we really can think *x*'s being black and not black at once, then we have contradicted ourselves and are again saying nothing meaningful. For we have said both that the law of contradiction binds our thought and that it does not, since we have successfully thought its opposite. Thus the theory that the law is a law of thought only, and not of things, cannot even be intelligibly stated.

The law of contradiction, then, is more than a statement about usage, more than a convention, and more than a law of thought. It is a statement about the nature of things. It says something about the real world. What it says is that truth is coherent in the sense that if two assertions are inconsistent with each other they cannot both be true. And if they cannot both be true, that is because the world about which they are reporting cannot itself have incompatible attributes. Truth must be consistent if the reality it describes is consistent. The laws of logic give us knowledge about the way things are put together.

(4) There is a current theory that denies this and urges a logic without ontology. It is a pragmatic theory which holds that the laws of logic are means to ends; they are not logically necessary, but only practically necessary, indispensable instruments in 'regulating the pursuit of human ideals'. What are these 'human ideals'? They are such things as the order, coherence, and systematisation of our knowledge. This is not, so far, very enlightening. For consistency is an essential part of ordered, coherent, and systematised knowledge, and so far as this is true, what we are told is that we should obey the law of contradiction—that is, should be consistent—because if we do we shall achieve consistency. The argument is thus circular. But the fact surely is that none of these things is the *ultimate* end of thinking. It is perfectly meaningful to ask why we should wish our conclusions to show order, coherence, or systematisation. And to this question the one natural and plausible answer is, because only thought that possesses these characteristics can be *true*. Thought as such and always aims at truth, that is, the grasp of things as they are. It is admittedly the pursuit of an end, and the laws of thought

regulate that pursuit; so far we agree with the pragmatists. But why this beating about the bush, this vagueness and circularity in their account of the end? Presumably because if they gave the natural answer, that the end of thought is to see things as they are, they would have to admit that logic is concerned with ontology after all. But then we *must* admit this, or else deny that the end of thought is to know. The ultimate reason why we should try to think consistently is that unless we do we shall not think *truly*, which means that we shall not see the world as it is.

The first step in our rational construction is thus that, whatever else it may be, the world is a consistent whole, in the sense that it harbours no real contradiction. But this is a very abstract and meagre bit of information. What else can be said about this whole?

THE WORLD A CAUSAL WHOLE

5 I think we may advance a step and say also that it is a *causal* whole. By this I mean not only (I) that every event is causally connected with some other, but (II) that every event is thus connected, directly or indirectly, with *every* other. Since both these propositions play important parts in the scheme of things I am outlining, I must develop their meaning more particularly.

6(I) Every event is causally linked with an event that precedes it and another that follows it. This needs some explanation and defence. What causal law connects is special characters of those facts or events. What causation connects is particular facts or events; Jones takes a country walk in August and on his return has a fit of sneezing; he suspects that something about the walk led to the sneezing, and he tries to single this out. His work would be vastly facilitated if he could see that the sneezing fit is the sort of effect that *must* follow from a certain kind of antecedent; but, as Hume pointed out, we do not possess such insight. We must proceed not directly by seeing what *must* be the cause, but indirectly by seeing what can*not* be the cause. We do that by taking for granted that the cause *A* and the effect *B* are connected through certain of their characters *a* and *b*, and that if one of two suspected characters happens without the other, they are not causally related. It could not have been taking a walk as such that caused the fit of sneezing, for Jones has often taken walks without sneezing afterwards; nor could it have been walking through this particular field, nor the smell of the pine woods, nor going bare-headed, for these things too he has been exposed to without any such result. Jones may soon reach the end of his resources and surrender the matter to a medical researcher, but the method of search would be the same. The researcher would go on eliminating suspected factors until he came to one—say the exposure to a certain saturation of ragweed pollen—that was regularly present when such attacks occurred and absent when they did not occur.

THE UNIFORMITY OF NATURE

7 Anyone who uses this method must admit on reflection that he is making two assumptions, and it will be to our advantage to state them explicitly. (1) The first is the uniformity of nature. This does not mean, of course, that nature is uniform in the sense that as a whole it repeats itself, or that it is not continually producing what is novel, unexpected, and in the light of existing knowledge unpredictable. The state of the world at this instant presumably never occurred before and will never occur again. What uniformity means is that if a thing acts in a certain way today it will under like conditions act in the same way at any other time. To say that nature is uniform is thus only another way of saying that things and events behave lawfully, that if an event occurs in accordance with a certain law today that law will not be suspended tomorrow. 'Same cause, same effect.' If nature were not thus uniform, if an attack of sneezing were produced today by exposure to ragweed pollen and tomorrow by an ice-jam in Behring Strait or the bribery of an official in Indonesia, it would be idle to search for *the* cause of anything, not merely because no method could find it, but because it was not there to be found. *The* cause is the uniform cause, the cause without which the effect never happens, and given which it always happens. For practical purposes it may be expedient at times to assume that the same effect can be produced by a plurality of causes or that the same cause can produce different effects, as when it is said that the sneezing may result from either ragweed or a cold, or that a given amount of alcohol produces different effects in different persons. But if nature is really uniform, there cannot be exceptions of this kind. One can only believe that if the sneezing in the first case is really the same in kind, a common element is present to account for it in the cold and the exposure to pollen. And if alcohol acts differently on different persons, that does not prove that the same cause has different effects, for the cause is *not* the same; the cause in one case is alcohol acting under organic conditions *abc*, and in the next case under conditions *xyz*. Uniformity demands that once the relevant conditions are fully and exactly stated the resulting law is invariant.

THE LAW OF CAUSALITY

8(2) Besides the uniformity of nature, there is another assumption that is commonly made by those who would explain events through causes. It is called the law of causality, and means simply that all events do have causes. If it were suggested to Jones that he might fail to find the cause of his sneezing fits because it was something recondite and technical, he would no doubt agree; but he would certainly flout the suggestion that he might fail because there was no cause to find. That he would regard as absurd. And if asked to say whether he thought this applied to all other events as well as to the particular event he was investigating, he would no doubt say yes again. Indeed he can see on reflection that his confidence that *this* event has a cause is based on the assumption that events *generally* have causes. What he is thus assuming is the law of causality. That law is the most general of all natural laws—a law of laws, to the effect that there *are* laws governing all particular events.

It was remarked above that an important part of the world view here being sketched is that the world is a causal whole, and that the meaning of this statement consisted in part of the law of causality, that all events have causes. We have now seen something of the role this law plays in the attempts of the plain man and the scientist to explain the world about them. Both use it daily and confidently as the cornerstone of their attempts at understanding. In this I think they are right; and in view of the importance of the law to my own scheme of things, I must reluctantly pause over it a little longer. Why should we believe it to be true? The mere fact that it is constantly and successfully appealed to does not prove its truth. Indeed when we reflect upon it further, we soon come upon difficulties that in the minds of many have seemed sufficient reasons for rejecting it. For it is not only (a) incapable of proof; it seems to be also (b) inconsistent with new developments in science, (c) inconsistent with miracles, and (d) inconsistent with free will. These points deserve consideration. But in accordance with the plan of this chapter, I can only set down my own views briefly and rather dogmatically.

OBJECTIONS TO THE SWAY OF CAUSALITY

9 (a) It is true that the law of causality cannot be established in the manner of other causal laws. Many attempts have been made to prove it in this way, but there is really no parallel between the types of arguments used. The scientific argument for A's causing B is: assuming that there is a law covering the occurrence of B, the dissociations I have found between B and all other possibilities than

A leave me no alternative to fixing upon *A* as the cause. This is perfectly valid reasoning. The corresponding argument for the law of causality would be: assuming that all events are governed by law, I may infer from the lawfulness of the events I have studied to the conclusion that *all* events are governed by law. And this is obviously circular; the conclusion is begged in the assumption with which the argument starts. So far as I know, all attempts to justify induction inductively have failed in similar fashion. The law of causality is the general principle used to justify generalisations from one case to others. Grant it, and the inference proceeds smoothly; call it in question, and reasoning cannot get underway. This suggests that if the law is to be established at all it must be by a priori rather than empirical argument. To this suggestion we shall return.

10 (b) There is an apparent conflict between the law of causality and the results of quantum physics. The causal laws with which we are familiar connect changes of observable things, but we now know that these things are composed of enormous aggregates of elements, so minute as to be far below the threshold of observation. Our familiar causal laws are thus statistical statements about the behaviour of vast aggregates of particles. But statistical statements throw little light on individuals. One could not argue from the fact (if it were a fact) that Americans who reached forty died on the average at sixty-three to the conclusion that Jones, aged forty, would die at sixty-three; he might have a stroke tonight or be still sprightly at ninety. Similarly, we cannot argue from the fact that an army of ten billion protons and electrons shows a majestic stability in its behaviour to the conclusion that its individual components will show a similar absence of skittishness. Indeed these components have so far resisted all attempts by physicists to catch their behaviour in formulae. Heisenberg showed that the more exactly one determines the velocity of a particle, the less exactly can one know its position; and it is notorious that when atoms were conceived on the analogy of the solar system, electrons had a baffling way of leaping from orbit to orbit without any assignable cause. Such discoveries have led many physicists to question whether, since causation connects only determinate events happening at determinate times, one can rightly speak of causation at all in the submicroscopic realm. A layman will be well advised not to rush into this vast and dimly lit region with a small and flickering candle. But there are certain things that he may justifiably say.

(i) Even those who hold that causality is suspended in the atomic realm still admit its sway in that world with which alone we are directly concerned.

(ii) There is a great disparity between the two realms, and since our experience is confined to events of the macroscopic order, we can only represent those of the atomic order through similes and analogies that cannot be accurately checked. Protons, electrons, and photons are not *things* in the sense in which tennis balls are things, yet it is hard not to think of them in this way. Thus we face an awkward alternative in construing the tenants of the atomic world. If we think of its members in terms of the things and changes we know, we are likely to talk nonsense, while if we regard them as wholly dissimilar, we can say nothing about them at all. Let us try to be clear about this.

Regarding the causeless leaping of electrons from orbit to orbit, C. D. Broad remarks: 'I see no objection to physicists using such language when about their own business, if they find them convenient ways of briefly expressing certain complicated facts or hypotheses. But, if the terms "electron", "nucleus", "orbit", "motion", and "jump" are taken literally, I have no hesitation in saying that such statements are, and can be seen by everyone to be, absurd.'[2] That a tennis ball or the planet Mercury should leap from one point to another without any cause whatever would certainly seem to the physicist incredible, and if he uses the same language of an electron, conceived as a thing whittled down in size, one can only say that it remains incredible.

On the other hand, if we hold that the entities of the atomic world, and their ways of behaving, are utterly unlike those of our familiar world, they become inconceivable. And again physicists would not accept that. They hold that at least the more abstract categories, those of logic and mathematics, apply to the atomic world, for these are their chief reliance in exploring it. Now causality is also a category, and though less abstract than these others, is, like them, a major means of understanding the world. It should not be abandoned except from absolute necessity. And it is not clear that this necessity has yet arisen.

(iii) The reply may come that whether it has in fact arisen is a matter to be decided by specialists, those with an intimate knowledge of physics and the philosophy of science, not by knight-errant philosophers. That is no doubt true. But if the issue turns into a battle of authorities, the names are not all on one side. Many names could be thrown into the scale against causality in the atomic world, but there are names on the other side too. Einstein, Planck, and Rutherford among physicists, and Broad and Nagel among philosophers of science, would, if I am not mistaken, agree with the statement of Russell that 'There is nothing whatever in the Principle of Indeterminacy to show that any physical event is uncaused'.[3]

11 (c) We now come to an objection to the law of causality of a very different kind. Most of the theologians whose views we have considered in this volume would decline to accept it because it leaves no place for miracles, miracles being conceived as suspensions of natural law by a supernatural power. To be sure, a miracle is not thought of as an uncaused event, but rather as one caused by God. Nevertheless the act of God is conceived as an intervention in the natural order, the overriding of a natural law to produce a result which, except for that intervention, would not have occurred.

Now it is easy to abolish miracles by definition; one need only define a natural law as universal to make any suspension of it self-contradictory. But we know too little about the causal connection to justify such dogmatism. It is not logically impossible, so far as we can see, for a man to walk on water or even for a decomposing body to come to life again. Hume was therefore right in saying that the decision whether an alleged miracle had actually occurred rested on the weighing of probabilities. And he thought that the evidence in favour of the 'law' would always outweigh the testimony in favour of its violation. It would always be more likely that there had been some deception, some error in observation, or some mis-reporting of the facts than that a generalisation firm enough to present itself as a law of nature had been violated. If the testimony for the miracle did seem to outweigh that for the law, it would always be more probable that the eccentric occurrence was governed by laws yet undiscovered, which supplemented and corrected laws already known, than that there had been a sheer break-through from a non-natural order. We can accept this, I think, though with some demurrer about the 'always'. A criterion of the occurrence of miracles should not be so framed as to exclude the acceptance of them even if they occurred. Still it is difficult to conceive an event, even the sudden disappearance of an advanced cancer or the reanimation of a dead body, that could not more credibly be assigned to unknown natural causes than to no natural causes at all. Regarding many of the miracles of healing recorded in the New Testament, for example, it is clearly possible to accept the facts while assigning them to laws now imperfectly known about the relation of mind and body. Regarding such miracles as Jonah and the 'great fish', Joshua and the halting of the sun, and the parting of the Red Sea, the probability that they are myths rather than actual suspensions of natural law is overwhelming. There is, indeed, no empirical way of disproving a miraculous factor in these or other events. That could only be done by showing that the laws alleged to be violated are necessary laws, and this is not now possible. Nevertheless the threat posed by miracles to the law of causality does not seem very alarming. The probability is that if they cannot be dismissed by the law they can, in the manner just suggested, be absorbed by it.

12 (d) For many persons the main objection to the law of causality is its apparent exclusion of free will. 'If all events are governed by causal law,' they would say, 'and my volitions are events, as they clearly are, then my volitions must be so governed, and everything I do or say must be already determined'. Now it is plain that the law of causality does imply determinism, for determinism is only the statement of that law as it applies to a special class of events called volitions. Many persons who would otherwise accept the law un-hesitatingly draw back from it when they realise that it commits them to this conclusion. I do not think that on reflection they should. For indeterminism is a less desirable and determinism a less undesirable position than these persons probably suppose.

If the law of causality is true, the state of one's mind and body and their surroundings at time t_1 completely determines the state of one's mind and body at time t_2. This the indeterminist denies. He holds that from the moment t_1 there may emerge some state of one's body or mind which is connected by no law with what went before and would therefore be unpredictable even by a complete knowledge of the circumstances at t_1. To anyone who believes that all events are caused, that is, occur in accordance with causal law, this is an arbitrary position. What has led the indeterminist to accept it? I think that two kinds of consideration have been uppermost, one drawn from fact and the other from assumptions in ethics.

The consideration drawn from fact is that when one makes a decision to act one commonly 'feels free' to act in any of a variety of ways. Even the determinist admits that he feels so. But this feeling does not stand up very well when put in the witness box. It is essentially the sense of the absence of any circumstances constraining one to act in this way rather than another. But this sense of the absence of constraining factors is clearly based on a lack of awareness of them; and this lack of awareness is inevitable and is quite com-patible with their presence.[4] When we make practical decisions, we are always forward-looking; we are engrossed with what our actions may lead to; and there would be no point at such a time in grubbing about in our subconsciousness for causal factors that may be acting on us. With our minds wholly engaged in one direction, we naturally have no eyes for what is going on in another. But if at a later moment we do turn our eyes in the other direction, we have no difficulty in bringing factors to light that were working on us at the time, and we can only suppose there were many more which retrospection can less readily find. This of course does not prove determinism, for one can never by empirical study exhaust the causes of an event, and there is always a loophole by which the indeterminist can escape. But it does show that the feeling of freedom, if offered as evidence of causelessness, has very little force.

For many reflective persons, however, the chief objection to determinism is the indignity that it seems to inflict on minds that like to think of themselves as moral and rational. To them it would make man a robot, as fully determined by mechanical law as the puppets of a Punch-and-Judy show. And of some forms of determinism it must be admitted that the charge is justified. Professor Skinner, for example, in his *Beyond Freedom and Dignity* sees so clearly that his behaviourism is incompatible with dignity as well as freedom in their traditional senses that he tries elaborately to deflate both. But this kind of determinism, which is built on the violent paradox of identifying consciousness with bodily behaviour, has little plausibility.[5] Determinism as accepted by the ablest moralists of this century—such writers as Rashdall and Moore, Ross and Prichard, Bradley and Bosanquet, Dewey and Broad—fully recognises that human motives affect the course of conduct. What makes determinism objectionable to most people is the sense that it dehumanises them, that it assimilates their behaviour to that of some mindless machine like a computer; and their antipathy to such crude reductionism is well grounded. Determinism in the hands of responsible thinkers rejects that position as emphatically as they do. And when they see that the line of causality runs, not around or beneath the human spirit but through it, so that every degree of elevation in their motives can still register itself in their conduct, the base of their suspicion largely disappears.

But not wholly, it will be replied. For those motives themselves will still be determined, and though it is less degrading perhaps to be a mental or spiritual robot then a mechanical one, it is still a deplorable state to be in. Now I think that when people take this view they are not considering the alternative. They object to their actions being determined; very well, consider the situation of the man whose actions are *not* determined. If not determined, they are of course uncaused. If they were uncaused, that means that *he* did not cause them, and that in any proper sense they are not his actions at all. Hence he is not responsible for them, and he can never be justly praised or blamed or punished for them. His attempts to form or improve his character may not only fail to improve his conduct but *must* fail, for if his actions are uncaused, whether at the stage of motives or of behaviour issuing from motives, they must remain unaffected by any measure taken to improve them. And if his own actions are thus undetermined, so are those of others; and his habitual predictions of what others will do from their behaviour in the past will be without foundation. If determinism has its undesirable aspects, none of them seems as undesirable as this detachment of one's conduct from one's past self and character, and its delivery over to chance. I say chance advisedly. For so far as an event issues from t_1 that is unconnected by law with what preceded, it is chance of the deepest kind—not merely the chance that is based on ignorance but the chance that means disconnectedness in the very nature of things.

The argument that the law of causality is to be rejected because it conflicts with free will thus seems to me to be based on factual and ethical misapprehensions, and to lose its force when these are removed. And with their removal, the last of the objections to the law of causality that we are considering has also been removed.

ALL EVENTS CAUSALLY INTERRELATED

13(2)   The causal monism proposed some pages back consists of two propositions. The first of these, the law of causality, we have considered. The second is the proposition that every event is causally connected, directly or indirectly, with every other.

This suggestion at first glance seems most improbable. We often think of a present event as if it were the last bead on a string that stretches straight and far into the past, or the final movement in a row of billiard balls in which each transmits its motion by impact to the next. From the last ball that has moved we can look back along the series and trace the line of causation as far as we care to go. The image is useful in suggesting that every event is only the most recent in a line of causes that stretches into an illimitable past and will continue into an illimitable future. But in an important respect it is misleading. The causation of an event is never merely a linear succession. We say that *the* cause of the ball's motion is the impact on it of another. But the cause of a motion includes everything without which it would not have happened. And when we ask what is essential in this sense to the motion of the ball, we clearly cannot confine ourselves to the impact of the ball before it, for the motion would not have been what it was without the retarding pressures of the air and the felt surface on which the ball rolls, without the minute tilt of the table, or the sudden breeze that came in at the door, or the given temperature of the atmosphere, or the gravitational attractions on the balls exerted by the earth, the sun, and indeed all the fixed stars. To pursue this last a little further, if the law of gravitation holds at all, we must suppose that, allowing for the time it takes for gravitational influence to travel, nothing in the universe is wholly irrelevant to the motion of the ball. The sun is exerting a pull upon it that varies directly as the sun's mass and inversely as the square of its distance; but so is the chair by the window, Mt Everest, Orion, and the Pleiades. Thus at one stroke we are taken out to numberless other things and events that would have to enter into the full causal story of this apparently trivial event.

These seemingly irrelevant factors are linked with the motion of the ball directly, for the gravitational influence from each is conceived as following a single causal line, like that of the light from a star. But every event that is gross enough for us to detect is the result not of a single causal line but of a convergence of such lines. Instead of following the gravitational track, for example, we could start, as we usually do, from the impact of the impinging ball, or again from the support exerted by the table, or the resistance of the air, or the friction of the felt surface, or the influence of the breeze through the door. Now just as the movement of the ball is the product of a pencil of forces, most or all of these causal factors would also be found to involve a pencil of forces each of whose radiating lines runs back indefinitely into the past and into remote spaces. The tracing of the full causation of an event is thus not like following the smooth path of a meteor, but rather like tracing the diverging roots of a tree.

14   This enables us to see what is meant by *indirect* causal connection. Events of importance are happening at every moment on the sun; it is believed, for example, to be losing mass at the rate of four million tons a second. Suppose that among these events there is happening at this moment an explosion of gases on the sun's surface. So far as direct causation is concerned, this event can have no influence on the present motion of the billiard ball, for there is an interval of some eight minutes between the occurrence of the explosion and the arrival of its effects on the earth. Are events on the sun and events on the earth therefore unrelated causally at any given time? Directly, yes. But indirectly, no; for the two sets of events have causal ancestors in common. The explosion of gases has a chemical and thermal history that runs through the five trillion years of the sun's biography. Take one state of the sun, say the one existing a million years ago. That state is a causal ancestor of the present explosion on the sun. But it is also a causal ancestor of the movement of the billiard ball, since without the light and heat made possible by that state of the sun, there would be no human life on the earth, and hence neither billiard players to wield cues nor billiard balls to be moved by them. The explosion on the sun and the movement of the ball, though neither is the direct cause or effect of the other, are thus clearly interrelated through their common causal ancestry.

Is this indirect relation strong enough to enable us to say that if either of the two events had not happened the other would not? I think we *can* say this, if not with certainty, at least with a presumption in favour of its truth. For consider: the motion of the ball is produced by a plurality of causal lines, which themselves tend to ramify out like the roots of an oak to a great depth and in many directions. Suppose that for a short time we follow one of these roots. The ball moved because it was struck by another; that in turn moved because it was struck by the cue; and the stroke of the cue followed a volition in the mind of the player. That volition sprang from the state of his mind and body at the moment before, which might be described generally as an interest in the game. What was it that conditioned this interest? The answer would have to include the means of the player, his residence, his education, his skill, his immediate opportunity, and much else. And these depend on what? His parentage, for example, which depends on his parents' parents, and their parents, in a line that could not be stopped short of the primeval woods and the still more primeval slime. And the woods and the slime were what they were, as we have seen, because of the light and warmth of the primeval sun.

Now let us make a contrary-to-fact supposition. Suppose that the player had *not* wielded his cue in the place, time, and manner that he did. If we believe in the law of causality, what would that commit us to? The denial of the consequent entitles us, of course, to deny the antecedent. We can say that if that effect had not happened none of the necessary conditions (the without-which-not conditions), either of the event or of those conditions themselves, could have happened as they did. And if one follows that through, it means not only that the man, his parentage, his community, and his nation would have had to be different in their history; it means that the story of life on earth would have had to be different. And since the warmth and light of the sun were indispensable conditions of the story's being what it was, they too would have had to be different. But if they were different, it could only be because the sun itself had a different constitution from that which it in fact had. Now start down the different line of causation governing the history of the sun. Every state of this history from that remote time to the present would likewise have had to be other than it was. The extent of the difference from what actually occurred, either at the start of the downward movement or at any later moment, is of course beyond calculation. One can only say that, in view of the ramifying lines of causation as one moves forward, the present total consequence in the state of the sun would have had to be massive. Indeed we could not say that *any* event now happening on the sun would be what it is.

In short, deny all the necessary causes of the movement of the billiard ball, work out all the changes involved in the replacement of one remote cause by another, and you cannot say with confidence that anything in the sun or on the earth would remain the same. Indeed by an easy extension of the argument we can say that if any event anywhere were cancelled every event everywhere would in some way and degree be affected by it. In the network of causal relations, nothing is wholly irrelevant to anything else.

It may be objected that we are overstating the implications of a change in the causal series. 'The player is playing billiards because he met Jones, who invited him to play; if he had met Smith and been invited by him instead, surely the game would have gone on just as it did; why this preposterous invocation of the sun and the fixed stars?' The answer is that on the large chessboard of the world you cannot in this nonchalant way replace one piece and assume that the other pieces will remain the same. If the billiards player had met Smith instead of Jones, the lines of causality both in Jones's life and his own would have had to be different not for a step or two but for millions of steps, and to suppose these steps different while their successors remained the same is to play fast and loose with causality. If we take the causal web seriously, the burden of proof would be on anyone who sets a limit anywhere to the radiating implications of any causal change.

CAUSALITY INVOLVES NECESSITY

15 We are now in a position to move forward. If the world is an interconnected causal system, can we say that it is a system in any further sense? It seems to me that we can. For I cannot accept the view that causal relations are merely contingent relations. If we know that A causes B, we know that the two are in some sense *necessarily* connected, and therefore that if the facts and events of the world are interconnected causally they are interconnected necessarily. I realise of course that this step from causality to necessity is controversial, and that it is to be taken only with care.[6]

Anyone who tries to take this step finds himself blocked at the outset by the burly figure of Hume. For Hume maintained, to the satisfaction of the now dominant schools of philosophy, that in no case of causation do we have any insight whatever into *why* the effect follows the cause. We see just as little necessity linking the blow of the hammer and the sinking of the nail, or the succession of one idea to another in our thought, as we do in the side-by-side appearance of a red leaf and a green one on an autumn tree. This doctrine has become part of the standard equipment of young philosophers.

And of course if one starts from the Humean premise that whatever is in our ideas must come from sensation, this conclusion does follow. The relation of necessity cannot be sensed. But to design a theory of knowledge that excludes necessary relations, even if they exist, and then say that inquiries made in accordance with that theory find no trace of them, is not inspired philosophising. The questions we have to ask are two: (1) Keeping our notion of experience broad enough to include necessary relations if they occur, does our experience of particular cases reveal the complete opaqueness to understanding that Hume claims to have found? and (2) When we analyse the notion of causality as such, do we find a priori necessity in it or not?

16(1)   The plausibility of Hume's view varies greatly as one passes from one type of case to another. In the field of purely physical relations, it is perhaps right. We do not know why the hammer sinks the nail or, to put it more technically, why the electrons moving around the nucleus of an atom repel the electrons of another atom. Electrons do act in that way, but why they do so is beyond our present understanding, and we can only accept the fact. This seems indeed to be true of all other instances of purely physical causation. Even laws of high generality are similarly opaque. Newton's law of the inverse squares, and the modification of it introduced by the theory of relativity, are statements of mathematical precision, but they are not statements of mathematical truth, and the question Why? can still be raised about them with no prospect of an early answer. The same is true of the action of body on mind. We know that if we stub our toe violently, we suffer pain, and that if a certain region in the brain is stimulated electrically, sensations of sound occur. No one has the least idea why.

Does this opaqueness remain as one passes to higher levels of causal experience? I do not think it does. It is true that one does not reach the simple and clear-cut necessities that belong to the abstractions of logic and mathematics, but neither does one remain in the darkness of mere conjunction. Take the influence, not of body on mind, but of deliberate volition on behaviour. A man decides to lift his arm and hold it out straight before him, and proceeds to do so. Can it reasonably be said that he is wholly in the dark as to why the arm behaved as it did? That hardly accords with his actual experience. He would be ready enough to admit that he does not know how a mental state affects the course of neural change. But I think he will also say that there is something about the causation of the movement that he *knows*, and does not merely infer with high probability from past conjunctions. He would say that, exceptional

circumstances apart, if his arm carried out th
that without that volition it would not have
far, the insight claimed is merely that the
condition of the movement, in the sense em
of difference. But the claim actually goes m
to some understanding of *why*, given that
arm followed, rather than a clenching of th
I do not think this insight a mere illusi...
admittedly limited. But it does go beyond the bare conjun...
which, on Hume's view, the knowledge of causation is confined.[7]

When we pass from psychophysical to psychical events, the conjunction theory is still less plausible. Mrs Jones receives a telegram
from the Secretary of Defence reporting that Private John Jones,
her son, has just been killed in action, and she is grief-striken as a
result. This, according to Hume, is a mere de facto sequence, in
which it remains as mysterious why the news should have produced
the result as it is why electrons repel each other. But it is surely not a
total mystery why that sort of loss should have produced that sort of
grief. Romeo receives a note from Juliet saying that she will meet
him at their trysting place tonight. He is excited and happy. Is
that wholly unintelligible? Othello, when he realises that he, 'like
the base Indian, threw a pearl away, richer than all his tribe,'
resolves to treat himself with the contempt that such fatuousness
deserves. Critics freely allow themselves to speak of the 'inevitability'
of the tragic denouement, and such language does not seem inappropriate. Much of the conviction carried by a great dramatist's
handling of human nature lies precisely in this inevitability; one
sees that a human being with such-and-such motives, passions, and
standards, confronted by such-and-such crises, *must* act in this way,
and would be acting incoherently if he acted in any other. The
literary critics show more perceptiveness here than the Humean
philosophers. If human conduct is not a highly rational achievement,
neither is it a mere refuse heap in which anything may be found
along with anything else. It is that peculiar kind of chaos that is
shot through with gleams of rationality, and the higher in the
scale it rises, the more intelligible the conduct becomes.

CAUSAL NECESSITY IN INFERENCE

17 Sometimes—and here Hume is most obviously wrong—the
nerve of necessity in a causal sequence shows itself nakedly. I have
argued this matter before, and may here be brief.[8] A course of
reasoning is a series of events, and therefore a process governed as
truly by causality as any physical process. In a logical deduction the

the premises precedes the presentation in one's mind of the
usion. If all members of the zoological class of insects have six
, and a spider does not have six legs, then (strangely enough and
against our prepossessions) a spider is not an insect. We cannot doubt
that the apprehension of the premises in their union was a cause
as well as an antecedent of the conclusion's emerging in our minds.
Is the emergence of that conclusion something as beyond our
understanding as the occurrence of pain when we step on a tack?
I do not think that anyone who says so can be looking attentively
at the facts. If we are asked, 'Why did that special conclusion emerge
in your mind rather than the suggestion, say, that Popocatapetl
might now be erupting?' we should reply unhesitatingly, 'Because
the premises I just had in mind required it,' and that answer,
though not a complete one, is, so far as it goes, correct. And if it *is*
correct, the causality that produced the conclusion has necessity
within it. Our thought moved along one line rather than another
because it was under constraint by the logical necessity linking the
contents.

It will not do, of course, to say that the conclusion emerged
because we *saw* that it was entailed by the premises, for we can only
see this if the conclusion is already in mind as one term of the nexus;
and then one is explaining the appearance of the conclusion by
presupposing this appearance. There is no escape, I think, from
saying that the timeless relation of implication between the content
of the premises and that of the conclusion is itself a condition accounting for the course of the inference. It is not a sufficient condition,
granted; for there are other factors, both conscious and unconscious,
that enter in; and these others may be such that the premises are
followed by the wrong conclusion or none at all. But it remains true
that when we have arrived at a certain conclusion we can often see
clearly and confidently that among the conditions of our doing so
was the relation of entailment between the premises we had in mind
at one moment and the conclusion that entered our mind at the next.

It is not true, then, that an empirical study of causal sequences
reveals nothing in them beyond conjunction. Hume's analysis
comes nearest to the truth in purely physical cases, but in mental
sequences, and particularly as we approach the level of thought and
action that is recognised as rational, we see with increasing clearness that necessity enters in as part of the causal strand.

A PRIORI ELEMENTS IN CAUSATION

18(2) The sense of necessity is stronger still when one turns from
an empirical study of cases to an analysis of the idea of causation.

Though most men would feel uneasy if told that in the action of one billiard ball on another there is no link stronger than succession, they find it hard to say precisely what this stronger link is. And when some neo-Humean presses his case by asking them whether there is anything contradictory in supposing that the second ball should refuse to budge or should fly straight up in the air, they are likely to admit that there is not, and to suppose that they were merely confused in supposing necessity to be present at all. But plain men are often right in their intuitions, even when faulty or helpless in formulating them. Fortunately, on this matter C. D. Broad has come to their aid. He was convinced that we have a priori knowledge even of physical causation. Assuming that causation is concerned with change, and that a change normally means the starting, stopping, or varying of a process, he asks whether we have any self-evident insight into the laws governing such occurrences, and concludes that we have such insight at four distinguishable points. (i) 'Every change has a cause.' (ii) 'The cause of any change contains a change as an essential factor.' (iii) 'If a change issues from a moment t, then all changes which are factors in its cause are changes which enter into t.' (iv) 'A given change in a given process issuing from a given moment cannot have more than one total cause.'[9] I agree with Broad that these are a priori insights, not empirical generalisations. If anyone were to offer empirical evidence that any of them was violated in a particular case, we should insistently disbelieve it, holding that the evidence must be mistaken or incomplete. Hume would deny that we have any such insights. And it is true that self-evident insights are to be accepted very gingerly. But they do exist, and when they present themselves as clearly as they do here, it is hardly possible to put them down as merely probable generalisations that experience may at any time rescind.

Nor do they exhaust our a priori knowledge of causality. I think we also know that if A causes B it is in virtue of its *character* as A. It is no accident that men do not gather grapes of thorns or figs of thistles. That is why causal laws, though holding of events, are always statements of connection between characters. Even though we do not know in the end why atropine dilates the pupil of the eye, we are so sure that the effect depends on something in the nature of atropine that if a liquid offered us as such did not dilate the pupil we should decline to admit that it was atropine. As H. W. B. Joseph said:

'If a thing a under conditions c produces a change x in a subject s . . . the way in which it acts must be regarded as a partial expression of what it is. It could only act differently, if it *were* different. As long therefore as it is *a*, and stands related under conditions *c* to a subject that is *s*, no other effect than *x* can be produced; and to say that the same thing acting on the same thing under the same conditions may yet produce a different effect, is to say that a thing need not be what it is. But this is in flat conflict with the Law of Identity. . . .'[10]

JOSEPH AND AYER ON CAUSATION

19 I think Joseph is substantially right. Though we do not know in advance of experience what effect *a* will produce, we do know that it will produce whatever it does produce in virtue of its being *a*; and this, so far as it goes, is necessary knowledge. Professor Ayer takes exception to this view, and his criticism should be noted, though it requires some lingering over technicalities; and if the reader is impatient, he should turn at once to the next section. If Joseph's view is accepted, Ayer says,

'I can no longer have any doubt that if the event I am observing really is an instance of *A* it will be succeeded under these conditions by an instance of *X*; but the trouble is that I must at the same time become correspondingly more doubtful whether this really is an instance of *A*. For the evidence which I formerly took to be sufficient to establish the truth of this existential proposition will *ex hypothesi* not be sufficient to establish it, now that I have widened the connotation of *A* by making it logically necessary that every instance of *A* should, in the relevant conditions, be conjoined with an instance of *X*.'[11]

This last is no doubt true. Even if we accept necessity in causation, our grasp of it will not enable us to predict with certainty that *A* will produce *X*, and hence we cannot be sure that the true cause of *X* is present until we find *X* present in fact. But this is not an argument against Joseph's view, and perhaps is not meant to be. Such knowledge as he claimed here was of the extremely general kind that is confined to the statement, 'if *A* causes *X*, it does so in virtue of its character'; and it is no objection to this view that we can never demonstrate what will follow from a particular given event and hence must wait for the effect before we can be certain. This is no evidence against either the presence of necessity or our knowledge of that presence.

Ayer goes further, however. He dismisses Joseph's theory on the ground that it is essentially a proposal to use words in a new and inconvenient way; its truth 'depends entirely upon how one chooses to construct one's language'. According to the theory, 'all causal expressions are treated as partial definitions of some general term'. But if we were to treat them so, 'we should have a language in which all synthetic causal propositions would take the form of singular existentials. We should not then be able to express at all what we now express by making causal propositions apply synthetically to an infinite number of possible cases. . . .' We should find, further, 'that it would not be possible for us, as it is at present, to abandon a "causal law" without making a change in our usage of words. There would, indeed, be nothing describable as "the abandonment of a causal law", except the redefinition of some term.'[12]

This criticism does not, I think, achieve its end. (a) To say that there is an element of necessity in A's producing B is not an attempt to *redefine* A. If a geometer discovers some new property which follows from a figure's being a circle, he is not proposing a redefinition of the circle; indeed if all that follows from a definition had to be included in the definition, we could never define anything. It may be replied that Joseph must have been attempting a definition, for he made A's very identity depend on its causal behaviour; if one says that A causes B in virtue of being A, B's absence commits one to saying that the apparent A could not have been really A. True; but this does not commit one to including all the consequences in the definition unless one holds that all necessary propositions are analytic of their subjects. Joseph would not have accepted that view, nor do I. Ayer seems to be contending that on a rationalist view of causality, if Julius Caesar produced a stream of effects lasting from his time to our own, these must all be parts of the very conception of Caesar, and therefore that none of his friends had a right to recognise him as Caesar until the scroll of history had unrolled. In one sense, no doubt, this is true; we do not fully understand the nature of anything until we understand what it entails, and hence our conceptions generally will be kept tentative and modifiable. But unless we could at least provisionally define things before knowing all that the definitions entailed, we could never develop these entailments. No sensible rationalist proposes that discursive reasoning be abandoned because everything it might discover is not provided in one packet at the outset.

(b) Nor does the truth of the rationalist view of causality 'depend entirely upon how one chooses to construct one's language'. That view is a theory of how nature is put together, and how nature is put together does not depend on how we put our words together. One can indeed order one's words appropriately if one knows the order of nature first, but it does not make sense to say that whether that order is of one kind or another 'depends entirely upon how one chooses to construct one's language'. The statement that causation in nature involves logical entailment is either true or not true, and it remains what it is, whatever language one uses about it. How otherwise could one choose between ways of constructing one's language? One can make language answer to fact; one cannot rearrange fact to suit one's linguistic preferences. These are truisms. But they have to be set down when questions about the nature of things are translated into questions about the use of words.

(c) Professor Ayer says that if we should adopt the necessity view, 'we should have a language in which all synthetic causal propositions would take the form of singular existentials. We should not then be able to express at all what we now express by making causal propositions apply synthetically to an infinite number of possible cases,' and 'it would not be possible for us, as it is at present, to abandon a "causal law" without making a change in our usage of words'. Ayer's admirable succinctness makes him somewhat cryptic here, and for fairness' sake it may be well to state in my own words what I take him to mean. (i) Why should he say that on the necessity view such a causal proposition as 'atropine dilates the pupil' is a 'singular existential'? Because if the atropine dilates the pupil in virtue of its nature as atropine, then so acting is part of its nature, and we cannot be sure it is atropine at all until we find it so acting. And we find it so acting only as we observe particular cases. Hence 'atropine dilates the pupil' must, if responsibly said, be only a report of one or more particular observations. (ii) Hence, again, it can no longer be what causal statements have commonly been, universal or general statements with application 'to an infinite number of possible cases'. And (iii) if we found a case in which atropine did not dilate the pupil, we should know that what we had could not be atropine, and, to be clear, we should have to find a new name for it. Hence we could not 'abandon a "causal law" without making a change in our usage of words'.

In all this there seems to me more subtlety than cogency. (i) Though it is true that on the necessity view you cannot be sure that you have atropine until you find it dilating the pupil, neither can you be sure beforehand on the empiricist view that what you conceived as the cause is really before you. Whether A produces x necessarily or only uniformly, you cannot be sure the A you meant is in operation without awaiting the result, and its being so is subject in both cases to the same veto through the non-appearance of the expected effect. (ii) It is hard to see that the statement 'atropine is *conjoined* with dilation of the pupil' should be a law capable of infinite applications and 'atropine *as such* dilates the pupil' should not. The latter is more obviously universal than the former, and if made with a little interpretation escapes the requirement of particular verification that Ayer would impose on it. What it means for the rationalist is something like this: in the substance called atropine, which has been found to dilate the pupil, there is something in virtue of which this effect will, under like conditions, be produced always and necessarily. This seems to me an a priori statement and, like all such statements, genuinely universal. (iii) Nor is it easy to see why on a rationalist theory we could not abandon a causal law without a change in our usage of words. That would follow only if the causal behaviour not only were necessary but were included in the very definition of the cause, which, as we have seen, it need not be. The word 'circle' does not have to be redefined and a new word found whenever a new property of the figure is discovered or an old one found to have been mistakenly deduced. If atropine failed in certain cases to dilate the pupil, the verbal way of dealing with this would be the same on either theory; we should say that atropine dilated the pupil only under certain conditions—e.g. when it was in liquid form, or when in a solution of three per cent or more, or if it had not been exposed to sunlight.

20 If what we have said is accepted, it is not unreasonable to hold that causal laws are also necessary laws. This does not mean, of course, that they are self-evident. We do not know that fire burns or water wets in the way we know that two and two make four. But in addition to our knowledge that necessity does in certain privileged cases enter into causation and our a priori grasp of some aspects of causality, we have what can only be called an invincible surmise that if events of certain kinds go uniformly together it is not by chance. Hume would have us think that no number of repetitions of fire's burning or water's wetting would affect the certainty or even the probability of their behaving the same way in the next instance. And on a theory of chance which rules out the possibility that the dice are loaded, there seems to be no way of avoiding this conclusion. If you throw a die ten thousand times and get ten thousand successive fives, it is no more likely, if loading is excluded, that you should get a five on the next throw than a two or a six. But the plain man would have no doubt in such a case that the die was loaded, and would regard it as absurd to rule that hypothesis out. He would take a roughly similar view about causation. One can point out to him that in an infinite run of cases no finite run can establish any probability, and hence that he has no right to expect anything rather than anything else; but he will go right on expecting as before, and —no one really doubts—with results that will confirm his expectation. The hypothesis of chance cannot be disproved, but once the hypothesis that more is at work is allowed, it is overwhelmingly supported by the course of events. We must admit that we do not in the end know why fire burns or water wets. But it will take more than Hume to convince men that it is merely a matter of chance; if fire burns and water wets, that is because of the distinctive nature of each.

Our conclusion so far is that the world is a unity in three senses. In the first place, it is a coherent world between whose facts there are no inconsistencies. Secondly, it is a causal unity, in the sense that all events are causally interrelated, directly or indirectly. Thirdly, its elements are also necessarily related, since causal relations, we have argued, would be seen as necessary if fully understood.

COMMON SENSE AND THE PERCEPTUAL WORLD

21 In discussing consistency, causality, and necessity, we have been dealing with abstract and general relations which, though they tell us little about individual things, tell us much of importance about the structure of the whole. Let us turn now from these general features to a more familiar scene, the perceptual world of common sense. Each of us at any moment is, or has, a field of consciousness in which the most conspicuous objects are such things as tables and chairs, rocks and roads, trees and animals and other people. This common-sense order is usually accepted without question as being what it appears to be. It is the base camp from which all the explorations of science or philosophy must start, and the haven to which all speculations must return when in need of empirical verification. It is the home base for everyone—the region where we feel most secure, where things and persons seem most stable and predictable, and doubt and mystery are at a minimum. It is a region where the speculations of the philosopher seem a luxury or an excrescence.

Some philosophers have come close to agreeing with this judgement of their work. A school of thought has appeared in recent decades which would make accordance with common sense the test of philosophy rather than make philosophy the inquisitor and judge of common sense. In his notable essay, 'A Defence of Common Sense', G. E. Moore offered a long list of beliefs that had been held by philosophers—the beliefs, for example, that matter did not exist, that space and time were unreal, that memory might be an illusion, that the existence of other minds was dubious; and he went on to assert that he *knew* these beliefs to be false on the ground that they outraged common sense. He was more certain, he said, that common sense was right about them than that any of the subtle arguments offered by philosophers against them were valid. Other philosophers, following what they took to be Moore's lead, developed a cult of 'ordinary usage', maintaining that so long as philosophers stuck to the standard meanings of words instead of warping and twisting them into new meanings of their own, they were on sure ground. The quagmires of philosophy consisted of verbal confusions.

These views found pleased acceptance among persons—and they were many—for whom the subtleties and ardours of philosophy held no attraction. We are all at times members of that camp. Nevertheless it had no tenable case. To suppose that common sense has the answer to sophisticated questions that it has never thought of raising is a strange position, to which Moore himself was unable to adhere. The common man takes it for granted, for instance, that matter exists, and that when he looks at a match-box, he is perceiving a material thing. Moore examined this perception and concluded that it may be interpreted in any one of three ways, between which, after a vast expenditure of pains and patience, he found himself unable to choose. Now common sense can hardly be a supreme court for philosophy if its pronouncements are so vague that it must thus rely on philosophers to tell it what they mean. Nor is the appeal to common usage in any better case. One can talk nonsense or falsehood in the most impeccable standard English. It is perfectly good usage, for example, to say 'I see a star'. But as understood by the plain man, that statement would abolish both modern physics and modern astronomy.[13] Common sense and common usage make a good beginning for philosophy, but if it must remain accountable to them to the end, they prove a mere ball and chain. It is true that anyone who departs from the common-sense view of things should be prepared to carry the burden of proof, but this burden is sometimes light.

THE PERCEPTUAL WORLD DEPENDENT ON MIND

22 That holds, I think, of the common-sense conviction that we are now about to examine, a conviction whose truth or falsity is of the highest importance to anyone trying to understand the world he lives in, even in broad outline. This is the conviction that we see things as they are, or, to put it a little more precisely, that what we are immediately aware of in perception is a physical world that exists apart from perception just as it is revealed to us. There is, I believe, no good ground for this conviction, and once that becomes clear, the world proves to be a very different place from the one common sense accepts.

The issue has been a controversial one for centuries. Even among philosophers of the present century there is a wide spectrum of opinions, reaching all the way from the extreme realism of E. B. Holt, who thought that even the objects of illusion had a subsistence independent of consciousness, to the solipsism of Christine Ladd-Franklin, who accepted the existence of nothing outside her own field of consciousness. It is impracticable to weigh all these theories, and I shall content myself with outlining my own position.

The crucial point is the fact of error. All men are realists, in the sense of believing that they perceive things directly and as they are, until perception misleads them, and sooner or later it always does. Straight sticks look bent in water; railway tracks seem to converge; santonin makes things look yellow; for alcoholics on lost weekends the wallpaper may squirm with bats' heads; water is warm to a cold hand and cold to a warm one; one man sees the signal in the road as green while his colour-blind partner sees it as grey. One or other of the conflicting impressions, if not both, must be in error. Here common sense and science agree, for they proceed on the same assumption, namely that no physical thing can have incompatible qualities. A surface cannot be green and grey at the same time, nor the same water hot and cold, nor the same rails parallel and converging, nor the same wallpaper quiescent and squirming, nor the same stick both straight and bent. Attempts have been made, indeed, to deny this. The most thoroughgoing of them was probably the theory offered by Russell in 1914 that a physical thing could be defined as the class of its actual and possible appearances, all of which were to be accepted as parts of it and independent of being perceived. This theory was given its coup de grace by Lovejoy in *The Revolt against Dualism*, and does not call for present discussion. We shall assume, with common sense and science, that physical things, if there are such things, cannot be characterised by qualities that are self-evidently incompatible.

This means that some at least of the qualities we seem to perceive in physical things cannot really belong to them. How do the errors arise? Take the case of the colour-blind man. Some twenty-four out of twenty-five men would agree in calling the signal green, and would accept this as its real colour. How does the twenty-fifth man come to call it grey? The answer in principle is clear. It is because the constitution of his eye is different, so that he does not respond in the normal way to the light waves that impinge on his retina. In his case, the colour he sees is not on the surface of the physical thing; it is a private impression produced by an abnormality in his nervous system. This is the standard account, which would be unanimously accepted, I think, by men of science.

23 Nevertheless it has surprising implications. If the immediate condition of one man's seeing grey is having a nervous system of a certain constitution, then the immediate condition of the normal man's seeing green must be his having a nervous system constituted slightly otherwise. Thus the immediate condition of seeing *either* grey or green is certain events in the nervous system, not the fact that a physical surface at some distance from us is coloured one way rather than another. If colour does exist in nature, we never see it. The experience of colour comes at the end of a long causal chain which contains as successive segments the movements of light waves, the occurrence of chemical changes in the retina, and the passage of electro-chemical pulses along the optical nerve. Have we any good reason for thinking that the colour appearing in the last event of this series is even *like* any quality in the object whose reflection of light formed the first event? None whatever. Of course the fact that a causal chain is interposed between sensation and physical thing does not prove their non-resemblance either. But it does, in sum, show two things. First, we never see the colour of anything in nature. Our experience of a colour is an event separated by time, space, and an elaborate causal mechanism from anything in the physical world that we suppose ourselves to see. Secondly, in view of this causal mechanism, there is no ground for supposing even a qualitative similarity between the object in nature and the appearance in our minds.

It is obvious that these considerations do not apply to colour alone. They apply in much the same way to pains, sounds, odours, and tastes, and also to felt hots and colds, wets and dries, smooths and roughs, hards and softs. There is no reason to believe that our experience of any of these qualities is a revelation of what exists in nature apart from us. Their appearances in our experience are always conditioned, as are those of colour, by the states of our brain, and without these states cannot be presumed to exist at all. Nor is there any more reason in their cases than in that of colour to suppose that the machinery of perception transmits a qualitative similarity along the causal chain.

24 We have said that sensations of certain qualities are conditioned by states of eye or brain. But eye and brain are physical things, and is it to be simply assumed that we can know them through perception? Science and common sense generally assume this without question. They assume that when a surgeon looks at the eye or the brain he is seeing an object in physical space, whose shape and size are directly presented to him. It is easy to see, however, that this cannot be the case. Our perceptions of shape, size, and motion are just as truly perceptions, and just as truly separated by a causal series from the physical objects they are supposed to reveal, as colours, sounds, or odours. No surgeon directly sees the shape or size of the eye or the brain he may be working on, and to suppose that he does would throw his theory of perception into hopeless confusion. He cannot consistently accept a causal theory for the 'secondary' qualities and a wholly different theory, instrumental or photographic, for the 'primary' qualities, for these two types of quality are plainly produced in his experience in the same way. It would not make sense to say that when he looks at an eye or a brain and sees a coloured shape, the colour diffused over that shape exists in his own experience only, while the shape over which it is diffused belongs to a different and material order. Both characters equally are contents of his perception, and if the appearance of one of them is conditioned by changes in his own brain, so is the appearance of the other.

This step also, natural as it is, has implications that carry us far. For if the shapes and sizes that we see belong to our private experience, then the whole spatial world of our immediate apprehension belongs likewise to our private experience. The extension occupied by these shapes and sizes *is* the space we perceptually live in. But this is not physical space, the space of stars and atoms. Perceptual space is a region where rails converge, spoons in water are bent, and one senses a variety of shapes as one walks around one's desk. There are no such things in the world of physics. The space we live in, the space of our perceptual world, is peculiar to each man; it is born with him and dies with him.

The same must be said of time. The time that enters into perception and memory is not the objective time of physics and astronomy. Perceptual time runs swiftly when we are amused and slowly when we are bored; time remembered seems long if it was crowded with events, and short if nothing happened; and memory may reverse the order of events. These accelerations, retardations, and reversals have no part in the impersonal time of science.

The conclusion from this line of thought is that the whole landscape of immediate experience, all sensed qualities and the time and space that they occur in, are of the stuff of consciousness. Many ingenious attempts have been made to avoid this conclusion, and if an adequate defence were to be offered, it would have to consider much else—the alleged distinction between act and object in sensation, the current objections to 'sense-data,' and the many attempts by naïve realists, critical realists, behaviourists, neutral monists, and others to preserve the plausibility of direct contact with the physical world. None of these attempts seems to me to have been successful, and some of the recantations made by their proposers are instructive. A single example will suffice. We have noted that Bertrand Russell in early life developed one of the most thoroughgoing forms of realism on record, holding that every sensed quality existed independently of experience. From this position he was compelled by criticism and reflection to beat a retreat, and after considering the matter for some forty further years, he wrote as follows:

'I hold . . . that whatever we know without inference is mental.' 'What I know without inference when I have the experience called "seeing the sun" is not the sun but a mental event in me. I am not immediately aware of tables and chairs, but only of certain effects that they have on me.' 'Among the things that I see at a given moment there are spatial relations which are a part of my percepts; if the percepts are "mental", as I should contend, then spatial relations which are ingredients of percepts are also "mental".'[14]

Such testimony is the more valuable as coming from a pioneer of realism, who would have clung to it if he could have found any plausible way of doing so.

25 'No man is an island,' said John Donne. 'Every Englishman is an island,' said Novalis. In our sense, both were short of the truth, for all men are islands. We never actually see the same chairs or tables, the same hills or sky, for we cannot share the contents of another's field of consciousness. In a way, we can cross the gulfs between us by throwing out precarious bridges in the way of words and signals, and using such assumptions as that if the thing in your field, called a chair, is related to the things around it in about the same way as something so named in my field, it is the same chair. Strictly speaking, it is not. One's knowledge of another's mind is always reached by inference, implicit or explicit, never by immediate insight. A possible exception is telepathy, which does seem to occur in certain cases and which, if it does occur, is philosophically important. But of its conditions almost nothing is known.

The world we have now reached is somewhat similar to Berkeley's, in which each person is confined to a field of consciousness of his own. Berkeley escaped a complete confinement of this kind by a leap of causal inference, and since this leap had in our judgement an a priori sanction, we should agree as to its validity. It is clear that when we open our eyes and see the sun, something other than ourselves is acting upon us. Berkeley could plausibly take this external cause as the will of God because he had ruled out the only important alternative, the action of matter. He ruled this out by the *esse est percipi* argument, which takes the very being of anything to lie in its being perceived. Indeed he thought this self-evident and unperceived matter to be a contradiction in terms. The argument is far from self-evident to me. I have no difficulty in conceiving even the blue of the sky and the greenness of grass as existing unperceived; and though I think they exist in fact only in consciousness, it is not on this ground that I think so. And just as Berkeley is unconvincing in his way of dismissing matter, so he is also in his alternative to matter. What we want in a causal explanation of perception is something that will explain why, when we open our eyes, we sometimes see a mountain and sometimes a postage stamp. Berkley would explain the appearance of these and of all other objects in nature in the same wholesale way; they are all impressed upon us by the divine will. But an explanation that applies equally to everything does not differentially explain anything.

SCIENCE AND THE PHYSICAL ORDER

26 Now science does attempt this differential explanation. Its accounts are detailed and elaborate, and though they fall short of demonstrable proof, they have been far too massively confirmed for philosophers to ignore. Philosophy and science form, or should form, one continuous, co-operative attempt to understand the world; and philosophy cannot afford to neglect the extraordinary success of science in correlating perceptions with inferred changes in the physical order. In 1906 a philosopher of distinction, McTaggart, could write that the existence of matter was 'a bare possibility to which it would be foolish to attach the slightest importance'. At present the foolishness would lie in writing that way at all. Protons and electrons, neutrons and positrons have never been perceived and presumably never will be, but at a time when scientists, by assuming that they exist and behave in certain ways, can harness them to such purposes as the driving of ships and the destruction of cities, they are hardly to be dispelled by a deprecatory waving of hands.

It must be admitted, however, that knowledge of them is as yet extremely tenuous. Nothing at all is known about their qualitative character. They are scarcely more than x's, arranged in dimly discoverable patterns and capable of motion. Though matter must be admitted to exist, it is neither the sturdy, solid matter of common sense nor the tiny atomic fragments of such matter envisaged by most materialists from Democritus, on, but a gossamer net of insensibles, or, as one theorist has put it, 'waves of probability undulating in nothingness'. There is no reason to believe that the chair I see, with its clean-cut lines and its hard and smooth brown surface, exists in nature. But we can form hypotheses as to the causes of our perception, and if these hypotheses are granted some degree of antecedent probability, they can be progressively verified. If we assume that there are light waves moving in independent lines from the various parts of the object to our eyes, that these parts are arranged in some sort of pattern that can be correlated with the parts of our percepts, that sensations of sound, odour, coldness, hardness, smoothness are produced by the motion of certain particles or waves, we find that these hypotheses can be confirmed, not only through continuing sensations of one's own, but through those reported by others. They may be further confirmed by batteries of tests made with cameras, scales, thermometers, reflectors, and other sensitive instruments. The confirmation is never complete, nor is it possible to assign the hypothesis a definite degree of probability, but when it enables us to predict how men and instruments will react to its presence, and the results all hang together as if the hypothesis were true, we are justified after a time in believing with an approach to certainty that it *is* true.

27 Epistemological idealism, if that means the view that all objects of sense experience are mind-dependent, seems to me unavoidable. What of ontological idealism, the view that everything is of the stuff of mind? That seems to me more dubious. There is of course something absurd in saying that the earth which produced us and our forefathers is a set of impressions in the minds of some of the creatures it has spawned. With the aid of telescopes we can see objects in the sky from which the light now reaching us began its journey before human minds appeared on the earth at all. Unless geology and astronomy are gross deceivers, matter long preceded such minds in the scheme of things.

Is it possible to say whether the constituents of matter—protons and electrons, neutrons and photons—independent as they are of *our* consciousness, are independent of consciousness *as such*? I do not know the answer to that question. The physicists who have considered it have held differing views. At a time when metaphysicians, who had furnished the chief support for idealism, were beginning to falter about it, physicists, who had not questioned the material character of atoms, began defecting in an idealist direction. Sir Arthur Eddington argued from the fact that the ultimate entities of physics, though independent of our own minds, were caught up in a web or system of mathematically formulable law to the conclusion that such a system and its terms must exist within a mind.[15] Sir James Jeans wrote: 'the universe can be best pictured, although still very imperfectly and inadequately, as consisting of pure thought, the thought of what, for want of a wider word, we must describe as a mathematical thinker.'[16] Professor E. A. Milne believed that the laws of the physical world formed so fully integrated a whole that they were capable of being stated as a deductive system, and he so far succeeded in constructing such a system as to convince himself of a rationalistic view of the world.

A philosophical rationalist can only be grateful for expert scientific aid, particularly in fields where his own light fails him. Eddington, Jeans, and Milne have been attacked for their thesis in terms suggesting that there is something perverse in trying to show that the physical world is intelligible. Needless to say, I have much sympathy with their endeavour. What gives me pause, however, is the assumption that if the universe could be shown to be an order governed by mathematical law it would thereby be shown to be not only intelligible but also mental, that is, to exist only in consciousness. This assumption may be true, but it is not self-evident to me, and I do not see how, except by self-evidence, it could be shown to be true. All the distinguishable things in the universe fall under the scope of arithmetic. Would the relations reported by arithmetical statements, for example $2 + 2 = 4$, remain in force if there were no human beings to apprehend them? Astronomers certainly believe that the planets pursued their courses round the sun before human life appeared, that these planets were different from each other, and that two of them and two others made four. Would this relation have held among them, even though no mind were aware of it? I do not know how to deny that it would. Man did not invent the multiplication table. He invented the words for it, to be sure, but not the relations it expresses; and if those relations, abstract and necessary as they admittedly are, can exist apart from his own consciousness, it is not clear to me that they must exist in another consciousness. It seems possible that the world should be a rational whole, in the sense that its parts are linked together by necessity, without being itself a mind. In short rationalism does not seem to entail idealism. In saying this, I do not mean to reject ontological idealism as demonstrably untrue. I mean that, unlike Eddington and Jeans, I see no straight path from the logical articulation of things to the conclusion that everything exists in consciousness. It may or it may not.

Our present position, then, is this. The universe is an order in which all events are interconnected by links of causation and necessity. In this universe there have emerged conscious minds, each limited in immediate awareness to the qualities and structures that appear in its own experience. From these qualities and structures it is possible to infer certain causes and certain abstract corresponding structures in the external world, though this world is cut off from direct access, and seems bound to remain only dimly and inferentially known.

CHAPTER XIV

HUMAN NATURE AND ITS VALUES

1   We have been sketching the world-view to which one rationalist seeking an alternative to traditional supernaturalism finds himself committed. It is a cosmic order in which seemingly chaotic facts and events are linked by causality and necessity into one all-embracing system, intelligible throughout, though at present only fragmentarily known. It is a system in which human minds are tiny islands in an apparently infinite universe, each occupying a perceptual world of its own, and making contact with the physical world and with each other by inference only.

We turn now from the dimly discerned vastness of the outer region to the better lighted area of our own consciousness and the human nature that finds expression through it. In a rationalist view of things, particularly one in which man must so largely build his world out of the materials of his own mind, the conception of human nature is important, and in the statement of our own view it is crucially important because, as we shall see, the place of values in the world depends upon it. Let us begin with what is most familiar, the content of our own consciousness. What do we find there?

We find not only the percepts we have been considering, but much else: memories, concepts, and beliefs; pleasure and displeasure, impulses, desires, and volitions; emotions in lush variety. These are all introspectable components in our field of consciousness. But it should be noted that there are dangers in so describing them. First, consciousness is not a static field, but a mass of events. A mind is, in the main, a set of drives or impulses restlessly seeking fulfilment. Secondly, the components of a mind are not parts of it, in the sense in which a brick is part of a wall, or even as a carburettor is part of an engine. These components inform or permeate each other in a unique way; in a desire, for example, you could not remove the element of idea, or of impulse, or of emotion, without changing the character of the others and of the whole. Thirdly, a mind is *one*. I look up from my desk and see a wall on which there are hundreds of books. These percepts are all mine in the sense that they belong to a single field in which attention can shift without break from one item to another. Again, two desires of mine may conflict, for example the desire for dinner and the desire to finish a letter; but they are felt as desires of a single self, and the decision between them is an action of the mind as a whole.

MIND AS A PACKET OF PROPENSITIES

2   A mind, then, is here conceived not as a static field of consciousness, but as a set of impulses unified in so intimate a way that they may partially overlap, and may enforce or inhibit each other. Now impulses can be adequately distinguished only by their ends. The impulses to fight, to flee, to make love, or to be with others can be marked off from each other only by the sorts of experience that would bring them respectively to rest. Some of them are instincts, that is, impulses whose courses are inborn, like the impulse to suck, to clasp, or to cry. But most of them are at the outset amorphous, experimental, and plastic, depending for the specific ends they come to adopt on the material that experience offers them. 'In the spring a young man's fancy lightly turns to thoughts of love,' but whether that fancy elects as its goal some dreaming Mary, some bustling Martha, or some shadowy Beatrice may well turn on the persons whom chance has appointed to cross his path.

Psychologists have in the past been much engaged with listing and classifying the original urges or instincts of human nature. E. L. Thorndike distinguished more than two hundred of them. William James had a more economical list of about fifty. McDougall, starting with a set of seven, expanded it later to twelve and then eighteen. Thouless recognised three, the self-preservative, the reproductive, and the gregarious; Freud distinguished two, sexuality and destruction, or love and death; Hobbes, Nietzsche, and Hocking made one drive supreme, the drive for power, though without agreeing how 'power' should be defined. These extreme variations do not necessarily show either arbitrariness or confusion. The drives of human nature may be taken at different levels according to the generality with which one conceives their ends. If one takes them at the bottom level, a large number of responses may naturally be grouped under a single common interest such as romantic or parental love. If one goes higher, and asks for an end toward which all these interests alike are directed, the answer is bound to be both vague and sweeping—Hocking's 'power', perhaps, or Dewey's 'growth', or Bradley's 'self-realisation'. It needs no great latitude of interpretation to find all these views consistent with each other and true.

Each of them brings out some aspect of the truth about human nature, namely that it is essentially dynamic, consisting of a set of drives toward ends. The classification of these ends, their organisation as a rational whole, and the consideration of the kind of conduct that would achieve them are, in my view, the task of ethics.

NEED AND IMPULSE AS THE BASIS OF VALUE

3 It is this connection with ethics that makes them important here. Man's fundamental drives are attempts to satisfy his needs, and in the fulfilment of those needs he finds his values. He is equipped by nature, for example, with promptings toward food, drink, sex, bodily activity, and companionship; if he were not, the race could not have survived; and in satisfying his primary hungers he finds the basic goods of life. Ascetic moralists have sometimes deprecated the seeking of these primal goods on the ground that they are animal-like and gross. But man, though more than an animal, remains an animal always; he carries his ancestry with him in both body and mind; and no ethics can be healthy that allows itself to forget the long roots of the present in the past.

Nevertheless a merely biological ethics is as absurd as a merely behaviourist psychology. Man's mind does not reduce to his body, however deep its biological roots. It has escaped into a world of objects beyond the range of bodily response; and the long ascent toward freedom is made through the same series of steps by the individual and by the race. Furthermore, the upward path that the mind follows on the intellectual side is strikingly parallel to that which it follows on the practical side. On the intellectual side the ascent is through a series of plateaux—sensation, perception, the free idea, and the linkage of free ideas in a system. On the practical side the ascent is through a similar series—impulse, desire, purpose, and moral choice. I have tried to trace these advances, the theoretical and the practical, in two earlier studies, *The Nature of Thought* and *Reason and Goodness*. It will serve to make clearer the conception of human nature and the closely related conception of value here proposed if this parallel advance is dwelt upon a little further.

COGNITIVE EVOLUTION

4 The career of mind on the cognitive side begins in sensation, perhaps with a pain or a sensation of touch. It is impossible to say when, or in what form, sensation first appears, either in the race or in the individual. And though it is the first step toward knowledge, it is not itself knowledge. It is not a state of mind in which anything is asserted, or denied, or taken as true or false. Knowledge begins with judgement, and the best test of the presence of judgement is the possibility of error. Sensation cannot err. There is no meaning in saying that a toothache is mistaken. The possibility of truth or error begins at the next level, the implicit judgement of perception, which is a taking of something to be present on the *warrant* of sensation. The child, on the strength of having found sugar sweet, takes the salt before him as also sweet, and forthwith gets a shock. He has used no words; he has not judged explicitly; but he must have done so implicitly, for he turns out to have been in error, and only a judgement can err.

Thought thus begins not in sensation but in perception. In the animal world it stays there. The higher animals obviously recognise things and persons; and since the nose of a dog or the eye of an eagle can detect much that to us is insensible, and these sensory differences may be freighted with meaning, the perceptual life of these lowly minds is in some regions richer than our own. Their great disadvantage is that they are immured in perception; their ideas or meanings are chained to what is given in sense; so that if they are confined in a cage, they are chafed and restless, but cannot sit down and think explicitly of their home on the range. A man can do that. He has escaped into the world of free ideas; he can look before and after, and dwell on what is absent and remote.

He goes a step farther when he can not only entertain free ideas but develop them reflectively. The animal in the cage can only claw at the lock; a man can sit down and consider the possible ways of escape: 'if I do A, the result will be B, and if I do C, the result will be D'. The pragmatists are no doubt right that reflective thought was first resorted to because of the pressure of practical need, but it does not remain dependent on that pressure. Natural science is an attempt by this 'if-then' way of thinking to determine the framework of law in the world around us. Philosophy is an extension of the same enterprise. It examines the assumptions that science starts with—the laws of logic, for example, or the law of causality—and tries to put together into a consistent whole the conclusions that science ends with. The theoretical impulse, the endeavour to understand, is continuous from the first employment of thought in perception to the last efforts of the metaphysician to articulate a system. It realises only gradually what business it is about. As we have seen in the study of mythology, the aesthetic, theoretical, and practical interests may work so intimately together in early thought that their diverse claims and ends are not distinguished. It is only as man moves up the reflective scale that he realises what sort of creature he is, and he does so by recognising and defining more explicitly the ends he is groping after. As for the impulse to know, he comes to see that the only end that would satisfy it is an understanding in which the question Why? would receive its final answer. And if that fulfilment is to be achieved, thought cannot halt short of a system in which there are no dark places, a system that would exhibit every fact as having its necessary place in one intelligible order.

CONATIVE EVOLUTION

5 This self-discovery of human nature proceeds by a similar evolution on its practical side. The ascent starts, not now with sensation, but with impulse. An impulse is a felt urge to behave in a certain way, but without awareness of any end that is subserved by so behaving. The newly hatched chick feels an urge to peck at the grains of wheat scattered around it, and apparently feels satisfied in doing so, but this urge cannot be guided at the beginning by any idea of the satisfaction that will emerge. The bird that builds its nest with apparent adroitness cannot be supposed to do so with a blueprint in its mind, or any explicit thought of the needs of its young. Presumably it merely feels an urge to gather threads and twigs and dispose them in a certain way, and feels satisfaction in doing it.

Impulsive behaviour is not likely, however, to remain purely impulsive. It soon passes over into the sort of behaviour that has acquired force and direction from the retained deposits of past success. When offered a choice of grains, the chick will peck with increased avidity at the kind it has found agreeable and avoid the bits of orange peel that have proved disagreeable. Just as, on the cognitive side, much of ordinary life consists of perception in which sensation is supplemented by meaning, so on the active side it consists largely of habits, in which impulse has been canalised along certain channels through finding these channels pleasant. Impulse is thus guided by desire. Such desire operates at first on a very low level, where the thought of an end is only implicitly present.

Desire that has broken free from this dependence on impulse is called by the same name, but it deserves a distinctive one; perhaps *purpose* will serve. It then becomes able not only to envision an end explicitly but to order present impulse with regard to it. The musician or athlete in training, the truck driver at his wheel, the captain of a ship, the surgeon in the operating room, the lawyer before the jury, are all acting from a clearly entertained purpose in the light of which some impulses are encouraged as relevant and others inhibited. Here, as in the use of free ideas, of which this indeed is one form, the mind is moving on an exclusively human level. The thought of an end, absent, remote, and desirable, which can be held steadily in view, and to which the veering impulses and desires of the moment can be made subservient, adds a dimension to man's life and gives him an overwhelming advantage over his animal rivals.

His world becomes larger still when he reaches the level of moral choice, which engages all his resources, cognitive and conative. When faced by important alternative courses, he must consider the long-run products of each of them and the by-products along the way; and he must manage to weigh this complex of goods against other like complexes in the light of some end to which all are conceived as contributory. It sounds impossible, and it *is* impossible except in loose approximation; yet we have to attempt it.

6 This is all rather general. The kind of calculation required will be clearer if we take an example and for simplicity's sake confine it to the agent's own good. Let us say that a young man comes into some money, and the question is how he shall use it. His particular passion at the moment is for boats and the sea, and he thinks with a thrill of what he could do with the new means available. He could buy a boat of his own that would run by either sail or power, and he begins exultantly to unroll the possibilities: he could drive it down inland waterways to Florida, bask there awhile in the sun, and then set sail for the islands of the Caribbean: he could make his way on through the canal to the Pacific, visit the coastal cities of the West, and—who knows?—if he learned his lessons well, he might venture on into the South Seas, visit the peoples down under, and come back in a year or so loaded with impressions of other cultures and memories of a hundred varied adventures. But there are competing possibilities. That same money would put him through a university. This prospect is less exciting to him. But would not the fruits be more enduring? What would these fruits be? New interests, he supposes, in the sciences, arts, and letters (and these exposures are important, for he is feeling about for a vocation); new knowledge, new friendships, new models of how to think, speak, and write, new proficiencies that would probably remain valuable through the years, a greater likelihood of economic success and all that this means in the way of comfort, health, and security. And these complex prospects must be somehow balanced against the plan that first suggested itself. Where the results are so far-ranging, impulse is helpless. All his intelligence and more is needed if he is to foresee even the major consequences and weigh them against each other.

MORALITY AND INTRINSIC VALUE

7 In such a calculation, what consequences are to count? Not physical changes, for these have no importance except as they make some difference to experiencing minds. Is it these experiences themselves that make up the relevant items? Yes. But if experiences are to be compared and appraised, it must be in some respect. What this respect must be is clear enough. The value, the intrinsic worthwhileness, the goodness or badness, of the experience is what counts. And it seems self-evident that if one's choice lies between two prospective experiences or sets of experiences, what one should choose to bring into the world is the larger value. There are apparent exceptions, well known to ethical theorists, that involve the keeping of promises, and above all, justice. This is not the place to explore these cases; I can only say that I am not convinced that they are true exceptions. The ultimate rule of conduct remains for me a synthetic a priori insight that one should produce the greatest good possible, or if one prefers this way of putting it, make the world as much better as possible.

THE NATURE OF GOODNESS

8 But in what does the goodness of an experience consist? That issue has been a battleground of ethics during the first half of the century; and Moore and Russell, who saw eye to eye about it at the beginning of that period, were poles apart at the end. Moore thought goodness undefinable. It could not be defined because it was simple and therefore could not be analysed. Though it was a property owned in common by every experience valued for its own sake, whether an intellectual insight or a sip of chianti, it was not a descriptive character like the clearness of the insight, or the bouquet of the wine; it was a unique 'non-natural' quality whose presence was apprehended not by the senses but by an intellectual intuition. Russell, agreeing at first about this quality, later professed himself unable to find it, and held that to call something good was not a statement at all, but the expression of a favouring attitude, normally a feeling, on the part of the speaker.

I cannot accept either view, though in certain respects I am near to both. The theory that to pronounce something good or right is merely to express a feeling is inconsistent with what seem to me the obvious facts that we often contradict each other on moral issues, that we argue about them, change our opinions about them, and make mistakes about them.[1] I still hold that a value 'judgement' is really a judgement. When we call an experience intrinsically good

—say the experience of the Fifth Symphony, or of understanding why E equals mc^2, or of a successful round on the golf links—we suppose ourselves to be saying something meaningful and true. But what exactly is this? Are we ascribing Moore's simple non-natural quality, identical wherever intrinsic goodness is found? Like Russell, I seem unable to find this in my thought. Its non-naturalness, its simplicity, its identity, I cannot verify.

9 We should not leap out of the natural world unless we have to, and I cannot think that in this case we must. Nor do I think goodness is simple and unanalysable; more about this shortly. What here concerns us is Moore's suggestion that the intrinsic value of music, of understanding, and of a game lies in an identical quality. There is something wrong here, and what is wrong is making goodness so unresponsive to human nature. For what we find good, as Aristotle saw, is bound up intimately with human needs. It is no accident that the table of intrinsic goods corresponds to the table of human drives. 'Of course it does,' the reply may come, 'for man would naturally direct his drives toward what he sees to be good'. But I am afraid this misconceives the order of dependence. Do not men find an experience good because it is fulfilling, rather than find it fulfilling because it is seen independently to be good?

I have slowly and somewhat reluctantly come to think that they do. Would food have any value if it did not satisfy hunger? Would understanding Einstein be a good to a mind without curiosity, or the Fifth Symphony to one without musical interest or responsiveness, or success in a game to one who was completely non-competitive and non-athletic? To hold, as Dean Inge and Nicolai Hartmann did, that the goods of these things are somehow eternal values laid up in the heavens and waiting for man's appropriation of them is to ignore the entanglement of these values with human impulses and longings. The beauty of the Fifth Symphony would no more exist in a world without aesthetic interest than the sound would exist in a world where there were no ears. Music is good because it fulfils this interest. Knowledge is good because it fulfils the impulse to know. Craftsmanship, adventure, physical prowess, poetry, love—sexual or parental—are good because they fulfil men's needs and urges; and if the course of evolution had at some remote juncture taken a different turn, so that instead of being super-simians we were super-reptiles or super-birds, how many of the activities in which we now find our good would have any sort of appeal? The fulfilment of the demands of nature is the condition of value.

Is it the only condition? No. For even though an experience fulfils, it may still lack value if fulfilment brings no pleasure with it. For the normal man it always does bring this bonus with it, as Aristotle again pointed out. But in certain abnormal conditions it does not, and then otherwise rich fruits have a way of turning to ashes in the mouth. Because they see this so clearly, hedonists have insisted that pleasure alone is good. They are wrong, as Mill virtually admitted in saying that it would be better to be Socrates than a pig, even though the pleasure in the two lives were equal. His defence was that Socrates' pleasure was higher in quality, a defence that in principle abandoned hedonism. If the Socratic life was really better, it was surely because intellectual and moral aspirations which in the mind of the pig had hardly begun to stir were in Socrates not only alive but magnificently fulfilled.

RATIONALISM IN MORALS

10 Thus intrinsic value has a twofold condition; it belongs to those experiences alone that fulfil and satisfy, i.e. realise a demand of our nature and bring pleasure in the realisation. We have described these as 'conditions' of goodness. But a defender of Moore's view could say that this way of conceiving them was quite consistent with taking goodness itself as a non-natural quality supervening on these 'good-making' conditions; they make anything good that has them, without *constituting* its goodness. I have admitted that I cannot find this quality of Moore's. I am inclined, therefore, to say that the possession of the two characters named gives the very meaning of intrinsic goodness—not the meaning that lies on the surface, but the meaning ultimately required by analysis and reflection. This is not an emotivist view. I should insist that the judgement of value is not an interjection; it is the statement that a certain experience is, in the senses indicated, fulfilling and satisfying, a statement that is either true or false. Nor is it an egoistic view, for under like conditions the experience of others has values equal to my own. It is clearly a rationalist view in the sense that both the calculation of consequences and the comparison and appraisal of these consequences are the work of reason. It prescribes as the ultimate rule of right conduct: So act as to produce the greatest net good of all affected by your action, the good consisting in experience that is at once fulfilling and satisfying.[2]

Though my ethical view, as intimated a moment ago, agrees with neither Moore nor the emotivists, it is in some ways close to both.. Like Moore's, it is an objectivist view. With the majority of moralists from Plato down, it holds that good rather than right is the primary notion in ethics, and that the rightness of competing courses of action must be determined by their tendencies to bring good into being.

Moore believed that the weighing of intrinsic values against each other was performed by intuition, which was itself a form of intelligence. Intelligence might be mistaken either in calculating or in weighing future goods, but Moore had no doubt that to the question whether an action was right or wrong there was a definite answer to be found and that this answer would provide truth as objective as anything in the sciences. I agree with him here, though I think the difficulty of the questions even greater than he did, since I hold that goodness involves two variables rather than one. There is some action, however hard it may be to discover, that would produce the largest amount of fulfilment and satisfaction to mankind of those now open to me; if I discover and do it, I am acting rightly; if I do anything else, I am acting wrongly. Of course with the best of motives I may make a mistake about what action is right, and it is therefore important to distinguish the moral goodness of an agent from the objective rightness of his conduct. An agent is morally good if he acts under the belief that his action is right, whether the consequences would bear him out or not. Fortunately, though there is always an objectively right act to be done, there is no duty to be infallible as to what this is.

11 On the other hand, the theory here offered is in one sense a subjectivist theory. Though the value of an experience or the rightness of an action is not a function of my feeling or judgement about it, it would have no existence at all apart from mind. That is obvious if goodness lies in the fulfilment and satisfaction of impulses and desires, for these things belong to minds alone. And it would hold whether we took these two as defining goodness or as merely conditions of it, for such goodness in either case would be mind-dependent. Is there any intrinsic goodness in the existence of a crater at a certain point on the planet Mars? One can see, I think, that the answer must be No, unless that crater falls within the notice and interest of a mind. Suppose someone suggests that in 1900 there was a rainbow in Spitsbergen which no one happened to see; was it not beautiful nonetheless? No, it was not. For if no one observed it, it not only satisfied no aesthetic interest but, as presumably devoid of colour, was not in the ordinary sense a rainbow at all.

It will be clear from this sketch of human nature and its values that ethics is in my view a secular study. Man does not depend on revelation for his knowledge of right and wrong, but on the sweet and bitter fruits of a long experimentation with diverse patterns of life. What makes these fruits sweet or bitter is not a divine sanction accorded to some and withheld from others, nor the presence on occasion of a unique non-natural quality. It is something more deeply rooted in human nature. The great goods of man correspond to the great needs of man; they are the food that quenches his persistent, fundamental hungers. Some experiences fulfil and satisfy these hungers; these are sought and prized; and the good man will try so to order his life that they will be in widest commonalty spread. Other experiences flout and shrink his nature, and these the good man will seek to prevent or limit. No man's good will be the same precisely as any other's, for no two men are constructed quite alike; nor is it likely that the good of any two periods in the biography of a man or of the race will be quite the same; for men grow, and human nature evolves. What sort of experience would prove most fulfilling we can sometimes conjecture, as we can in the field of cognition, through extrapolation from our own increasing fulfilments.

The religious literature of the world, full of 'the still sad music of humanity,' is rich with deposits of past experience as to the ways of life that have proved fruitful and others that have been ashes in the mouth. It would be foolish to disregard this storehouse of practical wisdom. But its counsel must be drawn on with discretion. Though its proverbs often come straight from human experience and would be endorsed to the full by a rational ethic, many of its maxims and mandates are derived from the supposed will of an inscrutable Deity and directed toward supposed consequences in a future existence. These injunctions also come in the end by a circuitous route from human nature, but too often from the fanciful, malicious or fearful parts of it. The religious injunctions to judge not, to resist not evil, to abjure the world and the flesh, to lay up treasures for the hereafter, to flee from the wrath to come, even to seek peace and ensue it and to have life and have it more abundantly, are most safely read by those for whom ethics is a rational discipline with a standard beyond the vagaries of faith or myth.

CHAPTER XV

GOODNESS AND THE ABSOLUTE

1 The account of value in the last chapter was a necessary preliminary to the problem now to be raised. Have we any valid grounds for saying that God is good, or that the universe is good? Indeed is there anything anywhere that is good outside the limits of man's consciousness? To answer such questions, one must know the condition under which goodness may appear. We have stated that condition in the last chapter. It is the existence of conscious minds with impulses capable of fulfilment and satisfaction. The question now before us is whether that condition exists apart from human experience.

The point of chief interest here is whether it exists in the power, if such there be, that governs the universe. But let us creep up on that momentous question by asking whether it exists anywhere in the universe outside our own minds. To that question there is a clear, even if limited, answer: it obviously exists in some animal minds. A dog that is starving or has lost its master in a crowd is unmistakably frustrated and suffering, even though the thought of what would bring its search to rest is less explicit than our own. If the dog finds food or is reunited with its master, its driving impulse gains fulfilment, and to deny that it is achieving its own humble good would be churlishly unreasonable. But animals are near to us; they are our biological cousins. What of the rest of nature? Our planet is a speck of stardust in a universe that stretches out in every direction for millions of light years. Life like ours is possible only within narrow zones of temperature; and at a rough computation, writes Sir James Jeans:

'these zones within which life is possible, all added together, constitute less than a thousand million millionth part of the whole of space.' The universe 'appears to be indifferent to life like our own. . . . Perhaps indeed we ought to say it appears to be actively hostile to life like our own. For the most part, empty space is so cold that all life in it would be frozen; most of the matter in space is so hot as to make life on it impossible; space is traversed and astronomical bodies continually bombarded, by radiation of a variety of kinds, much of which is probably inimical to, or even destructive of, life.'[1]

So far as we know, the crew of our small space-ship is alone in the universe, and if life and mind appear on other celestial bodies, they are probably so different from our own that we should not know where to begin in establishing communication with them. We can only say of these hypothetical beings that if they do have values it is because they have needs and wants that find fulfilment in certain experiences, though both the wants and their fulfilment may be unimaginably different from our own.

GOD AND THE ABSOLUTE

2 What has concerned religious thinkers in the past, however, is not whether other specks of stardust support minds but whether the universe itself is governed by a being with values more or less like our own. In the religious tradition of the West, two very different notions have been entertained of the ultimate nature of things and, in consequence, of the ultimate government of the world. One belongs to the strand of thought that runs through Spinoza, Hegel, Green, Royce, Bradley, and Bosanquet, and identifies God with an absolute mind embracing all things in an intelligible whole. The other is the specifically Christian strand of thought which conceives God as a Person distinct from the world, though its creator and sustainer. It will be clear from what has been said that the present work belongs in the first of these traditions rather than the second, whatever departures may have been made from it at particular points. We have argued that ultimate reality is an all-inclusive system, whose parts are necessarily related. It is this whole to which one is driven back in the end, even if, in the manner of Rashdall, Brightman, and other theologians, one holds to a finite Deity limited in power but not in goodness. For God, so conceived, remains one person among others in an infinite universe, and is not himself the ultimate reality. Many questions would still force themselves upon us regarding his origin, his relations to the space and time of science, and the authority to be attached to his thought and will. In trying to answer such questions, we should be carried back inevitably to the Absolute of which he is one component. Without suggesting that these questions lack interest or importance, we shall make no attempt here to deal with them. For us the ultimate reality in the universe is to be found in no part of it, however great, but only in the whole. It is the universe itself, not indeed as a scattered litter of items but as the one comprehensive and necessary order that a full understanding would find in it. Hence if we are asked whether in our view God is good, we shall perhaps be excused if we translate it into the question whether ultimate reality is good. In short, is the Absolute good?

We have already confessed to a doubt whether this all-inclusive system can be described with self-evidence as a mind or consciousness. In any case, if we now ask whether this Absolute has a scale of values to which ours may and should approximate, or a will for us which we should try to discover and obey, it is difficult to give any clear meaning to the question. For if we put it in terms of the theory stated in the last chapter, it becomes: may we ascribe to the Absolute a set of needs, wants, or desires in whose fulfilment and satisfaction its goods consist? The answer seems to be clear enough: an absolute being is not one that can need or seek fulfilment; and hence its experience could not be good in our sense.

THE ABSOLUTE AS FULFILMENT

3 This is not the conclusion of Bradley and Bosanquet. They hold, and I follow them in holding, that the universe is a system which, as apprehended in thought, would provide a final satisfaction of man's theoretical impulse, since then the question Why? could at no point be raised again. This question is raised at all only on the assumption that there is an answer to it. That the system which would satisfy the theoretic impulse is also the system which constitutes the nature of things is the assumption of thought at every level of its inquiry, and I conceive that rationalists have been justified in accepting this assumption, not as a demonstration that the world is rational, but as a working hypothesis dictated by the nature of the quest.

But such writers as Green, Bradley, and Bosanquet have gone far beyond this. They have assumed that just as the Absolute, conceived as an intellectual structure, is that which would satisfy the theoretic impulse, so on the side of value it is that which would satisfy completely such interests as the moral and the aesthetic. But the cases are not comparable. The search for truth is the search for an order that we do not make, but find. The attempt to embody the moral ideal or to create ideal beauty is the endeavour to realise something that we do not find, but make. The poet, the artist, the musician do not assume that the beauty of the poem or picture or melody they are creating is already there in nature, and that in creating it they are only following the lines of an existent structure.

It would not occur to the moral reformer to say that what he was attempting to reform was a world already perfect. Indeed that assumption, instead of encouraging and justifying his endeavour, would make it pointless. Thus while it is the natural assumption of the cognitive quest that its ideal is already realised, the natural assumption of the other major quests is that it is *not* realised, and that such realisation as may be achieved must be the work of our own hands.

I cannot agree, therefore, with the school of thinkers from whom I have perhaps learned most, the humane and distinguished group that includes Green, the Cairds, Bradley and Bosanquet, Royce and Joachim, that the Absolute in which our theoretical questions are presumed to have their answer is one in which the other values we strive for must also be realised. It may be insisted that the two cases are parallel after all, for is not truth itself a value, and if so, must not this and the other values be treated alike? The answer is No; truth is not in strictness a value; there is no intrinsic goodness in the truth that $2 + 2 = 4$. The goodness lies in the *knowledge* of truth, and this, like other values, is an achievement of our own. It would be absurd to maintain that we bring into being the truth or the fact that $2 + 2 = 4$ as we bring into being the happiness of a comforted child or the beauty of a well played melody. Admitting, then, that knowledge, like other forms of fulfilment, is intrinsically good, we must add that it has a character which other fulfilments lack: as the knowledge of something, it has an object and correlative in the world beyond itself. In this it is unique among the forms of value.

BRADLEY

4 Bradley at times seems to hold the view of goodness here accepted. 'Good, in the proper sense,' he writes, 'implies the fulfilment of desire';[2] 'desire is not an external means, but is contained and involved in goodness, or at least follows from it necessarily'.[3] Does such desire exist in the Absolute? No, he replies, for in desire there is a divorce between idea and existence, between the thought of something desired and its realisation in fact; and in the Absolute all such rifts are closed. Hence neither desire nor good, as we think of them, exists in the Absolute. Yet Bradley at other times speaks as if our desires and goods did exist in it. Indeed he says that there is nothing in it except the experiences of finite beings. 'Outside of finite experience there is neither a natural world nor any other world at all.'[4] 'The Absolute . . . has no assets beyond appearances.'[5] But if nothing exists in the Absolute but finite minds, and the desires of such minds are admitted to be unfulfilled, how can they also, in that Absolute, be fulfilled completely? Bradley never makes clear how this feat is accomplished. He can only say that if you could put together an enormous number of striving, discontented finite minds and see them in their true relations to each other, you would behold a thorough transmutation; they would 'somehow' all be fulfilled and satisfied.

I cannot accept this conclusion. Indeed, if taken seriously, it would undermine the moral life. We are told that if we could see things as they really are, we should recognise that all our desires were already realised and the world already perfect. Of course there are items of experience that would seem rather less than perfectly good: animals are casually torn to pieces by others to make a dinner; innocent children are afflicted with excruciating and deadly diseases; and there are the nightmare snakepits of Buchenwald and Belsen. We do not ordinarily call these good, but our sense of values must be confused. Bradley writes: 'we may even say that every feature in the universe is thus absolutely good.'[6] But if such things as these are absolutely good, why talk any longer about good and evil at all, or struggle to replace one by the other?

If anyone protests, Bradley is able to point out that something very like this view has been traditional in Western religion. 'For religion all is the perfect expression of a supreme will, and all things therefore are good.'[7] 'As a function of the perfect universe . . . you are perfect already.'[8] Evil then cannot be real, and yet we must fight against it as if it were. In dealing with evil, the maxim of the religious man, says Bradley, is: 'Because it is *not* really there, have more courage to attack it.'[9] Evil must be assumed for moral purposes to be a formidable reality, though for faith it is assumed to have been overcome. 'The moral duty not to be moral is, in short, the duty to be religious.'[10] Religion is condemned to a perpetual oscillation between the two sides of the contradiction, for it cannot abandon the moral struggle, nor can it abandon the conviction that, under God, 'all's right with the world'.

It is only philosophy, Bradley thinks, that can deal with the paradox, and the philosopher sees that where there is a contradiction one side or the other must go. The side that Bradley sacrifices is the side that for most minds is the more indubitable reality. He chooses to brand as unreal not the Absolute, in which all desires are extinguished in an ineffable blaze of fulfilment, but the moral enterprise itself. Good as we know it is appearance only; evil as we know it is appearance only; desire, with which good is bound up, is appearance only; the whole struggle between good and evil is nothing but an unreal seeming. It is hard to see that this is any great advance over the religious attitude that Bradley has just condemned. The religious man believes that he is committed to a life-and-death battle with evil and at the same time that the victory is somehow won. This is rejected as incoherent. What we are offered instead is the suggestion that the battle never really happened. It is all an illusion of finite mind.

But this way of thinking is itself based on an illusion. It proceeds on the assumption that the cognitive and the other impulses of human nature are to be dealt with in the same way, that just as the theoretic impulse is justified in postulating a world which, as intelligible, would fulfil and satisfy the desire to know, so the aesthetic and moral impulses are justified in assuming that the world is perfectly beautiful and perfectly good. Now in assuming that the world is intelligible, even though much of it is puzzling to us, there is no contradiction and scarcely even a paradox. It is wholly in accord with our logical sense to say that the law of contradiction really reigns in the world in spite of much that seems to us incoherent. The assumption that truth is a consistent whole belongs as essentially to the quest for knowledge as the recognition that our actual knowledge falls short of this. The corresponding assumption, we must repeat, is *not* involved, either overtly or implicitly, in the quest of non-cognitive values. 'It fortifies my soul to know/That though I perish, truth is so.' No doubt. But if Clough and other striving souls were to perish, would any virtue or beauty, anything good or evil, be left in the universe? That depends, we have said, on whether outside our tiny celestial stockade there exist 'in the distant places of creation' other minds with needs and desires. We know of none. And the Bradleyan Absolute is not well calculated to relieve our loneliness.

For consider; our desires exist in it, since all phenomena exist in it; but those desires are fulfilled, and desire that is fulfilled is no longer desire; so our desires do *not* exist in it. To be sure, they must do so, for there is nowhere else for them to exist, and to exist outside the Absolute would be too gross a contradiction. But since they are self-contradictory themselves (for thought and existence, the *what* and the *that*, cannot be sundered in reality), they are unrealities that can*not* be included in the Absolute. What is included instead is what they would achieve if perfectly fulfilled. But if our desires as such are not included, it is false to say that the Absolute is all-inclusive. Furthermore, the Absolute is not in time, and desires with no possible future fulfilment are not desires as we know them. The list of contradictions and paradoxes could easily be extended.

Such an Absolutist as Bradley would have a ready reply. He would say that contradictions were inevitable in the attempt of ordinary thought to construe its world; indeed Bradley devotes most of

528 REASON AND BELIEF

Appearance and Reality to riddling with contradiction the world we actually live in and the very bricks and mortar with which the intellect constructs it. The ramshackle incoherence of this structure is evidence, he would say, that we must look beyond its world of shadows to the coherent Absolute that lives behind it. But even to talk about this final coherence must be incoherent, at least for Bradley, since coherence is a relation, and he has declared all relations to be unreal. It is difficult to see any reply that would not be open to Sidgwick's criticism that 'he had never been able to make out' how the Absolutists 'managed to distinguish the contradictions which they took to be evidence of error from those which they regarded as intimations of higher truth'.[11]

5 What concerns us here is the moral implications of an Absolute in which there are no needs, impulses, or desires. In the absence of such things, the root of value is cut, and there could be neither good nor evil. The good and evil of our finite life would disappear in it, the good because it is not the good that would satisfy in the end, the evil because in the Absolute there would be no frustration. Good and evil would thus be transcended in a transformation that is spoken of sometimes as 'total', sometimes—because good is somehow closer to reality than evil—as one of degree. But there is no way of measuring how completely any particular good or evil is transcended in the Absolute; we can only be sure that what we now regard as such is not what it seems. This view shakes the foundation of both morals and religion; it leads us back toward the moral and religious nihilism of Mansel and Kierkegaard, of Brunner and Barth. We argued many pages ago that if there exists the discontinuity they alleged between divine and human standards of good and evil, no moral judgement could be trusted. A similar conclusion seems inevitable if their Deity of the 'wholly other' is replaced by a Bradleyan Absolute.

Bradley, to be sure, is less contemptuous of morality than Kierkegaard; he would take no satisfaction in contemplating murder as a divine command; and he finds in what we call goodness and beauty a nearer approach to the Absolute than in evil and ugliness. But we never know how near that approach is; and in any case, by abolishing impulse and desire in his Absolute, Bradley has abolished with them what we have found to be essential conditions of value. Furthermore, if there is no intrinsic goodness, there is no moral goodness either, for moral goodness is a bent of the will toward producing intrinsic goodness. And in the Absolute there is not only no intrinsic goodness in our sense, but no bents, no will, and no production, for these all belong to the unreal world of time. If reverence is based on moral goodness, we cannot worship a being to whom it would be contradictory to ascribe such goodness. A non-moral Absolute is no substitute for the God of religion.

6 Those who have attempted to retain in the Absolute some traces at least of what we call morality have struggled gallantly with the problem of evil. They have pointed out that there are things that even omnipotence cannot do, such as making a stone so big that it cannot lift it, or making a world in which courage is a virtue although there is nothing to fear. It cannot do what is logically impossible. But advocates of a morally perfect Absolute have still maintained that this is the best of *possible* worlds. Royce, for example, admitting of course that sin is evil, holds that any morality worth the name must know the temptation to sin if it is to win its most significant triumph; and when he turns to non-moral evil, he takes the same line. What of the evil that has nothing to do with man's will, and has neither the aesthetic value of tragedy nor any lesson to teach, but, so far as we can see, is mere pointless misery, loss, and pain? What about cities wiped out by earthquakes? What about Shelley and Schubert, their genius snuffed out at thirty? What about the incalculable toll of animal pain collected by nature in its ordinary course? What about the horror of hereditary disease, which so often, as Royce concedes, carries mental and moral degeneracy with it? In the face of these things, can we call the Absolute good?

'Can our chance be by any possibility his rationality; our chaos his order, our farce his tragedy, our horror his spirituality? Yes, even this may come home to us if we remember that he at least, in his absoluteness, does not find these things as foreign facts, forced upon him from without. He endures them, as we do; he condemns them as we must; but he *knows* them, as we in our finitude cannot. And so, if knowing them he wills these horrors for himself, must he not know wherefore? . . . He who solves all problems, shall he not solve this one also?'[12]

In view of the extent and intensity of the admitted evils, this is a singularly lame conclusion. It throws the issue back into the lap of faith. But faith is no solution; it has often proved mistaken; the question is whether it is a faith to which we have any rational right; and Royce has not, I fear, shown that it is. The right to a faith that the world is rational, in the sense that it is an intelligible system, we grant him as a working postulate of his inquiry. But the rationality of the world in the further and very different sense that the world is perfectly good is not to be thrown in as if it were an obvious corollary; it is anything but obvious; it must be argued for separately and on the evidence. And the evidence, as Royce agrees, includes evils of vast extent, of extreme intensity, and such that the reflective human eye can see no purpose served by them or any compensating circumstances, either in the short run or in the long. We are to have faith nevertheless that these evils are necessary parts of a world that is perfectly good.

Now one who talks this language is caught in a vice, and caught equally whether he starts from the Absolute or from the particular facts. If he starts from the Absolute and the assurance that he lives in a perfect world, the natural result, we have suggested, is quietism; why struggle to improve a world that is perfect already? If he starts from the facts of evil, the result is much the same. He relies at the outset on a moral judgement that seems to him as certain as anything can be, a judgement that the world is grossly imperfect. Since that view is religiously unacceptable, however, he replaces it with the conclusion that what seems unmitigatedly evil is really good. But then his judgement that it is evil must be a mistake. And if the clearest and most certain of his value judgements is unreliable, no such judgement can any longer be depended on. But this is to solve the problem by denying its existence. For if the most certain of value judgements cannot be relied on, we cannot be sure that there is any real evil to explain, or that there is any good either; the distinction between the two is lost in a dense and paralysing fog.

BOSANQUET

7 This kind of either-or approach has seemed too uncompromising to some defenders of a moral Absolute. Granting that there is much apparent evil in the world, they would say that it is neither so widespread nor so intense as to veto the conviction that the universe is on our side, that its standards are in the main ours, and that we are safe from at least the worst extremes of evil. This belief sprouts out in an unlikely place, Bosanquet's *Logic*.

'The writer is aware of a strong prejudice in his own mind,' he writes, 'that a disastrous earthquake in London is an exceedingly improbable occurrence . . . such a degree of inconstancy as to tempt an enormous heavily built city to be erected, and then to turn and rend it, would seem malicious on the part of Nature.'[13]

Bosanquet referred to this belief indeed as 'a psychological curiosity,' but it is clear that he regarded it as more than this, for he refused to withdraw it under criticism or to accept the belief 'that the world-system is wholly indifferent to the interests of civilisation'. He clearly thought 'the world-system' could absorb existing evils without forfeiting its goodness. But it is clear also that his faith was not of the type to which evidence is of no concern and which would continue to believe in a beneficent Deity no matter what evils piled up. The destruction of London would obviously give him pause. He wrote his words before the two world wars; would their multiple destruction of cities, their genocide, their pouring down the drain of youth, talent, and goodness—would these things have made any difference to Bosanquet's serene confidence that 'the world-system' embodied goodness? He could not fall back on uncaused human conduct to exculpate his Absolute, for quite rightly he did not believe in this kind of freedom. His own words suggest that he might have thought it reasonable under pressure to reverse his field and declare this epidemic evil to be 'malicious on the part of Nature'.

Would this be any more reasonable than on the former evidence to pronounce nature benevolent? I cannot think so. Both ascriptions seem to me equally projections on the universe of values that are not there. As soon as one studies the source of value in human experience, its inextricable entanglements with human nature, human needs, human desires, and human fulfilments, such invocations of the universe as the sponsor of one's values seem both uncritical philosophically and factually premature. The first point we have laboured enough. The second deserves a further word, and that word must be drawn from science. If the universe may be said to have a scale of values in any degree like our own, it must be concerned to maximise intrinsic goodness and to minimise intrinsic evil. Does the universe as revealed to us by modern science exhibit either concern? I cannot see that it does. It has, to be sure, generated value on one planet. But as if to cut off any inference to its benevolence, it has also provided the second law of thermodynamics, the law of increasing entropy, which tells us that energy at higher levels inevitably sinks to lower, so that our sun will end as a dark, cold cinder, and all life like our own be rendered impossible. An Absolute interested in the maximising of intrinsic goodness would presumably provide generous lodgements for it, but we have no evidence that life, mind or value exists anywhere except in one spot, and we do know that throughout the greater part of the visible universe they seem to be excluded. The reply may be made, and often has been, that the mere expansion of the known universe has no relevance to the place of values in that universe. But this is untrue. Values as we know them are dependent on minds, and minds as we know them dependent on bodies, and bodies in turn dependent on conditions of light, heat, and air. If these conditions are withheld through all but an in-

creasingly tiny fraction of the known universe, the suggestion that
that universe is bent on the production and conservation of value
becomes progressively improbable.

8 This classic problem whether God is good, here translated into
the question whether the Absolute is good, is so crucial that it may
be well to put our views on it in a more formal and summary way.
When a reflective person says that the world or the universe or the
Absolute is good, what does he mean? Presumably one of three
things.

IS THE ABSOLUTE MORALLY GOOD?

9(1)   The most obvious and probable meaning is that the Absolute
is *morally* good, that it is actively concerned about the welfare and
happiness of conscious beings. Whether this is true may be considered from either (a) the theoretical or (b) the empirical point of
view.

(a) The theoretical question is whether it makes sense to say that
the universe can feel 'active concern' about anything. Feeling, as
we know it, is always connected intimately with the nervous system,
and though Fechner and others have suggested that the galaxies
may be the cells in a world brain, the analogy is not close enough to
provide a base for serious argument. And that the Absolute, in the
sense of the ordered totality of things, should love or hate others or
have moral relations with them is precluded by the fact that there
are no others. These attitudes and actions would have to be directed
on beings that are parts of itself; and that the universe as a whole
should love or hate a part of itself, or should deal generously or
unjustly with it, is hardly intelligible.

(b) On the empirical question whether the universe presents a
scene arranged by perfect moral goodness, perhaps enough has been
said already. One would expect of such a being (i) that moral
goodness among men would be recognised in some way in which
wickedness was not, either by outward signs or by the happiness of
the agent; (ii) that if evil existed, it should not be pointless or fruit-
less; and (iii) that the intrinsic goods of the world or at least the
capacity to achieve them should be justly distributed.

As for (i), it appears to be true that moral goodness tends to
happiness and vice to unhappiness, though, as Sidgwick showed,
the pairs exhibit no firm correlations; the only way to establish
them would be to invoke a new world to redress the balance of the
old, and that would be turning from evidence to faith and hope.
So far as knowledge goes, the heroes who die for others in line of

duty gain nothing proportional to their sacrifice. And there are
wicked persons who notoriously flourish like the green bay tree.
(ii) As for gratuitous evil, we have seen that it exists in many forms
and in prodigal abundance. This too is sometimes denied by those
who hold

> That not a moth with vain desire
> Is shrivell'd in a fruitless fire,

but this, as the poet recognised, is less a conclusion from evidence
than a passionate leap of faith. The evidence that the shrivelling
fire is fruitful for the moth is not forthcoming. (iii) Nor is there
evidence of a concern for justice in the distribution of goods, or of
the opportunity or capacity for them. Does the power that orders
the universe exemplify justice in allotting to some Pacific and African
peoples a brief life of starvation and disease, and to other peoples a
life of longevity and plenty? One may grant that nature was
generous to Beethoven in spite of his deafness and to Milton in
spite of his blindness, but can one doubt that among the millions of
youth that have been led to the slaughter in this tormented century
there may have been Miltons who remained mute and Beethovens
who wrote no score because a tide in the affairs of men happened
to be running against them? And for that matter, what had the
young Beethoven or Milton done, or the local thalidomide or
mongoloid infant left undone, that the first should be endowed with
imperial genius and the second with hopeless disfigurement?
Justice does not appear to be nature's first law.

IS THE ABSOLUTE INTRINSICALLY GOOD?

10(2) Sometimes when it is said that God, meaning again the
Absolute, is good, what is meant is that the experience presumed to
constitute the Absolute is of transcendent intrinsic value. So far
as this is based on the notion that the Absolute must realise all
human capacities and desires, we have seen that the conclusion rests
on a false analogy. But the claim is sometimes based on another
ground. If the universe is, as we have held it to be, a perfect system
on the intellectual side, how could it be less than perfect on the side
of goodness?

I do not see the force of this consideration. Let us suppose that,
being hungry, I need and desire a square meal but fail to get it.
This is a very simple but also typical case of evil, consisting of
frustrated need and desire. Now one who holds that the world is an
intelligible system will hold that the frustration is caused, and since

causation involves necessity, that it is also necessitated. Given the rest of the universe, this even *had* to occur as it did. And what is alleged is that if this evil event were included it would disrupt the necessary system. But why? The frustration occurred; it is an event and as truly as any other event it has its explanation; why should it form an unassimilable cyst in the explanatory system? One can only suspect a confusion between two meanings of 'perfect'. Perfect intelligibility implies a system that is at once all-inclusive and fully integrated, in the sense that there is nothing in it that is contingent or arbitrary. A conscious state that is perfectly good is one in which impulse and desire are wholly fulfilled and satisfied. Is there any straight line from an experience that is perfect in the first sense to one that is perfect in the second? I do not see that there is. It is to be remarked, furthermore, that a distinguished succession of idealist thinkers has held that the world is rational, and since they applied this same term 'rational' to conduct that was morally right, they led others, and sometimes themselves, to believe that the two senses were somehow equivalent, that a universe which is rational in the sense of being articulated logically must also be rational in the sense of being flawless morally. But the two senses are clearly different, nor does either seem to be derivable from the other.

A NEUTRAL WORLD

11(3) Sometimes when it is said that God or the Absolute or the world is good, what is apparently meant is that the world is, or contains, more good than evil. This may well be true. The ordinary life of most men and presumably most animals affords a constantly renewed fulfilment of at least those impulses and desires that are necessary to maintaining life, so that the tone of most lives is one of mild satisfaction, punctuated by occasional extremes of exhilaration or distress. But considering how minute a fragment of the world we know, and how minute a fragment of that fragment we know directly, any pretence to exactness or certainty in our estimates would be absurd. About all we can say is that the scene does not suggest the support by absolute power of either good or evil. What it does suggest far more strongly is that the universe is indifferent to good and evil alike.

If the rationalist pursues this line of thought, where does it leave him with regard to the governance of the world? It leaves him in very different positions on the intellectual side and on the moral. His endeavour on the intellectual side is to construe the world in such a way as to find to his reiterated question Why? an intelligible answer. We have found nothing to veto his hope, and much to encourage it. When we turn on the other hand to the place of values in the universe, we have found two independent lines of thought converging to one conclusion, namely that the universe is indifferent to man's ideals. One such line runs through an analysis of the nature and conditions of intrinsic goodness, which shows such goodness to be dependent on a striving mind. The other line runs through the actual distribution of good and evil, and shows that there is no way, short of a faith that defies the evidence, by which the inequity of the apportionment can be reconciled with the moral government of the world. The two lines meet upon one tragic result. The moral life, the realm of value, the kingdom of ends has its throne in the human mind.

12 I say 'tragic' because the conclusion destroys so much that has supplied a trellis for human hope. It requires a revision of the very meaning of religion as accepted in the West. For Christianity is not merely the pursuit of the good life. It is that, to be sure, but it is far more. It has in fact been the pursuit of the good life in the confidence that the power which governed the universe was also involved in one's own battles, that an invisible, heavenly host was marching at one's side. The moral struggle, the struggle so make the world over, even to make oneself over, is infinitely demanding, and one knows well enough what the result will be if one must fight alone. It will be defeat and death, not improbably with a humiliating loss of faculty and perhaps in desolating pain. Millions of men and women have been enabled to face these horrors with equanimity by the assurance that they were not alone. Did they not have it on high authority that the hairs on their head were numbered, that everlasting arms were beneath them, and that even in the valley of the shadow of death they need fear no evil?

> Halts by me that footfall:
> Is my gloom, after all,
> Shade of his hand, outstretched caressingly?

Compared with this conviction that the power that governs all things cares, the prospect offered by rationalism is bleak. It admits that the world is governed by logic; it finds insufficient evidence that it is governed by love. The nature of things is not patterned to the heart's desire, though that desire has written itself large across every heaven that men have lived under. Religion and the philosophies animated by religion, holding that the heart has its reasons that reason does not know, have constructed a fabric in which the work of reason and that of feeling are intricately entangled with each other. We have seen already in our reflections on myth in religion how natural this entanglement is. We have also seen something of the long process by which an advancing reason has separated the strands of objective thought and anthropomorphic feeling. The understanding of how desire fashions belief was better understood after the explorations of Strauss and Feuerbach, of Freud and Frazer: and the shock of disillusionment was made more tolerable by the imaginative sympathy with which sceptics like Renan and Santayana could deal with the faith they had lost. The work of these men was iconoclastic, but in spite of defects of temper and insight it was in the main true.

13 We have admitted that this truth carries tragedy with it. But there are gains in it also. There is a notable gain in honesty. Pascal's reasons of the heart would not cut an impressive figure in astronomy or the stock market, and it is not clear why they should be thought reliable in speculative thought. There is more sober guidance in Bishop Butler's 'Things are what they are, and will be what they will be; why should we seek to deceive ourselves?' And it is surely self-deception to hold that because a view of the world is desirable, it must be true, or that feelings—even the noblest of feelings—are valid evidence as to the nature of things. Furthermore, if the religious view of the West is the product in part of noble feeling, that feeling has been mixed at times with others that are far from noble. The religion of the West has reflected the nationalism, the bigotry, and the cruelty of the worshippers as well as their idealism. It was under supposed divine sanction that witches were sent to the stake, Jews and Moslems massacred, thoughtful men broken on the wheels of the inquisition for the crime of such thought, French Protestants hunted down by Catholics on St Bartholomew's night, and the Catholic More and Campion martyred by Protestants in Britain. The religion of Aquinas and still more the religion of Luther, though they represented the world as governed by a God of love, made it also a nightmare in which the majority of men were denied even the grim blessing of extinction, and were kept alive for indefinite and terrible torture. When the charge is laid against rationalism that it wipes the smile from the face of the universe, the footnote should be added that it wipes away also an implacable frown that terrified souls as stout as Dr Johnson's. To anyone who has reviewed these by-products of Western religion, the remark of Julian Huxley is at least intelligible: 'For my own part, the sense of spiritual relief which comes from rejecting the idea of God as a supernatural being is enormous.'[14]

This supernaturalism is in decline. If we have given it fuller consideration in this work than most philosophers would consider necessary, it is because of the immense importance it has held, and still holds, in the life of the West. It has been taught as such infallible truth, it has been bound up so intimately with the inculcation of the highest ideals, that its loss seems to many like the end of morality itself. Nevertheless it is becoming clearer to reflective persons that a religion of this kind is neither intellectually tenable nor required as a moral sanction. Theologians themselves feel increasing embarrassment over it. More of them perhaps than would care to say so publicly have sympathised with the Bishop of Woolwich in the misgivings of his *Honest to God*, and those theologians who have read Professor Wisdom's essay on 'Gods' or followed the struggles of the analytic philosophers over the requirements of meaningfulness may doubt whether some of the central dogmas of traditional theology have any clear significance.

A like change has been taking place in the relation conceived to hold between religion and morality. Much of the reluctance to abandon a supernaturalist theology has sprung from the conviction that it is a necessary support for morals; and, as Mill said, 'It is a most painful position to a conscientious and cultivated mind, to be drawn in contrary directions by the two noblest of all objects of pursuit, truth, and the general good'.[15] But with the decline of supernaturalism, the dependence of morals on theology is coming to be seen as the reverse of the truth, in that it bases the more certain upon the less. Men are far more confident of the wrong of stealing or killing than they are even of such central dogmas as the incarnation, the atonement, or the Trinity, so that if dogma is necessarily linked to morals, it would be more likely to involve morality in its own uncertainty than to give it additional strength. Non-sectarian moralists, though deeply divided on many issues, are now generally agreed that moral obligation is independent of theological belief and is equally binding on atheist and devotee.

CHAPTER XVI

RELIGION AND RATIONALISM

THE TENSION BETWEEN SUPERNATURALISM
AND RATIONALISM

1 In the last three chapters a view of the world has been emerging very different from that of traditional religion. The world appears to be a closely knit, intelligible order, but an order neutral to good and evil. Good and evil, so far as is known, are confined to one planet, and to one strand in the history of that planet, namely the evolution of striving minds. As regards value, the universe presents the appearance of a great plain stretching to the horizon on all sides, but exhibiting at one point an extraordinary phenomenon —a tower that is being slowly thrust upward into the sky. This is the tower of purposive endeavour, begun in palaeozoic mud, pushed slowly upward through aeons of biological struggle, and rising more rapidly in its later stages through conscious human effort. In that solitary column all the values in the universe, so far as we know, have had their precarious career. The sky above it is not inhabited, as traditional religion has imagined, by a magnified, non-natural man who fixes a continual gaze, jealous, hortatory and punitive, upon man's comings and goings. The world cares nothing for man. His sky is now a vaster and colder expanse, an infinite impersonal network of qualities in relation. If religion is the adjustment of the man as a whole to what he holds to be ultimately true and good, then any proposed alternative to the religion of the past must rest on an understanding of that ancient upward thrust of which it is an essential part.

On the intellectual side we have seen something of what that aspiring thrust has meant. The powers that govern nature are personified in myth; little by little they are moralised and fused into one; and the character of Deity is gradually purified as man's conception of his own moral ideal is refined and made consistent. That process reached its acme in Christian theism. This theism took the form of an elaborately wrought supernaturalism, some expressions of which, both Catholic and Protestant, have fallen under review in this study. We have seen that it is a difficult view to defend, either morally or cosmologically. Some philosophical exponents of Christianity, particularly the line of distinguished idealists from Hegel to Royce, failed to find the alleged rift between natural and supernatural and insisted that the universe was a seamless whole. In this whole, described as the Absolute, all man's potentialities were somehow realised. Just as his intellectual impulse would be found fulfilled in a system in which all things were interconnected, so his moral and aesthetic impulses must be fulfilled in a whole of perfect goodness and unflawed beauty. This has been one of the great recurrent visions of philosophy. We have been able to accept it only with an important modification. There is good reason, indeed, to think the universe an intelligible system, but there is no reason to think that beyond the human horizon it is either good or beautiful. The cosmos of modern science and reflective thought is one that invites and incites man's intellect but cares nothing for the yearnings or aspirations of his heart.

2 If this is true, the theology of the future will have decreasing use for the theology of the past. That theology has pursued an uneasy and vacillating course, constrained by conflicting demands from the head and from the heart. Over and over again in our study we have seen that this double allegiance cannot be maintained without disaster. Theology should, in our view, recognise this frankly, concede that there is only one criterion for truth, and merge its efforts with those of science and philosophy, which recognise, at least formally, that their interest is in truth alone. The sort of world view that might emerge from such a pursuit we have ventured to sketch in the three preceding chapters.

To anyone who accepts the traditional faith, either Catholic or Protestant, this view must be bleak and forbidding; to accept it is to move from a Father's house into an infinite impersonal web of causality and logic. Nevertheless it may be doubted whether, to most men, the shock would be very great. Even in those ages in which supernaturalism had its fullest sway, men for the most part did it lip-service rather than the service of whole-hearted belief, and such belief as they had has been slowly crumbling for centuries. Does this mean that religion is threatened with extinction? Not if religion means what we have taken it to mean. Man's attempt to adjust himself to the ultimate truth about the world on the one hand and to the demands of ideal goodness on the other is certain to go on. But the centre of religious interest is slowly shifting from creed to conduct. The cosmology of religion is becoming less dogmatic, more honest, and more tentative. It is the ethical side of religion that now seems most important, and most likely to grow in importance. And the moral ideal is itself in course of development. Any projection of the religious future must here follow the graph of past moral advance, the line of man's long struggle to formulate his ends and to use them in the ordering of his life. We have spoken of his erecting a tower of purposive behaviour on a vast non-purposive plain. Let us return to that briefly, in preparation for our final question, whether the rational ordering of life is an adequate continuant or substitute for traditional religion.

THE PURPOSIVE ROOT OF MORALITY

3 The appearance of purpose in the world is a fact that has proved stubbornly inexplicable. No one knows when purposive behaviour began, or how, or why. Some have thought that it never began, that the existence of consciousness and the efficacy of purpose are both illusions, and that the universe is a physical whole governed throughout by purely physical law. We shall not stop to argue the matter. The evidence that I am a conscious being is that at the present moment I am aware of writing this line. The evidence that I am a purposive being is that I am aware of my using some words rather than others because they bear on my present purpose. There have been philosophers who held that purposive behaviour never began, but for an opposite reason, namely that it is present always and everywhere. Empedocles, Stout, and Whitehead held that even in the iron filing that moves toward the magnet there is some dim rootlet of what eventually becomes desire. It may be so, though it is hard to see how the position could be established. Suffice it to say that purposive behaviour is now a fact, that it has a long evolutionary history, and that it is enormously important, since all that we know of values—intellectual, moral, or other—belongs to this development and all we can hope to become must be achieved through its continuance.

Through most of this long history, the use of purpose has been intermittent, groping, and half blind. On the animal level purpose operates only when pushed by impulse and organic need, when the animal is hungry, for example, or is aroused by fear, sex, or anger. When impulse is in abeyance, there is no power to plan deliberately, or to defer lesser goods to later and greater ones, or to organise ends into a pattern of reciprocal support. The advance of purpose through animal agents is like the progress of a snail, pushing out tentative experimental horns in this direction and that, and inching along in the direction of least rebuff. The snail does not know where it is going; neither do the higher animals; neither, with any definiteness, does man. It is only in the later stages of the journey, when the purposes that have been half-consciously guiding him begin to assume explicit form, that man attains some rough idea of what he is seeking and what would bring him true fulfilment.

If one looks back along the line of man's advance, a certain sense of its gist and direction soon makes itself felt, a sense confirmed by fuller study. The central factor in human development is the advance of *thought*. It is advance in the free use of thought, in the firmer mastery of thought, in fuller submission to the laws of thought, in subjecting the protean miscellany of human impulses and feelings to unification and direction by thought. We may well follow in a little more detail how thought proceeds in raising the level of human nature and conduct. It adds three dimensions to life, which we may call length, breadth, and coherence.

THOUGHT AND LENGTH OF VISION

4(1) The advance of mind in the dimension of *length* means the ordering of life by what is more and more remote in time. The animal lives in the immediate, hunting when hungry and ceasing when satisfied, but taking no pains to lay up stores of provisions against the day when hunger returns and there is no prey to be found. We have admitted that there are apparent exceptions; the squirrel in secreting nuts does seem to be provisioning himself against the winter. But whatever may go on in his puzzlingly provident little mind, he never shows in laying up his treasures the far-flung strategy that man shows constantly. Man can not only provide for tomorrow or next winter; he can foresee the onset of old age and provide security for those who survive him; he can arrange a career of posthumous beneficence by placing his funds in trust for a hospital, college, or library. He may be able to speak almost in person to later generations, for as Milton pointed out, a book is the 'life-blood' of a mind, 'treasured up on purpose to a life beyond life'. To be sure, thought as a mental event is as truly confined to the passing moment as any other event; but in range of reference it has gained a freedom that has no bounds, and is able to order present action in the light of long past engagements or of consequences far in the future.

THOUGHT AND BREADTH OF VISION

5(2) Thought adds to conduct a further dimension of *breadth*. There is no such thing as a really 'single-track mind'. A mind is a composite of dispositions, each of which tends to realise itself in an impulse of its own, and these impulses, unless controlled from a single source, would go off each in its own direction. The self, in Plato's simile, is like a charioteer driving a team of horses, though the horses are not two, as he suggested, but many, and unless kept abreast by bit and rein, they are likely to tear the self apart. In animal behaviour some one instinct—the hunting, the maternal, the pugnacious—is likely at a given time to have clear dominance, to be succeeded by some other when the first has been more or less satisfied. If two of them compete, there will be an almost visible tug-of-war between them, resulting perhaps in a rapid alternation in dominance. The squirrel that is offered a nut gives a pretty exhibition of the shift from appetite to fear, first approaching hungrily, then turning timidly back, then approaching a little nearer, and finally, when it sees an unexpected movement, scurrying off in panic.

Man, through his ability to take thought, has escaped the necessity of that almost mechanical alternation. He can drive many horses abreast. A man who is in the market for a new house can specify in his own mind what he wants of it: he would like a house that is near a church, a supermarket, and a golf course; and it should have bookshelves, oil heat, a play-room, and a room that will hold a piano. Here he is planning the satisfaction of seven principal interests at once—religious, nutritional, athletic, intellectual, hedonic, paternal, aesthetic. His impulses are not acting singly, like scouts taking turns in leading the file; at his best they behave like an army advancing on a wide front under unified command. Nor is he confined in his consideration to the array of his own impulses. He can include in his thought the minds of others as centres of value like himself, and use them as models, counsellors, or allies. Here again his power of thought gives him a range of concern far beyond that of his animal predecessors. The concern of a cat for other members of its species is virtually confined to its own family, and that of a dog to its pack.[1] Man, through his power of thought, can recognise that any man anywhere has ends and values akin to his own, and that if he is to be consistent he must treat others accordingly.

THOUGHT AND COHERENCE OF AIM

6(3)   It is plain from the growing length and breadth of his concern that man is living in an enlarging world opened to him by thought. We must now look at the third aspect of this world, its increasing coherence.

The advance of thought, as we saw in the last chapter, is governed by an implicit end of its own. If one protracts into the future the line of its past advance, one can see fairly distinctly the goal toward which it is moving. Thought is seeking an understanding of the world that is both comprehensive and systematic. 'Comprehensive' is clear enough; what is meant by 'systematic'? Two things. First, the ideal system will be such that all its parts are consistent with each other; second (a much harder condition to fulfil), the parts will be so interlinked that none will be isolated, contingent, or arbitrary; each will be required and rendered intelligible by its relations with the rest.

When thought concerns itself with the structure or relations to be found among its concepts, it is commonly known as 'reason'. Now reason is as truly operative among purposes as among concepts. Rationality is not confined to logic, or mathematics, or natural science, or philosophy; it may display itself in conduct, and indeed is present in degree in the conduct of everyone. To be sure, the names of logical relations will carry appropriately modified meanings when applied to the realm of action. Two purposes may be consistent in the sense that both may be realised without inhibiting each other; one's interest in food and in seeing an old friend may both be satisfied simultaneously by having lunch with him. Two purposes may be inconsistent, as when a man's interest in buying an expensive motor car stands in the way of his desire to feed his family. One purpose may imply another in the sense of furthering and supporting it, as when a golfer's love of sport and his love of health work hand in hand.

We have seen that a desire is an impulse with awareness of its end, and that a personality may be conceived as a body of impulses belonging to a single conscious centre. We can now see what is the natural end of a personality so conceived. It is the realisation or fulfilment of its desires. But to fulfil them all is not practically possible, since many desires are so related that the realisation of one is bound to frustrate another. The amended aim of a reflective person is thus the *rational* fulfilment of desire, which means the completest fulfilment possible in practice. And since, as we have also seen, a man's experience of intrinsic goodness lies in the fulfilment of impulse, together with the pleasure that normally attends it, it follows that in such rational fulfilment he will find the greatest good open to him.

But this must at once be amended further. For Robinson Crusoe, such a sketch of his possibilities would perhaps serve. But no man lives alone. He is surrounded by others, in whom he recognises powers and interests very like his own; and the conditions that make an experience worth having are identical for everyone. If he uses his reason, he will see the inconsistency of holding that a certain experience is good as it occurs in himself while denying that an experience of the same quality and intensity is good when it occurs in someone else; the locus of an experience is irrelevant to its intrinsic goodness. If a man is rational, the system of goods that concerns him will include those of all who are affected by his conduct. Hence if he is to behave rationally, he will be alive not only to the consistencies, the inconsistencies, and the implications between his own goods but also to these relations as they obtain between his own goods and those of others. Reason thus introduces him to a world of immensely widened horizons in opportunity and duty.

THE MORAL REPUBLIC

7 The rational man, as Plato recognised, will thus be a citizen in a republic that exists only in men's minds when they are united by the common acceptance of an ideal good. The laws of that republic will not be laid down by any de facto legislature but by practical reason itself, operating among men's purposes and appointing their obligations and their rights. This practical reason is at once the ultimate legislature and the ultimate court of appeal, for it supplies the aim of actual and responsible law-makers, and it delivers the only verdict that is without appeal on whether laws are just or unjust. Politics is applied ethics. Its rights and duties all rest on the fact that the state is a necessary means to the ethical end. But the ethical republic itself has no geography, no national bounds, no visible existence. It is a country of the mind in which the qualification for citizenship is a certain level of thought. One must be able to recognise a general good of which one's own good is only a part, for on the recognition of that good one's moral duties and rights depend. One's duties: for duty consists in trying to promote this good. One's rights: for a right is the other side of a duty, and it is the duty of others to take one's own good into account.

There is nothing original in this way of conceiving the moral life. Indeed it belongs to a strand in ethical thinking that has been dominant through most of Western history. It is a teleological ethics, the ethics that recognises man as essentially a pursuer of ends, a seeker after good, and it makes the rightness of conduct depend on its contributoriness to those ends. It was developed with power and subtlety by Plato, and in the main accepted by Aristotle and Aquinas. In modern times it forms the trunk of the ethical tree. Though textbooks find great differences between the self-realisation theories of Green and Bradley and the theories of the utilitarians, and marked differences again between the pleasure-utilitarianism of

Mill and Sidgwick, the 'ideal' utilitarianism of Rashdall and Moore, and the 'rule' utilitarianism of some present-day writers, they were all teleological moralists whose practical judgements would generally agree. Even such critics of the tradition as Prichard and Ross accept it as providing a valid ground for most moral decisions; and though the emotivists would regard all such decisions as matters of feeling rather than argument, still when they do argue, which is not seldom, they usually do what Russell did and take a broadly utilitarian line.

Now when one suggests the appeal to reason as a substitute for the appeal to authority in the guidance of practical life, it is important to define the method of reason in a way that would have some kind of consensus among thoughtful men. There is no method of ethics that would command universal concurrence. But if there is any method to which the opinions of thoughtful persons tend to converge, it is this. Its major rules are simple enough. So act as to produce the greatest net good. Take into account the good of everyone affected by your action, and in your calculations give to each man's good an importance equal to the like good of anyone else. Treat all goods as commensurable. Assume that an objective better and worse, and therefore right and wrong, are to be found. Be as impartial as you can in trying to find the right and the good.

Every moralist knows how easy it is to set gun in rest and shoot holes in these principles as vague and ambiguous; and there would certainly be many differences of detail in interpreting and applying them. I have developed my own interpretation in *Reason and Goodness*. But I am not concerned now with detail. I am concerned with the question whether there is available for those who can no longer accept a revelational ethics an accredited rational alternative. That alternative, I think, exists.

THE RELIGIOUS PROTEST

8 When a secular ethics is proffered as an alternative to religious ethics, one vigorous objection may be expected, and indeed it has been offered to the first volume of these lectures. The objection is that such an ethics is a down-grading of the moral life. It is a surrender of the spiritual man to the natural man, an acquiescence in being driven *a tergo* by impulses surviving from an animal past rather than being drawn *a fronte* by envisioned nobilities. Conscience was once regarded with reverence as a divine voice in man; goodness was invested with the vast and powerful sanctions that connected it with an eternal destiny; the natural man was something to be transcended and kept under by the spiritual man. This insight into the war in our members between nature and spirit, indeed all that gave religious support and significance to morality, is now to be discarded—in the interest of what? A morality based on the wants of the natural man and on instincts shared with the animals. What an abasement of a great vocation!

I can understand the sad urgency with which this objection is pressed by persons for whom the moral life has been inseparable from religion, and by others for whom the human mind, on its moral as well as its intellectual side, is an embodiment in degree of the Absolute. And since in writing on the theory of knowledge I have defended the idea of an Absolute, I may be thought especially vulnerable to this criticism. I own that I am sensitive to it.

THE THEOLOGY OF EVIL

9   But (1) I am not wholly insensitive either to the evil in the world, and the moral morass into which it has drawn religion. The more I have thought about religion and evil, the less willing I have become to tie ethics to religious belief. Let me explain.

The treatment of evil by theology seems to me an intellectual disgrace. The question at issue is a straightforward one: how are the actual amount and distribution of evil to be reconciled with the government of the world by a God who is in our sense good? So straightforward a question deserves a straightforward answer, and it seems to me that only one such answer makes sense, namely that the two sides can *not* be reconciled. Many attempts at reconciliation have been made: evil was introduced by man's free will, and became general through inherited original sin; it is offered to test us or to educate us or to strengthen us; it is really an illusion, and if seen in perspective would vanish away; it represents some inexplicable impotencies (unfortunately conjured up ad hoc) in the divine power; and so on, and on, and on. These theories break down so promptly and notoriously that theologians commonly give up and fall back on faith to justify a belief that eludes support by evidence.

Some theologians, aware of this conflict, have at certain points resorted to open revolt against human reason and its morality. We have studied this revolt in the theological line that runs from Luther through Kierkegaard to Brunner and Barth, and seen that it is self-destructive. For my own part, I am ready to stand correction for the ignobility of my naturalistic ethics, but not from theologians of this stripe. If their ideal of goodness is the will of a Deity who could inflict or permit the evil we know in the world, they have no consistent standard at all. How can anyone of clean conscience call good in the Deity what he would regard as intensely evil in man? To tie ethics to the will of such a being is not to exalt one's ethics but to reduce it to incoherence. I do not doubt that in many respects morals have profited by their association with religion. But I cannot admit that anyone who holds to traditional doctrines of original sin, the atonement, or eternal punishment is standing on ground that entitles him to call a naturalistic ethics degrading. It was his own great authority who said that one should remove the beam from one's own eye before attacking the mote in another's.

TWO-STORIED MAN

10(2)   The charge of degrading morals is usually made from a two-world theory of man's condition, the theory that there is a spiritual order to be set over against the natural, man being a member of both. In our studies of theologians, we have noted various forms of this division, commonly based on the Pauline theology. In all these theories we found that once human nature is broken in two, the parts are not easily united again. The non-natural truth disclosed by revelation will not dovetail into the system of natural reason. The Kierkegaardian divine imperative shocks the ordinary sense of duty. If the natural man surrenders to the non-natural, he is divided against himself, for he cannot divest himself of the nature with which he was born, and this nature cannot assimilate beliefs that would wreck his logic and his ethics. On the other hand, if the non-natural man surrenders to the natural, he is likely to feel, as do our present critics, that he has sold his birthright for a mess of pottage.

The way to put a truce to this ancient warfare is surely not to proclaim a victory for one side or the other, but to deny the division between them. The gigantic crack that is said to run through human nature is not there. Man does not own two intellects, for one of which religious dogma is intelligible and for the other not; there is a single growing intelligence, pursuing an identical end from the first judgements of perception to the highest speculative flight. There are not two consciences, a lower one pronouncing on pleasures and pains and an exalted non-natural one promulgating the moral law; the apprehension of good and bad is a continuous growth from the first fulfilment or frustration of appetite to the fulfilment or frustration of a scholar's interest in knowledge, or a patriot's in his country, or a saint's in humanity. Indeed if there is continuity in the growth of intellect, there must be a like continuity in the advance of conduct, since, in the second as in the first, an unfolding intelligence is at the heart of the advance.

I do not mean to deny that the warfare of flesh and spirit has any reality; it has; and the description of it by St Paul has been verified by far too many witnesses to be cavalierly dismissed. What I do mean to question is the sharp division he made between two strata in man. Human nature has been split in this fashion on many grounds. Sometimes the ground is the alleged incommensurability of the good pursued on the different levels, as when Newman declared that no good of the lower nature, however great, weighed anything in the scale against the smallest venial sin.[2] Sometimes the division is between achievements that are voluntary and others in which we seem to be passive instruments of a will not our own; James concludes his *Varieties* by accepting such a division and holding that the subconscious self may be permeable to an oceanic consciousness that somehow envelops us. Sometimes again the division is between that part of the self which is capable of mystical visions, ineffable and super-rational, and the part that belongs to the workaday world. Sometimes, as in Kierkegaard's tax-collector, who talks and acts like everyone else but is secretly one of the elect, the higher self seems hardly connected with the lower at all; it is a theological *x*, defined by its capacity for a non-natural faith, an eternal salvation, and a love unlike any merely human affection.

11   Such contrasts serve a useful purpose in marking the extremes of which man is capable. But do they prove the existence of two world orders, a natural and a non-natural, of which man is simultaneously a member? I do not think so. For (a) no one as yet knows the limits of human nature, and therefore no one can say with certainty, when a man begins to 'speak with tongues', or write automatically, or experience a sudden inexplicable peace, or achieve a mystical exaltation, or even when he executes the astonishing right-about-face of religious conversion, that these things are beyond natural explanation. In some cases his performance does seem so disconnected with his past that the suggestion of a break-through from another world is inevitable. Yet we know that many experiences which would have been so construed without hesitation in the time of Luther or George Fox would now give small difficulty to a psychopathologist. James himself provides a convincing explanation of how sudden conversion may occur, based on his knowledge of the subconscious; and such knowledge has greatly expanded since he wrote. I do not know how his theory of subconscious intercourse with an 'oversoul' is to be refuted, but I suspect that he would prefer to explain even this through the operation of natural laws that are imperfectly known than through a leap out of nature altogether.

(b) The variety of grounds on which a non-natural self has been recognised makes it extremely hard to know what is to be included in that self. If the test is incommensurability of goods, many supernatural demi-souls will qualify besides that recognised by Newman. Many persons have claimed a clear insight that no natural gains, however great, could justify telling a lie, or for that matter eating beef, or marrying endogamously, or committing other unforgivable sins. More sensible moralists, like Rashdall, have maintained that such incommensurability is a myth. They are right, I think, and if so, this form of the two-level theory is without ground. If apparent control of the will from without attests the presence of the non-natural, the facts of control by evil forces as well as by good must be acknowledged, and then one will be on the road to a revived demonology. Similarly of the mystic. If visions accredited as mystical are to be accepted as true non-natural insights, one will have to accept the assurances of the Sufi mystic that God is one and of St Teresa that God is three. Since this is impossible and both are well accredited mystics, it seems more likely that both visions are naturalistically explicable than that one is revelation and the other delusion.

I conclude that a two-storied cosmology and a two-level anthropology will stand or fall together. Just as increasing knowledge of the continuity of nature is filling in the chinks and cracks that angels and demons once peeped through, so an increasing knowledge of the cavernous depths of human nature is making less credible, because less necessary, the two-tier theory of man. We draw back from a non-natural account of aberrations from normality, whether their direction is up or down. We are reluctant to turn to the non-natural before exhausting the resources of nature. These tendencies, drawn from science, do not of course disprove the occurrence of invasions from without into the natural order. But they suggest that Lecky's 'declining sense of the miraculous' is more than a passing fashion. It is based on the surmise, increasingly confirmed, that nature and man form a single order.

THE TRANSFORMATION OF INSTINCT BY THOUGHT

12(3) 'Nevertheless,' it may be insisted, 'your ethics still levels down. The intrinsic values you recognise are fulfilments of impulses shared with the animals. If such impulses are to determine the range of human goods, they will tie a ball and chain to man's aspiration. The ends of the artist, saint, and thinker are not set by animal needs, and hence will not be recognised as goods at all. And without such ends man would have no stars to steer his boat by. Surely there is more in human life than this business of being pushed along from behind by ancestral instincts. You leave out the process that is man's peculiar distinction, that of being drawn forward by ideals that carry him up and out of the animal realm to satisfactions —moral, aesthetic, intellectual—that have nothing to do with instinct. Man at his best has wings. You cut them off.'

I have put the criticism sharply because it is a not unnatural inference from my evolutionary way of putting the case, because it has been made by persons I respect, and because it is clearly important. If it is true, my moral theory is deeply flawed, and should be rejected. But I think the criticism rests on misunderstanding.

Man does inherit a large instinctive equipment from the animals, which gives him his continuity with them and a certain understanding of them. But it would be absurd to say that the instinctive response of the animal appears unchanged in man. As it appears in the human mind, its object is profoundly transformed and its characteristic feeling is transformed accordingly. The instinct of curiosity, for example, is displaying itself in the dog that gingerly explores the bristles and possibilities of the first porcupine it has seen. The 'same' instinct of curiosity is at work in a Leibniz and an Einstein. Does that commit us to denying the chasm between its earlier and later manifestations? The sex instinct in man is notoriously inherited from far down in the animal scale, from the level for example of the cat that caterwauls on the back fence. But it would be absurd to stretch this instinctive behaviour to cover Romeo's affection for Juliet or Dante's for Beatrice. Or, not to labour the point further, does it follow that if a peacock displays some glimmer of aesthetic response to the gorgeous dress of another, there is nothing further in the aesthetic response of a Leonardo?

These questions answer themselves. There is about as much resemblance between the instinctive life of an animal and that of a reflective man as there is between a seedling and a flower. And the main instrument in this transformation is thought. Instinctive behaviour, as McDougall pointed out, normally involves three elements, an afferent, a central, and an efferent—an object responded to, a characteristic emotion, and an impulse to take action about the object. Of these three elements, the key is the first, the object. Now the object, at the human level, is a construction of thought. Some perceptual thought is no doubt involved even in the dog's investigation of the porcupine, but it is microscopic compared with the intellectual sweep required even to see the problems that engage the curiosity of the physicist or the philosopher. Dante loved Beatrice. But the Beatrice who was the object of Dante's love was no mere woman of flesh and blood; she was a woman transfigured by the poet's thought into an embodiment of goodness and wisdom. Again, the objects of aesthetic response, supposed sometimes to be relatively simple in their appeal, may be informed and saturated with thought, as was the beauty of *La Gioconda* for Pater—a 'beauty into which the soul with all its maladies has passed'.

13 How is this enlargement of the object effected? Partly through the larger range of perceived similarities made possible by growing intelligence. For example, the tenderness felt instinctively for children may extend itself to all who, like them, are weak and helpless, including the large assortment of pets that human beings dote on. Similarly fear aroused in a child by an unhappy encounter with a dog may extend itself to all dogs or even all animals. Again, objects may change their character through association. Loud sounds are instinctively feared when they are first heard, but if thunder keeps repeating itself with no ill effect it comes to be accepted placidly; the snake that is at first repulsive may seem to the herpetologist who has studied its ways an object of attraction and even affection.

More significant is the transformation of the object by its reflective development in thought. Consider the difference, for example, between the attitude of a small boy toward a soldier in uniform and that of a Tolstoy or a Gandhi. Their attitude was so complex that one could not fully understand it without entering into the reflections of a pacifist philosopher about all that the soldier stands for in government and society. Or take a simpler object and observe how the widening context of knowledge about it transforms both the object and the emotions it arouses. A handkerchief lies on the floor. A dog looks at it; does he perceive a handkerchief? No. He sees a white patch, but a handkerchief is more than that. It is a piece of cloth made by man to perform certain functions, and only a creature who can bring to bear in its perception the thought of these functions can perceive what we perceive. But the object as we commonly see it is still relatively simple; let us complicate it. Suppose that the man who is looking is Othello and that the handkerchief is the one he gave to Desdemona as a mark of their mutual devotion. He looks at it and breaks into a storm of passion in which jealousy, rage, sorrow, and love all have their eloquent parts. In spite of its complex and torrential character, his response is intelligible and indeed has the inevitability of great tragedy. As seen by Othello, that handkerchief is the conclusive piece of evidence in the web of disloyalty and deceit that has been weaving itself about the head of Desdemona, so that his final and terrible response is not to any one thing or person but to the whole complex situation which his misguided thought has constructed. And there is yet a further stage of complexity. When the reflective critic of Shakespearean tragedy—A. C. Bradley for example—contemplates all that centred in that fateful handkerchief, he places it in the context not only of the play as a whole but of human nature and human experience, of man and woman, good and evil, as we know them. We see in the end that the small white square, which is all that is given to sense, lies not so much on a floor as at a crossroads of humanity, from which the intersecting roads run out to the horizon in all directions. Its significance has no limits except those of the mind that seeks to understand it.

SENTIMENTS

14 Thus advancing intelligence transforms the world man inhabits. The instinct of curiosity in the animal mind becomes in man the drive to approximate his system of thought to the nature of things, and in the course of the attempt he constructs first the world of common sense and then the world of science. To these new environments the rest of our instinctive drives must adjust themselves. But while cognition is accommodation, the other drives are attempts to make things over in the interest of their own special ends. Self-assertion and submission, sexual and parental love, gregariousness and pugnacity are urgencies to do rather than to know. How are all these impulsions to be organised? They never do get organised wholly; even the wisest and best of men are torn at times by the conflicting demands of love and anger, of self-assertion and sympathy. Nevertheless there is one agency of unification that has scored remarkable successes, at least at intermediate levels. This is what is called by psychologists a *sentiment*.

A sentiment is a cluster of impulses—or the dispositions to them—around a single object. A child, for example, arouses the mother's solicitude. But it also organises around it many other of her dispositions; she is fearful if it is in danger, angry if it is threatened, depressed if it is ill, pleased in sympathy with its own pleasure. There are men whose whole life is thus organised around a cause they have espoused, as Garrison's was around his crusade against slavery, or Gibbon's around *The Decline and Fall*. Such organisation may render an otherwise feeble life an engine of great force. Unfortunately a man's drives may be organised around foolish and irrational ends as well as rational ones, and then he becomes a fanatic, as McCarthy was with his obsession about communists and Hitler with his obsession about the Jews.

THE RELIGIOUS SENTIMENT

15 Is there any way of organising the interests and drives of a life which would carry a safeguard against such miscarriage? It is often urged that religion is the only enthusiasm equipped with such a safeguard, since even fanaticism, if it takes the form of religious dedication, is still an instrument of good. And it must be agreed that religion has often taken divided and apparently feeble personalities and turned them into astonishingly effective agents of benevolence and mercy; witness Francis of Assisi and Francis Xavier, John Bunyan and John Woolman. But to say that religious devotion is a safeguard against fanaticism would be notoriously untrue; indeed religious fanaticism has been one of the major curses of Western history. It massacred the Albigenses, burned witches, organised vain crusades, bloodied the borders between north and south Ireland, India and Pakistan, and found sanction in its heart and its Scriptures for destroying Bruno and Savonarola, Huss and Zwingli, Joan of Arc and Thomas More.

Is there any sentiment capable of unifying the anarchic energies of human nature while defusing their destructive power? Certainly religion as traditionally conceived, the religion whose thought on reason and belief we have been reviewing in this book, is not, on its record, a reassuring candidate. Why not? Because, as we have so often seen, it believes it has a source of guidance superior to reason itself. It has exalted two sentiments, the love of God and the love of man, into the primacy in human life, but the first has been used to block the second. The love of man, in its rational interpretation, we have accepted as a necessary principle in any valid account of the good life, sacred or secular. The love of God is in a different position. Whereas the love of man granted to intelligence freedom to devise fresh channels of benevolence, the love of God did not grant a parallel freedom to the exercise of criticism. Man's mind was held back by a cramping ethics of belief; he was burdened with a body of dogmas offered him as revealed certainties, though they were irreconcilable with his thought. The Christian love of man which, when allowed free flow, has been so noble and powerful an agency of good, has often been stopped short by signs of 'thus far and no farther' when it has sought to free itself from theological prepossessions about the world, the flesh, and the devil, to throw off Pauline shackles on woman, to recognise at their true value such goods of the natural man as physical fitness, art, play, sex, and science. All too often, though less often now than formerly, when a great church takes its stand on such a problem as abortion, its ultimate ground is not the promotion of human good but conformity to a theological dogma, which has perhaps laid down the point in pre-natal life when an immortal soul is joined to the body. Whether the moral policy is right or not, this sort of defence will not prove it right. Nevertheless such dogmas have much weight with many minds because they belong to a system of thought guaranteed by the church and supposed to carry the seal of divine approval.

THE SENTIMENT OF RATIONALITY

16   There is only one agency in human nature that is competent to deal with such claims. No reader will be surprised at this stage to learn what that agency is. The main thrust of our long study has been to show that when dogma conflicts with reason reason has the right of way. There is nothing arbitrary in such a priority, as if the two authorities stood logically on the same footing. One cannot deny the ultimate authority of reason without appealing to that authority in the very denial; to think at all is to bow to logic, and the laws of logic are the canons of reason. The authoritarian who tries to repudiate reason can codify and develop his own view only by accepting the reason he repudiates.

What holds in theory holds in practice. The court of final appeal when nations or men or impulses conflict is likewise reason. We need not stop to examine how the reason employed in conduct differs from that employed in mathematics or in natural science; for present purposes all that is needed is the acceptance of some form of cognition competent to deal with rightness and wrongness. It is reason in this sense to which all conflicts about conduct come back in the end, and that supplies the authority recognised in such conflicts. When two nations or two men submit their dispute to a court of law, they are appealing to reason, if only to discover how the law applies to their particular case. Even when there is no court or law that covers their case, or when they reject the existing law, it is still to reason that they appeal as the only authority that can offer real justification. (Of course they may take the law into their own hands and appeal to force, but that justifies nothing.) Now the final authority in settling the conflicts of nations and men is also the final authority in conflicts between the impulses or sentiments within the individual man. Surrender to the strongest feeling is essentially an appeal to force and, like it, settles nothing. The only competent government of impulse is one that can mobilise past experience, crystallise it in rules, apply these to the present case and, if necessary, suspend the rules in the interest of a greater good. In short, the ultimate authority in practice is practical reason.

Is it an infallible authority? Yes and no. The same answer must be given here as to the parallel question about theoretical reason. When the question Why? is raised, the final answer is that which would be offered by reason when pushed through to its goal. To reject that answer would be mere incoherence. In the same way, what I should do at this moment in the face of conflicting impulses (shall I give the soft answer or the lie direct?) or a conflict of sentiments (shall I give priority to love of country or to professional success?) is what a reason fully aware of the implications of each alternative would pronounce to be the right course. To deny that verdict would in effect be to deny that conduct is, or can be, rational at all, including that bit of conduct that consists in raising the question. We can only hold that if we had the ultimate answer of reason to any question of theory or practice, that answer would be infallible; to say otherwise would be to say that a perfect understanding could be imperfect. At the same time we must admit that our understanding is not perfect. The criterion of truth and rightness that we actually apply is never what reason in its complete fulfilment would give us, for that insight is never available, but only such approximation to it as limited powers and circumstances will allow. And *this* criterion is always fallible.

Nevertheless it is the best we have, and the best we have ever really had. Though the certainties of an infallible revelation are no longer open to us, it is better to have a warranted probability than an unwarranted certainty. We are following the only authority that could have unseated one claiming infallibility, and our attitude toward it is essentially that of Luther's 'I can no other'. Luther would of course have disowned us; he thought of himself as an enemy of 'the harlot reason'. But so far as his protest was valid at all, it was the voice of his own critical reason protesting against what was irrational, because unjust and wrong, in the ecclesiastical world of his time. And in protesting against Luther's own world, the reflective man of our day is following that same voice, however far from the Lutheran path it may lead him.

THE RATIONAL IMPULSE IN RELIGION

17 Religion is man's attempt to live in the light of what he holds to be ultimately true and good. It has often been claimed that through revelation he has received direct disclosures of ultimate truth and reality. But no finite being has ever actually stood in that austere presence. We are all prisoners in Plato's cave, studying the real world through shadows on the wall, and such light as we have is always filtered through our own blurred understanding. *Quidquid recipitur recipitur ad modum recipientis*. Religion is not loyalty to the ultimately true and good, but only to what we *hold* to be such. It has always been this, however much more it may have claimed to be. The character and dictates of the Mosaic tribal god were projections of the character and moral ideals of his worshippers. In the God worshipped by Jesus, that character and will had been transformed by a morally more sensitive mind, though traces of the old nationalism remain, and of the primitive vengefulness of eternal punishment. The advance of theology has been a continuous endeavour of man's reason to construct a more rational account of the divine mind and character, punctuated by occasional anachronisms such as Kierkegaard and Barth, who would impose the visions of one epoch on all succeeding times.

So our rationalist alternative is not, we should hold, an abandonment of religion, but a return to what, in spite of much self-misunderstanding, religion has always been. Piety, Santayana remarked, is loyalty to the sources of our being. The sources of our being lie in the struggle of an animal nature to achieve rationality in thought and action. An illuminating history of theology could be written to show how the inner pressure of reason has been continually at work in revising and remodelling the creeds, trimming off the dead wood of discredited dogma and grafting new shoots of insight on the old trunks. Illuminating accounts of ethics have been written to show how a similar pressure of reason has remoulded the moral ideal.[3] One may venture to say that at all the growing points of morals and religion reason will be found at work, whether its part is recognised or not. Western ethics and Western philosophy virtually began together with Socrates' insistence that life should be ordered by reason. All four of the political revolutions of modern times were made in the name, at least, of reason, and with philosophers in the background—Locke behind the American Revolution, Voltaire behind the French, Marx, prompted by Hegel, behind the Russian and the Chinese. But reason does not wait for an invocation by name to enter and do its work. Conscience is largely reason protesting against inconsistency between principle and practice. The private monitor of Marcus Aurelius, the 'inner light' of the Friends, the mystical leadings of Loyola and Xavier, the missionary call of Schweitzer, the non-violent protest of Gandhi and Martin Luther King were all agents under an alias of such reason as they had, speaking out on the needs and injustices of their time. We have suggested that the voice of Jesus himself was not the voice of a 'wholly other', that his major innovation in morals was the extension across boundaries of sex, class, and nation of an attitude already accepted by the Jewish prophets as binding among their own people.

18 Confinement of revelation *ad modum recipientis* is not a denial of revelation. All knowledge is revelation in the sense that thought is under the constraint of its object. If the world is, as we have held it to be, an intelligible system, then to the extent that our thought is comprehensive and coherent, that world is revealing itself to us. Rational thought is an activity of our own in the sense that we can choose to think or not to think, to attend loosely or intently. But the more rigorous we are in our thinking, the more aware we are that the lines our thought is following are not of our own creation but belong to the real world, and that the secret of following them faithfully is a 'wise passiveness'. That revelation occurs in the same sense in the sphere of morals is more questionable. Indeed if what is 'revealed' is a world that is morally perfect, as it is logically coherent, such a revelation would, as we have seen, not only be inconsistent with any honest dealing with the problem of evil but make nonsense of moral effort. Yet to the extent that moral insight is reasonable and does not thus overreach itself, it may fairly be regarded as revelatory here also. The intuition that knowledge is better than ignorance and justice than injustice is, as Socrates maintained, objectively true and an insight into the nature of things; we can no more alter the truth of these insights by our own thought or will than we can decree that two and two shall make seven. Such goods, so far as we know, exist only in human minds, but their relations of better and worse are as little open to our manipulation as the laws of nature themselves. The rise of rationality in morals does in this sense, like the advancing understanding of nature, involve a better adjustment to the real world.

That real world, it is here suggested, is one to which reason is the key, both in the progress of knowledge and in the conduct of life. 'And when you propose your rationalist alternative,' it may be asked, 'are you suggesting that reasonableness should take the place of faith, that reason shall replace revelation as the guide of thought and life?' Yes, that *is* what I am proposing and I had almost added that whatsoever is more than this cometh of evil. When faith has been encouraged to leap ahead of reason, it has often indeed painted a picture of the world that has given new heart and hope to its holders. But too often that picture has been painted on the clouds, and its disintegration in the winds of increasing knowledge has left scepticism and cynicism behind. In some quarters, as the winds rise, there appears a correspondingly desperate effort to keep the picture intact and to repudiate the science and philosophy, the anthropology and textual criticism that threaten to dissolve it. Locally and in the short run this may succeed. In the long run it will fail, and hysterical effort to block the advance of critical thought will make defeat, when it comes, more complete. Accommodation to reason betrays nothing in religion that deserves loyalty. Indeed there is much in the religious tradition that any rational critic would wish to retain.

Critics are not necessarily enemies. They may be animated not by malignance but by a genuine interest in finding what is true.

19 'But what of the vast motive power of religion? Is that now to be lost, and deliberately? Surely a pale and consumptive "sentiment of rationality" is not going to propel any Franciscans out among the lepers or any Xaviers across the sea. These men were not living by the wan light of their own thought, but by another kind of light entirely; they were obeying what for them was the will of God, and their everlasting destiny hung on whether they heeded that will or not. The drive wheel of their lives was attached to a powerful motor behind the scene, and it is idle to suppose that the power will still be available when the connecting belt has been broken.' This is fair criticism. But it raises two very different questions: One is: Is not the motive of being reasonable quite different from that of being moral? and can such a motive supply the driving force necessary to the good life?

As for the first question, the motive of life according to reason is actually purer morally than the religious motive itself. To do something because it will achieve an eternal reward or avoid an eternal punishment is not acting morally at all; the moral man acts in a certain way because he thinks it is right, not because it is self-serving. If a man acts as he does because he believes God wills it, his motive is higher, but still not the highest. What is that highest motive? Presumably the motive that would lead God himself to will it. But *he* cannot will it because he wills it; that makes no sense. He must be presumed to will it because it is right, and that is what should move man too.

But is not the idea of being moral one thing, and the ideal of being rational quite another? Certainly a man may consider what it is reasonable to do in buying a house or settling a bill without feeling any moral problem at all; and equally certainly the good man may be in no sense an intellectual. It remains true, however, both that the objectively right act is the one that a fully instructed reason would approve, and that the subjectively right act is the one approved by such insight as we can now command. The view that moral action means reasonable action has been accepted by thinkers as far apart as Kant on the one hand and Sidgwick and Moore on the other. I do not myself accept Kant's way of using reason in morals because it seems to me too formal and abstract, and hence too insensitive to the circumstances of the particular case. Reason tells us that we ought not to lie or steal, but to make these into universal mandates admitting no exception would in marginal cases demand what is absurdly irrational. The application of reason to conduct is made, I think, in a different way. In determining duty the main office of reason is (a) to develop in thought the values in terms of fulfilment and satisfaction that are involved in the actions proposed, and (b) to balance the net goods against each other.[4] If the attempt to be reasonable in this sense were fully successful, one would see and do what was right; the right and the rational would coincide. The ideal of rationality in conduct is thus also the moral ideal, though with emphasis now placed on the instrument of its achievement.

20   It must be admitted that the foresight and the maturity of judgement necessary to see with certainty what is objectively right are not granted us, and that we must make do with such limited vision as we have. Does not that mean that 'rationality' in practice is, after all, a state of anarchy in which each man does what is right in his own eyes? The appeal to reason is a sorry guide if every prophet with a new nostrum can preface his sales talk with 'it stands to reason'.

There is very little force in this criticism. It offers the unreal alternative of perfection or nothing. Reasonableness, to be sure, is an infinitely exacting ideal, which we shall never fully realise, but this does not mean that we are all equally far removed from it, or that we cannot move nearer it if we try, or that if we do try, we shall not reach fuller agreement about what it requires. In any but benighted communities there are some persons who stand out above others in their concern for dealing justly with their fellows and whose counsel is sought for its fairness and ripeness of judgement. And to say that persons who prize such things do not tend to agree as they cultivate them is virtually to deny that there are objective standards at all.

To be sure, there are persons who pride themselves on this denial as a mark of sophistication. There has been much talk in recent years about ethical and cultural relativism by persons who think they can dispose of objective standards merely by pointing to diversities of custom. They would not argue this way in other fields. They would not hold that since masses of Chinese people believe that the moon goes into eclipse because a celestial dog bites a piece out of it, while Western astronomers deny this, there is no such thing as an objective standard in astronomy. They would scout the idea of a Russian and an American physics, or of a French and an Indian chemistry, each contradicting the other but with equal claims to validity. There is simply physics or chemistry, with one universal standard of truth, to which place, time, and nationality are irrelevant.

I believe that, similarly, there is one universal standard of morality, set by the fundamental needs, and therefore ends, of human nature. This standard is at work in men's minds implicitly long before it is given explicit shape; its demands become firmer and clearer as it is acted upon, and more generally accepted as social intercourse widens. That its existence is really recognised is attested by such bodies as the United Nations and the World Court, which assume that when a protest is brought before them in the name of justice the term has a common meaning, and that with patience and good will a rational judgement may be achieved. It is true that reasonableness in morals is more difficult and elusive than reasonableness in mathematics; emotions are more deeply engaged and the appraisal of human values calls for richer resources of imagination and sympathy. Reasonableness in the concrete is indeed infinitely and impossibly difficult. Fortunately it is not one's duty to be infinitely and impossibly rational. It is one's duty only to be as reasonable as one can. If even that were seriously accepted, the world would be strangely different tomorrow morning.

REASONABLENESS AS A MOTIVE

21 This brings us to the second question: Is it not unrealistic to the point of absurdity to exalt the respect for reasonableness into such a position of primacy? How could so feeble and special a motive carry the weight here loaded upon it? 'The love of truth', said Housman, 'is the faintest of human passions'. 'Many of us,' says F. L. Lucas, 'having read our Freud, have grown more sceptical than ever; seeing reason no longer as a searchlight, but usually as a gust-swept candle guttering amid the winds of emotion and the night of the Unconscious'.[5] With many men, perhaps most, the felt obligation to be reasonable is so weak that it is pushed aside daily by jostling competitors from the cellars of the mind—selfishness, resentment, fear, envy, jealousy. Look closely and one will see that even the best of lives are spotted and fly-specked with petty prejudices, capricious likes and aversions, and other assorted irrationalities. The very attempt to be reasonable turns out at times to be the rationalisation of something irrational; Freud would regard all the flights of theological reflection that we have been reviewing in this book as so many desperate attempts to replace an earthly by a heavenly father on the part of minds in need of security; and there are contemporary philosophers who would say that even attempts at philosophical rationality are likewise self-deceptions. But this is clearly going too far, for it is self-destructive. It is itself an attempt at rational speculation, and if all such attempts are deluded, it too must be deluded.

The demand for reasonableness in belief and conduct is not to be evaded. One must comply with it in some measure even to stay alive. To comply with it in high degree is an all but universally admitted virtue. Yet reasonableness for most men has singularly little attraction; it remains the great grey virtue. Nor is it hard to see why. The first effect of reflection is normally the restraint of impulse, and that is bound at the time to be disagreeable. To most minds reasonableness seems negative and bloodless; it belongs to the spectator of life rather than to the active participant; it is formal, cool, collected, correct. And in all this there is nothing to stir the pulse. If the prospect of a way of life is to make men love and follow it, it must promise action, excitement, and if possible drama. Men will answer en masse a call to live adventurously, even dangerously; they will march under the banner of a Churchill or even a Hitler. But where has one seen a crowd marching, with band and streamers, under the banner of Spinoza? Surely if there is one mass movement against which we may feel safe, it is a stampede toward rationality.

There is much sense in this, but also a grave misconception. The role of reason in conduct is very far from that of the prim school-mistress. Plato was nearer the mark in making it that of the charioteer directing the course of spirited horses. The reins and the bit are less for the purpose of holding them back than of helping them forward in concert, so that they can reach their goal without getting in each other's way. The purpose of the rational control of conduct is precisely the more abundant life, and its momentary restrictions are for the sake of a release of energy and activity in the longer range. They are, in fact, the necessary means to freedom. 'It is ordained in the eternal constitution of things,' said Burke, 'that men of intemperate minds cannot be free'. The only true freedom, as the greater philosophers have noted, lies not in the surrender of reason to impulse but in the surrender of impulse to rational control.

THE REASONABLE TEMPER

22 There is no denying, however, that the ideal of reasonableness in thought and action involves reflectiveness and self-criticism, and therefore has never appealed to the many. Has it appealed with real effectiveness to anyone? Examples would seem called for to prove it a practical possibility. Happily there have been many great personalities whose comparative freedom from prejudice and pettiness, whose reasonableness of temper and habitual fairness of judgement have gained the admiration of all who knew them. If it is natural, for a student of philosophy, looking for personalities of this kind, to turn first to the philosophers, he must do so with a double admission. First, if one knew enough, examples could no doubt be drawn from any field; and secondly, philosophers have varied greatly in reasonableness of temper; some of them, and not the least brilliantly endowed, have been anything but balanced minds and have even lived on the ragged edge of sanity. Still, others among them have shown in exemplary measure what reasonableness as a conscious end can achieve. They belong to no one school of thought. Rationality in temper is happily not confined to rationalists in theory.

The father of this admirable tribe was Socrates, and his *Apology* is one of its classics. Of the modern line the father is Spinoza. Bertrand Russell has said of him that he is 'the noblest and most lovable of the great philosophers. Intellectually, some others have surpassed him, but ethically he is supreme.'[6] Then there is the sober and honest John Locke. It may surprise many who have read his writings to learn that 'Beneath their calm, unruffled surface there is a turbulent, fiery spirit. . . . But he knew how to keep the emotional side of his nature in check lest truth should suffer. . . .'[7] David Hume has always been an embarrassing figure to those who so reprobated his philosophy that they thought he must be himself a reprobate. 'Upon the whole,' said Adam Smith, who knew him well, 'I have always considered him, both in his lifetime and since his death, as approaching as nearly to the idea of a perfectly wise and virtuous man, as perhaps the nature of human frailty will admit'.[8] The name of John Stuart Mill should be added. Of Mill a critic wrote: 'The thinker was greater than the thought. It is the mental and moral quality of the "saint of Rationalism" . . . his infinite candour and teachableness, which gave his reputation its unique character . . .'[9] From my own limited knowledge, I should say that if one wants white light, uncoloured by any tinge of prejudice and offered invariably with a single eye to the evidence, one can turn with advantage even from such models as these to the thought and writing of Henry Sidgwick.

23 'To be rational in anything is great praise,' remarked Jane Austen; and the rational temper, difficult enough in thought, is more difficult by far in practice. Mere reasonableness is so difficult even for heads of state that Gibbon could describe history as 'little more than the register of the crimes, follies and misfortunes of mankind'; and many of those who fill most space in the record—Attila, Napoleon, Hitler—have been self-willed and power-drunk. But men's admiration has been arrested occasionally by a very different type of leader. There is some rashness in naming names where knowledge is so limited and partiality so nearly inevitable. But the name of Caesar, though controversial, can hardly be passed over. His quiet objectivity about himself and his almost effortless adequacy to every situation have invested him with a kind of fascination held by few other men in history. 'There Caesar, graced with both Minervas, shone; Caesar, the world's great master, and his own.'[10] But the exact ratio of fact to legend in his story will presumably never be known. In this curious quietude on a pinnacle, his only rival in the ancient world was Marcus Aurelius, whose *Meditations* remain a wistful classic of the ordering of life by reason. In modern times, the rational temper in men of affairs has had examples who, if less dramatic, come closer to where we live. American colonial life seems to have produced two of them in Franklin and Jefferson. British public life of this century has produced some others, of whom perhaps the most notable was H. H. Asquith. Asquith was recognised by both friends and foes alike as embodying the rational temper in an unusual degree. He was possessed, said Desmond MacCarthy, of 'a Roman aequanimitas'. 'Mr Asquith's character is a national asset,' said a political foe, Lord Birkenhead; 'he fights cleanly, wins without insolence and loses without rancour'. He had 'the best intellectual apparatus, understanding and judgement', said Lord Haldane, 'that I ever saw in any man'.

These men differed greatly from each other, but were alike in their devotion to reasonableness and in their success in retaining the reasonable temper through practical storm and stress. They were also men of unusual powers, and it may be wondered whether such success is limited to rare individuals, exceptionally endowed. The reassuring fact is that it has also marked certain communities as wholes, though apparently always small ones. The Athenian youth of the fourth century BC who fell under the spell of Socrates and the Academy seem to have been such a community. There were circles in Diderot's Paris and Hume's Edinburgh that exhibited the same attitude—an attitude easier in the eighteenth century than in most other times. There was another such community in the Cambridge of the early days of this century, a community of which Moore and Russell, McTaggart and Lowes Dickinson, Maynard Keynes and Roger Fry were leading spirits. And no doubt many other less luminous communities of the kind have sprung up and had their day, usually in academic centres.

24 Is education a condition of the rational temper? Formal education facilitates it, or ought to; but it is worth recalling that Mill never attended a university, and that many who did have acquired no tincture of the state of mind here considered. Let us be clear what this state of mind is. Reasonableness is not knowledge or learning, though this may help. It is not intelligence, which is in the main a native gift, most unevenly distributed, though if present this too will help. It is not skill in abstraction or in analysis or in argument or in expression, though again these are valuable aids. The reasonableness we are talking about is, rather, a settled disposition of mind. It is a disposition to guide one's belief and conduct by evidence, a bent of the will to order one's thought by the relevant facts, and to order one's practice in the light of the values involved. It is the habit of using reflective judgement as the compass of one's belief and decision. Since it is a habit, it is not native, but acquired; as something independent of great natural endowment, it can be acquired in degree by any normal person with sufficient interest in acquiring it.

25   Is it possible that interest in, and emulation of, the reasonable temper should exist not only in small communities but in a society as a whole? Stranger things have happened. If a quality of character comes to seem so important that one identifies one's self-respect with having it, the chances are that one will get it. The Stoics felt that way about bearing pain. Christians have felt so about loving-kindness. Soldiers have felt so about their honour. The French aristocrats of the old regime felt so about chivalry—and it is hard to forget Burke's apostrophe to what that chivalry had achieved: that 'unbought grace of life,' 'that sensibility of principle, that chastity of honour, which felt a stain like a wound . . . which ennobled whatever it touched, and under which vice itself lost half its evil by losing all its grossness'. No doubt all of these ideals had a touch of the extreme and the visionary in them, but their hold was widespread nevertheless. Is it an entirely impractical dream to suppose that the respect men have felt for hardihood, for the love of friend and enemy, for honour, for chivalry, they might come to feel for the habitual appeal to reason? John Dewey thought that the dream was not wholly visionary. 'One of the few experiments in the attachment of emotion to ends that mankind has not tried is that of devotion, so intense as to be religious, to intelligence as a force in social action.'[11] There have been psychologists who have thought that such an experiment might succeed. A specialist on the herd instinct, W. Trotter, has written:

> 'if rationality were once to become really respectable, if we feared the entertaining of an unverifiable opinion with the warmth with which we fear using the wrong implement at the dinner table, if the thought of holding a prejudice disgusted us as does a foul disease, then the dangers of man's suggestibility would be turned into advantages.'[12]

26 The question whether respect for rationality will ever become general, rather than the property of a small group of devotees, is no doubt beyond answer. In any case the question now most likely to present itself is of a different kind. We have suggested the respect for reason in belief and conduct as a possible alternative to traditional supernaturalism. To many who hold to this tradition, the suggestion will seem incredibly shallow and unimaginative. 'It is too hopelessly cerebral,' they will say; 'you have caught nothing of the depth of feeling, or of what is specifically religious in traditional Christianity. You have forgotten that religion has been the custodian of the noblest of human attitudes, those that have given man his outlook into "the eternities and immensities", that have humbled his pride, that have given him a perspective in which he can see himself as he is. Respect for reason? Why, yes, of course, as a supplement, a garnish, a grace note. But as a *replacement* for religious devotion? Absurd! There is vastly more in religion than merely being reasonable. It means such things as faith, which assures man that the power that governs the universe sees and cares. It means reverence, which keeps the vision of perfection before him, and humility, which is the one true antidote for his complacency and pride. These were of the essence of traditional Christianity. Are they now to be thrown away?'

FAITH

27 As for faith, one must admit that it would be unseated from its old primacy. Faith demands going beyond the evidence; 'blessed are they that have not seen, and yet have believed'. No ethics of belief that stands for the equating of belief to evidence could comply with that demand. If a readiness of assent is required in religion that would be unacceptable in other fields, it must be either because such assent is imposed by authority or because it is presented as a means to some great and special advantage. In earlier parts of this study we have examined both these inducements to belief and found them wanting, the first logically, the second morally. The new loyalty to reason would seldom call for a declaration of certainty, and it could admit every degree of likelihood and unlikelihood in belief. What it would exclude is any tempting, threatening, or coercing of belief by sticks or carrots other than evidential. When all forms of coercion are removed and the mind is permitted to play freely over the range of traditional dogmas, a winnowing out will follow; that is inevitable. Those tenets that remain will have a new and better base of accreditation. Those that fail of accreditation may be an emotional loss, but their loss will not be accounted by a rational mind as wholly tragic.

For many persons the real reason why faith is so much prized and reluctantly let go is that faith means in practice far more than belief. Most dogmas these persons could perhaps lose with equanimity. They would be more reluctant to part with the by-products of faith: the hopefulness, the confidence in facing the future, the heartening sense that all will come right in the end, the poetry—as St Francis felt it, or Chesterton—in a world brimming with the divine, the sweetness of a childlike trust.

> I know not where his islands lift
> Their fronded palms in air;
> I only know I cannot drift
> Beyond his love and care.

It must be admitted that the idyllic quiet and serenity of Whittier's world would not rest undisturbed under rationalism. Some of the glow on the world's face would be lost undeniably. Those attitudes that are treasured fruits of belief can hardly be expected to remain and ripen when their supporting trellis has been snatched away. Still, part of the traditional faith consists of moods or attitudes that are independent of belief and may well persist without dogmatic support. Courage, hopefulness, dutifulness, sunniness of temper, delight in the world and in man are not tied to any articles of belief and are quite at home in the rational mind—more so, one would have thought, than in a mind struggling to adjust itself to a formidable and inscrutable Deity. And to suggest that poetic feeling is rooted in dogma or confined to the world's intellectual immaturity is plainly untrue. If Francis Thompson, Christina Rossetti, and T. S. Eliot were great poets, as they were, so were Lucretius and Shakespeare and Shelley and Keats and Housman and Swinburne. Music in the soul need not be the echo of some projected music of the spheres.

REVERENCE

28 Reverence has a more secure position in a rationalist world than faith, though its objects will not remain unchanged. Its traditional object has been a Deity conceived as morally perfect, and toward such an object reverence is the wholly appropriate attitude. However, that attitude has been confused and rendered ambivalent by conflicts within the object itself. The Deities presented in the Old Testament and in the New are not consistent, and the God of the New Testament combines the tenderest of loving-kindness with the readiness to inflict eternal misery on his creatures. For the rationalist there is an internal block against reverencing a will in conflict with itself. Can his reverence, then, be accorded to nature, or the world, or the government of the world? This is difficult again, for reverence belongs to moral goodness, and while the world or the Absolute includes moral phenomena as well as others, there is no evidence, as we have seen, that it is itself a moral being.

These considerations do not mean, however, that the world of the rationalist lacks room for reverence. Two types of object remain that will engage and deserve it. One is the moral ideal itself, which will still be exalted and infinitely exacting. It was none other than Kant, the arch-rationalist in morals, who insisted most strongly on reverence for the moral law. Though Kant attempted—unsuccessfully—to connect morals with the existence of God, it is clear that reverence for ideal goodness does not depend on the existence in fact of a perfect being. And even if goodness, to be properly revered, did have to exist in fact, reverence in a rationalist world need not be starved. The world is not morally perfect; no man has achieved perfection; true. But in this respect some men nevertheless stand out like lighthouses in a grey sea. Of these, Jesus of Nazareth is the prime example. Such persons need not be pre-eminent in knowledge or power, but they stand out in the purity and elevation of their idea of goodness and in the degree to which they realised it in their lives. Comte was surely right in maintaining that genuine human goodness is an appropriate object of reverence; indeed in the religion in which such goodness is most esteemed, reverence for the divine has been commonly identified with reverence for its embodiment in the character of Christ. And that character remains what it is, whether framed or not in the elaborate dogma of the incarnation.

HUMILITY

29 There is another religious attitude whose fate in a rationalist order may arouse concern. Religion has to do with man's relation to the infinite whole of which he is a minute part, and in his attitude toward that whole an essential element is humility. For Schleiermacher religion was a sense of infinite dependence; and the genuinely religious spirit is felt by everyone to exclude pride and complacency. Humility is also essential in the moral life—not indeed for every level of morality, since Aristotle's great-souled man was not exactly humble—but for the receptiveness and teachableness that are conditions of moral growth. Some would go farther in their estimate of humility. 'Humility', said Burke, 'is the low but deep foundation of all true virtue'; for Butler, 'vice in general consists in having an unreasonable and too great regard for ourselves in comparison with others'; for A. E. Taylor, humility is 'the most exquisite flower of the moral life'. A disposition that can be so described is not one to be readily let go.

Now I suspect that this attractive virtue may have better justice done to it by the rationalist than by the supernaturalist. At any rate, for the rationalist it is a prime duty to see things as they are, while for the theologian this admirable virtue has often been construed to be a seeing of things as they are not. Here, for example, is Jonathan Edwards:

> 'I have greatly longed of late, for a broken heart, and to lie low before God; and, when I ask for humility, I cannot bear the thoughts of being no more humble than other Christians. It seems to me, that though their degrees of humility may be suitable for them, yet it would be a vile selfexaltation in me, not to be the lowest in humility of all mankind.'[13]

Edwards was apparently willing to sacrifice to humility both truth and consistency. If he accounted himself the lowest of mankind, and considered it self-exaltation not to do so, both of which he was trying to believe, he would be assenting to untruths which he could hardly fail to recognise as such. And if he 'cannot bear the thoughts of being no more humble than other Christians,' his pride in his own humility is peeping through in ironic fashion. Similarly St Francis must have for himself the most wretched scrap of bread, the most dilapidated robe, the hardest bed. This is a charming reversal of the attitude of most men. But if Francis really believed that these things were his true deserts, he was purchasing moral merit by self-deception. He was not the worst of men, and if he really was not, are we to regard it as a virtue in him to believe that he was? Whatever the defects of the rationalist, he values truth more than this. The difficulty he finds with supernaturalism, at least of the 'wholly other' variety, is that it plays fast and loose with truth. In earlier pages we have found it calling in question man's natural reason and conscience, and attempting to replace their verdicts by beliefs and imperatives before which he is encouraged to prostrate himself, whether they are consonant with truth or not. And if he murmurs that they seem to him irrational, he is denounced for preferring pride in his own reason to submission to true authority. Pride and humility thus change places. It is pride to say that, by such light as he has, he cannot see that a belief is valid. It is humility to say that one is in receipt of divine direction superseding both reason and common sense.[14]

This kind of humility the rationalist will eschew. The first interest of rationality is to see things as they are, and one's self happens to be among these things. But it would be a sad day for humanity if the grace of humility, which has been a genuine glory of religion, were to be denied to anyone in virtue of loyalty to truth. Nor need it be. Since humility has played so large a role in the religious attitudes of the past, it may be well to see how large a role it may still have in the rational mind.

30 First, then, we have seen that human nature is built on animal nature. The main difficulties of the moral life are those of regulating desires based on powerful and ancient impulses. Among these desires the most insistent are those that preserve and exalt the self. One's own life, success, dignity, and reputation are so naturally and generally man's prime concern that when any ethics challenges it—even an ethics not the highest, like utilitarianism—it seems to most men too exacting. It is easier to accept the ethics of Hollywood, the primitive ethics that sanctions revenge for any affront to one's pride, even if it happens to rest on truth. That the goods or the sufferings of other people are as important as one's own, that the goods and ills of other people taken together are almost infinitely more important than one's own and should be taken into constant account, is clear to the rational mind, even if to no other. To place oneself in that perspective and live in it is a humility based on truth, not on the sacrifice of it. A rational humility escapes the besetting egoism of the natural man without falling into the masochistic self-depreciation of the misguided 'saint'.

Note in the second place that a certain kind of humility is prized for its moral sensitivity, and that such humility is a requirement of the rational mind. It is notorious that those who have gone farthest in any discipline feel most keenly how far they have still to go, that it is Newton, not the freshly created Doctor of Philosophy, who insists that he has only picked up a few pebbles on the shore, that it is the sensitive publican rather than the mechanical Pharisee who prays 'Be merciful to me a sinner'. This does not mean, we may repeat, that the good man will regard himself with contempt. 'A man who does not think well of himself,' said Hazlitt, 'generally thinks ill of others, nor do they fail to return the compliment'. Still it is the instructed and reflective mind that is most likely to see the difficulties of doing anything as it should be done, and to have the sharpest eye for its own shortcomings. Harold Prichard, one of the most acute of moral philosophers, doubted whether he had ever done a really right act in his life; and Sidgwick, in a two-sentence service prepared for his funeral, described himself as 'a sinful man who partly tried to do his duty'.[15] A rational humility depends on the breadth of the recognised interval between what one is and what one might be, and the clearer one's vision, the fuller one's awareness of that breadth.

Thirdly, as Rashdall remarked, 'true humility is but one aspect of true love of one's neighbour'. When a person perceives that he has some advantage over his neighbour in gifts or wealth or good fortune, and contemplates the difference, one or other of two feelings is likely to dominate in him. One is satisfaction that he is on the upper side of the gap; the other is regret that his neighbour is on the under side. A gracious aspect of humility is the prominence of the latter feeling. And this feeling is certainly open to the rational man. To be sure, the passionate humility of the devotee—'My richest gain I count but loss and pour contempt on all my pride' —is hardly achievable by the secular mind. But that mind is at least not open to the suspicion of using its humility as a part-premium on a policy of everlasting insurance. And even if religious humility is free of any such taint, it is not the only genuine humility. There is no enmity between love of reason and love of neighbour; nor is a clear head necessarily swollen. Those who long ago listened to the socialist candidate for the presidency, Eugene V. Debs, often came away unconvinced by his socialist conclusions while convinced that there was such a thing as secular saintliness. 'As long as there is a lower class,' said Debs, 'I am of it; as long as there is a soul in prison, I am not free'.

We may note another and final element in religious humility that is equally the property of the rational man. Humility has been prized for its teachableness; it is open to correction and therefore growth. The man who is incapable of revering others as having far outstripped him may be doing them no harm, but he is handicapping himself through forfeiting much that he might have learned. Traditional Christianity has shown a notable openness and docility on the moral side; its special genius has lain there; it caught the passion of the Hebrew prophets for purity of heart and concentrated its energy on the quest with an almost fierce humility. But while morality may be three-fourths of life, as Arnold said, it is not all of it, and Christianity was too indifferent to the remaining fourth. There too, however, humility is of the essence. The rational man knows that he must move to his ends along many roads, and that all of them lead toward receding goals. If the moral ideal is for him infinitely far off, so is that of understanding and of taste; and humility is the order of the day in philosophy, science, and art. 'There is no sin,' said F. H. Bradley, 'however prone to it the philosopher may be, which philosophy can justify so little as spiritual pride'.[16] A similar attitude befits the scientist in a rapidly expanding world. We have already heard Huxley's 'Sit down before fact as a little child . . . or you shall learn nothing.' So also of the artist. There is an essay of Pater's on Raphael in which it is contended that the painter achieved what he did through the humility that took him to the feet of all the better artists of his time and kept him there till he had absorbed to the full what each had to give. Nor does humility end with apprenticeship. T. S. Eliot says of the artist: 'What happens is a continual surrender of himself as he is at the moment to something which is more valuable. The progress of an artist is a continual self-sacrifice, a continual extinction of personality.'[17] A hard saying, no doubt, but at any rate truer than the gospel of idiosyncrasy and whim now popular in some quarters.

31 We have been sketching a rationalist alternative to the traditional supernaturalism. Much that was desirable in the older attitude can be retained in the new. Reverence for goodness and humility before excellence will remain, if not in their lyric and passionate Franciscan forms, still in a form that will restrain egoism and encourage growth. Of the attitudes comprised in the older outlook, it is faith that will be most altered. In traditional faith belief has been subservient to the will to believe—the need, the desire, the duty, to believe. In religion as we conceive it, belief will be subservient to nothing but its own immanent ideal of reason. In the light of that ideal, with its demand for evidence and consistency, the old dogmatic structure is decaying.

For the last time the recurrent question arises: does that carry with it the decay of religion? Of religion as the traditional supernaturalism, Yes. Of religion in our wider sense, No. Religion we have conceived as the attitude of the whole man to what he regards as ultimately true and ultimately good; and religion in that sense will remain, however the conception of its object may change. This way of interpreting religion is of course a departure from that of traditional Christianity. Rationality, or the attempt at it, takes the place of faith. Ultimate truth and goodness of course remain the same through all men's changing conceptions of them, as Everest remains what it is in spite of the swirling mists through which it is seen. But it is those changing conceptions themselves that we must live with, for they give us the only available object of belief at any given time.

Traditional faith has accepted a body of belief as delivered once for all to the saints. But nothing given to man's mind is ever delivered once for all. It comes to him through his own evolving mind, through his own struggling and growing reason. Why should he not make a virtue of his necessity? If reason is his one dependence for shaping the object of belief, why not recognise it for what it is? It will at no stage give him finality, but he will approach his goal by means of it or not at all. The proposal here urged is as simple as it is sweeping. Take reason seriously. It has been from the beginning the unrealised architect of religion, of conduct, of the world, but almost always doing its work under the interference of interests alien to its own. Give it its head. Let it shape belief and conduct freely. It will shape them aright if anything can.

NOTES

1 For an English translation of the pronouncements of the Council, see Walter M. Abbott, S.J., ed. *The Documents of Vatican II* (N.Y., Guild Press, The America Press, 1966).

2 John Henry Newman, *Apologia pro Vita Sua*, 67 (Everyman).

3 'Eadem sancta mater ecclesia tenet et docet, Deum rerum omnium principium et finem naturali humanae rationis lumine e rebus creatis certo cognosci posse . . .' (session III, chap. 2). The Council added in its uncompromising way: 'Si quis dixerit, Deum unum et verum, creatorem et dominum nostrum, per ea, quae facta sunt, naturali rationis humanae lumine certo cognosci non posse; anathema sit' (ibid., Canones II). I am reluctant to burden the text with footnotes, but when one is criticising a position, it is essential to have it correct, above all at crucial points. For the Latin text of official pronouncements by popes or councils I have mainly relied on Mirbt's *Quellen zur Geschichte des Papstums und des Römischen Katholizismus* (3rd edn., Tübingen, Mohr, 1911).

4 M. C. D'Arcy, *Belief and Reason* (Burns, Oates & Washbourne, 1944), 49.

5 Decree of Vatican Council I, session III, chap. 4. 'Hoc quoque perpetuus ecclesiae catholicae consensus tenuit et tenet, duplicem esse ordinem cognitionis, non solum principio, sed obiecto etiam distinctum: principio quidem, quia in altero naturali ratione, in altero fide divina cognoscimus; obiecto autem, quia praeter ea, ad quae naturalis ratio pertingere potest, credenda nobis proponuntur mysteria in Deo abscondita, quae, nisi revelata divinitus, innotescere non possunt.' Mirbt, *Quellen*, 360.

6 '. . . ratio ad humanum fastigium Thomae pennis evecta, iam fere nequeat sublimius assurgere . . .' Mirbt, 376. This passage occurs in a much longer passage of unqualified panegyric for Aquinas.

7 The twenty-second error condemned by Pius X in this decree of 1907 was that 'Dogmata quae ecclesia perhibet tamquam revelata, non sunt veritates a coelo delapsae, sed sunt interpretatio quaedam factorum religiosorum quam humana mens laborioso conatu sibi comparavit.' Mirbt, 408.

8 Vatican II, Constitution on Divine Revelation, chap. 3, sec. 11. This repeats the words of Vatican I, 'spiritu sancto inspirante conscripti Deum habent auctorem.' Session III, chap. 2.

9 1545–63.

10 Tobias, Judith, Wisdom, Ecclesiasticus, Baruch, and First and Second Maccabees.

11 A. E. Taylor, *The Faith of a Moralist* (London, Macmillan, 1930), II, 209.

12 Constitution on Divine Revelation, chap. 2, sec. 9.

13 Matt. 16:18.

14 '. . . sedis vero apostolicae, cuius auctoritate maior non est, iudicium

a nemine fore retractandum, neque cuiquam de eius licere iudicare iudicio.'
Vatican Council I, Session IV, chap. 3.

15 'Neque enim Petri successoribus spiritus sanctus promissus est, ut eo
revelante novam doctrinam patefacerent, sed ut, eo assistente, traditam per
apostolos revelationem seu fidei depositum sancte custodirent et fideliter
exponerent.' Session IV, chap. 4.

16 '... hanc sancti Petri sedem ab omni semper errore illibatam per-
manere. . . .' Session IV, chap. 4.

17 Encyclical *Providentissimus Deus*, 1893.

18 *Summa Theologica*, pt I, q. 32, art. 4: 'Indirecte vero ad fidem pertinent
ea ex quibus negatis consequitur aliquid contrarium fidei; sicut si quis
diceret Samuelum non fuisse filium Helcanae; ex hoc enim sequitur Scrip-
turam divinam esse falsam.'

19 Constitution on Divine Revelation, chap. 3, sec. 11.

20 *Contra Gentiles*, I, chap. 4.

21 Vatican I, session III, chap. 4: 'Verum etsi fides sit supra rationem,
nulla tamen unquam inter fidem et rationem vera dissensio esse potest; cum
idem Deus, qui mysteria revelat et fidem infundit, animo humano rationis
lumen indiderit; Deus autem negare seipsum non possit, nec verum vero
unquam contradicere.'

22 *Contra Gentiles*, I, chap. 7.

23 Vatican I, session III, chap. 3: 'nemo tamen evangelicae praedicationi
consentire potest . . . absque illuminatione et inspiratione spiritus sancti. . . .
Quare fides ipsa in se . . . donum Dei est. . . .'

24 'Hanc vero fidem . . . virtutem esse supernaturalem, qua, Dei aspirante
et adiuvante gratia, ab eo revelata vera esse credimus, non propter intrin-
secam rerum veritatem naturali rationis lumine perspectam, sed propter
auctoritatem ipsius Dei revelantis, qui nec falli nec fallere potest.' Ibid.

25 *Summa Theologica*, pt II, II, q. 4, art. 5.

26 E. Gilson, *Reason and Revelation in the Middle Ages* (N.Y., Scribner's,
1938) 73–4.

27 Vatican I, Canones III, 5: 'Si quis dixerit, assensum fidei christianae
non esse liberum, sed argumentis humanae rationis necessario produci . . .
anathema sit.' Cf. Aquinas: 'Credere autem, ut supra dictum est, non habet
assensum nisi ex imperio voluntatis; unde, secundum id quod est, a volun-
tate dependit. Et inde est quod ipsum credere potest esse meritorium; et
fides, quae est habitus eliciens ipsum, est secundum theologium virtus.'
De Veritate.

28 'Quoniam vero sine fide impossibile est placere Deo . . . ideo nemini
unquam sine illa contigit iustificatio, nec ullus, nisi in ea perseveraverit
usque in finem, vitam aeternam assequetur.' Vatican I, session III, chap. 3.

29 Canon George D. Smith, ed., *The Teaching of the Catholic Church* (N.Y.,
Macmillan, 1949), I, 17.

30 See fn. 27 above.

31 'Liberum cuique homini est eam amplecti ac profiteri religionem, quam
rationis lumine quis ductus veram putaverit.' Mirbt, 353.

32 Cf. the words of St Ignatius Loyola: 'In order to be entirely of one mind
with the Catholic Church, we must—if it declares that something which to

our eyes appears white is black—confess that it is black. . . .' Quoted by
C. J. Cadoux, *Catholicism and Christianity* (London, Allen & Unwin, 1928;
N.Y., Dial Press, 1929), 122 fn.
33 E. Gilson, *The Spirit of Mediaeval Philosophy* (Sheed & Ward; Scribner's,
1936), 6.
34 *De Veritate*, xiv, 1.
35 E. Gilson, *The Philosophy of St. Thomas Aquinas* (2nd edn, Cambridge,
Heffer, 1929), 48.
36 Ibid., 52–3.
37 Smith, ed., op. cit., I, 1.
38 Vatican I, session III, chap. 4.

CHAPTER II: REASON AND REVELATION

1 'There can be no falsehood anywhere in the literal sense of Holy
Scripture.' *Summa Theologica*, pt I, q. 1, art. 10.
2 'Si quis autem libros ipsos integros cum omnibus suis partibus, prout
in ecclesia catholica legi consueverunt et in veteri vulgata latina editione
habentur, pro sacris et canonicis non susceperit . . . anathema sit.' Session
IV. Mirbt, *Quellen*, sec. 356.
3 '. . . omnes libros tam veteris quam novi testamenti, cum utriusque
unus Deus sit auctor . . . pari pietatis affectu ac reverentia suscipit et venera-
tur.' Ibid.
4 Session III, chap. 2.
5 *Providentissimus Deus*, 1893, 'Etenim libri omnes atque integri, quos
Ecclesia tamquam sacros et canonicos recipit, cum omnibus suis partibus,
Spiritu Sancto dictante conscripti sunt; tantum vero abest, ut divinae
inspirationi erro ullus subesse possit, ut ea per se ipsa non modo errorem
excludat omnem, sed tam necessario excludat et respuat, quam necessarium
est, Deum, summam Veritatem, nullius omnino erroris auctorem esse.'
Denzinger, *Enchiridion Symbolorum* (edn 33, Herder, 1965), 641–2.
6 Vatican II, Constitution on Divine Revelation, chap. 3.
7 In the Vulgate Bible, commonly used by Catholics, the ten references
just given would be to the following books: II Kings, I Paralipomenon, II
Kings, II Kings, I Kings, II Paralipomenon, I Kings, II Paralipomenon,
I Kings, I Kings, chapter and verse remaining the same.
8 For the complete prohibition, Mark 10:2–12, Luke 16:18; for the
qualification, Matt. 5:32 and 19:3–9.
9 Renan, in explaining his reasons for abandoning Catholic belief, says
that these arose from the study of the Biblical text; 'they were in no degree
metaphysical, political, or moral. These last kinds of ideas seemed to me
pretty nebulous and capable of being turned in any direction. But the
question whether there are contradictions between the fourth gospel and
the synoptics is a question that can be definitely settled. I see these contradictions with an evidence so absolute that I would stake my life upon it, and
hence my eternal salvation, without a moment's hesitation.' *Souvenirs
d'Enfance et de Jeunesse* (Paris, Nelson; Calmann-Lévy, n.d.), 216.

10 'Ad quem pestem avertendam . . . ut gregem vestrum a lethiferis hisce pascuis amovere. . . .' *Ubi Primum*, Mirbt, sec. 481. For many similar prohibitions, see Cadoux, *Catholicism and Christianity*, 260 ff.

11 Nor is this method open to those who follow Papal injunctions strictly. In *Pascendi Gregis*, Pius X adverts to 'certain writers in recent times who somewhat restrict inspiration, as, for instance, in what have been offered as so called *tacit citations*. But in all this we have mere verbal conjuring.'

12 *Summa Theologica*, pt I, q. 1, art. 10.

13 Constitution on Divine Revelation, chap. 3, sec. 12.

14 *Lamentabili*, props. 12, 11.

15 Council of Trent, session IV; Vatican I, session III, chap. 2; and cf. *Providentissimus Deus*: 'it is absolutely wrong and forbidden, either to narrow inspiration to certain parts of Holy Scripture, or to admit that the sacred writer has erred.'

16 Cf. Cardinal Newman: 'whether or not the last verses of St Mark's, and two portions of St John's gospel, belong to those Evangelists respectively, matters not as regards their inspiration; for the Church has recognised them as portions of that sacred narrative which precedes or embraces them.' *Nineteenth Century*, Feb. 1884, 196; quoted by Cadoux, op. cit., 334.

17 The count was made by a librarian of the Bodleian library, Dr James, who wrote a paper about it.

18 For a fuller account, see George Salmon, *The Infallibility of the Church* (2nd edn, London, J. Murray, 1923), 226–9.

19 'Quinque Moysis,' Council of Trent, session IV.

20 *Catholic Encyclopedia*, article 'Moses'.

21 Called 'Q' from the German *Quelle*.

22 The decree *Lamentabili* condemns the proposition that 'the narrations of John are not properly history . . .' and that 'in reality he is only a distinguished witness of the Christian life, or of the life of Christ in the Church, at the close of the first century.' I suppose most critics would say that this is exactly what he was.

23 In the London *Daily Telegraph*, Oct. 8, 1875. Quoted by G. G. Coulton, *Romanism and Truth* (London, Faith Press, 1930), I, 6.

24 See chap. 3 for illustrative cases. This constraint here mentioned is referred to in Catholic manuals in gentler terms; e.g. 'so deep is the reverence in which the Church holds the inspired word of God that she guards it most jealously; encouraging scholars, indeed, in their endeavours more profoundly to penetrate its meaning, but keeping upon them a salutary check, lest human ingenuity should corrupt the wisdom that is divine.' Canon G. D. Smith, ed., *The Teaching of the Catholic Church*, I, 31.

25 *Providentissimus Deus*, 1893; Denzinger, 3291. For the two citations following, see Denzinger 3650 and 3405.

26 Council of Trent, session IV.

27 1 Samuel (1 Kings) 15:3.

28 2 Samuel (2 Kings) 24:15.

29 Deuteronomy 19:21.

30 Exod. 21:2; Lev. 25:44–6.

31 The matter is further complicated by the fact that Jesus himself is recorded as having ascribed the 110th Psalm to David, an ascription which most modern critics find it impossible to accept. If the record of his having said this is in error, Scripture can err; if it is correct, how is one to escape the conclusion that he himself could err?

32 '. . . docemus et divinitus revelatum dogma esse definimus: Romanum pontificem cum ex cathedra loquitur, id est, cum omnium christianorum pastoris et doctoris munere fungens pro suprema sua apostolica auctoritate doctrinam de fide vel moribus ab universa ecclesia tenendam definit, per assistentiam divinam, ipsi in beato Petro promissam, ea infallibilitate pollere, qua divinus redemptor ecclesiam suam in definienda doctrina de fide vel moribus instructam esse voluit; ideoque eiusmodi Romani pontificis definitiones ex sese, non autem ex consensu ecclesiae irreformabiles esse.' Session IV, chap. 4.

33 Pope Leo wrote of Pope Honorius: '. . . Honorium, qui hanc ecclesiam non apostolicae traditionis doctrina lustravit, sed profana proditione immaculatam fidem subvertere conatus est.' For the three texts referred to, see Mirbt, *Quellen*, 80, 90.

34 The following Protestant theologians have cited a great variety of such cases: James Martineau, *The Seat of Authority in Religion*, bk II, chap. 1; Karl von Hase, *Handbook to the Controversy with Rome*, vol. I, chap. 1; C. J. Cadoux, *Catholicism and Christianity*, pt III; George Salmon, *The Infallibility of the Church*, lect. 14. All these books are by able and careful scholars. In the case here cited I follow Martineau, who supplies sources and fuller detail.

35 Martineau, op. cit., 141.

36 von Hase, op. cit., I, 33-4.

37 Janus (a pseudonym for the distinguished scholar von Döllinger and others), *The Pope and the Council* (Eng. trans., 2nd edn, 1869), 51. The book cites many other cases of conflict in authoritative pronouncements.

CHAPTER III: REVELATION AND NATURAL KNOWLEDGE

1 Vatican I, session III, chap. 4. The statement continues: 'cum idem Deus, qui mysteria revelat et fidem infundit, animo humano rationis lumen indiderit; Deus autem negare seipsum non possit, nec verum vero unquam contradicere.'

2 *The Christian Philosophy of St. Thomas* (N.Y., Random House, 1956), 20.

3 Canon G. D. Smith, ed., *The Teaching of the Catholic Church*, I, 36.

4 'falsam illam doctrinam Pythagoricam, divinaeque scripturae omnino adversantem, de mobilitate terrae et immobilitate solis, quam Nicolaus Copernicus . . . et Didacus . . . docent. . . .' Mirbt, *Quellen*, 282.

5 The story has often been told, sometimes unscrupulously. I follow two older writers who give it in careful detail: Andrew D. White, in *A History of the Warfare of Science with Theology in Christendom* (N.Y., Braziller, 1955), I, 130-70, and Salmon, *The Infallibility of the Church*, 229-52.

6 In Sermon XIV of *Sermons on the Theory of Religious Belief*.

7 It is not the Old Testament only that raises difficulties of this kind. For a parallel New Testament example, consider the following: Luke

23:44–5, reports an eclipse of the sun at the time of the crucifixion. These events are reported as occurring at Passover, which itself occurred at the time of the full moon. But modern astronomy tells us that an eclipse at the time of the full moon never does or can occur.

8 Henri Fesquet, *The Drama of Vatican II* (trans. by B. Murchland, N.Y., Random House, 1967), 486. Paul VI has, however, permitted the republication of a life of Galileo by the Rev. Pio Paschini, earlier banned by the Holy Office.

9 Smith, ed., op. cit., I, 207. Pope Paul VI, addressing a group of theologians in 1966, said: 'The theory of evolutionism will not seem to you acceptable whenever it does not accord decisively with the immediate creation by God of each and every human soul, and does not hold decisive the importance that the disobedience of Adam, universal protoparent, has had for the lot of humanity.' *New York Times*, 30 Sept. 1966, p. 6.

10 Smith, op. cit., I, 92.

11 Ibid., 205.

12 Ibid., 204.

13 Ibid., 206 ff.

14 Cf. the encyclical *Humani Generis*, 1950: 'Non enim christifideles eam sententiam amplecti possunt . . . Adam significare multitudinem quamdam protoparentum; cum nequaquam appareat quomodo huiusmodi sententia componi queat cum iis quae fontes revelatae veritatis et acta Magisterii Ecclesiae proponunt de peccato originali, quod procedit ex peccato vere commisso ab uno Adamo, quodque generatione in omnes transfusum, inest unicuique proprium.'

15 Pope Pius IX wrote of 'Darwinism': 'A system which is repugnant at once to history, to the tradition of all peoples, to exact science, to observed facts, and even to Reason herself, would seem to need no refutation, did not alienation from God and the leaning toward materialism, due to depravity, eagerly seek a support in all this tissue of fables . . .' White, op. cit., I, 75. Fortunately for the church, this was given as a personal opinion, not as a formal pronouncement.

16 I add a specimen of his thinking on this head. It has been drawn to his attention, he says, that 'complures utriusque sexus personae, propriae salutis immemores et a fide catholica deviantes, cum daemonibus, incubis et succubis abuti, ac suis incantationibus, carminibus et coniurationibus aliisque nefandis superstitiosis, sortilegis excessibus, criminibus et delictis, mulierum partus, animalium foetus, terrae fruges, vinearum uvas, et arborum fructus . . . suffocari et extingui facere et procurare; ipsosque homines, mulieres, iumenta . . . doloribus et tormentis afficere et excruciare; ac eosdem homines, ne gignere, et mulieres, ne concipere, virosque, ne uxoribus, et mulieres, ne viris actus coniugales reddere valeant, impedire. . . .' Mirbt, *Quellen*, 182.

17 *The Rise and Influence of Rationalism in Europe* (3rd edn, London, Longmans, Green, 1866), I, 8 fn. Lecky's account is detailed. A passage he cites from the French theologian Thiers supports our point: 'On ne scauroit nier qu'il y ait des magiciens ou des sorciers . . . sans contredire visiblement les saintes lettres, la tradition sacrée et profane, les lois canoniques et civiles et

l'expérience de tous les siècles, et sans rejeter avec impudence l'autorité irréfragable et infaillible de l'Église. . . .' *Traité des Superstitions* (1741), I, 132.
18 *New York Times,* Dec. 18, 1972, p. 9.
19 White, op. cit., II, 118.
20 *New York Times.*
21 C. C. Martindale, in article 'Fatima,' *Catholic Encyclopedia,* Supplement II (1951), Vol. 18, sec 1.
22 An independent inquiry into the facts is reported in Paul Blanshard's *Freedom and Catholic Power in Spain and Portugal* (Boston, Beacon, 1962), 233 ff.
23 *New York Times,* May 14, 1967.
24 *Outspoken Essays* (London, Longmans, Green, 1919), 164.
25 From a review of Anne Roe's *The Making of a Scientist, New York Times Book Review,* Dec. 20, 1953.
26 *Time,* June 7, 1954.
27 I say 'perhaps' because I think that some components of the law of causality *can* be seen to hold a priori. The case is argued in my *Reason and Analysis* (London, Allen & Unwin, 1962), 466–71.
28 *Hibbert Journal,* April 1950, 241. There is an effective reply to this article by P. H. Nowell-Smith in the same journal for July 1950.
29 Ibid., 245.

CHAPTER IV: CATHOLICISM ON THE MARKS OF THE CHURCH

1 See the concluding paragraph of chap. 1.
2 'Et unam, sanctam, catholicam et apostolicam Ecclesiam.'
3 Essay on von Ranke's *History of the Popes.*
4 Moorfields Lectures (3rd Am. edn), I, 63.
5 I, 28. Cf. Vatican Council I, session IV, chap. 3: 'Neque enim Petri successoribus spiritus sanctus promissus est, ut eo revelante novam doctrinam patefacerent, sed ut, eo assistente, traditam per apostolos revelationem seu fidei depositum sancte custodirent et fideliter exponerent.'
6 Pius IX in *Qui Pluribus,* 1846, repeated by Pius X in *Pascendi Gregis,* 1907.
7 Martineau, *Seat of Authority,* 143–4. Zosimus reversed his own reversal a year or two later.
8 G. G. Coulton, *Papal Infallibility* (London, Faith Press; Milwaukee, Morehouse, 1932), 62–3.
9 *The Infallibility of the Church,* 213.
10 Matt. 25:41.
11 *Eternal Hope* (N.Y., Dutton, 1878), 201–2.
12 *What Is of Faith as to Everlasting Punishment?* (Oxford, Parker, 1880), 38. Pusey himself never joined the Roman Church.
13 'Sequitur deinde: in ignem aeternum, quod quidem alterum poenarum genus, poenam sensus Theologi vocarunt: propterea quod sensu corporis percipiatur, ut in verberibus et flagellis, aliove graviore suppliciorum genere: inter quae dubitari non potest, tormenta ignis summum doloris sensum efficere; cui malo cum accedat ut perpetuum tempus duraturum sit,

ex eo ostenditur damnatorum poenam omnibus suppliciis cumulandam esse. . . .'

14 '(Sacrosancta Romana ecclesia) firmiter credit, profitetur et praedicat, nullos intra catholicam ecclesiam non existentes, non solum paganos, sed nec Iudaeos aut haereticos atque schismaticos aeternae vitae fieri posse participes, sed in ignem aeternum ituros, qui paratus est diabolo et angelis eius, nisi ante finem vitae eidem fuerint aggregati.' Mirbt, *Quellen*, sec. 326.

15 Gibbon, *Decline and Fall*, Milman's edn (Philadelphia, Lippincott, 1867), III, 343.

16 The attitude of thoughtful men toward this doctrine of hell varies strangely. John Stuart Mill said that 'compared with the doctrine of endless torment, every objection to Christianity sinks into insignificance.' Nicolas Berdyaev says similarly: 'I can conceive of no more powerful and irrefutable argument in favour of atheism than the eternal torments of hell. If hell is eternal, then I am an atheist.' London, *Times Lit. Sup.*, Nov. 24, 1950. Again, George Sand wrote: 'L'Église Romaine s'est porté le dernier coup: elle a consommé son suicide le jour où elle a fait Dieu implacable et la damnation éternelle.' *Spiridion*, 302 (quoted by Cadoux, op. cit., 547). On the other hand, the kindly Martin D'Arcy, admitting that theologians talk about the fire of hell, writes: 'The first and main reason is that Christ so frequently chooses the word "fire". The Church rightly keeps to the language and thought of Revelation, and finds that both in terms of love and philosophy the language is well-suited.' *Belief and Reason*, 74 fn. The more sceptical minds here show the greater imagination and moral seriousness.

17 Salmon, op. cit., 206.

18 *An Essay on the Development of Christian Doctrine* (11th ptg, Longmans, Green, 1900), 389.

19 *The Teaching of the Catholic Church*, II, 1146.

20 Ibid.

21 'When Herman Schell (in 1893) argued that such children might enter heaven, his statements called forth a storm of protest, and his book was placed on the Index.' Cadoux, op. cit., 541.

22 *The Teaching of the Catholic Church*, II, 1169–70.

23 Ibid., 1158–9.

24 Ibid., 977.

25 Cadoux, op. cit., 488–9.

26 *The Infallibility of the Church*, 209.

27 From an encyclical of 27 October 1904, quoted by Dean Inge, *Outspoken Essays*, 143.

28 *The Infallibility of the Church*, 21.

29 Rt Rev. William Shaw Kerr in *The Churchman* (London) vol. 65 (1951), 8. Charles Davis, the British Catholic theologian, cited the impossibility of believing these dogmas to be revealed truth as among the reasons for his leaving the church in 1966.

30 Article 'Tradition' by George M. Sauvage, *Catholic Encyclopedia*.

31 *Essay on Development*, 17.

32 'Newman began his *Lives of the Saints* with such a bias in favour of the miraculous that even Roman Catholics with a healthy stomach for such fare

could not digest the feast of legend which he prepared with such gusto. "They scrupled," so Newman told a friend, "to receive the account of St Winifred carrying her head".' Arnold Lunn, *Roman Converts* (London, Chapman & Hall, 1924), 86.

33 *New York Times*, March 7, 1967.

34 Ibid., 13 Feb., 1967.

35 *Human Society in Ethics and Politics* (London, Allen & Unwin, 1954), 67.

36 Quoted from a letter of Acton's by Arnold Lunn, *Roman Converts*, 116.

37 Cadoux, op. cit., 176.

38 Martineau, *Seat of Authority*, 163; italics his.

39 The question might be asked, further, whether unity in a field where desires are strongly engaged offers as effective a witness as in science, where normally they are not. Newman has left it on record that an important factor in determining his own religious opinion was the thought, *securus judicat orbis terrarum*. Sidgwick commented on this maxim: 'Instead of *securus judicat orbis terrarum* must we not say *orbis terrarum vult decipi et decipietur?*' A. and E. M. Sidgwick, *Henry Sidgwick: a Memoir* (London, Macmillan, 1906), 407.

40 W. R. Inge, *Protestantism* (Garden City, Doubleday, Doran, 1928), 12.

41 In the pages that immediately follow, I owe a special debt to Bishop Charles Gore's *Roman Catholic Claims* (11th edn, London, Longmans, Green, 1920) and Dr Cadoux's *Catholicism and Christianity* (London, Allen & Unwin, 1928). The latter book is, I suppose, the most comprehensive criticism in English of the Catholic position.

42 Sabatier, *Religions of Authority and the Religion of the Spirit* (1904), 120.

43 Alfred Fawkes, article 'Papacy' in *Encyclopedia of Religion and Ethics*.

44 Gore, op. cit., 91–92.

45 Irenaeus, *Contra Haereses*, III, 3 (Migne).

46 See Tertullian's *De Pudicitia*, chap. 21.

47 *Religions of Authority*, 118.

48 Coulton, *Papal Infallibility*, 10.

49 Cf. W. J. Sparrow Simpson, *Roman Catholic Opposition to Papal Infallibility* (London, J. Murray, 1909), 271. Newman's attitude is worth recording by reason of his careful study of the fathers. In a letter to Bishop Ullathorne printed 7 April 1870, he wrote: 'I . . . pray those early doctors of the Church, whose intercession would decide the matter (Augustine, Ambrose, and Jerome, Athanasius, Chrysostom, and Basil), to avert this great calamity. If it is God's will that the Pope's infallibility be defined, then it is God's will to throw back the "times and moments" of the triumph which He has destined for His kingdom; and I shall feel that I have but to bow my head to His adorable inscrutable Providence.' (Quoted by Salmon, op. cit., 21–2.) In the end Manning seems to have prevailed over the saints.

50 Decrees of Council of Chalcedon, chap. 28. Mirbt, sec. 161.

51 Decrees of the Sixth Ecumenical Synod, Actio XIII. Mirbt, sec. 188.

52 Matt. 16:28; 24:42 ff; Mark 9:1; 13:30; 14:62.

53 Proposition 52 in the Syllabus of Errors; for the text see Mirbt, sec. 558.

54 Gore, op. cit., 96–7.

55 Sabatier, op. cit., 119.

>582 REASON AND BELIEF

56 A. M. Fairbairn, *Catholicism, Roman and Anglican* (N.Y., Scribner's, 1899), 38.
57 Newman, *The Idea of a University* (London, Longmans, Green, 1912), 136–7.

CHAPTER V: REASON AND FAITH IN LUTHER

1 W. E. H. Lecky, *The Rise and Influence of Rationalism in Europe*, I, 66.
2 Jaroslav Pelikan, *Luther the Expositor* (St Louis, Mo., Concordia, 1959), 37.
3 A. C. McGiffert, *Martin Luther: the Man and His Work* (N.Y., Century, 1911), 333.
4 Quoted by McGiffert, op. cit., 152, from Luther's pamphlet *Against the Traitor at Dresden*.
5 Lucien Price, *Dialogues of Whitehead* (Boston, Little, Brown, 1954), 236, for the Whitehead and Livingstone quotations.
6 McGiffert, op. cit., 151.
7 Ibid., 188.
8 Schlaginhaufen, *Aufzeichnung*, 74, quoted by H. Grisar, *Luther* (St Louis, 1916), V, 391.
9 McGiffert, op. cit., 233.
10 Heroes and Hero-Worship (Everyman), 365–6.
11 J. A. Froude, *Short Studies on Great Subjects* (1885), I, 62. Froude's vivid pictures of the sixteenth century in this work, in his *Life and Letters of Erasmus*, and in the second and third volumes of his history are too little read. Few historians have suffered so much from unjust criticism.
12 'Address to the German Nobility,' in *First Principles*, ed. by Wace and Buchheim (1885), sec. 25.
13 From an open letter to the city councils of Germany, 1524, quoted in McGiffert, op. cit., 270.
14 McGiffert, op. cit., 61. Cf. the same author's comment in another work: 'Of intellectual curiosity he had scarcely any; of interest in truth for truth's sake none at all.' *Protestant Thought before Kant* (N.Y., Scribner's, 1911), 20.
15 On Galatians, 3:6.
16 In this connection Professor B. A. Gerrish quotes the following pronouncement of Luther's: 'Mathematica est inimicissima omnino theologiae, quia nulla est pars philosophiae, quae tam pugnat contra theologiam.' *Grace and Reason* (Oxford, Clarendon, 1962), 54 fn.
17 For example: 'Omnis caro est creatura. Verbum est caro. Ergo verbum est creatura.' Gerrish, op. cit., 53.
18 J. A. C. F. Auer, *Humanism States Its Case* (Boston, Beacon Press, 1933), 38–9.
19 Roland H. Bainton, *Here I Stand* (N.Y., Abingdon-Cokesbury; copyright by Pierce and Smith, 1950), 370.
20 *Commentary on . . . Romans*, trans. by J. T. Mueller (Grand Rapids, Mich., Zondervan Publishing House, 1954), 30.

21 Julius Köstlin's paraphrase in *The Theology of Luther* (Philadelphia, Lutheran Publication Society, 1897), I, 481. This is a valuable work, both for the development of Luther's thought and for its systematic exposition.

22 *De Servo Arbitrio;* Köstlin, I, 492–3.

23 Quoted in Köstlin, I, 494–5.

24 'Fides, inquiunt, infusa (quam proprie vocant fidem in Christum) non liberat a peccatis, sed fides formata charitate. . . . Profundae sunt abominationes blasphemae huius doctrinae.' *Commentarium in Epistolam S. Pauli ad Galatas* (Erlangen 1843–44), I, 214–15 (2:17).

25 *On Galatians,* 5:10.

26 Ibid., 3:6.

27 Ibid.

28 'On Christian Liberty,' in *First Principles,* ed. by Wace and Buchheim, 137.

29 'Das ist religio falsa,' he says, mixing his German with his Latin, 'quae concipi potest a ratione.' *Werke* (Weimar), vol. 40, pt I, 603.

30 Ewald M. Plass, *What Luther Says* (St Louis, Mo., Concordia, 1959), I, sec. 1401.

31 *On Galatians,* 2:16.

32 Ibid.

33 *Werke* (Weimar), vol. 6, 138.

34 For these and further relevant citations see Gerrish, op. cit., 115–16.

35 *On Galatians,* 3:6.

36 'Eiusmodi sanctos diligit Satan. . . .' 'Mundus tunc omnium pessimus quando optimus.'

37 'Et quidem omnes prophetae viderunt hoc in Spiritu, quod Christus futurus esset omnium maximus latro, homicida, adulter, fur, sacrilegus, blasphemus etc., quo nullus major unquam in mundo fuerit . . .' *Commentarium . . . ad Galatas,* II, 14 (3:13).

38 Ibid.

39 Köstlin, op. cit., II, 236.

40 *Briefe,* I, 228; quoted by Köstlin, op. cit., I, 322.

41 Genesis 12:4–5; Acts 7:2.

42 Genesis 46:27; Acts 7:14.

43 *Rational Religion and Rationalistic Objections* (London, Whittaker, 1861), 25–6.

44 The second paragraph of the long decree of the Council on original sin begins as follows: 'Si quis Adae praevaricationem sibi soli, et non eius propagini, asseret nocuisse; et acceptam a Deo sanctitatem, et justitiam, quam perdidit, sibi soli, et non nobis etiam eum perdidisse; aut inquinatum illum per inobedientiae peccatum, mortem et poenas corporis tantum in omne genus humanum transfudisse, non autem et peccatum, quod mors est animae; anathema sit.'

45 Article IX reads in part: 'Original sin standeth not in the following of Adam (as the Pelagians do vainly talk), but it is the fault and corruption of the nature of every man, that naturally is engendered of the offspring of Adam, whereby man is very far gone from original righteousness, and is of his own nature inclined to evil, so that the flesh lusteth always contrary to the

spirit, and therefore, in every person born into this world, it deserveth God's wrath and damnation.'
46 Romans 5:12, 18–19.
47 F. R. Tennant, article 'Original Sin' in *Encyclopedia of Religion and Ethics*; see also his *The Origin and Propagation of Sin*.
48 Köstlin, op. cit., I, 147.
49 *Irrationalism and Rationalism in Religion* (Duke Univ. Press, 1954), 55.
50 *The Faith of a Moralist*, I, 165.
51 *Sceptical Essays* (N.Y., Norton, 1928), 108–9.
52 *The Search for Good Sense* (London, Cassell, 1958), 119.
53 *Rationalism in Europe*, I, 404 and fn. 'The God that holds you over the pit of hell, much as one holds a spider, or some loathsome insect, over the fire, abhors you, and is dreadfully provoked: his wrath towards you burns like fire. . . . You are ten thousand times more abominable in his eyes than the most hateful venomous serpent is in ours.' From Edwards' sermon, 'Sinners in the Hands of an Angry God.'
54 Quoted in Köstlin, op. cit., II, 49.
55 E. M. Plass, *What Luther Says*, III, sec. 4895.
56 For reference to many passages see Köstlin, op. cit., II, 348 ff.
57 Noel Annan, summarising Leslie Stephen on the point: 'To accept the doctrine of Original Sin was to turn one's back on the scientific spirit . . . and ultimately to despair of making a better world; it was to despise reason, art and endeavour as vanities and delusion.' Noel Annan, *Leslie Stephen* (London, MacGibbon & Kee, 1951; Harvard Univ. Press, 1952), 194.
58 W. K. Clifford, *Lectures and Essays* (Macmillan, 1901), II, 221.
59 *On Galatians*, 3:6.
60 *The Table-Talk of Martin Luther*, trans. by William Hazlitt.
61 *Werke* (Erlangen), vol. 22, 183; quoted by Köstlin, op. cit., II, 262.
62 *On Galatians*, 3:6.
63 Ibid.
64 Köstlin, II, 264. See the references in this work for many other ways in which Luther stated the point.
65 Quoted in Köstlin, II, 290–1.
66 Quoted in ibid., 307.
67 Ibid., 464.
68 Ibid., 304–5.
69 *Werke*, Weimar ed., vol. 10, pt III, 306.
70 Plass, *What Luther Says*, III, sec. 4862. This work is a useful selection and translation of the most important passages from Luther's work, topically arranged.

71 Ibid., sec. 4864.   **72** Ibid., sec. 4848.
73 Ibid., I, sec. 1413.   **74** Ibid., sec. 1425.
75 Ibid., sec. 1436.   **76** Ibid., sec. 1378.
77 Ibid., 1375.   **78** Ibid., 1376, 1393.
79 Ibid., 1387.   **80** Ibid., sec. 1397.
81 *Table-Talk*, sec. 618.   **82** Ibid., sec. 593.
83 Ibid., sec. 577.
84 *Charles Kingsley*, ed. by his wife (N.Y., Scribner, Armstrong, 1877), 360.

85 *Table-Talk*, sec. 109.
86 Ibid., sec. 303.
87 Bainton, *Here I Stand*, 379.
88 *Werke* (Weimar), vol. 51, 196.
89 *Table-Talk*, sec. 817.
90 Ibid., sec. 381.
91 Ibid., sec. 427.
92 Ibid., sec. 454.
93 Ibid., sec. 466.
94 Plass, op. cit., I, sec. 1400.
95 Ibid., sec. 1378.
96 Ibid., sec. 1445.
97 Ibid., sec. 1448.
98 *Werke*, Weimar, vol. 6, 529: 'nulla peccata eum possunt damnare, nisi sola incredulitas.'
99 For the public expression of unbelief, Luther thought that the state itself might well begin the punishment that Providence was to continue. 'In 1530 Luther advanced the view that two offenses should be penalized even with death, namely sedition and blasphemy.' Among the offences that were to count as blasphemy was the rejection of an article of the Apostles' Creed. Bainton, op. cit., 376.
100 McGiffert, *Luther: the Man and His Work*, 62.
101 Plass, op. cit., I, sec. 1192.
102 Lecky, *Rationalism in Europe*, I, 66.
103 Köstlin, op. cit., II, 334.
104 Bainton, op. cit., 27.
105 Lecky, op. cit., I, 67.
106 In the example 'Omnis caro est creatura; verbum est caro; ergo verbum est creatura,' it seems plain enough to a secular eye that one *is* reasoning validly if the terms are used in the same sense. Luther can deny the conclusion only by taking 'the Word' that is flesh in a different sense from 'the Word' that is a creature. But then the false conclusion is *not* reached validly, but through the fallacy of four terms.
107 *The Works of the Rev. John Wesley*, Journal for 15 June 1741 (N.Y., Harper, 1827), I, 350.
108 Owen Chadwick, Inaugural Lecture, *Creighton on Luther* (Cambridge Univ. Press, 1959).
109 Stephen Zweig, *Erasmus of Rotteram* (N.Y., Viking, 1934), 16.

CHAPTER VI: REASON AND FAITH IN KIERKEGAARD

1 Karl Barth, *The Knowledge of God and the Service of God* (London, Hodder & Stoughton, 1938), 126.
2 Emil Brunner, *The Theology of Crisis* (N.Y., Scribner, 1930), 63.
3 Harald Höffding, *Sören Kierkegaard als Philosoph* (Stuttgart, Frommanns, 1922), 89.
4 Kierkegaard, *Either/Or* (London, Humphrey Milford, Oxford Univ. Press; Princeton Univ. Press, 1944), I, 20.
5 Ibid., 30–1.
6 Ibid., II, 175.
7 'My either/or does not in the first instance denote the choice between good and evil, it denotes the choice whereby one chooses good *and* evil/or excludes them.' Ibid., 143.

8 *Concluding Unscientific Postscript* (Princeton Univ. Press, 1944), 186 and cf. 517. Henceforth *CUP*.

9 I owe a correction on this point to Professor Louis Dupré.

10 It may help readers unfamiliar with Kierkegaard's style to gain some idea of the difficulties facing the interpreter if we quote two sentences in which he tries to bring these two stages into sharp contrast: 'Religiousness A is the dialectic of inward transformation; it is the relation to an eternal happiness which is not conditioned by anything but is the dialectic inward appropriation of the relationship, and so is conditioned only by the inwardness of the appropriation and its dialectic. Religiousness B, as henceforth it is to be called, or the paradoxical religiousness, as it has hitherto been called, or the religiousness which has the dialectical in the second instance, does on the contrary posit conditions, of such a sort that they are not merely deeper dialectical apprehensions of inwardness, but are a definite something which defines more closely the eternal happiness (whereas in A the only closer definitions are the closer definitions of inward apprehension), not defining more closely the individual apprehension of it, but defining more closely the eternal happiness itself, though not as a task for thought, but paradoxically as a repellent to produce new pathos.' *CUP*, 494.

11 *Fear and Trembling*, trans. by Robert Payne (Oxford Univ. Press, 1939), 66.

12 *Efterladte Papirer*, IX, 503; quoted by Regis Jolivet, *Introduction to Kierkegaard* (N.Y., Dutton, n.d.), 158.

13 *Fear and Trembling*, 67.   **14** *CUP*, 387.

15 Ibid., 406.   **16** Ibid., 256.

17 Ibid., 389.   **18** Ibid., 390.

19 Ibid., 412.

20 These passages from various later writings are cited by Jolivet, op. cit., 155.

21 *CUP*, 412.   **22** Ibid., 405.

23 Ibid., 474–5.   **24** Ibid., 163.

25 Ibid.

26 *The Journals of Søren Kierkegaard*, trans. by A. Dru (Oxford Univ. Press, 1938), 1061.

27 Ibid., 1025.   **28** *CUP*, 259.

29 Ibid., 491.   **30** Ibid., 413.

31 Ibid., 82–3.   **32** Ibid., 242.

33 Ibid., 448.   **34** Ibid., 431.

35 Ibid., 125.   **36** *Either/Or*, I, 27.

37 Walter Lowrie, *Kierkegaard* (Oxford Univ. Press, 1938), 103.

38 *CUP*, 80.   **39** Ibid., 118.

40 Ibid., 201.   **41** Ibid., 99.

42 Ibid., 506–7.   **43** Ibid., 267.

44 Ibid., 290, 292.   **45** Ibid., 267.

46 Ibid., 107.   **47** Ibid., 205.

48 Ibid., 26.   **49** Ibid., 304.

50 Ibid.   **51** Ibid., 306.

52 Ibid., 262.   **53** Ibid., 85.

54 Ibid., 280.

55 To defend this statement adequately in the light of recent developments in ethics would take much space. I may perhaps refer to my *Reason and Goodness* (London, Allen & Unwin, 1961), where I have attempted to work it out in detail. See especially Chapter 13.

56 *CUP*, 284.

57 Reidar Thomte, *Kierkegaard's Philosophy of Religion* (Princeton Univ. Press, 1948), 127–8.

58 Ibid., 211.		**59** *CUP*, 342.	
60 Ibid., 141.		**61** Ibid., 181.	
62 Ibid., 115.		**63** Ibid., 116.	
64 Ibid.		**65** Thomte, op. cit., 117.	
66 *CUP*, 288.		**67** Ibid., 117.	
68 Ibid., 176.		**69** Ibid., 178.	
70 Ibid., 282.		**71** Ibid., 433.	
72 Ibid., 320.		**73** Ibid., 201.	
74 Ibid., 181.		**75** Ibid., 182.	
76 Ibid., 187.		**77** Ibid., 154–5.	
78 Ibid., 206.		**79** Luke 23:14.	
80 Ibid., 23–4.		**81** *CUP*, 290.	
82 Ibid., 179.		**83** Ibid., 38.	
84 Ibid., 339.		**85** Ibid., 189.	
86 Ibid., 337.			

87 *Fear and Trembling*, trans. by Payne, 74.

88 *CUP*, 182.

89 *Papirer*, IVa, 109; quoted by Thomte, op. cit., 144.

90 *Fear and Trembling*, trans. by Walter Lowrie (Princeton Univ. Press, 1968), 37.

91 Ibid., 31.		**92** Ibid., 64.	
93 Ibid., 35.		**94** Ibid., 47.	
95 Ibid., 57.		**96** *CUP*, 121.	

97 H. J. Paton, *The Modern Predicament* (London, Allen & Unwin; N.Y., Macmillan, 1955), 120.

98 Emil Brunner, *Revelation and Reason* (London, Student Christian Movement Press, 1947), 310.

99 *Fear and Trembling*, 49–51.

100 *CUP*, 209.		**101** Ibid., 290.	
102 Ibid., 38.		**103** Ibid., 159.	
104 Ibid., 495.		**105** Ibid., 496.	
106 Ibid., 339.		**107** Ibid., 181.	
108 Ibid., 116.		**109** Ibid., 117.	

110 *Journals*, 275.

111 *Christian Discourses* (Oxford Univ. Press, 1939), 90. Quoted also by L. H. DeWolf in *The Religious Revolt against Reason* (Harper, 1949), 98—a book from which I have profited.

112 *Journals*, 444.

113 *Fear and Trembling*, 54.

114 Paton, *The Modern Predicament*, 120.

115 D. F. Swenson in E. Geismar, *Lectures on the Religious Thought of Søren Kierkegaard* (Minneapolis, Augsburg Publishing House, 1937), xvii.

116 R. Niebuhr, *The Nature and Destiny of Man* (N.Y., Scribner's, 1949), I, 263; I, 182 fn.

117 W. Kaufmann, ed., *The Will to Power* (N.Y., Random House, 1967), 53.

118 Lowrie, *Kierkegaard*, 5.

119 *Mind*, April 1946, 179.

CHAPTER VII: REASON AND REVELATION FOR EMIL BRUNNER

1 Wilhelm Pauck in *The Theology of Emil Brunner*, ed. by C. W. Kegley (N.Y., Macmillan, 1962), 37.

2 *Dogmatik* (Zürich, Zwingli-Verlag, 1956), II, 61–2.

3 Ibid., 65.

4 Ibid., 67.

5 *The Theology of Crisis*, 60.

6 *The Divine Imperative* (London, Lutterworth Press, 1937), 155.

7 *The Theology of Crisis*, 101.

8 *Divine Imperative*, 146.

9 *Theology of Crisis*, 73.

10 *Divine Imperative*, 150.

11 *The Word and the World* (N.Y., Scribner's, 1931), 81.

12 *Divine Imperative*, 155.

13 *Theology of Crisis*, 78.

14 *Divine Imperative*, 57.

15 Ibid., 186, 185.

16 *Theology of Crisis*, 104.

17 *Divine Imperative*, 203.

18 *Theology of Crisis*, 102.

19 Ibid., 106, 107.

20 *Divine Imperative*, 146.

21 Ibid., 156, 157.

22 Ibid., 158.

23 *Theology of Crisis*, 61.

24 *The Word and the World*, 71.

25 Ibid., 66.

26 *Theology of Crisis*, 65.

27 *The Word and the World*, 74.

28 Ibid., 72.

29 *Theology of Crisis*, 83.

30 *Divine Imperative*, 164.

31 Ibid., 163.

32 Ibid., 162.

33 *Theology of Crisis*, 76.

34 *Divine Imperative*, 76.

35 *Theology of Crisis*, 83–4.

36 *Divine Imperative*, 81.

37 Ibid., 161.

38 *The Word and the World*, 64.

39 *Divine Imperative*, 79.

40 Ibid., 176.

41 Ibid., 134.

42 Ibid., 79.

43 Ibid., 78.

44 Ibid.

45 Ibid., 134.

46 Ibid., 83.

47 Ibid.

48 Ibid., 287.

49 Ibid., 192.

50 Ibid., 191.

51 Ibid., 194.

52 Ibid., 117.

53 Ibid., 196.

54 *Theology of Crisis*, 71.

55 *Divine Imperative*, 162.

56 Ibid., 204.

57 Ibid., 206.

58 *Revelation and Reason*, 371.

59 Ibid., 16.

60 Ibid., 44.

61 Ibid., 39.
63 *The Word and the World*, 33.
65 Ibid., 45.
67 *Revelation and Reason*, 213.
69 Ibid., 33.
71 *Theology of Crisis*, 65.
73 Ibid., 290.
75 *The Word and the World*, 80.
77 Ibid., 46.

62 Ibid., 278.
64 Ibid., 126.
66 Ibid., 68, 71.
68 *Theology of Crisis*, 44.
70 *The Word and the World*, 95.
72 *Revelation and Reason*, 61.
74 Ibid., 206, 208.
76 *Divine Imperative*, 88.

78 *The Theology of Emil Brunner*, ed. by Kegley, 331.
79 *Revelation and Reason*, 383. For further reflections on this point, see H. D. Lewis, *Morals and Revelation*, 42 ff.
80 *Revelation and Reason*, 204.
81 *The Theology of Emil Brunner*, 334.
82 *The Word and the World*, 45.

83 Ibid., 74.
85 Ibid., 61.
87 Ibid., 61.
89 *The Theology of Emil Brunner*, 11.
90 *Divine Imperative*, 162.
92 *The Word and the World*, 81.
94 *Divine Imperative*, 46.
96 Ibid., 57.
98 *Divine Imperative*, 43.

84 *Theology of Crisis*, 83–4.
86 *Revelation and Reason*, 217.
88 Ibid., 392.

91 *Theology of Crisis*, 101.
93 Ibid., 71; *Divine Imperative*, 157.
95 Ibid., 84.
97 *Theology of Crisis*, 78.
99 *Theology of Crisis*, 84.

100 *Mysticism* (4th edn, London, Methuen, 1912), 115.
101 *Revelation and Reason*, 220–1.

CHAPTER VIII: REASON AND REVELATION FOR KARL BARTH

1 *Nein! Antwort an Emil Brunner* (München, Kaiser, 1934), 63.
2 *Von Glauben und Offenbarung* (Jena, E. Diederichs, 1923), 11.
3 *The Knowledge of God and the Service of God*, 26; hereafter referred to as *Knowledge of God*.
4 *Credo* (N.Y., Scribner's, 1936), 185–6.
5 *Knowledge of God*, 194.
6 *The Word of God and the Word of Man* (Boston, Pilgrim Press, 1928), 17.
7 *Knowledge of God*, 146 fn.
8 Ibid., 154.
9 O. C. Quick, *The Ground of Faith* . . . (Nisbet, 1931), 100.
10 *Knowledge of God*, 127–8.
11 *Epistle to the Romans* (Oxford Univ. Press; London, Humphrey Milford, 1933), 33 ff.
12 Ibid., 458.
13 *Knowledge of God*, 178.
15 Ibid., 212.
17 Peter H. Monsma, *Barth's Idea of Revelation* (Somerville, N. J., Somerset Press, 1937), 138.

14 *Epistle to the Romans*, 258.
16 Ibid., 238.

18 *Knowledge of God*, 71. **19** Ibid., 67.
20 Ibid., 30. **21** Ibid., 106.
22 Ibid., 96. **23** Ibid., 135.
24 Ibid., 83, 84 fn. **25** Ibid., 103–4.
26 A. C. McGiffert, *A History of Christian Thought* (N.Y., Scribner's,1932), I, 5.
27 *Knowledge of God*, 138–9. **28** Ibid., 135.
29 *Divine Imperative*, 120. **30** *Knowledge of God*, 21.
31 *Divine Imperative*, 175. **32** Ibid., 71.
33 *Knowledge of God*, 107. **34** Ibid., 91.
35 *Advance*, 13 June 1956, 20.
36 Sydney Cave, *Hinduism or Christianity?* (N.Y. and London, Harper, 1939), 37.
37 John Baillie, *Our Knowledge of God* (London, Oxford Univ. Press; N.Y., Scribner's, 1939), 16.
38 *God and the Astronomers* (London, Longmans, Green, 1933).
39 H. J. Paton, *The Modern Predicament*, 54.
40 Herbert Paul, *Life of Froude* (N.Y., Scribner's, 1906), 25.
41 Paton, op. cit., 58.
42 *On Selfhood and Godhood* (London, Allen & Unwin; N.Y., Macmillan, 1957), 14–15.
43 J. B. Pratt, *Can We Keep the Faith?* (Yale Univ. Press, 1941), 80.

CHAPTER IX: RATIONALISM AND CHRISTIAN ETHICS (I)

1 W. R. Inge, *Christian Ethics and Modern Problems* (N.Y., Putman, 1930), 55.
2 Hastings Rashdall, *Theory of Good and Evil* (2nd edn, Oxford Univ. Press; London, Humphrey Milford, 1924), II, 293.
3 Henry Sidgwick, *The Methods of Ethics* (2nd edn, London, Macmillan, 1877; p. 355), bk III, chap. 13, sec. 3.
4 Ibid. (2nd edn, p. 356).
5 J. S. Mill, *Essay on Liberty* (Everyman), 109.
6 Bertrand Russell, *Why I Am Not a Christian and Other Essays*, ed. by Paul Edwards (N.Y., Simon & Schuster's, 1957), 56.
7 For an account of early Christian asceticism, see W. E. H. Lecky, *History of European Morals from Augustus to Charlemagne*, II, 101–40, and Inge, op. cit., chap. 3.
8 Paul Elmer More, *Christianity and the Problems of Today* (N.Y., Scribner's, 1922), 92.
9 Adam Smith, *Theory of the Moral Sentiments*, pt IV, chap. 1.
10 James Seth, *Essays in Ethics and Religion* (Edinburgh and London, Blackwood, 1926), 65.
11 Percy Gardner, *Evolution in Christian Ethics* (London, Williams & Norgate, 1918), 236.
12 W. R. Inge, *Freedom, Love and Truth* (Boston, Hale, Cushman & Flint, n.d.), 2.
13 W. R. Inge, *Vale* (Longmans, Green, 1934), 93.

14 Lucien Price, *Dialogues of A. N. Whitehead*, 262.

15 Ernest Renan, *The Life of Jesus* (N.Y., Burt, 1897), 154.

16 W. E. H. Lecky, *Rise and Influence of Rationalism in Europe*, II, 149.

17 Bishop Henson points out, however, that the English versions leave out the essential word of the Latin text, which reads, 'arma portare et *justa* bella administrare.' H. H. Henson, *Christian Morality* (Oxford, Clarendon Press, 1936), 255.

18 Neither were the persons of whom Bertrand Russell, not very fairly, wrote as follows: 'The First World War was wholly Christian in origin. The three emperors were devout, and so were the more warlike of the British Cabinet. Opposition to the war came, in Germany and Russia, from the Socialists, who were anti-Christian; in France, from Jaurès, whose assassin was applauded by earnest Christians; in England, from John Morley, a noted atheist.' *Why I Am Not a Christian*, 203–4.

19 Inge, *Christian Ethics and Modern Problems*, 41.

20 Warner Fite, *Jesus the Man* (Harvard Univ. Press, 1946), 114.

21 F. H. Bradley puts the point more uncompromisingly: 'Universal love doubtless is a virtue, but tameness and baseness—to turn the cheek to every rascal who smites it, to suffer the robbery of villains and the contumely of the oppressor, to stand by idle when the helpless are violated and the land of one's birth in its death-struggle, and to leave honour and vengeance and justice to God above—are qualities that deserve some other epithet. The morality of the primitive Christians is that of a religious sect; it is homeless, sexless, and nationless. The morality of today rests on the family, on property, and on the nation. Our duty is to be members of the world we are in; to be in the world and not of it was their type of perfection. The moral chasm between us is, in short, as wide as the intellectual. . . .' *Collected Essays* (Oxford, Clarendon Press, 1935), I, 173–4.

22 Cf. the following from Archbishop William Temple: 'Force is entrusted to the state in order that the state may effectively prevent the lawless use of force; and from the moral standpoint the use of force to uphold a law designed for the general well-being against any who try to use force contrary to the general well-being is in a totally different class from the force which is thus kept in check.' *Christ and the Way to Peace*, 15.

23 The gospels, however, are contradictory on the point; cf. the denial in John 4:2, with the double affirmation in the previous chapter, John 3:22, 26.

24 Lecky, *History of European Morals* (London, Longmans, 1882), II, 66.

25 Edward Westermarck, *Christianity and Morals* (N.Y., Macmillan, 1939), 335.

26 L. T. Hobhouse, *Morals in Evolution* (5th edn, Chapman & Hall, 1925), 199.

27 A. E. Garvie, article 'Womanliness,' in James Hastings, ed., *A Dictionary of Christ and the Gospels*. Cf. Lecky: 'The change from the heroic to the saintly ideal, from the ideal of Paganism to the ideal of Christianity, was a change from a type which was essentially male to one which was essentially feminine.' *History of Europeans Morals*, II, 362.

28 Pius IX in the bull *Ineffabilis* describes Mary as 'the safest refuge for all who are in peril, the most trusty aid, and with her only begotten Son, the most powerful mediatrix and reconciler of the world.'

29 Inge, *Christian Ethics and Modern Problems*, 80.
30 Bernard Shaw, Preface to *Androcles and the Lion*.
31 The passage from Tertullian is quoted from Westermarck, *Christianity and Morals*, 338.
32 Lecky, *History of European Morals*, II, 338.
33 Ibid., 339–40.
34 B. Russell, *Marriage and Morals* (Garden City Pub. Co., 1929), 60–1.
35 H. L. Mencken, *Treatise on Right and Wrong* (London, Kegan Paul, Trench, Trubner, 1934), 41.

CHAPTER X: RATIONALISM AND CHRISTIAN ETHICS (II)

1 Warner Fite, *Jesus the Man*, 103.
2 George F. Thomas, *Christian Ethics and Moral Philosophy* (N.Y., Scribner's, 1955), 248.
3 H. C. King, *The Ethics of Jesus* (N.Y., Macmillan, 1912), 38.
4 Friedrich Paulsen, *A System of Ethics* (N.Y., Scribner's, 1899), 71.
5 Francis W. Newman, *On the Defective Morality of the New Testament*, 19.
6 Fite, op. cit., 117.
7 Inge, *Christian Ethics and Modern Problems*, 246–7.
8 A. C. Benson, *Thy Rod and Thy Staff* (London, Smith, Elder, 1912), 161–2.
9 F. W. Newman, op. cit., 10.
10 Percy Gardner, *Evolution in Christian Ethics*, 201–2.
11 Paul Tillich, *Systematic Theology* (Univ. of Chicago Press, 1963), III, 135.
12 Adolf Harnack, *What IS Christianity?* (1901), 67, 70.
13 John Dewey, *A Common Faith* (Yale Univ. Press, 1934).
14 See above chap. 6, secs. 40–41.
15 This view is developed and defended in my *Reason and Goodness*, chaps. 11–13.
16 H. Sidgwick, *The Methods of Ethics*, bk III, chap. 10, sec. 2 (2nd edn, 309).
17 King, op. cit., 207 ff.
18 Albert Schweitzer, *The Psychoanalytic Study of Jesus*.
19 George Santayana, *Reason in Religion* (N.Y., Scribner's, 1916), 13.
20 J. A. Froude, *Short Studies on Great Subjects*, IV, 286.
21 Albert Schweitzer, *The Quest of the Historical Jesus*.
22 Reported by White, *Warfare of Science with Theology*, II, 369.
23 'Camus argues that "capital punishment, in fact, throughout history has always been a religious punishment. . . ." He finds humanism more humane than theism.' Walter Kaufmann, *Religion from Tolstoy to Camus*, 41.
24 Fite, op. cit., 108.
25 D. C. Simpson in *The History of Christianity in the Light of Modern Knowledge* (London and Glasgow, Blackie, 1929), 162.

26 H. Sidgwick, *History of Ethics* (4th edn, Macmillan, 1896), 124.
27 Fite, op. cit., 136.
28 Eduard Zeller, *Strauss and Renan*, 75.
29 H. Sidgwick, *Miscellaneous Essays and Addresses* (Macmillan, 1904), 8 fn.
30 Leslie Stephen, *Essays on Freethinking and Plainspeaking* (N.Y., Putnam, 1908), 391.
31 Russell, *Why I Am Not a Christian*, 18.

CHAPTER XI: THE ETHICS OF BELIEF

1 W. E. H. Lecky, *The Rise and Influence of Rationalism in Europe*, II, 38.
2 T. H. Huxley, *Science and Christian Tradition* (London, Macmillan, 1894), 310.
3 B. Russell, *A History of Western Philosophy* (N.Y., Simon & Schuster, 1945), 816.
4 W. K. Clifford, *Lectures and Essays*, II, 175.
5 D. M. Baillie, *Faith in God* (Edinburgh, T. & T. Clark, 1927), 10 ff.
6 Isaiah 7:9.
7 Psalms 106: 24–5; 78:22.
8 Mark 16:16.
9 Matt. 8:13.
10 Mark 9:17 ff.
11 E.g. Mark 10:52; Luke 7:50; 8:48; 17:19.
12 1 Cor. 3:18, 19.
13 1 Cor. 1:19, 20.
14 2 Cor. 5:7.
15 E. Westermarck, *Christianity and Morals*, 133.
16 James 2:20, 19.
17 Hebrews 11:1, 3, 6.
18 Romans 14:23.
19 Canon C. E. Raven, *Jesus and the Gospel of Love* (N.Y., Holt, 1931), 20.
20 Ibid., 26.
21 G. Santayana, *Reason in Religion*, 118.
22 Bull delivered by Pope Gregory at the Feast of the Assumption in the church of St Maggiore. Lecky quotes further relevant passages, op. cit., II, 76.
23 E. Westermarck, *Ethical Relativity* (N.Y., Harcourt, Brace, 1932), 203.
24 Lecky, op. cit. II, 95–6.
25 Jacques Maritain, *The Dream of Descartes*.
26 De Maistre, *Soirées de St Pétersbourg* (2nd edn, Lyon, 1831), I, 6me Entretien, 436, 452.
27 W. L. Sperry, *Yes, But—* (N.Y. and London, Harper & Bros, 1931), 18.
28 For a recent critique of the psychoanalytic approach see W. P. Alston, 'Psychoanalytic Theory and Theistic Belief' in *Faith and the Philosophers*, ed. by John Hick (N.Y., St. Martin's Press, 1964), 63–102.
29 W. James, *The Will to Believe* (Longmans, Green, 1897), 14, 8.
30 Cf. Henry Sidgwick on a similar proposal: 'I am so far from feeling bound to believe for purposes of practice what I see no ground for holding as

a speculative truth, that I cannot even conceive the state of mind which these words seem to describe, except as a momentary half-wilful irrationality, committed in a violent access of philosophic despair.' *The Methods of Ethics*, 468.

31 Cf. Santayana on James: 'To be boosted by an illusion is not to live better than to live in harmony with the truth; it is not nearly so safe, not nearly so sweet, and not nearly so fruitful. These refusals to part with a decayed illusion are really an infection to the mind. Believe, certainly; we cannot help believing; but believe rationally, holding what seems certain for certain, what seems probable for probable, what seems desirable for desirable, and what seems false for false.' *Character and Opinion in the United States* (N.Y., Scribner's, 1920), 87.

32 J. S. Mill, *Autobiography* (N.Y., Holt, n.d.), 153–4.

33 Insincerity is of course a difficult charge to sustain. Cf. F. L. Lucas: 'are we to tax a writer with insincerity because he says things which we think he must himself have seen to be preposterous? We know little of human nature if we try to set limits of this sort to its powers of self-deception, of seeing only what it wants to see. The gifted Newman could believe in prodigies like the liquefaction of the blood of Saint Januarius, and the aerial transport of the Virgin's house from Palestine to Loreto.' *Style* (London, Cassell, 1955), 146.

'Let us maintain before we have proved,' said Newman in Tract 85. 'This seeming paradox is the secret of happiness.' Referring to an article by Newman in *Nineteenth Century*, Feb. 1884, Dr Cadoux writes: 'Newman professed his belief that the Ten Commandments were actually written by the finger of God on the tables of stone without the use of a human medium: it was the only part of Scripture, he said, which was so written.' *Catholicism and Christianity*, 310.

In the light of such views, it is not surprising that many who have studied Newman should have been puzzled and repelled as well as fascinated by him. A few illustrative comments may be added for their intrinsic interest. ' "Where shall I be most safe?" was the question that haunted him as he hesitated between his Mother Church and the Church of Rome. Fear, not love, was the basis of his creed. His was a God who encourages us to play for safety and to avoid the adventure of the mind.' (Sir Arnold Lunn, *Roman Converts*, 74.) Again, 'in spite of his controversial skill he failed as a philosopher, as everyone must fail who steadily forms his conclusions first, who steadily discounts reason, and who looks on argument not as an instrument for carrying the mind forward to truth, but as a fence for restraining the mind within the dogmas received by faith.' (Ibid., 80). 'Hardy talked rather interestingly of Newman. . . . He said very firmly that N. was no logician; that the *Apologia* was simply a poet's work, with a kind of lattice-work of logic in places to screen the poetry.'(A. C. Benson, *Diary* [3rd edn, London, Hutchinson, n.d.], 29 April 1904.) 'He is by nature a poet, by necessity rather than choice a metaphysician and historian.' (Principal A. M. Fairbairn, *Catholicism, Roman and Anglican*, 119.) 'I have just read the life of Newman, who was a strange character. To me he seems to have been the most artificial man of our generation, full of ecclesiastical loves and hatred.

... In speculation he was habitually untruthful and not much better in practice. His conscience had been taken out, and the Church put in its place. Yet he was a man of genius, and a good man in the sense of being disinterested. Truth is very often troublesome, but neither the world nor the individual can get on without it.' (Benjamin Jowett in letter to Margot Asquith printed in her *Autobiography* [2nd edn, Butterworth, 1921], I, 123–4.) 'That man is the slipperiest sophist I have ever met with.' (T. H. Huxley in his *Life and Letters*, ed. by his son [1900], II, 226.) The Cardinal's brother, Professor Francis W. Newman, spoke of 'his apparent forgetfulness in the hymn against "Private Judgment," that *evidence* plays or ought to play any part in religious convictions.' And again, 'He seemed unable to understand the force of gentleness and modesty. His admirers tell me he was very *Christian*. My life has been a long sadness that I never could see it in him.' (... *Early History of Cardinal Newman*, 118, 117.) Finally Henry Sidgwick: 'The Cardinal interests me—always has interested me—as a man and a writer rather than a reasoner. I delight in the perfect fit of his thought to its expression, and the rare unforced *individuality* of both; but as a *reasoner* I have never been disposed to take him seriously, by which I do not of course mean that I treat his views with levity, but that, regarding him as a man whose conclusions have always been influenced primarily by his emotions, and only secondarily by the workings of his subtle and ingenious intellect, I have never felt that my own intellect need be strained to its full energies to deal with his arguments; they always seemed to me to admit of being referred without much difficulty to certain well-known heads, to which the *generic* answers were known.' (*Henry Sidgwick: a Memoir*, 507.)

34 Though Santayana was a somewhat unsympathetic critic of James, he was a shrewd one, and is worth quoting further. For James 'the degree of authority and honour to be accorded to various human faiths was a moral question, not a theoretical one. All faiths were what they were experienced as being, in their capacity of faiths; these faiths, not their objects, were the hard facts we must respect. We cannot pass, except under the illusion of the moment, to anything firmer or on a deeper level. There was accordingly no sense of security, no joy, in James's apology for personal religion. He did not really believe; he merely believed in the right of believing that you might be right if you believed.' *Character and Opinion in the United States*, 76–7.

35 *Pensées*, Fragment 223.

36 T. H. Huxley, *Life and Letters*, I, 219.

CHAPTER XII: MYTH IN RELIGION

1 E. B. Tylor, *Primitive Culture* (1883), I, 424.

2 S. Freud, *The Future of an Illusion* (N.Y., Liveright, 1953), 43.

3 F. D. E. Schleiermacher, *On Religion* (1893), Second Speech, 35.

4 W. R. Inge, *Faith and Its Psychology* (London, 1909), 67.

5 B. Blanshard, *Reason and Goodness*.

6 Tylor, op. cit., I, 385. The larger part of this admirable old book is devoted to an account of animism.

7 Isaiah 14:10.

8 Ecclesiastes 9:10.

9 If we were considering the advance of religion generally rather than of the intellectual factor in it, we should have to introduce magic and ritual at this point.

10 G. Santayana, *Reason in Religion*, 79–80.

11 Matthew Arnold, *Literature and Dogma* (N.Y., Macmillan, 1903), 171.

12 Santayana, op. cit., 98.

13 E. W. Barnes, *The Rise of Christianity* (London, Longmans, Green, 1947), 70.

14 W. R. Inge, *Outspoken Essays*, 149.

15 See the passages assembled by Pusey, *Eirenicon*, pt II, 79 ff.

16 J. B. Mayor, 'Mary' in Hastings' *Dictionary of the Bible*, III, 289.

17 Charles Gore, Bishop of Oxford, *Roman Catholic Claims*, 71.

18 The views of about a hundred and fifty of these are cited in Pusey's *Eirenicon*.

19 Mayor, op. cit.

20 The facts are summarised in C. J. Cadoux, *Catholicism and Christianity*, chap. 16.

21 L. R. Farnell, *The Attributes of God* (Oxford, Clarendon Press, 1925), 15.

22 Sir James Frazer, *Adonis, Attis, Osiris* (New Hyde Park, N.Y., University Books, 1961), I, 301 ff.

23 Pusey's *Eirenicon* contains much information about the gradual change.

24 Cited by Mayor, op. cit., 290.

25 Both the passages last cited are from Pusey's *Eirenicon*, pt I, pp. 102–6, where many similar passages are given.

26 Ibid., 103.

27 Cadoux, op. cit., 365.

28 Bull *Ineffabilis Deus*, 8 December 1854.

29 Joseph Duhr, S.J., *The Glorious Assumption of the Mother of God* (N.Y., P. J. Kenedy, 1950), 78.

30 See the Apostolic Constitution, *Munificentissimus Deus*, of Pius XII.

31 See his *Dream of Descartes*.

32 Cf. White, *Warfare of Science with Theology*, I, 234–5.

33 Ibid., 75–6, for the opinions on Darwin's theory of the reigning Pope, Pius IX.

34 A fuller account of the incident is given in ibid., II, 341–8.

35 Bishop E. W. Barnes, author of the Gifford Lectures of 1927–29, on *Scientific Theory and Religion*.

CHAPTER XIII: COSMOLOGY

1 R. Carnap, *Logical Syntax of Language*, xv.

2 C. D. Broad, *Examination of McTaggart's Philosophy* (Cambridge Univ. Press, 1933), I, 236.

3 Bertrand Russell, *The Scientific Outlook* (London, Allen & Unwin, 1931), 110.

4 I have discussed this somewhat more fully in Sidney Hook, ed., *Determinism and Freedom* (1958), chap. 1.

5 I have paid my respects to behaviourism in *The Nature of Thought*, I, chap. 9; in *Reason and Analysis*, 209–20; and in John E. Smith, ed., *Contemporary American Philosophy*, chap. 1.

6 The issue has been argued more fully than is possible here in *The Nature of Thought*, II, 492 ff.

7 Cf. Broad's discussion of this point, op. cit., I, 243–4.

8 E.g. in *The Nature of Thought*, II, 495–9, and in Sydney and Beatrice Rome, eds., *Philosophical Interrogations* (1964), 238–41.

9 Broad, op. cit., I, 232–3.

10 H. W. B. Joseph, *An Introduction to Logic* (2nd edn. rev., Oxford, 1916), 408.

11 A. J. Ayer, *The Foundations of Empirical Knowledge* (London, Macmillan, 1940), 201.

12 Ibid., 202.

13 These strands of contemporary thought are more fully examined in *Reason and Analysis*, chaps 7 and 8.

14 Bertrand Russell, *Human Knowledge: Its Scope and Limits* (Simon & Schuster, 1948), 201–2 224, 225.

15 See Eddington's Gifford Lectures on *The Nature of the Physical World*.

16 Sir James Jeans, *The Mysterious Universe* (new rev. edn, Macmillan and Cambridge Univ. Press, 1932), 168.

CHAPTER XIV: HUMAN NATURE AND ITS VALUES

1 The case against emotivism in various forms is developed in *Reason and Goodness*, chap. 8.

2 Many questions of course arise about distribution, the commensurability of values, distinctively moral goodness, the idea of duty, the nature of evil, and the relations of thought and desire. I have tried to deal with these in the last-named book.

CHAPTER XV: GOODNESS AND THE ABSOLUTE

1 Jeans, *The Mysterious Universe*, 6, 4.

2 F. H. Bradley, *Appearance and Reality* (2nd edn rev. London, 1908), 403.

3 Ibid., 409.		**4** Ibid., 279.	
5 Ibid., 489.		**6** Ibid., 412.	
7 Ibid., 440.		**8** Ibid., 508.	
9 Ibid., 443.		**10** Ibid., 441.	

11 *Henry Sidgwick: a Memoir*, 586, fn. With much admiration for Bradley, I confess that I prefer a more modest approach than his to questions of ultimate difficulty. Cf. the following: 'We hold that our conclusion is certain, and that to doubt it logically is impossible. There is no other view, there is no other idea beyond the view here put forward. It is impossible rationally even to entertain the question of another possibility. Outside our main result there is nothing except the wholly unmeaning. . . .' Bradley, op. cit., 518–19.

12 J. Royce, *The Spirit of Modern Philosophy* (9th edn, Houghton, Mifflin, 1897), 469–70.

13 B. Bosanquet, *Logic* (2nd edn Oxford, Clarendon, 1911), II, 220, fn.

14 J. Huxley, *Religion without Revelation* (new and rev. edn, N.Y., Harper & Bros., 1957), 24.

15 J. S. Mill, *Three Essays on Religion* (1875), 71.

CHAPTER XVI: RELIGION AND RATIONALISM

1 In a recent moving picture of the behaviour of a pack of African wild dogs made by Jane Goodall and her husband, there is a horrifying sequence showing how a bitch, herself with puppies, came across a nest of puppies belonging to a mother that had been ostracised by the pack. She systematically destroyed them.

2 J. H. Newman, *Certain Difficulties Felt by Anglicans in Catholic Teaching* (Longmans, Green, 1901), I, 240.

3 For example, L. T. Hobhouse's excellent *Morals in Evolution* and T. H. Green's chapter on 'The Origin and Development of the Moral Ideal' in his *Prolegomena to Ethics*.

4 There is a further use of reason which should be mentioned, though to state it adequately would call for more space than we can here afford. Many students of Mill, Sidgwick, and Moore have noted that if the rightness of an act is made to depend on its good and evil consequences apart from any further considerations, some acts would have to be judged right that reflection would clearly condemn, e.g. the conviction of an innocent ne'er-do-well by a secretive judge acting for the community's advantage. I think Joseph (following Plato) is right that we cannot account for our judgements in such cases without taking into consideration the 'form of life', the complex of interrelated rules, to which the given act belongs. It is the goodness of this form of life as a whole that is the ultimate justification of the particular act. And the discernment of this whole is an office of practical reason.

5 F. L. Lucas, *The Greatest Problem* (London, Cassell, 1960), 145.

6 B. Russell, *A History of Western Philosophy*, 569.

7 R. I. Aaron, *John Locke* (Oxford Univ. Press, 1937), 53.

8 From a letter of Adam Smith to William Strahan, Green and Grose's edition of Hume's *Essays* (1889), I, 14.

9 Wilfrid Ward, *Men and Matters* (1914), 177. It was Gladstone who called Mill 'the saint of rationalism'.

10 Pope, 'The Temple of Fame'.

11 John Dewey, *A Common Faith*, 79.

12 W. Trotter, *Instincts of the Herd in Peace and War* (T. Fisher Unwin, 1923), 45.

13 *Representative Selections* (rev. edn, N.Y., Hill & Wang, 1962), 70–1.

14 There are some pointed remarks on this paradox by Professor H. D. Lewis in *Philosophy* (Jan. 1949), 41.

15 A. and E. M. Sidgwick, *Henry Sidgwick: a Memoir*, 599.

16 F. H. Bradley, *Appearance and Reality*, 7.

17 T. S. Eliot, *The Sacred Wood* (2nd edn, London, Methuen, 1928), 52–3.

ANALYTICAL TABLE OF CONTENTS

PART I: REASON AND FAITH: THE CATHOLIC VIEW

Chapter I: Catholic teaching on faith and reason
1 The central Catholic dogmas remained almost untouched through Vatican II.
2 In the support of those dogmas reason holds a high place,
3 but its authority is limited by revelation.
4 Revelation is held to be received through Scripture, tradition, and Papal pronouncement,
5 and Scripture to be inspired throughout.
6 Revelation is held to be above reason but not opposed to it.
7 Faith is assent to what the intellect does not understand,
8 and involves a divinely assisted act of will.
9 Grounds of assent are supplied by 'motives of credibility' and 'notes of the church.'
10 A division is made between philosophy and theology,
11 a division that most philosophers reject;
12 but Catholic respect for reason makes dialogue possible.

Chapter II: Reason and revelation
1 Harmony with reason requires internal consistency.
2 Catholic teaching holds Scripture to be inerrant,
3 but it contains many inconsistencies
4 which reflect doubt on church authority.
5 Since the church is the interpreter of Scripture,
6 such inconsistencies are not adequately dealt with (1) by distinguishing authentic from quoted statements;
7 or (2) by distinguishing literal statements from metaphorical,
8 which was encouraged, though incoherently, by Vatican II;
9 or (3) by recognising corruptions in the text,
10 a recourse that the church has severely limited;
11 or (4) by confining inerrancy to faith and morals.
12 Since this is not open to Catholics,
13 and in the narrower field inconsistencies still abound,
14 the notion of a revelation so limited is morally incoherent.
15 The conditions of Papal infallibility are not precise,
16 but official Papal pronouncements have shown inconsistency,
17 as have the teachings of the councils.

Chapter III: Revelation and natural knowledge
1 Despite official claims, revelation and natural knowledge conflict
2 (1) in astronomy, as witness the case of Galileo,
3 from which the church has found no mode of extrication;
4 (2) in biology, as witness a resistance to the theory of evolution,

599

5 which has restricted the freedom of the Catholic biologist;
6 (3) in psychology, as witness the survival of demonology.
7 Science has not accepted the potency of relics
8 or the 'visitations' at Lourdes and Fatima,
9 nor is the appeal to reason an appeal to faith.
10 Science renders miracle increasingly improbable.
11 Do miracles exemplify trans-natural law?
12 No; for (1) the moral implications of this view are unacceptable,
13 (2) it attributes inconsistency to Deity,
14 and (3) if applied fairly, it is self-refuting.
15 The notion of causality entails that of law.
16 Summary.

Chapter IV: Catholicism on the marks of the Church
1 Four authenticating marks of the true church have been recognised:
2 (1) Its *unity* means the unchanging persistence of 'the deposit of faith,'
3 but this unity has been impaired (a) by inconsistencies
4 and (b) by additions to the deposit.
5 Though eternal punishment was accepted from the beginning,
6 the doctrine of purgatory is a later accretion,
7 as are the dogmas of 1854 and 1950 about the Virgin.
8 Newman's theory of development abandons the unity required.
9 (c) The deposit has also changed by subtractions.
10 (2) The *sanctity* of the church means a unique goodness,
11 but the purest goodness does not rest on supernatural sanctions,
12 and such sanctions have been inhumanely misapplied.
13 (3) The *universality* of the church implies a common body of doctrine,
14 but this community is factitious.
15 (4) *Apostolicity*, in its first sense, connotes an unbroken chain of authority,
16 but its first link is frail, for
17 (a) the authenticity of 'Thou art Peter' is questionable;
18 (b) the Apostles showed no awareness of Peter's primacy;
19 (c) nor did the church fathers,
20 (d) nor the early general councils.
21 (e) The founding of an enduring church does not consist with the imminence of the second coming.
22 (f) The secular primacy of Rome largely accounts for its religious primacy.
23 Apostolicity, in its second sense, connotes the reproduction in essence of the primitive church,
24 a claim that is tragically contrary to fact.
25 The authoritarian is left in an embarrassing dilemma.
26 But Catholicism has been sustained by (a) human need, and
27 (b) congeniality of the intellectual climate.
28 But the climate of the modern world is uncongenial.
29 Dogma must be judged by its coherence with systematised experience.
30 Miracle suits ill with a world of law,
31 and a two-world theory with the integrity of thought.

32 We may legitimately ask of religion consistency with science
33 and, still more, coherence with experience as a whole.

PART II. REASON AND FAITH: THE LUTHERAN SUCCESSION

Chapter V: Reason and faith in Luther
 1 Modern Protestantism stems from Luther,
 2 who accepted from Catholicism more than he rejected.
 3 Luther's character was deeply flawed,
 4 but with flaws that made him formidable.
 5 His humility was joined with vast self-confidence
 6 and the sense of a divine mandate to reform the church,
 7 which was then sunk in corruption.
 8 Luther regarded reason as an enemy of faith
 9 on a variety of grounds.
10 The Christian creed was foolishness to reason,
11 and God's ways in conflict with our ethics.
12 Indeed he appears to be responsible for all evil.
13 Faith for Luther (1) is essentially belief,
14 (2) i.e. a certainty that we have been divinely forgiven,
15 (3) made possible by grace alone.
16 (4) It is faith that saves, not works,
17 (5) though good works follow from faith,
18 a view that Luther states incoherently.
19 Scripture, not the church, was for him the ultimate authority,
20 though its authority varied greatly from book to book
21 and depended, circularly, on faith for its perception.
22 His theory of levels of inspiration was arbitrary.
23 He undermined the appeal to reason by fear,
24 holding that in religion it was sinful pride.
25 (I) Original sin was central in Luther's theology,
26 but (1) the doctrine implies a mythical past.
27 (2) It has no adequate basis in the Bible.
28 (3) Sin is not heritable,
29 (4) nor can anyone be responsible for ancestral sin,
30 (5) which the doctrine magnifies beyond bounds.
31 (6) Sin cannot precede moral choice.
32 (7) If there is original sin, why not original goodness?
33 (8) Luther's doctrine was not consistent with his determinism,
34 (9) nor was it coherent with the character he ascribed to God.
35 (II) The incompetence of reason in theology was central in his teaching,
36 but what is false in philosophy cannot be true in theology.
37 The resort to semantics is an evasion,
38 as was Luther's attempt to distinguish two separate realms,
39 since his theology made free use of the reason he abjured
40 and is riddled nevertheless with contradiction.
41 (III) 'Justification by faith' was central in Luther's teaching,

42 but this 'faith' is alien to human nature,
43 and the doctrine is a depressant to morality.
44 Faith, for Luther, was belief exercised by 'the heart.'
45 Has such belief proved reliable?
46 No; it clearly misled Luther himself.
47 He confused emotive with cognitive certainty,
48 assuming that feeling can know
49 and that satisfactoriness to desire is evidence of truth.
50 For Luther, disbelief was the supremely culpable moral act,
51 a view that unduly extends responsibility,
52 strains intellectual integrity,
53 and depreciates the love of truth.
54 In manifold ways
55 Luther was a powerful engine of reform,
56 but his reason too generally echoed his passions.

Chapter VI: Reason and faith in Kierkegaard
1   The revival of Kierkegaard was due to his anti-rationalist strategy.
2   The Biblical view of nature had been undermined by science,
3   and the traditional creed by rationalist criticism.
4   Liberalism was an appeasement of the rationalists,
5   but Kierkegaard led a determined revolt against them.
6   He recognised three 'stages on life's way':
7   The aesthetic stage is devoted to the goods of the senses.
8   Escape from it raises the problem of 'either/or.'
9   The ethical stage demands moral perfection,
10 a demand which Kierkegaard misreads.
11 The religious stage has two levels, A and B,
12 of which A, the first, is marked (1) by resignation;
13 (2) by suffering,
14 on which Kierkegaard's stress is morbid and unchristian;
15 (3) by a sense of profound guilt,
16 which is natural to the religious man's morality
17 but, as conceived by Kierkegaard, is hardly sane,
18 and which suppressed the Hellenic in the Hebraic tradition;
19 (4) by humour, which sees man in perspective
20 though Kierkegaard's account of it is illogical and cynical.
21 Level B has three chief characteristics:
22 (1) It transcends objective knowledge, which is inadequate, since
23 (a) it is confined to universals
24 and hence is unable to grasp existent individuals,
25 but thought does deal with these on its way to the universal
26 and has achieved some understanding and control of them;
27 (b) objective knowledge fails of the certainty necessary in religion,
28 But Kierkegaard's argument for this necessity is incoherent;
29 (c) religious belief is an act of will, not of intellect,
30 but his separation of thinking and willing is untenable.
31 (2) Religion at its highest demands 'subjectivity,'

32 which is (a) active, (b) passionate, (c) incommunicable,
33 and in religion (d) identical with truth.
34 But this is to eviscerate belief of its meaning
35 And to fall into manifold confusion.
36 Subjectivity takes its character from thought.
37 To equate it with truth destroys truth.
38 (3) Religion demands a leap of faith,
39 which for Kierkegaard is a commitment to the unintelligible
40 and, in the case of Abraham and Isaac, to immorality.
41 Such a view entails moral nihilism
42 since it denies the validity of man's clearest insights
43 and exalts him to sainthood for no apparent reason.
44 It makes rational theology impossible.
45 Kierkegaard's thought was twisted by his morbid temper
46 and by a mismanaged romance.
47 His manner and personality impose special difficulties,
48 and at the summit of his thought lies incoherence.

Chapter VII: Reason and revelation for Emil Brunner
1 The last half-century is notable for its revolt against liberalism.
2 In this revolt, Brunner and Barth upheld the Lutheran tradition.
3 (1) Brunner's view of man is that of St Paul,
4 for whom human nature had been corrupted by the fall.
5 Since man is helpless to escape,
6 his state is one of despair.
7 (2) Faith, a supernatural gift, is man's only escape.
8 Brunner is ambiguous as to its mode of achievement.
9 (3) The good life lies in obedience to divine imperatives.
10 (4) Revealed and natural knowledge are different in kind.
11 If each keeps in its own sphere, conflict is needless.
12 Reason is held incompetent to deal with revelation,
13 but it must be more competent than Brunner allows,
14 for he relies on it in describing the state of faith.
15 At times he makes its relevance a matter of degree,
16 but his theory is still disastrous for psychology
17 and for history.
18 The relation between his two realms is baffling
19 and full of paradoxes.
20 Theology is given the right of dictation to philosophy,
21 but when these conflict, natural reason must take precedence,
22 for (1) the abandonment of logic is self-destructive, and
23 (2) the choice between proffered revelations requires reason.
24 Brunner's ethics involves discontinuous moral orders,
25 a theory which, for the natural man, leads to moral scepticism.
26 Moral sanity rests on the acceptance of natural morality.
27 Brunner's theory would undermine such sanity
28 and has grave dangers in practice,
29 for sincere minds may be mistaken in their 'intuitions,'

30 which makes sharp separation of the two realms impracticable,
31 as does the resemblance of faith to certain natural experiences.

Chapter VIII: Reason and revelation for Karl Barth
 1 Barth marks the culmination of the Lutheran line of thought.
 2 He regards the incarnation as the central fact of history,
 3 holding that revelation is not through nature or speculation
 4 nor through conscience
 5 nor through the Bible as rationally interpreted
 6 nor through immediate experience
 7 but directly to a divinely conditioned faith.
 8 Barth turned the tables on rationalism with an adroit strategy,
 9 holding not merely that understanding is limited
10 but that natural knowledge is overridden by revelation.
11 To accept this, however, is disastrous to reason
12 and entails metaphysical irrationalism.
13 Barth's practice is inconsistent with his theory,
14 which would expropriate philosophy from its traditional province
15 and make theology unintelligible.
16 Barth's ethics depreciates natural virtue
17 and has strange philosophic affinities.
18 It provides no intelligible standards of practice.
19 Barth admits no community between Christian and other religions.
20 His theology inculcates despair of aspiration and effort.
21 At times he regards science as neutral to religion,
22 but his theology accords ill with science,
23 as does his ethics of belief with scientific standards.
24 His indictment of philosophy for pride recoils upon itself.
25 Irrationalism is tempting
26 but disastrous.

PART III: ETHICS AND BELIEF

Chapter IX: Rationalism and Christian ethics (I)
 1 Christian morality may be examined independently of dogma,
 2 though the ethics of Jesus was in fact affected by his eschatology.
 3 His teaching is discernible only through many veils.
 4 It rejected the ethics of mechanical conformity
 5 and made certain inward attitudes all-important
 6 which were detailed in the Beatitudes.
 7 The gospel of love has been taken as an ultimate ethic,
 8 and the principle of benevolence is indeed rationally founded.
 9 But in the Christian ethics some great goods were ignored.
10 It showed little interest in the pursuit of knowledge
11 or in the goods of the natural man;
12 and its opposition to wealth was scarcely rational,
13 nor did it care much for aesthetic goods.

14 Christian ethics, unlike the Greek, did not stress civic duty.
15 It repudiated violence so generally as to
16 (1) underrate the importance of courage,
17 (2) sacrifice public safety,
18 and (3) veto international government.
19 Jesus was not unaffected by the nationalism of his people,
20 and early Christianity seems to have acquiesced in slavery.
21 Jesus had a notable sympathy for women,
22 though without any reported sexual interest.
23 He was an opponent of divorce.
24 His attitude toward his mother is puzzling.
25 Paul's teaching about women was irrational
26 but unfortunately became the official view of the church.

Chapter X: Rationalism and Christian ethics (II)
1 In the ethics of Jesus, justice is a secondary virtue,
2 to which Deity himself appears not to conform.
3 Christianity overlooks the preventive side of justice,
4 and the conception of justice implied in some parables is primitive.
5 Jesus rates surprisingly low the importance of work
6 and of family ties.
7 For him the 'love of God' was a natural motive,
8 which is not thus natural for modern man.
9 Such love he thought a necessary part of morality,
10 but a high morality is possible without it.
11 Christian humility does not require self-deception,
12 but it is not presented consistently,
13 and is at odds with the cosmic claims attributed to Jesus.
14 The issue whether Jesus is God or man is unavoidable.
15 The hypothesis of his humanity is the less vulnerable.
16 That of his deity is not defensible historically
17 for, as to knowledge, there is evidence of ignorance and error
18 and of manifold inconsistencies.
19 Nor was his cast of mind that of an intellectual.
20 As to his power, that too was sharply limited.
21 As to his moral teaching, it was marked by limitations,
22 as was his originality.
23 And his character in the gospels is not without flaw.
24 Christianity was deficient in its respect for reason, since
25 (1) it tied its ethics to a mythical cosmology
26 and (2) thereby distorted human motives,
27 (3) it adopted a mistaken ethics of belief,
28 and (4) misconceived the place of reason in morality.
29 Jesus was a moral genius, not a philosopher.

Chapter XI: The ethics of belief
1 Common views on the morality of belief are confused.
2 The ethics of thought demands adjusting belief to the evidence.

3   This has been denied on the ground that belief is involuntary.
4   But belief can, in a measure, be controlled indirectly.
5   It is a matter of social importance,
6   and the manner of its formation still more important.
7   But this does not entail the right of social control.
8   We hold some men responsible for their beliefs,
9   and justly.
10 Hence an ethics of belief is necessary.
11 In science exceeding the evidence is not permissible.
12 In religion it has been approved, both in the Old Testament
13 and in the New,
14 and unequivocally by St Paul.
15 For the church fathers disbelief became deadly sin.
16 The emancipation of reason came with Descartes and Locke.
17 Our present concern is not with faith as self-validating.
18 Restriction of belief to evidence seemed to James churlish in religion,
19 since it overweighted the value of truth.
20 Here he is on strong ground,
21 but (1) we prize truth more than he admitted,
22 and (2) though doubt may be repressed by pragmatic arguments,
23 such repression generates a divided mind.
24 (3) The 'will to believe' offers no rational halting-place.
25 Pascal justified belief by the calculation of chances,
26 but his argument is both cynical and incoherent.
27 Religious problems engage feeling as scientific problems do not.
28 The questioning mind is bound to imperil belief,
29 but truth should be its only pole.
30 Morality does not stand or fall with theological belief,
31 nor, in general, does happiness.
32 The appeal to authority is often justifiable.
33 Certainty on ultimate issues is seldom possible.
34 Probability has served many as a guide of life,
35 and honesty may admit of nothing more.

Chapter XII: Myth in religion
1   Religion has often been confined to one side of human nature,
2   but it necessarily involves thought, feeling, and will,
3   though in its history these elements have varied in prominence.
4   It began in animism.
5   In primitive thought the soul is a double of the body.
6   Myth-making is an advance beyond animism.
7   (a) It is a first effort at scientific understanding,
8   (b) though, as incipient art, it must also satisfy feeling,
9   (c) thus opening the conflict of reason and feeling in religion.
10 The most influential Western mythology is that of the Hebrews.
11 Its history was one of progressive moralisation.
12 It paved the way for the ethics of Jesus,
13 which approached a morals without mythology.

14 The conception of God reflects changes in the moral ideal,
15 and this ideal was purified in the teaching of Jesus.
16 Christian inwardness and Greek intelligence needed each other,
17 but the church fathers embedded Jesus in a framework of dogmas
18 whose mythical character may be exposed by their history.
19 The Biblical account of the Virgin, e.g., is meagre and inconsistent,
20 but she was gradually exalted by speculation within the church,
21 by pressures from the pagan world,
22 and by the victory of Athanasius at Nicaea.
23 She has reached virtual deification.
24 Dogmatic systems appear as increasingly improbable,
25 and wither in a climate of rational inquiry.
26 Dogmatic Christianity was weakened by both rationalism and empiricism,
27 as well as by science,
28 biblical criticism,
29 and the criticism of Christian ethics.
30 Scepticism continues to spread.

PART IV: A RATIONALIST ALTERNATIVE

Chapter XIII: Cosmology

1   Reason has proved a better critic than architect,
2   but our negations have had positive bases.
3   The law of contradiction reveals the world as a coherent whole.
4   Subjectivist interpretations of this law have failed.
5   The world is also a causal whole
6   in which (I) all events are linked with others through their characters.
7   It is assumed (1) that nature is uniform
8   and (2) that all events have causes,
9   though (a) this cannot be inductively proved
10 and (b) it has been questioned by quantum physicists,
11 (c) by theologians in defense of miracles
12 and (d) by metaphysicians in defense of free will.
13 (II) All events are causally interconnected, either directly
14 or indirectly.
15 Causation involves necessity, for
16 (1) it is not, as Hume maintained, always opaque to understanding,
17 and in some cases of inference necessity is plainly at work.
18 (2) Analysis of the idea of causation reveals necessity,
19 though this has been questioned by Ayer.
20 Actual frequencies of conjunction rule out chance.
21 Common sense has proved an unreliable guide,
22 for it is mistaken about what is revealed in perception.
23 All sensed qualities are dependent on mind,
24 as are perceived space and time.
25 And all men are islands.

26   Science, with strong grounds, accepts a physical order
27   whose mathematical framework does not entail its being mental.

Chapter XIV: Human nature and its values
 1   A mind is a unique kind of dynamic and purposive whole,
 2   whose main components are impulses or drives.
 3   The evolution of mind advances through a series of plateaus.
 4   The plateaus in the evolution of thought
 5   correspond to those in the evolution of will.
 6   Moral choice may involve a complex calculation of values,
 7   the end being the production of the greatest good.
 8   What makes an experience intrinsically good? Opinions differ.
 9   We hold it to be the fulfilment and satisfaction of impulse.
10   This is both a rationalist and an objectivist view,
11   though it makes good and evil mind-dependent.

Chapter XV: Goodness and the Absolute
 1   In only a small part of the universe are the conditions of value known
to be realised.
 2   Is the Absolute good?
 3   Some idealists have said Yes, though on dubious grounds.
 4   Bradley's answer is not coherent.
 5   The Absolute is not, in our sense, good.
 6   Royce's attempt to exhibit its goodness is self-defeating,
 7   as is Bosanquet's faith that the world system embodies goodness.
 8   That the Absolute is good has various meanings:
 9   (1) its moral goodness is not indicated by fact or theory;
10   (2) its intrinsic goodness is not entailed by its logical completeness;
11   (3) its being more good than evil is compatible with its indifference.
12   The loss of belief in the moral government of the world is tragic,
13   but the passing of the old supernaturalism is not wholly so.

Chapter XVI: Religion and rationalism
 1   Supernaturalist belief is waning,
 2   and religious interest shifting to the moral life.
 3   In the development of morality thought has played the central role,
 4   adding to it new dimensions of (1) length,
 5   (2) breadth, and
 6   (3) coherence.
 7   The rational man is a citizen of an ideal republic.
 8   A merely rational ethics has been held debasing to the spiritual life,
 9   But (1) so, in its attitude toward evil, is traditional theism;
10   (2) the Pauline division of natural and spiritual man is artificial
11   for no clear boundary is discoverable;
12   (3) in man the object of animal response is transfigured by thought
13   and may be enlarged without limit.
14   Man's impulses are organised in sentiments.
15   The religious sentiment has been powerful but divisive.

16 The sentiment of rationality, though fallible, is man's best guide,
17 and has been the active principle in the evolution of religion.
18 Reason is itself revelation.
19 To be rational is to be moral,
20 and, despite differences of practice, the moral standard is objective.
21 Rationality imposes immediate restraint for ulterior freedom.
22 The rational temper is well illustrated in certain men of thought
23 and in certain men of action.
24 Since it is an acquired disposition,
25 it could be widely diffused.
26 How would the rational temper affect faith, reverence, and humility?
27 It would deprive faith of its primacy.
28 It would leave ample occasion for reverence.
29 Religious humility has sometimes sacrificed truth.
30 True humility is required by the rational mind.
31 Religion in our sense will endure.

Aaron, R. I., on Locke 562
Abortion, Catholic resistance to 95
Absolute: God and the 523; as the complete fulfilment of desire 524; Bradley on 525; difficulties in his view 526 ff.; Royce on the 529–30; failure of his conception 529; Bosanquet on the 530; he does not show it to be good 531; is it moral? 532; is it intrinsically good? 533; two senses of 'rational' 534; the world as neutral 534; tragedy involved in this 535; the relief involved 536
Acton, Lord 96, 103
Adam and Eve in Catholic theology 63, 64, 65
Adrian VI, Pope 66
Aeterni Patris 26, 81
Alexander VI, Pope 96
Alexander VIII, Pope 59
Alston, W. P. 593
Andrews, C. F. 304
Animals, theology and treatment of 96
Animism, origin of religion in 436
Annan, N. 584
Anne, mother of Mary 69
Apostles, attitude toward Peter 101
Apostolicity as note of church 98; (A) continuity of succession 98; criticism of this conception 98–106; (B) reproduction of original community 106; criticism of this conception 106 ff.
Aquinas, Thomas 106, 108, 334; Leo XIII on 26; on Scripture 29, 38, 42; on truths beyond reason 29, 31, 32; on faith 30–2; on the devil 67; on hell 84; estimate of 466
Aristotle, on slavery 341; as complement to Christianity 453
Arnold, M., on religion 434; on Jesus

and philosophy 451; on conduct 590
Asquith, H. H. 563
Astronomy, Scripture and 59
Athanasius, Saint 102
Atonement and justice 362
Augustine, Saint 30, 97; on science and theology 58; on hell 84; on Peter 102; on love of God 370; on heresy 414
Austen, Jane 502
Authentic *v.* quoted Scriptural passages 41
Authority in religion: its dialectic 108; tested by coherence with experience 114; in morals 430
Ayer, A. J., on causation 498

Bacon, F. 416, 441
Baillie, D. M. 412
Baillie, John 311
Bainton, R. H. 134, 175, 585
Barnes, Bishop E. W. 456, 471
Barth, Karl: his Gifford Lectures 288; the thrust of neo-orthodoxy 289; revelation not through thought or conscience 290; nor through the Bible, critically read 292; nor through mystical experience 293; revelation known only to faith 293–4; revelation and reason conflict 296; but to desert reason is disastrous 297; and Barth genuinely does this 299; He expropriates philosophy from its own province 301; God as wholly other 302; for Barth the real Christ is incognito 303; which overshoots the mark 305; Barth's affinity with positivism 305; with Stoicism 306; the inapplicability of his ethics 306; his ostracism of other religions 308;

Barth, Karl (*cont.*)
the futility of moral effort 309; neo-orthodoxy and science 311; its view here unconvincing 313; and demands violation of scientific method 313; the sin of pride 316; the seductiveness of the irrational 316–17

Beatitudes 329

Behaviourism 597

Belief, ethics of, chap. 11; is belief a moral matter? 400; yes, because partly voluntary 402–4; and habits of belief are influential 404; social control of belief 407; case of the inquisitors 408; the scientific standard 410; the religious standard 411; gospel stress on belief 412; Paul's teaching 413; heresy as wickedness 414; rise of rationalism 416; the open conflict 416; James on right to believe 418 ff.; criticism of James 421–4; importance of religious belief 427; truth as sole compass of thought 428; morality does not rest on dogma 429; the uses of authority 430; certainty *v.* probability 431

Bellarmine, Cardinal 81

Bello, Francis 72

Benedict XV 38, 50, 70

Benson, A. C., on work 366, 593

Berdyaev, N. 580

Bettelin, Saint 91

Bible Society, British and Foreign 40

Biblical Commission 46, 48, 63, 104

Biology, revelation and 62

Birkenhead, Lord 502

Blanshard, Paul 579

Bosanquet, B., on the Absolute 523 ff; 530

Bradley, A. C. 551

Bradley, F. H. 523 ff.; on pride 317; on the Absolute 525; its character contradictory 527; it undermines finite goodness 528; on Christian ethics 591; his claim to certainty 597

Bradshaw, M. 310

Brandes, G. 245

Brightman, E. S. 523

British Medical Council 69

Broad, C. D. 90, 486

Brooks, Phillips 304

Browning, Robert, quoted 337, 367; on doubt 423

Brunner, Emil: on unimportance of proof 284; on Kierkegaard 239; compared with Barth 249; his view of human nature 251; of man's fall and corruption 252; the illusion of progress 254; the new birth 255; his account of this incoherent 257; the nature of the good life 257–60; revelation and reason contrasted 260; the conflict between them 261; causes of the conflict 262; Brunner's attack on reason 264; though he employs it in theology 265; his 'law of contiguity' 268; which would destroy psychology 268; and fill history with gaps 270; Brunner unable to relate his two orders 271; his account self-contradictory 273; neo-orthodoxy as criticism of philosophy 274; reason as inescapable 275; even in the choice of a faith 277; divine imperative not rational 278; and involves return to moral nihilism 279; it makes havoc of theology 279–80; and threatens moral sanity 280; 'divine leading' may be deceptive 282; the damaging analogy of mysticism 285; quoted 302

Burke, on intemperate minds 185; on honour 344; on chivalry 564; on humility 567

Butler, Bishop 536, 567

Cadoux, C. J., quoted 98, 577, 581, 594

Caesar, Julius 562

Caird, J. and E. 290, 407, 525

Calvin, J. 365, 467

Campbell, C. A., on the appeal to reason 319

Camus, A., on Christian injustice 362

Carlyle, T.: on Luther 127; on Mrs Fuller 380; on Darwin 470

Carus Lectures, preface 9–10

Causality: as a postulate 115; law of 484; objections to the law 484 ff.; it is empirically unprovable 484; questioned in quantum physics 485; difficulty about miracles 487; difficulty about free will 488; all events interconnected 490; indirect causal connection 491; causality involves necessity 493; cases of partial grasp 494; necessity a cause in inference 495; a priori elements in causation 496; Joseph and Ayer on causality 498

Causal whole, the world as 482
Cave, Sydney 311
Certainty, two kinds of 177; *v.* probability 431
Chadwick, O., on Luther and Erasmus 184
Chalcedon, Council of 56, 102, 166
Charles, R. H., on Sermon on the Mount 390
Chrysostom: on hell 85; on Peter 102
Church, Dean R. W. 304
Civic duty, Christianity and 341
Clement VIII 47
Clifford, W. K.: on original sin 159; on ethics of belief 411
Clough, A. H. 527
Coherence as ultimate test of truth 114–15
Common sense and its world 502
Conation, evolution of 515
Conscience, reason in 556
Consciousness, field of 511
Contradiction, law of, its meaning 479; not a statement about language 479; nor a convention 480; nor merely a law of thought 480; but a truth about the nature of things 481
Contradictions: in revealed truth 39; regarding God 50 ff.; in papal pronouncements 55 ff., 82; in conciliar pronouncements 57; in Luther's Bible 146; in his use of reason in religion 163; in Brunner on the new birth 257; in Brunner on the two orders 273; between reason and revelation in Barth 296
Copernicus 59
Corruptions in Scriptural text 46
Cosmology of a rationalist 477 ff.
Coulton, G. G. 83, 102–3
Councils: inconsistencies in statement 57; on primacy of Peter 103
Courage, Christianity and 344
Custom as determining belief 112
Cyprian, Saint 414
Cyril, Saint, on Peter 102

Dante, on hell 85
D'Arcy, M. C. 25; on divine punishment 580
Davis, Charles 580
Debs, E. V. 570
Demonology 67
Denifle, H., on Luther 126

Descartes 31, 334, 436, 468
Development, Newman on 128
Devil, Pope Paul VI on the 67; Luther and the 122–3, 125, 171, 174, 182–3
Dewey, John, on Greek depreciation of labour 367; on 'religiousness' 373; on intelligence as social force 564
DeWolf, L. H. 587
Divorce, Christian teaching on 354–5
Döllinger, J. J. I. von 103, 577
Dogma, as rooted in desire 110; ultimate test of 114–15; and modern world 116; and myth 454, 455
Duhr, J., on the Virgin 463
Dupré, L. 586

Eddington, Sir A. 509
Edwards, Jonathan: on humility 568; on an angry God 584
Eichinger, Bishop, on Galileo 61
Eliot, T. S., quoted 228, 591
Emerson, R. W.: on courage 345; on prayer 373
Emmet, D. 428
Erasmus: on freedom 135; Luther on 166; and Socrates 334
Erikson, Erik, on Luther 147, 271
Error and realism 504
Ethics: a secular study 520; rational, in outline 544; religious objection 545; this is without standing 546
Ethics, Christian, chaps 9 and 10; creed and morals thought interdependent 323; Christian ethics may be separately examined 324; is it an *Interimsethik?* 325; source of knowledge of it 326; its negative side 327; classification of Christian ethics 328; an ethics of inward attitude 329; love as settled good will 329–30; the claim to finality 330; meaning of Christian love 331; undervalued the good of knowledge 333; as means as well as end 335; undervalued good of natural man 335; differing here from the Greeks 336–7; Christianity, wealth, and poverty 337; Christianity and art 340; and civic duty 341; and non-violence 342; and courage 344; and political force 345; and war 346; and nationalism 348; and slavery 350; and the position of women 351; feminine traits in Jesus 353; his teaching on lust 354; on

Ethics, Christian (*cont.*)
divorce 354–5; his coolness toward his mother 355–6; attitude of Saint Paul 356; attitude of the church 357–8; teaching on justice 360 ff.; and divine condemnation 361; and the atonement 362; on prevention of wrong 362–3; parables on justice 263–5; Christianity and work 365; ambiguous on family relations 367; the love of God: meaning? 369; essential in ethics of Jesus 371; but morally ambiguous 372; humility 375; Jesus: human or divine? 558 ff.; as limited in knowledge 381; inconsistencies in teaching 384; limitation in power 388; originality 390; his character not flawless 391; adequate respect for reason lacking 394; his ethics tied to false cosmology 394; ethics and theology must be rational 398

Eugene IV, Pope 84
Euhemerus 444
Evil, Luther on 134
Evolution: and Catholicism 75 ff.; cognitive 513

Faber, F. W. 87
Fairbairn, A. M.: on primitive church 107; on Newman 594
Faith: as distinct from reason 26; necessary for the Catholic 30; involves will 31; a gift of grace 31; a free act 31; and morally defensible 32; the lure of 34; scientific and religious 72; no single Protestant view 121; Luther on faith and reason 136; meaning of faith for Luther 136 ff.; as awareness of being forgiven 137; as a divine product 138; and works 138; essential to salvation 139; as interpreter of Scripture 141; as consisting of belief 171; as 'knowledge of the heart' 171–2; this widely misleading 174; Luther's anti-Semitism 175; faith and intellectual integrity 182; conflict of faith and reason 184; faith and belief 412, 417; as working hypothesis 432; can reasonableness replace? 565; its fate under rationalism 565; prized for its by-products 566

Family relations, Christian teaching on 367
Farnell, L. R. 460
Farrar, Dean, on eternal punishment 84
Fathers, church 89, 94; attitude toward Peter 101; their mythology 453; distortion of figure of Jesus 454
Fatima 91
Fawkes, A. 100
Fesquet, H. 578
Fite, Warner: self-assertion and Christianity 344; an overstress of love 360; on Christian injustice 364; on the Pharisees 385
Florence, Council of, on hell 84, 579
Forgiveness, may be refused by God 361
Fox, George 270
Francis of Assisi, Saint 92, 93, 428, 568
Franklin, B. 563
Frazer, Sir J. 105; on date of Christmas 460
Freedom of belief, Catholic restrictions on 44–6
Freud, S. 105; on religion 434, 560
Friends, Society of, Dean Inge on 107–8
Froude, James Anthony: on early saints 91; on fifteenth-century church 128; on Newman 317, 379; his history of England 582
Fulgentius 414

Galileo, case of 59 ff.
Gandhi, on non-violence 343–4
Gardner, Percy, on Christian ethics 341
Garvie, A. E., on feminine traits in Jesus 353
Gelasius, Pope 54
Gerrish, B. A., quoted 133, 582
Gibbon, E. 85, 105, 562
Gifford Lectures, preface 9–10
Giles, Prof., on original sin 157
Gilson, E., quoted 31, 32, 33, 58
Gleitman case 95
God: varying scriptural conceptions 50 ff.; and the Absolute 523
Goethe: on Luther 126; on Christian ethics 330
Goodall, J. 598
Goodness, intrinsic, defined 517, 519; objective 519
Goose, P. H. 52–3
Gore, Bishop Charles 102, 105, 581; on Virgin Mary 458
Grattan, H., on intolerance 410

Greeks: on love of knowledge 333; on good of natural man 335
Green, T. H. 523 ff.
Gregory I, Pope 85
Gregory XVI, on liberty of conscience 415

Haldane, R. B. 563
Happiness, belief and 430
Hardy, Thomas, on Newman 594
Harnack, A., on Barth 249; on the love of God 373
Hase, Karl von 57, 577
Hazlitt, W. 569
Hegel, G. W. F. 303
Hell in Catholic teaching 83-4
Henson, H. H. 591
Herbert, George 367
Hick, J. 593
Higher criticism 470
Hippolytus, Saint 102
Hobhouse, L. T., on position of Jewish women 352; on the good life as rational 556
Holland, Canon Scott 304
Holt, E. B. 503
Honorius, Pope 54, 577
Hopkins, Mark 429
Housman, A. E. 560
Humani generis 63, 64, 65, 578
Hume, D., view of causation rejected 494; his reasonable temper 562
Humility, Christian 375; its position under rationalism 567; pride masked as 568
Huxley, J. 536
Huxley, T. H., on ecclesiasticism 68; on ethics of belief 410-11; on Newman 595

Idealism, mind-dependence of observed things 503; epistemological and ontological 509
Immaculate conception 88, 458-9
Immortality, for Kierkegaard 227
Impulses, their variety 512
Indulgences 87, 128-9
Inerrancy, see Infallibility
Infallibility of Pope, its conditions 59, 103; inconsistencies in papal pronouncements 55
Infallibility of Scripture 28, 38; difficulties 38-57; on faith and morals 119 ff.

Inference, necessity at work in 495
Inge, Dean W. R.: on Catholicism 71; on Society of Friends 107-8; on Luther 126; on thermodynamics 313; on Christian ethics 341, 357; on the gospel of work 365; on the Virgin birth 456
Innocent I, Pope 83
Innocent VIII, Pope 54, 66, 578
Intellectual climate and belief 111
Irenaeus, on Peter 102; on original sin 153
Isaiah 46

James, W. 94; on mysticism 285; on will to believe 419; criticism of 421-4; on instincts 512; on an oversoul 548
Januarius, Saint 69
Jastrow, J., on the 'emotion of conviction' 177
Jeans, Sir J. 509, 522-3
Jefferson, T. 563
Jerome, Saint 46, 358
Jesus, his character and ethics, chaps 9 and 10; attitude toward Old Testament 52; attitude toward Peter 99, 103; attitude toward creed 108; his remoteness from modern church 107; divine or human? 377; nature of the alternative 380; his limitation in knowledge 381, 576-7; inconsistencies in teaching 384; difficulties with his language 387; limited in power 388; borrowed much, yet unique 390; perfect character open to question 391; deficient respect for reason 394 ff.; ethics linked to mythical cosmology 395; and a dubious ethics of belief 398; misprized reason in ethics and theology 398; independence of his moral insights 449; his greatness 452; distortions by the church fathers 454; attitude toward his mother 457
John XXII, Pope 83
John XXIII, Pope 24
Joseph, H. W. B.: on causation as necessary 498; on intrinsic goodness 598
Jowett, B., on Newman 595
Joyce, G. H. 92
Julius II, Pope 66
Justice, Christian, reviewed 360-5

Kant, I., on religion 434
Kaufmann, W. 592
Keble, J., on doubt 422
Kegley, C. W. 588, 589
Kerr, Rt Rev W. S. 88
Kierkegaard, S., why he was revived 187, 190–1; stages on life's way 192; aesthetic stage 192; ethical stage 194; its demand for perfection 195; religious stage A 197; this demands (a) total resignation 198; (b) suffering 199; (c) guilt 203; about which he was a 'sick soul' 207; (d) humour 209; which in K. was inhumane 210; religious stage B 212; requiring (a) abandonment of objectivity 213; objective thought deals with abstractions 213–15; but also, contra K., with existents 216; objective thought and religious certainty 219; belief as commitment to action 220; confusion of this notion 221–2; (b) subjectivity: its meaning 223; subjectivity as truth 225; incoherence of this notion 227; subjectivity as passion; its errors 229–32; (c) the leap of faith 232; this not made on evidence 233; crucial case of Abraham and Isaac 234; which destroys rational ethics 236; and rules out a rational theology 240; evidence of pathology 242; concluding unhappy postscript 245; Brunner's debt to Kierkegaard 278; Kierkegaard's style 586
King, H. C., on Christian ethics 361, 376
Kingsley, Charles, on Luther 174; his debate with Newman 424
Köstlin, J. 583

Ladd-Franklin, C. 504
Laird, J., on Kierkegaard 245
Lamb, C. 330
Lamentabili Sane Exitu 45, 50, 104, 576
Lang, A. 444
Lecky, W. E. H.: on witchcraft 66; on asceticism 94; on Luther 121; on Jonathan Edwards 157–8; on slavery 351; on the father's view of women 358; on repression of freedom of mind 415; on the feminine ideal 591
Leo I, Pope 106
Leo II, Pope 54
Leo XII, on Bible reading 40

Leo XIII 26, 46, 120; on inspiration 38, 50; on Scripture and science 58; on proofs of revelation 80–1
Lewis, H. D. 589
Liberalism, decline of 189, 190, 248, 294–5
Liberius, Bishop of Rome 102
Liddon, H. P. 383
Livingstone, Sir R., on Luther 126
Locke, J.: on the love of truth 416; his reasonableness 562
Loisy, Abbé 45, 456
Lourdes, miracles at 90
Louvet, Abbé 87
Love, Christian: interpreted 330; love of God ambiguous 369–70; its distortion of love of man 550
Lucas, F. L.; on theism and punishment 157; on irrationalism 560; on sincerity 594
Lunn, Sir A. 25; on miracles 75; on Newman 594
Luther, Martin, chap. 5; his inherited faith 122; on Copernicus 122, 166; centred in theology 122–3; his character 124; contrasted with Erasmus 125; his lack of moderation 125; his self-confidence 127; his antipathy to reason 129, 131; his two realms 131; his rejection of reason in morals 197; in theology 135–6; his conception of faith 136–8; on faith and works 138; his view incoherent 140; his attitude toward Scripture 141; unevenness of Bible 142; his circular defence of Scripture 144; his distinctions within Scripture 146; their failure 146–7; his disservice to the free mind 148–9; reliance on reason as arrogance 149; an original sin 150; this doctrine false and immoral 151–6; and makes an ogre of Deity 156; his depreciation of reason in religion 159; his two incongruous realms 161; which lead to many inconsistencies 163 ff.; on justification by faith 167; a doctrine incoherent and unethical 168; faith as belief 171; his faith often in error 174; confusing two kinds of certainty 176; his ethics of belief 179; summary on 184; on free thought 415; his implicit appeal to reason 555; his lack of interest in truth 582; on mathematics 582; on the death penalty 585

Macaulay, T. B.: on the antiquity of the church 81–2; on George Fox 270
MacCarthy, D. 563
McDougall, W. 512, 557
McGiffert, A. C. 127, 131, 181, 305
Macintosh, D. C. 318
McTaggart, J. M. E. 430
Maistre, J. de, on free thought 416
Manning, Cardinal, on infallibility 49
Mansel, H. L. 295
Marcus Aurelius 330, 563
Maritain, J.: on Luther 126; on Descartes 468
Mark 99; concluding verses 46
Marks, see Notes
Martineau, J. 56, 83, 98, 304, 577
Mary, see Virgin Mary
Mencken, H. L. 344, 359
Metaphorical v. literal interpretation 38 ff.
Mill, J. S.: on Christianity and utilitarianism 308–9; on Christian morality 332, 471; on habit of clarity 403; on freedom of belief 407; on F. D. Maurice 422; on qualities of pleasure 519; on truth and goodness 537; as 'saint of rationalism' 562; on hell 580
Milne, E. A. 509
Milton, J. 541
Mind: as a set of propensities 512; non-terrestrial 522–3
Miracles 68–79; profusion of Catholic 68–9; at Lourdes 69; at Fatima 70; the logic of belief in 72; and probability 74; the concept of 75; difficulties in 76 ff.; and accident 78; some cases explicable 389
Mithraism 460
Mivart, Saint G. 66
Monophysite controversy 56
Monsma, P. H. 589
Montaigne 409
Montesquieu 442
Moore, G. E., on intrinsic goodness 517
Morality 92 ff.; not based on authority 92, 94; or on creed 323–4, 429–30; but on intrinsic goods 517; rationalism in 518; ultimate rule in 519; as implicitly evil 526
Moses 46
Motives of credibility 32, 81
Müller, Max 444

Myth in religion 434 ff.; primitive idea of soul 438; supported by dreams and death 438; birth of mythology 439; myth as incipient science 440; as incipient art 441–2; it is the product of no one faculty 442; early Hebrew mythology 445; moralisation of myth 447; Jesus' freeing of morality from myth 449; possible union of Greece with Palestine 453; mythology of the church fathers 454; their transfiguration of Jesus 454; the mythology of the Virgin 456 ff.; absorption of dogma into myth 464; influence of rationalism 468; influence of empiricism 468; influence of science 469 ; influence of higher criticism 470

Nagel, E. 486
Nationalism, Christianity and 348
Neo-orthodoxy, rise of 248
Nestorians 56
Newman, F. W.: on defending one's rights 363; on virtue of industry 366; on J. H. Newman 595
Newman, John Henry 24, 30, 71; on purgatory 85–6; on the Virgin Mary 88; on the development of dogma 89; criticism of his theory 90 ff.; on early saints 91; on primacy of Peter 103; on coherence of thought 118; letter to Manning 316; his anti-rationalism 317; a sermon at Saint Mary's 379; his breaches in rationality 380; his intellectual timidity 422; his suppression of scepticism 423; on incommensurability of values 548; on ending of Mark 576; on miracles 581; on infallibility 581; appraisals of 594–5
Newton, Sir I. 427
Nicaea, Council of 103, 461; primacy of Peter 103
Nicholas III, Pope 83
Niebuhr, Reinhold 245, 317
Nietzsche, F. 330, 471, 512
Noble lectures, preface 9–10
Notes or marks of true church 33, 110 ff.; their variety 81; four chief notes enumerated 81
Nowell-Smith, P. H. 579
Nygren, A.: on irrationality 317; on love of God 370

Objectivity: rejected by Kierkegaard
213; in morals 519
Origen, on hell 84; on Peter 102
Original sin, meanings of 150; its base-
lessness 151; its immorality 154 ff.
Ottaviani, Cardinal 43, 113

Pacifism and Christian ethics 507 ff.
Paley, W. 250, 396
Parables, puzzling: of the householder
363; of the buried treasure 364; of
the talents 364–5
Parousia and a permanent church 103
Pascal: his fear of disbelief 148–9; his
'knowledge of the heart' 173; on
'thinking well' 186; his 'gamble' on
belief 424–5; criticism of 425 ff.
Pascendi Gregis 45
Pater, W. 551, 591
Paton, H. J.: on Kierkegaard 239, 245;
on theological arrogance 316; on
irrationalism 319
Patterson, R. L., on original sin 155
Pauck, W., on neo-orthodoxy 247
Paul V, Pope 59
Paul VI, Pope 24, 67, 71, 578
Paul, Saint: on knowledge 534; on civic
duty 342; on slavery 350; on woman
356; the soul as two-storied 547; incredibility of this theory 548 ff.
Paulsen, F.: on justice 363; on religion
434
Pelagius 83
Pelikan, J. 125
Perceptual world as mind-dependent
503; illusion and its implications 504;
primary and secondary qualities
505–6; Russell's retreat from realism
506–7; the Berkeleian universe 507;
perception and physics 508; epistemological and ontological idealism 509
Perpetua, Saint 86
Peter, Saint 27; 'upon this rock' 99;
attitude of Apostles toward 101; of
the fathers toward 101; of the Coun-
cils 103; primacy of 103; difficulty
of second coming 103; rise of Papacy
naturalistically explicable 104
Physics, world of contemporary 505–7
Pius VI, Pope 86
Pius VII, Pope 87
Pius IX, Pope 32, 85, 96, 112; on pro-
gress 82; on Darwinism 578
Pius X 50, 87, 104; on 'tacit citations'
576; on modernism 45
Pius XI, Pope 68, 70
Pius XII 68, 70, 112; on mental evolu-
tion 63
Plass, E. M. 584
Pleasure, place of in goodness 518–19
Pliny 330
Poverty, Christianity and 339
Pratt, J. B. 319
Prichard, H. A. 569
Prophets, function of Hebrew 447
Providentissimus Deus 28, 38, 50, 575
Psychology: Catholicism and 66; its
invasion by neo-orthodoxy 268–9
Purgatory, Catholic teaching on 55
Purposive root of morality 540
Pusey, E. B.: on eternal punishment
84; on the Virgin 464

Quanta Cura 32
Qui Pluribus 82
Quick, O. C. 292

Rashdall, H.: on finality of Christian
ethics 330; on a limited God 523;
on humility 590
Rationalism: modern advance of 188
416; no single view 478; does not
entail idealism 509–10; in morality
519; two senses of 'rational' 534; and
religion, chap. 16; tension with supernaturalism 538; as an alternative to
religion, chap. 16
Rationality: sentiment of 552; as a
motive 558, 560; its greyness 561
Raven, Canon C. E. 414
Reason: Catholic respect for 3 ff.; and
revelation, chap. 2 (and see Revelation); 'above reason': its meaning 37;
faith in, and in religion 72; and
authority in religion 108–9; Luther's
contempt for 129; the creed as foolishness to 132; Luther's rejection of
in morals 133; his attack on philosophy 147; this involves either scepticism 159; or two incoherent worlds
161; reasons of the heart and their
dangers 173; Luther's sacrifice of
intellectual integrity 181; Brunner's
criticism of 264; appeal to it unavoidable 267; as the ultimate authority
276; its conflict with revelation in
Barth 295 ff.; his abandonment of it
disastrous 297; at work in moral

Reason (*cont.*)
 sense 362; defective respect for in
 Christianity 394; the answers of
 reason tentative 472; reason in religion: meaning 477; reason in conduct 543; as court of final appeal
 554; and revolution 556; in religious
 advance 555; as revelation 557; as
 the replacement of faith 557
Reasonable temper: examples of 561-
 2; an acquired disposition 564
Reimarus, H. S. 349
Relics, claims to efficacy 68-9
Religion as a threefold response 434
Renan, Ernest: on Christian ethics 342;
 his *Vie de Jésus* 450, 470; on scriptural
 contradiction 575
Republic, the moral 544
Revelation: and astronomy 59; and
 biology 62; and psychology 84; two
 standards of truth impossible 114;
 reason as revelation 557
Revelation for Catholics 26 ff.; through
 Scripture 27; through tradition 27;
 through Papal pronouncement 27-8;
 its content 28; never irrational 30,
 35-6; paradox of a veiled 52; and
 natural knowledge chap. 3
Revelation for Protestants, pt II, *passim*
Reverence under rationalism 566
Riddell, Rev J. 84
Rightness: objective 519
Robinson, Bishop J. A. T. 371, 537
Roe, Anne 72
Royce, J., on the Absolute 529
Russell, Bertrand 96; on the importance of knowledge 335; on Christi-
 anity and women 359; on the character of Jesus 392; on the ethics of
 belief 411; on values 517; on Christianity and war 591

Sabatier, L.-A., on primacy of Peter
 100-2; on primitive church 107
Salmon, G. 59, 576, 577; on additions
 to dogma 83, 88; on purgatory 85,
 87
Sanctity of the church: defined 92;
 criticised 92 ff.; a flawed ideal 93;
 Acton on 97
Sand, George, on hell 580
Sanity, meaning of 207
Santayana, G.: 93; on reverence 379;
 on sceticism 414; on ascepticism

448; on dogma 455; on piety 556;
 on James 594, 595
Schell, Herman, on hell 580
Schleiermacher, F. E. D., on religion
 434
Schweitzer, A. 304; his *Interimsethik*
 355, 396-7; his psychoanalytic study
 of Jesus 378; his *Quest of the Historical
 Jesus* 381
Science: revelation and science, chap. 3;
 conflict of revelation with astronomy
 59; with biology 62; with psychology
 66; and Catholic education 72; and
 miracles 96 ff.; Catholicism and
 scientific mind 115-16; as challenge
 to theology 188; as challenge to
 Scripture 188-9; and neo-orthodoxy
 311; implicit in myth 440
Scripture: as inspired throughout 38;
 contradictions in 39; as interpreted
 by church 40-1; defences against
 charge of contradiction 41 ff.; inconsistent ideas of God 50-1;
 Luther's view of 141; his defence of
 Scripture circular 144
Sentiments 552; the religious sentiment
 552-3; the sentiment of rationality
 554
Seth, J. 341
Shaw, Bernard, on Paul 357
Sidgwick, Henry: on benevolence 331;
 on humility 376; on charity 390;
 on the sinlessness of Jesus 392; on the
 value of belief 421; on the Absolute
 528; as example of reasonable temper
 562; on himself 569; *securus judicat*
 581; on truth 593-4; on Newman
 595
Simpson, D. C. 390
Simpson, W. J. S. 103
Sixtus V, Pope 47
Skinner, B. F., on determinism 489
Slavery and Christian ethics 350
Smith, Adam: on poverty and happiness
 339; on Hume 562
Smith, Canon George Duncan 31, 34,
 58, 62 ff., 82, 86, 576
Socrates 354, 442-3, 452, 562
Soul: primitive idea of 438; Saint Paul's
 two-storied 547; its incredibility 548
Speculatores Domus Israel 59
Sperry, W., Dean 417
Spinoza 562
Spiritus Paraclitus 38, 50

Stapleton, Thomas 81
Stephen, Leslie: on divinity of Christ 392; on Newman 424; on original sin 584
Strauss, D. F. 455
Subjectivism in ethics 520
Suenens, Cardinal 113
Suhard, Cardinal 48
Summis Desiderantes 66
Supernaturalism *v.* rationalism 538 ff.
Swenson, D. F. 245
Swinburne, A. C. 330
Syllabus of Errors 85

Tacitus 330
Taylor, A. E.: on the Bible 27; on original sin 157; on humility 568
Teilhard de Chardin 66
Temple, W., Archbishop, on force 591
Tennant, F. R.: on Saint Paul 153; on original sin 155
Teresa, Saint 286, 549
Tertullian: on Peter 102; on women 357–8; on belief 414
Tetzel 128
Theology, line between it and philosophy 33
Thomas, George, Christian stress on the personal 360
Thomte, R. 223
Thorndike, E. L. 512
Thought: in perception 514; the evolution of 514–15; central in human evolution 541; and length of vision 541; and breadth of vision 541–2; and coherence of aim 542–3; transformation of instinct by 549
Thouless, R. H.: on instincts 512
Tillich, P.: on the love of God 372
Torquemada 408
Trent, Council of: on inspiration 38, 46, 49; on hell 84; on virginity 358–9; on original sin 583
Trotter, W. 564
Truth, Catholicism's two standards 115–16; a double standard unworkable 116–17; as the one compass of thought 428
Tylor, E. B.: on religion 434; on animism 437

Underhill, Evelyn 286
Uniformity of nature 483
Unity of the church: defined 81; its failure in consistency 82–3; failures through addition 83 ff.; failures through subtraction 91
Universality as note of church 97; criticised 97–8
Urban VIII, Pope 59

Values: based on needs and impulses 513; calculation of 516; morality and intrinsic 517; intrinsic, defined 517; non-cognitive values 524; truth not a value 524; values in the Absolute, chap. 15
Vatican I: on faith and reason 26, 35; on authority of Papacy 27; on deposit of faith 28; on infallibility 28, 53; on inspiration 28–9; on consistency with reason 29–30; on gift of faith 30–1; faith a free act 31–2; required for salvation 32; on Scripture 38; *nulla vera dissensio* 58; on the unity of church 113; revelation complete 579
Vatican II 68, 113; significance of 1 ff.; on inspiration of Scripture 28–9; its untenable compromise 49; on Galileo 61–2; its attempt at accommodation 43
Vigilius, Pope 56, 83
Vincent of Lerins 83
Virgin birth 113; evidence inconsistent with it 456
Virgin Mary: appearance at Lourdes 69; at Fatima 70, 74, 77; immaculate conception unknown to early church 88; as was also her bodily assumption 88–9; Jesus' coolness toward her 355; myth of the Virgin studied 456 ff.; her son's attitude 457; status in early church 458; doctrine of immaculate conception 459; influence of other religions 459–60; influence of Nicaea 461; her gradual exaltation 461–2; her glorification by the church 462–3; Vatican I and the two dogmas 463; the larger issue stated 464–6; as mediatrix 592
Vulgate Bible 46

War and Christian ethics 346
Wealth, Christian view of 337
Webb, C. C. J. 316
Weber, Max, on Luther 126
Wesley, John: on Luther 184; on knowledge 334–5

Westermarck, E.: on Jewish polygamy 351; on Saint James 414; on orthodoxy 415
Whewell, W. 470
Whistler, J. McN. 335
White, A. D., on science and theology 59, 68, 577
Whitehead, A. N. 4; on Luther 126; on Christian ethics 341; on striving in nature 540
Whittier, J. G. 566
Wilde, O. 429

Will to believe 418; criticism of doctrine 421 ff.
Wisdom, J., on 'Gods' 537
Wiseman, Cardinal 82
Witchcraft 66, 578
Witches' Hammer 94
Women in Christian ethics 351 ff.
Work, Jesus' attitude toward 365

Zeller, E., on character of Jesus 392
Zosimus, Pope 83
Zwingli, Luther and 133